Current Perspectives in Banking

Current Perspectives in Banking

Operations, Management and Regulation

Second Edition

Edited by

Thomas M. Havrilesky
Duke University

John T. Boorman
International Monetary Fund

AHM Publishing Corporation
Arlington Heights, Illinois 60004

ISBN: 0-88295-405-9
Library of Congress Catalog Card Number: 79-55734
PRINTED IN THE UNITED STATES
OF AMERICA

Contents

Preface to the Second Edition

Since the appearance of the first edition of this collection, innovations in the operation and management of banks and other financial institutions have not diminished. However, the regulatory reform that had been anticipated at the time of the first edition has not occurred. Conflict between operational innovation on the one hand and resistance to regulatory reform on the other has brought about dramatic changes in the management of and competition between financial institutions. Two areas of change—electronic funds transfer systems and international banking—are the subjects of entire new sections in this edition. Other areas of continuing change, such as new developments in Federal funds activity, the prime rate, and large negotiable certificates of deposit, are represented by new articles in other sections.

Another result of the clash between continuing innovation and the absence of concomitant regulatory reform has been that managers, regulators, and scholars have grown more reflective regarding the failure of reform and have come to approach the matter cautiously, seeking feasible reform on a piecemeal basis. Several new readings in the last three sections of this edition reflect this pattern.

In order to focus on these new developments yet maintain a reasonably priced book, we had to delete some material. Two criteria were used. As with the original edition, we first considered the relevance of the material to contemporary issues in banking and we second determined whether the material was now adequately treated in available textbooks.

We would like to thank Harold Black, John Boyd, Kalman Cohen, Robert

Eisenbeis, William Hendorf, Edward Kane, Manfred Peterson, and Robert Schweitzer for their suggestions and comments; Maureen Trobec for production assistance; and our editors, Harlan Davidson and Roger Williams, for their advice, encouragement, and cooperation.

THOMAS M. HAVRILESKY
Durham, North Carolina

JOHN T. BOORMAN
Washington, D.C.

April 1979

Preface to the First Edition

Few industries have undergone more sweeping change in the last decade than commercial banking. For example, bank management and bank regulatory bodies function today in an environment that has been dramatically altered by new methods of liability management and capital financing, by an accelerating use of credit cards, by an exciting technology of electronic funds transfer, and by a much-expanded role for international banking. In addition, the skills of the banking specialist have been enriched by new tools of analysis provided by economists and management scientists.

Propelled by progressive management, and a somewhat less restrictive regulatory environment, the banking industry has, in the same ten-year span, witnessed tremendous growth in branching, mergers, the chartering of new banks, and the formation of bank holding companies. Some banking firms have had difficulty coping with such a rapidly changing environment—and a number have failed. This has suggested to some observers that the banking revolution has weakened the ability of the system to withstand severe shocks and, in turn, has prompted extensive examination of the proper role of bank regulatory bodies.

The environment of rapid change has resulted in an outpouring of analysis from industry, governmental, and academic sources. Traditional textbooks have had difficulty in keeping up with, not to mention effectively assimilating, this valuable lode of material. It remains for a set of readings garnered from diverse contemporary sources to transmit this new knowledge to students of banking.

The material herein was selected first for its genuine contemporary relevance; we avoided readings that, however skillfully prepared, merely supplemented the standard fare of the textbook. In addition, readings were chosen on the basis of their lucidity and their complementarity with one another. Finally, an important criterion was the potential of the reading for generating critical reflection and discussion.

The conceptual structure of these readings was devised primarily for the student of banking as a business enterprise. For this reason considerable attention has been paid not only to new developments in banking operations but also to contemporary issues in bank regulation and to new analytical methods in bank management.

This book is suitable for use in courses in money and banking, bank management, financial markets, and the management of financial institutions. It can also profitably be used by individuals who seek a convenient means of self-study of recent developments in the field. The material has been used effectively in courses at Duke University at the undergraduate and graduate level.

We are grateful to the copyright holders for granting permission to reprint these articles and congratulate them for their contribution to scholarship.

We would like to thank Kalman Cohen, Robert Eisenbeis, Edward Kane, Manfred Peterson, and Robert Schweitzer for their suggestions and comments; James Johnson, Steven Happel, Paul Funk, Linda Giberson, Katie Frye, Maxine McGee, Jean Peek, Annie Sarino, Ziska Lalamentik, and Maureen Trobec for production assistance; and our editors, Harlan Davidson and Harry Metzger, for their advice, encouragement, and cooperation.

THOMAS M. HAVRILESKY
Durham, North Carolina

JOHN T. BOORMAN
Jakarta, Indonesia

November 1975

Asset Management

I

A general rule of financial management for all firms is that asset policy should shape financial and capital policy—the liability and capital mix should reflect the risk, maturity, and liquidity of investments. However, banking firms traditionally have been viewed as possessing only a limited ability to control their liabilities, meaning that asset management is affected to some extent by the sources of a bank's funds. But while asset management in banking, as suggested by the readings that follow, focuses upon the trade-off between liquidity and profitability and liquidity needs may be met by reserve adjustments and the conversion of earning assets to cash, the acquisition of new liabilities, as discussed in Section II, is also an important source of liquidity. Within these three categories adjustment patterns are determined by the preferences of bank management, subject to market, technological, and regulatory constraints.

The first article, by Leonall C. Andersen and Albert E. Burger, serves as a traditional introduction to this trade-off and then tests whether banks' portfolio activity reflects profit-maximizing behavior or a simple accommodation of customer demands. In the second reading Thomas Havrilesky and John Boorman focus exclusively on the short-run aspects of asset management with a simplified neoclassical model of the sources and uses of bank liquidity.

As indicated by the model presented by Havrilesky and Boorman, the Federal funds market is an important source of funds for banks' short-term borrowing needs; in addition, banks with excess liquidity may make short-term loans in the Federal funds market. The third article, by Charles M. Lucas, Marcos T. Jones, and Thom B. Thurston, describes the origins, development, and continually evolving innovations in this market. When read in conjunction with the selections on liability management in Section II, it indicates the breadth of banking innovation in recent decades.

Readings 4 through 6 deal with bank management of earning assets. Ronald D. Watson provides a fine analysis of strategies for selecting the maturity distribution of securities in the face of uncertainty regarding top management's preferences as well as market constraints. In Article 5 Stuart A. Schweitzer examines what banks do to try to make sure that they have sufficient resources to absorb loan losses. The sixth essay, by Randall C. Merris, describes recent innovations in the structuring of the prime rate, the interest rate charged by banks on business loans to their most creditworthy customers.

The final reading in this section deals with a new approach to bank balance sheet management—the management of the bank's entire balance sheet rather than just its assets. Alfred Broaddus explains in a most understandable fashion how linear programming can be applied to asset management.

In closing, it is important to point out that this section, in addition to providing selections that cover analytical approaches to real-world banking problems, also gives examples of three approaches to modeling bank behavior—the traditional portfolio-theoretic approach of Andersen and Burger, the neoclassical (marginal cost–marginal return) approach of Havrilesky and Boorman, and the linear programming approach of Broaddus.

Asset Management and Commercial Bank Portfolio Behavior: Theory and Practice

Leonall C. Andersen
Albert E. Burger*

This paper reports the results of an investigation we have conducted regarding two aspects of commercial bank portfolio management. With regard to the first aspect, two alternative hypotheses regarding bank behavior are tested. These are the "accommodation principle" implied in the commercial loan theory of banking and the "profit maximization principle" implied in recent developments in bank portfolio theory and related research. The second aspect is an investigation into the proposition that there has been a significant change in bank portfolio behavior in recent years.

Knowledge of the first aspect of commercial bank behavior is important for monetary management. The accommodation principle implies that the demand for bank loans determines bank portfolio behavior. On the other hand, the profit maximization principle implies that commercial bank responses to market forces determine their portfolio behavior. Expectations of bank response to actions of the Federal Reserve System differ according to which principle is accepted.

For example, under the accommodation principle, Federal Reserve open-market operations slowing growth in the reserve base could have little effect on growth in the

Reprinted from *Journal of Finance* 24, no. 2 (May 1969): 207-22, by permission of the American Finance Association and the authors.

* Vice president and economist, respectively, Federal Reserve Bank of St. Louis. The views expressed in this article are the views of the authors; they do not necessarily represent the views of either the Federal Reserve Bank of St. Louis or the Federal Reserve System.

volume of bank loans if the demand for such loans, at given interest rates, was expanding rapidly. Such would be the case if economic activity was expanding rapidly. Thus, loans could continue to rise at the previous rate or even to accelerate if demand should strengthen. Banks would tend to accommodate such demand by shifting out of investments. By comparison, in such circumstances of Federal Reserve restraint, profit maximization would induce banks to reduce the rate of growth of both loans and investments, at given interest rates, with loan growth continuing at its previous rate only if interest rates on loans rose relative to interest rates on investments.

Changes in bank portfolio behavior, the second aspect of this investigation, have important implications for monetary management. A change in commercial bank portfolio behavior may be reflected in a shift in a function, a change in the shape of the function, or both. For example, with regard to bank loans, a shift in the function explaining the desired level would be reflected in a change in its intercept. A change in its shape would be a change in the elasticity of the desired level of loans with regard to one or more of its arguments.

Monetary authorities, when attempting to forecast the asset behavior of banks in response to a given change in monetary policy, must take into consideration empirical evidence bearing on these questions. If the central bank attempts to forecast bank behavior based on a set of relations estimated from past observations of dependent variables such as borrowings, excess reserves, and loans, and a set of independent variables, and if the conditions under which these estimated relations are proposed to represent bank asset behavior no longer hold, then the predictions of the response of commercial banks to monetary policy actions may be far from satisfactory. Furthermore, during different periods of time, banks may change their behavior, perhaps from accommodating business loan demand to responding more to market forces such as the relationship between short- and long-term interest rates.

This report consists of four sections. First, recent literature and research into commercial bank asset behavior is surveyed with a view to delineating the accommodation and the profit maximization principles. Then, a model of bank asset behavior is constructed which provides the basis for testing these two principles. Next, the two rival hypotheses of bank asset behavior are tested. Last, evidence is presented bearing on the proposition that there has been a significant change in bank behavior in recent years.

I. Review of Literature on Bank Asset Behavior

The study of commercial bank portfolio behavior is important for at least two major reasons:

1. Commercial bank portfolio behavior is an important explanatory factor for the magnitudes and changes in the magnitudes of the aggregate economic quantities (the money stock and bank credit).

2. At a less aggregate level, bank portfolio behavior is a key determinant of the cost and flow of credit to specific sectors of the economy.

For the purpose of discussion, monetary theory is defined as the set of theories concerned with the influence of the quantity of money in the economic system, and monetary policy as policy employing the central bank's control of the stock of money as an instrument for achieving the objectives of general economic policy. If one believes that changes in the magnitude of the money stock are an important explanatory variable for changes in real output, employment, and prices which are the goals of economic policy, then the study of factors determining the money stock becomes of crucial importance. Especially if one is interested in monetary policy, knowledge about the linkage between operations that may be performed by the monetary authorities and changes in the magnitudes of economic quantities such as the money stock and bank credit becomes primary.

Recent research in the field of monetary theory has shown that, given the institutional structure in the United States, the magnitudes of the stocks of money and bank credit are determined jointly by the actions of the Federal Reserve, commercial banks, and the public.[1] The Federal Reserve, by its actions alone, does not determine the magnitude of the money stock. The immediate impact of a Federal Reserve operation, such as a purchase or sale of Government securities, may be to increase or decrease the money stock. However, the equilibrium magnitude of the money stock is determined by the conjunction of the Federal Reserve action and the behavioral reactions of the commercial banks and the public to that action.

The behavioral responses of the banks and the public may be viewed as a portfolio adjustment process. The ability to predict the effect of a given action by the monetary authorities on the magnitudes of money and bank credit depends on being able to predict the behavioral responses of the banks and the public as they adjust their portfolios of financial and real assets.

In this section we present a summary review of some recent developments in the study of commercial bank portfolio behavior incorporating the profit maximization principle. This summary is followed by a brief analysis of the accommodation principle. Due to limitation of space and the nature of the content of the rest of our article, we concentrate primarily on bank portfolio behavior as it affects the holdings of excess reserves, borrowings from Reserve banks, and the volume of loans outstanding.

IA. Profit Maximizing Principle

At the micro-level, the individual commercial bank is viewed as an economic unit whose goal is to maximize profits. The commercial bank holds a portfolio of assets

---

[1]We might mention at this point that actions of the government sector, specifically actions by the Treasury in financing the debt, may enter as an explanatory variable in the actions of the monetary authorities. However, the actions of the monetary authorities determine the effect of a Treasury financing operation on the money stock.

and, given the characteristics and distribution of its liabilities, the commercial bank attempts to structure its portfolio of assets in such a manner as to yield the greatest return subject to these constraints. The assets held by a bank may be divided into two broad classes, frequently called earning assets and nonearning assets. Earning assets are the two balance sheet items called loans and investments. Nonearning assets consist of the total reserves of the bank. Total reserves are then frequently partitioned into required reserves and excess reserves.

In most studies of bank portfolio behavior it is assumed that given such factors as the present and expected levels of market interest rates, loan demands and cash demands, the level of the discount rate, and actions by the Federal Reserve System, the individual commercial bank has a desired distribution of assets in its portfolio. If the existing distribution of assets held by the commercial bank is not the distribution desired, then the bank will attempt to adjust its portfolio of assets by increasing its holdings of some assets and decreasing its holdings of other assets.

Federal Reserve actions such as an open market purchase or sale of Government securities, a change in the legal reserve requirements on member bank demand and/ or time deposits, or a change in the discount rate have their initial impacts in the commercial banking sector on total reserves. A purchase of Government securities by the Federal Reserve System leads to an increase in total reserves of the commercial banks. An increase in reserve requirements alters the composition of total reserves leading to an increase in required reserves and a decrease in the actual level of excess reserves. A change in the discount rate alters the cost for member banks of borrowing reserves from the Federal Reserve Banks.

Given that, before the action by the Federal Reserve System, commercial banks were holding their desired distribution of assets, these actions by the monetary authorities lead to a portfolio adjustment process on the part of the individual banks. For example, if an individual bank finds its total reserves increased as a result of the purchase of securities from the public by the Federal Reserve System, the bank will no longer be holding its desired distribution of assets. The proportion of nonearning assets to earning assets will be greater than the desired level. The bank will have an incentive to expand its earning assets by extending additional loans and/or purchasing securities.[2]

Assuming that the proportion of assets held in the form of required reserves is determined by the existing legal reserve requirements against commercial bank demand and time deposits, a commercial bank faces the decision of allocating its portfolio of assets between earning assets (loans and investments) and nonearning assets (excess reserves). Having chosen the desired distribution between earning and nonearning assets the commercial bank then decides what portion of its nonearning assets to hold in the form of free reserves (excess reserves less borrowings from Reserve banks). For member banks this involves a decision as to the level of borrowings from the Federal Reserve banks they desire to maintain.

---

[2]Since interest rates are usually entered as an explanatory variable in bank demand functions for assets, the interest rate impact of the open market operation will also affect the adjustment process.

Given the de jure and de facto status of the majority of their liabilities, and given that the individual bank cannot predict with certainty future deposit flows, loan demands, interest rates, and actions by the monetary authorities, commercial banks desire to have a portion of their portfolio of assets represent a stock of liquidity to act as a buffer against changes in these factors. One form in which commercial banks may hold this stock of liquidity is excess reserves. However, also available to banks are other assets, such as Treasury bills, which under most circumstances can be converted into cash with little loss of time or value, and unlike excess reserves yield an interest return to the bank. Also, member banks may borrow from Federal Reserve banks to meet reserve demands; they also may acquire reserves in the Federal funds market.[3]

A considerable amount of research in the field of commercial bank portfolio behavior has been devoted to the question of what factors determine a bank's desired holdings of excess reserves. As recent research has highlighted, there are definite costs to the individual commercial bank in adjusting its portfolio of assets to meet changes in deposit flows, loan demand, and actions by the Federal Reserve System.

Although excess reserves yield no interest return as do other assets, they implicitly have a positive yield for the commercial banks. Excess reserves act as an immediate source of liquidity, and hence enable the individual bank to minimize the adjustment costs associated with restructuring its portfolio. Commercial banks' desired holdings of excess reserves are postulated to depend on (1) the yield on Treasury bills which are the main alternative to holding excess reserves for liquidity purposes and hence represent the primary opportunity cost of excess reserves, and (2) the adjustment costs involved in restructuring the bank's portfolio. Such adjustment costs are the costs of alternative sources of funds to cover reserve demands. The primary alternative sources of short-term funds are borrowings from Federal Reserve banks and borrowings in the Federal funds market. Recent research by Peter Frost indicates that banks will permit their holdings of excess reserves to fluctuate within certain limits and adjust their holdings only when the return from doing so exceeds the potential cost of not making the adjustment.[4]

Sometimes the Federal Reserve discount rate is used as a proxy for the adjustment cost. However, as pointed out by several authors, the actual level of the discount rate may not fully represent the actual cost to a member bank of using this means to make adjustments in its portfolio.[5] Federal Reserve banks do not always set the discount rate and then allow member banks to determine the volume of the borrow-

---

[3]The difference between these two sources of reserves is that by borrowing from the Federal Reserve Banks total reserves of all commercial banks may be increased, while by borrowing in the Federal funds market reserves of the borrowing bank are increased and reserves of the lending bank are decreased with no change in total reserves of the system.

[4]Peter Frost, *Banks' Demand for Excess Reserves,* unpublished UCLA dissertation, 1966, University Microfilms: Ann Arbor, pp. XIV-XV, 279-287.

[5]See Stephen Goldfeld and Edward Kane, "Determinants of Member Bank Borrowing: An Econometric Study," *Journal of Finance,* September, 1966, pp. 499-514; and Murray E. Polakoff and William L. Silber, "Reluctance and Member-Bank Borrowing: Additional Evidence," *Journal of Finance,* March, 1967, pp. 88-92.

ings at that rate. They also "administer" the discount window and subject the use of borrowings of member banks to careful surveillance. This so-called "discipline of the discount window" has probably at times made the cost of borrowing from Reserve banks less attractive and hence raised the implicit return to commercial banks from holding excess reserves.[6]

Recent research by Stephen Goldfeld and Edward Kane has brought into question the assumption that all banks react in the same manner to changes in factors such as short-term market interest rates, the discount rate, availability of reserves, and new loan demand. Goldfeld investigated commercial bank portfolio behavior using a stock adjustment model.[7] He fitted the structural model with quarterly, seasonally adjusted time series data from the third quarter of 1950 to the second quarter of 1962. Goldfeld concluded that for both country and city member banks the major determinants of excess reserve holdings appeared to be interest rate considerations (the differential between the bill rate and the discount rate) and changes in the availability of reserves (as measured by a potential-deposit variable). However, the portfolio responses of the two classes of banks to changes in interest rates, deposit flows, and new loan demand were markedly different. In the management of excess reserves the city bank sector was found to be more responsive to interest rate considerations than country banks. With respect to changes in borrowings to meet new loan demand, Goldfeld found that city banks increased their borrowings by $12 for each $100 of new loan demand while country banks' borrowings rose only about $6 per $100.[8]

Kane and Goldfeld presented and estimated a model of member bank borrowing from Reserve Banks.[9] Banks were assumed to maximize utility, which was postulated to be a function of the cost of acquiring reserves and borrowing. Utility declines as this cost of borrowing rises. Kane and Goldfeld suggest that, following an exogenous disturbance, banks may effect desired changes in their security portfolios through a series of partial adjustments. In the short run a bank may prefer to borrow from the Federal Reserve rather than immediately liquidating its securities. Hence, banks may borrow more in the short run than a static model would imply. They estimated the dynamic version of their model using weekly data on reserves and borrowings for four member bank categories from July, 1953 through December, 1965. The results using both seasonally adjusted and unadjusted data supported the importance of a distributed lag response. Also, they found that the speed of portfolio adjustment for country banks was slower than the speed of city bank portfolio adjustment.[10]

---

[6]The effect of Federal Reserve surveillance is extremely difficult to quantify. However, the existence of periods such as the middle of 1966, when the spread between the discount rate and the Federal funds rate rapidly widened while member bank borrowings did not increase, lends some credulence to the assertion of the existence of such an effect.

[7]Stephen Goldfeld, *Commercial Bank Behavior and Economic Activity: A Structural Study of Monetary Policy in the Postwar United States*, Amsterdam: New Holland Publishing Co., 1966.

[8]Goldfeld, pp. 149–152.

[9]Goldfeld and Kane, *op. cit.*, pp. 499–514.

[10]Goldfeld and Kane, p. 512.

IB. Accommodation Principle

The accommodation principle of commercial bank behavior stems from an older concept of the proper role of banking in economic life. This older concept is known as the "commercial loan theory" or the "real bills doctrine" of commercial banking. According to this theory bank earning assets should be limited to short-term, self-liquidating loans related to the production and distribution of goods and services. Proper banking practice is to accommodate the "legitimate credit demands" of business, commerce, and agriculture.

This principle of banking is imbedded in the Federal Reserve Act.[11] Accordingly, the accommodation principle has been used as a basis for Federal Reserve supervision of banks, eligibility requirements for collateral for borrowing from Reserve banks, and Federal Reserve collateral for its issue of currency.

The accommodation principle has also played an important role in monetary management. The real bills debate over the proper types of securities for Federal Reserve open-market transactions points to the importance given this principle by monetary authorities. The Federal Reserve still views, to a considerable degree, its actions as accommodating loan demand.

The accommodation principle holds that commercial banks should primarily make business loans and agricultural production loans. The use of the term "accommodation" implies that the *demand* for such loans would mainly determine bank behavior regarding borrowing from Reserve banks, holdings of excess reserves, and the division of earning assets between loans and investments.[12] Thus, the response of demand for loans to such economic variables as interest rates and economic activity would also determine bank behavior regarding the above mentioned balance sheet accounts.

II. Model of Banking Portfolio Behavior

Bank behavior regarding assets is viewed in this paper as a process of allocating a given amount of wealth (defined as total deposits) between nonearning assets (required and excess reserves) and earning assets (loans and investments). Once this allocation is determined, earning assets are allocated between loans and investments.

---

[11]See Clifton B. Luttrell, "Member Bank Borrowing: Its Origin and Function," *Quarterly Review of Economics and Business,* Bureau of Economic and Business Research, University of Illinois, Autumn, 1968, pp. 56-65.

[12]Some discussions of the Federal Reserve-M.I.T. Econometric Model seem to indicate that an accommodation hypothesis of bank lending behavior was assumed in constructing the model. For example, "Banks are assumed to accommodate short-run changes in loan demand by their business customers partly by changing their free reserve position." Frank de Leeuw and Edward Gramlich, "The Federal Reserve-M.I.T. Econometric Model," *Federal Reserve Bulletin,* January, 1968, p. 14. Also see Robert Rasche and Harold Shapiro, "The F.R.B.-M.I.T. Econometric Model: Its Special Features," *American Economic Review,* May, 1968, p. 139, and footnote 19.

We now proceed to set forth the factors influencing bank behavior with regard to this allocation process.

Since this study is concerned only with the behavior of member banks of the Federal Reserve System, the special considerations regarding the reserve requirements imposed on these banks will be applied. The following discussion is based on the assumption that banks are profit maximizers. Their behavior based on the accommodation principle will be presented later. Aggregate member bank behavior is used in the remainder of this article.

IIA. Bank Behavior Under the Profit Maximizing Principle

Total Deposits Member bank total deposits (D) are constrained by their total reserves (deposits at Reserve banks and vault cash) and the average reserve requirement ratio. This relation may be expressed by the following identity:

$$D = \frac{1}{\bar{r}} R$$

In the above expression, R is member bank total reserves and $\bar{r}$ is the average reserve requirement ratio. R consists of nonborrowed reserves (NB) and borrowings from Reserve banks (B). The term $\bar{r}$ is the average reserve requirement which takes into consideration the distribution of deposits between demand and time accounts and between reserve city and country banks.

The identity may be expanded to:

$$D = \frac{1}{\bar{r}} (NB + B)$$

With $\bar{r}$ constant, borrowing from Reserve banks or as a result of the Federal Reserve System increasing nonborrowed reserves, member banks as a group may expand their deposits, thereby allowing them to have more earning assets.

Borrowing Member bank borrowing from Reserve banks, although relatively small compared with NB, is an important aspect of bank behavior. It is a liability item which allows banks some flexibility in their asset management within the constraint imposed by nonborrowed reserves.

The desired level of borrowings from Reserve banks (B*) is postulated as follows:

$$B^* = f_1 (i_s, i_d, i_F, C_b, D)$$

In this relationship, i_s is the short-term interest rate, i_d the Federal Reserve discount rate, i_F the Federal funds rate, and C_b other costs of borrowing. B* is postulated to be positively related to i_s, i_F, and D, and negatively related to i_d and C_b.

Excess Reserves   Holdings of excess reserves, other things constant, result in holdings of fewer earning assets; therefore banks hold excess reserves for returns other than earnings. Holdings of excess reserves constitute a buffer stock which allows banks to meet sudden withdrawals of deposits without requiring a reduction in earning assets. The desired level of excess reserves (ER*) is given by the following function:

$$ER^* = f_2 (i_s, i_d, i_L, C_{er}, D)$$

ER* is postulated to be negatively related to i_s and i_L and postively related to D, i_d, and C_{er} (costs of managing excess reserves).

Loans   Earning assets in the form of bank loans consist mainly of loans to businesses, households, and financial institutions. The desired level of loans (L*) is given by the following relationship:

$$L^* = f_3 (i_s, i_d, i_L, C_1, D)$$

L* is postulated to be negatively related to i_L, i_d, and C_1 (transaction costs of lending), and positively related to i_s and D.

Investments   Earning assets classified as investments consist mainly of holdings of government securities. The desired level (I*) is expressed as:

$$I^* = f_4 (i_s, i_d, i_L, C_i, D)$$

Investments are considered a residual item in this study; however, I* is postulated to be negatively related to i_s, i_d, and C_i (transaction costs of investments) and positively related to i_L and D.

IIB. Bank Behavior Under Accommodation Principle

Under the accommodation principle, bank behavior would mainly reflect the demand of customers for loans. For example, a rise in the demand for loans from banks (supply of this form of earning asset) would be met, subject to the deposit constraint, by reductions in investments and excess reserves and an increase in borrowings from Reserve banks. This implies that the factors influencing the demand for bank loans affect L*, I*, ER*, and B*.

The following equation is postulated as determining the supply of loans (viewed as earning assets of banks):

$$L^* = g (i_s, i_L, GNP, W)$$

L* is postulated to be negatively related to i_s and positively related to i_L, the level of economic activity (GNP), and to private nonbank wealth (W). These signs are the ones commonly developed on the basis of business maximization of profits and household maximization of satisfaction, subject to wealth and income constraints.

As stated above, the function g would be the relevant one for examining bank behavior under the accommodation principle. Incorporation of this principle into the functions for B*, ER*, L*, and I* in place of the profit maximization principle, introduces GNP and W into each function and reverses the signs for i_s in the B*, ER*, L* equations, and the sign for i_L in the L* equation.

IIC. Stock Adjustment Model

A stock adjustment framework is used as the basis of constructing the model of bank portfolio behavior. It is assumed that banks have a desired level of each of the balance sheet items under consideration (B*, ER*, L*, and I*) and that the stock of the item held is changed at a certain rate to close the gap between the actual and the desired level. This may be expressed as two equivalent equations:

$$X_t - X_{t-1} = \lambda(X^*_t - X_{t-1})$$
$$X_t = \lambda X^*_t + (1 - \lambda) X_{t-1}$$

In the above equations, X_t is the stock on hand at time (t); X^*_t is the desired stock; X_{t-1} is the stock in the previous period; and λ is a speed of adjustment coefficient. The desired stock depends on the economic factors spelled out in the preceding discussion. The speed of adjustment coefficient may range from zero to plus one. The closer it is to one, the faster the speed of adjustment.

III. Testing Two Rival Hypotheses

IIIA. Two Rival Hypotheses

Frequently, policy makers are confronted with conflicting policy advice. For example, one group of policy advisers starting from the assumption that banks passively accommodate business loan demand might predict one set of consequences for a policy action taken by the monetary authorities. Another group of advisers, assuming that banks behave as profit maximizers, might predict an alternative result for the same policy action. The policy results predicted by both policy advisers depend on whether initial assumptions about bank portfolio behavior do in fact represent the behavioral reactions of commercial banks.[13]

In this section we provide evidence on these two alternative assumptions about bank portfolio behavior. To compare the two hypotheses we first state each hypothesis so that it can be confronted with empirical evidence. Also, the two hypotheses

---

[13]See Albert E. Burger and Leonall C. Andersen, "The Development of Explanatory Economic Hypotheses for Monetary Management," *Southern Journal of Business* (forthcoming).

must be stated in such a form that the available empirical evidence can discriminate between them. They must not, however, be formulated so that the empirical evidence is in good agreement with both. In section IIIB the regression equations used in the formulation of the two hypotheses are presented. As we have formulated the two proposed explanations of commercial bank portfolio behavior, each of the two alternative hypotheses implies certain signs for the coefficients in the regression equations. These signs are presented in Exhibit 1 and discussed in section IIIC. The implied signs are used as the basis for testing the hypotheses.

EXHIBIT 1

	i_s	i_L	GNP/D
Profit-Maximizing Hypothesis:			
B/D			
Expected sign	+	+,0	0
Sign of Regression Coefficient			
1953–1960	+	−	0
1961–1967	+	0	0
ER/D			
Expected sign	−	−	0
Sign of Regression Coefficient			
1953–1960	0	−	0
1961–1967	−	0	+
L/D			
Expected sign	+	−	0
Sign of Regression Coefficient			
1953–1960	+	−	0
1961–1967	+	−	0
Accommodation Hypothesis:			
B/D			
Expected sign	−	+,0	+
Sign of Regression Coefficient			
1953–1960	+	−	0
1961–1967	+	0	0
ER/D			
Expected sign	+	−	−
Sign of Regression Coefficient			
1953–1960	0	−	0
1961–1967	−	0	+
L/D			
Expected sign	−	+	+
Sign of Regression Coefficient			
1953–1960	+	−	0
1961–1967	+	−	0

IIIB. Estimation Procedures

Multiple regression analysis, using monthly observations for the period 1953–1967, is used to determine which of the two alternative explanations of commercial bank asset behavior, i.e., the profit maximization or accommodation principle, is in better agreement with the empirical evidence. Lack of suitable data resulted in dropping the wealth variable and variables reflecting transactions and other noninterest costs. Also, the Federal funds rate was omitted. Another variable, the ratio of country bank deposits (DCB) to total member bank deposits, was introduced to take into consideration the possibility of differences in behavior between classes of member banks.

It was assumed that each function is homogenous with regard to deposits; hence, each variable measured in dollars was divided by D. The stock adjustment model thus becomes one involving the closing of a discrepancy between desired and actual ratios.

$$\frac{B}{D} = f_1\left(i_s, i_d, i_L, \frac{GNP}{D}, \frac{DCB}{D}, \left[\frac{B}{D}\right]_{-1}\right)$$

$$\frac{ER}{D} = f_2\left(i_s, i_d, i_L, \frac{GNP}{D}, \frac{DCB}{D}, \left[\frac{ER}{D}\right]_{-1}\right)$$

$$\frac{L}{D} = f_3\left(i_s, i_d, i_L, \frac{GNP}{D}, \frac{DCB}{D}, \left[\frac{L}{D}\right]_{-1}\right)$$

In the above equations, all variables are for the current period except the lagged ratios. All of the variables are seasonally adjusted monthly averages. Monthly data for GNP were developed by a straight line interpolation of quarterly GNP centered on the mid-month of each quarter. The 91-day Treasury bill rate was used as a proxy for the short-term interest rate, and the corporate Aaa bond rate was used for the long-term interest rate. Regressions were run using logarithms, thereby providing elasticity estimates. Two variables, i_s and i_L, were considered endogenous within a more complete model of bank behavior; hence, the two-stage least-squares estimation procedure was used.[14]

The regression results are reported in Table 1. The regression equations were run for the entire period 1953 through 1967. However, application of the Chow test indicated a significant structural change between the period 1953–1960 and

---

[14]A complete model includes stock adjustment equations for demand deposits held by the public, currency in the hands of the public, and the public's holdings of time deposits. Also, there are balance sheet identities for demand deposits held by the public and bank total earnings assets. In addition to the exogenous variables in the equations presented above, there are the lagged stocks of demand deposits, time deposits, and currency. Exogenous variables derived from the balance sheet identities include the factors affecting nonborrowed reserves and average reserve requirements for member banks. The balance sheet identity for private demand deposits is developed in Leonall C. Andersen, "A Study of Factors Affecting the Money Stock: Phase One," *Staff Economic Studies,* Board of Governors of the Federal Reserve System, October, 1965. The identity for earning assets is a slight alteration of the private demand deposit one.

Table 1.   Regression Results—Member Bank Behavior Borrowed Reserves, Excess Reserves, and Loans (variables in natural logarithms)

Intercept	i_s	i_L	i_d	GNP/D	DCB/D	Lagged Dependent Variable	Standard Error	R^2
B/D								
1953–1960								
− .715	1.717*	− 1.047*	− .709*	− 3.434	− 2.499	.517*	.197	.94
	(.246)	(.399)	(.235)	(1.549)	(3.958)	(.069)		
1961–1967								
− 14.660	1.557*	− 1.978	.174	1.879	− 12.034	.622*	.268	.93
	(.632)	(1.032)	(.738)	(2.937)	(6.260)	(.122)		
ER/D								
1953–1960								
.131	− .103	− .289*	.118	− .271	.956	.746*	.079	.89
	(.063)	(.141)	(.095)	(.849)	(1.585)	(.079)		
1961–1967								
− 10.704	− 1.246*	− .286	.319	5.258*	− .505	.040	.094	.93
	(.223)	(.182)	(.240)	(1.033)	(2.213)	(.112)		
L/D								
1953–1960								
.702	.044*	− .041*	− .043	− .169	.479*	1.006*	.007	.99
	(.009)	(.015)	(.011)	(.136)	(.176)	(.033)		
1961–1967								
− .038	.033*	− .019*	.015	− .008	.040	.878*	.004	.99
	(.007)	(.007)	(.013)	(.036)	(.098)	(.030)		

Numbers in parentheses are standard errors of the regression coefficients.
*Statistically significant at 5 percent level.

1961-1967. The F-value of the Chow test was 2.83 for B/D, 9.98 for ER/D, and 3.01 for L/D. All of these values are statistically significant at the 5 percent level. Therefore, the observation period 1953-1967 was split into two periods, 1953-1960 and 1961-1967. Only the results of the regressions for the separate periods are reported in Table 1.

IIIC. Expected Signs of the Regression Coefficients

Following the above discussions, Exhibit 1 presents the expected signs of the coefficients of the independent variables considered most relevant for the testing of the two hypotheses about commercial bank asset behavior. These variables are i_s, i_L, and GNP/D.

Exhibit 1 also presents the calculated signs of the regression coefficients. If the calculated t-value of a regression coefficient was not significant at the 5 percent level, a zero value for that coefficient is entered in this table.

An examination of Exhibit 1 reveals that the results of the regression analysis do not support the hypothesis that the factors influencing the demand for bank loans are the primary determinants of bank asset behavior. In neither period is it observed that bank behavior responds in the manner prescribed by the hypothesis that banks passively accommodate the demand for bank credit. However, the results tend to support the hypothesis that bank behavior responds to changes in i_s, i_L, and GNP/D in a manner that is consistent with the hypothesis that banks attempt to manage their asset portfolios in a way that is consistent with a profit maximizing explanation of commercial bank behavior.

In both periods, as the short-term interest rate rises, banks respond by increasing the ratio of loans to deposits. As the long-term interest rate rises, making investments more attractive relative to loans, banks restructure their asset portfolios by reducing the proportion of loans to investments in their portfolios. Lending behavior is not directly related to changes in GNP. These findings are consistent with the profit maximization hypothesis.

In both periods, as the opportunity cost of holding excess reserves increases (i.e., market interest rates rise), we find that banks respond by decreasing their holdings of excess reserves relative to deposits. This behavior is consistent with profit maximization. In the first period the long-term rate of interest is more important than the short-term rate in determining the behavior of ER/D; in the more recent period the roles on the interest rates are reversed and the short-term rate becomes a more important factor in determining changes in ER/D. In the period 1953–1960 our regression results show that GNP/D does not enter as a significant influence on banks' excess reserves to deposit ratio. In the period 1961–1967, GNP/D appears as a significant influence on excess reserve behavior. The positive sign on the coefficient of GNP/D, indicating an increase in excess reserves given an increase in GNP, is clearly not in good agreement with the expected sign under the accommodation hypothesis. However, such a large positive influence on excess reserve behavior is also surprising given the expected sign of the coefficient under the profit maximizing hypothesis of bank asset behavior.

With respect to borrowing behavior, we find that in both periods banks are sensitive to changes in interest rates in a manner consistent with the profit maximization hypothesis. A rise in short-term interest rates in both periods leads to a rise in borrowings by member banks from Reserve banks. Tentatively, these results indicate that banks may not be unaware of the profit opportunities inherent in a situation where the discount rate lags a rise in the short-term rate. In the period 1953–1960, as the discount rate rises, member banks reduce their ratio of borrowings to deposits. In the latter period, 1961–1967, our statistical tests indicate that the coefficient for i_d is not statistically different from zero. This may reflect the development of alternative sources of short-term funds in the more recent period. In neither period do we find that the independent variable GNP/D enters as a significant influence on commercial bank borrowing behavior.

IV. Change in Bank Behavior

Since about 1960, many new developments have occurred in the area of commercial banking. Observers of bank behavior since then have suggested that banks have become more aggressive competitors among themselves and in their relationships with other financial intermediaries. They appear to have become more profit-oriented, i.e., basing to a greater extent than previously their decisions on assets acquired and liabilities offered on cost and yield considerations.

New liability forms have been developed, such as marketable and consumer type CDs. This development suggests that banks have become more willing to compete for funds from many sources on the basis of rates paid. Asset adjustments, when required, appear to be made more on the basis of cost considerations. The development of the Federal funds market has created an important source of short-term funds for banks, and the proposition is frequently advanced that member banks now rely less on borrowing from Reserve banks for short-term adjustment purposes. Banks in their quest for profits have entered into new lending areas such as municipal bonds and mortgages. Recently, bank credit cards and a practice similar to overdraft checking have been started. Holdings of U.S. Government securities by banks have reached a low level.

The Federal Reserve System has also altered the economic environment of commercial banking. Open-market transactions since 1960 have been conducive to fairly long periods of quite uniform rates of expansion in bank credit and money. Furthermore, the period since 1960 has been characterized by a general economic expansion only interrupted by two mild plateaus, the first in 1962 and the second in the first half of 1967.

In response to these developments, economists have speculated about the impact of this new environment on commercial bank behavior regarding their holdings of excess reserves borrowing from Reserve banks, and acquisition of loans and investments. Such changes in bank behavior would involve shifts in functions and changes in the shapes of the functions.

Testing for Changes in Bank Behavior   Evidence presented in Table 1 is consistent with the view that a significant change in bank behavior has occurred. The Chow test, as mentioned previously, indicates that the set of parameters estimated for 1961–1967 are significantly different from those estimated for 1953–1960.

With regard to borrowing behavior, there was a downward shift in the function but no change in its shape. The intercept changed from $-.715$ to -14.660. Application of the test for differences in parameters of the independent variables indicates that there is no statistical significant difference for any of these parameters between the two periods. The downward shift in the borrowing function is consistent with the proposition that the development of the Federal funds market and the increased use of time deposits as sources of funds have led to a decreased preference for borrowing from Reserve banks as a source of funds.

The regression results for excess reserve behavior indicate both a downward shift in the function and a change in its shape. Its intercept changed from .131 to

— 10.704. There was a statistically significant change in the parameters for i_s, GNP/D, and the lagged ratio. The downward shift is consistent with a lower preference for excess reserves as a buffer stock as a result of the development of the newer sources of adjustment funds discussed under borrowing behavior. The elasticity of excess reserves to i_s increased from − .103 to − 1.246; this is consistent with the proposition that banks have become more sensitive to the opportunity cost of holding excess reserves. The change in the coefficient for the lagged ratio indicates that in the latter period there was almost instantaneous adjustment to a discrepancy between desired and actual excess reserves, compared with a much longer adjustment period earlier. The coefficient for GNP/D also changed, but no explanation is offered here.

Bank lending behavior also underwent a marked change between the two periods. The intercept decreased from .702 to − .038. One explanation of this downward shift is the expansion of bank participation in the growing municipal bond market. The adjustment period decreased moderately, as indicated by the decrease in the coefficient for the lagged ratio. In the first period the coefficient for the discount rate is significant, but in the period 1961-1967 the coefficient for i_d is not statistically significant. The negative sign on the coefficient for i_d in the first period indicating a rise (fall) in L/D given a decline (increase) in i_d is consistent with a profit maximizing explanation of bank behavior. In the period 1961-1967, the absence of a significant effect of i_d on L/D may reflect, as discussed earlier, the institutional change reflected in the development of the Federal funds market.

REFERENCES

LEONALL C. ANDERSEN. "A Study of Factors Affecting the Money Stock: Phase One," *Staff Economic Studies,* Washington, D.C.: Board of Governors of the Federal Reserve System, October, 1965.

ALBERT E. BURGER and LEONALL C. ANDERSEN. "The Development of Explanatory Economic Hypotheses for Monetary Management," *Southern Journal of Business* (forthcoming).

FRANK DE LEEUW and EDWARD GRAMLICH. "The Federal Reserve-M.I.T Econometric Model: Its Special Features," *American Economic Review,* May, 1968, pp. 123-149.

PETER FROST. *Bank's Demand for Excess Reserves,* unpublished dissertation—UCLA, 1966, University Microfilms: Ann Arbor, pp. XIV-XV, 279-287.

STEPHEN GOLDFELD. *Commercial Bank Behavior and Economic Activity: A Structural Study of Monetary Policy in the Postwar United States,* Amsterdam: New Holland Publishing Company, 1966.

STEPHEN GOLDFELD and EDWARD KANE. "Determinants of Member Bank Borrowing: An Econometric Study," *Journal of Finance,* September, 1966, pp. 499-514.

CLIFTON B. LUTTRELL. "Member Bank Borrowing: Its Origin and Function," *Quarterly Review of Economics and Business,* Bureau of Economic and Business Research, University of Illinois, Autumn, 1968, pp. 55-65.

MURRAY E. POLOKOFF and WILLIAM E. SILBER. "Reluctance and Member Bank Borrowing: Additional Evidence," *Journal of Finance,* March, 1967, pp. 88-92.

ROBERT RASCHE and HAROLD SHAPIRO. "The Federal Reserve-M.I.T. Econometric Model: Its Special Features," *American Economic Review,* May, 1968, pp. 123-149.

A Note on Liquidity Management

Thomas M. Havrilesky
John T. Boorman

2

There are two basic aspects to bank balance sheet management. One aspect is that assets are managed with explicit recognition of the relationship between risk, rate of return, and liquidity. The other is that the type of financial intermediation carried out by a commercial bank encourages it to give considerable attention to liability management. Specifically, in order to meet customer loan demands and satisfy liquidity needs, a bank can attract funds from a wide spectrum of sources. A useful way to view this process is to see the bank as attracting funds from deposit and other sources until the marginal cost of attracting those funds (marginal cost includes interest, advertising, and service charges borne by the bank) is equal to the marginal return on investments (this marginal return is adjusted downward to reflect legal reserve requirements, if any, on each source of funds). With the total level of funds so determined and the optimal scale of bank operations thus derived, management would allocate funds across alternative classes of loans and investments until their respective marginal returns were equal. This is the neoclassical model of bank behavior.[1]

Reprinted, with revisions, from Thomas M. Havrilesky and John T. Boorman, *Monetary Macroeconomics* (Arlington Heights: AHM Publishing Corp., 1978), pp. 83–86.

[1]The neoclassical approach is only one of several possible analytical frameworks that may be used to model bank behavior. Examples of neoclassical models of bank behavior, aside from this note, include John H. Wood, *Commercial Bank Loan and Investment Behavior* (New York: John Wiley and Sons, 1975), and, at a simplified level, Thomas M. Havrilesky and John T. Boorman, *Monetary Macroeconomics* (Arlington Heights: AHM Publishing Corp., 1978), Appendix to Chapter 3. Tradi-

In this note we present a simple neoclassical model of banking liquidity management. Profit maximization is assumed to be the goal of bank management, with the present net worth, loans, and deposits of the bank assumed given over its short-term planning period.[2]

We assume the following balance sheet:

$$\bar{L} + V_s + \bar{RR} + FF = \bar{DD} + \bar{TD} + \bar{NW} \tag{1}$$

where $\bar{L}$ = loans, V_s = short-term government securities, $\bar{RR}$ = required reserves, FF = Federal funds borrowing, $\bar{DD}$ = demand deposits, $\bar{TD}$ = time deposits, and $\bar{NW}$ = net worth. (A bar over a variable indicates that it is given at the beginning of the period.)

We assume that required reserves are fixed proportions ϱ of demand deposits and b of time deposits:

$$RR = \varrho DD + bTD, \qquad 0 < \varrho, b < 1. \tag{2}$$

The legal reserve requirement is an important constraint on bank portfolio management because it requires a bank to hold a certain amount of its assets in a nonearning form.

Other important constraints on bank management have to do with the volatility of deposit shifts and currency withdrawals and variations in customer loan demand. These random factors lead to expected cash drains that determine the bank's short-term liquidity needs. In a more sophisticated model we could assume that there exists a probability distribution of expected cash drains and that the cost associated with an expected level of cash drains rises with the level of deposits and falls with the level of reserves. In such a model there could be implicit and explicit costs to the bank that vary directly with expected cash drains. Explicit costs might include the penalty rate at which banks with reserve deficiencies can borrow reserves from the Federal Reserve. Implicit costs might include the "embarrassment" felt at borrowing from the Fed.[3] However, in the present case our model will be a bit simpler.

Short-term liquidity management is viewed as an ongoing process that occurs *within* the context of an intermediate-term planning period. Expected cash drains that arise from expected deposit shifts and currency withdrawals and from expected variations in loan repayments and loan demand determine a bank's liquidity needs.

tionally, bank asset management was conceived as a portfolio-theoretic problem. This mode of analysis is still useful. See Leonall C. Andersen and Albert E. Burger, "Asset Management and Commercial Bank Portfolio Behavior: Theory and Practice," *Journal of Finance*, Vol. 24, No. 2 (May 1969), pp. 207–22. More recently, linear programming models have been applied to bank asset as well as bank balance sheet management. See Alfred Broaddus, "Linear Programming: A New Approach to Bank Portfolio Management," Federal Reserve Bank of Richmond, *Monthly Review* (November 1972). Editor's note: Each of these articles is reprinted in this section.

[2]Longer term balance sheet management will not be considered.

[3]See Michael Klein, "A Theory of the Banking Firm," *Journal of Money Credit and Banking*, May 1971, pp. 205–18.

The bank then satisfies its net short-term liquidity needs from the multiplicity of sources: excess reserve balances, Federal funds purchases, borrowing from the Fed, offerings of short-term negotiable CDs, issues of bank-related commercial paper, Eurodollar borrowing, and the sale of short-term Treasury bills. Net liquidity needs are met from each source until the rising marginal cost of obtaining liquidity from each source is equal to the (fixed) penalty cost, including all implicit costs perceived by the borrowing bank, at which the bank borrows from the Fed.

A highly simplified model of short-term liquidity management might be sketched as follows: Assume that expected cash needs vary in direct proportion to the level of demand deposits and the level of time deposits. Let these factors of proportionality be α and β, respectively. Assume further that expected cash needs also vary proportionately with the level of loans by a factor γ. The *gross* liquidity needs of the banking firm Q_g are therefore

$$Q_g = \alpha \cdot \overline{DD} + \beta \cdot \overline{TD} + \gamma \cdot \overline{L}, \tag{3}$$

where the bars indicate intermediate-term equilibrium values.

Assume for simplicity that instead of the wide array of sources of liquidity cited above, there are only three: required reserves, RR; short-term government securities, V_s; and Federal funds purchases, FF. Thus the *sources* of the banking firm's gross liquidity are

$$Q_g = RR + V_s + FF. \tag{4}$$

As required reserves are defined in Equation (2), we may substitute Equation (2) into Equation (4) and the result to Equation (3). Rearranging allows us to equate *net* liquidity needs, Q_n, to the means by which these net needs may be met.

$$Q_n = \overline{DD} \cdot (\alpha - \varrho) + \overline{TD} \cdot (\beta - b) + \overline{L} \cdot \gamma = V_s + FF. \tag{5}$$

Net liquidity needs may be met either by the bank's selling short-term securities, V_s, or by its borrowing in the Federal funds market, FF. A short-run optimum position is obtained where the increasing marginal (interest-opportunity and transactions) cost of selling securities is equal to the given rate at which Federal funds may be borrowed. If considerable liquidity is needed for only a few days, it might be quite costly to sell (and then repurchase) short-term securities. Conversely, if funds were needed for a longer period, repeated Federal funds borrowing might be more costly than the sale of short-term securities.[4]

Within an intermediate-term planning period there are a number of short-term planning periods. Deposit and customer loan variability and the various interest rates will change between short-run periods. Thus, for example, the bank could be a lender of Federal funds and a purchaser of short-term securities in one short-term

[4]See Donald DePamphilis, "A Microeconomic Econometric Analysis of the Short-Term Commercial Bank Adjustment Process," Federal Reserve Bank of Boston, *Research Report* 55 (April 1974).

period and a borrower of Federal funds and a seller of short-term securities in another.

The distinction between short-term and long-term planning periods is an artificial one, but it has the advantage of simplifying our discussion. In reality, the bank's balance sheet undergoes a dynamic adjustment to shocks. For example, if a bank is successful at increasing its level of deposits, it may first hold excess reserves and then loan out these reserves in the Federal funds market. Next, if the new level of deposits persists, it may purchase short-term securities. Finally, if in the intermediate term it regards these deposits as secure, it may fully adjust its portfolio by increasing its loans.[5]

To describe the pattern of short-run adjustments more specifically would require a model that is richer in detail (see footnote 4). Such a task is beyond the scope of this note.

[5]The process of dynamic portfolio-theoretic adjustment to exogenous forecasted changes in deposits using a variety of estimation techniques is dealt with in Donald D. Hester and James L. Pierce, *Bank Management and Portfolio Behavior* (New Haven: Yale University Press, 1975).

Federal Funds and
Repurchase Agreements

Charles M. Lucas
Marcos T. Jones
Thom B. Thurston

3

The markets for Federal funds and repurchase agreements (RPs) are among the most important financial markets in the United States. Using these instruments, many banks, large corporations, and nonbank financial firms trade large amounts of liquid funds with one another for periods as short as one day. Such institutions provide and use much of the credit made available in the United States and typically manage their financial positions carefully and aggressively. The interest rate on overnight (one day) Federal funds measures the return on the most liquid of all financial assets, and for this reason is critical to investment decisions. That is, financial managers compare this rate to yields on all other investments before choosing the combinations of maturities of the financial assets in which they will invest or the term over which they will borrow.

The Federal funds market is also important because it is related to the conduct of Federal Reserve monetary policy. The interest rate on Federal funds is highly sensitive to Federal Reserve actions that supply reserves to member commercial banks, and the rate influences commercial bank decisions concerning loans to business, individual, and other borrowers. Moreover, interest rates paid on other short-term financial assets—commercial paper and Treasury bills, for example— usually move up or down roughly in parallel with the Federal funds rate. Thus the rate also influences the cost of credit obtained from sources other than commercial banks.

Reprinted, with deletions, from *Quarterly Review,* Summer 1977, pp. 33–48, by permission of the Federal Reserve Bank of New York and the authors.

Frequently, the Federal funds market is described as one in which commercial banks borrow and lend excess reserve balances held at the Federal Reserve, hence the name Federal funds. While banks often use the Federal funds market for this purpose, growth and change in the market have made this description highly oversimplified. Many active market participants do not hold balances at the Federal Reserve. These include commercial banks that are not members of the Federal Reserve System, thrift institutions, certain agencies of the United States government, and branches and agencies of foreign banks operating on United States soil. Moreover, this broad set of market participants borrows and lends amounts far beyond the modest total of excess reserve balances. Currently, borrowings of Federal funds outstanding average $45 billion to $50 billion daily.

A closely related market for short-term funds is the market for RPs involving U.S. government and federal agency securities.[1] This market includes many of the same participants that trade Federal funds, but it also includes large nonfinancial corporations, state and local governments, and dealers in U.S. government and federal agency securities. The RP market has expanded rapidly of late, and its workings are perhaps less widely known than those of the Federal funds market.

Although the Federal funds and RP markets are distinct, they share many common features. Both, for example, primarily involve transactions for one business day, although transactions with maturities of up to several weeks are not uncommon. In both markets, commercial banks that are members of the Federal Reserve System can acquire funds not subject to reserve requirements. A lesser known but nevertheless very important common element is the fact that transactions in both markets are settled in what are known as "immediately available funds." Indeed, some observers see the two markets as so closely related that they might appropriately be grouped together under a broader designation—"the markets for short-term immediately available funds."

The main purpose of this article is to review major recent developments in the markets for Federal funds and RPs. The most significant changes are the dramatic growth of the volume of transactions and of the number and type of institutions active in these markets. At the same time, the language of the market has been changing, mostly because of the evolution in market practices. It is, therefore, necessary to begin with definitions of some terms most frequently used by market participants.

Federal Funds

Federal funds transactions are frequently described as the borrowing and lending of "excess reserve" balances among commercial banks.[2] This description of Federal

---

[1]The term "federal agency" is used here in its popular meaning, which refers both to federal agencies, such as the Commodity Credit Corporation, and to federally sponsored quasi-public corporations, such as the Federal National Mortgage Association.

[2]A fundamental difficulty with this notion of Federal funds borrowing is that the use of the term "excess reserves" is very imprecise. No distinction is made between the actual excess reserves held in a bank's reserve account and what might be called "potential" excess reserves. Clearly, an individual bank can

funds was accurate years ago but is now seriously deficient, even though it still appears in the financial press. While such commercial bank use of the market persists in substantial volume, Federal funds transactions are no longer confined to the borrowing and lending of excess reserve balances. Moreover—and this is a key point—a Federal funds transaction does not necessarily involve transfer of a reserve balance, even though such a transfer usually does occur. For example, a commercial bank can borrow the "correspondent balances" held with it by other banks. The execution of such a transaction involves only accounting entries on the books of both the borrower and lender.

The most useful description of Federal funds has several elements, some based on regulations, others simply on market convention. In practice, Federal funds are overnight loans that are settled in immediately available funds. Only a limited group of institutions are in a position to borrow in this fashion, mostly commercial banks and some other financial institutions such as agencies of foreign banks. If a member bank borrows Federal funds, Federal Reserve regulations do not require it to hold reserves against the borrowing, as it must for funds acquired in the form of demand or time deposits. But, under Federal Reserve regulations, member banks are permitted to borrow reserve-free funds only from a certain group of institutions. This group includes other commercial banks, federal agencies, savings and loan associations, mutual savings banks, domestic agencies and branches of foreign banks, and, to a limited degree, government securities dealers. Market convention has adjusted to these regulatory restrictions, and a Federal funds borrowing has come to mean an overnight loan not just between two commercial banks but between any two of the group of institutions from which member banks may borrow free of reserve requirements. A savings and loan association, for example, can lend Federal funds to an agency of a foreign bank.

This description makes it easy to see that the Federal funds market is by no means limited to the lending of excess reserves. Many of the institutions that participate in the market are not members of the Federal Reserve System and, therefore, do not have reserve accounts. Moreover, the excess reserves of individual member banks are normally very small in relation to their total reserves. The excess reserves characterization of Federal funds borrowing suggests that total activity in the market is likewise rather modest. While this was once true, it no longer is. In recent years, daily outstanding borrowings by member banks in the Federal funds market have approached $50 billion, or about 40 percent more than the *total* reserves they hold. Some individual banks continually borrow as much as four times their required reserves in the Federal funds market.

Fairly recently, banks have begun to borrow immediately available funds for periods longer than a single business day. This form of borrowing was developed by agencies of Canadian banks located in the United States. The transactions are arranged among the same institutions which participate in the overnight market and

---

control the amount of excess reserves it has available to sell in the Federal funds market most easily by selling assets and converting the proceeds into balances at a Federal Reserve Bank. In this sense, the potential excess reserves of an individual bank are nearly as large as its total earning asset portfolio.

are similar in all respects except maturity. For these reasons, the transactions have come to be called "term Federal funds" transactions.

The Federal funds and term Federal funds transactions described above are normally "unsecured." This means that the lending institutions have no guarantee of repayment other than the promise of the borrower. For this reason, unsecured Federal funds transactions are done only by institutions that enjoy a very high degree of mutual confidence. At times, however, a lender of Federal funds will ask that the transaction be "secured." This means that the borrower must pledge an asset, usually a government or federal agency security, as "collateral" against the loan. The borrower may either set aside the collateral in a custody account or actually deliver it to the lender. However, secured Federal funds transactions are not very common.[3]

Repurchase Agreements

A repurchase agreement (RP) is an acquisition of immediately available funds through the sale of securities, together with a simultaneous agreement to repurchase them at a later date. RPs are most commonly made for one business day, though longer maturities are also frequent. The funds that a member bank acquires in this manner are free of reserve requirements so long as the securities involved are those of the U.S. government or federal agencies. When an RP is arranged, the acquirer of funds agrees to sell to the provider of funds U.S. government or federal agency securities in exchange for immediately available funds. At the maturity of the agreement, the transaction is reversed, again using immediately available funds. Market insiders use different terms to describe the RP, including "repo" and "buy back."

Those who supply or acquire funds view RPs as involving little risk. Transactions are usually arranged only among institutions enjoying a high degree of confidence in one another. In addition, contracts are usually of very short maturity. Protection against any residual risk can be incorporated in an RP contract by establishing a differential—called a margin—between the quantity of funds supplied and the market value of the securities involved. The margin can protect either party to the transaction, but not both. It protects the supplier of funds if the value of the securities exceeds the quantity of funds supplied. It protects the taker of funds if the securities are of less value than the amount of funds supplied. The supplier of funds generally considers the consequences of default by the other party to be minor, because the securities acquired are obligations either issued or guaranteed by the federal government. Another element of risk arises from the possibility that the price of the securities may fall between the time the RP is arranged and the time of any default. For this reason, the margin is most often set to protect the supplier of funds.

---

[3]Banks chartered in certain states face regulations that require collateral to be provided for the portion of an individual Federal funds transaction in excess of some proportion of the lender's combined capital and surplus.

This article is concerned with RPs involving only U.S. government and federal agency securities, but it should be noted in passing that an RP can involve any sort of asset which the supplier of funds is willing to accept. RPs involving other assets are executed to a limited degree, for example using certificates of deposit of large banks.

Transactions are executed in several ways, but two approaches are most common. One approach is for the securities to be both sold and repurchased at the same price, with charges representing the agreed-upon rate of return added to the principal at the maturity of the contract. The second approach involves setting a higher price for repayment than for selling.

The term "reverse repurchase agreement" is sometimes thought to be quite different from an RP. In fact, it refers to exactly the same transaction viewed from the perspective of the supplier of funds rather than the recipient. Compare the two views of the transaction: The recipient of funds sells a security to obtain funds, and "repurchases" it at maturity by redelivery of funds. In a reverse RP, the supplier of funds buys a security by delivering funds when the agreement is made and "resells" the security for immediately available funds on maturity of the contract. From the perspective of the party acquiring funds, the term "repurchase agreement" seems apt, and from that of the supplier of funds, the transaction is exactly the "reverse." However, whether funds are acquired or supplied, the transaction is usually referred to in the marketplace simply as an RP.

The Markets for Federal Funds and RPs

There is no central physical marketplace for Federal funds; the market consists of a loosely structured telephone network connecting the major participants. These participants, as already mentioned, include commercial banks and those other financial institutions from which, under Federal Reserve regulations, member banks can buy reserve-free Federal funds. The market also includes a small group of firms that act as brokers for Federal funds. These firms neither lend nor borrow but arrange transactions between borrowers and lenders in exchange for a very small percentage commission.

All major participants employ traders. These individuals make the actual telephone contact on behalf of lending or borrowing institutions, making offers to borrow or lend at specific interest rates. They also negotiate any differences between the rate bid by a borrower and that offered by a lender. Transactions are usually executed in lots of $1 million or more. Frequently, but not always, settlement of the transaction requires transfer of funds over the Federal Reserve wire transfer network, first when the agreement is reached and again the next day when repayment is made.

Many banks, particularly medium-sized and large ones, frequently borrow and lend Federal funds on the same day, thereby performing an intermediary function in the Federal funds market. Such banks channel funds from banks with lesser need for funds to banks with greater need for them, frequently borrowing from smaller banks and lending to larger ones. Over the past decade, more medium-sized regional banks have begun to act as intermediaries. In addition, many more banks during this period have come to borrow significantly more than they lend; that is, they have become continual net borrowers.

In recent years a growing portion of the market has consisted of large banks' borrowing of correspondent balances from small banks. Historically, these correspondent balances earned no interest. But both large and small banks have come to regard correspondent relationships as convenient bases for arranging Federal funds transactions. Small banks now intentionally accumulate large balances, selling off daily the excess not needed for the clearing of checks or for other purposes. In such cases, it is not necessary to transfer funds over the Federal Reserve wire transfer network, and reserve balances need not change ownership. Rather, bookkeeping entries are posted by both the borrower and lender to reflect the fact that a noninterest-bearing correspondent demand balance has been converted into a Federal funds borrowing.

No central physical marketplace for repurchase agreements exists either. Transactions are arranged by telephone, largely on a direct basis between the parties supplying and acquiring funds but increasingly through a small group of market specialists. These specialists, mostly government securities dealers, arrange a repurchase agreement with one party to acquire funds and a reverse repurchase agreement with another party to supply funds. They earn a profit by acquiring funds more cheaply than they supply them.

Large banks and government securities dealers are the primary seekers of funds in the RP market. Banks use the market as one among many sources of funds, but have a distinct advantage over other institutions as acquirers of funds because they hold large portfolios of U.S. government and federal agency securities. Moreover, because the supplier of funds receives securities, and because member banks acquiring funds need not hold reserves against RPs regardless of the source of funds, the RP market attracts a wider array of participants than does the Federal funds market. Government securities dealers use the market as a source of funds to finance their holdings of government and agency securities. Many types of institutions supply immediately available funds in this market, but large nonfinancial corporations and state and local governments dominate.

Typically, participants on both sides of the RP market have lists of customers with whom they routinely do business. Each of the largest participants uses an "RP trader," an individual whose job it is to contact other traders and to negotiate the best arrangements possible. A trader begins the day with information on the amount of funds he must supply or acquire. His objective is to arrange transactions at the maximum return obtainable if he is to provide funds and at the minimum cost possible if he is to acquire funds.

With these definitions and descriptions in mind, it is possible to discuss in some detail the roles of the major institutional participants in the markets for immediately available funds. It is appropriate to begin with an examination of the role played by commercial banks, who are currently the most important of those who obtain funds in these markets. Moreover, the reserve position adjustments that banks make in the markets for immediately available funds are important links in transmitting the effects of monetary policy throughout the financial system.

Commercial Banks and Immediately Available Funds

Commercial banks are the largest and most active participants in the markets for immediately available funds. Banks use these markets for several purposes, among which is the day-to-day adjustment of reserve positions. Large banks have made such adjustments in the Federal funds market for over fifty years and continue to do so in substantial volume. But commercial bank use of both the Federal funds and the RP markets is best understood in the much broader context of how banks obtain and use funds. In addition, bank operations in the Federal funds and RP markets have been heavily influenced by changes in the regulations that govern bank activities.

The traditional view of banks has been that they accept deposit liabilities from customers and use the funds to lend or invest. In the process, they make a profit by earning more in interest on loans and investments than their cost of operations, including interest they pay on deposits. This approach has undergone significant modification over the past decade at least, particularly at large banks. In place of a passive stance, banks have become active solicitors of funds in the open markets. Moreover, they have developed liabilities in addition to standard demand and savings accounts. Fifteen years ago, for example, banks developed and began to exploit the negotiable certificate of deposit (CD). More recently, Eurodollars, commercial paper issued by bank holding companies, and other instruments have been developed and used as sources of funds. Large banks set a target for the total amount of liabilities they will attempt to secure, basing that target on the total of loans and investments thought to be profitable. The overall approach, summarized here in its barest outlines, is generally known as "liability management."

The spread of the practice of liability management has had two related effects on commercial bank activity in the Federal funds market. First, instead of just engaging in relatively small trades for the purpose of making daily reserve adjustments, today banks may rely on this market to meet a desired proportion of liabilities. Thus, they at times borrow amounts that are large relative to their total assets or liabilities. Second, instead of individual banks lending as often as they borrow, some banks are continual net borrowers, while others are continual lenders. The borrowers use the market both to offset the impact on their reserve holdings of day-to-day inflows and outflows of deposits and as an ongoing source of funds to finance loans and investments. The lenders, usually smaller banks, treat Federal funds as a highly liquid interest-earning short-term asset.

Origins of the Federal Funds Market

Commercial banks were entirely responsible for the origination and early development of the Federal funds market. The market began among a small number of
New York City banks in the early 1920s. Some banks frequently found themselves
in reserve deficit positions and, therefore, were forced to borrow from the Federal
Reserve discount window. Others frequently had unanticipated excess reserve holdings, and these balances did not earn any interest. Under these circumstances, an
obvious opportunity for mutual benefit existed, and bank managers devised a
mechanism to realize these benefits. They exchanged drafts drawn on Federal
Reserve balances and so created the Federal funds market. A lending bank made
payment by delivering a draft on the day a borrowing was arranged. Such drafts,
in contrast to a common check, could be collected on the day they were presented
to the Federal Reserve. To accomplish the repayment, the borrowing bank gave a
clearinghouse check made out to the lender to be collected the following day. The
repayment check was for a slightly larger sum to reflect the interest due.

This practice spread to other cities in subsequent years, but the amounts traded
remained small, and the markets remained largely confined to local areas. Only
large banks participated in the market, and transactions were undertaken only to
adjust for relatively small deficits or excesses in reserves. Many individual banks
found that they were able to lend in the market one day, but had to borrow the
next.

Toward the end of the 1920s, the market began to expand to include interregional
as well as intracity transactions. Trading of funds between regions was made possible by the Federal Reserve wire transfer facilities, which permitted the movements of
funds from one city to another without the use of drafts. By this time, daily borrowing reached about $250 million. With the 1929 stock market crash and the ensuing
depression, however, interest rates fell substantially and banks developed a strong
preference for holding cash, reflected in large holdings of excess reserves. These
developments cut short the growth of the Federal funds market, but the brief appearance of wire trading of Federal funds in the late 1920s set the stage for rapid
development of the market after World War II.

Federal Funds in the Postwar Era

In the three decades since the end of World War II, the Federal funds market has
changed in at least two fundamental respects. First, both the number of banks participating in the market and aggregate trading volume in Federal funds have grown
enormously. Second, most large banks, which formerly alternated between borrowing and lending, have become continual net borrowers, while small banks not
previously active in the market have entered the market, primarily as continual
lenders.

The changing role of the large banks is evidence that liability management has been added to daily reserve position adjustment as a motive for participation in the Federal funds market. A continuous and steady supply of funds is available to large banks once they have established market contacts with sellers. As a result, Federal funds have become an important source of liabilities because of their availability and the low cost of executing transactions over the Federal Reserve wire network, and because these funds are not subject to reserve requirements or interest rate ceilings.

Smaller banks have been introduced to the market primarily through correspondent relationships with large banks. Immediately after World War II, small banks held relatively large amounts of their assets in cash. The practice was understandable at that time, because interest rates were very low and because a high value was placed on liquidity due to the vivid memories of the prewar depression. Interest rates began to rise in the 1950s, however, increasing the interest earnings foregone by holding large amounts of cash. With large banks willing to borrow and interest rates rising, a few small banks began to lend their cash balances to large banks in the form of Federal funds. Such overnight lending provided virtually the same liquidity as cash.

By the early 1960s, banks of all sizes and types had become familiar with the advantages of participation in the Federal funds market. Two major rulings by bank regulators in these years also served to encourage trading of Federal funds.

In 1963, the Comptroller of the Currency issued rulings that eliminated restrictions on the amounts that a nationally chartered bank could lend to any one bank. Formerly, unsecured lending to a single borrower in Federal funds had been restricted to 10 percent of the lending bank's combined capital and surplus. Though this limit applied to all nationally chartered banks, it effectively restricted the activities only of the small banks in this group. The 1963 ruling declared Federal funds transactions to be purchases and sales, not borrowings and lendings. In so ruling, the Comptroller effectively removed the restrictions that had kept small banks from placing relatively large amounts of funds in the Federal funds market.

In 1964, a ruling by the Federal Reserve Board made it clear that member banks could legally purchase correspondent balances of nonmember banks as Federal funds. Prior to this ruling, the practice of purchasing correspondent balances had not been as widespread.

Together these rulings served to encourage the sale of Federal funds by small banks, and to reinforce the spread of liability management techniques among large correspondent banks. Small banks were now in a position to ask their correspondents to engage in Federal funds transactions under the threat that their funds would otherwise be moved to a competitor. Faced with a potential loss of balances, large correspondent banks began to buy Federal funds regularly in large amounts from small banks.

The net purchases of Federal funds by large commercial banks have increased enormously since the regulatory changes. . . . Spurts of rapid growth in this market have generally taken place during periods when short-term interest rates were either rising rapidly or at high levels. The Federal funds rate . . . has reached several postwar peaks in the last fifteen years. At such times, large banks sought funds most aggressively. They put considerable effort into developing new correspondent relationships and into attracting larger amounts of funds from existing ones. Smaller banks were induced to increase their lending by the high interest rates offered. The volume of funds traded in the market declined somewhat during periods of lower short-term interest rates, but once developed, the correspondent relationships have tended to remain active.

The rapid postwar development of the Federal funds market led to a reversal in 1965 of the long-standing relationship between the Federal funds rate and the Federal Reserve discount rate. Prior to that time, the discount rate had served as an effective ceiling on the Federal funds rate. This was because many banks borrowed Federal funds only occasionally and in relatively small amounts, and were therefore able to accomplish such short-term adjustments at the discount window as an alternative to Federal funds borrowing. This use of the discount window occurred whenever the Federal funds rate approached the discount rate. As banks turned to the discount window, demand for Federal funds diminished, and upward rate pressures slackened.

With the rise in liability management practices in the early 1960s, banks borrowed Federal funds more frequently and in larger amounts. Such borrowing could not be done at the discount window, which has always been available only for short-term adjustments by individual banks. As a result, banks using the Federal funds market for liability management purposes continued bidding for Federal funds as the rate rose to and exceeded the discount rate. This happened for the first time in 1965, when tightening monetary policy pushed the Federal funds rate upward. The Federal funds rate has been above the discount rate for much of the period since.

Another significant change in the market came in 1970. Federal Reserve Regulation D, which specifies those deposits of member banks that are subject to reserve requirements, had previously exempted Federal funds borrowing from reserve requirements so long as the lender was a commercial bank. An amendment to the regulation, along with a formal interpretation, extended the exemption to several other types of nonbank institutions, including agencies of the U.S. government, savings and loan associations, mutual savings banks, as well as agencies and branches of foreign banks operating in this country. By 1970, some banks had already begun to borrow Federal funds from these nonbank institutions, and the regulatory change removed any doubt that the practice was acceptable. This change was particularly important, for it provided explicit regulatory approval for banks to borrow Federal funds from selected lenders outside the banking community, just as banks do by issuing CDs, demand deposits, or any other type of liability.

Commercial banks are able to obtain immediately available funds through repurchase agreements as well as through Federal funds transactions. The growth of RP activity by commercial banks, like that of Federal funds, has been influenced by regulatory changes. In 1969, Federal Reserve Regulation D was amended to restrict the exemption from reserve requirements only to those funds raised through RPs involving U.S. government or federal agency securities. This action practically eliminated bank trading in those RPs which involve other sorts of financial claims. At the same time, however, it removed any question about the status of RPs involving government securities.

Recent Developments in the Banking Sector

Some rather dramatic events occurred in the markets for immediately available funds beginning in 1973. Monetary policy was tightened that year in response to rapid inflation and a booming economy. The tightening placed severe pressure on the banking system—which had a limited supply of funds and faced strong demand for loans, particularly from businesses. Under these circumstances, banks with a strong liability management orientation turned to any and all potential sources of funds. In early 1973, large banks began to borrow heavily in the CD market. This borrowing was facilitated by the suspension in May 1973 of interest rate ceilings on all maturities of large denomination CDs. From early 1973 through mid–1974, CD borrowing jumped by about $38 billion. Large banks sought short-term open market funds to meet loan demands much more heavily than before, taking in about $18 billion of additional Federal funds and RPs during the same period.

The United States economy went through a sharp recession between late 1973 and early 1975. Demand for credit from commercial banks as well as other lenders remained strong for a time, but progressively weakened through the later stages of the downslide and into the recovery which began in mid-1975. With loans contracting, large banks gradually reduced their lending rates and also sought liabilities with lessened intensity. Their CDs dropped sharply, falling by $28 billion between early 1975 and late 1976. Commercial bank acquisition of Federal funds and RPs, however, did not follow the pattern set in the CD market. Holdings of these funds declined by only about $4 billion in late 1974 and 1975, then grew by about $17 billion in 1976. This reflected a continuing basic growth of the markets for Federal funds and RPs.

The basic growth also was manifest in the continuing entry of banks into the markets for immediately available funds. Call reports of member banks of the Federal Reserve System show that in 1969 about 55 percent of all member banks either bought or sold Federal funds. By 1976, the proportion of member banks that was in the market had climbed to 88 percent. Most of the new entrants to the market were small banks.

Thus, even in the early 1970s many commercial banks were newcomers to the markets for immediately available funds. These markets broadened and deepened in stages which typically occurred in periods of high interest rates. The concentration of entry in such periods is due at least partially to sizable start-up expenditures for trading in immediately available funds. Start-up costs are incurred mostly by borrowers, and mainly involve expenses of finding and establishing a trading relationship with potential suppliers of funds. The expenditures are more easily justified when interest rates (and potential earnings) are high. Once established, trading relationships tend to remain active even after interest rates fall.

Other developments also contributed to the greater acquisition of Federal funds and RPs by banks during 1975 and 1976. In 1974, the Treasury changed the way it handled its deposits at commercial banks (tax and loan accounts). Such accounts had been held at banks for decades. Beginning in August 1974, however, most of these balances were transferred to the twelve Federal Reserve Banks. This reduced the volume of government and agency securities that commercial banks were required to hold as pledged collateral against Treasury deposits. Once free from this purpose, these securities were available for use in the market for repurchase agreements.

With loan demand light in 1975, commercial banks began to accumulate large amounts of additional government and agency securities. The process was significantly aided by the large amounts of new government securities the Treasury sold in order to finance the sizable deficits the federal government was running. These securities were heavily used by large banks to acquire funds in repurchase agreements since they could be financed in this way at a cost below their interest yield. At about the same time, the effects of the recession led corporations to reduce inventories and expenditures for fixed plant and equipment. This enabled corporations to begin to rebuild their liquidity, partly through the purchase of government securities and also by supplying funds to the RP market. The use of RPs grew rapidly as corporations increasingly came to view repurchase agreements as income-generating substitutes for demand deposits at commercial banks.

Quite separately, small banks and nonbank financial institutions were also increasing their offerings of immediately available funds. Both types of institutions experienced a decline in loan demand from corporate and other borrowers with the onset of the recession. But individuals stepped up their savings in the form of deposits with small banks and with nonbank thrift institutions. With increasing deposit inflows and declining demand for loans, these institutions looked for alternative investments and became active suppliers of immediately available funds.

The Role of Government Securities Dealers

Government securities dealers are the second major group of participants active in the markets for immediately available funds. Dealers are in the markets primarily to acquire funds, but they also supply funds under some circumstances. In some ways dealers act as financial intermediaries, but their operations also have speculative features. Dealers earn income in two ways: "carry income" and "trading profits." Carry income (or loss) refers to the difference between the interest yield of a dealer's portfolio and the cost of the funds which support that portfolio. Trading profits refer to the gain (or loss) a dealer earns by selling securities for more (or less) than he paid for them.

Government securities dealers often hold sizable positions in U.S. government and federal agency securities. These positions are highly leveraged in that the dealers borrow a very high percentage of the cost of purchasing securities. The search for low cost money to finance his position is a central part of the operations of any successful government securities dealer. This search led the dealer community to promote the use of the repurchase agreement shortly after World War II. RPs were offered mainly to large corporations, which found them attractive because the short maturities of the RP contracts made them much like demand deposits, with the added advantage of earning income. The use of RPs by dealers has expanded ever since, in part because more corporations and others have come to accept the repurchase agreement as a reliable short-term money market instrument. Dealers have also come to vary the size of their positions much more than before, in response to the greater variability of interest rates and securities prices in recent years. These larger swings in position . . . have been accompanied by higher average positions, which in turn have contributed to the increased use of RPs by dealers.

Because of greater interest rate variability, and in an effort to broaden their activities, government securities dealers have developed new trading techniques and expanded the use of others. One of the greatly expanded techniques enables dealers to act essentially as brokers in the RP markets. They obtain funds in exchange for securities in one transaction and simultaneously release funds in exchange for securities in a separate transaction. When the maturities of the two transactions— one a repurchase agreement and the other a reverse repurchase agreement—are identical, the two are said to be "matched." The dealer profits by obtaining funds at a cost slightly lower than the return he receives for the funds he supplies. After arranging such a pair of transactions, a dealer is exposed to credit risk (the possibility of default), but not to market risk (changes in the value of the portfolio due to changes in market prices).

A commonly used variant of the "matched" agreement gives the dealer greater opportunity to try to take advantage of movements in interest rates. A dealer may deliberately not "match" the maturity of an RP with the maturity of a reverse RP. Usually the RP is for a period shorter than the reverse RP, establishing what is called a "tail." The "tail" refers to the difference in the maturities of the two transactions. If during this period the dealer is able to refinance the reverse RP with an RP at a lower cost, he makes a profit; if not, he loses money.

Another use of the reverse RP has been developed more recently. Reverse RPs are now used frequently to facilitate "short sales" of government and federal agency securities.[4] In the past, dealers wishing to establish such positions had to borrow securities from commercial banks, usually at an interest fee of 50 basis points ($\frac{1}{2}$ percent). Now dealers often acquire securities elsewhere under reverse RPs and frequently through this device reduce the cost of obtaining securities for the purpose of short sales.

Use of the reverse RP to facilitate the short sale has led to the appearance of a new

---

[4]The dealer does not own the securities that he promises to deliver in a short sale. He "covers" the short by buying in the open market the particular security he has promised to deliver. Trading profits can be earned during periods of falling securities prices if the securities that were sold short become available at below-contract prices prior to the agreed-upon delivery date.

subsector of the repurchase agreement market, known as the "specific issue market." The subsector has developed because, for purposes of a short sale, a dealer tries to obtain the exact issue whose price he expects to fall. In a usual reverse RP, the specific securities to be exchanged are rarely discussed (though their maturity should exceed that of the reverse RP), since the parties to the agreement are primarily concerned with the cost of the money involved. The placement of securities in the specific issue market is advantageous for both principals to the transaction. Since it is apparent that the dealer is interested in a particular issue, the holder of the securities is able to negotiate with the dealer and can often get funds at a slightly lower cost than if he were to place the securities in the overall RP market.

Corporations and the RP Market

Up to this point, the analysis has concentrated on the major demanders of Federal funds and RPs. The discussion of major nonbank suppliers begins with nonfinancial corporations. They have been supplying funds through RPs against government and agency securities for about thirty years.

The principal reason corporations hold cash and other short-term liquid assets is to bridge timing gaps between receipts and expenditures. Large quantities of funds are accumulated in anticipation of payments for dividends, corporate taxes, payrolls, and other regular expenses. In addition, corporations also accumulate short-term liquid assets in anticipation of expenditures for plant and equipment. In general, corporate liquidity is related to economic conditions and expectations about the future course of the economy and interest rates. Liquidity is often low—i.e., corporations have small amounts of liquid assets and large amounts of short-term borrowing—in periods of rapid economic expansion. Liquidity is rebuilt by reducing short-term borrowings and acquiring liquid assets during an economic slowdown or the early stages of an expansion.

Corporations have traditionally held significant amounts of their liquid assets in the form of demand deposits at commercial banks. Such balances have not earned interest since 1933, but this was not of great significance during the low interest rate periods of the depression and just after World War II. Interest rates began to climb in the late 1950s, and the higher rates have had a significant impact on how corporations handle their liquidity positions. They constituted an inducement to develop "cash management" techniques in some ways parallel to the "liability management" techniques adopted by banks during the same period. Cash management consists of a variety of procedures designed to achieve four goals: to speed up the receipt of payments due; to slow down the disbursement of payments owed; to keep a corporation's demand deposits to a minimum because they earn no interest; and to earn the maximum return on liquid asset holdings.

Repurchase agreements are particularly useful as tools of cash management. They generate income for the supplier of funds and are generally regarded as secure. Their key advantage is flexibility, primarily because they can be arranged for periods as short as one day. Few if any other income-generating assets have this feature. Regulations prevent banks from issuing CDs with maturities of less than thirty days; commercial paper and bankers' acceptances can be obtained for shorter periods, but as a practical matter not for one day. None of these instruments are viewed as being quite as secure as repurchase agreements, where there is a margin between the amount of funds supplied and the value of the securities. Corporations can buy government securities or other financial assets and hold them for short periods, but the transaction costs can be relatively high and the possibility of capital loss reduces the attractiveness of such alternatives. The overnight feature of RPs means that corporations treat them as if they are income-earning demand deposits.

Corporations make heavy use of a particular form of RP known as the "continuing contract." Under such a contract, a corporation will agree to provide a specific volume of funds to a bank or a dealer for a certain period of time. However, during the life of the contract the repurchase agreement is treated almost as if it were reestablished each day. That is, earnings are calculated daily, often related to the prevailing overnight RP rate. Either party has the right to withdraw at any time, although this right is seldom used. The principal advantage of the continuing contract over the daily renewals of an RP is that securities and funds are exchanged only at the beginning and at the end of the contract. The continuing contract therefore significantly reduces transactions costs, compared with daily RPs. An additional feature of the continuing contract RP is the seller's right of substitution, under which securities of equal value may be used to replace those originally involved in the RP. This option does not appear in all continuing contracts but, where it does appear, it is frequently exercised.

Another RP arrangement rather similar to the continuing contract specifies neither a definite period nor a fixed amount. Arrangements are made by banks chiefly for their corporate customers. The corporation concentrates all its demand balances in a single account at that bank daily. Before the bank closes its books each day, the corporation's balance in this account is determined, and any excess over a specified minimum is automatically converted into an RP. The following morning the funds are moved from the RP back to the corporation's demand balance for use during the day. Such automatic arrangements for the conversion of demand deposits to RPs are often included in packages of services offered by banks to their corporate customers. Among the services in such packages are lines of credit, payroll administration, and the use of safekeeping facilities. Payment for such service packages is usually not made on the basis of a stated fee. Instead, average or minimum demand deposit balances—called compensating balances—are usually required.

RPs also can be used to provide liquidity for somewhat longer periods, for example, to allow the accumulation of funds for a tax or dividend payment. This option is particularly attractive to corporations if the income that can be earned on a longer RP exceeds that available on an overnight RP. One or several RPs can be written, as liquidity is accumulated over the period prior to a payment date, with the contracts maturing on the day disbursements must be made. The RP has less commanding advantages over other money market assets for longer periods, however. Commercial paper can frequently be tailored to mature on a specific day, and Treasury bills that mature very close to the desired date can often be purchased. RPs are nevertheless used very frequently for such purposes, primarily because they can be arranged easily and quickly once a corporation has established a routine trading relationship with market participants.

The volume of corporate RPs has grown dramatically in the 1970s. This growth has not been smooth, but has occurred in bursts. Monetary policy was quite restrictive through 1969 and into 1970, and again in 1973 and early 1974. During these periods, interest rates, particularly on short-term instruments, reached very high levels. The interest income foregone by holding demand deposits was obviously very high, and corporate treasurers responded by accelerating the development of cash management techniques in general and increasing the use of RPs. In effect, the periods of high interest rates helped corporations meet the cost of developing these new techniques, and the high rates then attainable explain the apparent paradox that corporations provided a growing volume of funds to the RP market when they were most strapped for cash.

Interest rates fell rather quickly once the economy entered the 1974–75 recession. For a time, as they had in the earlier periods of declining interest rates, corporations reduced their supply of funds to the RP market. By early 1975, however, corporations began to expand their RP activity rapidly. The apparently atypical increase in RP activity was brought on by the combination of several forces. Most important, the RP became widely accepted as an instrument of cash management for corporations. During preceding periods, many corporations did not participate in the RP market due either to restrictions in their by-laws or to lack of familiarity with the instrument among corporate treasurers. But by the mid-1970s, by-laws of many corporations had been changed, and the instrument had become widely accepted. Coincidentally, by 1974 many corporations felt that their liquidity had reached dangerously low levels, and rebuilding liquidity thus became a high priority. Reductions in capital expenditures and inventories were possible as the economy turned downward, thereby reducing corporate borrowing needs and contributing to improved cash flow. Corporations were able to begin to accumulate liquid assets as soon as cash flow began to improve after the worst of the recession was over, a process that has continued since. Significant portions of the new-found corporate liquidity were placed either in outright purchases of government securities or in repurchase agreements against such securities.

State and local government units have entered the RP market only in recent years but have quickly become major suppliers of funds. The RP is particularly well suited to their needs. These governments usually are required by law to hold their assets in the most secure form, generally in bank deposits or government and federal agency securities. The RP provides a way of meeting these requirements while earning income on short-term investments.

Tax receipts of state and local governments never match exactly the timing pattern of their expenditures, thereby creating the need for them either to borrow or to invest for short periods at various times of the year. Until recently their major investment alternative to deposits has been Treasury bills. As the advantages of the RP have become more widely recognized, these governments have switched more of their liquid investments into RPs.

In 1972, the Congress passed revenue-sharing legislation which increased the total volume of federal money flowing to states and localities. The revenue-sharing payments are concentrated at the beginning of each calendar quarter, and state and local governments have invested large portions of these funds in RPs until needed.

The Role of Nonbank Financial Institutions

Several types of nonbank financial institutions are active in the markets for immediately available funds. These include mutual savings banks, savings and loan associations, branches and agencies of foreign banks that operate on U.S. soil, and Edge Act corporations. (The latter are affiliates of United States commercial banks empowered to engage in international or foreign banking in the United States or abroad.) All of these institutions are active primarily in the market for Federal funds, and generally do not enter into repurchase agreements in volume. They generally lend Federal funds to commercial banks, although under certain circumstances agencies and branches of foreign banks will borrow from banks or other nonbank lenders.

The appearance of all these institutions in the Federal funds market has occurred relatively recently. Their entry has dramatically changed the function of the Federal funds market, allowing the banking system to draw funds from a wide array of institutions, instead of just reallocating reserves. The expanded borrowing ability of banks serves to integrate more closely the United States financial structure, and to help break down the barriers which have traditionally existed among various types of financial institutions.

The agencies and branches of foreign banks have also become active participants in the Federal funds market. These institutions deal with or represent foreign commercial banks, which trade in both the money markets of their home countries and in the Eurocurrency markets. Through the Federal funds market, the agencies and branches of foreign banks provide a link between the various markets abroad and the United States commercial banking system.

The participation of these institutions in U.S. financial markets mirrors the activities of U.S. commercial banks overseas. In the last three decades, overseas branch networks of U.S. banks have grown significantly in both the scale and range of their operations, and these networks have provided U.S. banks with easy access to foreign and international financial markets. Entry into the Federal funds market by agencies and branches of foreign banks, therefore, has contributed to the continuing integration of credit markets and banking in the United States and abroad.

The Role of the Federal Reserve

The Federal Reserve is important to the markets for Federal funds and RPs for two quite different reasons. One is that Federal Reserve regulations play a very important role in the markets by limiting the type and terms of transactions member banks may undertake. A second is that actions taken by the Federal Reserve in the normal conduct of monetary policy have a major influence on the levels of interest rates in general and on the Federal funds rate in particular. Federal Reserve monetary policy is oriented toward achieving steady and sustained growth of the economy, along with reasonably stable prices. Such a sound economy depends on a multiplicity of factors, one of which is the capacity of the commercial banking system to extend loans and create deposits. These capacities, in turn, are strongly influenced by the interest rate on Federal funds and the supply of reserves to member banks.

The Federal Reserve controls the supply of reserves through open market operations, mainly via outright purchases and sales of government and federal agency securities. An outright purchase of securities provides reserves permanently, while a sale permanently reduces the total supply of reserves. But the Federal Reserve also needs to provide and absorb reserves for short periods, mainly to accommodate the seasonal needs of banks for reserves and to offset the effects on reserves of day-to-day changes in currency in circulation, in the Treasury's balance at Federal Reserve Banks, and in Federal Reserve float. Reserves can be supplied temporarily by use of repurchase agreements, and absorbed temporarily through "matched sale-purchase transactions," which most market participants call reverse RPs.

A full historical treatment of Federal Reserve use of the RP and matched sale-purchase transaction would require another article, but a few highlights are important because they have influenced the development of the RP market. Federal Reserve use of the RP dates back to 1917, but extensive use of the instrument began only in the postwar period. Matched sale-purchase transactions were first used to absorb reserves in 1966. The technique was introduced at the time of a sudden, temporary increase in float arising from a widespread interruption of airline service. The amount of reserves needed to be absorbed at that time was too large to be handled by *outright* sales of securities by the Federal Reserve without disturbing the financial markets.

Until 1972, Federal Reserve RPs were executed at a rate fixed by the Federal Reserve, usually the discount rate. In that year the Federal Reserve instituted a competitive bidding procedure whereby the rate on RPs was set as a result of government securities dealer offerings of securities in relation to Federal Reserve needs to provide reserves. Shortly thereafter, dealers were permitted to offer to the Federal Reserve any securities they obtained in separate transactions with other market participants. Until 1975, RPs were done by the Federal Reserve only with nonbank government securities dealers. At that time, the practice was changed to include commercial bank government securities dealer departments. All these changes contributed to the acceptability, flexibility, and utility of the RP.

Federal Reserve use of RPs and matched sale-purchase transactions for temporary reserve adjustment has grown sharply in the past few years, but for generally different reasons than those which explain the increase in the use of RPs by banks and others. The increase has arisen in large part from a change in Treasury procedures for handling its cash balances. Prior to August 1974, the Treasury received payments into accounts at commercial banks, and generally moved funds into its balance at the Federal Reserve only as funds were needed to make payments on behalf of the federal government. Under this scheme, Treasury balances in commercial banks fluctuated widely, but the Treasury balance at the Federal Reserve was reasonably stable. In August 1974, the Treasury began to move its balances more quickly into its accounts at the Federal Reserve Banks, which climbed by several billion dollars over a period of several months. This policy has led to much wider fluctuation in these accounts. This in turn has created greater variability in the supply of reserves available to the banking system which the Federal Reserve usually offsets by temporary adjustments to reserves through RPs or matched sale-purchase transactions.

Some Major Implications

The Federal funds and RP markets have grown dramatically since World War II, but particularly in the past few years. This growth is due in part to changes in the regulations which govern the operations of commercial banks, but is more basically due to the changing practices and behavior of all participants in these markets. The circumstances influencing each group of market participants have differed in detail, but for all, the quite high interest rates since the mid-1960s have provided the major motivation.

In addition, technological development has made participation less costly. Growth—both in trading volume and in the number of institutions participating in the markets—has not been even. Periods of most rapid growth in these markets have occurred when interest rates were rising toward or stood at postwar peaks. For the most part the markets for immediately available funds have contracted as interest rates fell from successive peaks, but never by as much as in the earlier periods of expansion.

The growth in the Federal funds and RP markets has several implications. Most importantly, the markets have expanded to include a broader range of domestic and international financial institutions and corporations. They use the markets as a link in a worldwide network that transfers interest-sensitive dollar balances to wherever they are in greatest demand. To be sure, mechanisms to move funds to high-demand uses have existed for some time, but the Federal funds and RP markets help make the task easier and more efficient by bringing interest-sensitive funds into a central marketplace from a broader arena. For example, most individuals who hold deposits at thrift institutions do not move their funds quickly from one investment to another in response to small interest rate changes. But thrift institutions can lend in the Federal funds market, in effect allowing the small deposits of individuals to be combined and placed directly in the national markets for short-term credit. Similar considerations apply with respect to international credit flows.

These developments have some implications for the conduct of Federal Reserve monetary policy. Policy actions significantly influence the Federal funds and RP markets, which commercial banks now use as sources of funds more extensively than ever before. Hence any change in the availability of funds in these markets probably has a more direct impact than before on the cost to banks of making loans and on the rates they charge. Moreover, many more small banks and nonbank financial institutions have become quite active in the markets. Through this mechanism, Federal Reserve monetary policy is felt more quickly and directly by a broader range of the financial institutions, including those that provide a major portion of the total credit available in the United States economy.

United States and international financial markets have also become more closely integrated in recent years. There are multiple linkages among the various markets, but they center on the activities in this country and abroad of multinational corporations and of United States and foreign commercial banks. These institutions borrow and lend sizable amounts in both the United States and international markets, and are sensitive to the margins between borrowing and lending rates in different countries. For example, if short-term interest rates in the United States were higher than abroad, the differential would quickly draw funds from other uses abroad and channel liquidity into the United States financial markets. These flows would tend to reduce the differential between interest rates abroad and in this country.

But the flows of credit induced by such interest rate differentials may not be in keeping with Federal Reserve policy objectives at the time. For example, a restrictive monetary policy works to reduce spending by individuals and businesses, partly because it makes borrowing more expensive and difficult to obtain. The effects of such policies on the domestic economy could be dampened if large corporations and financial institutions can readily obtain credit elsewhere.

While high interest rates and inflation have encouraged growth of the Federal funds and RP markets, the evolution of technology, particulary the use of computer facilities, has also played an important part. The new and changing technology speeds the transfer of funds, reduces the cost of record keeping, and increases the availability of information concerning investment opportunities. It seems certain that technological change will continue at a rapid rate, thereby reducing further the costs of arranging and executing financial transactions and reinforcing the already strong trend toward aggressive financial management.

The rapid growth of the markets for Federal funds and RPs in recent years can be viewed as part of a pervasive trend in all United States financial markets toward more aggressive portfolio management by holders of financial assets. This trend will clearly continue to be a strong influence on the markets. Participants will no doubt devise new trading techniques, refine existing ones, and attract others into the marketplace. But the Federal funds and RP markets are only two of many markets for short-term financial claims, and their growth relative to others will be heavily influenced by the regulatory and legal framework in which they operate. These markets could be significantly affected by several proposals for financial reform that have been put forth in recent years, some in the form of legislative proposals introduced in the Congress.

Of particular note in this respect are the increasing number of arguments heard in favor of relaxing or eliminating prohibitions against the payment of interest on demand deposits and the payment of interest on member bank reserve accounts. Such proposals, if enacted, would probably have minor effects on the Federal funds market insofar as it is used by banks for reserve adjustment purposes, but would more heavily affect the use of both the Federal funds and RP markets as sources of funds on a continuing basis by banks. The effect any legislation will have on the markets will, of course, depend on the exact provisions. But one fact seems clear: legislative and regulatory changes can channel the pressure emanating from aggressive financial management into or away from the Federal funds and RP markets, but it is unlikely that financial management itself can be forced to return to the tamer posture of a decade and more ago.

Bank Bond Management: The Maturity Dilemma

Ronald D. Watson

4

Had Gilbert and Sullivan been as familiar with managing bank investments as they were with policemen and pirates, they might well have intoned "a banker's [policeman's] lot is not a happy one."[1] The meter of this change of phrasing might have caused them some problems, but those difficulties pale when compared to the headaches of managing millions of dollars of government securities investments in today's financial markets. Recently bank investment officers have become aware that this complex job requires more than simply understanding the financial markets in which they ply their trade. They must also discern how their superiors will measure the success of their bond management performance. Recent developments in banking research suggest that the bond management script may need to be rewritten before future performances. At a minimum there are ways to make the leading role—that of the bond account manager—easier to play.

Setting the Stage: Bank Liquidity Management

Banks, just like any other business, come upon times when they could use more hard cash. When a bank wants money, say to meet a cash outflow, it has many sources to

Reprinted from the Federal Reserve Bank of Philadelphia, *Business Review*, March 1972, pp. 23-29, by permission of the publisher.
[1]William S. Gilbert and Arthur Sullivan, *The Pirates of Penzance; or the Slave of Duty*, Act II.

tap. Cash balances not currently held to meet reserve requirements might be reduced, additional deposits solicited, loan outflows curtailed, temporary borrowings made from the Federal Reserve Bank, or portions of the bond portfolio sold. As this incomplete list of possibilities indicates, management can convert earning assets into cash or acquire new liabilities to meet cash demands. The choice depends on the relative cost of the alternatives. This process is called *liquidity management.*

Before the mid-1960s, techniques for managing bank liquidity focused on *selling assets,* such as bonds, to generate additional cash. However, considerable attention has been devoted recently to solving these liquidity problems exclusively by *buying short-term liabilities* in the money markets as funds are needed. This strategy is known as *liabilities management.* Awareness and use of this option has added a new dimension to managing a bank's liquidity. Bankers now have more flexibility in meeting unexpected cash demands because this borrowing power enables them to avoid selling bonds or other assets when they find that prices are unfavorable.

However, the simple fact that these money markets are now well-developed sources of financing doesn't make them the most economical method for alleviating every financial pinch. The credit crunches of '66 and '70 showed the folly of presuming that money markets can accommodate all the banking community's liquidity demands at the borrowing rates it is willing to pay. Thus, bank assets, particularly government securities, and the men who control them continue to play key roles in bank liquidity management.

The Role of Government Bonds   Cash, U.S. Treasury securities (bills, notes, and bonds), government agency bonds, municipal bonds, and loans all have some value for meeting liquidity needs. Just as a playbill lists actors in order of appearance, the balance sheet ranking above suggests the probable order in which assets would be converted to cash and applied to satisfying a liquidity problem.

Cash is the most readily usable liquid asset, but much of a bank's cash is likely to be tied up meeting legal reserve requirements. Justifying an increase in the cash account beyond minimums required for reserves and daily business is difficult because the bank receives no income from this asset. At the other extreme, loans are a costly source of liquidity. There is no formal market in which to dispose of these obligations cheaply and easily. Hence, using loans to meet a liquidity pinch is impractical except as a last resort.

The assets which remain—the bank's portfolios of government securities—are a more practical source of liquidity. These bonds are formal obligations of borrowers who are financially sound, which can be traded in relatively well-organized markets. Some are more marketable than others, of course, but all can be converted into cash with little difficulty. The Treasury security, because of its ready marketability, has become the most common source of asset liquidity used by the men who manage bond portfolios at commercial banks.

The Role of the Bond Portfolio Manager   The man running the bond portfolio show has to be a first-rate director. His job is balancing the bank's liquidity requirements against bank earnings. An important part of this balancing act involves shaping the *maturity distribution of bonds*—the balance of short-, intermediate-, and long-term issues—in the securities portfolio.

There are no easy rules that will allow a banker to set a maturity distribution which enables him to meet cash outflows at a minimum cost. Sometimes short-term borrowings will be the cheapest and easiest source of funds. At other times the banker may be unable to use that market at all. Irregularities in the securities markets may make it advisable to raise cash by selling long-term rather than short-term bonds. A desire to take capital gains or capital losses for tax purposes may affect the selection of maturities to sell. Further, the choice of bonds to sell might depend on what the banker wants to leave in his securities portfolio for future liquidity protection. Despite the diverse circumstances, a bond portfolio manager's job in shaping the maturity distribution of the portfolio ultimately comes down to matching returns against risks.

Act One: the Uncertain World of the Account Manager

The curtain rises with the bond manager at his desk scratching his head over the bewildering choice of bond maturities before him. In choosing which assets to hold and how long to hold them, he is out to achieve the highest possible returns for the bank without exposing it to unwanted risks. But this task is easier said than done. It is a simple fact of life that a portfolio which offers the expectation of above-average returns—either in the form of interest or capital gains—normally brings higher risks. The uncertainty of future interest rates lies behind much of this problem of balancing risks and returns.

A Problem with Interest Rates   Changes in interest rates cause changes in bank earnings and in the value of the portfolio. Thus, the vagaries of interest rates involve the portfolio of the manager in two kinds of troublesome risks: 1) the variations occurring in the interest income earned on bond investments, and 2) the capital losses resulting from an upward shift in market interest rates.[2] Managing these risks can be particularly difficult because reducing the portfolio's exposure to one often increases exposure to the other.

For example, suppose an account manager seeks to reduce exposure to the first risk, fluctuating interest income. He may be able to do this by putting more of his portfolio in longer-term maturities. Long-term bonds offer a steady flow of coupon or interest income as long as they are held. And since their rates tend to fluctuate less than short-term rates, reinvestment income is also more stable.

But what happens if interest rates in the market shift upward after this move to long-term bonds is made? Our manager has that unsettling experience of seeing his

---

[2]Falling interest rates create capital gains. However, this form of income instability is not viewed as a "problem" by portfolio managers.

portfolio drop in value. This change in interest rates results in a loss because more interest income could now be earned with the same investment in a newly issued bond. Hence, no one would pay the old price for the bond, and its market price would be bid down until its effective yield matched the current market rate. Whether or not the account manager has to record or "realize" this capital loss would depend on whether he has to sell any long-term bonds to cover cash drains on the bank. If he does have to sell, say, a 15-year bond yielding 5 percent in a market where the current yield has risen to 6 percent, he will have to swallow a capital loss of nearly 10 percent.

Thus, by attempting to avoid the first risk of interest income fluctuation, our account manager falls victim to the second risk, capital loss, all because of the fickle nature of interest rates. Consequently, a portfolio manager's outlook for interest rates must necessarily shape his selections for the government bond account. Honing the accuracy of his interest rate predictions allows him to reduce capital losses or increase capital gains while still meeting the bank's liquidity demand. Moreover, top management could help by making its interest rate expectations clear. Senior management can hardly set the level of future interest rates by decree. However, interest rate forecasts have a strong impact on the maturity distribution appropriate for the portfolio. It only makes sense to insure that top management's expectations are considered in formulating portfolio policies so that these policies are consistent with those followed in other areas of the bank's operations.

To the extent that the portfolio manager is uncertain about future interest rates, he's likely to "hedge" his bets when balancing risks against returns by planning for a variety of contingencies.[3] The manager hedges by putting some of his assets in long-term bonds while keeping others in short-term bonds. This provides some income stability plus a ready supply of emergency liquidity free of capital loss risk. In short, the hedging manager won't lose big, but he won't win big either.

Uncertainty for Top Management   Not only does an account manager run into uncertainty from interest rates but also from top management. Portfolio managers may be unsure as to how their bosses weigh the risks of unstable portfolio income as opposed to capital losses—that is, how much management is willing to forego in potential earnings to avoid or reduce exposure to each type of risk.

Quite likely those evaluating a bond manager's performance will be less than elated by significant capital losses, and some will be even more unhappy if the capital losses have to be "realized." These bankers usually try to keep realized losses at a

---

[3]An important element of the portfolio maturity decision is the structure that is assumed for future interest rate movements. Until recently it had been common to presume that bond yields would generally rise as the maturity of the bond increased. Such an assumption implies that there will be a long-term improvement in a portfolio's income (after capital gains and losses) if maturities can be lengthened. In the last few years, short-term yields have exceeded long-term rates so frequently, that some bond managers are beginning to doubt the wisdom of trying to extend the portfolio's average maturity. The longer-term bonds still seem to offer an opportunity for more stable income flows, but their net return may not be higher. To the extent that one believes that interest rate movements will more closely mirror the recent past than the overall experience since 1951, the following discussion will have to be modified. Funds normally invested in long-term bonds, because their yield was expected to be high, might be shifted into shorter maturity issues.

minimum, because such losses stand out in the income statement. Thus, reporting them creates unfavorable publicity and embarrassment. This forces the portfolio manager to hold enough short-term securities (for instance, Treasury bills which are virtually free of capital loss risk) to cover any cash outflow likely to come down the pike.

Other portfolio managers may have to please bosses (or possibly stockholders) who are more concerned with the steadiness of the bank's overall income than with capital losses. This will encourage the portfolio manager to select more long-term bonds for the account. However, as income stability improves, the risk of capital losses climbs. Therefore, he will lengthen his maturities only as long as the combined effects create a more stable net income.

But often an account manager is uncertain as to the weight management attaches to these alternative forms of risk. As in the case of uncertainty about future interest rates, the manager is likely to shape the maturity distribution of the portfolio to hedge his bets. He will hold a supply of short-term securities sufficient to cover most cash drains without severe capital losses. He will also keep some longer maturities to steady the portfolio's interest earnings. Thus uncertainty about management's views on risk poses a difficult problem for the account manager in terms of balancing risks against returns.

Act Two: Management Techniques

Surrounded by the uncertainty of which risks his bosses most want to reduce along with a great deal of uncertainty about what the future holds for interest rates, the account manager seeks some method to guide him in plying his trade. The technique often chosen for selecting the bond portfolio is the "liquidity reserve classification system" (see below).

The Liquidity Reserve System for Portfolio Management

The most common scheme for managing the bond portfolio's distribution is the reserve system. It is characterized by the wide variety of bond maturities included in the portfolio. According to this method of portfolio management, both the kinds of liquid assets available for bank investment and the sources of instability in the bank's cash flows are grouped into several categories. Assets needed for maintaining the bank's liquidity can be safely allocated to cash, short-term government securities, other short-term securities that are also highly liquid, and long-term government bonds. Paralleling this asset structure, sources of cash flow uncertainty are divided into daily, weekly, seasonal, and cyclical cash flows. Net cash inflows represent a liquidity problem for the bank only in an opportunity-cost sense, but net outflows are presumed to have specific causes and are met from specific sources of reserve funds.

The *primary reserve* is the part of a bank's cash account that exceeds its legally required reserves: ready money for meeting net outflows that occur in the normal course of the bank's daily activities. This reserve must be large enough to allow the bank to meet its current obligations without encountering embarrassing cash shortages. Yet primary reserves must be kept at a working minimum because they earn no interest.

The *secondary reserve* is composed of short-term, highly marketable government securities. Paramount is the requirement that these assets be readily convertible into cash at little or no risk of capital loss. Generally, the most suitable security for this purpose is the Treasury bill. However, Treasury notes of less than two years to maturity or even government bonds which mature in the near future satisfy these requirements. This reserve provides a useful source of liquidity for seasonal cash outflows such as crop cycles, holiday periods, and tax deadlines.

A *tertiary reserve* might be held by the bank for protection against major cyclical outflows associated with either loss of deposits or with the heightening of loan demand, both phenomena occurring over a long period of time. The reserve for this kind of outflow need not be as liquid as the primary or secondary reserves, so it is generally composed of securities of somewhat longer maturities and higher yields. Government securities with maturities of two to five years could normally qualify for this reserve designation.

To the extent that bonds of still longer maturities have a reserve function, they are said to be part of the *investment reserve*. Securities of this type can be held to provide an additional cushion in case of severe financial stress. Combining assets held for each of these reserve purposes produces a spaced maturity portfolio.

Seldom is this one-to-one correspondence of reserve to function followed very rigorously in the banking community. Any sensible banker needing to convert a portion of his reserves to cash would analyze his portfolio to determine the most advantageous sale. However, the liquidity reserve system provides a banker with a rough tool for measuring his reserve needs for cash outflows and for protecting himself from serious losses in bond account dealings.

Liquidity Reserve Approach   Under the most common form of this system, each kind of investment is categorized (primary, secondary, tertiary, and investment) according to how liquid it is. Cash, of course, is the most obvious source of liquidity, but most of it is needed to meet the bank's reserve responsibilities. The short-term Treasury bill becomes part of the bank's secondary reserves which are held as the next line of defense against outflows. Long-term bonds are an investment reserve to be sold or "cashed in" when the bank is under the pressure of extended funds outflows.

Under this layered system of reserves the greatest concentration of invested funds occurs in the short-maturity Treasury bills and notes. However, some reserve funds are spread over a wide range of maturities to increase the average return on the portfolio and to stabilize the flow of interest income. By advocating an extension of a portion of the portfolio's investment funds into intermediate- and long-term securities, this management approach assumes that, on the average, short-term yields will be lower than long-term ones. Moreover, it implicitly assumes that stabilizing interest income is desirable as long as capital losses are under control. Avoidance of losses is the key to this philosophy as evidenced by a heavy concentration in short-term securities. Attaining a "reasonable" level of income without incurring high capital loss risks, rather than seeking high income, is the name of the game.

The problem with the liquidity reserve approach is that it is not designed to find a bank's *best* bond maturity distribution. It serves only to suggest one that will *suffice*. Therefore, the portfolio manager may be missing chances for higher returns that would not increase the bank's risks. Another difficulty encountered in following the liquidity reserve system is deciding which intermediate and long maturities to include in the portfolio. Specialists in the field sharply differ in their willingness to include maturities of more than five years because of the heavy capital losses that can occur in ten- and fifteen-year bonds. If long-term government bonds are held only as a backstop against catastrophic outflows, the longest maturities are suitable. "Forced sales" and hence realized capital losses will rarely occur. However, if these bonds are to be used frequently in absorbing cyclical liquidity demands, the chances of realizing capital losses are higher, and some authorities are reluctant to suggest commitments longer than five to seven years. In either case, the liquidity reserve approach yields a portfolio that is hedged with intermediate maturities.

Split Maturity Strategy Some recent research may result in an eventual rewriting of the script for portfolio managers. It has uncovered a *split maturity strategy* as an alternative to the *liquidity reserve approach* to bond management. This recent addition to the banker's repertoire was uncovered by computer analysis, using techniques from operations research.[4] The preliminary results merit careful analysis for they contradict the liquidity reserve system under certain assumptions.

This research discloses that the bond maturity distributions which produce the most attractive combinations of risks and returns are structures comprised of either all short-term bonds, all long-term bonds, or combinations of the two (split maturity

---

[4]A detailed description of this research can be found in Charles R. Wolf, "A Model for Selecting Commercial Bank Government Security Portfolios," *Review of Economics and Statistics,* 5 (1969): 40–52 (a nonlinear mathematical programming model); Dwight B. Crane, "A Stochastic Programming Model for Commercial Bank Bond Portfolio Management," *Journal of Financial and Quantitative Analysis,* 6 (1971): 955–976 (a probabalistic linear programming model); Ronald D. Watson, "Tests of Maturity Structures for Commercial Bank Securities Portfolios—A Simulation Approach" (unpublished D.B.A. dissertation, Indiana University, Bloomington, Indiana, 1971) (a simulation model).

structures).[5] These maturity distributions contain no bonds maturing between five and fifteen years. This result depends heavily on the presumption that there is a yield advantage to investing in long-term bonds.

Split maturity strategies contradict the basic approach of the liquidity reserve system. Rather than trying to produce a "sufficient" return without heavy capital loss risks, the split maturity structures result from attempts to earn the highest return possible while controlling *probable* losses. These results suggest that it may be more efficient for a manager to control capital loss risks by investing only in the shortest maturities available and to seek income by investing in the maturity offering the highest expected yield rather than spreading investments over many maturities. The manager would then be investing in a portfolio of "balanced risks and returns" rather than one that is hedged with intermediate maturities.

A further point highlighted by this split portfolio research is the importance of the account manager's measure of risk. When the risk measure used in the analysis was "capital gains and losses," the entire short-term portion of the portfolio was invested in the shortest available maturity. However, altering the concept of risk to include both capital value changes and income instability made it more efficient to spread the short-term investments over a range of short maturities (up to four or five years to maturity). Extension of some short-term investments over several years increases the portfolio's capital loss risks, but it more than compensates by reducing interest income uncertainties. But even with this concept of risk, there remains a gap between the short and long maturities in the portfolio.

The split maturity strategy may help the portfolio manager improve his perform-ance in the face of changing interest rates, but it isn't a cure-all. He must still weigh the risks of capital losses versus income stability in allocating his investable funds. He must also make the decision of how risky he wishes his portfolio to be (relative to the bank's liquidity requirement). Finally, he must incorporate expectations of future interest rates into the managing of the bond account's maturity distribution. These decisions can be simplified when top management makes the ground rules clear, but it's still a delicate balancing act.

Finale

Again, to paraphrase slightly Messrs. Gilbert and Sullivan, the portfolio manager's lot is certainly not a happy one. The performance of his bond portfolio is subject to forces beyond his control—the bank's liquidity requirement and the vagaries of inter-est rates. Estimating both of these is a tricky business. He may also face the dilemma of having his performance rated by a criterion that is unknown to him.

[5]For purposes of this discussion short-term bonds are defined as those being less than five years to maturity, intermediate from five to ten, and long-term from ten to fifteen years. In addition, this result is predicated on: 1) the bank's management being averse to taking risks, 2) the unequal trade-off of capital losses and increasing bond maturities, 3) the assumption that long-term interest rates normally exceed short-term rates.

A bank's top management has a responsbility to reduce the difficulty of this job by helping the portfolio manager cope with this uncertainty. It should first decide how his performance will be evaluated (with a full understanding of the implication of each criterion) and make him aware of the decision. Then it should work out with the portfolio manager a set of interest rate projections to be used in managing the bond account. These two acts will enable the bond account manager to devise a strategy that is consistent with the objectives and expectations of the bank as a whole. When the plot has unfolded, the strategy could well be a split maturity structure. However, the important point is that the bond account manager should understand the constraints under which he must make his decision. If this can be done, the portfolio manager's lot will be a much more happy one.

Bank Loan Losses: A Fresh Perspective

Stuart A. Schweitzer*

5

Nobody likes to be in default on a loan. Yet, even the best-intentioned borrowers are sometimes unable to pay their debts. And when they have difficulty paying their debts, their troubles fall right into the laps of their creditors. No wonder, then, that analysts of banks and the banking system pay particular attention to bank loan losses.

Loan loss rates at commercial banks have been on the rise for some time. And some bank experts say there's apt to be a record volume of loan defaults this year, as recession brings financial misfortune to many. That brings to the fore the issue of bank defenses against potential loan losses.

Analysts generally focus on a bank's "reserves for possible loan losses" as its principal defense against uncollectable loans. Yet, over the past five years banks haven't built up their loss reserves as rapidly as they have increased their vulnerability to loan losses. While this has distressed some observers, there is a line of reasoning which leads to the conclusion that there probably isn't that much real cause for concern. The logic goes something like this: Until recently, bank loan loss reserves have been unnecessarily large. In addition, most banks have substantial earnings

Reprinted, with deletions, from the Federal Reserve Bank of Philadelphia, *Business Review*, September 1975, pp. 18–28, by permission of the publisher.

* Dr. Schweitzer, formerly a Senior Economist at the Federal Reserve Bank of Philadelphia, is now Assistant Economist at Morgan Guaranty Trust Company of New York. This article was prepared while the author was associated with the bank.

streams and capital resources which can also be used to cover potential loan losses. Thus, according to this reasoning, loan losses themselves pose much less of a threat to bank soundness than the danger of public overreaction to those losses.

Bank Loan Losses: Background and Foreground

When the record books are finally closed on 1975, the year's loan losses just may set some records. Many bank watchers expect the dollar volume of bank losses to hit an all-time high in 1975. And some argue that the rate of such loan losses, as a fraction of bank loans outstanding, will be higher than at any time since the 1930s. These analysts could turn out to be right. But it's important to place the current situation in perspective. The rate of bank loan losses is nowhere near its high water mark, set in 1934. At the depths of the Depression, commercial banks "charged off" over $3.40 of every $100 of bank loans as uncollectable. In 1974, by contrast, about 38 cents of every $100 of loans met a similar fate. Whatever may happen to loss rates in 1975, they have little chance of approaching their 1930s levels.

Upward Pressure on Loan Losses In the context of the postwar period, those predictions of record loan losses for 1975 have a lot going for them. Loan loss rates have been on the rise for about 25 years now. And the recession of 1974–75 is quite likely to accentuate this trend.

An upward path of loan losses since 1950 is unmistakable. While loan losses in the 1950s amounted to less than 7 cents per $100 of bank loans, the loss rate rose to just above 16 cents in the 1960s and to about 31 cents for the 1970–74 period. A trend as strong and as longstanding as that is not quickly reversed. While the renewed emphasis on conservatism in banking which emerged in 1974 may eventually lower the loss rate, that won't happen overnight.

On top of this longstanding trend is the 1974–75 recession. As a downturn cumulatively worsens, the profitability of the business community can seriously erode, forcing many firms to absorb operating losses out of stockholders' equity. The next step for such firms may be bankruptcy, since some of them may become unable to pay their outstanding debts. Bank loan losses would then rise accordingly. Likewise, as unemployment grows during a downturn, personal borrowers may also fail to meet their debt-repayment obligations.

No one, of course can be sure about the impact of a recession on bank loan losses. Conventional wisdom dictates that recession and a higher rate of loan losses ought to go together, although that hasn't been true in all postwar recessions. Nonetheless, the latest recession has been more severe than other postwar downturns. Problems with loans for real estate development, for example, are particularly severe this time around. These forces could mean that loan losses will surge upward this year, as many Wall Streeters say, but this will be known for sure only in hindsight.

Loan Losses in the Public Eye It is only natural, therefore, that public attention is now sharply focused on the loan loss problem. Even banks are forewarning their shareholders about higher losses in 1975. Eyebrows are thus now raised over the question of adequacy of bank defenses against high loan losses. And most of the questioners are concerned with the volume of funds banks have set aside as reserves for possible loan losses.

Setting and Subdividing the Loss Reserve

Most firms and individuals maintain reserves of some sort to assist them in managing their financial affairs. These reserves may be only a few dollars set aside in a cookie jar or millions of dollars invested in income-producing assets. But, in either case, they help tide the household or business over any financial rough spots that may occur. Since banks are forever advising the general public to "put something aside for a rainy day," it is only fitting that most banks do the same. Loss reserves are the device that most banks use to build protection against normal variation in loan losses. Banks usually plan to rely on their earnings and capital accounts to cover extraordinary loan losses.

A bank that adopts the "reserve method" for covering its loan losses makes an addition each year to its loan loss reserve.[1] The bank doesn't earmark particular assets as part of its loss reserve. Rather, the loss reserve becomes a claim upon the assets of the bank generally, as are the bank's liabilities and capital accounts. When a loan held by the bank proves uncollectable, the decline in the value of the bank's loan assets can be "charged off" against the loss reserve. That way, as long as losses don't exceed reserves, the bank's earnings do not have to absorb loan losses directly. Earnings are buffered from the potentially wide swings in loan losses from year to year. And the reserve helps to cushion the bank against insolvency as well.

Taxes and Accounting for the Loss Reserve   Besides offering smoother earnings and an insolvency cushion, the reserve method also offers banks small tax bills. A bank may take tax deductions for the funds it transfers to its loss reserves instead of for its actual loan losses. And the tax law's generous standard regarding the size of the loss reserve permits banks thereby to reduce their tax payments (Box 1).

Box 1   *The Tax Advantages of Building Loss Reserves*

U.S. tax laws give recognition to the fact that a portion of the interest received by a bank eventually will be needed to cover its losses on uncollectable loans. Ever since 1921, banks have been permitted to deduct from taxable income a "reasonable" volume of transfers to a reserve for loan losses. Of course, since these tax deductions reduce a bank's taxes, it has always proven difficult for banks and the Government to agree as to what is reasonable. For a long while banks were

---

[1]Banks aren't required to use the reserve method for covering their loan losses. They are also permitted to be on the "direct charge-off method," whereby they use current earnings to meet loan losses as they occur.

permitted to build a reserve consistent with bank loss experiences during the 1930s. The last vestige of this was a U.S. Treasury ruling in 1965 permitting banks to maintain reserves in an amount up to 2.4 percent of their "eligible loans."[2] Tax reform has since sent this percentage lower.

The U.S. tax system is heading toward application of the principle that a bank should be able to shelter from income tax only those contributions to a loan reserve which are consistent with its recent loss experience. That principle is a part of the Tax Reform Act of 1969, but will not be fully effective until 1988. In the meantime, banks are permitted to shelter a reserve whose ratio to eligible loans is either based on the bank's loss experience or else is subject to a stipulated maximum.[3] The maximum ratio currently is 1.8 percent, but will drop down to 1.2 percent in 1976. It will drop further to 0.6 percent in 1982. Not until 1988 will banks be required to be on an "experience basis" for their loan loss reserves. Beginning in 1988, under current law, banks will be limited to a tax-free reserve no larger, as a fraction of their eligible loans, than the ratio of uncollected loans to eligible loans on an average basis over the prior six years.

Thus, under current law, the tax benefit to a bank from handling its loan losses via the reserve method will gradually decline. For a time, however, the size of the tax saving will continue to be substantial. The U.S. Treasury estimates that over one billion dollars of tax receipts will be lost to the Government in fiscal 1975 because of the generous allowance for loan loss reserves at banks and savings and loan associations combined. The tax loss is expected to remain close to that level in fiscal 1976. But it should decline after that, as the maximum ratio of the reserve to eligible loans drops to 1.2 percent on January 1, 1976. That reduction will have its impact in fiscal 1977.

The tax deduction gives banks the incentive to transfer the maximum amount allowed by law to their loan loss reserves, and most do just that. But they usually don't report all of those tax deductions as operating expenses in their published financial reports. Although it may seem unusual, it's quite legal for a bank to report larger expenses to the Government than to its shareholders. The tax authorities permit a bank to "pay" for a transfer to its loss reserve partly by provisions from operating expenses and partly by provisions from retained earnings. Either way, the bank's transfer to its loss reserve is tax-deductible. But the bank's operating earnings aren't reduced when retained earnings are used to build the reserve.

[2]According to IRS rules, not all bank loans are eligible to serve as a basis for the reserve computation. The loans which are ineligible include Federal funds sold, loans backed by U.S. Government securities or bank deposit balances, and loans guaranteed by the U.S. Government.

[3]Regulations limit the size of the deduction for a transfer to the loss reserve during any single year to 0.6 percent of eligible loans.

The Three Parts of the Loss Reserve   In actual practice, most banks charge both retained earnings and operating expenses for transfers to their loss reserves. This leads to a loss reserve which has three components—a valuation reserve, a contingency reserve, and a deferred tax reserve. But the bank can't cover loan losses out of all of these components.

When a bank charges its operating expenses to provide for estimated loan losses, accountants record the result as an addition to the bank's *valuation reserve.* When a transfer is made from retained earnings to the bank's loss reserve, that's recorded as an addition to the bank's *contingency reserve.* When the bank cuts its tax bill by taking tax deductions for additions to its contingency reserve, its tax saving is recorded in the bank's *deferred tax reserve* (see Box 2 for a numerical example). In principle, this account is used only for holding funds that will eventually be paid to the Government as taxes.

Box 2   *The Three Parts of a Loss Reserve*

All of the dollars in a bank's loan loss reserve are not created equally. Instead, each dollar comes from one of three sources—the bank's revenues, its retained earnings, or the taxes that it owes to the U.S. Government. An example will clarify just how this all happens. But first, it may be useful to know why things need be so complicated.

The answer is our tax laws. It's already been noted that banks are allowed to accumulate, free of corporate income taxes, more loan loss reserves than can be supported by loan loss experience. While banks are entirely willing to save on their taxes, they want to do so in a way which doesn't reduce the profits that they report to their shareholders. This requires some financial gymnastics, but it can be done. What it requires is that banks sort their loss reserves into three segments—the valuation, contingency, and deferred tax portions of the overall loss reserve.

An example will help clarify this. Consider the status of the mythical Small-Loss National Bank. Small-Loss National had revenues last year of $1,000. Its operating expenses, before any provision for loan losses, were $700. Its loan portfolio equals $10,000, and its average annual loan-loss ratio equals 0.2 percent.

Small-Loss National has decided to "charge" its revenues with a $20 addition to its bad debt reserve ($20 equals 0.2 percent of $10,000). This $20 represents an addition to the bank's *valuation reserve*—it meets the tests of being "charged" against revenue as a bank expense, and that's what's required of funds added to the valuation reserve. The bank thus reports its net income before taxes as $280 ($1,000 minus $700 minus $20).

This $280 figure is what Small-Loss National tells its shareholders and the public generally that it actually earned last year. In an effort to use legal means to reduce its tax liability, however, it tells Uncle Sam something else. Remember, the U.S. Government usually permits a bank to add more to its loss reserves—and therefore shelter more income from current taxation—than the bank may need to cover loan losses. Suppose that in Small-Loss National's case, the Government will permit a $50 deduction for transfers to its loss reserve this year. Since it's only willing to take $20 for its loss reserve out of revenues, but it can shelter a total of $50 if it wants to, the bank looks elsewhere for the other $30.

Here's how the bank does it. Whereas shareholders were told that the bank actually earned $280, the Government hears a different story. Taxable income is reported to the Government as $250 ($280 less $30). That reduces Small-Loss National's tax obligation by $15 (assuming, for simplicity, that the bank's tax rate is 50 percent). This $15 tax saving is an addition to the *deferred tax* portion of the bank's loan reserve.

Now, only another $15 is needed to make the bank's total addition to its loss reserve equal to $50. That final $15 is the other half of the $30 the bank is looking for. It represents the shareholder's half of the difference between the bank's reported profit of $280 and its taxable profit of $250. This $15 would have gone into the bank's retained earnings if it hadn't been added to the loan loss reserve. It is assigned by accountants to the *contingency portion* of the loss reserve.

Of the three reserve components, accounting principles permit loan losses to be charged only against the valuation portion. While the contingency and deferred tax items are part of the bank's total loan loss reserve, they represent transfers made for Federal income tax purposes only. If a bank's loan losses should exhaust its valuation reserve, the bank's next resource would be its earnings rather than the other loss reserve elements.[4]

The 1969 Agreement on Valuation Reserves   The principle that the valuation reserve be the only reserve element available to cover a bank's loan losses is a longstanding accounting axiom. It became a banking rule, however, only after a 1969 agreement among the Securities and Exchange Commission, the Federal banking agencies, and the accounting profession. Under that agreement, the *entirety* of each bank's loan loss reserve as of January 1, 1969, became a valuation reserve. Additions to the valuation reserve had to be charged to the bank's income statement as expenses only beginning with 1969. And only since 1969 have the other elements of the valuation reserve been ineligible to cover loan losses.

---

[4]A bank could regain use of its contingency reserve by restoring that reserve to retained earnings and making a tax payment in the amount of the deferred tax reserve. But this would only be useful if the bank had exhausted both its valuation reserve and its earnings and was charging retained earnings to cover further loan losses.

Choosing the Size of the Valuation Reserve   The success of the reserve method as a device for handling loan losses depends on a bank's ability to anticipate its losses. Ideally, a bank should set aside funds which, over time, will just equal the loan amounts that end up being uncollectable. To do this, the bank must accurately assess the risk of loss on each loan it holds. This is quite simple for some kinds of loans—consumer loans, for example, generate highly predictable loss experiences. But some kinds of lending, often involving large loans to business, generate a more erratic flow of loan losses. It's quite difficult to compute a proper addition to the valuation reserve for such loans.

How large do a bank's valuation reserves need to be? Obviously, they need to be large enough to cover the normal losses which may be expected on the basis of actuarial principles. In addition, the valuation reserve might include a cushion against unusual losses which may occur irregularly over time. But it would be impractical and unnecessary to make the valuation reserve large enough to cover . . . the bank's unusual losses. Current earnings and equity capital are always available to backstop the loss reserve. Translating these principles into action isn't simple, of course. And critics have been quite vocal in criticizing the quality of bank judgments about the size of their valuation reserves.

Valuation Reserves Fail to Keep Pace

Current regulatory rules require each bank on the "reserve method" to make a minimum addition to its valuation reserve during each year, equal to its average rate of loan losses for the last five years, applied to its volume of loans outstanding on average during the current year.[5] This is only a minimum addition to the bank's loan loss reserve, however. Banks are instructed to reserve more than the minimum amounts if they anticipate loan charge-off rates significantly higher than their five-year average. That is where bank judgment comes into play. And critics quickly point out that bank judgment has produced declining loan loss coverage by valuation reserves over the past several years.

After 1969, when the agreement on expensing of the valuation reserve was reached, and through 1973, most banks provided only the minimum amounts required as an addition to their valuation reserves. In 1974, many banks altered this pattern and provided extra amounts above and beyond the minimum set by bank regulators. Evidence from quarterly earnings reports indicates many banks are continuing to provide extra amounts for loan losses in 1975. In fact, the formula for loan loss provisions seems to be playing a small part in banks' decisions about how much to provide for their loss reserves this year.

[5]Regulations do permit banks to be only partially on the reserve method. That is, it would appear that banks can build a tax shelter from some of their income but still be on a direct charge-off basis for covering actual loan losses. Banks doing this will be considered *not* to be on the reserve method for the purposes of this article.

Between 1969 and 1974, while they were reliant on the formula, banks charged off nearly as much in uncollectable loans as they added to their valuation reserves. Hence, the valuation reserve as of year-end 1974 was only about 1 percent larger than it was at the start of 1969. This relative constancy of bank valuation reserves contrasts sharply with the rapid growth of bank loans and loan losses. Bank loans have nearly doubled since the start of 1969 while the dollar volume of bank loan losses has risen nearly fourfold.

How could valuation reserves have fallen relatively so far behind? It's principally because banks' entire loan loss reserves were defined as valuation reserves when the accounting rules were changed in 1969. That change left the average bank with valuation reserves of nearly 2 percent of loans outstanding, which was enough to cover ten years of loan losses at the rate at which such losses occurred in the 1960s. Thus, even as loans and loan losses grew substantially after January 1969, few banks felt the need to charge their revenues with more than the minimum required amounts. The valuation reserve cushion that banks had when the '69 rules change was enacted left them comfortable with the small contributions made from '69 through '73.

It is notable that even during 1974, when many banks for the first time reserved more than the minimum amounts required under the '69 rules, the ratio of valuation reserves to loans continued to decline. And the ratio of these reserves to new loan charge-offs fell off even more. It is thus important to focus on the relative protection against loan losses afforded by valuation reserves and banks' other defenses, and to assess whether there's been a material weakening of banking soundness in this area.

Losses Outpace Loss Reserves: What Are the Implications?

The failure of bank valuation reserves to keep pace with bank loans and loan losses since 1968 is indeed striking. But this development may say more about the meaningfulness of banks' prior earnings reports than it does about any changes in the industry's vulnerability. Bank valuation reserves smooth out a bank's earnings record and make that record more meaningful to investors in the face of irregular loan losses. But, as guarantors of bank solvency, they are quite limited. A bank's earnings and equity capital are more significant defenses against unusual loan losses.

Effects on Earnings   When a bank employs the reserve method, its earnings in any year are considerably insulated from its actual loan loss experience during that year. The bank's reported earnings in each year are reduced by that year's contributions out of revenues to its valuation reserve. As long as the bank follows the regulatory formula to compute its current minimum provision for loan losses—that is, if the bank bases its loan loss provision upon its latest five-year rate of charge-offs—a given year's loan loss will have an effect only 20 percent as large on the bank's earnings in that year.[6] Actual losses in a given year may be above or below the year's addition to the valuation reserve; if so, the valuation reserve will absorb the difference between the year's loss provision and the year's actual losses.[7] In this way, annual variations in a bank's loan loss experience which will end up offsetting one another within a five-year period have their biggest impact on the valuation reserve rather than on earnings.

The valuation reserve does more than just smooth out a bank's earnings record. The reserve also helps make that earnings record more meaningful as a statement of the bank's underlying profitability. That is, the buffering function of valuation reserves helps to prevent erroneous signals about bank profitability from being conveyed to the public because of a one-time change in the charge-off rate. But this only holds when banks adhere rigidly to the principle of the reserve method. Suppose a bank boosted its interest revenue by extending more risky loans. Since the loans are riskier than those the bank had been issuing, the fraction of those loans likely to prove uncollectable a year or two hence is higher than the bank has been charging off recently. If the bank takes proper account of this, it will provide extra amounts for its valuation reserve concurrent with its receipt of higher interest payments. That is, it will reduce its reported net income to reflect more meaningfully the profitability of its current operations.

Has this feature of the reserve method actually worked in the past few years? Apparently not. Until recently, banks have not felt compelled to build up their valuation reserves in order to handle their growing loan losses. The 1969 rule change left them with plenty of loan loss coverage. Now, to the extent that many banks have since used up the valuation reserve cushion that the rule change gave them, income statements will now begin to reflect relatively larger charges for the loan loss reserve than in the past. That is, banks' net operating earnings apparently have been somewhat overstated since 1969 because funds that might ordinarily have been "spent" to build loan loss reserves have not been expended.[8] Crude estimation suggests that during 1969–74, banks were spared enough loan loss expense to boost their net earnings after-tax by nearly 8 percent (see box 3). Now that valuation reserves seem no longer to be inflated, bank profits will no longer contain this bonus.

This may hold some implications for the success that banks will have in raising funds in both the debt and equity markets. While lenders and shareholders are, of course, concerned with bank soundness per se, they are also keenly interested in bank

---

[6]An example may help here. Suppose a bank has had loan charge-offs equal to 20¢ per $100 of loans during each of the past five years. Imagine that its current year charge-off rate was $1 per $100. Then its latest five-year average would equal $(4 \times 0.20 + 1 \times 1.00) \div 5 = .36$. The bank would have to boost its valuation reserves this year by 36¢ for every $100 of loans outstanding. That's only 16¢ per $100 higher than last year's requirement of 20¢ per $100. And it's only 20 percent of the 80¢ per $100 runup in this year's loss ratio.

[7]Continuing with the above example, suppose the bank has $1,000 in loans outstanding. Its charge-offs this year are 1 percent of $1,000, or $10. Its contribution to the valuation reserve is 0.36 percent of $1,000, or $3.60. Thus, the valuation reserve will decline this year by $6.40.

[8]Bank profits were overstated before 1969 as well. The focus here is on considerations following the 1969 rule change, however.

profitability. For one thing, sustained profitability is itself an indicator of bank soundness. For another, bank profits are a measure of the bank's ability to make additional interest or dividend payments. Thus, to the extent that banks lose the profits advantage they held in the years after 1969, they may also now lose some of their attractiveness to investors. Of course, investors may have previously recognized any overstatement of bank earnings and entered that into their analyses. If so, elimination of the artificial boost to profits from loss reserve provisions won't significantly affect bank fund-raising efforts.

Box 3   1969 Ruling on Valuation Reserves Boosted Bank Profits

Computing the "right" volume of loan loss reserves for a bank to maintain is a very tricky procedure. But let's take an intellectual "giant step." Suppose that, for the banking system as a whole, valuation reserves ought to equal—as they did at year-end 1974—about 1 percent of loans outstanding. Many banking observers think a valuation reserve ratio of 1 percent is about right for the industry as a whole, so the assumption may be all right. We'll come back to this assumption shortly.

The valuation reserve ratio which the banking system held as of the start of 1969 was just under 2 percent. This high ratio was attained because banks were permitted to classify the entire loan loss reserve as a valuation reserve on January 1, 1969. This gave them $5.22 billion of valuation reserves as of that date.

Over the years since 1969, banks have added a net of only $.06 billion to their valuation reserves. That is, additions to bank valuation reserves have exceeded loan charge-offs against these reserves by only $.06 billion. This small addition to bank valuation reserves was concurrent, of course, with substantially increased loan and loan loss volumes. Banks got away with so small a net increase only because they had so much in valuation reserves to start with.

Now back to that assumption. Imagine that banks had been assigned the "right" volume of valuation reserves back in 1969. Instead of $5.22 billion, they would have had only $2.65 (1 percent of $265 billion in loans) billion at that time. Then, banks would have had to work harder in order to reach the "correct" level of valuation reserves by year-end 1974. The banks would have had to charge their earnings with—and reduce their profits by—a total of $2.57 billion more than they actually did over the 1969-74 period. This amounts to nearly 6 percent of bank operating earnings, pretax, and nearly 8 percent of bank net earnings, aftertax, during 1969-74. If valuation reserves are now at the "right" ratio to loans, then this profit bonus will no longer be available to banks.

Loss Reserves as Solvency Insurance   While there is no substitute for loss reserves as an earnings stabilizer, earnings and equity capital are effective substitutes for loss reserves as solvency insurance. A bank with uncollectable loans runs the risk of insolvency. But if a bank should "run out of" valuation reserves in meeting a calamitous loan loss, its earnings and capital accounts could still absorb the loss.

A bank's net operating earnings would be its next line of defense should its valuation reserves be exhausted. And, for the banking system as a whole, there's a lot of room to cover loan losses out of earnings. Earnings, before tax, in 1974 were over four times as great as charge-offs. This meant that valuation reserves and earnings together were over 7.5 times as great as charge-offs. Furthermore, the banking system's equity capital represents an amount 30 times as great as 1974 charge-offs. And equity capital is what a bank turns to if its earnings are exhausted. While each of these multiples is substantially less than their values of a few years ago, it's difficult to argue that they aren't *now* high enough.

Thus, the combination of loan loss reserves, operating earnings, and equity capital appears sufficient to protect most banks from loan losses well above those they've been experiencing. Of course, those defenses may not be adequate to keep all banks afloat, should loan losses jump. But judgments about the adequacy of reserve provisions shouldn't rest solely on whether each individual bank is sound. A more important issue is whether the *banking system* as a *whole* is safe. If too many individual banks got into trouble from loan losses, that could endanger the entire system. But the dimensions of the capital, earnings, and loss reserve protection now existing render this most improbable.

Capital as the Ultimate Insurance against Loan Losses   It's good to know that the banking system is well buffered from loan losses. But it's troublesome to consider all of the attention that's been placed upon loss reserves by students of this issue. Loss reserves are one of the guarantors of bank solvency, but their role is small in comparison to that played by bank capital. The real issue surrounding the industry's ability to withstand higher loan losses is the same as that surrounding its ability to withstand higher losses in other areas—the adequacy of bank equity capital. True, there's lots of controversy over how much bank capital is needed. But that's where there ought to be controversy, for loss reserves are just a variation on the bank capital theme.

Appearances Are Deceiving

As banks have expanded their roles as department stores of finance, their exposures to the risk of loan losses have also grown. With a severe recession on the books for 1975, the likelihood of particularly high loan losses at banks this year has raised questions about the ability of the industry to handle such losses.

While a recession needn't necessarily bring higher loan losses to commercial banks, the issue of adequate loan loss coverage is still meaningful at this juncture. Valuation reserves—the loan loss reserves out of which a bank normally "covers" loan losses—have grown very little over the past five or six years. Meanwhile, the volume of bank loans and loan losses has risen substantially. Thus, the degree of loan loss coverage which valuation reserves can provide has fallen substantially.

Banks are aware that they must have the resources to absorb loan losses internally. Otherwise, they realize, they can get into the same kind of financial hot water as their defaulting borrowers. Do banks need to cover more than three years' worth of losses with valuation reserves? That's how much coverage they had at year-end 1974, and it may be enough for all but a few institutions. Besides, loan loss reserves may not be the best measure of a bank's ability to remain solvent in the face of unusual losses. Loan loss reserves help stabilize a bank's earnings and are the bank's first line of defense when faced with loan losses. But the bank's earnings and equity capital are typically far more meaningful than loss reserves as resources in the battle against unforeseen loan losses. These resources must be available to cover a wider set of contingencies than just a bank's loan losses. But their sheer size relative to the historical experience which commercial banks have had with loan losses is reassuring indeed. Potential loan losses don't appear as overwhelming when viewed in the perspective as they would if loan loss reserves were a bank's principal defense.

The Prime Rate

Randall C. Merris

. . . Determining its prime rate is one of many decisions a large bank makes in the continuous process of managing its balance sheet—i.e., its asset portfolio and liability holdings. Three broad categories of market rates provide major inputs into these decisions: (1) rates on nonloan bank assets, (2) rates on bank-acquired liabilities, and (3) rates on corporate debt claims issued in lieu of bank borrowing. Because bank loan contracts remain in effect until specified future dates, bankers' expectations concerning the future course of market rates are more important than current rates in the prime-setting decision. Other important considerations are expected growth in deposits—the major source of bank funds—and expected loan demand.

Several institutional characteristics of bank administration also have a profound influence on the prime-setting process. A decision to alter the prime rate involves adjustments in a bank's schedule of business loan rates. Nonprime rates typically are determined by tying them directly and formally, or indirectly and informally, to the prime. Thus, a bank must consider expected demand for nonprime loans in establishing its prime rate.

A bank's "customer relationships"—the arrangements whereby a bank provides a variety of services to its long-established clientele—also must be considered in setting the prime. A banker must be concerned with the long-run profitability of the "total

Reprinted, with deletions, from *Economic Perspectives,* July/August 1977, pp. 17–18, and May/June 1978, pp. 14–16, by permission of the Federal Reserve Bank of Chicago and the author.

customer" and, therefore, is loath to make frequent rate adjustments that might jeopardize customer loyalty. The usual customer relationship includes two features that are especially relevant to prime rate decisions—compensating balance requirements and a bank credit line.

Role of Compensating Balances

Compensating balances are minimum average checking account balances that bank customers agree to maintain as partial remuneration for an array of bank services. Although compensating balances earn no interest return, typically they do qualify business customers for credit lines—prearranged agreements whereby banks extend credit on demand up to specified amounts.

Compensating balance requirements also serve to raise "effective" loan rates. Although requirements usually are stated as percentages of dollar amounts of credit lines, many arrangements require the deposit of additional balances when credit lines are activated or used. Nominal loan rates at banks are quoted in terms of the dollar size, or principal, of the loan. If a borrower uses part of the loan proceeds to meet compensating balance requirements, the "effective" loan rate on the funds actually available for the borrowers' use will exceed the stated rate because the borrower is paying loan interest on funds committed to remain in his deposit account. By increasing compensating balance requirements, banks can raise "effective" loan rates and thereby ration credit without changing prime rate quotations.

Other methods whereby banks can trim the flow of credit without altering loan rate schedules include reclassifying borrowers from lower- to higher-risk classes (ones carrying higher loan rates) and varying one or more nonprice loan terms—maturities, collateral requirements, or even loan sizes. Because of these practices, coupled with the ongoing uncertainty that surrounds future events—specifically, future credit conditions and market interest rates—the prime rate has tended to be more inflexible, or "sticky," than most other short-term interest rates. As a consequence, most banks have been satisfied simply to follow prime rate adjustments initiated by a few "leader banks."

Managing Bank Liabilities

During the late 1940s and throughout the 1950s, large commercial banks were able to accommodate the growth in business loan demand by reducing their large stock of liquid assets—mainly, short-term U.S. Government securities accumulated during the war. Because of the favorable earnings potential of loans vis-à-vis these securities, banks found it advantageous to reduce their U.S. Government security holdings in order to finance more business credit. Because of banks' highly liquid positions, there was little pressure for increases in the prime rate and adjustments occurred only infrequently.

Faced with reduced liquidity in the early 1960s, large banks began to direct more attention to the liability side of their balance sheets. In their competition for funds to meet expanding credit demands, large banks began to rely relatively less on such traditional sources as demand deposits and regular time and savings deposits and to rely more on marginal sources of funds, including large-denomination negotiable certificates of deposit (CDs), federal funds, and Eurodollars. Negotiable certificates of deposit are bank time deposits with various stated maturities, and Federal funds are overnight loans between banks made in immediately available funds. Eurodollars for domestic bank lending mainly are funds acquired by U.S. banks from their foreign branches.

During the 1960-65 period favorable margins between loan returns and costs of market-sensitive funds enabled large commercial banks to meet expanding credit demands while holding the prime rate at $4\frac{1}{2}$ percent. As markets for CDs, Federal funds, and Eurodollars matured and competition intensified, however, spreads between the prime rate and rates on bank liabilities narrowed. By December 1965 the Eurodollar rate had risen above the prime rate, and the 90-day CD rate and the Federal funds rate had climbed to within less than $\frac{1}{2}$ of 1 percent of the prime.

Beginning in the 1960s, large banks became increasingly sensitive to competition from commercial paper—unsecured promissory notes issued by large corporations either directly or through dealers and sold to large-volume investors, including other large corporations. Competition from the commercial paper market placed unusual pressures on banks in the acquisition and use of funds. During the 1960s, the volume of commercial paper outstanding nearly tripled and the number of participants in the market grew considerably. Historically, the prime rate had exceeded the 90-day commercial paper rate by one percentage point or more. This differential narrowed in the early 1960s, as more and more corporations came to view commercial paper as a close substitute for bank credit.

Commercial paper began to compete strongly for investment funds with commercial bank CDs. Top-quality corporate paper and bank-issued CDs were sold in large denominations and short maturities, and each type of claim carried minimal default risk. Because of these similar characteristics, the same groups of investors—mainly large corporations—constituted the major markets for both commercial paper and CDs. Over time large investors grew increasingly sensitive to interest rate differentials; widening and narrowing spreads between CD and commercial paper rates prompted large quantities of funds to shift between these markets. As a result of this high degree of substitutability, the rate on 90-day commercial paper moved in close harmony with the 90-day CD rate during the 1960s.

In the latter part of the decade banks themselves came to view commercial paper as a ready source of loanable funds. They began to borrow extensively in the paper market by having their affiliates (i.e., holding companies and subsidiaries) issue bank-related paper, and then channel the acquired funds into the bank via loan sales. By December 1969 the volume of bank-related commercial paper outstanding amounted to more than $4 billion and accounted for over 13 percent of the total volume of commercial paper. After reaching $7.8 billion in July 1970, however, the volume of bank-related paper fell sharply, primarily because of the Federal Reserve's imposition of reserve requirements on this type of paper. By October 1971, when the formula prime was introduced, bank-related paper totaled $1.9 billion and accounted for less than 6 percent of all commercial paper outstanding.

The Formula Prime

On October 20, 1971, a few large banks announced that they were considering the feasibility of a formula, or "floating," prime rate—i.e., prime rate quotations adjusted in direct response to variations in the rates on one or more money market instruments. Although the prime rate and market rates always had been related and generally moved together over time, banks had never attempted to explain in detail the connection between them.

The next day, October 21, First National City Bank (Citibank), the largest bank in New York, announced the first prime rate formula. The essence of the formula was that the prime rate was to be reviewed weekly, adjusted by minimum steps of ⅛ percentage point, and kept approximately 50 basis points above the average rate on 90-day commercial paper placed through dealers. The choice of the commercial paper rate reflected the high degree of substitutability between bank loans and commercial paper. Moreover, because of its relatively large volume, commercial paper was considered fairly well insulated from unusual disruptive influences on both domestic and foreign credit markets, resulting in a reliable indicator of the "free market rate" for short-term business credit.

By the end of 1971 a few other commercial banks had introduced their own formulas. While differing from Citibank's formula in minor respects, these other formulas followed it in relating prime rate quotations to average rates on top-quality 90-day commercial paper. Banks differed in their choices of which side of the dealer-placed market to use—the rate charged issuers or the rate offered investors. Some banks chose longer intervals than a week for appraising prime rate adjustments, and some selected ¼ percentage point rather than ⅛ percentage point as the minimum step for prime rate adjustments. One New York bank based its formula rate on two alternative money-market criteria—the issuer rate on 90-day commercial paper (plus .50 of 1 percent) or the 90-day CD rate (plus .65 of 1 percent).

Why a Formula Prime?

Although its adoption by some of the largest banks was an important event, the idea of a formula, or a "floating," prime rate for business loans was not a new one. Bankers had searched for a long time for some means of insulating prime rate changes from political criticism. And two major political incidents were fresh in the minds of commercial bankers when the formula prime was introduced.

- In December 1964 several banks boosted the prime rate from 4½ to 4¾ percent. Although this was the first prime rate movement since August 1960, banks began to rescind their rate hikes two days later, following Presidential urging that rates be held down.

• In June 1969 the prime rate again came under close political scrutiny when banks undertook a full percentage point increase, from 7½ to 8½ percent, at that time a record high. This move kindled immediate Congressional response, and ten days later hearings were convened by the House Committee on Banking and Currency for the specific purpose of investigating prime rate increases. On this occasion, however, banks did not rescind their increases, and the 8½ percent rate remained in effect until March 1970 when it was lowered to 8 percent.

In the fall of 1971 signs pointed toward a renewed round of political concern. Phase I of the wage-price control program had been unveiled two months earlier and Phase II was due in about a month. The Committee on Interest and Dividends (CID), organized under the Economic Stabilization Program, had taken initial steps to monitor interest rate developments. On October 20, 1971, just one day before Citibank announced its formula rate, the CID requested that all lending institutions keep records of their loan rate schedules, retroactive to August 16, 1971. This CID action suggested to commercial banks that closer scrutiny of prime rate revisions might be approaching. . . .

Formulas and Rate Spreads

Citibank's first formula called for setting its prime rate approximately ½ percentage point above the rate on three- to four-month commercial paper subject to weekly review. Since then, Citibank has exercised considerable latitude in tempering the formula prime concept to the financial and political environment—rounding up or down from the formula, temporarily discounting the formula in 1973, intermittently ignoring weekly rate changes implied by the formula, and revising the formula itself. The current Citibank formula, and the only one now publicized nationally, calls for a prime rate that is 1¼ percentage points above the three-previous-week average of the 90–119 day, dealer-placed commercial paper rate. The present Citibank prime-setting method is the culmination of four changes in the differential between the formula prime and the commercial paper rate since the CID ended. The formula spread was increased from ¾ to 1 percentage point in October 1974, from 1 to 1¼ to 1½ percentage points in January 1976, and then was lowered to 1¼ percentage points in June 1977.

Although other large commercial banks do not presently issue formula-prime quotations, some acknowledge that they use the commercial paper rate as an informal indicator for prime rate revisions. Some banks also admit to using Citibank's prime as a benchmark for their own prime rate revisions, although clearly they do not have a simple follow-the-leader allegiance to Citibank's prime. Industry-wide prime quotations have tended to stay within ¼, or at most ½, percentage point of Citibank's rate.

Even though prime bank loans and commercial paper are both tailored to borrowers' needs and are close substitutes for short-term business financing, a historical spread exists between the respective rates. The basic spread depends on differences in administrative costs and nonprice lending terms involved in issuing and servicing each type of debt contract. Differences in interest cost calculations—discount method for commercial paper and typically bond-yield method for prime loans— also contribute to the spread. . . .

An Update

A widely reported development in commercial bank lending over recent years has been the extension of business credit at interest rates below prime. If these ''super-prime'' loans become widespread, they could signal structural, or long-range, changes in bank lending and the concept of the prime rate itself.

Since it originated in 1933, the modern prime rate has come to serve three major functions for banks:

- It is the interest rate applicable to a bank's most creditworthy customers.
- It is a base rate to which are tied, formally or informally, the higher interest rates on nonprime bank loans.
- It is an index rate for floating-rate bank loans—contracts that allow interest charges to vary up and down with market rates over the durations of the loans.

  Bank borrowers have found their own meanings for the prime rate, and intentionally or otherwise, banks have fostered these ideas:
- Qualifying for the prime is a symbol of business success and a sign of a healthy enterprise.
- Qualifying for the prime in some cases is a reward to a customer of longstanding for allowing one bank to handle all his banking needs.

In short, the prime rate is expected to serve several functions—a lot to ask of a single interest rate.

Banks have tried to adopt lending practices over time that would allow the prime rate to perform its multiple tasks. But difficulties with the concept of a prime rate have been accumulating since the early 1960s. Borrowers in the prime category have become increasingly heterogeneous, and the idea of a ''most creditworthy customer'' has been broadened to the limit. The floating-rate function of the prime was once fairly minor. But with the increased variability of interest rates since the early 1960s, that has become one of the most important functions. At least half of the dollar volume of business lending at many large banks is now made under floating-rate provisions. The growth of long-term bank lending has contributed vitally to the importance of this prime function. New long-term lending at many banks has been predominantly at floating rates.

Recent Lending Experience

Conflicts between the functions of the prime rate have arisen several times in recent years. But the problems became especially severe in 1976 and 1977, when demand for business loans was slack at large money-center banks. During that time banks saw the demand for loans from business in general and prime-rate borrowers in particular fail to respond to declining loan rates. Many large banks, however, were able to identify submarkets of prime-rate customers that might borrow more if bank rates were lowered.

Under these circumstances, banks were faced with a dilemma. If they lowered the prime rate, most loan customers would not borrow more. The primary effect would be simply to reduce total loan revenue. If they did not lower the rate, a large amount of loan business would be lost from submarkets that were responsive to lower rates. To complicate the problem further, there was a conflict with the function served by the prime in floating-rate contracts. If the prime was lowered, banks stood to forfeit revenue from all loans already on the books at rates tied to the prime.

One way to entice borrowers that were receptive to lower loan rates was to relax other loan terms. Some banks allowed these borrowers to "double count" compensating balances. The same noninterest deposit balances were used both to compensate the bank for a credit extension and to reimburse the bank for the nonloan services it provided business customers.

The most obvious method was to lend at special rates below prime to the subcategories of borrowers that seemed receptive to lower rates. But banks moved quietly and reluctantly in this direction. Below-prime rates for some customers could lead to disgruntled prime-rate borrowers. They could lead also to reactions from other banks, either in the form of a general reduction in loan rates or charges of unsound banking practices. But even if below-prime pricing might not have been good strategy for these reasons, it was good economics under the circumstances.

Basic price theory can be used to show how a firm can maximize profits in a situation in which one segment of a market is fairly unresponsive to a lower price (in this case, interest rate) and another is fairly responsive. Demand in the first submarket is termed relatively price inelastic, and demand in the second submarket is said to be relatively price elastic. The solution is to separate demands in the two submarkets and establish different prices for each. The submarket with the relatively elastic de-

Percent of Dollar Amount of New Short-Term Business Loans at Floating Rates, 48 Large Banks

1977 During the Week of	All Sizes of Loans	Loan Size Category (in Thousands)					
		$1-24	$25-49	$50-99	$100-499	$500-999	$1,000 and Over
February 7-12	66.5	42.0	55.3	56.7	63.5	72.4	68.4
May 2-7	63.7	43.6	49.8	53.8	54.0	60.3	68.0
August 1-6	61.6	44.4	53.6	55.1	61.1	66.9	62.2
November 7-12	71.5	38.5	48.8	61.4	67.6	77.2	74.3

Percent of Dollar Amount of New Term Loans at Floating Rates, 48 Large Banks

1977 During the Week of	All Sizes of Loans	Loan Size Category (in Thousands)			
		$1-99	$100-499	$500-999	$1,000 and Over
February 7-12	74.6	59.5	76.7	84.0	74.8
May 2-7	66.9	66.1	76.4	67.2	65.9
August 1-6	81.3	65.1	76.2	67.5	84.5
November 7-12	69.0	81.0	80.7	80.9	64.2

Source: Survey of Terms of Bank Lending, Board of Governors of the Federal Reserve System. Included are commercial and industrial loans other than construction and land development loans. Short-term loans have original maturities of less than one year, and term loans have maturities of one year or more.

mand, then, receives a lower price than the other submarket and a lower price and a larger volume of sales (here, loans) than would be the case if both submarkets were treated together to establish a common price.

Theory also is useful in identifying the submarket with the most elastic demand. it is the customers with the most or best substitutes for the product or service. Prime-rate borrowers with the best alternative sources of funds were identified as corporations that issue commercial paper and multinational companies with access to the Eurocurrency credit markets. These are often the same companies.

Commercial paper is unsecured debt issued by large corporations either directly or through dealers and sold to large-volume investors. Eurocurrency credits are over-seas bank loans extended and repayable in currencies other than the currency of the lending bank. Both the commercial paper and the Eurocurrency markets have grown dramatically since the early 1960s, measured in terms of either the volume of credit or the number of participants.

By not letting the prime rate fall as fast as the three-to-four month commercial paper rate, bankers allowed the prime-paper rate spread to increase to over 1 percentage point in early 1975 and to 1½ percentage points by early 1976. The spread has narrowed again since last summer. But through the first quarter of 1978, it was still about 1¼ percentage points. And as a result, competitive pressures for below-prime lending to issuers of commercial paper have persisted.

Special Rates

Since November 1977, two large money center banks have offered new lending programs to approved lists of corporations that issue commercial paper. Loans under these programs allow corporations to postpone new issues of paper in anticipation of lower paper rates or when the market for a particular maturity is weak. Under one program, loans are granted in maturities up to ten days. Under the other, maturities go up to 29 days.

Under both programs, loan rates are based on the incremental cost of funds to the lending bank and are kept competitive with commercial paper rates. Loans under one program have fixed-rate interest charges. Under the other, floating-rate charges are revised daily. The first rate quotations for one of these programs last November were a little over ¼ percentage point above the three-to-four month commercial paper rate and nearly 1 percentage point below the 7¾ percent prime rate in effect at the time.

In March 1978, another large bank announced it had initiated a program several months earlier to provide credit to multinational corporations at special rates and in maturities competitive with commercial paper. This newest program is in contrast to plans at the other two banks, which are aimed only at corporate financing for less than a month before commercial paper sales. By offering maturities on loans from a day to 180 days or longer, the program of this third bank provides a direct substitute to commercial paper for short-term corporate financing.

All three banks have emphasized that they do not consider their new lending programs as temporary measures dependent only on current money-market conditions. Since these plans were announced, some other large commercial banks have disclosed informally that they are also making special efforts to attract commercial paper issuers as borrowers. Included in these efforts are special lending rates.

One factor determining whether banks with special lending programs expand them and whether other banks formally announce such programs will be the spread between the prime rate and the commercial paper rate. If banks narrow the spread soon, the need for the special lending programs could disappear for a while. But because the basic conflicts between the functions of the prime rate are endemic to modern banking, the problems of 1976 and 1977 are apt to reappear.

Linear Programming:
A New Approach to Bank
Portfolio Management

Alfred Broaddus

Perhaps the most important and most difficult problem facing any commercial bank's senior management on a continuing basis is asset portfolio management. Portfolio decisions made at any given time directly affect a bank's current income and profits. Moreover, current decisions may significantly influence income and profit flows in future periods. What makes asset selection difficult is that alternative courses of action invariably present trade-offs between profits, liquidity, and risk. Evaluating and weighing these factors is an inherently complex task. The problem has been compounded during recent years by the pressure on commercial banks to maintain adequate profits in the face of increased competition for funds both from nonbank financial institutions and from various money market instruments.

As a result of this increased pressure, the commercial banking industry has begun to seek more sophisticated approaches to portfolio management. Management scientists are assisting the industry by devising improved decision techniques that can be understood and effectively employed by bankers.[1] One technique receiving considerable attention is linear programming. Linear programming is a basic analytical procedure, or "model," employed extensively in management science and operations

Reprinted from the Federal Reserve Bank of Richmond, *Monthly Review,* November 1972, pp. 3-11, by permission of the publisher and the author.

[1]Two management scientists, Kalman J. Cohen and Frederick S. Hammer, have been instrumental in this effort. Their published work in this area, on which the present article draws extensively, is listed in the accompanying references.

research. Although the theory underlying the technique involves advanced mathematics, the model's structure is straightforward and can be understood by management personnel having only minimal training in mathematics. The purpose of this article is to describe the technique in a nonmathematical manner and to indicate how it can be used in the bank portfolio management process. Section I outlines two currently popular approaches to asset management and points out some of their principal deficiencies. Section II describes the linear programming model and uses a highly simplified numerical example to indicate the model's applicability to bank portfolio decisions. Section III discusses how banks might employ the model in practice and attempts to suggest the model's proper role in the overall portfolio decision process. Section IV summarizes the technique's advantages in banking applications and points out some of its limitations.

I. Current Approaches

The typical bank's balance sheet lists a variety of assets and liabilities. Liabilities, such as demand and savings deposits, are sources of bank funds. Assets, such as business loans, consumer installment loans, and government securities, are uses of bank funds. The essence of the asset management problem is the need to achieve a proper balance between (1) income, (2) adequate liquidity to meet such contingencies as unanticipated loan demand and deposit withdrawals, and (3) the risk of default. The problem arises because assets carrying relatively high yields, such as consumer installment loans, are generally less liquid and riskier than assets having relatively low yields, such as short-term government securities.

The "Pooled-Funds" Approach   During the early postwar period, funds were generally available to banks in ample supply at low cost. Consequently, most banks followed what has been termed a "pooled-funds" approach in deciding how to allocate funds among competing assets. Under the pooled-funds concept, a bank begins its asset selection procedure by arbitrarily defining a fixed liquidity standard, usually some target ratio of reserves and secondary reserve assets to total deposits. Using this standard, the bank then allocates each dollar it attracts, from whatever source, in identical proportions among various categories of assets. A principal deficiency in this procedure is its failure to take into account variations in liquidity needs that arise from variations in the structure of liability and loan accounts.[2]

The "Asset Allocation" Technique   The pooled-funds approach served most banks reasonably well during the late 1940s and early 1950s when funds were relatively plentiful and the majority of bank liabilities were noninterest-bearing demand deposits. Since that time, the financial environment in which banks operate has

---

[2]The "structure" of an individual bank's liabilities refers to the proportionate allocation of total funds among various liability categories such as demand deposits, savings deposits, and certificates of deposit. Similarly, the structure of a bank's loan accounts refers to the allocation of total loans among various classes of loans.

changed dramatically. Nonbank financial institutions, particularly savings and loan associations and mutual savings banks, began to compete vigorously with individual commercial banks for deposits during the 1950s. In addition, corporate treasurers, motivated by sharp increases in the yields of such money market instruments as Treasury bills and high-grade commercial paper, began to trim their working balances held in commercial bank demand deposits to bare minimums. The banking industry has responded to these deposit drains by developing new sources of funds, notably negotiable certificates of deposit, commercial paper issued through affiliates, and Eurodollar borrowings. While these innovations have permitted the banking industry to grow at an adequate rate, they have proved costly, resulting in increased pressure on bank profits. Therefore, a premium has been placed on efficient bank balance sheet management.

The management tool developed to meet the need for more sophisticated portfolio management was the so-called Asset Allocation technique.[3] The distinguishing feature of this procedure is that it takes explicit account of a bank's liability structure in guiding asset choice. More specifically, the Asset Allocation approach recognizes that the velocity of various types of liabilities differs systematically from one liability category to another.[4] The procedure specifies that funds obtained from liabilities with rapid turnover rates (such as demand deposits) should be invested relatively heavily in assets of short maturity, and, conversely, that funds obtained from low-velocity liabilities (such as certificates of deposit) should be invested relatively heavily in long-term assets. In its most extreme form, the technique divides a bank into subsystems by liability classes: for example, a "demand deposit bank," a "time deposit bank," and a "Eurodollars bank." Funds flowing into each of these "banks," that is, funds obtained from each liability source, are then allocated proportionately among alternative assets using formulas that reflect liability velocities. For example, the demand deposit formula might specify relatively high proportions of short-term government securities and short-term business loans, while the time deposit formula might specify a relatively high proportion of mortgages.

Faced with an ever-widening range of diverse sources of funds, many bank portfolio managers have adopted the Asset Allocation approach because of its explicit attention to asset-liability linkages. But while the method represents an improvement over earlier procedures, it possesses several fundamental weaknesses.[5] First, velocity is a poor guide to the liquidity requirements imposed by a given class of liabilities. A far more relevant consideration is account stability, that is, the net daily variation of an account's total balance. It is widely recognized that no correlation necessarily

[3]The Asset Allocation or "conversion of funds" procedure was originally devised by Harold E. Zarker. See Harold E. Zarker, *Conversion of Commercial Bank Funds* (Cambridge, Massachusetts: Bankers Publishing Company, 1942).

[4]The velocity of a given liability account is the ratio of the dollar flow within that account during some specified time period to the average stock of dollars in the account during the same period. The reciprocal of velocity is then the length of time an average dollar remains in the account.

[5]For a more extensive critique, see Kalman J. Cohen and Frederick S. Hammer, ed., *Analytical Methods in Banking* (Homewood, Illinois: Richard D. Irwin, Inc., 1966), pp. 45-53.

exists between stability and velocity.[6] Second, the technique is arbitrary and inflexible. It is arbitrary because no clearly defined bank goal (such as some form of constrained profit maximization) guides the determination of the various fund conversion formulas. It is inflexible because no systematic procedure is provided for altering the formulas in the face of changing external conditions, such as shifts in particular asset yields. Third, by compartmentalizing a bank into various subsystems, the method diverts attention from the overall goals of the bank's operations and fails to recognize important interactions between various bank activities. The linear programming approach described below avoids these difficulties.

II. The Linear Programming Model: An Example

Linear programming is a general mathematical procedure for maximizing target variables subject to constraints.[7] The linear programming model has been extensively applied in industrial production analysis, where the objective typically is to maximize profits by achieving the proper product mix within the constraints imposed by technical production procedures, resource availability, and resource costs. This section presents a simple numerical example designed to illustrate how the model can be used by bank portfolio managers. The example employs a set of graphs to assist readers unfamiliar with the model in grasping the essence of the technique's substantive content. While graphs are a useful explanatory device, their employment restricts the scope of the illustration. Consequently, the example is a necessarily artificial and unrealistic representation of the actual portfolio decision process. Nonetheless, the illustration conveys the flavor of the technique and demonstrates its applicability to bank balance sheet decisions.

Consider a hypothetical bank that holds two classes of liabilities, demand deposits (DD) and time deposits (TD), and that can choose between two classes of assets, loans (L) and securities (S). Hence, the bank's balance sheet takes the following form:

Assets	Liabilities
L	DD
S	TD
	Capital Accounts

Assume that the rate of return on loans is 10 percent during some relevant decision period, but that no loan matures and no loan can be sold during the period. Assume

---

[6]See George R. Morrison and Richard T. Selden, *Time Deposit Growth and the Employment of Bank Funds* (Chicago: Association of Reserve City Bankers, 1965), p. 12.

[7]A comprehensive treatment of linear programming is contained in G. Hadley, *Linear Programming* (Reading, Massachusetts: Addison-Wesley Publishing Company, Inc., 1962).

further that securities yield 5 percent during the period and can be liquidated at any time without the risk of capital loss. Total funds available to the bank are fixed at, say, $100 million, distributed as follows: $45 million in demand deposit accounts, $45 million in time deposit accounts, and $10 million in capital and surplus. Finally, assume for illustrative simplicity that the bank incurs no costs in attracting and maintaining deposits.

The bank would like to select an asset portfolio that maximizes its total return over the period. If this were all that were involved, the optimal asset selection decision would be obvious: channel all available funds into loans, the asset yielding the higher return. The bank recognizes, however, certain constraints upon its actions. In reality, the constraints are numerous. The present example will consider three.

Total Funds Constraint As indicated above, the bank has $100 million to allocate between loans and securities. Consequently, the sum of its loan and securities balances cannot exceed $100 million. This constraint can be expressed mathematically as:

$$L + S \leq 100 \text{ million} \tag{1}$$

where the symbol $\leq$ means "less than or equal to."[8] Figure 1 depicts this restriction graphically. Any point on the graph represents some combination of loans and securities. For example, point X corresponds to a loan balance of $60 million and a securities balance of $70 million. The diagonal line AA' (the graphical representation of the equation $L + S = 100$ million) is the locus of points at which loans and

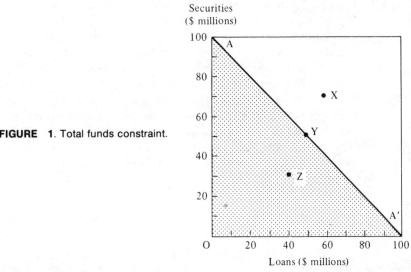

FIGURE 1. Total funds constraint.

[8]The opposite symbol $\geq$ means "greater than or equal to."

securities total $100 million. At point Y, for example, the loan balance is $50 million, the securities balance is $50 million, and total assets are therefore $100 million. At any point above and to the right of line AA', such as X, total assets exceed $100 million. At any point below and to the left of the AA', such as Z, total assets are less than $100 million. The total funds constraint requires that the point representing the bank's asset portfolio either fall on AA' or within the shaded region below and to the left of AA'.[9]

Liquidity Constraint   The bank recognizes that, because loans cannot be liquidated during the time period under consideration, some quantity of negotiable securities must be held to meet unanticipated deposit withdrawals. Therefore, the bank makes it a rule always to maintain some minimum ratio of securities to total assets. Assume that, with $45 million of demand deposits and $45 million of time deposits, the bank always maintains a securities balance equal to or greater than 25 percent of total assets. The mathematical expression for this constraint is:

$$S \geq .25 \, (L + S), \tag{2}$$

or, equivalently and more conveniently, as:

$$S \geq .33 \, (L). \tag{3}$$

Constraint (3) is depicted graphically by Figure 2. It requires that the bank's asset portfolio fall on line OB or at some point in the shaded region above the line.

On the presumption that time deposits are generally more stable than demand deposits, the bank's management varies its liquidity ratio inversely with shifts in the ratio of time to total deposits. Hence, an increase in the ratio would cause line OB to rotate downward, thereby enlarging the shaded area of acceptable portfolio. Conversely, a reduction in the ratio would rotate OB upward, diminishing the area of acceptable portfolios. The effects of such shifts will be considered below.

Loan Balance Constraint   Because the bank considers lending its most important activity, it imposes certain restrictions on its loan balance. Specifically, the bank attempts to satisfy all the requests for loans submitted by its principal customers. Assume that the aggregate demand of these customers totals $30 million during the period. This constraint is depicted by Figure 3. The restriction requires the bank's portfolio to fall on or to the right of line CC'. The mathematical statement of the constraint is:

$$L \geq 30 \text{ million.} \tag{4}$$

[9]Strictly, with total funds equal to $100 million, the balance sheet identity requires that L + S equal exactly $100 million, that is, that the point representing the bank's asset portfolio fall *on* line AA'. For the purpose of illustrating the linear programming technique, it is helpful to treat the constraint as an inequality rather than an equality. This deviation will not affect the example's solution.

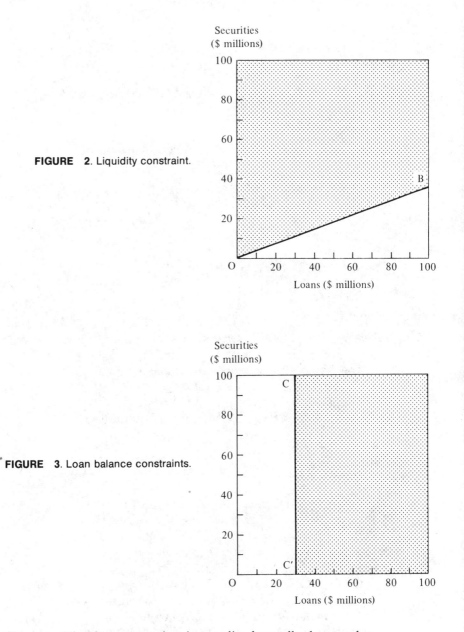

FIGURE 2. Liquidity constraint.

FIGURE 3. Loan balance constraints.

The Feasible Region   The three constraints just outlined are all relevant when the bank's management meets to allocate available funds between loans and securities. Figure 4 shows how the constraints taken as a group restrict the bank's range of choice. Any asset portfolio represented by a point outside the shaded region EFG violates one or more of the constraints. Conversely, any portfolio represented by a point within or on one of the boundaries of this region satisfies all of the constraints.

Securities
($ millions)

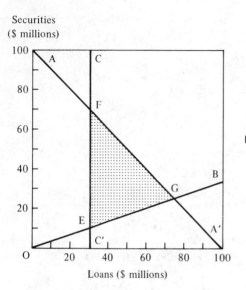

FIGURE **4**. The feasible region.

Loans ($ millions)

Therefore, the portfolio selected must lie within the region or on one of its boundaries. For this reason, the area is called the "feasible region."

The Objective Function   The reader will recall the assumption that loans yield
10 percent and securities 5 percent during the relevant time period. Consequently,
the bank's total income during the period equals 10 percent of its loan balance plus
5 percent of its securities balance.[10] Mathematically:

$$\text{Income} = .10(\text{L}) + .05(\text{S}). \tag{5}$$

Expression (5) is called the objective function of the linear programming problem.
Figure 5 depicts the "family" of objective functions represented by equation (5).
Each member of the family, that is, each of the parallel lines on the graph, corresponds to some unique income level. On the graph, the line closest to point O corresponds to income of $1 million, the middle line to income of $3 million, and the
outermost line to income of $5 million.[11] Hence, the bank's income increases as the
objective function shifts upward and to the right.

The Optimal Asset Portfolio   All of the elements relevant to the bank's portfolio
decision have now been developed. The linear programming problem is summarized
by the following mathematical statement:

[10]For simplicity, the possibility of loan default is ignored.
[11]The reader can easily confirm that *any* point on one of these lines represents a portfolio that yields the
designated income.

Maximize income $= .10(L) + .05(S)$ (6)
Subject to:

$$L + S \leq 100 \text{ million}$$
$$S \geq .33 (L)$$
$$L \geq 30 \text{ million.}$$

The solution to the problem is depicted graphically by Figure 6, which reproduces the feasible region of Figure 4 along with several members of equation (5)'s family of objective functions. From what has been said, it should be clear that the bank can find its income-maximizing portfolio by pushing the objective function outward as far as possible without going beyond the point where some part of the function lies within the feasible region. Clearly, the income-maximizing objective function in this case is line NN'. This line barely touches the feasible region at point G. Any line to the right of NN', such as PP', lies entirely outside of the feasible region. Lines to the left of NN', such as MM', may contain points within the feasible region but correspond to income levels less than that represented by NN'. The solution to the problem is given at point G. The bank can maximize its income, while observing all constraints, by choosing the combination of loans and securities represented by point G: that is, by allocating \$75 million to loans and \$25 million to securities.[12] This portfolio would yield \$8.75 million of income during the period. The linear programming model has provided the bank an objective procedure for determining its opti-

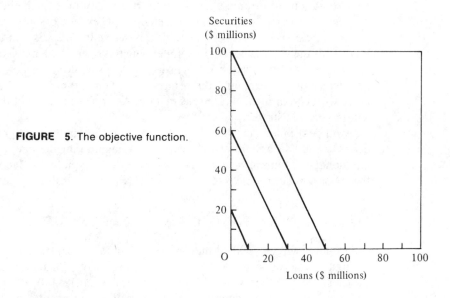

Securities
($ millions)

FIGURE   5. The objective function.

Loans ($ millions)

---

[12]For simplicity, the solution values are rounded to the nearest million.

Securities
($ millions)

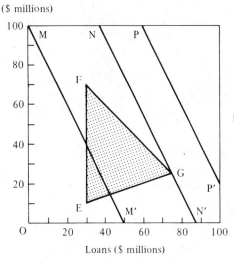

FIGURE 6. The optimal asset portfolio.

Loans ($ millions)

mal portfolio. The model has taken explicit and simultaneous account of the various factors assumed relevant to the decision.

Analytical Uses of the Model   The linear programming model can perform a number of useful analytical tasks for the bank in addition to suggesting reasonable approximations to income-maximizing portfolios. In particular, the model can specify how the bank's optimal portfolio changes when one of the constraints changes. Through analysis of this sort, the bank can determine the costs, in terms of foregone income, of the various constraints under which it operates. Knowledge of these costs, in turn, can assist the bank in such diverse tasks as deciding how much interest to pay depositors, determining the rate of return on capital, and deciding whether to borrow or lend in the federal funds market. A simple extension of the above example will serve to illustrate.

It will be recalled that the bank's deposits total $90 million: $45 million of demand deposits and $45 million of time deposits. Imagine that the bank gain access to an additional $10 million of *time* deposits. These additional time deposits affect two of the constraints in problem (6). First, the total funds constraint is eased to:

$$L + S \leq 110 \text{ million.} \tag{7}$$

Second, it will be recalled that, by assumption, the bank's management varies the minimum ratio of securities to total assets inversely with the ratio of time to total deposits. Assume that, with $55 million of time deposits and $45 million of demand deposits, management considers a 20 percent liquidity ratio constraint adequate. Under these conditions, the restriction becomes:

$$S \geq .20(L + S), \qquad (8)$$

or:

$$S \geq .25(L). \qquad (9)$$

With these modifications, the mathematical statement of the bank's problem is changed from (6) to:

Maximize income $= .10(L) + .05(S)$ (10)
Subject to:

$$L + S \leq 110 \text{ million}$$
$$S \geq .25(L)$$
$$L \geq 30 \text{ million}.$$

Figure 7 depicts the altered situation graphically. EFG is the feasible region of the preceding problem. E′F′G′ is the extended feasible region of the new problem that results from the easing of the total funds and liquidity constraints attendant upon the $10 million increase in time deposits. Point G′ represents the solution to the new problem, with the objective function in position QQ′. As indicated by G′, the bank's new income-maximizing portfolio contains $88 million of loans and $22 million of securities. Since yields have not changed, the bank's income is now $9.9 million.

The solutions to problems (6) and (10) can assist the bank in determining how much to pay depositors for the $10 million increment of time deposits. Comparing

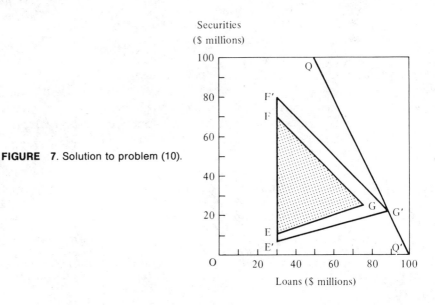

FIGURE 7. Solution to problem (10).

incomes in the two cases, it is clear that the additional deposits produce $1.15 million of additional income ($9.9 million − $8.75 million), or $.115 per additional time deposit dollar. Consequently, the bank can afford to pay up to a rate of 11.5 percent for each additional time deposit dollar.[13] At first glance, management might consider it ridiculous to contemplate incurring additional deposit costs at a rate that exceeds the available return on either loans or securities. The reason it is profitable to do so is that the additional time deposits have both a direct and a secondary effect on the bank's income. The direct effect in this case is the additional income resulting from the investment of the extra funds. The secondary effect is the additional income generated by the reallocation of the bank's original $100 million of funds to a higher proportion of loans made possible by the eased liquidity constraint. The linear programming technique takes account of such secondary effects automatically. This illustration demonstrates the potential usefulness of the comprehensive decision framework that characterizes the model.[14]

III. Applying the Model in Practice

The example presented in the preceding section has conveyed something of the flavor of the linear programming technique. This section builds on the example to describe more fully how the model might be applied to portfolio management in practice. The section concludes with a few remarks regarding actual use of the technique at one large commercial bank.

Decision Variables and Constraints   The example developed above considered only two decision variables: that is, only two variables over which the bank had direct control. These were the bank's loan and securities balances. In reality, of course, bank balance sheets break assets down into far more detailed categories. (They also show a much wider variety of liabilities than the twofold deposit classification used in the example.) To exploit the model fully, a bank should define as many asset decision variables as there are assets of significantly different yield, liquidity, and risk in its portfolio. The model is capable of handling any number of decision variables. Problems containing more than two or three variables cannot be solved using graphs. Several standardized solution procedures (known as algorithms) exist, however, for solving large problems.[15]

In addition to handling as many decision variables as necessary, the linear programming model can accommodate as many constraints as bank managers consider relevant to the portfolio decision process. Specifically, detailed and realistic sets of

---

[13]It should be emphasized that this conclusion applies only to *additional* time deposits, not to deposits already held. A bank could pay a higher rate for additional deposits by, for example, issuing a new certificate of deposit.

[14]In actual linear programming applications, questions of the sort just discussed are analyzed in a more sophisticated manner, using the so-called "dual" linear program. For an elementary treatment of duality in linear programming, see William J. Baumol, *Economic Theory and Operations Analysis,* 2nd ed. (Englewood Cliffs, New Jersey: Prentice-Hall, Inc., 1965), pp. 103–28.

[15]The most widely used algorithm is the so-called "simplex" method. See Baumol, *op. cit.,* pp. 82–97.

liquidity constraints can be built into the model reflecting liability and capital structures, cash flow patterns, seasonal fluctuations in loan demand, and miscellaneous restrictions imposed by management on the basis of experience.[16] A variety of other constraints is conceivable, taking account of such operating factors as legal reserve requirements, corresponding balances, and the use of certain assets as collateral to support government deposits.

Dynamic Considerations The section II illustration was static. That is, the bank's decision process was cast in terms of a single time period. Actual portfolio management is anything but static, and no rational portfolio manager can confine his attention myopically to the present. For example, current portfolios should provide adequate liquidity to accommodate anticipated future loan demand. As a second example, loan decisions in the current period may affect deposit levels in future periods. One of the distinct advantages of the linear programming framework is its capacity to treat such intertemporal linkages explicitly. In portfolio decision applications, the model can be designed in such a way that it takes account of anticipated future conditions and generates optimal portfolios for several future periods as well as for the current period. The reader should not infer that management would, at some point, use the model to suggest desirable portfolios for, say, the next five quarters, and then slavishly follow the prescriptions for each quarter as time passes. Obviously, the model should be updated and solved again as forecasts are superseded by knowledge of actual events. Rather, the value of explicit attention to the future lies in the resulting clarification of the factors relevant to current decisions.

Bank Goals It was assumed in the illustration that the bank's objective was to maximize gross income during the single time period considered. Obviously, actual banks must define more refined objectives. First, deposit interest and other operating expenses have to be considered. In the terminology of the model, the variable maximized should be net income in some form. The model can easily meet this requirement by treating bank expenses as negative increments in the objective function. Second, if, as suggested earlier, a multiperiod time framework is employed, management must select a means of discounting future income to present value equivalents. A number of alternative procedures are available, any of which can be explicitly incorporated in the model.[17] The model cannot itself select an objective; however, the model forces management to define some operating goal. Moreover, the model is structured in such a way that each specific portfolio decision has a definite quantitative effect on the goal variable and can be evaluated on this basis.

Use of the Model at Bankers Trust Company During the 1960s, a group of management scientists developed a linear programming model at Bankers Trust

---

[16]In their pioneering application of the linear programming method to bank portfolio management, Chambers and Charnes developed a detailed system of capital adequacy-liquidity constraints using some of the bank examination criteria employed by the Federal Reserve System. See D. Chambers and A. Charnes, "Inter-Temporal Analysis and Optimization of Bank Portfolios," *Management Science*, 7 (July 1961), 393–410.

[17]For a comparative discussion of these alternatives, see Kalman J. Cohen and Frederick S. Hammer, "Linear Programming and Optimal Bank Asset Management Decisions," *The Journal of Finance*, 22 (May 1967), 159–62.

Company in New York to assist that bank's management in reaching portfolio decisions.[18] The model is quite detailed. It employs a multiperiod decision framework, a large number of balance sheet categories as decision variables, and numerous constraints of the type described above.

Perhaps the most interesting aspect of the Bankers Trust experiment is the role played by the model in the overall decision process. The model has not served in any sense as a substitute for the judgment of management. Rather, its principal function has been to clarify the consequences of alternative decisions. An excellent example is provided by management's use of the model to analyze liquidity ratio constraints.

When the consulting team initially formulated the model, they included no constraint on the ratio of government securities to total assets. The bank's executive management was troubled by this omission. They feared possibly adverse consequences in the market for the bank's stock should the Bankers Trust balance sheet show a much lower ratio than the balance sheets of other large New York banks. Informed of this criticism, the consulting team reformulated the model to include a minimum ratio of 16 percent. Subsequently, the scientists used the model to specify the effects on profits of small reductions in the ratio. The model indicated that quite small reductions could increase profits significantly. Management was unaware of this sensitivity. On the basis of this information, a more flexible policy was adopted.

This experience demonstrates the kind of informative dialogue that can develop between a bank's executives and a team of management scientists using a relatively sophisticated linear programming model. It is precisely in such interchanges that the model's value to management lies.

IV. Conclusions

This article has described the linear programming technique and has indicated how it can be applied to bank balance sheet management decisions. A few cautionary remarks and a brief summing up are now in order.

Although the linear programming model is a powerful analytical tool, it is in no sense an automatic procedure for generating optimal portfolio decisions. The complex and continually changing conditions faced by banks cannot be fully specified by a set of equations. It is unlikely that any bank will ever know, precisely and definitively, its optimal portfolio at a point in time. At best, techniques such as linear programming can only suggest a range within which the "best" portfolio is likely to fall.

Nor is the model a substitute for the judgment of experienced portfolio managers. While it is unnecessary for executives to understand in detail the mathematical theory underlying the model or its computational procedures, management must be

---

[18]Kalman J. Cohen served as a principal consultant in the Bankers Trust project. The following remarks summarize his description of the model and its application. See Cohen, "Dynamic Balance Sheet Management: A Management Science Approach," *Journal of Bank Research*, 2 (Winter 1972), 11-18.

directly involved in the construction and application of any operational model. Specifically, management must define the objectives of the bank's operations so that the model can reflect these objectives. Further, management must specify the constraints it considers relevant to asset selection decisions in order that these constraints can be built into the model. Finally, management must determine the specific questions that the model is used to analyze. In short, the model does not reduce the need for managerial judgment. On the contrary, it challenges that judgment in a very comprehensive manner.

With due attention to the proper role of the model in the decision process, it seems clear that the linear programming approach has several distinct advantages over many alternative asset management tools, such as the Asset Allocation method described earlier. First, the structure of the model forces a bank's management to establish a definite operational objective and provides a convenient framework for considering factors relevant to portfolio choice. Second, the model simultaneously determines each element of a bank's optimal portfolio, given the particular goals and constraints specified by management. Because of its simultaneous approach, the model automatically takes account of trade-offs between decisions with respect to one element of the portfolio and decisions with respect to another element of the portfolio. Third, the model provides a convenient tool for evaluating (1) the comparative consequences of alternative decisions, (2) the effect of alternative constraints on bank profits, and (3) how portfolios should be adjusted when economic and financial conditions change.

The application of linear programming to asset management appears to be one of the more important recent developments in banking.[19] Small banks may find the costs of constructing and operating linear programming models prohibitive. If the technique becomes widespread among larger banks, however, small banks may find themselves exposed to the procedure through the portfolio management services provided by correspondents. Consequently, all bankers should be aware of the technique and its implications.

REFERENCES

I. GENERAL TREATMENTS OF LINEAR PROGRAMMING

Two excellent and relatively nontechnical introductions to linear programming are:

BAUMOL, WILLIAM J. *Economic Theory and Operations Analysis.* 2nd ed. Englewood Cliffs, New Jersey: Prentice-Hall, Inc., 1965, pp. 70–128.
DORFMAN, ROBERT "Mathematical or 'Linear' Programming." *American Economic Review,* 43 (December 1953), 797–825.

[19]In this regard, it should be pointed out that linear programming is only one, and by no means the most advanced, of the modern quantitative models currently being employed in private industry. It is quite possible that in the future one or several of the other techniques may prove more useful in banking applications than linear programming.

Advanced treatments of the technique are:

GASS, SAUL *Linear Programming: Methods and Applications.* New York: McGraw-Hill Book Company, 1958.

HADLEY, G. *Linear Programming.* Reading, Massachusetts: Addison-Wesley Publishing Company, Inc., 1962.

II. APPLICATIONS OF LINEAR PROGRAMMING TO BANK PORTFOLIO MANAGEMENT

CHAMBERS, D. and A. CHARNES "Inter-Temporal Analysis and Optimization of Bank Portfolios." *Management Science,* 7 (July 1961), 393–410.

COHEN, KALMAN J. "Dynamic Balance Sheet Management: A Management Science Approach." *Journal of Bank Research,* 2 (Winter 1972), 9–19.

COHEN, KALMAN J. and FREDERICK S. HAMMER "Linear Programming and Optimal Bank Asset Management Decisions." *Journal of Finance,* 22 (May 1967), 147–65.

COHEN, KALMAN J., FREDERICK S. HAMMER, and HOWARD M. SCHNEIDER "Harnessing Computers for Bank Asset Management." *Bankers Magazine,* 150 (Summer 1967), 72–80.

Liability Management

Traditionally, most bank funds have taken the form of deposits from individuals located in the bank's market area. While these sources can still be relied upon, competition from thrift institutions and the prospect of interest payments on demand deposits have meant that traditional deposit sources cannot be taken for granted. Over the past decade, therefore, banks have turned to purchased liabilities, including large-denomination certificates of deposit, Federal funds and acceptances, and, in the case of bank holding companies, Eurodollar loans and commercial paper. These sources are volatile and not reliable under all economic conditions. As discussed in several of the readings in Section I, the proper management of these sources can be an important source of liquidity in addition to that provided by effective asset management.

Article 8 by Stuart A. Schweitzer not only surveys the competitive benefits of bank liability management but also considers the potential costs to the public as well as ways in which regulators might deal with these costs. Many of the regulatory reforms discussed by Schweitzer are examined in greater detail in the final section of this book, "The Role of Regulatory Institutions."

Among the various sources of investable short-term funds, large negotiable certificates of deposit (CDs) are extremely important. A good example of banking innovation, no other vehicle for liability management has been subject to as many regulatory changes. Article 9 by William C. Melton assesses the rapid emergence of the negotiable CD over the past two decades and its enormous impact on financial markets.

A more traditional and less volatile instrument for liability management is member bank borrowing from the Federal Reserve. Elijah Brewer succinctly surveys all of the relevant aspects of member bank borrowing in Article 10.

The next reading centers on compensating balance arrangements. Article 11 is a survey and analysis by Joseph E. Burns of the characteristics of compensating balances and their benefits to banks and bank customers.

Aspects of liability management are also discussed in many of the readings in Section I—particularly those by Merris and Lucas, Jones, and Thurston.

Bank Liability Management:
For Better or for Worse?

Stuart A. Schweitzer

With the financial collapse of 1933 almost forgotten, today's byword for banks is competition. Banks no longer stand back from the financial fray, waiting for the public to come to them. A rising aggressiveness propels them into the financial markets where they are scrapping for business like everyone else. As an example, bank assets at one time consisted largely of cash items and U.S. Government securities, and bank lending activities were limited. Now, however, banks vie among themselves and with other lenders to extend credit to businesses and households. Similarly, while they once relied for their loan funds upon people's willingness to keep large balances in interest-free checking accounts, banks today offer double-digit interest rates to attract funds from diverse sources.

In a nation whose economic system is based upon the principle that competition is the best way to achieve efficiency, word of banks' new competitiveness should be good news to the public. But some observers think otherwise. They argue that banks' enterprising behavior makes the banking and financial system less secure, and monetary policy less effective, than if banks were more conservative in their behavior. Bank regulators have a duty to preserve the basic soundness of the financial system, but they must carefully avoid stifling the competition that breeds efficiency and service for bank customers.

Reprinted from the Federal Reserve Bank of Philadelphia, *Business Review*, December 1974, pp. 3-12, by permission of the publisher.

Bankers Join the Fray

Bankers have always faced a basic cash management problem. On the one hand, they must be ready at all times to make good on the checks written by their depositors. To succeed at this they either need to hold an abundance of cash or must be able to raise cash quickly. As bankers would say, they need to have liquidity. On the other hand, bankers also want to earn as large a profit as possible. And to do that they have to make interest-bearing loans and investments which can be hard to turn into cash on short notice.

The last three decades have produced a major shift in bankers' willingness to trade off liquidity for earnings. Banks entered the post-World War II period with large holdings of Government securities that they had acquired as a part of the war financing effort.[1] They also held fresh memories of the loan losses and bank failures of the 1930s. As the postwar years went on, however, the strengthened national economy and the avowed U.S. Government commitment to full employment made another depression seem increasingly unlikely. That made loans a more attractive alternative to Government securities. At the same time, as the pace of economic activity accelerated, so did the volume of business requests for bank loans. Most bankers chose to accommodate their customers' loan demands—accepting reduced liquidity in exchange for higher profits.

A "Shortage" of Funds   The growth in bank loans to business in the 1940s and 1950s was facilitated by stored-up liquidity—that is, banks' cash assets and U.S. Government securities, which represented roughly three-fourths of their assets in 1946. By the end of the '50s, however, bank lending capacity was largely depleted. Although deposits had grown by about 50 percent in the postwar period, total bank loan volume had tripled. The loan-liquidity gap was widened further in the early '60s, when corporations began paring their demand deposit balances. Whereas corporate treasurers had formerly held large sums of idle money in interest-free checking accounts, they were now withdrawing these funds to purchase interest-bearing assets such as Treasury bills and commercial paper.

Tapping New Markets   Faced with further loan growth and a shortage of funds, banks sought new sources of liquidity. Money market banks in New York, as well as large banks in other cities, began issuing negotiable certificates of deposit (CDs) at competitive interest rates. These CDs were time deposits, and hence carried fixed maturity dates. They were made particularly attractive, however, by the development of a secondary market for CDs $100,000 and larger, which meant these instruments could be sold before maturity if an investor needed his funds.

The CD innovation was successful, and banks learned that liquidity could be found on both sides of the balance sheet. A bank needing funds could choose to go to the money market either with its assets or with its liabilities for sale. Banks choosing to practice "liability management"—that is, issuing liabilities at competitive rates

---

[1]In 1940, even before the United States' involvement in World War II, over 60 percent of member banks' assets were in cash items and U.S. Government securities.

to fulfill cash needs—could combine asset liquidity with liability liquidity to support further loan growth.

Along with CDs, banks in the 1960s began issuing a multitude of other manage-able liabilities. Federal funds trading, which had previously occurred in limited vol-ume, grew rapidly. Banks borrowed Eurodollars from their foreign branches, and bank holding companies sold commercial paper and loaned the proceeds to their bank subsidiaries. The effect is that, while virtually none of the funds at large banks were derived from liability management in 1960, nearly 30 percent originate with this source today. Banks are now vigorous competitors in the market for loanable funds. However, the increasing reliance on liability management as a source of bank liquid-ity is raising concern as to whether the practice is in the public interest.

Aggressive Banking: Too Much of a Good Thing?

Critics of bank liability management contend that, while the practice may offer some benefits to society, it may also have some costs that outweigh the public's gains. Competition may make the public better off, but opponents charge that the potential for reduced monetary policy effectiveness and greater bank riskiness offset these gains.

Competition and Public Gains   The chief benefit to society at large from bank liability management is that the practice has brought stiffer competition to financial markets. Compared to the period before 1960, when banks avoided competitively bidding for loanable funds, the public now has additional financial options. Savers with funds to invest in short-term assets can now buy not only Treasury bills and commercial paper but also bank CDs. Borrowers whose loan needs might not have been accommodated at the banks can, because of liability management, choose be-tween bank loans and other types of credit. With public use of these added options high, it is safe to conclude that the banks' terms are attractive and that the public has gained from their availability (see box below). However, if liability management creates significant offsetting costs to society, the public could wind up worse off despite the benefits liability management creates.

For Large and Small Alike?

It's a truism that anyone who voluntarily conducts his business with a bank, when he could conduct that business with some other borrower or lender, is glad to have that bank around. Liability management is one device that banks have used to make themselves available for borrowing and lending. But does the little fellow gain as much from this availability as the big one? Let's look at savers and investors sepa-rately.

Savers The small saver has not reaped many benefits from liability management. After all, it is the corporations, wealthy individuals, and governmental units that can come up with the funds to buy a $100,000 CD, not the little guy. Large CDs paved the way for the savings certificates available to the small saver, but those certificates carry lower rates than do large CDs.

A key element of liability management is the payment of competitive rates on savers' funds. Now, liability management has not produced the same sorts of gains for small savers as for large savers, not because banks are unwilling to compete for small savers' funds, but rather because of Federal Reserve and FDIC ceilings on the rates banks can pay on small deposits.

These regulations serve a purpose which the nation values highly, protecting thrift institutions (mutual savings banks and savings and loan associations) from a wholesale loss of funds. But the regulations, and not discriminatory bank behavior, are what stand between liability management and enlargement of small savers' financial options.

Borrowers What would borrowers' options be if there were no liability management and, in particular, no CDs? It seems plausible to assume that savers who now buy CDs would instead buy commercial paper. The funds now available to borrowers through bank loans would then be available through the commercial paper market. Very large businesses could borrow directly in that market. Other businesses and individuals could not issue commercial paper, but could borrow from finance companies, which can. As above, those who actually borrow at banks when they have the choice of these other methods reveal themselves to be better off than they would be if banks couldn't loan to them.

Another issue is whether loan customers of small banks suffer indirectly because of the liability management practices of large banks. The problem is that small banks are net lenders of Federal funds to large banks. Federal funds are excess reserves loaned for short periods by one bank to another. Many large banks, as part of their liability management activities, bid aggressively for Federal funds on a continuing basis. When large banks bid these funds away from small banks, the effect is for loanable funds to flow from the rest of the country to the major financial centers in the nation's large cities. Individuals and small firms that are borrowers from the small lending banks may well suffer in such cases.

It might be suggested that this could all be prevented by appropriately regulating the Federal funds market. The Federal funds market occupies so special a place in the transmission of Federal Reserve monetary policy, however, that this would be impractical. Besides, any restrictions on the flow of Federal funds would probably be circumvented

> somehow. Banks are very innovative, and if it were profitable for the
> funds to flow to the big cities, the banks would find a way to get them
> there. Furthermore, the effect of inhibiting the funds flow would be to
> subsidize rural area firms and individuals whose borrowing opportuni-
> ties are affected. If society wants to subsidize these firms and individ-
> uals, it can probably find a more efficient way.

Monetary Policy and Any Losses?　Critics of bank liability management argue
that it allows banks to circumvent a restrictive monetary policy. In the past when
monetary policy tightened and market interest rates moved up, rates on CDs and
other bank deposits lagged behind because of restrictions on the rate bankers were
permitted to pay. Since banks were less able to compete for funds because of these
restrictions, bank credit shrank. During the 1960s, however, banks began to issue
unregulated obligations on which they paid market interest rates. They borrowed
from Eurodollar, Federal funds, and commercial paper lenders. Aggressive liability
management kept funds flowing into the banks for relending.

This process clearly permitted banks to use liability management to insulate themselves from some of the impacts of tight monetary policy. Indeed, the process continues to work today, especially since all interest rate ceilings on large CDs have been
suspended. But a more important issue is whether liability management lessens the
impact of monetary policy on the economy. Many believe that liability management
merely allows banks to get a bigger share of the credit pie without influencing total
credit in the economy. Without liability management, they argue, funds would simply by-pass banks, going through other financial firms or directly from ultimate
lender to ultimate borrower. With liability management, the argument goes, banks
are in a better competitive position to attract and relend funds, but the volume of the
total credit flow is, for the most part, unchanged. If so, the effectiveness of restrictive
monetary policies probably is not impaired by the bank credit growth that liability
management permits.

In addition, many claim that liability management does not affect the impact of
tight policy on the economy because Fed policy works through changes in the money
stock and not through changes in credit. An important ingredient of the money stock
is, of course, demand deposits—a particular kind of bank liability.[2] This raises the
question of whether bank liability management makes control of money more difficult. Doesn't liability management allow banks to obtain more funds which they can
then use to support more demand deposits?

In our economy, the ultimate restriction on the banking system's ability to create
demand deposits is the availability of reserves. Because member banks are required
to hold reserves equal to a fraction (designated by the Fed) of outstanding deposits,
the amount of these deposits they create is limited by the availability of reserves. So

---

[2]Authorities differ on what ought to be counted as money. A popular view is that money consists of the
public's demand deposits and currency holdings. Many believe, however, that savings deposits at commercial banks should be included in money as well.

using an oversimplified illustration, if the reserve ratio is 20 percent and reserves amount to $30 billion, deposits cannot exceed $150 billion (20 percent of $150 billion is $30 billion). If the Fed increases reserves to $31 billion, demand deposits could rise to $155 billion. The world is more complicated than this simple example suggests because the reserve ratio fluctuates. First, the required reserve ratio is different for different banks. Second, actual reserves held exceed required reserves on demand deposits by varying amounts.[3] But the example does point out how the Fed can control demand deposits generally. As long as the demand deposit/reserve ratio is fairly predictable over time the Fed can control demand deposits through reserves. Banks' use of liability management techniques will not impair the Fed's ability to manage the nation's money stock, unless it makes the demand deposit/reserve ratio more erratic. There is no evidence that this has happened to date.

Overall, therefore, the impact of liability management on monetary policy effectiveness doesn't seem substantial. Bank credit growth is facilitated by aggressive bank competition for loanable funds. But total credit is probably unaffected. Moreover, the Fed's ability to control the nation's money stock does not appear to be unduly hampered by the advent of liability management.

Bank Riskiness and Public Losses   The principal argument offered today, however, by those who oppose liability management is that it has reduced the soundness of numerous individual banks and therefore threatens the stability of the entire banking system. Most critics do not question the industry's use of liability management *per se,* but contend that many banks have grown too reliant on the practice and do not maintain sufficient liquid assets to meet unforeseen cash needs. They claim that these banks are "illiquid."

The danger in being illiquid is clear—an otherwise solvent bank can be pushed into failure if it can't meet its cash needs. For even though a bank's assets might appear to exceed its liabilities, those assets might not hold their value if the bank had to sell them hurriedly to meet impending cash needs. If a forced sale made asset values decline by an amount greater than the level of bank capital,[4] the bank would become insolvent and then fail.

The evidence on *asset liquidity* at the nation's banks is consistent with the critics' position. Throughout the postwar years, the proportion of bank funds invested in cash and other liquid assets has gradually declined. At the same time, loans—which are of lesser liquidity—have been a growing component of bank portfolios (see Figure 1). A large proportion of the liquid assets that banks still have is already committed to meet reserve requirements and requirements to hold collateral against government deposits. They are, therefore, largely unavailable to meet other cash needs.

---

[3]This results partly because banks hold reserves in excess of requirements and in part because reserves are required against other bank liabilities.

[4]An issue closely related to whether banks have ample liquidity is whether they have enough capital. See Ronald D. Watson, "Insuring Some Progress in the Bank Capital Hassle," *Business Review* of the Federal Reserve Bank of Philadelphia, July-August 1974, pp. 3-17.

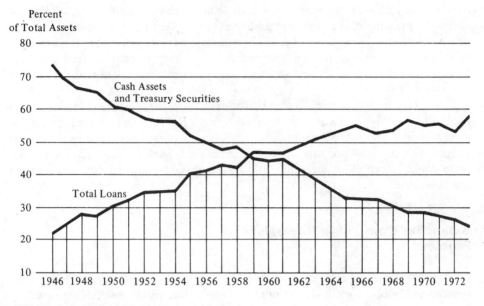

FIGURE 1. Asset liquidity falls by the wayside.

Note: Data are as of December 31 of each year and apply to all commercial banks.
Source: Federal Reserve Bulletin.

The evidence on *liability liquidity* is less clear. The fact that banks already have substantial volumes of manageable liabilities on their books tells us nothing about how much liability liquidity they have left. It does, of course, tell us of their need to turn regularly to lenders to "roll over—or refinance—maturing liabilities. What we need to know, however, is whether banks can count on being able to roll over existing liabilities and sell new obligations when cash needs arise.

A bank's ability to sell its liabilities depends in part on market conditions and on its willingness to pay market interest rates. The most important factor, however, is whether lenders think the bank is sound. Lenders have recently become particularly sensitive to the issue of bank safety. The high interest rates banks were paying for funds and the financial difficulties of the Franklin National Bank combined to make investors wonder whether other banks that use liability management for liquidity were still sound. Whereas in the past lenders often accepted bank soundness on faith, many became anxious about the creditworthiness of the banks whose CDs they bought. Some of these lenders responded by shifting their funds into larger banks. As a result, the nation's largest banks now pay an interest rate below that paid by other liability-managing banks. Indeed, some lenders will now lend only to the largest banks, regardless of interest rate.

Moreover, tight-credit periods make it particularly difficult for banks to expand their use of liability management. Lenders might interpret a rapid build-up of a bank's manageable liabilities as a sign of stress at the bank, limiting the usefulness of liability management as a source of additional liquidity. Furthermore, it could even be counterproductive in such an environment for a bank to offer more than the rate paid by banks of similar size to attract new funds. Lenders might read the higher rate as an admission of great risk and scramble to get their funds out before the worst had a chance to happen.

Thus, while it can't be proved that bank liquidity on average is now too low, there is certainly justifiable concern about its adequacy. Reliance upon liability management as a principal source of liquidity could at some point leave some banks unable to cope with liquidity pressures. Society's losses from bank failures that might then occur could indeed offset the gains from the competition that liability management has generated.

Balancing Competing Interests: The Problem

As might be expected, a close appraisal of liability management reveals both public benefits and public costs from the practice. The public gains from having access to financial markets that are more competitive than they would be without bank liability management. But the public also loses from the increased potential for bank failures and from the possibility of a reduction in the effectiveness of monetary policy.

Everyone has a stake in a stable and secure financial system—one that facilitates rather than impedes productive activity. Only if banks kept 100 percent reserves against their liabilities, however, would there be absolutely no risk of bank failure from illiquidity. But if banks did that, there would be less competition to issue loans, which would impose costs on the public in other ways. Most would agree that 100 percent reserves are not needed, and that with a bit less liquidity, banks could start competing in loan markets without becoming unsound. The problem is to identify the best amount of liquidity for a bank.

Ideally, from society's standpoint, the right amount of bank liquidity is that which produces the greatest net benefits for society—that is, which maximizes the difference between the public's benefits and its costs. Identifying that amount is a tricky business, since the public's costs and benefits are not readily measured. Attaining it is even trickier, however, since the costs that banks respond to are the ones that affect their stockholders' profits, and these amounts may not include all the costs which are important to society at large.[5] That is where bank regulators—the Federal Reserve, the Comptroller of the Currency, the FDIC, and the 50 state banking departments—come in. An important part of their job is to balance the interests of society and the banks, insuring that banks respond to social as well as private considerations.

---

[5]When a bank fails, its stockholders lose whatever they have invested. But the public may lose the uninsured portion of its deposits and other bank debt, and the failure may undermine confidence in other banks as well.

Balancing Competing Interests: Methods

Many argue that, although liability management has been profitable for the banks, its heavy use has reduced liquidity below where the public's net benefits are greatest. Indeed, many banks have already begun reducing their reliance on liability management, in response to signals from the market and from regulators that they ought to do so. But whether banks will end up acquiring enough liquidity to reach the socially "right" position depends on the framework regulators establish to promote that end.

The Framework Today   Market forces and regulatory pressures currently play a role in limiting bank reliance on liability management. The role of market forces, on the one hand, is limited by the fact that investors know relatively little about the soundness of individual banks. They cannot efficiently respond, therefore, to changes in the creditworthiness of borrowing banks. Bank regulators, on the other hand, conduct periodic examinations of all insured banks. Armed with hard facts about a bank's condition, a regulatory agency can press for changes which it deems advisable. However, regulators have proceeded cautiously in this area because they don't have clear standards against which an individual bank's liability management activities can be judged.

At present, the limits on bank liability management are not at all firm. Bankers get some signals about how far they should go, but those signals may not always be strong enough to curb their behavior. It is possible, therefore, for *individual banks* to get into a liquidity bind even though the *banking system as a whole* is sound. To protect confidence in the banking system from the possible excesses of a few banks, the Federal Reserve stands ready to meet its responsibility as "lender of last resort."[6] A founding purpose of the Fed was to prevent general liquidity crises, and it has traditionally stood ready to lend to solvent but illiquid banks when no one else would do so. At the same time, however, "lender of last resort" loans from the Fed's discount window are intended to protect banks from illiquidity *only while* they make appropriate asset and liability adjustments. Discount window loans are not designed to insulate banks from the need to make those adjustments.[7] The window's function is to insure bank safety for the public's benefit, not to provide a subsidy to bank stockholders.

Therefore, while the "lender of last resort" function is a valuable safety valve, it is not a substitute for regulatory and internal bank management policies that insure adequate liquidity for banks. The problem is to build into the banking system measures that will bring these policies about and to balance the benefits properly against any reduction of financial market competition. There's no quick way to do so, how-

[6]See, for example, "Maintaining the Soundness of Our Banking System," an address by Arthur F. Burns, Chairman, Board of Governors of the Federal Reserve System, at the annual convention of the American Bankers' Association, Honolulu, Hawaii, October 21, 1974.

[7]The discount window also extends credit to member banks to help with significant seasonal outflows of funds, and to provide long-term help to overcome some "emergency" situations—such as those occurring from natural disasters that affect the communities they serve—as well as for short-term "adjustment" credit.

ever, for the regulators' short-run options are few. It will take new approaches to achieve these kinds of results.

Should the Banks Stand Alone?   One approach that is frequently suggested, but which seems seriously flawed, is to let failing banks fail. In such a world, if a bank assumed too much risk and couldn't meet its obligations, the Fed wouldn't extend it credit. Advocates say that banks, knowing there would be no one around to bail them out, would plan accordingly. The discipline of the market would then be all that was needed to produce the "right" mix of conservatism and risk taking in banking.

There is some merit in the notion that banks should either stand on their own or fail. That would encourage greater efficiency in banking, since inefficient and poorly managed banks wouldn't have much chance of survival. The problem with this approach, however, is that it might be difficult to isolate bank failures and keep them from spreading. One bank's failure could easily beget deposit outflows at other banks. That might well cause those other banks to fail and seriously undermine confidence in the entire banking system.

Should the Regulators Set the Standards?   Another way for bank regulators to insure that banks maintain an ideal reliance on liability management is for them to impose their standards on banks directly. Once those standards were met, banks would be able to meet cash needs with less strain, which would do much to reduce the pressure of deposit runoffs. The regulators may not have the means to enforce their standards, however. The record of bank innovation in response to regulatory actions is that traditionally banks have found loopholes faster than regulators could plug them. If regulators were to limit bank reliance on one or more kinds of liabilities, banks would probably devise a new method of attracting funds.

But even if regulatory standards could be enforced, it's not clear what those standards should be. What is the *ideal* liquidity ratio for a bank? To what extent should banks be allowed to trade off liquidity for earnings? Until light is shed on these issues, the regulators could easily adopt improper standards. The public could incur significant costs if the standards were wrong, without the regulators ever knowing it. It would seem preferable to seek solutions which protect the public by allowing the interplay of economic forces to reflect changing preferences.

Closing the Information Gap   Still another approach, which employs the discipline of the market, would be to give the investing public better information than it now gets about banks' financial health. As matters stand now, the information lenders have on the banks they deal with is typically quite sketchy. Thus, they often proceed on intuition, rules of thumb, and, worst of all, rumor.

There's no more effective way to prevent rumor than to present the facts. If the public knew key elements of an up-to-date examiner's report on every bank, it could make an informed selection among borrowing banks. But the key is that the facts would have to be current. National banks are now examined roughly every eight months, and state-chartered banks approximately once a year. That sort of timetable leaves plenty of opportunity for major changes in a bank's condition to occur between examinations. If bank examinations were updated at, say, quarterly intervals, this could not happen.[8] Then, if the examiner's quarterly summary of each bank's capital, asset, and management quality were available to the public, rumor might not readily sweep the financial market.[9]

An important advantage of this plan is that bank soundness would have the profit motive on its side. Investors wouldn't lend to banks that had anything less than a clean bill of health, unless they were paid premium interest rates. That would add an extra incentive for banks to curb their risk exposures and to maintain greater liquidity. Furthermore, while this idea may be new in banking it is applied every day in the bond market. Bond market investors are able to rely on the published ratings of bond issues, which are based on extensive information collected by private agencies. The proposed release of examiners' ratings would afford that same benefit to investors in short-term bank debt. The only difference would be that risk information would come from public regulatory agencies instead of private firms.

Such an approach could not be implemented overnight, of course. For one thing, the release of examiner's ratings is now illegal. It would take an act of Congress to change that. What's more, the regulators would need time to gear up for more frequent examinations.[10] The banks would also need time to prepare for their new environment. Those banks which now have less than the best possible examiner's report, and which may now be working with the regulators to correct their problems, should be given time to get their houses in shape for public scrutiny. If it were announced, say, that banks have two years to get ready, that might do the trick. The banks would have time to correct any adverse situations, and conditions would start improving immediately.

Liability Management: It's Here to Stay

In comparison to ordinary deposit banking, liability management is a more aggressive way to run a bank. That aggressiveness has meant added options for the public, but many feel that heavy use of the technique has also harmed the public by making the achievement of monetary policy objectives more difficult. They also say that it has made the banking system less liquid and therefore potentially less stable than it should be. True, liability management can provide banks with liquidity beyond that available in their assets, but liability liquidity is found in a bank's ability to issue and

---

[8]On November 12, 1974, Comptroller of the Currency James E. Smith announced new procedures to update periodically his office's information on national bank loan quality and liquidity. Henceforth, he announced, all national banks will be required to provide the Comptroller with regular reports of past-due loans. The 200 largest national banks, furthermore, will be required to supply quarterly reports on asset and liability maturities.

[9]It would also help if the number of rating categories used were large enough and their definitions narrow enough to reveal small changes in a bank's circumstances. That way, the user of an examiner's report could readily distinguish major and minor changes in bank condition.

[10]In part, this time would be needed to take on and train the additional examiners required to meet the more frequent examinations timetables. The regulators would also need time, however, to coordinate their examination activities in order to insure comparability of their examination reports.

sell *new* liabilities. Those obligations that are already on a bank's books only increase its needs for liquidity, not its supply of liquidity.

The banks are aware of their greater vulnerability to shifts of financial market sentiment when they rely on liabilities for liquidity. They are unlikely to curtail their operations, however, unless market forces or regulatory actions compel them to do so. As long as reduced liquidity and expanded liability management are profitable for the banks, they will continue to pursue these practices. The market currently provides some incentives for banks to stay liquid, and many bankers have recently begun to take account of these incentives. However, it is largely up to the regulators to promote greater bank liquidity. The regulators can try to do this administratively by telling the banks what liquidity ratios they must attain. Or they can tell the public what they know about each bank's health and let investors and the banks work things out between themselves. That way, there is a substantial chance that the competitive benefits of liability management can be preserved, while the threat of bank failures can be reduced.

The Market for Large Negotiable CDs

William C. Melton

During the last fifteen years "liability management" has become accepted by large banks as a principal strategy for adjusting their lending capabilities. In tapping the domestic pool of short-term investable funds for the purposes of liability management, large negotiable certificates of deposit (CDs) are even more important to banks than trading in federal funds or engaging in repurchase agreements (RPs) for Treasury bills. Because of the heavy bank reliance on the CD market, the monetary authorities have on numerous occasions used a wide variety of policy measures to influence bank use of CDs. In fact, since its introduction in 1961 no other vehicle for liability management has been subject to as many changes in regulations.

The Mechanics of CDs

As its name suggests, a certificate of deposit is simply a receipt certifying that a certain amount of money has been deposited at the bank issuing the certificate. The certificate also specifies the rate of interest to be paid and the date on which the principal and interest may be withdrawn (the maturity date). Large-denomination CDs, those in amounts of at least $100,000, are the ones used in liability management.

Reprinted from *Quarterly Review,* Vol. 2, No. 4 (Winter 1977–78), pp. 22–34, by permission of the Federal Reserve Bank of New York and the author.

They are generally negotiable, i.e., the owner may sell title to the deposit to another investor prior to the maturity date.

Because CDs are time deposits, they are subject to Federal Reserve Regulation D, which requires time deposits to have a minimum maturity of thirty days. Time deposits are covered by deposit insurance up to the first $40,000 of principal, and this is usually only a small fraction of the face value of large-denomination certificates. Therefore, investors must evaluate the likelihood of default by the issuing bank when considering purchase of a CD.

Since computation of reserve requirements for deposits issued on a discount basis is cumbersome, CDs are almost always issued at par and traded on an interest-bearing basis. (Most other money market instruments, such as bankers' acceptances, commercial paper, and Treasury bills, are traded on a discount basis.) Should a CD be sold prior to maturity, the seller receives payment from the buyer for the principal—adjusted to current market value—and for all interest accrued from the original issue date to the date of the sale. If the buyer holds the CD to maturity, he of course receives both the principal and the full amount of interest indicated on the certificate.

Interest on CDs is computed on the basis of a 360-day year instead of the 365-day year used for bond yields. Issuing banks post rates for CDs of various maturities—30 days, 60 days, 90 days, etc.—but the actual rate is often negotiated between the issuer and the buyer (i.e., the depositor) and is affected by the reputation of the issuing bank, the amount of funds it needs, the size of the CD, as well as its term to maturity. The new-issue market is called the primary CD market, and interest rates paid on newly issued CDs are primary rates. Transactions involving outstanding CDs take place in the secondary (dealer) market at what are termed secondary rates.

CDs are normally paid for in immediately available funds on the day of purchase, and they are redeemed in immediately available funds on the day they mature.[1] To facilitate settlement, CDs of many non-New York banks are often issued and redeemed through the issuer's correspondent bank in New York.

CDs are an attractive short-term, liquid investment for individuals, business firms, municipalities, and other organizations with large amounts of temporarily investable cash balances. Since CDs—unlike Treasury bills—are subject to at least some risk of default, they typically yield more than do bills of the same maturity. Thus, they are a tempting alternative for an investor willing to accept slightly more risk in return for a higher yield. Another advantage of CDs is that they may be issued for any desired maturity (of at least thirty days), whereas a Treasury bill maturing on a specific day, e.g., a tax-payment day, may be difficult if not impossible to locate. Also, legal restrictions on the investment powers of state and local governments force many to hold their temporarily investable funds in either government obligations or deposits in local commercial banks. Thus, these restrictions often make CDs the only instrument on which municipalities can obtain returns on

[1]See "Federal Funds and Repurchase Agreements," Federal Reserve Bank of New York, *Review* (Summer 1977), pp. 33–48, for a description of immediately available funds.

Original Purchasers of Large Negotiable CDs (in Percentage of Total)

Type of Purchaser	December 5, 1962	June 30, 1964
Business	69	67
State and Local Governments	16	11
Foreign Official Institutions	6 ⎱	
All Other Foreign	1 ⎰	12
Individuals	3	2
Others	6	9
Total	100	100

Numbers may not add to totals because of rounding.
Sources: 1962, Board of Governors of the Federal Reserve
System: 1964, American Bankers Association.

short-term investments that are greater than those available on Treasury bills or other time deposits.

The present distribution of CDs among different types of investors is known only in broad outline. Some detailed information is available from surveys conducted in the early 1960s when there was only about $10 billion of large CDs outstanding, compared with about $70 billion at present. The results of those surveys, summarized in the table, showed that, as one would expect, business corporations were by far the largest original purchasers of CDs, while the remainder was bought, in about equal amounts by state and local governments, foreigners, and "others." The surveys also showed that smaller banks tended to sell relatively more of their negotiable CDs to individuals and to state and local governments and that these CDs were smaller on average than those issued to other types of investors.

The only recent source of information on the distribution of CD holdings is the breakdown of weekly reporting banks' outstanding CDs into those issued to individuals, partnerships, and corporations (IPC) and those issued to all others. In recent years, the share of CDs issued to IPC holders has been about two thirds. This suggests that the proportion of CDs originally purchased by businesses and individuals has not changed much from that shown in the table.

In liability management, banks actively seek more flexibility in expanding their lending capability in line with their profitable lending opportunities instead of adjusting their lending to deposits received more or less passively. Banks can do this by increasing their CDs when loan demand is strong and by allowing them to run off when loan demand turns sluggish. Only money-center and large regional banks have the ability to market their CDs effectively. The one hundred largest commercial banks with deposits in excess of $1 billion account for about 90 percent of all large-denomination CDs issued.

On occasion, even a large bank may not issue all of its CDs directly to investors. For example, when a bank's liability management strategy requires it to market a large amount of CDs quickly, it may attempt to issue the CDs to dealers who are willing to purchase them for later sale or who are able to reach a broad array of potential investors quickly. When banks issue CDs into the secondary market in this way, the distinction between the primary (new-issue) and secondary (dealer) market becomes rather blurred.

CDs resemble other short-term money market instruments such as Treasury bills and bankers' acceptances in that they may be traded in a secondary market. The existence of such a market enhances their liquidity and makes them attractive relative to both non-negotiable instruments and negotiable instruments having poorly developed secondary markets. However, the secondary market rate generally exceeds the interest rate at which CDs are originally issued. The reason is that the CDs available in the secondary market may not match the maturities or be issued by the banks desired by investors, and investors have the option of buying CDs of any desired maturity of at least 30 days from preferred issuing banks. As a result, yields in the secondary market must often be increased relative to primary yields to induce investors to purchase them.

Generally, the spread between rates bid and asked in the secondary market averages about 10 basis points for maturities in the three- to six-month range and is somewhat greater for shorter maturities. These spreads, however, are representative only for CDs of the top twelve to fifteen banks whose certificates are traded regularly by the handful of dealers who maintain markets in CDs; bid-asked spreads for CDs issued by banks whose CDs are less frequently traded are naturally somewhat wider.

Moreover, there is generally a tiering (differentiation) of market rates according to market perception of the strength of the issuing bank and of the liquidity of its CDs. Less favored banks must pay somewhat higher rates on their CDs than the most favored money market banks.

In addition to issuing CDs in the domestic market, United States banks with foreign branches have the ability to secure time deposits from holders of offshore dollar balances—Eurodollars. Funds deposited in branches can then be re-lent by them to their United States head offices or lent abroad. Like the CD market, the Eurodollar market is a wholesale market in which the average denomination of deposits is quite large. A further similarity between the Eurodollar and CD markets is that some London branches of United States banks issue London dollar CDs (i.e., dollar-denominated CDs redeemable only at the London branch of the issuing bank), which trade in a secondary market much as domestic CDs do. Since large banks have the option of selling CDs or similar liabilities in either the U.S. domestic money market or in the Eurodollar market, they change their relative reliance on the two markets according to where effective costs are lowest.[2]

---

[2]Two important differences between Eurodollars and CDs are (1) Eurodollar deposits have no minimum term to maturity, while CDs have a minimum of 30 days, and (2) net Eurodollar borrowings of head offices of United States banks from their foreign branches currently are subject to a 4 percent reserve requirement, while CDs are subject to reserve requirements of 1 to 6 percent, depending on their original term to maturity.

Beginnings of the CD Market

The negotiable CD came into prominence only seventeen years ago. The conditions that fostered a large market for CDs were the gradual rising trend of interest rates during the 1950s and 1960s as well as the related development of sophisticated money management techniques by corporate treasurers. Since banks were prohibited from paying interest on demand deposits and since most were unwilling to pay interest on corporate time deposits, corporate treasurers actively began to use their temporarily investable balances to purchase short-term money market instruments. This investment strategy inhibited the growth of corporate deposits at large money market banks. In addition, the unavailability to banks of a flexible instrument with which to augment their conventional deposit sources meant that, in periods of monetary restraint, the share of bank credit in total credit flows to nonfinancial sectors (business, state and local governments, housing, and consumers) declined.

Responding to this state of affairs, the First National City Bank of New York (now Citibank) began to offer CDs to domestic business corporations, public bodies, and foreign investors in February 1961. The primary objectives were to increase corporate deposits and to allow banks greater discretion over their sources of funds, so that in a period of rising loan demand and increasing interest rates they could accommodate increases in short-term credit demands by expanding their CDs. Otherwise, they would have to turn down profitable loan applications or sell some of their investments, possibly at a substantial loss. The ability of banks to "buy" funds by paying market rates of interest added greatly to their flexibility and was the key element in their ability to shift to liability management.

CDs had existed in negotiable form for years prior to 1961, but they could not become an important source of funds for banks until they could compete with other short-term money market instruments. To do so, they had to be readily marketable and to pay a market rate of return. The crucial innovation in February 1961 was the secondary market for large negotiable CDs (provided initially by the Discount Corporation of New York, a dealer in United States Government securities). The secondary market made CDs a truly liquid money market instrument by establishing a means through which an investor could sell his holdings quickly and at low cost prior to maturity. Other large banks promptly began to issue CDs, and other dealers soon entered the secondary CD market.

The expansion of CDs in the early 1960s was rapid and steady (Chart 1). The smooth and impressive growth of outstandings from February 1961 through the middle of 1966 reflected increasing acceptance of this new money market instrument. However, the CD rates which member banks—virtually the only banks issuing CDs—could pay were subject to the interest ceilings of the Federal Reserve's Regulation Q. The 1 percent ceiling rate on time deposits of less than three months' maturity prevented CDs in this range from being issued. Moreover, the market for longer term CDs was affected in late 1961, when three-month Treasury bill rates edged upward and exceeded the 2½ percent ceiling rate in effect for three- to six-month

CHART 1. Large Negotiable Certificates of Deposit Outstanding at All Commercial Banks (Not Seasonally Adjusted)

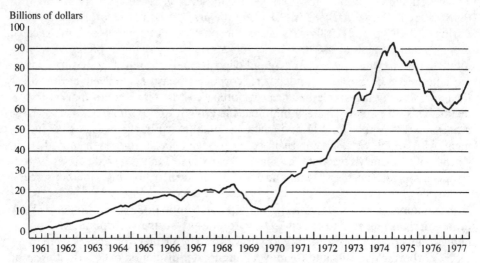

Source: Board of Governors of the Federal Reserve System.

CDs. At that point, only CDs of six-month or longer maturities on which the ceiling rate was 3 percent could be sold by banks, and these also became difficult to sell as the six-month Treasury bill rate approached 3 percent.

At the beginning of 1962, the Federal Reserve raised the ceiling rate for CDs of six- to twelve-month maturity to 3½ percent and that for CDs of twelve-month or greater maturity to 4 percent.[3] As a result of this change, banks were able once more to market CDs in the longer maturity range but were effectively prevented from issuing shorter maturities. A year and a half later, in July 1963, ceiling rates for CD maturities of three months and longer were fixed at 4 percent.

Meanwhile, the ceiling on one- to three-month CDs was deliberately held at an uncompetitive 1 percent level. This stimulated the growth of the secondary market which was then still in its infancy. The large spread between ceiling rates on long- and short-term CDs allowed dealers and corporations to buy long-term CDs, to hold them until only a short term to maturity remained, and then to sell them in the secondary market without fear of being undercut by banks offering competitive rates on newly issued short-term CDs. In additon, since long-term CD rates generally exceeded short-term CD rates, while both remained relatively stable, dealers profited during the first half of the 1960s by buying long-term CDs, holding them in inventory, and then selling them as short-term CDs. As long as rates were stable, this investment strategy—called "riding the yield curve"—increased their total interest

[3]In addition, time deposits of foreign official institutions were made exempt from Regulation Q interest rate ceilings in October 1962.

CHART 2. Dealer Transactions in Large Negotiable Certificates of Deposit (Monthly Averages of Daily Figures; Not Seasonally Adjusted)

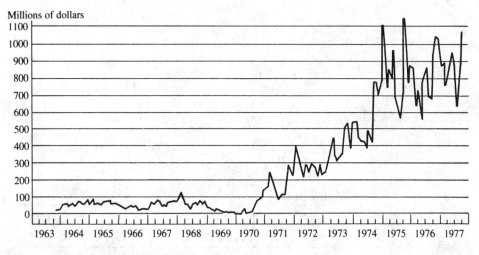

Source: Federal Reserve Bank of New York.

return by an amount depending on the spread of the long-term CD rate over the short-term CD rate.

The artificially low Regulation Q ceiling on short-term CDs remained in effect until November 1964, when the maximum rate on CDs of 30- to 89-day maturities was raised to 4 percent, and the rate on longer term CDs was raised to 4½ percent. This change allowed banks to make competitive rate offers on CDs in the 30- to 89-day range for the first time. It thus put an end to the artificial stimulus to the growth of the secondary market. From the end of 1963 to the middle of 1966, the value of CDs outstanding nearly doubled, reaching $17.8 billion, while the daily average of gross dealer transactions changed little and remained at a modest level (Chart 2).

First Crisis: 1966

In response to rising interest rates, the existing Regulation Q ceiling rates were raised to a uniform 5½ percent for all CD maturities in December 1965 (Chart 3) in order to prevent banks from encountering difficulty when renewing (rolling over) their existing CDs. However, other market rates soon exceeded the new ceiling, and the CD market reacted immediately. Issuance of CDs began to slow, and outstandings started to fall.

Rates on CDs with longer maturities ran up against the ceiling in about the middle of 1966. Consequently, new issues of such maturities were greatly reduced, and the average maturity of outstanding CDs began a sharp decline (Chart 4). Shortly afterward rates on short-term CDs ran up against the ceiling, and new issues of short-term CDs also started to decline. The runoff of CDs from August to December 1966 reached a sizable $2.9 billion (Chart 1), a decrease of about 16 percent from the

CHART 3. Interest Rates on Large Negotiable Certificates of Deposit

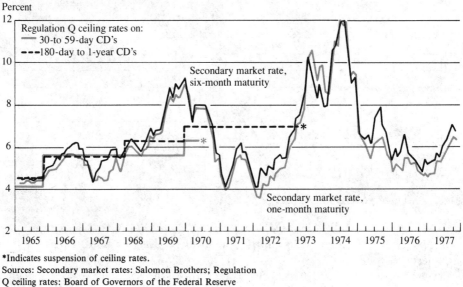

*Indicates suspension of ceiling rates.
Sources: Secondary market rates: Salomon Brothers; Regulation
Q ceiling rates: Board of Governors of the Federal Reserve
System.

CHART 4. Average Maturity of Outstanding Large Negotiable Certificates of Deposit (Weekly Reporting Banks; Not Seasonally Adjusted)

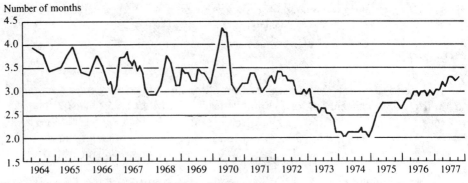

Source: Board of Governors of the Federal Reserve System.

August level. In the five years since the introduction of negotiable CDs, banks had never undergone a comparable experience.

The effects were also significant in the secondary market, where a rapid rise in rates—to which Regulation Q, of course, did not apply—resulted in considerable book losses for holders of outstanding CDs. Investors reacted by cutting back purchases of new CDs and holding to maturity the CDs already in their portfolios; thus market transactions as well as dealer positions were greatly reduced. Gross transactions in the secondary market declined to a level even lower than that observed in 1963, when data first began to be collected.

The pressures in the CD market caused by Regulation Q ceilings abated in December 1966, when interest rates started to decline rapidly. Pressures resumed in 1967 as rates on longer maturities again rose to the ceiling rate and made the average maturity of outstandings contract sharply. Early in 1968, when other market rates declined and the Regulation Q ceiling for longer term CDs was raised to 6¼ percent, pressures on the CD market were relieved once more.

During the 1966 "credit crunch," banks found that CDs were a potentially unreliable source of funds. In reaction, some large banks began to develop alternative sources of funds, particularly Eurodollars, on which rates were not subject to regulation. A few United States banks had used Eurodollars prior to 1966, but in that year gross borrowings from foreign branches rose to about $2 billion for the first time. It was also in the same year that the London dollar CD was introduced by the London branch of Citibank. The establishment of facilities for tapping the Eurodollar market during the 1966 credit crunch proved to be important during the 1969–70 crunch, when banks faced an even greater runoff of CDs.

In much of the postwar period, Regulation Q interest rate ceilings for member banks were set below the rates that thrift institutions specializing in housing finance were paying. In this way, *cross-intermediation,*—i.e., the shift of deposits from thrift institutions to commercial banks—was prevented. It was widely thought that preventing such a shift would encourage home building.

The increase in time deposit rates paid by commercial banks after the December 1965 adjustment of Regulation Q ceiling rates appeared to observers to have contributed to outflows of deposits from thrift institutions in 1966. Accordingly, the monetary authorities were in part blamed for the difficulties of the housing market in that year. In response, the authorities requested, and the Congress promptly passed, legislation permitting different ceiling rates for time and savings deposits according to their size and, for the first time, also extending ceilings to rates paid on time and savings deposits by thrift institutions. In September 1966, the ceiling rate on commercial bank deposits smaller than $100,000 was reduced to 5 percent while the ceiling rates for savings deposits and large negotiable CDs were left unchanged at 4 percent and 5½ percent, respectively. Although these actions may have reduced the threat of cross-intermediation, later events showed that rigid reliance on interest rate ceilings made both commercial banks and thrift institutions more susceptible to serious *disintermediation*—i.e., the withdrawal of time and savings deposits to purchase higher yielding money market instruments.

Second Crisis: 1969–70

Early in 1968, in response to rising market interest rates, Regulation Q ceiling rates were set at 5½ to 6½ percent, according to maturity. However, despite the change in the ceilings, rates on new issues of CDs with shorter maturities were uncompetitive throughout most of 1968, and toward the end of that year the same happened to longer term CDs. In 1969, as monetary policy attempted to dampen inflationary pressures, market rates rose rapidly to the vicinity of 8 percent, which far exceeded Regulation Q rates. The ceilings were left unchanged, for the monetary authorities hoped that restriction of bank access to the CD market would both reduce the overall expansion of credit and cause banks to reduce the rate of their expansion of credit to business and thereby to lessen the financial squeeze on other sectors, such as housing and state and local governments. Consequently, between December 1968 and December 1969, banks were buffeted by the largest involuntary runoff of CDs ever, as investors sought more attractive returns available on other money market instruments. Outstandings declined by $12.6 billion, a loss of more than 50 percent from December 1968. Thereafter, outstandings stabilized at a depressed level during the first half of 1970.

The CD runoff during 1969–70 would have been even larger had not banks begun to take advantage of the exemption of deposits of foreign official institutions from Regulation Q ceilings. During the second half of 1969 and the first quarter of 1970, banks were able to increase CDs issued to foreign official institutions by about $2 billion, which offset some of the decline of CDs held by other investors.

The composition as well as the level of CDs was affected by the runoff. With the severe fall in new issues of CDs, the average maturity of outstandings actually rose sharply in the first half of 1970 (Chart 4) as large amounts of short-term CDs matured without being rolled over. (Because of the large proportion of short-term CDs, a runoff increases the average maturity of outstandings.)

While banks faced an unprecedented drop in outstanding CDs, the secondary market virtually dried up. Average daily gross dealer transactions dropped to the lowest levels since the inception of the market and were practically zero during the second half of 1969 and the first part of 1970. At the same time, dealer positions were almost completely eliminated. Hence, any potential investors in CDs were doubly deterred: the interest rates on alternative money market instruments substantially exceeded rates permitted on primary CDs, and the liquidity that had contributed to the earlier attractiveness of CDs no longer existed.

To compensate for the heavy loss of CDs, banks sold government securities, restricted lending to business, and sharply cut back purchases of municipal obligations (large banks were actually net sellers of municipals during the second half of 1969). Although the rate of expansion of bank lending to business was substantially reduced, business spending was not commensurately curtailed because many large firms were able to obtain funds by selling liquid assets and by utilizing sources of nonbank funds, e.g., by selling commercial paper.

Eurodollars—a Substitute for CDs

In addition to restraining lending and liquidating investments, banks also greatly increased their reliance on borrowings from their foreign branches. In fact, large New York banks, which had the best developed access to the Eurodollar market, were able to replace their CD losses almost dollar for dollar with such borrowings. As a result, Eurodollar borrowings from foreign branches soared in late 1968 and 1969; they reached an all-time high of $15 billion in October 1969.

Eurodollar borrowings were a highly attractive source of funds just then. In contrast to CDs, which were subject to Regulation Q ceilings, Eurodollar rates were unregulated. U.S. banks could therefore secure funds to offset their CD losses if they were willing to pay high interest rates, and their access to funds was potentially more reliable for the same reason. In addition—and again in contrast to CDs—the cost of Eurodollar borrowings was reduced somewhat because they were not subject to reserve requirements.

In October 1969, a 10 percent reserve requirement was imposed on net borrowings of U.S. banks from their foreign branches that were above a reserve-free base, defined in a rather complicated way. In essence, the base was equal to at least 3 percent of a bank's total deposits less its deposits due to foreign banks in any current four-week period. For banks that had average Eurodollar borrowings in excess of the 3 percent formula in the four-week period ended May 16, 1969, the base was raised to the May average. However, the base was automatically reduced if average borrowings fell below the May average in any subsequent four-week period. But in no case could the base be lower than that given by the 3 percent formula. The 3 percent formula was intended to avoid discriminating against banks which had been slow to enter the Eurodollar market and consequently did not have large levels of borrowings. The reserve-free base was adopted in order to motivate banks to refrain from reducing Eurodollar borrowings abruptly. Some banks were thus undoubtedly induced to maintain their borrowings for longer than they would have otherwise, and the net liability of U.S. banks to their foreign branches remained flat in the latter part of 1969 and declined only gradually in early 1970.

Because reserve requirements now applied to borrowings from foreign branches, banks turned to other sources of funds. The most important of these was outright sales of loans to bank affiliates, which in turn generally sold commercial paper to pay for the loans. Loan sales to affiliates at large weekly reporting banks increased from about $2.1 billion in May 1969 to $3.0 billion by the year-end. In the first six months of 1970, loan sales doubled, and they reached an all-time high level of $8.1 billion at the end of July.

Meanwhile, in January 1970, the Board of Governors of the Federal Reserve

System raised Regulation Q ceilings somewhat. The action was designed to limit outflows of CDs and other time deposits from commercial banks, but its impact was very modest. Even though market rates declined slightly around that time, they were still well above the new ceilings.

Effects of the Penn Central Crisis

On Friday, June 19, 1970, efforts to induce the U.S. government to grant emergency credits to the Penn Central Transportation Company collapsed. Two days later, on Sunday, June 21, Penn Central filed its bankruptcy petition. The railroad then had in excess of $80 million of commercial paper outstanding, and the prospect of imminent default on this paper generated fears of a general liquidity crisis. For this reason, on Tuesday, June 23, the Federal Reserve took a variety of supportive actions, among which was suspension of the Regulation Q ceiling rate on CDs maturing in 30 to 89 days. The effect was to allow banks to reenter the short-term CD market, which they did with great alacrity. The massive acquisition of funds through new issues of CDs was crucial to banks' efforts to meet the financial needs of business. Many firms were unable to issue commercial paper during the weeks immediately after the Penn Central bankruptcy petition, and total commercial paper outstanding promptly contracted by about $3 billion.

Restoration of banks' access to the CD market also reduced their need to sell loans to affiliates and to raise funds indirectly through commercial paper. Accordingly, loan sales declined slightly in August, and they began to fall sharply after September, when reserve requirements were placed on bank-related commercial paper used to fund bank lending. By the end of 1970, outstandings of loans sold amounted to only $2.7 billion, well below the peak of $8.1 billion.

As banks resumed issuing CDs, the average maturity of outstandings declined rapidly from the all-time high of more than four months in early 1970 to a more normal range of about three months. In addition, the secondary market recovered almost immediately, and daily average transactions and dealer positions soon attained levels far exceeding all previous ones. A significant longer term effect was that participants in the financial markets assumed that the suspension of Regulation Q ceilings on the shortest maturities meant that the Federal Reserve would no longer employ rigid ceilings on CD rates as a tool of quantitative credit control.

After the Regulation Q ceiling on short-term CDs was suspended, deposits at foreign branches were 2 to 3 percentage points more expensive than domestic CDs. Thus, it was no longer attractive to maintain existing levels of Eurodollar borrowings, and banks began to pay them down rapidly. The Federal Reserve Board raised the reserve requirement applying to net borrowings from foreign branches to 20 percent in January 1971. In addition, it announced that, if a bank defining its reserve-free base of Eurodollar borrowings as 3 percent of deposits reduced its borrowings below the reserve-free level, its base would be reduced accordingly. The intention was that the threat of higher reserve requirements on future borrowings would stimulate banks to maintain their current borrowings, thus counteracting the abrupt turnaround in international capital flows resulting from the reduction of borrowings from foreign branches. However, the inducement offered was evidently inadequate, since banks continued to repay them.

The Boom of 1973-74

Credit demand began to revive in 1972, particularly demand for bank loans. Business loans increased rapidly during late 1972 and early 1973, in part because the prime rate was being held to a relatively low level under the influence of the Committee on Interest and Dividends in line with the price and wage control apparatus then in force. In May 1973, as interest rates on CDs with maturities of 90 days and more approached Regulation Q ceilings, these ceilings were suspended, an act that terminated Regulation Q ceilings on *all* large negotiable CDs. Thus the market's earlier assumption that, after the 1969-70 credit crunch, ceilings on CDs were no longer to be used as instruments of monetary policy turned out to be right. Had the ceiling on longer term CDs not been removed, the average maturity of CDs would have declined—an outcome that the authorities wished to avoid. As a result of their continued access to the CD market in 1973-74, banks were able—for the first time in the postwar period—to maintain their share in total credit flows to nonfinancial sectors during a period of monetary restraint.

In June 1973, the Federal Reserve attempted to slow the rapid rate of expansion of bank credit by introducing a marginal reserve requirement on CDs similar to the one applied earlier to Eurodollar borrowings. The existing 5 percent reserve requirement on a bank's base of CDs (defined as the amount of CDs outstanding on May 16, 1973) was continued. For CDs in excess of this base amount, the marginal reserve requirement was increased to 8 percent by addition of a supplementary reserve requirement of 3 percent.[4] At the same time, the authorities reduced the reserve requirement on Eurodollar borrowings by head offices of U.S. banks to 8 percent and announced a gradual elimination of the reserve-free base. This put reserve requirements for CDs and Eurodollars on a roughly equal basis. In September 1973 the Federal Reserve attempted to counteract expectations of an imminent easing of monetary policy by announcing an increase in the marginal reserve requirement on CDs to 11 percent beginning October 4. The new reserve requirement, whatever its effect on market expectations, had little obvious effect on banks' utilization of CDs, for the volume of outstandings continued to increase. When strains on the credit markets temporarily eased in December 1973, the marginal reserve requirement was reduced to 8 percent again.

In September 1974, shortly after money market rates began to decline from their record highs, the authorities restructured CD reserve requirements by removing the

---

[4]This supplementary reserve requirement did not apply to banks with less than $10 million of CDs outstanding.

3 percent supplementary reserve requirement for CDs with an original maturity of four months or more. Thus, CDs in excess of the base amount that had an original maturity of less than four months continued to be subject to an 8 percent reserve requirement, while longer term CDs became subject to a reserve requirement of only 5 percent. This was the first time reserve requirements had been related to the maturity of CDs. The Federal Reserve wanted to induce banks to lengthen the average maturity of their CDs—by now reduced to an all-time low of slightly more than two months—by lowering somewhat the effective cost to banks of longer term CDs.

Other modifications to the reserve requirements came in December 1974. The marginal reserve requirement for CDs was eliminated, and reserve requirements were set at 6 percent for CDs with an original maturity of less than six months and at 3 percent for those with an original maturity of six months (180 days) or more. One problem with such a structure of reserve requirements is that banks may find themselves able to reduce their required reserves with adjustments of their CD maturities that leave the average maturity of CDs essentially unchanged. For example, issues of six-month CDs—which have a low reserve requirement—might be increased while issues of five-month CDs are reduced. This sort of change will reduce required reserves but will increase maturity only very slightly.

It is difficult to assess with precision the effect of these new reserve requirements on the maturity structure of CDs. However, the timing of changes in the average maturity of CDs sheds some light on the question. The average maturity of CDs actually declined slightly following the September revision and increased rapidly beginning in early 1975. Since the December revision in fact weakened the incentive banks had to lengthen CD maturities, the abrupt increase in the average maturity in early 1975 seems primarily attributable to the sharp runoff of CDs which began at that time.

Moreover, the actual changes in the spread of the six-month CD rate over the one-month rate were far greater than could have been produced by the modifications to reserve requirements. Simple calculations show that, all other things being equal, the change should have been an increase of 25–30 basis points in the spread of the six-month rate over the one-month rate. However, the spread increased by about 125 basis points from late 1974 to the end of 1975 and then was in large part reversed by the end of 1976 (Chart 3). This roughly followed the pattern of changes in the structure of interest rates in other markets. The actual behavior of the spreads thus suggests that market forces have a determining influence on the structure of interest rates in the CD market, while the influence of the differential reserve requirements is difficult to isolate.

A Multitier Market Emerges

Though the CD market underwent a variety of shocks during the 1973–74 boom, it performed quite well. Unlike earlier booms, when Regulation Q ceilings precipitated a runoff of CDs and a severe thinning of the secondary market, in 1973–74 banks were generally able to market their CDs successfully—though they had to pay quite costly interest rates—and no discernible transactions decline occurred in the secondary market. The principal change was the advent of a "multitier" market, in which the rates paid by banks on CDs were tailored according to investors' perception of the riskiness of the issuing banks.

The collapse of the United States National Bank of San Diego in October 1973, followed by Herstatt in Germany and the Franklin National Bank in New York in 1974, had significant ramifications. For the first time since the 1930s, the specter of possible failure of even major financial institutions arose, making investors more sensitive to relative risk in evaluating CDs issued by different banks. Accordingly, investors did demand noticeably higher rates on the CDs of banks viewed as less stable. Since the early years of the CD market, distinctions had typically existed between rates paid by banks then classified as prime and nonprime, but the multitier market introduced a rather more refined differentiation. For the most part, in the new tier structure, the larger banks pay lower rates.

Bank size affected rates paid on CDs in two ways. Liquidity considerations favored the CDs of the large money market banks, since the secondary market for them is the most developed. And banks that attempted to place issues of their CDs beyond the circle of regular customers who knew them well had to pay a premium. For both reasons, regional banks trying to tap new sources of funds with their CDs in 1974 generally had to pay higher rates than did large money market banks. In 1975, when public attention began to focus on the financial crisis in New York City, even some large New York City banks found their CDs being less favorably received by investors than before. That change in the structure of CD rate tiers has since moderated significantly.

The development of a tiered market in CDs may betoken the maturation of the CD as a money market instrument. The earlier, relatively crude differentiation between prime and nonprime CDs was a rather peculiar feature of the CD market. A refined structure of tiered borrowing rates has, for example, long been a standard feature of the bond and commercial paper markets. In response to the development of tiering in the CD market, some banks may very well have changed their approach to lending or investing funds obtained through CDs, thus giving more emphasis to asset management relative to liability management. It is probably safe to conclude that banks are now far more conscious of the impact of their incremental CD exposure on their total cost of purchased funds than they were prior to 1974.

Another indication of the maturation of the CD market is that, as banks on the whole faced sluggish loan demand from the beginning of 1975 until relatively recently, they allowed their CDs to run down. At the same time, they restructured their balance sheets by expanding their investment portfolios considerably. This is the first time since 1961 that banks in the aggregate voluntarily reduced their CDs to any significant extent; earlier contractions had occurred when market rates exceeded Regulation Q ceilings. At other times CDs were always growing, even when loan demand was sluggish. This altered behavior may mean that the rapid growth stage of CDs has ended. From now on CDs will probably expand and contract in step with the movements of loan demand.

Developments in borrowings of United States banks from their foreign branches were less dramatic during 1973–74 than in 1969. Such borrowings were subject to reserve requirements during 1973–74 and, since Eurodollar rates typically exceeded CD rates, Eurodollars were generally a more expensive source of funds for United States banks than were CDs. Equally important, since the last remaining Regulation Q ceiling on CD rates was suspended in May 1973, CDs remained available—though they were extremely expensive—even during the tightest money market conditions in 1973–74.

Under these circumstances, banks relied very little on Eurodollars for domestic lending. In 1973, net borrowings from foreign branches remained in the neighborhood of $1.5–$2 billion, far below the peak of over $15 billion in 1969. An unexpected tightening of the money market in early 1974 led to a rapid increase to about $3 billion, a level maintained through the summer. But a general weakening of demand for credit then became apparent, and starting in October net Eurodollar borrowings were rapidly repaid. Since February 1975, U.S. banks on balance have been net lenders to their foreign branches.

Lessons of the Past and New Developments

The lessons of the seventeen-year history of CDs primarily concern experience with the two means employed by the monetary authorities to influence the CD market: Regulation Q interest rate ceilings and reserve requirements.

While Regulation Q interest rate ceilings did restrict bank lending to business somewhat during the 1969–70 period, overall credit extended to business was affected much less. The rigidly maintained CD rate ceilings succeeded in preventing deposits from flowing from thrift institutions to commercial banks, but as a result both suffered severe deposit losses which greatly increased uncertainty in domestic financial markets. The further evolution of the financial system since that time and the increased ability of borrowers to secure funds from outside the banking system make it even more doubtful that Regulation Q can be used constructively as a means of monetary control in the future.

As to the various forms of reserve requirements applied to CDs, there is little evidence that they have had any appreciable effect on the market. This holds true for the marginal reserve requirements as well as for the current reserve requirements that are differentiated according to original maturity.

Further alterations of reserve requirements do not appear to be a promising means of increasing the average maturity of CDs. The demand for long-term CDs is mainly affected by three factors: the short period of time for which many investors have funds available, the thinness of the secondary market for long-term CDs, and the spread of the long-term CD rate over the short-term CD rate. Current reserve requirements influence the latter factor by penalizing short-term CDs. Given the tendency of the other factors to favor the purchase of short-term CDs, it seems likely that reserve requirements would have to incorporate a considerably greater differential to stimulate the issuance of long-term CDs. The legal limit on the range of reserve requirements that may be applied to time deposits, 3–10 percent, does not appear to allow much scope for creating such a differential.[5]

Of course, given the increased use of term loans in bank lending to business, there is a presumption that banks should lengthen the maturities of their deposits so as to maintain something of a balance between the maturities of their assets and their liabilities. In fact, the average maturity of CDs has recently tended to vary directly with the cyclical increase in the proportion of term loans in the portfolios of large banks. But, judging by the timing of maturity changes, very little of this variation appears to be attributable to the lowering of reserve requirements for long-term CDs in September and December 1974. The balancing of asset and liability maturities thus appears to take place over the business cycle independently of changes in reserve requirements.

The most interesting developments in the CD market in the last few years have been the innovations introduced by banks to extend the maturities of CDs. During early 1975 the variable-rate CD was introduced. It has a minimum maturity of 360 days, and its interest rate, pegged at a specified spread over the issuing bank's current rate on 90–day CDs, is adjusted every 90 days. With such an instrument an investor can increase his total interest return over that obtainable by successively renewing short-term CDs without being committed to a fixed rate. The attraction to the issuing bank is that, on average, the total interest paid on a variable-rate CD will be less than that on a conventional (fixed-rate) CD of the same maturity. The reason is that the investor and the bank in effect split the risk premium included in the spread of the long-term conventional CD rate over the short-term CD rate. It is impossible to determine how many variable-rate CDs have been sold. The amount cannot be very large, since demand for long-term CDs is restricted by the scarcity of long-term investable funds and the relative illiquidity of long-term CDs.

Another recent innovation has the potential of altering somewhat the character of the market as well as lengthening maturities. It is the rollover CD introduced by Morgan Guaranty Trust in late 1976. The rollover CD was designed to overcome the limitation on a bank's ability to issue long-term CDs, due to six months being about the maximum maturity traded regularly in the secondary market. Investors are naturally reluctant to purchase long-term CDs if they in large part lack the liquidity provided for short-term CDs by the secondary market. The rollover CD attempts to deal with the problem by packaging a series of six-month CDs into a commitment to roll them over for a longer period of time, e.g., three years. Any one of the six-month CDs may be sold in the secondary market if the investor needs liquidity but, if he does so, he is nevertheless committed to roll over the CD by redepositing equivalent funds at each maturity date.

The rollover CD allows long-term CDs to be structured so as to be able to take advantage of the existing secondary market. Still, it is not so liquid as a conventional

---

[5]Reserve requirements for specific kinds of time deposits have recently been set below 3 percent, but a bank's reserve requirement for all of its time deposits must nevertheless be at least 3 percent.

six-month CD, since the investor cannot at present sell his rollover commitment in the secondary market and since the rate of interest is fixed for the entire term of the commitment. Even so, the innovation could enhance considerably the liquidity of long-term CDs. A disadvantage to the issuing bank of the rollover CD, compared with a conventional long-term, single-maturity CD, is that the bank takes the risk, however small, that an investor may default on his future commitment to roll over the six-month CD. The additional risk may well limit the attractiveness of rollover CDs to banks until experience indicates that the risk is negligible or that it can be reduced to reasonable levels through careful management. The future of the roll-over CD is still uncertain, and only a moderate amount has been sold by Morgan Guaranty.

The Federal Reserve has continued to encourage banks to lengthen the average maturity of their CDs by lowering reserve requirements for time deposits (including CDs) with long original terms to maturity. For example, in October 1975 the reserve requirement applying to CDs with original terms to maturity of four years or longer was reduced to 1 percent from 3 percent.[6] Since only a minute fraction of CDs outstanding at present have this long an original maturity, the effect of the change on the average maturity of CDs was probably nil. In January 1976 the reserve requirement applying to time deposits with an original maturity of at least 180 days up to four years was lowered to 2.5 percent from 3 percent. It seems unlikely that this small change had any appreciable effect on the average maturity of CDs.

It appears that the structure of reserve requirements on time deposits could well be simplified by eliminating different requirements for different maturities. As noted, it seems unlikely that these reserve requirements have had any significant effect on the average maturity of CDs, and they complicate considerably the calculation of banks' required reserves. There is also reason to question whether influencing the maturity structure of CDs is a desirable policy objective. If it is, consideration should be given to ways to encourage innovations such as the rollover CD; liquidity is likely to be more important to potential investors than the small extra return that might be created by low reserve requirements on long-term CDs.

Another possible policy initiative would be to eliminate the 30-day minimum maturity of CDs. It is difficult to point to any important purpose served by this requirement, and its removal would probably contribute modestly to the smooth functioning of the market. Although removal would require a change in the legislation governing time deposits, such action is not inconceivable in light of recent trends toward payment of interest on demand deposits (NOW accounts, telephone transfers, etc.).

The availability of very short-term CDs would make CDs more attractive in investors' portfolios relative to finance company commercial paper, which often has only a few days' maturity. Most investors would probably find very short-term CDs

---

[6]Morgan Guaranty initially hoped that rollover CDs of four years and longer maturity would be subject to the 1 percent reserve requirement applying to conventional CDs of such a maturity. But a recent Federal Reserve ruling held that, for calculation of required reserves, a rollover CD is equivalent to a six-month CD and thus is subject to a higher reserve requirement.

attractive at only a modest spread over the RP rate. Very short-term CDs would also give banks a somewhat more flexible instrument for short-term adjustment of reserve positions than RPs, which must be backed by Treasury securities if they are to be exempt from demand deposit reserve requirements. Elimination of the 30–day minimum maturity would thus remove the artificial stimulus to secondary market trading in CDs of less than 30 days remaining maturity, much as was done for 30- to 89-day maturities by the November 1964 increase in the applicable Regulation Q ceiling from its earlier uncompetitive level. Finally, the availability of very short-term CDs would considerably simplify the cash management policies of munici-palities, whose legal investment alternatives tend to be few.

Prospects for CDs

An assessment of prospects must recognize that the CD market probably has reached maturity. Rates have become tiered to reflect investor perception of the relative riskiness of issuing banks—a standard feature of other financial markets. Perhaps more revealing of market maturity is the banks' voluntary reduction of outstanding CDs beginning in 1975, the first sustained voluntary retrenchment ever. There is thus little likelihood that bank reliance on CDs will increase at anything like the steady rate observed during much of the 1960s, when Regulation Q ceilings were not binding. The outlook, rather, is for CDs to behave much as they did in 1973–76; in that period, issues expanded in line with increased loan demand and contracted as loan demand declined.

Without a return to Regulation Q ceilings on CD rates or some other quantitative constraint on banks' liability management, U.S. banks' reliance on borrowings from their foreign branches as a source of funds will probably reflect primarily the relative cost of funds in the CD market and the Eurodollar market. Unless Eurodollar rates should at times get to be abnormally low relative to U.S. CD rates, such borrowings from now on should chiefly provide a source of funds with maturities of less than 30 days. Substitution between domestic CDs and Eurodollar time deposits at foreign branches will most likely be of appreciably smaller im-portance than it was in the past. For this reason, borrowings from foreign branches will probably grow much less than CDs whenever banks seek to expand their discre-tionary liabilities in response to growing loan demand.

Some Insights on Member Bank Borrowing

Elijah Brewer

10

The amount of member bank borrowings at the Federal Reserve banks has averaged about $1.2 billion for the past six months, ranging between $500 million and $1.7 billion on a weekly average basis. This compares with the less than $100 million level that prevailed between late 1975 and early 1977.

Because member bank borrowings are usually higher in times of monetary restraint, concern occasionally arises that the *discount window* amounts to a leak in the Federal Reserve's control over commercial bank reserves and money.

This article focuses on the major elements affecting the volume of borrowings, both over the interest rate cycle and in the short run. It also explains why borrowing is not a significant obstacle to the achievement of policy goals.

Under current Federal Reserve procedures and regulations, three factors influence the volume of borrowings:

- The cost of borrowing from the Federal Reserve (the discount rate) relative to the cost of short-term funds from other sources.
- The volume of funds the Federal Reserve makes available to the banking system through open market operations relative to the total amount of required reserves.

Reprinted from *Economic Perspectives,* November/December 1978, pp. 16–21, by permission of the Federal Reserve Bank of Chicago and the author.

- Federal Reserve administration policy regarding the extension of credit to member banks.

Providing for Bank Reserves

The Federal Reserve system provides aggregate reserves to the commercial banking system through both open market operations and loans to individual member banks.[1] While the former are undertaken at the initiative of the System, the latter are at the initiative of the member banks.

There is an incentive for banks to borrow when the discount rate is below the cost of buying funds in the Federal funds market—a major avenue through which reserves supplied by open market operations are distributed among banks.[2] Although some borrowing is clearly related to the size of this rate incentive, the very process of policy implementation under current regulations virtually ensures that borrowing will increase when the Fed funds rate rises. This would be true even if the discount rate were tied to the Fed funds rate so that a rate incentive could not develop.

Because of the way the discount window is administered, borrowed reserves are temporary and self-constraining. Not only are they taken into account when the *Desk* (the securities department at the Federal Reserve Bank of New York) determines its operational strategy in conducting open market operations, but they reflect operational problems.

Member bank reserve accounts at Federal Reserve banks serve as working balances through which many transactions, such as check clearings, are channeled. Banks with a greater value of checks written on their deposits than the value of checks deposited with them pay the difference by drawing down their reserve accounts.

Normal deposit flows between the thousands of commercial banks in the United States result in significant shifts in the distribution of deposits among banks. Banks hold funds on deposit at Federal Reserve banks to cover these day-to-day shifts.

In addition, banks are required to hold on average for each weekly reporting period (Thursday through Wednesday), a proportion of their deposits as reserves at

---

[1]There are also other factors that cause changes in the reserves of the banking system. The three principal factors are (1) changes in Federal Reserve float; (2) flows of currency between banks and the public; and (3) changes in Treasury balances at Federal Reserve banks. These outside factors, which often affect reserves by hundreds of millions of dollars in a single day, are offset or supplemented by open market operations in accordance with overall reserve needs.

[2]The interest rate on the bulk of member bank borrowing is the base rate applicable to loans secured by paper "eligible" for discount or purchase by the Reserve banks under the provisions of the Federal Reserve Act. This is generally referred to as the "discount rate" even though loans are not made on a discount basis. An additional one-half of 1 percent is required on loans secured by other collateral satisfactory to the lending Reserve bank. Since 1974, a special discount rate has been applied to member banks requiring exceptionally large loans extended over a prolonged period of time. This rate has typically been set at one to two percentage points above the basic rate.

**Member Bank Borrowings Tend to Vary with
the Spread between the Federal Funds Rate
and Discount Rate**

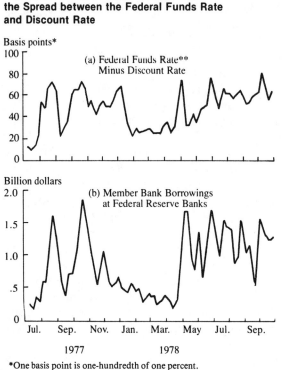

*One basis point is one-hundredth of one percent.
**Weekly averages of daily effective federal funds rate.

the Federal Reserve banks. Because the amount of reserves required to be held in the current week is based on deposits two weeks earlier (*lagged reserve requirements*), every bank knows at the beginning of a statement week what its reserve balance will have to be on average for that week. Also, the Federal Reserve knows the aggregate of required reserves that all member banks will have to hold.

Reserve Availability—
Controlling the Fed Funds Rate

In supplying reserves to the banking system to influence bank deposits and credit, the Federal Reserve pursues its monetary objectives through its influence on the price of reserves in the market—the Fed funds rate. The policy decisions involve estimates of the level of this key money market rate that would be consistent with the rate of monetary expansion being sought. If deposits are growing faster than the Federal Reserve wants them to, the flow of reserves to the banking system is slowed through open market operations. The Fed funds rate rises, discouraging banks from expanding deposits and their holdings of loans and investments.

Because of lagged reserve requirements, however, constraints on total reserves are limited in the short run. If the amount of reserves supplied to the banking system falls short of the amount needed, the banks in deficit bid up the Fed funds rate. As the rate rises, some banks will respond to the rate differential by borrowing at the discount window. Regardless of the differential, however, enough has to be borrowed to cover the overall reserves shortage. If more reserves are supplied through open market operations than required, the Fed funds rate falls relative to the discount rate and both the need and cost-savings incentive for banks to borrow are reduced.

By supplying through open market operations either more or less reserves than required to meet reserve needs overall, the monetary authorities can achieve the Fed funds rate they believe is consistent with the rate of monetary expansion they seek. Member bank borrowings serve as a residual source of reserves that equates the supply of reserves overall to the amount of required reserves, which is fixed in advance.

Shortages of reserves created in the process of pushing the Fed funds rate up force borrowings to rise as the funds rate rises. But the tighter conditions—with respect to both availability of reserves and their cost—also discourage credit and money growth in the weeks that follow.

Borrowing Complements
Open Market Operations

While the lagged reserves rule gives the Desk advance knowledge of the average amount of reserves that will have to be held each week, there is less certainty about the amount that will be supplied from outside sources and, therefore, the volume of transactions needed to cover required reserves at a particular level of monetary ease or restraint.

Changes in purely technical factors, moreover, can make the necessary offsets hard to achieve. These operational difficulties can happen because of shortages in collateral, delivery problems, and constraints on interest rates.

Movements in aggregate borrowing at the discount window give clues to whether non-borrowed reserves are sufficient, deficient, or excessive during the reserve settlement week. Member bank borrowings reflect not only the response of monetary authorities to the strength of credit demand and monetary growth but also to imbalances in the supply and demand for bank reserves brought on by day-to-day operational problems. These imbalances can result from errors in projecting reserves and from temporary inabilities to implement the actions intended.

In conducting operations to implement monetary policy, the Federal Reserve attempts to offset potential disturbances to the money market and changes in credit availability caused by other factors that affect bank reserves. These include changes in Federal Reserve float, currency in the hands of the public, and especially shifts of funds out of private deposits into Treasury balances at Federal Reserve banks.

Such changes are estimated in advance, but the estimates are subject to error. The most likely amount of member bank borrowing is also estimated on the basis of recent experience and the spread between the Fed funds rate and the discount rate. Based on the net effect of all these elements, projections are made of the amount of reserves that will be available during the period and the probable need to add or drain reserves so that the total supply equates to the total required, allowing for some minimal amount of excess reserves.

To the extent open market operations fail to compensate for a net reserve drain from other elements affecting reserves during the settlement week, member banks in the aggregate will have to borrow from Federal Reserve banks to cover the reserve deficiency. Such borrowing will be necessary by the end of the settlement week, regardless of the reason for the deficiency—whether it is an unexpected increase in currency in the hands of the public, a sharper decline in float than had been expected, or a delay in the cashing of Treasury checks.

The only question is *who* will do the borrowing. As in a game of musical chairs, the net deficiency nationwide will impact on some individual bankers when the settlement period ends.

The uncertainties banks face also affect their borrowing. When normal deposit patterns are expected to change or reserves are expected to be less available, some banks borrow in anticipation of the change in their needs. A bank may borrow over a long holiday weekend, for example, to make sure reserve needs are covered. The Federal Reserve's discount facility, therefore, is an important mechanism for meeting the needs of bank liquidity arising from uncertainties about deposits. Such uncertainties are naturally greater in periods of monetary restraint. To the extent that such borrowing overcompensates for actual shortages in availability, the Federal Reserve may have to take offsetting open market action to absorb reserves.

Even when the Desk's estimates of reserve needs nationwide are reasonably accurate, implementation of monetary policy is not simple. The Federal Reserve controls the supply of reserves over the long run mainly through the outright purchase and sale of government securities. An outright purchase of securities permanently provides reserves. A sale permanently reduces reserves. But the Federal Reserve also has to provide or absorb reserves for short periods, often just a day or so within the reserve settlement week. Repurchase agreement transactions (RPs) with government securities dealers are particularly useful in providing reserves to offset temporary reserve drains resulting from factors other than Desk operations. Matched sale-purchase transactions in government securities can be used to withdraw reserves on a temporary basis.

RPs involve the purchase of government securities by the Federal Reserve and commitments on the part of dealers to repurchase the securities at a specified date and price. The Federal Reserve pays for the securities by crediting the reserve accounts of the dealers' clearing banks, which receive an equal increase in customer deposits. Such transactions are effectively short-term loans by the Federal Reserve to the dealers, collateralized by government securities.

Conversely, if the Federal Reserve is withdrawing reserves from the banking system, it enters into matched sale-purchase agreements with securities dealers. These contracts involve the sale of blocks of securities to dealers for immediate delivery with a simultaneous purchase for delivery at a specified later date. The securities sold by the Federal Reserve are paid for by debits to the reserve balances of the dealers' banks, with the result that bank reserves decline.

The ability to provide reserves through open market operations depends, however, on the ability of government securities dealers to pledge collateral. Collateral is no problem when reserves are being withdrawn. But the success of the Federal Reserve in negotiating enough repurchase agreements to achieve reserve objectives depends on the ability of securities dealers to draw collateral from their customer networks.

When interest rates are rising, dealers tend to keep their inventories low and collateral is not as readily available as when interest rates are declining. This makes a large open market operation difficult. At other times, when dealers have substantial inventories of government securities, it is fairly easy to inject a large volume of reserves into the banking system as needed to meet predetermined reserve requirements.

In weeks when the Federal Reserve is not successful in providing needed reserves through open market operations, loans to member banks rise. Such increases can be quite sharp, but they are usually only temporary. In the interim, of course, the fed funds rate also tends to rise.

Constraints through Window Administration

Borrowed reserves, even in times of tight money, are only a small part of total bank reserves. Federal Reserve policy regarding loans to individual banks is an important constraint on expansion in borrowing. While this policy is applied consistently, whether money is tight or easy, its impact is felt mainly during periods of restraint, when member banks need to borrow.

If the discount window actually represented an open line of credit to member banks, the difference between the Fed funds rate and discount rate would be much more important in determining the level of borrowing. The privilege of borrowing, defined by Federal Reserve Regulation A, is not freely available to member banks on a continuing basis.

Borrowing by member banks is intended to cover unusual short-term needs. Administration of the discount window imposes an implicit cost in the form of surveillance of member banks that use the window for extended periods. Because borrowings today tend to reduce the willingness of the Federal Reserve to accommodate future borrowings, banks tend to use the window sparingly, reserving their access for times or urgent need.

**Borrowed Reserves Account for a Small
Proportion of Total Reserves, Even in Periods
of Monetary Restraint (Average of Monthly
Figures Includes Seasonal Borrowings since
1973)**

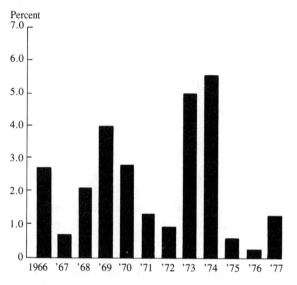

Banks borrow only to cover reserve deficiencies during the reserve settlement week. They do not borrow to obtain excess reserves. As long as a bank's performance shows its intentions to operate within the limits of its own resources, it can usually arrange for credit to meet its needs. A bank can use the discount window, for example, for temporary aid in working out portfolio adjustments to meet unexpectedly strong local credit demands.

Continuous borrowing at the window is considered inappropriate, for whatever purpose. Continuous borrowing suggests the bank is using Federal Reserve funds to supplement its capital resources. It also indicates the bank has basic difficulties with its reserve position, which ought to be corrected through portfolio adjustments. Federal Reserve surveillance, including frequent contact with borrowers, tends to discourage extended use of the discount window, constraining the growth in total borrowings.

An exception to the rule is the *seasonal borrowing privilege,* created in 1973 through revision of Regulation A. The authority for Federal Reserve banks to accommodate small banks in covering shortfalls in deposits relative to loans was intended to assist banks, especially those serving agricultural or resort areas, to meet the credit needs of their communities. While credit can be arranged for several months under this program, the total outstanding has usually been less than $200 million. The desk managing open market operations knows the amount in advance.

Large Banks Dominate Profile

In periods of monetary ease, borrowing tends to bounce along at very low levels. With open market operations taking care of the supply of reserves, member bank use of the window results mainly from frictional problems that distort the distribution of reserves to small banks.

When the economy is sluggish, the Federal Reserve, in freely accommodating a fairly modest rate of growth in bank credit and deposits, supplies reserves faster than they are being absorbed by deposit growth. These are conditions associated with a low fed funds rate and a low volume of member bank borrowing at the discount window.

The Fed funds rate was consistently below the discount rate in 1976 and early 1977 and, although occasional bulges reflected problems at the end of settlement weeks, member bank borrowing was minimal. The volume of borrowings began increasing substantially about mid-1977, however, as did the volatility.

With credit demands accelerating and deposits growing faster than desired under monetary policy objectives, the Federal Reserve ceased accommodating all the associated reserve demands through open market operations. Demand for reserves rose faster than the supply, and money market interest rates rose. The Fed funds rate has been persistently above the basic discount rate since April 1977, although progressive increases in the latter have kept the margin fairly narrow.

Peak Demand for Credit at the Discount Window Reflects Residual Pressures on Large Banks

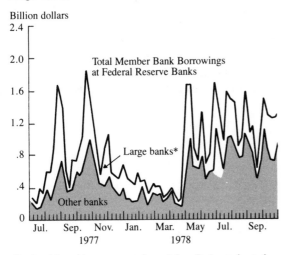

*Banks with weekly average net demand deposits (gross demand deposits minus cash items in process of collection and demand balances due from domestic banks) greater than $400 million.

In times of monetary restraint, member banks of all sizes come to the discount window in increasing numbers and with increasing frequency, especially when the discount rate lags the rise in money market interest rates. Even then, however, the number of borrowers is a small proportion of member banks. Less than 10 percent of member banks borrowed at the window in any single week in the second quarter of 1978, and probably no more than 25 percent borrowed at any time during that quarter.

Small banks step up their use of the discount window as their deposit growth fails to keep up with loan demands. This is because many small banks do not have access to money market sources of funds. Peak demands for Federal Reserve loans reflect the convergence of residual pressures on the large banks in major cities. There are comparatively few large banks and they do not borrow as often as the small borrowers. When they do borrow, however, a large amount of credit often is involved. The sharp short-run fluctuations in total member bank borrowings reflect the intermittent borrowings of large banks, some of which have required reserves of more than a half billion dollars.

It is on these large banks that the net pressures in the money market converge at the end of the reserve settlement week when there is a shortfall in the overall supply of reserves below the required level. This is partly because of the role these banks play in accommodating the needs of smaller correspondent banks.

Borrowing by large banks tends to be concentrated on Wednesdays and they rarely borrow for more than a day at a time. The average daily volume of member bank borrowing in 1977 was $454 million, while the average for Wednesdays only was $737 million, including some Wednesdays at more than $2 billion.

The sharp but irregular Wednesday spurts in borrowings clearly reflect shortages in the aggregate supply of reserves relative to required reserve levels, whether the shortages were the result of policy moves or operational problems.

The pattern of member bank borrowing at Federal Reserve banks suggests strongly that the large commercial banks come to the window, not because of a rate differential, but mainly because reserves are not available in the money market. Any benefits they receive from a favorable discount rate are largely fortuitous.

Compensating Balance Requirements Integral to Bank Lending

Joseph E. Burns

11

A businessman seeking a loan at a commercial bank may well be asked to keep an amount on deposit at the bank equal to some specified percentage of the loan. Such an arrangement is known as a compensating balance requirement.

Compensating balance requirements are not new. As early as 1924, Glenn C. Munn, in his *Encyclopedia of Finance and Banking*, referred to compensating balances. But the mutual satisfaction with such requirements is becoming increasingly important in the negotiation of bank loans. Evidence suggests that compensating balances have become much more common in recent years. And indications are that they may become even more common in the years ahead.

Of more than 100 banks recently surveyed in the Eleventh Federal Reserve District, nearly 60 percent require compensating balances on some types of loans. Also, marked changes have been underway. While large banks have long employed compensating balances to some degree, many smaller banks indicated they had initiated the practice only in recent years.

Reasons for the changes are many and sometimes complicated by changing conditions in the credit market. In some cases, however, compensating balances may involve advantages to both parties in a loan negotiation.

Reprinted, with deletions, from the Federal Reserve Bank of Dallas, *Business Review,* February 1972, pp. 1–8, by permission of the author and the publisher.

From the Borrower's Standpoint

There are several circumstances under which a borrower finds it advantageous to accept such a requirement. The most obvious is one in which he ordinarily holds deposits at the lending bank anyway. And if these deposits are sufficient to meet the compensating balance requirement, it is, of course, to his advantage to accept the requirement—provided that by so doing he can obtain a lower interest rate on the loan or receive bank services that would not be available without using a compensating balance. If, however, the borrower has no deposits at the bank or less on deposit than is needed to meet the balance requirement, he must assess the cost of obtaining the additional funds against the benefits of borrowing under these conditions—such as a reduced rate of interest on the loan or additional bank services.

If the borrower wants to withdraw the full proceeds of the loan but does not have enough funds on deposit to meet the balance requirement, he must either liquidate some assets or borrow to make up the deficiency in deposits. In some cases, the bank may be willing to increase the size of the loan to cover the balance requirement. In others, the borrower may have to find a third party that can provide the needed funds.

Under this arrangement, called *link financing,* a third party deposits enough of its own funds in the bank to meet the requirement. Finance and insurance companies, or sometimes even construction or manufacturing firms, are usually willing to undertake such link financing. The borrower then has to pay interest to the third party in addition to his interest payments to the bank.

The borrower's choice, then, to take a loan under an arrangement requiring a compensating balance depends partly on the cost and availability of funds from each of the three alternative sources—liquidating assets, borrowing from the bank, or borrowing from a third party. In some cases, the cost of these alternative sources of funds may be more than he wants to pay and he must look elsewhere for the loan. In some cases, he may not have access to these alternatives or even be aware of them. This might be particularly true of small borrowers.

Small borrowers also may be confused or alienated by the requirement and, therefore, deterred from borrowing. But since compensating balances are used mainly by large banks in connection with sizable loans to fairly large businesses and finance companies, such situations are probably not common. Borrowers encountering compensating balance requirements are typically quite knowledgeable regarding the sources and costs of funds.

From the Bank's Standpoint

A bank's decision to use compensating balances depends partly on its estimate of its relative profit position, with and without such requirements. In a short-run, static sense, it might seem unprofitable at first for banks to use compensating balance requirements.

For example, if a bank charged the same effective rate of interest on its loans—say, 8 percent with a 20 percent compensating balance requirement or 10 percent with no compensating balance requirement—it would earn more interest income on loans in a fully loaned-up position if it did not use balance requirements. The reason, of course, is that the bank must hold reserves against the deposits used to satisfy the balance requirements. This keeps the bank's lending capacity below the level needed to generate as much interest income as could be earned if no balance requirements were used.

The widespread use of compensating balances—and the reasonable supposition that bankers are interested in profitability—seems to indicate, however, that this is an altogether too simple view of the role of compensating balances in banking. The relationship between a bank and its customers has a whole host of dimensions other than the customer's outlay of interest and the bank's interest income on loans. Within this complex of relationships, compensating balance requirements can be reasonable.

To begin with, the use of compensating balance requirements can increase the flow of deposits and reserves into the bank. Not every borrower is already a depositor at the bank. Nor does every borrower raise all the funds he needs to meet the requirement at the lending bank. Where the customer has to borrow from a third party or liquidate an asset, the lending bank may gain the use of deposit funds it would not otherwise have had.

But if the use of compensating balances can lead to net inflows of deposits and reserves at the lending bank, it can also lead to net outflows at another bank. Another reason for compensating balances, then, is to offset net clearing drains to other banks using compensating balances. In fact, in some cases, balance requirements may be used simply as a defensive measure because competing banks require them.

Compensating balances also tend to reduce fluctuations in deposits and, in so doing, probably increase bank profits. To meet deposit drains, banks must reduce cash reserves, sell assets, or borrow funds in, say, the Federal funds or some other money market. All these options involve costs to the bank. In addition, more predictable deposit flows may allow banks to invest in longer-term assets, which are usually higher yielding than short-term investments.

Table 1. Use of Compensating Balance Requirements, Eleventh Federal Reserve District

Bank Deposit Size (Million Dollars)	Total Respondents In Category	Percent Requiring Compensating Balances
$500 or more	6	100%
$100 to $499	17	82
$50 to $99	24	63
Less than $50	62	45
All respondent banks	109	58%

Profitability can also be enhanced by compensating balances raising the effective rate of interest on a loan without altering the stated contract rate. At times there are psychological or legal ceilings on the permissible contract rate.

The traditional stickiness of the prime lending rate provides a case in point. Because the prime rate changes only infrequently, it is sometimes out of line with the cost of bank credit that would otherwise reflect market forces of supply and demand. By changing its compensating balance requirement, a bank can alter the effective interest rate over time, bringing it more in line with the actual market cost of bank credit.

Sometimes a borrower may suffer from "interest illusion," not realizing that compensating balance requirements raise his effective interest cost. In such cases, a bank may be able to make a loan that could not have been made had the borrower been aware of the actual interest cost. Such situations are probably rare, however, as compensating balances are typically used in connection with loans to fairly large borrowers—who are well aware of the impact of these balances on the effective rate of interest they pay.

More common probably are situations where the borrower has no illusions about the effective rate but, for his own reasons, may seek a lower contract rate. Prestige, for example, may require that a borrower obtain credit at the lowest contract rate, without great regard for the effective rate. In such cases, a borrower that might not otherwise qualify for the prime rate may, through use of a compensating balance, obtain a loan at the prime rate.

Banks may employ compensating balances to reduce the risk associated with some loans, assuming that if the customer defaulted, some of the loss would be offset by the compensating balance. This may not always be the case, however, since customers are usually required to keep only an average balance to compensate for the loan. If the customer drew down his balance before defaulting, the requirement would do little to reduce the default risk.

The requirement helps a bank improve its competitive position by giving it a way of rewarding customers that keep working balances at the bank. If, in the normal course of business, a customer keeps enough deposits at the bank to meet the compensating balance requirement, he can usually obtain a loan at a lower effective cost than borrowers that do not maintain such balances. Use of this device to arrive at a preferential lending rate also, of course, encourages borrowers to seek future loans at the bank where they keep balances. This tends to limit customer business with other banks—a development that is desirable from the standpoint of the lending bank.

Some borrowers have special characteristics that encourage the use of compensating balances. Finance companies, for example, usually maintain large lines of credit with banks. And although they are prone to borrow large amounts, much of this borrowing is at infrequent intervals and for only short periods. As a result, these companies borrow, on average, only a small amount of the total credit available to them. The cost to the bank of maintaining such volatile lines of credit and borrowing is very high compared with the interest income the loans actually generate. Compensating balances help increase bank earnings on these fairly costly loan arrangements.

Profits aside, most banks are also interested in increasing their total deposits. Larger deposits increase the size of a bank, extending its market power and enhancing its prestige. To this end, compensating balance requirements can, of course, be highly effective.

All these reasons for employing compensating balances are probably not in the minds of all bankers at all times. Nevertheless, it is very likely that each of these reasons, from time to time, has been used by bankers as a rationale for balance requirements.

Who Uses Compensating Balances?

To gain some insight into the characteristics of compensating balances at banks in the Eleventh Federal Reserve District, more than 100 commercial banks in the area were surveyed in September 1971. And their responses indicate the importance of compensating balance requirements as a part of bank lending practices in the District.

Results of the survey show compensating balances are used more commonly at large banks in the District than at small banks (Table 1).The proportion of banks requiring compensating balances drops noticeably, in fact, with the size of banks. All six of the banks in the District with deposits of $500 million or more regularly require compensating balances on some types of loans. But of the 62 responding banks with deposits smaller than $50 million, fewer than half use such balance arrangements.

One reason for the difference is the type of loans handled by banks of different sizes. Compensating balances are most often used on business loans and loans to finance companies. And because these loans make up a greater share of the total loan portfolios at large banks, the largest banks could be expected to use compensating balances more than smaller banks do.

Some of the smaller banks reporting that they do not use compensating balance requirements indicated, however, that they sometimes grant lower interest rates to borrowers that are also depositors at their banks. Thus, while these banks require no strict minimum balance, they employ a practice closely akin to the use of compensating balances to encourage customers to hold deposits with them.

Where the largest banks in the District have used compensating balances for many years—since before 1950, in fact—smaller banks have taken up the practice only in fairly recent years (Table 2). Almost 80 percent of the banks with deposits less than $50 million that reported use of compensating balances have started the practice since 1961. Thus, while large banks are still the main users of compensating balances, more and more small banks are apparently beginning to employ such requirements.

Table 2. Length of Use of Compensating Balance Requirements, Eleventh Federal Reserve District

Bank Deposit Size (Million Dollars)	Percent of Banks Initiating Compensating Balances			
	Before 1950	1951–60	1961–65	Since 1965
$500 or more	100%	0	0	0
$100 to $499	62	23	8	8
$50 to $99	36	45	9	9
Less than $50	5	16	47	32
All respondents requiring balances	39%	22%	22%	16%

Why Do They Use Them?

Compensating balances, while becoming more common among smaller banks, are still not used, however, by half the banks with deposits less than $100 million. Nearly two-thirds of the banks not using compensating balances stated a preference for making adjustments in their interest rates to accommodate needs of the situation. Most felt that compensating balance requirements complicate the loan contract unnecessarily, making it hard for customers to understand and accept.

This is particularly true of small banks, especially those with deposits less than $50 million. Some of these banks felt that the cost of administration is too high. And in light of customer resistance, possible loss of good will is too great to integrate compensating balance requirements into their loan contracts, especially since few of their competitors require compensating balances. Under these circumstances, such banks do not have to concern themselves with possible problems of net deposit outflows to competing banks using compensating balances.

Banks using compensating balance requirements, on the other hand, saw significant advantages in them—especially in increasing total deposits (Table 3). Almost

Table 3. Reasons for Using Compensating Balance Requirements, Eleventh Federal Reserve District (Percentage of Respondent Banks Requiring Compensating Balances, by Deposit Size)

Reason for Requirements	All Size Banks	Bank Deposit Size (Million Dollars)			
		$500 or More	$100 to $499	$50 to $99	Less than $50
Increase deposits	73%	83%	76%	67%	71%
Increase earnings	71	100	86	67	61
Increase lending capacity	54	67	64	67	39
Keep contract rate unchanged	27	17	29	27	29
Allow more borrowing at prime rate	22	0	43	20	18
Because other banks use them	14	50	14	0	14

three-fourths of the banks using compensating balances took this position, and the response was fairly uniform for all sizes of banks. Nearly that many banks also thought compensating balances increase net earnings, although the importance attached to this advantage declined with the size of the bank.

More than half these banks indicated a belief that compensating balances enhance their lending capacity—although, here again, this response was least prevalent among the smallest banks. Also, well over a fourth of the banks felt that compensating balances are useful in allowing them to change the effective rate of interest on loans without changing contract rates. The importance of this consideration was frequently mentioned in connection with the stickiness of the prime lending rate.

More than a fifth of the banks reported compensating balances as being important in allowing more borrowing at a prime contract rate (for "prestige" reasons) than would have been possible without balance requirements. Not one of the six largest banks responded in this manner, however, probably because more of their customers actually qualify for the prime rate than customers at small banks.

Although half the largest banks indicated use of compensating balances because their competitors employ such requirements, only 14 percent of all banks using compensating balances reported this to be a significant reason. This finding was reasonable, of course, since more large banks than small banks require compensating balances and large banks are more likely to encounter competitor banks using such balances.

General Characteristics

Most of the banks approach compensating balance arrangements with a great deal of flexibility (Table 4). More than 80 percent of the banks using compensating balances negotiate requirements with each customer individually. Many stated, however, that while these requirements are open for negotiation, they try to maintain guidelines that can serve as a point of departure in the negotiations. Here again, however, there is a difference in the practice at different size banks, the degree of flexibility diminishing somewhat with bank size. A larger proportion of banks with deposits of less than $100 million set compensating balances in advance of negotiations—and hold to them—than is the case with larger banks.

The difference may be due to customers of large banks being in a stronger competitive position than customers of small banks—stronger in the sense that they probably have several alternative sources of credit and are in a better position to bargain for preferential lending terms. Borrowers at small banks may not have such options. Alternatively, or in addition, small banks may not want to bother with the negotiation of compensating balances on each loan contract, preferring instead the simplicity of uniform requirements.

Banks use compensating balance requirements more often in negotiating lines of credit than in negotiating direct loans. This is particularly true of larger banks. Where almost 90 percent of the banks with deposits of $50 million or more use

Table 4. Characteristics of Compensating Balance Requirements, Eleventh Federal Reserve District (Percentage of Respondent Banks Requiring Compensating Balances, by Deposit Size)

Description	All Size Banks	Bank Deposit Size (Million Dollars)			
		$500 or More	$100 to $499	$50 to $99	Less than $50
Compensating balances are:					
Negotiable	81%	83%	86%	80%	78%
Set in advance	19	17	14	20	22
Compensating balances are used mostly in:					
Lines of credit	75	83	100	80	57
Direct loans	25	17	0	20	43
Compensating balances can be held in:					
Either demand or time deposits	65	100	50	53	71
Demand deposits only	35	0	50	47	29
Requirement is met by					
An average deposit	87	100	100	80	82
A minimum deposit	13	0	0	20	18

balance requirements more frequently on lines of credit, only 57 percent of the banks with deposits of less than $50 million do so. This difference, however, may indicate only that more of the loan business of small banks is associated with direct loans than with lines of credit.

About two-thirds of the banks reported that customers could meet their compensating balance requirements with either demand deposits or time deposits. All banks with deposits of $500 million or more accept this arrangement—which, again, could reflect the stronger bargaining position of borrowers at these banks.

Allowing such balances to be held in time deposits might appear at first to represent a considerable concession on the part of banks, since they may have to pay interest on time deposits. But the bank's seeming sacrifice in paying interest on compensating balances held in time deposits may be offset, at least in part, by either higher contractual interest rates on loans or reduced rates on the time deposits. Moreover, the greater stability of time deposits may also allow banks to use balances held in this form more profitably than those held in checking accounts. Also, reserve requirements are lower on time deposits than on demand deposits.

Most of the banks also allow compensating balance requirements to be satisfied by an average balance maintained over the length of the loan contract, rather than merely by some minimum balance. This flexibility can be an important source of liquidity for customers, since it allows the borrower some discretion in drawing down his balance temporarily. The longer the period over which a customer is allowed to average his balances, the greater the liquidity of such balances. The borrower can draw down larger amounts simply because he has more time to make up the deficit.

Types of Borrowers

Compensating balance requirements are applied systematically to only a few types of borrowers (Table 5). All banks using compensating balances require them in connection with commercial and industrial loans. Requirements on these loans vary widely, ranging from 10 percent to 30 percent of the loan. The most often cited requirement, however, is 20 percent. And except for the smallest banks, which are about equally divided in reporting their requirements at 15 percent and 20 percent, only infrequently is the requirement other than 20 percent, regardless of bank size.

All banks indicated extensive use of compensating balances on loans to finance companies. Here, the requirements are somewhat less uniform than those for business loans, however—the most common being from 15 percent to 20 percent. Again, other requirements were reported—some as low as 5 percent and some as high as 30 percent.

Although some banks reported no compensating balance requirement on security loans, most banks ask that borrowers maintain balances against these loans. And while some requirements are as high as 30 percent, most are from 10 percent to 20 percent.

Most banks do not employ compensating balances on agricultural, consumer, or real estate loans. A few banks, however—particularly the smallest banks—reported that they use compensating balances for such loans. The requirement is usually 5 percent to 15 percent. Some banks, however, do not consider such balances as a requirement but merely as a "suggestion" that borrowers keep whatever deposits they have at the lending bank rather than at some other institution. The concern here seems not so much with the amount of deposits as with their being held at the lending bank.

There are few systematic differences in requirements based on either the size of the borrower or the size of the loan. Some banks pointed out that larger applicants for large loans might often be more creditworthy than small borrowers and, therefore,

Table 5. Most Typical Compensating Balance Requirements, Eleventh Federal Reserve District (Percentage Most Often Cited, by Respondent Bank Deposit Size)

Type of Loan	Bank Deposit Size (Million Dollars)			
	$500 or More	$100 to $499	$50 to $99	Less than $50
Commercial and Industrial	20%	20%	20%	15-20%
Finance company	20	15	20	15
Security	20	20	10	15
Agricultural	0	0	0	0
Real estate	0	0	0	0
Consumer	0	0	0	0

more able to negotiate lower balance requirements. At banks of all sizes, however, requirements tend to be fairly uniform for various size borrowers and loans.

The most common compensating balance requirement on lines of credit—usually to businesses and finance companies—is 10 percent. Once the line is used, however, the requirement on the amount of credit borrowed is typically raised to that prevailing on direct loans. The requirement on the unused portion of the line remains unchanged.

Cyclical Variations

Policies regarding the level, generality of use, and enforcement of compensating balance requirements tend to vary with changes in monetary conditions. During periods of rising interest rates and generally tight credit conditions (Table 6), banks usually raise their compensating balance requirements, apply these requirements to a larger proportion of their loans, and enforce the requirements more rigorously. During periods of falling interest rates and increased credit availability, the reverse is generally true.

The most important policy change during periods of tight money seems to be more rigorous enforcement of compensating balance requirements. More than 60 percent of the banks indicated that they enforce their balance requirements more strictly during periods of tight money. The proportion is much higher for larger banks, probably because these banks usually suffer more deposit losses in periods of tight money than smaller banks do.

More than half the banks reported that they apply compensating balance requirements to a larger proportion of their loans during such periods. Of the very largest banks, however, only 17 percent indicated they take such action. This could be the result of small banks having more leeway for such action than larger banks, which probably apply such requirements fairly uniformly all the time.

Only a few banks in each size category increase their requirements across the board in times of tight money. Some banks pointed out, however, that they tend more to raise compensating balance requirements on loans to new customers than to change agreements on outstanding loans.

Table 6. Compensating Balance Requirement Policies, Eleventh Federal Reserve District
(Percentage of Respondent Banks Requiring Compensating Balances, by Deposit Size)

		Bank Deposit Size (Million Dollars)			
Requirements During Tight Money Periods	All Size Banks	$500 or More	$100 to $499	$50 to $99	Less than $50
Enforced more rigorously	62%	83%	93%	53%	46%
Applied to more loans	51	17	71	60	43
Increased	17	17	29	13	14

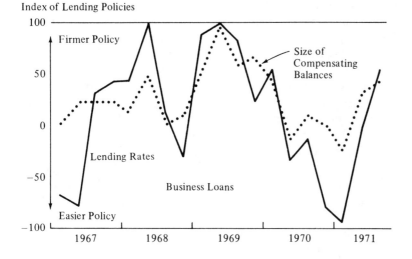

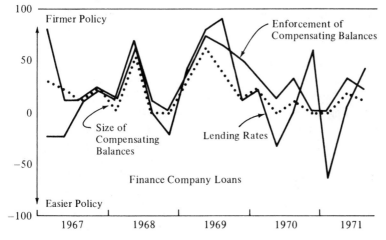

FIGURE 1. Use of compensating balances in the District varies over the business cycle.

Note: The index is computed as the sum of the percentage of banks in each response category after multiplication by the weight in each category. The weights used were: much firmer (2), moderately firmer (1), essentially unchanged (0), moderately easier (− 1), much easier (− 2).

Some indication of the relationship between changes in bank policies regarding compensating balances and those on lending rates can be obtained from the Quarterly Survey of Changes in Bank Lending Practices published by the Board of Governors of the Federal Reserve System. In this survey, a sample of large banks is asked about policies regarding interest rates and the size of compensating balances on loans to businesses and finance companies, as well as the enforcement of balance requirements on finance company loans. The banks are asked to indicate whether these policies are much firmer, moderately firmer, essentially unchanged, moderately easier, or much easier than those reported in the previous survey.

A weighted index of responses from banks in the Eleventh District (Figure 1) shows that large banks in the Southwest tend to firm policies regarding lending rates and the size and enforcement of compensating balances during periods of generally rising market rates of interest and reduced credit availability—such as the first half of 1968 and most of 1969. The index also shows that these banks have eased their policies in periods of generally falling market rates of interest and increased credit availability—such as the last half of 1968, late 1969, and 1970.

Changes in policies regarding compensating balances usually coincide with changes in lending rates. The extent of the changes, however, is generally less than for changes in lending rates, particularly during periods when these policies are eased.

This suggests that there may be some minimum *normal* level of compensating balance requirements that banks want to maintain. During periods of tight money, banks seem willing to increase these requirements roughly in line with firmer lending rates. But during periods of easy money, they seem unwilling to reduce the requirements below this presumably normal minimum. And this reluctance to lower requirements could account for the greater ease in lending rate policies compared with compensating balance requirement policies in such periods. Nevertheless, it remains clear that there have been significant changes in policies on compensating balance requirements in recent years and that these changes have been a major factor in variations in bank lending practices over the course of the business cycle.

It appears, then, that compensating balance requirements are an important element in bank lending policies and that these requirements can benefit both banks and their customers. Through the use of compensating balances, some customers may be able to reduce their effective interest cost and banks may be able to increase their earnings, deposits, and lending capacity, as well as develop a closer working relationship with their customers.

It also appears that compensating balances may become even more important in the years ahead as the interaction between banks increases through the spread of holding companies and correspondent bank relationships. As more banks become aware of the potential advantages of compensating balances, the requirement of these balances will doubtlessly continue to increase. Necessary to this expansion, of course, will be customer understanding and acceptance of compensating balance arrangements.

Bank Capital Adequacy

Perhaps the most controversial area of concern in banking in recent years has been bank capital adequacy. Rapid expansion has required heavy reliance on external debt; equity financing has been shunned because of possible dilution of earnings and the more attractive financial leverage provided by debt financing. Increased fixed-interest expenses, however, raise the risk of fluctuations in earnings at the same time that the debt-financed expansion raises credit risk.

Regulators tend to view bank capital as a "cushion" to absorb loan and security losses and thereby avoid insolvency and bank failure. However, industry sources argue that a large amount of capital in banking cannot arrest large-scale bank failure but can seriously reduce current and retained earnings and loan loss reserves, which in themselves are important "cushions" for absorbing losses and preventing insolvency.

In the opening selection, Ronald D. Watson provides a thorough economic critique of both regulatory and industry views as well as a penetrating exposition of a proposed means for resolving this problem—deposit insurance premiums that vary to reflect the risk assumed by the insured's bank. Next, an excerpt from George J. Vojta's seminal work on bank capital adequacy outlines in an analytical fashion an industry view of the subject. In the essay that closes this section, Ronald D. Watson takes an instructive look at the problems and prospects associated with debt, equity, and internal financing. The three articles in this section could be profitably followed by reading George R. Juncker's review of the new method of bank rating used by all three federal supervisory agencies (see Section X).

Insuring Some Progress in the Bank Capital Hassle

Ronald D. Watson

12

What do bank managers want less of, bank regulators want more of, and ordinary depositors seldom care a whit about? The size of a bank's capital account (see Box 1). The generalization is too broad, but it captures the flavor of a problem that has long been a bone of contention between bankers and regulators.

Box 1   What Constitutes Bank Capital?

It's axiomatic in corporate finance that a company must have *some* capital to remain in business over any extended period. In this respect, banks are no different from other corporations. A bank must have a minimal amount of capital as a legal prerequisite to receiving its charter. Furthermore, capital protects the bank's solvency by absorbing losses which occur in the normal course of business. The key *capital* questions are "how much?" and "what kind?"

The basic building block in a bank's capital account is *common stock*—money invested by the bank's shareholders in the hope of making a profit. All banks employ some of this permanent source of funding. In fact, they need minimal amounts of common stock before regulators will grant them a charter to begin operation as a commercial bank.

Reprinted from the Federal Reserve Bank of Philadelphia, *Business Review*, July–August 1974, pp. 3–18, by permission of the publisher.

A second source of equity funds is *preferred stock,* although this is becoming less and less common for banks. In addition, any bank that has been profitable has probably augmented its capital account with some *retained earnings.* The high cost of issuing new common stock often makes retention of earnings the least expensive and most practical way for a bank to increase its capital account.

Less obvious sources of capital are the *reserves* normally set aside for losses on securities investments and on bad loans. These two reserve accounts may not appear explicitly as capital on the bank's balance sheet, but they can be treated as capital. In the absence of special reserve accounts, a bank's capital accounts would serve the same function of absorbing operating losses.

The final source of capital to a bank is intermediate- and long-term *debt* (usually subordinated to the claims of other creditors and sometimes convertible into common stock). Adoption of this form of financing is a relatively recent phenomenon and is generally available only to larger banks (although some small banks have been successful in selling debt to the general public or to their major correspondents). However, debt has characteristics that make it riskier than equity, so there are important public policy questions concerning the appropriateness of treating debt capital as a substitute for equity capital.

Aggressive banks have repeatedly tried to extend the frontiers of "prudent management policy" by operating their banks with less and less capital—often in defiance of regulatory guidelines (see Box 2). Supervisory authorities—on guard against bank failures—continue to resist this decline of capital.

Box 2   A Minihistory of Bank Capital

For well over a century this country's bankers have been steadily reducing the proportion of capital they use in operating commercial banks. In the early 1800s banks relied heavily on long-term capital for the money used in lending and investing activities. A bank raising more than half of its funds from capital sources was not at all unusual. However, permanent capital is usually a more expensive source of money than deposits or other short-term borrowed funds. It stood to reason that a bank could increase its profits if deposits could be increased relative to capital funds—subject, of course, to preserving the safety and stability of the bank's operations.

Over the years, then, competition and desire for greater profits have led bankers to whittle away at their capital accounts—not by reducing the size of the capital account, but by failing to augment it at the same rate that the bank's assets were expanding. As a result, very few banks in operation today count on capital to provide more than 10 percent of their funds. For some the proportion is even below 5 percent.

While today's banks may be much better managed than those of 40 to 50 years ago, the basic reason that banks have been able to reduce their reliance on capital as a source of working funds is the increasing stability of the commercial banking industry. Creation of the national banking system and the Federal Reserve System made banking a more sound industry. The Federal Deposit Insurance Corporation (FDIC) was also instrumental in stabilizing the industry. This insurance increased the public's confidence in banks and made deposits a less volatile source of funds to the banks. If bankers can count on their deposits to provide a large and stable proportion of their operating funds, they can reduce their reliance on the more expensive alternative source—capital. Continuing expansion and the stability of the economy since the Depression have enabled bankers to reduce their capital accounts to very low levels relative to their asset holdings.

Expansion into new bank-related activities through the holding company organization has injected another element of uncertainty into the banking business. The Federal Reserve Board has recently been applying pressure to the most aggressive banks and their holding companies to increase their capitalization. No one is positive that capital positions have been reduced to their absolute minimum working levels, but Federal Reserve authorities are unwilling to take additional risks in this area.

While corporations with large uninsured deposits may be concerned about bank capital, most small depositors are oblivious to the whole issue. To them the safety of their money depends, not on the size of that bank's capital account, but on the FDIC membership sticker displayed in the bank's front window. Who cares how much capital the Ninth National Bank has as long as its deposits are insured?

Clearly, the bankers and supervisors care a lot—both have something at stake. But the general public *should also care,* because it has something equally important at stake. Capital is a scarce resource, and society's best interests dictate that it be used efficiently. If banks are forced to use more capital than the market requires, their operating costs and, therefore, prices may be higher than necessary. However, bank failures resulting from inadequate capital can impose costs on the bank's depositors, investors, and the whole society. In the long run everyone's interests are best served (and capital may be used most productively) when each bank holds the amount of capital which just balances the social costs of its failure with the losses which result from carrying more capital than the market requires.

Setting the "proper" amount of capital for commercial banks entails weighing the costs and benefits to all parties involved. Regulators and bankers each offer a solution to the "adequacy" problem. Unfortunately, there is little common ground, because each sees his *own* objectives as being of primary importance. However, since a basic reason for enforcing capital adequacy standards is to protect the nation's deposit insurance reserves, compromise may be possible. If the FDIC were to level deposit insurance premiums according to the risk associated with each institution, bank managers could be given the freedom to reduce their capital as long as they were willing to pay the cost of insuring this higher risk. In effect, it may be possible to substitute deposit insurance for some of a bank's capital without harming the interests of society.

The Seed of the Controversy

Regulators and bank managers may differ widely on the issue of capital adequacy, but both embrace the same basic objectives for the commercial banking system. *Both* want banks to be safe, to serve the interests of the general public and the economy, and to be profitable. They differ on capital adequacy questions—and may always differ—becuase each attaches different priorities to accomplishing these objectives.

The Regulator's Priorities   There are many reasons for regulating banks, but the most important one is protecting the public's best interests. In broad terms, this means trying to assure that the banking community uses its resources efficiently and that the social costs associated with banking are borne as equitably as possible. On the one hand, bank regulators want banks to compete, because competition will stimulate the industry to be as efficient as possible. On the other hand, bank failures can have a very high cost for society, and regulators must try to prevent the costs of bank failures from exceeding any benefits that might be gained from competition.

On an operating level, the bank supervisor doesn't *always* prefer more capital to less. He knows that excessive amounts of capital can prevent a bank from earning the return necessary to stay in business and attract new capital for growth. However, while his charge is to protect the public interest, this broad objective tends to be translated into the more easily measured (and less appropriate) goal of trying to prevent banks from failing. A banking industry with very few failures inspires public confidence.

It also gives the appearance that the regulator has done his job well. His performance is not measured by his ability to hold the combined costs of regulation and bank failures to a minimum. Instead, he is judged by the number and size of the banks that fold.[1] Regulators suffer a high personal cost when a bank's capital turns out to be *inadequate,* but none when it's too high.[2]

The Banker's Priorities   The bank manager finds himself in the opposite position. His goal is sizable profits for the bank's stockholders. His salary and promotions

---

[1]In the minds of some critics, the occurrence of a bank failure is presumed to be sufficient reason for closer regulatory control. Seldom is concern shown for balancing the costs of more supervision with the probable benefits it would yield.

[2]It isn't clear that supervisory authorities have been successful in their attempts to make banks employ more capital than the banks feel they need. (See Sam Peltzman, "Capital Investment in Commercial Banks and Its Relationship to Portfolio Regulation," *Journal of Political Economy,* 78 [1970]: 1-26.)

depend on making profits—not simply on avoiding bankruptcy. Naturally, success in the long run requires that the banker protect the interests of depositors and share-holders by maintaining the bank's solvency. He must also safeguard its solvency to protect his own reputation, future job prospects, stock options, and pension. How-ever, solvency is a constraint on the manager's decisions rather than a primary objec-tive.

A rational banker will want additional capital if his current capital base is insuffi-cient. A bank wanting to add new services, open additional offices, or move into new markets may need more capital before tackling these activities. All are risky and would require capital and extensive management attention. Even a management that is strongly profit-oriented may judge the added risks to be too great for existing capital to support and would then have an incentive to get more capital. However, adding more capital is designed to achieve that combination of risks and profits that management feels is *ideal* for the bank rather than simply to avoid risks.

What Is an Unusual Loss?   A crucial difference in the way regulators and bank-ers treat capital is the magnitude of the losses each expects it to absorb. Both pre-sume that the capital account should be sufficient to cover any and all of the com-mon losses that banks face. Operating expenses may be unexpectedly high, bonds may have to be liquidated to meet deposit withdrawals or to adjust the maturity structure of the portfolio, and some loans will certainly sour. That's the nature of the business. However, with few exceptions these losses should be small enough that they can be covered out of current earnings. A profitable operation is clearly the bank's first line of defense against occasional losses.[3]

It's the question of covering *unusual* losses that brings out differences of opinion. Aggressive bankers believe that they should be responsible for handling any losses resulting from an economic recession or from a mild natural disaster but should not be prepared for another depression or the losses resulting from a collapse of financial markets. They argue that the Federal Government is officially committed to pro-grams of economic stabilization. What's more, the economy has been able to stay on a "reasonably" steady course since the 1940s. In light of this experience, it may be wasteful to plan the industry's liquidity and capital requirements around another depression.

Regulators don't really want capital adequate for another depression,[4] but they clearly want banks to be prepared for emergencies worse than anything experienced since the 1940s. The formulas used by bank supervisors (see Box 3) to define capital adequacy are based, in some sense, on a pessimistic psychology. In effect, they as-sume that the bank is sold to pay the depositor's claims with all expected losses from asset liquidation made up from capital. If liquidation were the standard way to handle an insolvency problem, this would be reasonable, but many banks—especial-

---

[3]In 1971, the worst year for loan losses that the industry has faced since World War II, the industry's ratio of net loan loss to aftertax earnings was just under 21 percent.

[4]Federal Deposit Insurance Corporation, *Annual Report—1957* (Washington: Federal Deposit Insur-ance Corporation, 1958), p. 49.

ly larger ones—that encounter problems are merged into other institutions.[5] In that case, the conservative valuation placed on bank buildings and certain loan categories may undervalue the assets and thereby overstate real capital needs—or so say the bankers.

Box 3   Measuring Capital Adequacy

Imagine trying to draw a precise blueprint with a stubby piece of charcoal. The tool just isn't up to the task. Much the same can be said about trying to "measure" the adequacy of a bank's capital account. Regulators have only the foggiest conceptual notion of what constitutes adequate capital. Finding numerical measures for capital adequacy just compounds the problem.

The commonest adequacy measures depend on analysis of financial ratios—primarily comparisons of accounts on the bank's balance sheet. The grossest of these tools are the ratios of capital to assets and capital to deposits. The capital-to-assets ratio implies that a bank's risks stem from its asset holdings. The greater the size of the capital account relative to total assets, the lower the chance that losses suffered on asset values will impair the bank's solvency or result in losses to depositors. Much the same information is gleaned from the capital-to-deposits ratio. The principal objective of this measure is to define the proportion of long- versus short-term funds being used by the bank. The more long-term funds employed, the lower the risk of losses to depositors.

Of necessity, a somewhat more sophisticated measure—a ratio comparing a bank's capital to its risky assets—was developed following World War II. During the war banks bought a large share of the newly created government war debt without increasing their capital accounts proportionately. This change in the asset structure of banks caused many of them to "fail" the basic capital adequacy tests. The problem focused attention on the economic fact that the composition of a bank's assets could have as much to do with its risk as the size of its assets. Accordingly, the capital adequacy ratios were revised to fit the new industry structure. The new measure of capital adequacy was *capital-to-risk assets,* where risk assets were defined as total assets minus cash, bank balances, and U.S. Government securities.

Still other refinements were in order—one of the most elaborate being an adjusted risk asset method developed in the Federal Reserve System in the early 1950s. Bank assets were categorized according to their probable risk and assigned a hypothetical capital reserve depending on

---

[5]Roughly half of the banks that have failed since 1945 were merged into other institutions. However, many banking problems are solved by the regulators prior to an *official* failure, by merging the weak bank or by finding new capital for the bank.

the amount of the asset held. The sum of these hypothetical reserves (with an additional adjustment for liquidity) set a standard for "adequate" capital in the bank being analyzed.[6]

Each succeeding refinement of the capital adequacy measures has added more surface realism to the analysis process. However, the implied precision of these refinements may lull users into assuming these tools have a higher level of accuracy than is really the case. Aware of the inherent fallibility of ratio measures and of the need for using seasoned judgment in evaluating capital adequacy, regulators try to temper their numerical analysis by considering other factors. In addition to an examination of a bank's capital position from its balance sheets, most supervisory authorities consider factors such as profitability, management quality, efficiency, fixed costs, and competitive environment. Ratios have an important place in this informal analysis, but bank regulators usually try not to be dependent on them for an "answer" to the question: "Is capital adequate?"

The "Proper" Approach to Capital Evaluation

Differences over the actual *amount* of capital a bank should have are the chief disagreements that arise between aggressive bankers and strict regulators, but they are not the only ones. Bankers and supervisors also have rather opposite philosophies of *how* capital needs should be calculated.

The Regulator's Ratios   In general, supervisory authorities have shown a strong preference for ratio analysis in measuring a bank's capital position.[7] Such affection is understandable. The objective numerical precision that ratio analysis offers is reassuring in an area fraught with uncertainties. Ratios also enable the analyst to compare a bank with others in the industry or with its own past record.

No regulator would suggest that ratio analysis should be taken strictly at face value without the benefit of judgmental modification. But the fact that ratios are the foundation of the evaluation indicates that many regulators find them useful and more defensible than any alternative measure.

Underlying this reliance on ratios is the belief that, for all their faults, they're the most workable analytical tool available. There is a body of historical information available about bank capital ratios. The analysis that has been done of historical experience used ratio analysis. In short, examiners feel comfortable in their beliefs about what capital levels have been adequate historically. Regulators argue that they

---

[6]This formula was revised in 1972.

[7]The Comptroller of the Currency's examiners claim that they rely only incidentally on formulas and ratio analysis to evaluate bank capital adequacy.

have been flexible in applying ratios, and that their perceptions of capital needs have changed in recent years. However, the regulator wants to minimize bank failures by sticking to "proven" methods of capital evaluation even though they may not be appropriate for fully evaluating "adequacy."

The Manager's Market Method While some regulators are wedded to ratio analysis, aggressive banks are equally committed to using the capital market's evaluation of their institution as the true measure of its soundness. Bankers hold that the investors who supply the bank with debt and equity capital are equipped to evaluate the risks inherent in their investment. Stockholders obviously want to avoid defaults and insolvency, but their interest in profits provides a balancing motive for economizing on capital. Bankers also claim that a stockholder is more likely to evaluate the bank as an ongoing organization and examine its ability to meet obligations through profits and liabilities management[8] as well as through asset liquidation. Factors such as management quality, liquidity, and growth prospects also enter into an investor's determination of a bank's capital adequacy in much the same way that they influence a regulator's.

The attractiveness of a bank's stock (its profit potential and risk) determines the price that the institution must pay for new capital. Shareholders are more vulnerable to loss than any of the bank's creditors or depositors. If either the current or potential stockholders feel that the bank's capital position is weak (and the bank, therefore, is too risky), the stock's price will fall. A falling stock price is a powerful signal to management to change its policies, because that price affects the cost of new equity capital and the value of the current shareholder's investment. Managers that are not responsive to the best interests of the shareholders may not be around long enough to pick up their retirement checks. Investors in a bank's debt capital can convey the same signal to management. As the bank's riskiness increases, the bond market will increase the interest rate that must be paid for new debt capital. Rising debt costs will lower residual profits for the common stockholders, and management will get the message in a hurry.[9]

Bankers don't argue that the market is always perfect in its evaluation of risks, but they do champion it over the regulator's analysis. Investors require that a bank's capital be adequate to meet its commitments with very high probability. But that probability need not be 100 percent. Unlike the regulator, stockholders are willing to risk insolvency because in doing so the bank can conserve on capital and realize a higher return.

Each Has Shortcomings Even with the alternative approaches so clearly drawn, choosing sides is difficult. While ratios are mathematically precise, easy to

---

[8]Liabilities management is a relatively new technique for bank liquidity managers. It involves meeting a need for cash by acquiring a new liability rather than by selling an asset. For instance, a large deposit withdrawal might be covered by selling new certificate of deposit liabilities rather than by liquidating an existing investment.

[9]Market discipline may be somewhat dulled if the regulatory agencies publicly guarantee the solvency and liquidity of banks that encounter difficulty.

use, and apparently of some validity as a historically proven guide, they are theoretically inadequate.

Primary objections to ratio analysis stem from its unreliability as a method for detecting potential bank failures. The criticism is a bit unfair because there are no statistics available to show the number of bank failures that were averted because regulators required additions to the capital of weak banks. However, statistical analysis has shown that capital ratios for banks that have failed are seldom materially different from those of banks that didn't fail. A crucial reason for this is that many banks failed because of fraud or bad management practices that aren't captured in the ratio comparisons. Two banks with apparently identical balance sheets can have very different insolvency risks, and, therefore, needs for capital.

Bank regulators include these incidental factors in deciding how vigorously to enforce the capital standards. Nonetheless, if judgmental factors become overwhelming considerations in the evaluation of capital, an elaborate ratio analysis scheme is rather pointless. Furthermore, regulators note that the market's stock analysts and securities rating agencies also use ratios in making their assessments of risk.

The *social costs* of bank failure represent the key reason why an unmodified "market discipline" rule is inadequate.[10] A bank's failure has an obvious cost to its investors, but their loss is limited to their investment. However, society may also pay a cost. Apart from the many inconveniences suffered by a local community when a bank that serves it fails, banks are a vital cog in the nation's economy—as savings and safekeeping institutions, lenders, and payments system intermediaries. If a large bank should fail—or more important, a number of large banks—the event could disrupt the public's confidence in the soundness of the industry. In the extreme, a 1930s-style "run" on the banks could develop with accompanying liquidity crises, contractions of reserves, and severe strains on the resources of the FDIC.

This scenario is highly unlikely. The Government's economic stabilization policies, deposit insurance programs, and the Federal Reserve's discount window are all designed to prevent it from happening. Refinement of bank management techniques also reduces the risk. But it is still as a *possibility* if the industry takes on too much risk relative to its capital position. Multiple failures are a cost which regulators are currently unwilling to pay—the cause of capital efficiency notwithstanding. Finding a merger partner for a troubled $10 million bank is one thing—for a $10 billion bank quite another.[11] Virtually any institution large enough to absorb such a big problem bank as a merger partner would be an illegal suitor for antitrust reasons.

---

[10]Many economists argue that there would be gains in the private sector's efficiency if more banks were allowed to fail, and these gains might outweigh the social costs of those failures. The difficulty, of course, is defining the limit where added efficiency becomes secondary to the uncertainty that increased failures create for all banks.

[11]Investors seeking to reduce or limit total risk can diversify their stock and bond holdings among a number of industries, thus avoiding some of the risk that their bank investments are undercapitalized. Regulators don't have the same option. The FDIC is diversified in the sense that it insures a wide spectrum of banks, but it cannot diversify against the risk that the entire industry is undercapitalized. This is why bank deposits cannot be protected by a private insurance company.

If all the costs *to society* of multiple failures could be included in the market's valuation of bank capital, supervisory authorities might be willing to let the market work. Sketchy information about the riskiness of bank investments and thin markets for bank stocks would not be problems of sufficient seriousness to force abandonment of the market as "chief disciplinarian." But since the full cost of banks taking risks is not entirely shouldered by the investor, regulators feel they have an obligation to impose a greater constraint on bank operations than the market will. Too large a segment of society can be harmed by the mistakes of a relatively small number of overaggressive banks for those banks to be free of any social responsibility for their policies.

A Better Solution?

Though the conflict between aggressive banks and regulators (with each trying to keep his own costs to a minimum) is understandable, official policies on bank failure should be selected with an eye to bringing the greatest net benefit to the whole society. Perhaps a solution to this conflict might be found in a compromise by both parties of their operating objectives.

Would society be better off with the private sector benefits of improved capital allocation and the social costs created by more bank failures *or* with fewer failures and some degree of overcapitalization? Many bankers opt for the first combination—regulators for the second. What is needed is a more objective basis for choosing the amount of risk a bank should take—a scheme which allows a banker to select any amount of capital he wishes as long as he pays the cost of protecting society against the risks his choice creates.[12]

Accordingly, regulators and legislators might consider several modifications of the FDIC's insurance system. First, banks could be charged a fee for their deposit insurance which varies with the risk of the bank. Banks currently pay a flat rate which is the same no matter how safe the bank is. Second, all *demand deposits* at banks could be fully insured by the FDIC rather than leaving deposits of more than $20,000 vulnerable to loss when a bank fails.

Using the Market   A central feature of this compromise approach to capital adequacy would be to make better use of markets to determine society's real preferences. Presently, only a portion of a bank's funds are sensitive to its risk. Stockholders and long-term creditors are very likely to demand a return which compensates them for their risks. However, only the largest and most sophisticated of the bank's depositors do, because the FDIC protects most deposit funds from loss. The cost of most of a bank's deposits does not respond to changes in its risk.

If the FDIC were to vary its insurance premium according to the risk of the bank rather than just the total amount of its deposits, the bank would have to pay an

[12]Several proposals are found in the literature. Suggestions from the work of Tussing, Jacobs, Mayer, Kreps and Wacht, and Robinson and Pettway (see Bibliography) are combined in this plan.

additional insurance fee for trying to reduce its long-term capital. An insurance rate that increased as the relative amount of long-term capital decreased would place an implicit risk premium on deposits of a low-capital bank. Since, everything else being equal, the risk of the low-capital bank failing is higher than that of a better-capitalized bank, it is only appropriate that the price for insuring its deposits be higher.

The cost of FDIC insurance might also be adjusted to reflect the asset composition, liquidity, profitability, and management of the bank as well as its mix of liabilities. This would further refine the price paid by the bank for engaging in riskier activities. The objective would not be one of preventing banks from increasing their risks but of making sure that they pay the appropriate cost to society of assuming these risks.

The obvious objection is that the artificiality of the capital adequacy evaluation might not be improved. It might even be argued that setting an explicit insurance fee according to the result of the evaluation compounds the problem. However, the importance of developing a rational fee structure that is actuarially sound would give bankers and regulators an incentive to work together to build a solid system for distinguishing various grades of risk. Once this rate structure was established it would have the advantage of giving greater decision-making flexibility to the banker. It would make the costs of each decision more explicit. If he thinks the benefits of adopting a riskier capital structure will outweigh the cost of insuring society against the risk, he is free to make that choice (see Box 4).

Box 4   Setting the Rate

Setting a proper insurance premium is a crucial element of the proposal. Without trying to minimize the difficulty of the task, it should be possible to do this with *sufficient* precision. The regulatory authorities have access to an enormous store of banking data extending over several decades. Since the 1940s, America's banks have managed to cope with several recessions and a couple of severe credit crunches. Careful analysis with the statistical tools currently available should enable regulators to set insurance rates that would accurately reflect the change in risk that the insurance fund must absorb if a bank changes its capital policies. Past experience may be a poor indicator of future developments, but it does define the current capabilities of the Government's stabilization policies and the effect that volatile interest rates and several credit crunches have had on the liquidity and solvency of the banking system. Virtually any method developed would be more rational than charging a very conservative, liquid bank the same rate for insurance as that charged a rather risky institution.

The Rate Setters   Specifically, a politically independent panel of experts might be charged with the task of determining the appropriate rate structure for insuring society against the risks of alternative levels of bank capitalization. Bankers, regulators, statisticians, banking scholars, and actuaries should all be represented on such a panel. Judgment and reason should be combined with rigorous statistical and economic analysis to set these rates.[13] Further, the panel might be reconvened at five-year intervals (or sooner, should the regulator feel it necessary) to revise the rate structure in light of new developments in the economy and the banking industry and new research findings.

The Rates It is unlikely that any "perfect" method could be found for setting the insurance fee schedule. However, with serious effort it should be possible to construct an internally consistent, rational set of rates that would be *at least as sound* as the present capital adequacy rules and, perhaps, much better because of the new flexibility given the banker.[14] At the outset it might be desirable to set the insurance fees rather conservatively, assigning relatively high social costs to management policies which are radically different from current standards. As regulators and bankers learned to live with the new plan, any artificial conservatism could be gradually done away with, thus increasing flexibility and discretion under this system to the greatest extent possible.

The Insurance Fund This does not mean that the FDIC's reserve fund must necessarily grow larger than it is now. No one knows exactly how large the fund must be to do its job, but its present size seems sufficient to satisfy the regulatory community.[15] (In fact, for many years the FDIC has been rebating a portion of each year's official insurance premium to its member banks.) There is no reason for the fund to increase further (*vis-à-vis* insured bank deposits) unless the risk associated with protecting those deposits increases. Under the proposal offered here, banks that are less risky than average would pay a lower premium for insurance, and those that are more risky than average would pay more—an amount equivalent to the cost of protecting society against the higher risk of that bank's operations.

Uncle Sam's Role The Federal Government should be ready to backstop the industry's insurance programs against the possibility of a depression, because it isn't practical for banks to pay the full cost of insurance or hold sufficient capital. The Government is committed to a program of stabilizing the economy—a commitment that bankers and

[13]The risk insurance fees should not be used as a tool for selective credit control.

[14]Given the same analytical resources and the correct objectives, regulators would be able to set capital adequacy standards just as rationally. However, improved goal specification and increased flexibility for all participants make this a better approach to the problem.

[15]The FDIC's insurance reserve fund presently has assets of over $5 billion and has an additional $3 billion of borrowing authority from the Treasury. Between 1933 and 1972 the corporation had suffered only $74.4 million of net losses as a result of bank failures. (While losses are only a small portion of the reserve, it must be remembered that no major bank has failed since 1940, and the FDIC has been very successful in disposing of failed banks at very small losses. Furthermore, the potential losses faced by the corporation from the failure of the United States National Bank in San Diego are well above $100 million.) Federal Deposit Insurance Corporation, *Annual Report—1972* (Washington: Federal Deposit Insurance Corporation, 1973), p. 28

> regulators both agree precludes the need for capitalizing banks to with-
> stand another depression. In the event of an economic disaster it would
> be in the nation's best interest to preserve the industry. Since the bene-
> fits of supporting the whole industry would fall not only to depositors
> but to everyone, the job of preserving the system rightly falls to the
> Government. When the public is the primary beneficiary, it should
> bear some of the costs.
>
> In some sense, this kind of commitment has already been formally
> acknowledged. The Treasury stands ready to provide the FDIC with
> several billion dollars should that agency's insurance reserves ever be
> exhausted.

The revised capital evaluation system would stress ranking the risk of each bank
against a wide spectrum of possibilities. There would not be any "adequate versus
inadequate" line—a subject of continual debate—but, instead, a choice between
increasing the bank's risks (and insurance costs) or decreasing them. With a variety
of risk classes and a similar spectrum of rates, bankers could make more rational
cost/profit decisions. The cost of *each* of the bank's sources of funds would respond
to management's policy decisions, thus bringing the discipline of the market into
each decision *without* imposing capital constraints which are rigid and artificial on
the banks and *without* forcing society to bear additional *uncompensated* risk. More
bank failures might occur under this plan, but higher insurance fees from the riskier
banks should cover the costs of these failures. Furthermore, if the regulator's insurance-premium rating for each bank were made public, this additional information
would aid the securities markets in setting costs for the bank's long-term funds.

The insurance-premium method for regulating risk would be superior to the bank
supervisor's determination of "adequate" capital, because it focuses the regulator's
objective more clearly on the broad goal of controlling the total cost imposed on
society by the banking system rather than the present narrower objective of preventing bank failures. Setting capital adequacy standards is now tantamount to preventing any bank from exceeding a risk limitation. Variable insurance premiums put the
regulator in the more appropriate position of a *risk* manager whose goal is to control
the total risk and cost that society faces rather than to limit the management discretion of each bank.

The second element of this plan to rationalize the bank capital problem is 100
percent insurance on demand deposits. While this is a retreat from the market discipline advocated for a risk-based insurance fee, it is intended to serve society by
making the entire banking system less vulnerable to financial panic. Depositor protection is an obvious but still secondary function of this plan. The prime objective is
to reduce the likelihood and the social costs of a major crisis caused by multiple bank
failures.

This proposal has always been rejected on the grounds that sophisticated depositors would not leave their funds in banks which had inadequate capital. A banker's

interest in attracting such money would force him to maintain adequate capital. Yet, while these uninsured deposits do encourage management to respond to market pressures, these funds may be very unstable during a period of financial uncertainty. The failure of one *major* bank could generate immediate deposit outflows at institutions throughout the industry which are otherwise quite sound. Full demand deposit insurance would obviate the need for short-term depositors to set in motion such chain reactions, thereby reducing the chance of this happening. The banking system's legal privilege of not paying time-deposit withdrawal requests as though they were demand deposits should provide the industry with sufficient flexibility to withstand any short-term financial crisis, if it is sound in all other respects.

Furthermore, the benefits of market discipline would still not be lost entirely. Not only would the cost discipline of an insurance fee based on risk be substituted for analysis by uninsured depositors, but the bank would continue to have to satisfy the market's standards on any funds raised through nondeposit sources. Since these funds sources are of great importance (especially to the major banks), the market would still have a strong influence on the kinds of risks bankers take.

Protect the Depositors, But Not the Bankers   In conjunction with the variable insurance premium and higher deposit insurance, the FDIC and the other regulators should continue their policy of trying to minimize the cost and inconvenience suffered by depositors when a bank fails. A very common solution to date has been the speedy merger of a distressed bank with a stronger institution. Where state law or antitrust considerations preclude such a merger, the strategy of finding new ownership and management has sometimes been explored.

This basic approach is laudable. One of the regulator's chief goals should be to prevent an isolated failure from jeopardizing the public's trust in all banks. Preservation of a distressed bank's ability to continue to serve its customers while it is being reorganized is vital to keeping that trust.

However, this protection should not be extended to either senior management, stockholders, or uninsured investors in the bank's debt. These persons either made the decisions that led to the losses that created the bank failure or invested in the bank with knowledge that there was some risk. Investors may not have been fully aware of the bank's policies, but taking those risks is part of the implicit contract they made when they invested. Before the market can impose any discipline on bank management's decisions to take additional risks, investors must be aware that they can and will lose their money if the risks prove too great. Regulators should be careful not to let their enthusiasm for saving a bank inadvertently cause them to shield former managers or investors from the adverse consequences of making bad decisions.

Adequacy and Equity

One of the theoretical roles of bank capital is to protect the interests of shareholders while the bank is in operation and both creditors and uninsured depositors upon liquidation. However, the minimum capital requirements that bank examiners try to enforce aren't needed as protection for these investors. A bank's stockholders and creditors should rely on their own financial savvy and the free market for capital to assure themselves of a competitive return for investing their money at risk. Furthermore, in the event of liquidation, capital adequacy requirements are only protection for some depositors since the bulk of the funds deposited by unsophisticated investors are insured by the FDIC.

Instead, a major function of the minimum capital rules is to limit the risk exposure of the FDIC and, thereby, the probable cost to the Government of "bailing out" the industry during a period of extreme financial stress. Since the regulator's objective should be to control costs incurred by the public sector rather than to maintain minimum capital standards as an end in themselves, there may be a way to dispense with these rules. If the regulators can charge a deposit insurance fee that varies with the riskiness of a bank's structure, yet covers the expected additional social costs of management opting for that extra risk, society's interests can be protected within a freer banking environment. Furthermore, if deposit insurance protection could be extended to all demand deposits, the risk to society of a financial crisis might be reduced appreciably. Naturally, bankers and regulators would continue to argue over how risky each bank is. But the important change is the substitution of a pricing mechanism for the "adequacy versus inadequate" capital rules. This will provide greater flexibility for bankers willing to pay the full cost of stretching their capital.

BIBLIOGRAPHY

COHEN, KALMAN J. "Improving the Capital Adequacy Formula." *Journal of Bank Research* 1(1970): 13-16.

COTTER, RICHARD V. "Capital Ratios and Capital Adequacy." *National Banking Review* 3(1966): 333-46.

DINCE, ROBERT R. and FORTSON, JAMES C. "The Use of Discriminant Analysis to Predict the Capital Adequacy of Commercial Banks." *Journal of Bank Research* 3(1972): 54-62.

INSTITUTE FOR FINANCIAL EDUCATION. "The Capital Adequacy Problem in Commercial Banks, 1974-1978." *Banking Research Report,* February 1974 (unpublished report).

KREPS, CLIFTON H. and WACHT, RICHARD F. "A More Constructive Role for Deposit Insurance," *Journal of Finance* 26(1971): 605-14.

LINDLOW, WESLEY. "Bank Capital and Risk Assets." *National Banking Review* 1(1963):29-46.

MANN, MAURICE. "Competitive Viability—A New Dimension for Capital Adequacy Requirements." Speech to National Correspondent Banking Conference. American Bankers Association, Washington, D.C., 6 November 1973.

MAYER, THOMAS. "A Graduated Deposit Insurance Plan." *Review of Economics and Statistics* 47(1965): 114-16.

MAYNE, LUCILLE S. "Supervisory Influence on Bank Capital." *Journal of Finance* 27(1972): 637-51.

MEYER, PAUL A. and PIFER, HOWARD W. "Prediction of Bank Failures." *Journal of Finance* 27(1970): 853-68.

PELTZMAN, SAM. "Capital Investment in Commercial Banking and Its Relationship to Portfolio Regulation." *Journal of Political Economy* 78(1970): 1-26.

REED, EDWARD W. "Appraising the Capital Needs of Commercial Banks." *Bankers Magazine* 147(1964): 73-83.

ROBINSON, ROLAND I. and PETTWAY, RICHARD H. *Policies for Optimum Bank Capital.* A study prepared for the Trustees of the Banking Research Fund—Association of Reserve City Bankers, 1967.

SHAY, JEROME W. "Capital Adequacy: The Regulators' Perspective." *Magazine of Bank Administration,* October 1974, pp. 22-25.

SHEEHAN, JOHN E. "Bank Capital Adequacy—Time to Pause and Reflect." Speech to National Correspondent Banking Conference, American Bankers Association, 6 November 1973.

STAATS, WILLIAM F. "Capital Adequacy of Commercial Banks." Ph.D. dissertation, University of Texas, 1965.

TUSSING, A. DALE. "Bank Failure: A Meaningful Competitive Force." Proceedings of a Conference on Bank Structure and Competition Sponsored by the Federal Reserve Bank of Chicago, 13 May 1968.

TUSSING, A. DALE. "The Case for Bank Failure." *Journal of Law and Economics* 10(1967): 129-47.

VOJTA, GEORGE J. *Bank Capital Adequacy.* New York: Citicorp, 1973.

VOJTA, GEORGE J. "Capital Adequacy: A Look at the issues." *Magazine of Bank Administration,* September 1973, pp. 22-25.

Bank Capital Adequacy

George J. Vojta

13

... Currently, regulatory opinion is deeply divided on the issue of capital adequacy. In essence, the Federal Reserve Board's adjusted risk asset/liquidity approach quantifies capital required to protect a bank under abnormal conditions. Additionally, non-balance sheet factors are weighed in judging the bank's capital position. The Federal Deposit Insurance Corporation continues to rely on a ratio of capital funds, net of investments in fixed and substandard assets, to average total assets. The Comptroller of the Currency deemphasizes static ratios, relying instead on guidelines for appraising management performance and viewing the bank as a going concern under normal conditions. Practice in state and various Federal Reserve jurisdictions varies widely, but in general is more in line with Board and FDIC standards than those of the Comptroller of the Currency.

An absolute standard of capitalization has not been characteristic of commercial banking, nor have regulatory approaches to capital adequacy converged to a generally accepted position. Levels of capitalization appear to have had no causal relationship to incidence of bank failure. The historical record documents a secular trend of asset and deposit growth in excess of levels of capital; bank capitalization has tended to adjust materially in periods of structural change in the economy or in the industry with regulatory standards adapting ex post facto. . . .

Reprinted, with deletions, from *Bank Capital Adequacy* (New York: Citicorp, 1973), pp. 12-30, by permission of Citibank and the author.

Toward a Redefinition of Capital Adequacy

Regulators presently perceive banks as core businesses of bank holding companies. Presently, the typical holding company is dominated by the balance sheet and profit and loss results of subsidiary bank(s); dividends from the bank(s) are a major factor in the holding company's cash flow, essential to the financing of acquisitions and to the servicing of dividend payments and debt. Over time the bank(s) ought to be viewed as an important business in a holding company portfolio, together with consumer finance companies, leasing companies, mortgage banks, etc. In the latter position, the financial condition of the holding company is strengthened by dividend payments from the larger investment portfolio; the long-run role of the holding company is to maintain appropriate levels of capital in subsidiary businesses, including banks, and to stand ready to provide additional support in case of need.[1]

The overriding objective of regulatory policy must be to prudently promote the evolution of banks and bank holding companies in procompetitive terms. Cognizance must be given to the fact that banks can only perform the intermediation function by competing against a formidable array of competitive bidders for funds in the money and capital markets. Success in the marketplace necessitates management of banks to prudently maximize earnings and return on capital. As appropriate, weight must be given to the supportive role of the parent holding company in determining capital adequacy for subsidiary bank(s).

From this point of view, the functions of bank capital are twofold: first to permit acquisition of the institutional structure necessary to perform the intermediation function and provide related services, and second in conditions short of total economic collapse to provide protection against unanticipated adversity leading to loss in excess of normal expectations. The capital provision against excessive loss permits the bank to continue operations in periods of difficulty until a normal level of earnings is restored.[2]

The first function is self-validating and consistent with the Board's current formulation. Capital funds permit an enterprise to acquire the physical and skill base to compete in the markets it chooses to enter. It is legitimate to expect the shareholders,

---

[1]Articulation of this position can be found in *Federal Reserve Bulletin,* August 1972, pp. 301 and 717.

[2]Stated another way, capital permits a bank to absorb losses while earning its way out of difficulty. The pivotal relationship between earnings and solvency is avowedly emphasized by these definitions of capital functions. Regulatory bias tends to view "profit maximization" as imprudent, because it leads banks to assume a higher than desirable level of risk which can cause future problems. Factual cases exist to illustrate the point. Excessive risk-taking and profit-maximizing managerial behavior are properly associated with institutions not recognized as business enterprises. Since banks now are compelled to compete as enterprises, risk taking and profit maximization must be accepted as integral to bank management processes. The regulatory psychology must empathize with management's view of the world in these terms. The postwar experience, particularly in the 50s, confirms that inhibiting risk-taking and profit-maximization functions at the regulatory level can only cause banks to lose ground to competition in the marketplace; and over time the demise of the banking system as a viable vehicle of intermediation is involved. Managers of banks are employed to assume and manage risks and they must be permitted to seek the verdict of the marketplace in validating or invalidating performance in this regard.

as principals at interest, to finance these requirements. Banks, as enterprises, require capital funds for the same purposes and it is the shareholders' responsibility to provide them.

The second function of capital requires precise definition. There are six generic risks in commercial banking which occasion loss, or stated another way, negative claims on earnings and capital. These are: *credit risks,* losses arising from externally—or internally—caused deterioration in the quality of earning assets; for purposes of this discussion, the proxy for credit risks is assumed to be the loss experience in the loan portfolio; *investment risks,* defined as losses in the principal values of bank investments, primarily the securities portfolio and fixed assets; *liquidity risks,* losses arising from financing mismatches in the tenor of assets and liabilities and from liquifying assets or switching liabilities in adverse market conditions to meet liquidity claims: *operating risks,* losses arising from operating errors, inefficiencies, and other contingencies which are uninsured and chargeable to earnings and capital funds; *fraud risks,* losses arising from the malfeasance or dishonesty of staff and customers; to the degree that these risks are not insured, contingent claims on earnings and capital are involved; and *fiduciary risks,* losses arising from the improper discharge of fiduciary responsibilities. In most businesses, risks of loss are both known and predictable and unknown and unpredictable in terms of frequency of occurrence and magnitude of exposure. Loss of both types inheres in each of the generic categories of risk.

Little progress has been made in systematically analyzing the recurrent loss experience associated with commercial banking. Instead, attention has focused on losses related to crisis periods. Incidence of loss in banking exhibits reasonably regular patterns. In stable market conditions portfolio and operating losses tend to occur within narrow ranges of amplitude, and losses related to the investment portfolio, management of the liquidity position, operating error, fraud, and fiduciary risks tend to be negligible. Unanticipated loss tends to rise in periods of instability in all categories of risk; more importantly, unanticipated loss tends to occur in random sequence. The concept of capital adequacy should properly derive from the analysis of risk dynamics and loss phenomena in the business. In these terms two general "tests" of capital adequacy can be suggested.

The first is the degree to which current earnings (after taxes, accounting provision for losses, other charges to reserves, and net of dividend payments) cover anticipated losses, estimated as a continuation of "normal," historical loss experience, on the assumption that stable business conditions prevail. A proposed "earnings test" for capital adequacy requires that annualized current earnings be equal to at least twice the amount of actual loss anticipated by management. The "two for one" earnings test warrants that earnings coverage to this extent provides a reasonable cushion. Actual loss is computed as the five-year moving average of total charges to loan and other contingency reserves expressed as a percentage of total risk assets net of cash and due from banks modified by a variable representing management expectations concerning departures from the historical mean as indicated by future business plans, as well as known factors in the environment.[3]

[3]A five-year moving average of net losses (defined as total net charges to all reserves) expressed as a percent of average total assets less cash and due from banks is the basis for estimating total net losses in the current year. The average loss factor is applied to average total assets less cash and due from banks for the current period in order to gain an estimate of total net losses consistent with historical experience. Management can recognize that actual net losses during the current year will show some variance with respect to the calculated value for average historical losses. To capture this variability, a multiplicative relationship can be established between historical loss and expected actual loss. For example, assume that by employing the moving average formulation net losses were determined to be $25 million. Using the assumption of a triangular distribution for the multiplicative factor, N, management can define its expectations for current net losses in terms of the average net loss value experienced historically. The distribution for N is described in terms of low, most likely, and high estimates equal to .8, 1.5, and 4, respectively. In numerical terms, management's expectations regarding actual net losses in the current period would range from a low of $20 million (.8 × $25MM) to a high of $100 million (4 × $25MM) with the most likely amount being $38 million (1.5 × $25MM). Expected actual loss in the current period is calculated by multiplying the expected value of N (E (N) is ⅓ (.8 + 1.5 + 4.0), equal to 2.1) times the value of average historical loss (2.1 × $25MM = $53MM). The expected value of N can be confirmed in a practical sense within a simulation framework and represents a valid proxy for the numerical value of N utilized to determine the expected actual loss.

In graphic terms the distribution for N is illustrated as follows:

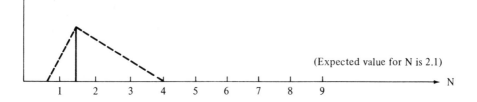

Probability – P(N)

(Expected value for N is 2.1)

P (N) on the vertical axis represents the probability of N. N is measured along the horizontal axis and management has said in effect that the probability of N falling between .8 and 4 is 1 or P $(.8 \leq N \leq 4) = 1$.

The curve as drawn evidences a triangular distribution pattern. Obviously this is an implicit assumption. A more sophisticated mathematical-statistical approach would be required to establish the true nature of the observed distribution of N. However, in the real world, management of an enterprise cannot totally risk business solvency by literal adherence to a theoretical formulation. Management has no choice but to anticipate risk in expectational terms based on past experience, what is known, probabilistically, about the future and allow for a prudent margin of error. Random values of N, within the limits imposed

The second proposed test of capital adequacy is the extent to which capital funds (capital, surplus, undivided profits, and all reserves except depreciation and amortization reserves) cover "unexpected" losses, expressed as a deviation from average historical loss expectations by a prudent margin, say a factor of two. Capital funds aggregating to twenty times twice the average value of historical loss experience (as computed above) can be regarded as providing a reasonable margin of protection against unanticipated loss.[4]

---

by the distribution, can be produced and evaluated within the confines of a simulation model. A simulation model also can provide a framework for evaluating extreme values of N since the probability of generating extreme values with a random draw mechanism is very low. Simulation techniques can be utilized as a cross-check on management's expectational assumptions as well as to permit management to work toward more precise insights about future loss experience. The case for the use of expectational considerations is not dependent upon theoretical satisfaction of the risk distribution question but the nature of the assumptions must be clearly understood. . . .

Another way to analyze the problem is to express net losses as a percent of average total assets less cash and due from banks. Suppose, on average, net losses equal 0.5% of average total assets less cash and due from banks. Using the previous range of values for N, expected actual net losses would range from 0.4 percent (0.8 × 0.5%) to 2 percent (4.0 × 0.5%) of average total assets net of cash and due from banks. The expected value of actual losses would be 1.05 percent (2.1 × 0.5%), representing $1.1 million of pretax losses for every $100 million of average total assets less cash and due from banks forecasted.

[4]The capital cushion or "rule of twenty" test can be illustrated in additive terms to the example utilized in Footnote 3. If average historical losses are $25 million and N is within a normal range, the "rule of twenty" test requires that there by sufficient capital to cover twenty times twice the average historical loss or N = 20 × 2 = 40. Capital in this instance would have to exceed $1 billion (40 × $25MM) to satisfy the "rule of twenty" test.

An illustrative example using the triangular distribution with the high value of N is outlined below:

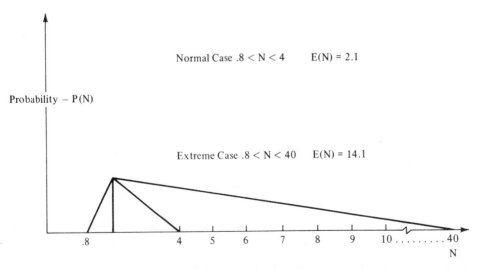

By moving the high value from 4 to 40 the expected value of N increases from 2.1 to 14.1 with the expected value of actual losses increasing from $53 to $353 million. The result of spreading out the distribution is to increase the probability that significant losses will be realized. For example, every $100 million of average total assets less cash and due from banks forecasted would result in expected losses of $7.1 million (14.1 × 0.5% = 7.1 × $100MM = $7.1MM) as opposed to $1.1 million in the normal case. In the extreme case (N = 40), the required level of capitalization could run quite high depending upon

The "rule of twenty" test applies as a minimal level of capital required provided a bank meets the following preconditions; first, the "two for one" earnings test is satisfied[5]; second, that management performance is rated superior by the regulators[6]; and third, that known adverse contingent claims on capital in the form of loans classified substandard, doubtful, or loss, and other known potential write-offs are not in excess of 50 percent of total capital funds.[7] A supplementary requirement of the "rule of twenty" test relates to asset/liability concentration factors. A proposed rule of prudence is that the total capital cushion must increase by 5 points for every risk asset/liability concentration by industry/customer group in excess of 10 percent of total nonbank private risk asset/liabilities respectively.[8] The two tests for capital adequacy and three preconditions operate subject to the constraint that total capital

---

loss experience. If loss experience reached the 1 percent level than the "rule of twenty" test would require capital equal to 40 percent (40 × 1.0%) of average total assets net of cash and due. This is excessive in real terms and tends to work against banks with small footings if a significant loss occurs. It is impractical to expect a 40 percent level of capitalization even though this in fact may be prudent to protect the smaller bank with a highly concentrated loan portfolio. In these cases the regulators may place an upper bound on the "rule of twenty" test which limits total capitalizations to 20 percent of average total assets net of cash and due, provided that other factors are favorable.

[5]Current earnings significantly in excess of the "two for one" test would obviously permit greater flexibility in management of the capital account and the cash flow of the bank. For example, assume average historical losses in year (t) are $20 million, and expected net earnings are $100 million, in excess of anticipated loss by a ratio of 5:1; aggregate capital funds required total $800 million (2 × $20MM × 20). At the end of the year management would have $80 million in surplus undivided profits. After allowing for forecasted earnings, losses, and asset growth in the following year (t + 1), management options then exist to increase dividends, build up capital, seek acquisitions, etc.; on the other hand, if earnings were 0 in the year t, and losses were $20 million, required capital would be deficient both in the current year (t) and in the following year (t + 1); management would doubtless have to raise capital in these instances.

Another possibility in the first case would be to temporarily reduce capital during year (t) in anticipation that earnings in year t would be retained to restore capital to the prudent limit of 40 times average historical losses. A strong earnings performance would permit this to occur without jeopardizing the capital position of the bank.

[6]Management "rating" in this sense involves assessments as currently made by the Comptroller of the Currency and the Federal Reserve Examiners. . . . Relevant considerations are the overall condition of the bank's liquidity position, earnings compared with banks of similar size, the adequacy of credit files, the effectiveness of collection efforts, quality and distribution of the investment account, the adequacy of internal controls, efficiency of operations, provision for management succession, and the bank's service to the community.

[7]This precondition is consistent with the approach of the Comptroller of the Currency utilized in assessing a bank's loan portfolio for capital adequacy purposes. The purpose of the requirement is to anticipate difficulty as it becomes known to management through external or internal audit processes. The proposal is that when substandard assets (assets classified substandard, doubtful, or loss), and/or other potential write-offs aggregate to 50 percent of capital funds, a review of the bank's capital account is triggered and appropriate remedial action is to be initiated. This "trigger condition" is broader in scope than the Comptroller's formulation since it includes potential losses arising from investment, liquidity, operational, fraud, and fidelity risks as well as from credit risks. The trigger condition is designed to assure the maintenance of timely audit coverage of the bank's operations and permit maximum lead-time to work out of emerging difficulties.

[8]As an illustrative case, a bank satisfying the earnings test, management performance, and "trigger" conditions would be required to maintain a capital provision of 20 times twice the average value of historical losses, provided the loan portfolio did not contain an industry loan/asset concentration in excess

requirement is not less than 5 percent of average total assets net of cash and due from banks and not more than 20 percent of total assets net of cash and due from banks.[9]

The proposed capital adequacy tests are applicable to banks operating in conditions short of total collapse of the financial system. It is recognized that regulatory opinion maintains that the level of capital must be sufficient to assure solvency in these conditions; reappraisal of this point of view is needed.

Prudence dictates that bank management anticipate recurrent crisis. In the absence of countervailing action by the monetary authorities, disaster conditions carry the risk of massive deposit/liability shrinkage and totally illiquid asset portfolios. In these circumstances capital funds aggregating to not less than 100 percent of total liabilities, held in cash, are required to prevent insolvency. Since the banking system operates on a fractional reserve basis, a capital cushion to this extent is, by definition, not available. It is time to draw the realistic conclusion that in environments which bring the financial system close to collapse, the only recourse of all institutions— including banks—is the capability of the authorities to manage the economy out of crisis. Public confidence is and must be retained by the general expectation that the authorities will not hesitate to act in this manner. In severe cyclical swings caused by economic policies, the authorities must assume responsibility for public confidence in the financial system. This does not mean that government is expected to bail out mismanaged institutions; but neither should financial institutions be expected to be so overcapitalized as to bail out government's mismanagement of the economy. As a matter of fact and practicality, the economic disaster case should be excluded as a relevant scenario for capital adequacy purposes. More positively, the range of condi-

---

of 10 percent of total nonbank private risk assets or a nonbank private liability concentration (from deposits or borrowings) of the same amount. If one such concentration existed, the rule of twenty requirement would require total capital funds to aggregate 25 times twice the average value of historical losses; if an asset/liability concentration exceeded 20 percent of risk assets, the test would require maintenance of 30 times twice the average value of historical losses.

In evaluating concentration factors in the asset/liability structure definitional precision and prudent regulator judgment would be required. Utilization of established business loan and liability classification formulae for reporting purposes would be a prudent point of departure. Personal credit extended to a widely diffused set of borrowers probably need not be given as much analytic weight in the regulatory judgment.

Clearly, concentration factors could escalate the capital cushion requirement to excessive impractical levels of capital on a formula basis. Again a maximum of 20 percent of capital to total assets net of cash and due from banks might be prudently accepted as a maximum condition for those banks deemed excessively vulnerable to solvency problems owing to concentration factors.

[9]The maximum ratio condition of capital funds not to exceed 20 percent of total assets net of cash and due from banks established a prudent limit to which bank capital can be extended by formula. A bank which is required, by formula, to maintain a higher level of capitalization is either substandard in risk terms or is not in a position to shift assets or defend against liquidity pressure to any significant degree. This is in fact the real world of banking. This degree of vulnerability would require careful continuing management attention, or the ready availability of external assistance should adverse conditions materialize. The minimum 5 percent condition is intended to set a prudent "floor" to assure that significant capital is maintained in the business. If actual losses over a five-year period are zero or trivial, obviously the proposed formulation will require only nominal capitalization. In practice most banks will fall within the ranges. Regulatory judgment at the extreme conditions will obviously be needed to establish reasonable standards for the particular banks involved.

tions which is operative for the proposed tests of capital adequacy extends from conditions of external stability or "normalcy" to conditional severity short of the peak pressures experienced in the credit crunch of 1969/70.[10]

The proposed capital adequacy tests are demonstrably responsive to the need of relating capital adequacy to the six generic categories of risk, referred to previously.

Credit Risk

Analytic software now permits banks to reconstruct historical loan experience over extended periods. Utilizing these techniques, loss occurrence, gross, and net of recov-

[10]The experience of the credit crunch of 1969/70 provides a basis to measure the capacity of the financial system to withstand crisis. Severe inflationary pressures, triggered by expansive monetary and fiscal policies associated with the Vietnam War, brought inflationary expectations to a peak. The attempt by the Federal Reserve to restrict growth in the monetary aggregates caused more sustained upward pressure on the interest rate structure. In time, more fundamental stress occurred which threatened the viability of the entire financial system. Severe commercial bank illiquidity resulted from operative interest rate ceilings on certificates of deposit imposed by Regulation Q. Massive disintermediation from the banking system forced money center banks to Eurodollar sources to offset the runoff of domestic CDs caused by Regulation Q ceilings. Ensuing crises in the international exchange markets, commercial paper market, and the stock market, and bankruptcy declarations by Penn Central and several major brokerage houses threatened the level of public confidence.

It was not until the monetary and fiscal authorities reestablished direct support to the credit markets, lifted Regulation Q ceilings, and suspended the convertibility of the dollar that public confidence was restored, and the level of inflationary expectations abated. The significance of the credit crunch experience is that in contrast to the 1930s, the authorities acted to stabilize the financial system and provide liquidity to maintain the credit base, while leading the economy out of danger. This policy mix permitted commercial banks and other financial intermediaries to survive. Had the Federal Reserve not stood ready to intervene in the markets, incidence of insolvency in the banking system, the brokerage houses, and among distressed corporations would have been high and the commercial paper market probably would have been near collapse. No level of capital would have been adequate to permit affected institutions to withstand general stress of this magnitude.

This is not to say that what is proposed is that the authorities permit banks to operate free of capital constraint in normal times and support banks in difficult periods. The point is that, in crisis, maintenance of solvency in the banking system necessitates official support to the credit markets if the system as a whole is to survive.

The nature and frequency of future crises cannot be predicted with any certainty. What is certain is that the viability of the system depends finally upon the successful execution of stabilization policy by the authorities. Individual institutions can and should be adequately capitalized to deal with relative and individual adversity but not to withstand a pervasive crisis as severe as the 1969/70 credit crunch.

Interestingly, incidence of bank failure in 1969 and 1970 was not excessive. Between January 1969 and March 1971, 19 commercial banks failed. The Honorable Frank Wille, Chairman of the Federal Deposit Insurance Corporation, testified before the House Committee on Banking and Currency on various aspects of these failures. The 19 closed banks had 126 thousand depositors with a total of $219 million in total deposits. Of the 19 banks, 4 were closed because of irregularities in loan or deposit records. The remaining 15 banks were closed because of weakness in management of the loan portfolio. Closings in 7 of the 15 cases were the result of losses on loans to borrowers outside the bank's normal market area. Elsewhere improper loans to bank officers, directors, or owners of the bank or their affiliated interests where volume and quality exceeded prudent limits produced failure. Of the 19 banks that failed, ranging in size from $1–$113 million in assets, only 6 were members of the Federal Reserve System. As of June 30, 1969, 212 commercial banks were identified as "problem banks" with 31 designated as "serious." On June 30, 1970, the number of problem banks had risen to 244 with 54 being designated as serious. During this period, 108 banks were declassified and 140 new ones were added. Source: *Recent Bank Closings; Hearing Before the Committee on Banking and Currency, House of Representatives;* March 9, 1971, U.S. Government Printing Office, Washington, D.C.

eries can be charted and correlated with parallel earnings experience and net changes in provisions for loan losses, criticized loans, and in the total reserve for loan losses. Historical loss experience provides a basis for estimating future loss experience within prudent ranges of expectational probability.[11]

Anticipated loss experience derived in this manner can be expressed as a weighted percentage of total assets, net of cash and due from banks.[12]

For capital adequacy purposes, the first line of defense against loss is current earnings. The appropriate focal relationship is the ratio of current earnings, after taxes, provisions for loan losses and dividends, to actual loss expectations.[13]

In the universe of banks, the possibilities can vary (see Figure 1) from an earnings stream which exceeds loan losses by a comfortable margin (because earnings are high and/or losses are low), to cases in which losses exceed earnings (because of low profit

---

[11]An internal staff study at Citibank focused on adverse loan experience over a 10-year period from 1962–1972. Charting the results of eleven National Bank Examiner reports, charge-off experience was recaptured for the 10-year period of total loans classified substandard, doubtful, or loss, excluding personal finance and charge card losses. Gross charge-offs ranged from 1.7 percent to 8.4 percent of loans classified, and net charge-offs after recoveries (often involving a time lag) ranged from 0 percent to 7.4 percent; the results also showed that gross charge-offs as a percentage of classifications was declining, with the exception of 1970, when the Penn Central bankruptcy occurred.

A computer data base consisting of the 10-year classification results was created to chart the course of each classified loan over time. The study showed that cumulative gross charge-offs ranged from 2 percent to 10 percent of classified loans over the time period extending from the date of original classification, with average net charge-offs in the 2 percent range. The study also showed that well over 80 percent of loans classified were ultimately paid or declassified, that most gross charge-offs occur within 2 years after classification, and that over time recoveries tend to reduce net charge-off.

The 10-year period shows that in no year did aftertax loan charge-offs exceed 13.1 percent of aftertax earnings, and that on average charge-offs in that period were 6 percent of annual earnings (notwithstanding changes in the accounting for loan losses). Average charge-offs as a percentage of loan loss reserve were 3.5 percent, with a peak experience of 7 percent. Aftertax loan losses averaged less than 0.5 percent of total capital accounts and in the worst year (the Penn Central bankruptcy) charge-offs aggregated 1.3 percent of total capital accounts. Charge-offs as a percentage of total assets net of cash and due from banks averaged .11 percent with a high of .26 percent.

Prudent expectations would hold that expected future losses would average 6 percent of annual earnings, 3.5 percent of reserves, 0.5 percent of capital accounts, and .11 percent of average total assets net of cash and due from banks. Peak/trough experience also is known.

During the same period charge-offs in personal and installment credit averaged between 0.5 percent–1 percent of outstandings and were fully absorbed by annual earnings on the portfolio. The quantitative results are not material, except to illustrate the facility with which this data can be captured and organized.

A comparable analysis on business loans was done by Wu for a stratified sample of 56 national banks, to assess the fate of criticized loans on bank balance sheets over time. The study was empirically oriented and cited the importance of the Examiner's role in identifying loan situations requiring additional management supervision. Citibank's results supported one of Wu's conclusions that a key factor in reducing loan losses was management's reaction to classification of loans by the Examiners. Generally, Wu's study also indicated charge-off experience on classified loans in line with the Citibank study. Wu, Hsin-Kwang, "Bank Examiner Criticism, Bank Loan Defaults, and Bank Loan Quality," *Journal of Finance*, Vol. 25 No. 4, pp. 637–651, June 1972.

[12]The analytic derivation of expected loss has been discussed in footnotes 3, 4, and 11.

[13]In the context of this discussion of credit risk, *loan* loss expectations are related to total loans, as a subset of the larger relationship of total expected loss and total expected assets less cash and due from banks in the general formulation. The subset relationship aggregates into the general capital adequacy tests.

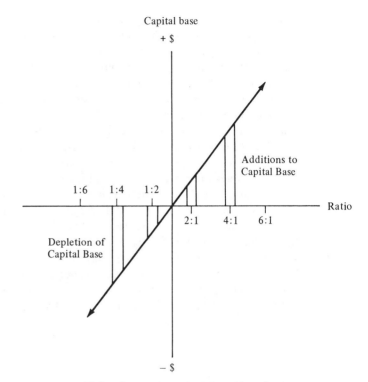

FIGURE 1.

Ratio of current earnings to net loan losses.

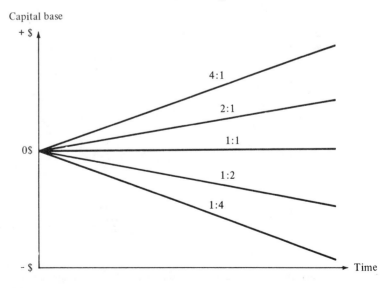

Effect on capital base of various ratios of current earnings to net loan losses over time.

performance and/or high losses). In the first set of cases the positive earnings gap will lead to a build-up of reserves and capital funds over time, assuming the incremental earnings are achieved and retained. In the second set, excess losses will reduce reserves and progressively erode the capital base.

A pattern of positive earnings growth in excess of net losses tends to validate the relative constancy of expected loss ratios and to reduce total capital requirements over time, because a larger cushion of current earnings exists to absorb losses. The obverse holds: continuous losses in excess of earnings produce a negative capital gap tending to increase expected loss ratios and capital requirements. Consideration of unpredictable loan losses, which of course might exceed normal expectations, is a more complex matter. An example of risks of this nature is an abrupt deterioration in the quality of the loan portfolio caused by adverse conditions in industries or markets in which the bank has an unduly large concentration of loans. A composite risk distribution curve, which represents loan losses, as an element of risk in the loan portfolio, is illustrated in Figure 2.[14]

The vertical axis plots the expectational probability of loss experience in the total loan portfolio, the horizontal axis the percentage of the loan portfolio which is expected to be written off. The shape of the distribution curve implies that in management's view there is a higher probability that loan loss experience will occur within

Probability

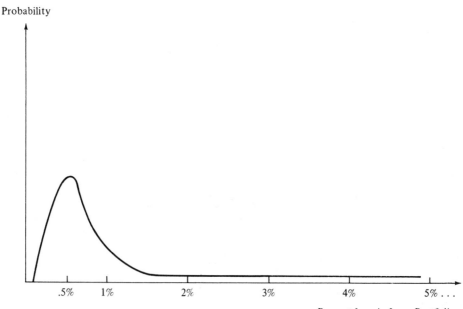

Percent Loss in Loan Portfolio

FIGURE 2. Distribution of the percent of losses in the loan portfolio.

[14]Again it is emphasized that the triangular distribution is assumed and in fact is a reasonable approximation for the major portion of the distribution shown in Figure 2.

the range of historical experience and a lower probability that loan losses will exceed historical experience by a significant amount.

The distribution curve defined in expectational terms will vary from bank to bank depending on the scope of operations, the number of customers, and the nature and degree of market/industry concentrations in the loan portfolio. A one-office bank with 5 million dollars in loans, all of which are extended to wheat growers in an immediate trading area, would be out of business if blight ruined the wheat crop; a money center bank with 20 billion dollars in loans at risk in 50 states in the United States and 80 countries abroad, with a loan concentration of .001 percent of total loans to wheat growers in the entire United States, would not be affected to any material extent by the same occurrence of blight. Unanticipated loan loss would occur for both banks; for the first bank the impact is ruinous, for the second bank it is negligible. Obviously, the smaller, undiversified bank must be more conservatively capitalized than the second bank because of the degree of industry concentration in relation to the total loan portfolio. There is a qualitative difference in the loss exposure dynamics of the two banks.[15]

The second line of defense against credit loss is the reserve for loan losses and of course other capital accounts after the reserve has been charged and exhausted. The second test of capital adequacy stipulates that provided the principal preconditions are satisfied, loan loss reserves and other capital accounts must aggregate to 20 times twice the level of historical loss, including loan loss, to provide a reasonable margin of safety.

Investment Risk

The investment account extends from the securities portfolio to commitments to owned real estate and major equipment installations. The earnings equation involving interest earned and interest paid can be represented as the "interest differential" business of a bank. Similarly, the earnings equation involving positive or negative differences between the cost/book values of investment securities and fixed assets and their respective market values constitutes a bank's "capital appreciation" business. Profit or loss occurs if yields or cost benefits exceed carrying charges and/or if liquidation of these assets produces values greater than/less than/cost/book values.[16] Yields on securities investments may exceed/be less than interest costs on funds

[15]In practical terms, it must be recognized that the small bank, with a loan portfolio totally committed to wheat growers, cannot survive the incidence of a ruinous blight—or in other words the destruction of its earning asset base caused by exogenous variables. In these and comparable cases, the only recourse would be to reorganize the bank, and protect depositors by pursuing remedies from public sector support.

[16]Again a "subset" relationship of income to carrying charges can be discussed in terms similar to the analysis of credit risk in the previous section. To avoid redundancy the process will not be repeated here or in the consideration of liquidity, operating, fraud, and fidelity risks to follow. The analytic approach is similar and all subset conclusions aggregate to the general formulations for capital adequacy discussed earlier. The purpose here is to segment the analysis to highlight the qualitative aspects of the risks.

utilized to carry the portfolio. Losses in this sense are covered by earnings and are measurable in capital adequacy terms by the proposed "two for one" earnings test.

Concerning investments in fixed assets, one of the valid functions of capital has been represented as permitting the bank to acquire the institutional structure necessary to commence and maintain a business presence. If investment decisions are correctly taken, earnings generated by these assets will more than cover depreciation expense and other carrying charges, permitting the institution to earn a residual profit. If the investment decisions are incorrectly taken, earnings will be insufficient to cover charges and a negative impact on earnings results. The capital adequacy implications of investment risks are covered by the proposed earnings and capital cushion tests. So long as total earnings comfortably exceed the costs of carrying securities/fixed assets, the bank is not in difficulty; negative earnings net of carrying charges require a build-up of capital funds over time.

Unexpected investment losses arise from forced liquidation in suboptimal market conditions. For example, in periods of tight money banks often sell securities in a rising interest rate environment. If securities are sold to finance expanding loan demand, the net effect on earnings is positive; if forced sales are necessary to meet liquidity pressures, a portfolio loss involving a negative charge on earnings occurs. Forced sales of fixed assets, the write-off of undepreciated equipment, investment premia, etc., can have similar negative earnings consequences.

In periods of instability both portfolio securities (including government securities in an unsupported market) and fixed assets have close to zero liquidity, and a considerable market risk of loss is involved. Losses arising from forced sales or other dispositions which cannot be covered by earnings can arise. These losses, to the extent that they exceed current earnings, would have to be charged against the capital account. The proposed "rule of twenty" capital cushion test is meant to apply to risks of extraordinary capital loss, by integrating loss experience in this area in the general formulation.

Liquidity Risks

The ability of a bank to obtain liquidity is directly dependent on reputation in the marketplace. Liquidity pressures require the institution to liquify assets or acquire incremental liabilities to refinance maturing claims; favorable/unfavorable market reputation influences the ability to finance liquidity, especially in periods of stress. The tenor mix of the asset and liability structure defines liquidity gaps which must be financed. Current and anticipated money market conditions and the time frame in which action can or must be taken are the important external variables.

At the peak of a money crunch, the range of available asset/liability choices is restricted. In these circumstances, a bank may find that all assets are illiquid and that the only method of refinancing liabilities is borrowing from the lender of last resort. In stable market conditions, with longer time periods in which to act, the array of options is broader, making liquidity management an easier task. The ability of banks to withstand liquidity pressures is a function of market reputation and business scope. Money center banks, operating on a global scale, can access every significant money market in the world. They are further supported by the financing power of the parent holding company which has broader options than does the bank itself. A small rural bank, experiencing comparable liquidity pressure, has a narrower scope of operations, fewer options available, and generally less time to react before reaching an extreme state of difficulty.

Regulatory tradition and current practice recognize the relationship between capital and liquidity. The Federal Reserve capital analysis approach views bank liquidity as a function of liability refinancing and asset liquification, and considers capital funds as the last line of defense. What is not recognized in the Board's capital adequacy formulation, but obviously is recognized in the formulation of monetary policy, is the fact that the history of monetary crisis indicates that a fractional reserve banking system cannot survive a prolonged period of liquidity pressure, unaided by the monetary authorities. In the 1930s, the operative cause of the massive incidence of bank failure was the withdrawal of official support to the credit markets, which had the effect of destroying the credit base of the economy. In the credit crunch of 1969/70, the ability of the authorities to intervene and maintain the credit base permitted the financial system to withstand the crisis.

The capital account of a bank is not adequate to maintain solvency in the event of a major liquidity crisis, nor can the capital account withstand the pressure of a major run once public confidence in the particular bank has been irretrievably lost. Effective defense against ultimate crisis comes from lenders of last resort. The admissible liquidity-related risks for capital adequacy purposes are the earnings risks associated with suboptimal asset liquification or liability refinancing. Negative effects on earnings and, if losses are major, on capital funds, can of course arise. For capital adequacy purposes, liquidity-related losses can be treated according to the proposed earnings and capital cushion tests of capital adequacy. Loss experience arising from liquidity-related risks need only be integrated with other loss experience in quantifying capital requirements to accomplish this.[17]

Operating/Fraud Losses

"Normal" operating losses are susceptible to historical analysis in the same manner as are other "normal" losses. Operating losses are charged directly to earnings or against reserves created by charges to earnings. Unanticipated major loss not covered by earnings occurrence is chargeable directly to capital funds. For capital adequacy purposes, the two for one earnings test covers expected normal loss and the capital cushion test covers extraordinary nonrecurring loss.

---

[17]Extraordinary capital losses from forced sales of securities would of course be treated as below the line losses, i.e., adversely affecting income after securities gains or losses as discussed in the previous section on investment risks.

Fraud losses of minor amount also are relatively predictable by management; nonrecurring major losses can eventuate. Since banks usually are insured to a degree against major fraud loss, capital implications tend to be minimized. The two tests of capital adequacy can embrace this category of risk with facility.

Fidelity Risks

The proposed rule of twenty test extends to loss exposure arising from trust operations. No separate provision need be made.

Loss experience, as understood in terms of the generic categories of risk incurred by commercial banks, can be dealt with by the two proposed tests for capital adequacy. The "earnings" and "capital cushion" tests are premised on a dynamic, "going concern" view of the bank operating in relatively normal conditions. In the revised formulations, capital provision is quantified on the basis of *actual* analysis of historical risk dynamics and prudent managerial expectations concerning future loss. Positive weight is assigned to earnings as a first defense against loss, and total capital funds are measured by the degree to which protection is afforded against extreme variations of the ongoing risk experience of the bank. The proposed new tests reward managerial competence in assessing and managing risks instead of penalizing it and are consistent with conditions in the business climate in which banks now compete.

Public Policy Implications

Commercial banks have been stimulated by changes in public policy to compete in the market place as viable businesses. This is the significance of the emergence of commercial banking in the holding company context. Public policy also stipulates that institutions performing the intermediation function and offering permissible related services to the public are to develop in a procompetitive direction. Commercial banking has been deemed a business to be professionally managed to achieve optimum rates of return on capital to the long-run benefit of the public.

The disciplines of the marketplace to which banks are now subject are worth emphasis. Services must be offered on a quality and price-competitive basis; capital must be acquired at least cost, on risk/reward terms prevailing in the marketplace, and employed to most productive uses. Business costs must be managed to minimal levels consistent with proper standards of internal control. Commercial banks and parent holding companies must by law and equity accept the discipline of fuller disclosure including the revelation of materially adverse loss exposure to customers and investors, in addition to regulators. These are the new rules of the game. Failure to follow the rules certainly will result in a competitive deterioration of the banking system and produce dysfunctional social effects in the long run.

Ultimately the marketplace must determine the extent to which both commercial banks and parent holding companies are capitalized. The market can be expected to assess the increasingly differentiated performance of banking enterprises, the appropriate new earning dynamics, and the progressive distinction between the financing power of parent holding companies and wholly owned subsidiary bank(s). If allowed to work, market forces will assure that appropriate cognizance of these factors is taken and will establish relevant capital standards for a restructured banking industry. The market also will vote substandard banks out of existence, relying on public policy and the regulatory structure to assure protection of the general public. Based on previous FDIC experience in liquidating substandard banks, this need not cause undue concern. As market mechanisms operate in this manner, banks can be expected to adapt and perform as the economy requires and to become more capably managed. The proposed tests of capital adequacy are not intended to substitute for the ultimate judgment of the marketplace, but are designed on an interim basis to permit banks to prudently maintain an adequate level of capital without compromising their ability to compete as charged. It is recognized that the capital adequacy tests now utilized by regulators are employed as aids to but not substitutes for judgment. They assist supervisors in assessing the overall condition of a bank. The proposed new tests are warranted as more appropriate aids to bank supervisors because they relate in a dynamic fashion the vital measures of a bank's strength—the ability to assume and manage risks and to achieve stable earnings in a competitive environment. It is time for regulatory policy to adapt a new perspective and adjust to a point of consistency with the new priorities. Regulatory policy which issues from the obsolete public policy context of the pre-1971 period can only frustrate achievement of the larger objectives explicit in the amended holding company legislation.[18]

This article has endeavored to delineate a new set of premises on which to base an approach to capital adequacy in the context of current conditions. New tests for capital adequacy have been proposed. Careful consideration of the capital adequacy issue in these terms is needed.

---

[18]Lucille Mayne writes that one way to view the regulatory role in the long run is that "bank supervisory agencies should abandon completely the use of capital adequacy standards in the examination process and concentrate instead on the competency of bank management. Implicit in this course of action is the premise that it is not possible to devise a generally applicable measure of capital adequacy since the essential function of capital is to serve as a defense against the occurrence of unpredictable events. Moreover, such a policy would imply that the key to soundness and success of a banking enterprise lies not so much in the amount of its capital funds as in the ability of its management to assess and absorb the risk inherent in its own particular operation and environment. Certainly, sound management would not wish to operate with less capital than a knowledgeable supervisor would specify. . . . Focusing primarily on management competency, therefore, may well be supervisory agencies' best assurance of banks' maintaining capital in an amount sufficient to protect the public interest." Mayne, Lucille S., "Impact of Federal Bank Supervisors on Bank Capital," The *Bulletin, New York University Graduate School of Business Administration, Institute of Finance,* Nos. 85-86, September 1972, p. 49.

Banking's Capital Shortage: The Malaise and the Myth

Ronald D. Watson

14

Is it possible that bank capital—like oil—is a scarce resource whose supply is in danger of being exhausted? To read the financial industry's trade journals a person might conclude that capital is a rare substance whose supply can grow only at a strictly limited rate. However, the current presumption that banks can't raise the funds they want for strengthening their capital positions and expanding deposits needs a lot of rethinking. Banks must have capital to inspire public confidence and absorb losses.[1] If they can't get the capital required to support their operations, maybe banks aren't serving the economy as effectively as is generally assumed.

Clearly, the banking industry must raise additional capital if it is to grow. Growth without new capital is possible, but only if bank regulators are willing to allow risks to increase, and that isn't likely. The "shortage" is occurring because banks are expanding their assets more rapidly than reinvested profits can boost capital. The obvious supplement to retained earnings is new capital from public issues of long-term debt and equity securities. But bankers claim that declining stock prices and higher interest rates have made the cost of this new money (especially the equity) too high. The problem is compounded by generally weak markets for bank securities,

Reprinted, with deletions, from the Federal Reserve Bank of Philadelphia, *Business Review,* September 1975, pp. 3-13, by permission of the publisher.

[1]Ronald D. Watson, "Insuring Some Progress in the Bank Capital Hassle," of the Federal Reserve Bank of Philadelphia, *Business Review,* July-August 1974, pp. 3-18.

especially in the wake of several failures of large banks in 1974. Most banks resort to outside financing only when other sources of funds are no longer readily available.

Restricting the industry's growth to the rate at which it can generate capital internally has been suggested, but most banks are reluctant to accept a policy that might mean losing ground to other financial intermediaries or even slowing the whole economy's growth. Yet further growth for banking appears to be stymied. Internal generation of new capital is too slow, outside capital seems too costly, and the regulators are closing off the alternative of expanding without additional capital.

This should not—and need not—be an impasse. If the problem looks insurmountable, it may be that we are zeroing in on the wrong target. The issue should not be one of "*how* to get capital for future expansion," but "are the profit opportunities of this expansion great enough to justify raising new capital at today's prices?" If the profits are there, banks can afford to pay the going rate for capital. If they aren't, then the capital should go to industries that have better opportunities to use it. Bank capital markets may be in poor shape, but that alone shouldn't change the way the decision to expand is made.

The Capital Chasm

The bank capital "shortage" has been brewing for several years, but recent projections of enormous capital shortfalls over the next decade have significantly pepped up discussions of the problem. There have been prophecies of a capital "gap" (differences between probable capital accumulations and capital demands of the industry) of $16.7 billion[2] by 1978 or $32.0 billion[3] by 1979. These projections have intensified the industry's awareness that the methods used for financing growth in the '60s may not be equal to the task in the '70s.

Bankers have normally considered it impractical to try to close this gap with outside sources of funds. Data on bank financing is very sketchy, but the industry has a long history of depending heavily on earnings retention for additional long-term funds (as have most corporations). Of the new securities issued by banks the bulk has been debt (subordinated notes and debentures) rather than common or preferred stock.[4] In general, internal funds are more appealing as a source of capital than external funds because their cost seems very low. Retained earnings almost always look cheaper than new common stock. A new stock issue may dilute the earnings of current shareholders, but retaining earnings never will. Furthermore, there are substantial transaction costs associated with floating new debt or equity issues publicly.

[2]*The Capital Adequacy Problem in Commercial Banks, 1974-1978* (Princeton, N.J.: The Institute for Financial Education, 1974), p. 8.

[3]Warren R. Marcus, *The Challenge to Banking: Capital Formation in the Seventies* (New York: Salomon Brothers, 1974), p. 6.

[4]"Report of Securities Issued by Commercial Banks and Holding Companies," Report #67, Corporate Financial Counseling Department of Irving Trust Company, New York, February 28, 1975.

Retained earnings may also seem less costly than long-term debt which carries an explicit obligation to pay interest.

Raising money through new issues of common stock has become even more expensive in the last few years because bank stock prices have declined dramatically even though earnings have been growing. Bankers accustomed to seeing their shares sell for 15 to 20 times earnings in the early 1960s were dismayed to see those prices drift into the 10 to 15 times earnings range in the late 1960s and early 1970s and then plummet to the 5 to 10 times earnings range in 1974.[5] As stock prices decline, the number of shares that must be sold to raise a fixed amount of new capital increases. When this occurs, the current stockholder's control of the bank is diluted and his future dividends diminish relative to what he would have received if the stock had been sold at a higher price. And each jump in equity cost has strengthened management's resolve to avoid paying the cost of raising funds with new stock issues.

Even debt capital has become more expensive in the last few years. Not long ago sound banks were able to sell their long-term obligations at an interest rate of 5 to 6 percent. However, an upward drift in rates and recent concern about bank soundness have made the going rate 8½ to 10 percent these days.

Current Remedies for Spanning the Gap: A Weak Bridge

Even though there is no universally accepted response to this problem, there have been any number of suggestions. Some have been directed toward loosening the regulatory constraint on expansion while other plans have been designed to reduce the industry's cost of capital. All of these proposals have some merit, but none constitutes a lasting solution to the problem.

Lower Capital Standards   Some effort has gone into convincing the regulatory agencies that banks don't really need all the capital that supervisors currently consider prudent. If capital standards were lowered, still more expansion could take place. Bankers point to the willingness of investors in the capital markets (until very recently) to advance debt funds to banks at interest rates nearly on a par with other high-quality corporate borrowers. This is interpreted as evidence that investors (who are the first to lose their money if banks fail) have considered banks to be good risks. If regulatory standards on capital are too conservative, reducing them would alleviate the current bind on growth. Reducing capital requirements might also enable banks to maintain the lower standard through retention of earnings. However, such a hope might be overly optimistic. A key reason that banks haven't maintained capital at the current standard through internal generation of profit is that they have

---

[5]*Keefe Bank Stock Manual* (New York: Keefe, Bruyette, and Woods Inc., 1974). Inflation and riskier bank portfolios have been important reasons for the rising cost of new debt and equity capital. However, many bankers claim that public statements by regulators warning of capital inadequacy problems have increased the cost of funds even to very conservative banks by making investors wary of all bank securities—not just banks that had been aggressive in using leverage.

been willing to sacrifice profits to achieve asset growth. If the regulator's capital constraint is relaxed without a simultaneous reexamination of the importance of maintaining profitability, the problem will just reappear in a couple of years. Asset growth will again be halted by the capital adequacy barrier, but this time it will be at an even lower standard.

More Debt   The second type of suggestion for closing the capital gap consists of plans for lowering the price that banks must pay for their capital funds. The most common proposal is that banks use more long-term debt as a substitute for equity capital. As long as debt hasn't been overused, it has a cost below that of equity and appears to be the cheapest way to raise outside capital. Debt is a particularly attractive form of capital in that it is the one form of long-term funds whose cost is a tax-deductible expense.[6]

Yet, substituting long-term debt for new equity is also only a partial solution. Long-term debt is an inadequate substitute for equity because it has legal characteristics which are different from those of common stock. Its claim to interest is secondary to that of depositors, so it backstops their claims. But interest and principal must be repaid on time if the bank is to avoid default, and operating losses cannot be charged against debt "capital" (except in liquidation) as they can against equity capital.

Accordingly, if banks' asset growth is financed with debt capital rather than equity, the chance of incurring a large loss that would wipe out the remaining cushion of equity capital grows. The greater the amount by which the growth of risky assets exceeds expansion of the equity cushion, the greater the risk of failure. Bondholders are also wary of this heightened risk of failure. As the investors' risks grow, the yield they demand on their investment also climbs. As a result, heavy use of "cheap" debt capital will eventually raise the cost of new equity and debt (both new and refinanced) by causing the market price of these securities to decline. This risk "spillover" reduces the cost advantage of new debt. It also hurts the financial position of the current shareholders whose investment has now dropped in value. If a bank's debt position becomes excessive by market standards, management will find that by cutting back on the use of debt the shareholders' risk will be reduced, the stock's price will tend to rise, and the overall cost of funds will be lower (even new equity issues become relatively less costly than additional debt).

New Securities   One of the problems preventing banks from using more debt capital is the poor marketability of these securities. Major banks that have market recognition are able to sell large amounts of debt at relatively low interest rates. However, smaller banks that lack this reputation aren't so fortunate. The market for their securities is normally restricted to their operating region, and borrowing costs may be higher than those of a large bank of the same risk. To overcome these disadvantages some smaller banks have borrowed debt capital from their big-city

---

[6]There have recently been legislative proposals that all dividend payments be treated as tax-deductible expenses in the same way that interest payments are now deductible. If this change in the tax codes were enacted, it would make stock a relatively more attractive way to finance corporations.

correspondents.[7] There have also been suggestions that smaller institutions use investment trusts (like mutual funds) to pool their securities. This device is intended to simplify the investor's diversification problems while providing a wider market for the securities of these banks.

Weakness in the stock and bond markets has prompted some authors to suggest that banks turn to convertible bonds for new capital. These are securities that can be converted into common stock if stock prices rise. Convertible bonds usually have an interest rate below that of nonconvertible debt. What's more, the price at which holders are allowed to convert their bonds into common stock can be set above the current market price of the stock. This type of security is supposed to give the issuer a cheap source of debt which will eventually be turned into equity at a better price than new stock issued right now—in a sense, the best of both worlds for the bank.

Investment trusts and convertible debt securities might be useful to a bank, but they won't make the cost of new capital *substantially* lower. Such a trust may improve the overall marketability of a bank's securities, making it easier for the institution to tap new sources of capital. However, an investor should be able to diversify his or her investments without the trust and has little reason other than convenience to accept a significantly lower return on pooled securities than for the individual issues.

Convertible bonds (and convertible preferred stocks) are also useful, but again they don't solve the problem. On the surface they look like a very cheap way to raise money. But this is not the case. If a bank offers a convertible bond, it may sell the securities at a low interest rate and attractive conversion price. However, it has still sold a debt issue, and debt is riskier for the bank than new equity. Holders of these bonds will only convert them to stock if the price of the bank's stock rises to a level *above* its conversion price in the future. If a bank really wants debt capital now and equity capital sometime in the future, it might be better off to float a bond issue initially, and then refinance it with a common stock issue later at the stock's higher price. In principle, there's no reason to expect a bank to be able to raise capital substantially more cheaply in the long run with convertible securities than with ordinary debt and stock.

Cut Dividend Payout   The high cost of new external capital has also prompted the suggestion that banks boost earnings retention by gradually cutting the proportion of earnings paid out as dividends. Retained earnings are an appealing way to build equity capital because the process doesn't create new shares which dilute earnings. The internal funds also increase the likelihood that there will be higher earnings in subsequent years.

But the suggestion that higher earnings retention be used when equity capital costs are high skips over some basic economics. If the cost of new equity is prohibitive, the cost of retained earnings should be treated as only "a bit less" than prohibitive. The cost of retained earnings is closely linked to the cost of new equity in the long run. In

---

[7]This may make the smaller bank's capital position look more sound, but it hardly enhances the stability of the banking system.

a world without taxes these costs would be identical except for the cost of underwriting new stock issues. Taxes make retained earnings slightly cheaper because investors whose profits are retained for reinvestment by the bank will avoid income taxes—at least until the reinvested profits produce higher dividends or until stockholders realize a capital gain on their investment. Realizing a capital gain would reduce the effective tax rate on the profits from reinvestment.

The connection between the cost of retained earnings and that of new common stock becomes clearer if we think of retained earnings as bank profits that are being reinvested within the organization for the *benefit of the shareholders* rather than being paid out to them in the form of dividends. Those same investors who want a very high return for investing in a new stock issue aren't likely to be happy to have their profits reinvested for them at significantly lower expected returns. If investors currently expect 15 percent as a return for investing in a bank's stock, they must feel that 15 percent is a competitive return given the risks of bank investment and the alternative uses they have for their money. If the bank can't earn enough profit on these retained earnings to give the shareholders that 15 percent return, it would make the investors better off by giving them the money as a dividend to invest as they see fit. In the long run, reinvestment of retained earnings at substandard rates will lower the bank's overall rate of return, and investors will bid down the price of the bank's stock. Therefore, reinvesting retained earnings when profit prospects don't warrant doing so is no solution to the capital problem.

Boost Earnings   The final proposal for closing the capital gap is one of speeding internal equity creation by increasing earnings margins. Greater profits would allow earnings to grow faster, equity to expand faster, and asset growth to be less impeded by capital. The proposal that banks raise their profit margins is the soundest and the most important of this crop of "solutions." It comes the closest to confronting the fundamental reason that the industry finds itself "unable" to raise adequate capital. It is also the basic component of a real solution.

The Fundamental Problem

The problem that banks face isn't a *shortage* of capital but an *unwillingness or inability to pay the "going rate."* There is no question that capital costs are high right now. By the historical standard of the last three decades, the only time they were higher was in the latter part of 1974 when long-term interest rates were above their present levels and stock prices were extremely depressed. Adjusting to these rising capital costs is difficult for all businessmen—and the reaction is likely to be slow. Many bankers have delayed raising capital hoping that a future drop in market rates will reduce these capital costs.

Beyond the argument that rates may soon drop, many bank managers are simply unwilling to tolerate the dilution of earnings per share that could accompany a new stock issue (spreading the existing earnings pool over a larger number of shares). Retained earnings may have a high implicit cost, but it's a difficult cost to pinpoint.

Diluted earnings, however, suggest that management may have made some errors somewhere along the line. That makes dilution a difficult path to accept. . . .

Bankers may also be unwilling to pay the high cost of new capital for the sound economic reason that they cannot reinvest it at a sufficiently high return. They may know that they need greater earnings to justify raising additional funds yet may be unable to increase their margins because competitive pressures are too strong. Any move to raise earnings will be hard to sustain if other financial institutions don't consider themselves to be under the same pressures. If only one bank in an area raises its loan rate, its competitors will have an advantage in selling their services. In all probability the first bank will lose some of its share of the market. It's only when all banks feel the pressure to build their capital (and no one has a clear cost advantage) that profit margins can be raised successfully. Even then, banks may lose some business to other nonbank financial organizations unless those firms are under equivalent pressure to boost earnings.[8]

In the long run, the banking industry can only pay a higher price for capital if it can pass these costs along to customers in the form of higher effective interest rates or higher fees for other services provided. The ability to pass costs along depends in great part on whether the industry can preserve its cost advantage over (or, at least, parity with) competing suppliers of financial services. If bank loan prices can't be competitive, profit opportunities will shrink and maintaining the industry's recent growth rate will be impossible.

The Fundamental Solution

The industry *can* pay the going rate for capital if it is careful to use sound methods in analyzing its costs of funds and return available on new investments. In the long run, solid financial analysis will be more effective in loosening the industry's growth constraints than plans to make bank securities more marketable. Management will also find that its own long-run interests are served by making sound financial decisions. Asset growth may be one measure of accomplishment, but consistent profitability over the long haul makes a banker's position more secure.

The Cost of Funds   One of the most basic problems that industry must confront is estimating the costs of its own sources of funds. Bank management must determine where new money is coming from, what its full cost is, and what effect decisions to change the bank's capital structure (and, thereby, its risk) will have on the cost of these funds. The cost of funds to a bank depends in part on the riskiness of its capital structure—the proportions in which it raises long-term versus short-term funds and

---

[8]This should not be interpreted as an approval of collusion to raise prices. Even though the entire industry has profits that are insufficient to attract new capital, each bank must respond to the problem individually. However, the more widespread the profits squeeze, the more likely that individual banks will follow a move to raise prices rather than try to increase their market share by maintaining current prices for loans and services. In the long run, competitive markets will generate equal prices from all suppliers, but at a level which covers the cost of all factors of production including equity capital.

debt capital versus equity. A bank may raise its *next* dollar of funds from any of several specific sources, but it must carefully maintain a balance of debt and equity as it grows over time. If this week's funds come from debt sources, they will soon have to be balanced with new equity. Since increasing risk makes it impractical to expand indefinitely using only short-term borrowings, bankers must include the cost of funds from all of the sources that will eventually be tapped when they estimate the real cost of additional funds.[9] To be profitable, any investment made by the bank should earn enough profit to pay for all the funds used to finance it.

Lending money at rates which cover only the cost of funds borrowed to make the loan will quickly lead to profit problems. The cost of the new equity that must be raised to keep risk exposure constant must also be covered in the rate charged on the loan. Otherwise, the cost of the bank's funds will rise even further. If the cost of new capital is increasing, the signal to management should be clear: either reduce the bank's overall risk or be prepared to earn a high enough return on assets to pay for this capital. Successful operation over a long period requires that investors be given an expected return on their funds that is as high as returns available from other comparable securities. The fact that markets for the capital of smaller banks are especially imperfect doesn't alter the fact that those banks must have equity to expand and must pay whatever the "going market rate" is for that equity.

A Minimum Return Once a bank has estimated the price it must pay for new funds it has a benchmark for judging alternative investments. A bank should only invest in loans or securities (or combinations of them) whose expected return is above the cost of the new funds required to finance them. That seems obvious. But the decision must be made on the basis of the current cost of *all funds* that will be raised during the next planning period rather than just the cost of a block of short-term debt which might be raised next week. It should also consider the full effect that any change in the bank's asset or liability risks will have on the cost of any funds raised. Furthermore, if the bank expects to have more funds than it needs to meet loan demand and liquidity requirements for an extended period, simply investing them in the highest yielding asset available may not be the best strategy. The investment must still yield enough to pay the full cost of these funds, or they should be returned to those who have loaned to or invested in the bank. This might be done by not replacing maturing debt issues or by paying extra dividends. In the long run, capital markets should eventually force a bank in the direction of managing its funds efficiently. (Limitations on entry into banking and imperfections in the market for bank securities may make market discipline less effective than it is in unregulated industries.)

---

[9]A common technique for estimating a corporation's cost of new funds is the weighted average method. A business evaluates the net cost of raising additional funds from debt and equity sources by estimating the cost of each source and weighting the cost according to the proportion that those funds will represent of any new money raised. If a bank expects to finance 80 percent of its growth with short-term debt costing 4 percent after taxes and the other 20 percent of the expansion with new stock costing 12 percent, its weighted average cost of funds is $.8 \times .04 + .2 \times .12 = .032 + .024 = .056$ (5.6 percent). . . .

Shrink, If Necessary   If investment prospects don't justify raising new funds, the institution shouldn't try to expand. Doing so isn't in the best interests of either shareholders or management. When the cost of funds exceeds the returns available to a bank, capital markets are giving management a signal that alternative uses for its shareholders' fund are relatively attractive. If the bank can't earn a competitive return on its equity, its stockholders can use the money for other investments. A bank that reinvests shareholder earnings when its return isn't on a par with other securities of similar risk is preventing shareholders from making better use of their own money. Eventually, the shareholders will sense this and try to sell their stock. The falling stock price will put pressure on management to correct the problem or answer to the stockholders.

The market is also signaling the bank that consumers and borrowers aren't sufficiently interested in its banking services to pay the prices that make the bank able to give investors a competitive return. Either another financial organization can provide that service at a lower cost or tastes have changed and people don't really want the service at all. Banks that can't afford to pay the going rate for funds (because they can't pass their higher costs on to their customers) should not expect to get additional money.

The Regulatory Constraint   If banks were unregulated and absolutely free to buy money and sell services in a competitive business environment, these market forces could resolve the "capital shortage" automatically. But the fact is, they're not free and, therefore, they do not work perfectly. The industry, in fact, is tightly regulated, and the regulations influence bank profits. Exclusive rights to issue demand deposits and limitations on entry into the industry are examples of implicit subsidies from Government to commercial banks. Conversely, capital adequacy constraints, reserve requirements, and portfolio limitations tend to lower bank profits. The point is not that these constraints are "wrong" or "unjust," but that they influence the profitability and competitiveness of banks *vis-à-vis* other financial service organizations.

Firms operating in an unregulated world have the right to raise their prices enough to compete for the higher-cost equity funds—as long as their customers are willing to pay those higher prices. Banks are free to make some price adjustments, but they may not be able to pass on higher money costs as effectively as unregulated financial corporations. If banking agency regulations or state usury statutes inadvertently hold earnings below the level needed to raise new capital, the industry's growth would be unnecessarily curtailed.[10]

There is no way to know, right now, whether this will be an important problem or not. Bank regulators must be vigilant in assuring that only the constraints that are necessary to promoting the financial system's stability are enforced. This problem

---

[10]It is also possible that their regulated environment gives banks an advantage as money costs rise. In that instance, regulations are giving banks an unearned competitive edge and allowing them to increase their market shares at the expense of nonbank businesses. This results in just as great a misallocation of society's resources as occurs when bank profits and growth are unnecessarily restricted.

becomes especially important as regulators weigh the pros and cons of changes in capital requirements and of expanded powers for both banks and thrift institutions.

Conclusion

Any projection of historical trends in bank growth, profits, and dividend payout practices suggests that the banking system's demand for external capital will expand rapidly in the years immediately ahead. Yet the capital "gap" will probably sow the seeds of its own resolution. If banks curtail their growth because of an inability to find profitable new investments (or to circumvent the regulator's capital constraints), the least attractive investments can gradually be culled from their portfolios. By concentrating available resources on the more profitable business that remains, banks will be taking steps to build capital internally. Better profits and stronger capital positions will cut risks, and banks will then be more able to compete for new external capital. Competition from the nonbank financial sector will remain, but these organizations must also pay high prices for additional capital. The key, however, is astute use by banks of the money available to them and prudence in raising only those funds that can be reinvested profitably. As long as the profit opportunities exist, banks will have the opportunity and the justification for raising whatever funds they need. When expected profitability is insufficient, the desire to expand must be held in check.

Regulators also face a challenge in the years ahead. They must not only protect the public's interest in its financial system but also try to keep the game "fair." The regulatory agencies can alter the competitive viability of the industries they regulate. If these industries are to serve society and their shareholders efficiently, they must be free to respond to their changing economic environment. The desire to expand banking's capital base rapidly is one development which can only be accomplished successfully if regulation doesn't prevent the industry from competing for funds, investing rationally, and passing rising costs along to customers who are willing to bear them.

Cost and Profitability

IV

Section I contained several readings on the recent applications of analytical tools to asset management. New analytical inputs are now being applied to the area of bank profit planning, the subject of this section. From 1970 to 1974, the rate of return on assets in the fifty-eight largest national banks declined by about 50 percent.[1] The readings in Section III indicated that profitability is the key to bank capital adequacy. Obviously, banks and bank holding companies cannot grow and prosper without paying attention to product cost control and pricing. Analytical tools will increasingly be applied in controlling costs and determining appropriate prices. Examples of these tools will be covered in this section.

The opening article by William A. Longbrake analyzes how data can be and have been used in estimating bank operating costs. Longbrake shows how estimated cost relations can be used for product costing, incremental costing, and cost forecasting. Article 16 by Ronald D. Watson shows how incremental (or marginal) cost analysis, even when based on data that are considerably more sketchy than the statistical cost functions proffered by Longbrake, can be a boon to bank profitability.

[1]Federal Deposit Insurance Corporation, *Operating Statistics* (Washington, D.C.: U.S. Government Printing Office, 1970 and 1974).

Tax considerations also loom as an elemental consideration in bank profit planning. Article 17 by Margaret E. Bedford examines the various approaches that commercial banks have taken to minimize their individual tax burdens and the aggregate effect of these approaches in lightening the tax burden of commercial banks as a whole in recent years. In some cases bank profits suffer because of improper use of cost and other data to price loans and other services. In Essay 18 Paul S. Anderson describes the functional cost analysis program of the Federal Reserve System and then shows the insights that it provides into banking operations, including the costs of various detailed activities.

If further reading in cost analysis is desired, the article by George J. Benston in Section VII carefully reviews both the results and the possible applications of a number of recent econometric studies of bank operating costs.

Statistical Cost Analysis

William A. Longbrake

Statistical techniques provide information useful in making many types of business decisions. For several reasons, however, statistical analysis is seldom used in analyzing production and other costs. Standard costing procedures, such as time and motion studies and direct costing procedures based on past experience and modified by anticipated changes, are sufficient in many decision-making situations.

Data limitations frequently hinder the employment of statistical analysis. To use it, data concerning costs, output, and product characteristics must exist for a sufficient number of time periods in one business firm or, alternatively, these data must be available for one time period for several firms producing essentially the same product. Another impediment is the general lack of knowledge about statistical cost analysis.

This article will demonstrate the use of statistical analysis for product costing, incremental costing, and cost forecasting. While the illustrations are developed specifically for use by commercial banks in making decisions about demand deposit operations, the basic techniques could be modified for cost analysis of products in other industries or products of a single firm.

Detailed cost accounting and production data exist for a sample of nearly 1,000 banks that have voluntarily participated in the Federal Reserve Banks' Functional

Reprinted from *Financial Management* 2, no. 1 (Spring 1973): 48-55, by permission of the Financial Management Association and the author.

Cost Analysis (FCA) program. Development of uniform accounting classifications and methods of allocating costs by the FCA has enabled participating banks to compare their performance with the average performance of similarly sized banks. As a result, the accuracy and consistency of FCA data is excellent. Hence, the data afford a good basis for demonstrating the uses of statistical analysis.

Methodology

Before statistical analysis can take place, it is necessary to construct a cost function that describes accurately all relevant factors. First, cost categories must be defined. For example, three types of costs are incurred in providing services to demand deposit customers—fixed maintenance costs, variable maintenance costs, and transactions costs. Fixed maintenance costs arise from routine operations performed on a regular basis for every account, e.g., carrying a master record of an account on a ledger card and preparing and sending monthly statements. Variable maintenance costs, such as FDIC insurance and "free" services, vary with the size of an account. Transactions costs vary directly with the volume of transactions.

Second, measurable variables must be found that explain variations in each general cost category.

Third, other factors that may indirectly influence the costs of providing demand deposit services should be identified, and variables should be defined that explain their effects. For example, to the extent that common production costs exist and cannot be allocated precisely, the level of time deposit operations may have an influence on demand deposit costs. Other factors arise when the cost behavior of several firms is being analyzed. For instance, legal organizational form—unit, branch, or holding company affiliate—may influence the organization of demand deposit operations and, therefore, influence operating costs as well. In addition, wage rates prevailing in local labor markets will have an important effect on demand deposit costs because of the large amount of labor required.

It may be impossible to determine the separate effects of each of these factors because of their complex interrelationships. Moreover, if the volume of output affects the unit cost related to any one of these factors, the accountant's use of standard costs may overlook important variations, that occur with changes in the level of output. Thus, a cost function may be a useful alternative to ordinary accounting practices.

Bell and Murphy [1] and Longbrake [2] have demonstrated that a log-linear cost function of the type defined in the following equation is appropriate for commercial banks and explains most of the variation in demand deposit operating costs among banks:

$$
\begin{aligned}
\log C = {} & \log H + \delta_1 \log N + \delta_2 \log S + \psi_1 \log T_1 + \psi_2 \log T_2 + \psi_3 \log T_3 \\
& + \psi_4 \log T_4 + \psi_5 \log T_5 + \psi_6 \log T_6 + \alpha_1 \log B + \alpha_2 \log M + \alpha_3 \log w \\
& + \alpha_4 \log I,
\end{aligned}
$$

where C is total *direct* operating costs allocated by a bank to the demand deposit function. A glossary of the symbols in the equation appears below. The reader is asked to peruse them before proceeding, and refer to them as necessary in company with the following exposition.

Glossary of Symbols

C	= total *direct* operating costs allocated by a bank to the demand deposit function
log H	= cost function constant
N	= average number of accounts per banking office
S	= average dollar size of a demand deposit account
T_1	= average number of home debits (items posted to the debit column in the ledger for each account) per account
T_2	= average number of deposits per account
T_3	= average number of transit checks (checks written on banks other than the home bank) deposited per account
T_4	= average number of official checks issued per account
T_5	= average number of checks cashed per account
T_6	= average number of transit checks cashed per account
B	= number of offices operated by a bank
M	= ratio of the number of regular checking accounts to the sum of both regular and special accounts
w	= average annual wage rate per demand deposit employee
I	= ratio of the dollar volume of demand deposits to the dollar volume of demand and time deposits, measures the effects of time deposit production activities on demand deposit costs
$\delta_i, \psi_i, \alpha_i$	indicate that percentage change in total cost that occurs when a particular variable changes by 1 percent, given that all other variables remain unchanged

Coefficients of the variables in the cost equation shown above—δ_i, ψ_i, and α_i—indicate that percentage change in total cost occurring when a particular variable changes by 1 percent, with all other variables unchanged. The effect on costs of the addition of a new account with characteristics *identical* to the existing "average" account is measured by the coefficient of log N. The indicated percentage change in costs will include additional fixed maintenance, variable maintenance, and transactions costs. The percentage change in costs caused by an increase in the average size of account S will indicate primarily increases in variable maintenance costs associated with account size. The percentage change in costs caused by an increase in T_1 will show the change in transactions costs due to a large number of home debits per account. Changes in the other transactions variables can be interpreted in a similar fashion.

If a regular account is substituted for a special account, the coefficient of log M will indicate whether costs increase or decrease. The change in costs may result from differences in either fixed maintenance, variable maintenance, or transactions costs for two accounts which are identical in all respects except that one is a special account and the other is a regular account. The coefficient of log w indicates the percentage change in costs which occurs when the wage rate changes. Differences in local wage rates or differences in the mix of personnel engaged in demand deposit operations could cause differences in total costs. Therefore, the effects of maintenance, transactions, and other factors on demand deposit costs are contained within the cost function. Although the cost of a specific demand deposit production operation may not be identifiable, the statistical cost function can be used to determine the costs which occur for a given set of production relationships.

Data for estimating the coefficients of the cost equation shown above were obtained from 964 banks that participated in the 1971 FCA program. These banks ranged in size from $5 million to $6 billion in total deposits. Regression analysis was used to estimate the coefficients; the results are presented in Exhibit 1. These results will serve as a base for developing illustrations of product costing, incremental costing, and cost forecasting below.

Product Costing

Accountants generally recognize two methods of product costing—job order costing and process costing. In job order costing, each job is an accounting unit to which

EXHIBIT   1.   Regression Results for the 1971 Demand Deposit Cost Function*

$$\log C = -1.7345 + .9503 \log N + .3936 \log S + .0467 \log T_1$$
$$(.1792) \quad (.0127) \qquad (.0248) \qquad (.0268)$$

$$+ .1427 \log T_2 + .0742 \log T_3 + .0583 \log T_4 +$$
$$(.0348) \qquad (.0126) \qquad (.0111)$$

$$+ .0183 \log T_5 - .0046 \log T_6 + 1.0150 \log B +$$
$$(.0105) \qquad (.0124) \qquad (.0092)$$

$$- .0626 \log M + .4312 \log w + .0113 \log I$$
$$(.0251) \qquad (.0470) \qquad (.0311)$$

$\bar{R} = .9630$
Standard Error of Estimate = .0998
F-Ratio = 2087.5

*Numbers in parentheses are standard errors of the regression coefficients.

material, labor, and other costs are assigned. However, in process costing, attention centers on total costs incurred by a department for a given time period in relation to the units processed. Dividing total costs by the quantity of units produced gives the average unit cost. Process costing is usually more appropriate for mass production.

Statistical analysis of costs is more applicable in process than in job order costing. Costs are accumulated over a period of time for a specific department, and data concerning production activities in the department are collected for the same time period. However, rather than employing traditional accounting methods to ascertain average unit costs, average unit costs are estimated through a statistical analysis of the cost-output relationship as defined in a cost function. Traditional accounting methods must assume a rather uncomplicated relationship between output and costs (or various categories of costs); however, if complex interrelationships prevail among the various factors influencing total costs, statistical methods may be more appropriate. It must be remembered that data are required for several time periods or for several firms producing essentially the same product before statistical analysis is feasible. Traditional accounting methods do not have such a requirement.

In many respects, servicing demand deposits in a bank is similar to a continuous production process in manufacturing and thus will serve as a good general illustration. Tellers perform several operations including counting cash, verifying deposit amounts, and issuing receipts. The proof department sorts checks by type and identifies questionable checks. The bookkeeping department posts deposits and checks to appropriate accounts. Furthermore, many other activities, in addition to those mentioned above, occur on a regular and continuing basis.

Two kinds of demand deposit accounts—regular and special—customarily exist in most banks. Special accounts have no minimum balance requirement whereas regular accounts do. As a result of the no minimum balance feature, special accounts tend to be held by individuals rather than businesses and they tend to be less active and have smaller average balances than regular accounts. Thus, regular and special accounts are distinct products; however, production operations for both always occur simultaneously. Consequently, the cost of servicing each type of account is not easily separable.

In Exhibit 2, it is shown how the total and average cost per $100 of an average regular and an average special account can be determined from the results of the statistical analysis shown in Exhibit 1. For convenience, values of the various account characteristics and bank characteristics have been selected that are approximately equal to the sample geometric means of these characteristics. In the cost computations for regular accounts, it is assumed that no special accounts exist. However, in the cost computations for special accounts, it is assumed that 1 percent of the accounts are regular. This assumption is required because the log of the mix variable (M) is undefined when there are no regular accounts.

The average regular account in Exhibit 2 is more than twice as costly to service as the average special account. However, the average regular account is only 29 percent as costly per *dollar* of deposits as the average special account. Product costs developed in this way can be used to develop pricing policy. In the case of banks, this kind

EXHIBIT 2. Computation of Average Unit Costs for Regular and Special Checking Accounts

	Regular Account				Special Account		
	(1)	(2)	(3) Cost Function Coefficient	(4) Product of Columns 2 and 3	(5)	(6)	(7) Product of Columns 3 and 6
	Value	Log of Value			Value	Log of Value	
Characteristics of average account							
S Account size	$2,100	3.32222	.3936	1.30763	$ 300	2.47712	.97499
T_1 Home debits/accounts	230	2.36173	.0467	.11029	100	2.00000	.09340
T_2 Deposits/accounts	40	1.60206	.1427	.22861	25	1.39794	.19949
T_3 Transit checks deposited/accounts	180	2.25527	.0742	.16734	20	1.30103	.09654
T_4 Official checks/accounts	3	.47712	.0583	.02782	2	.30103	.01755
T_5 Checks cashed/accounts	30	1.47712	.0183	.02703	30	1.47712	.02703
T_6 Transit checks cashed/accounts	14	1.14613	− .0046	− .00527	16	1.20412	− .00554
Bank characteristics							
N Number of accounts	3,250	3.51188	.9503	3.33734	3,250	3.51188	3.33734
B Number of offices	3	.47712	1.0150	.48428	3	.47712	.48428
M Regular accounts/all accounts	100%	.00000	− .0626	.00000	1%	− 2.00000	.12520
w Annual wage rate	$5,700	3.75587	.4312	1.61953	$5,700	3.75587	1.61953
I Demand deposits/total deposits	40%	− .39794	.0113	− .00450	40%	− .39794	− .00450
H Cost function constant				− 1.73447			− 1.73447
Total cost (log)				5.53860			5.23084
(antilog)				$345,623.00			$170,054.00
Average cost per account				$ 35.45			$ 17.44
Average cost per $100				$ 1.69			$ 5.81

of information is useful in establishing service charge schedules. It should be noted that the average unit cost of an account need not be the same for each set of account characteristic and bank characteristic variables. Any bank which knows its values for the variables in Exhibit 2 may determine its average unit costs by following the demonstrated computational procedure.

This method of product costing would be useful in any business enterprise that produces more than one product on a regular and continuing basis using essentially the same types of resources. For example, different types of telephone service—private, party, or commercial—could be costed using the methods described above. Other possible applications might include the manufacture of canned and processed foods, book publishing, manufacture of apparel, manufacture of consumer durable goods such as automobiles, refrigerators, television sets, appliances, lawn mowers, and so on.

Incremental Costing

Incremental or differential costs are the increases or decreases in total costs, or the changes in specific elements of cost, that result from some variation in operations. An incremental costing approach to decision making is important when certain costs are fixed and, as such, are not influenced by changes in operations. Ordinarily such a situation occurs in the short run when scale of operations cannot be changed. When the decision is whether or not to accept another order or expand output from a given level, and certain costs are fixed or are relatively inflexible, use of standard costs or average unit costs may lead to the wrong decision. This could happen because the incremental cost of the additional output may differ from the change in total costs indicated by multiplying the additional output by the average unit cost.

Situations in which an incremental cost approach to decision making may be appropriate include: taking on new orders; increasing, decreasing, or eliminating production of certain products; replacing old equipment with new; and so forth. In commercial banks, it may be useful to know the incremental costs of a new demand deposit account, especially if it is tied to a loan arrangement, so that an appropriate pricing strategy can be developed. Incremental costs can also be developed for specific types of demand deposit accounts that differ in various respects from the average account.

The usual accounting approach to differential costing is to identify variable and fixed costs. Then, in a particular situation the affected variable costs can be used to determine the differential cost. However, if variable costs cannot be determined easily or if variable costs do not remain constant per unit of output at various levels of output, the usual accounting techniques may prove to be insufficient.

Statistical cost analysis may improve the accuracy of incremental cost determination in such circumstances because estimates of incremental (marginal) costs can be derived directly from the cost function for every variation in the basic product that might exist. For example, incremental costs can be determined for each type of transaction that is identified in the demand deposit cost function. Thus, the incremental cost of one additional home debit per account is the change in total cost, C, which results from an increase in home debits per account, T_1, while all other variables in the cost equation shown above remain unchanged. This incremental cost is computed by taking the partial derivative of total cost, C, with respect to home debits per account, T_1. In the present instance, the incremental cost of one additional home debit per account is equal to the cost function coefficient of T_1 (ψ_1) times total cost (C) divided by T_1. Thus, the incremental cost of an additional home debit per regular demand account is computed in column 3 of Exhibit 3 by multiplying the appropriate cost function coefficient in column 1 (.0467) by total cost ($345,623) and then dividing by the number of home debits per regular account (230). Incremental cost per unit, shown in column 4, is obtained by dividing the incremental cost figure in column 3 by the number of regular accounts (9,750). Incremental costs for other variations in the product are calculated in a similar fashion and the results are shown in Exhibit 3.

The incremental cost of an additional regular demand deposit account that is *identical* to the average regular account is $33.69. This is less than the average unit cost of $35.45 for an existing regular account as indicated in Exhibit 2. However, the incremental cost of an additional special account is slightly larger than the average unit cost of a special account. Thus, increases in the number of regular accounts would reduce average unit cost, but increases in the number of special checking accounts would increase average unit cost. To the extent that unutilized capacity exists, management may wish to promote regular rather than special accounts.

An additional dollar in a special account is more than three times as costly to service as an additional dollar in a regular account. This indicates that the cost of providing extra services to small special checking accounts is greater per dollar than the cost of providing additional services to large regular checking accounts. This also implies that the incremental cost associated with an additional dollar of deposits most likely depends on the size of the deposit, i.e., fixed account maintenance costs can be spread over more dollars in large accounts. Home debits are associated with

EXHIBIT   3.   Incremental Costs for Various Characteristics of Regular and Special Accounts

		Regular Accounts				Special Accounts		
		(1)	(2)	(3)	(4)	(5)	(6)	(7)
	Characteristics	Cost Function Coefficient	Value	Incremental Cost	Incremental Cost per Unit*	Value	Incremental Cost	Incremental Cost per Unit*
N**	Account	$\delta_1 =$ .9503	9,750	$ 33.69	$33.6867	9,750	$ 17.67	$17.6664
S	Account size	$\delta_2 =$ .3936	$ 2,100	64.78	.0066	$ 300	223.11	.0229
T_1	Home debits/accounts	$\psi_1 =$ .0467	230	70.18	.0072	100	79.42	.0081
T_2	Deposits/accounts	$\psi_2 =$ .1427	40	1,233.01	.1265	25	970.67	.0996
T_3	Transit checks deposited/accounts	$\psi_3 =$ .0742	180	142.47	.0146	20	630.90	.0647
T_4	Official checks/accounts	$\psi_4 =$ .0583	3	6,716.61	.6889	2	4,957.07	.5084
$(T_5 - T_6)***$	Nontransit checks cashed/accounts	$\psi_5 =$ .0183	16	210.83	.0216	14	103.73	.0106
T_6	Transit checks cashed/accounts	$\psi_6 = -$ .0046 $\alpha_2 = -$ .0626	14	97.27	.0100	16	54.84	.0056
C	Total Costs		$345,623			$170,054		

*Incremental cost per unit is determined by dividing incremental cost by 9,750 accounts.

**The number of accounts variable (N) includes both regular and special accounts. However, the mix variable also contains both regular and special accounts. Let $N = (N_R + N_S)/B$ and $M = N_R/(N_R + N_S)$. Then, the incremental cost of another regular account $= (\delta_1 - \alpha_2) [C/N_R + N_S] + \alpha_2(C/N_R)$. The incremental cost of another special account $= (\delta_1 - \alpha_2) [C/N_R + N_S]$.

***Nontransit checks cashed per account equals $(T_5 - T_6)$ while transit checks cashed equals T_6. The sum of these two categories is total checks cashed (T_5). The incremental cost of nontransit checks cashed $= \psi_5(C/T_5)$. The incremental cost of transit checks cashed $= \psi_5(C/A_5) + \psi_6(C/T_6)$.

highly routinized operations which may explain why there is little difference in the incremental costs of home debits in regular and special checking accounts. With the exception of transit checks deposited, incremental costs of changes in other account characteristics are greater for regular accounts than they are for special accounts. There are only one-ninth as many transit checks deposited annually in special accounts as in regular accounts. The difference in incremental costs for transit checks deposited in regular and special accounts may occur if the cost of handling the first few transit checks is high while the cost of handling each additional transit check declines.

Suppose management wishes to know the cost of a specific regular checking account that differs in identifiable ways from the average regular account. Incremental cost analysis can be used to help determine the cost of this *example* regular account. Characteristics of the example regular account to be costed are shown in column 1 of Exhibit 4 and characteristics of the average regular account are contained in column 2. Column 3 is the difference of the first two columns. The incremental cost in column 5 is the product of the figure in column 3 and the incremental cost per item in column 4, which was computed in Exhibit 3.

Although the cost of the example regular account in Exhibit 4 is considerably greater than the cost of the average regular account, the cost per $100 is lower because of the larger balance. This result suggests that service charge rates should be based on account size and the number of various types of transactions. Knowledge of incremental costs can be used to establish variable rate service charge schedules which reflect the actual cost incurred in servicing a particular account more accurately than using average unit costs or some kind of standard costing procedure.

EXHIBIT 4. Computation of the Cost of a Regular Checking Account Which Differs from the Average Regular Checking Account

	Characteristics	(1) Value Example Account	(2) Value Average Account	(3) Difference (1) − (2)	(4) Incremental Cost per Item	(5) Change in Average Cost per Account
S	Account size	$5,000	$2,100	$2,900	.0066	$19.14
T_1	Home debits/accounts	400	230	170	.0072	1.22
T_2	Deposits/account	50	40	10	.1265	1.26
T_3	Transit checks deposited/account	300	180	120	.0146	1.75
T_4	Official checks/account	5	3	2	.6889	1.38
$(T_5 - T_6)$	Nontransit checks cashed/account	20	16	4	.0216	.09
T_6	Transit checks cashed/account	20	14	6	.0100	.04
Total						$24.88
Cost of Average Regular Account						+ 35.45
Cost of Example Regular Accounts						$60.33
Cost per $100 of the Example Regular Account						$ 1.21

Such an approach to pricing may be useful in nonfinancial firms that produce a product or service capable of being differentiated or varied in several ways. For example, the incremental costing method may be useful in establishing the cost of selling particular types of merchandise in retailing firms or in determining the cost of handling particular types of customer credit accounts.

Cost Forecasting

When management contemplates or expects some change in operations at a future date, it is important to forecast the effects of this change on costs. The use of statistical analysis in forecasting, especially for forecasting sales, is well established. However, cost forecasts ordinarily are based on a nonstatistical evaluation of the production facilities, equipment, labor, and materials required to produce enough to meet the sales forecast. When statistical methods are used to forecast costs, it usually involves either a simple regression analysis of volume and cost or, in rare cases, a multiple regression analysis.

The principal danger inherent in statistical cost forecasting is that future behavior may differ substantially from past cost behavior, thus making forecasts unreliable. Changes in plant and equipment, materials, products, production techniques, personnel, internal organization, prices paid for materials and labor, and many other factors will tend to impair the reliability of statistical cost forecasts. Nevertheless, in some circumstances statistical cost forecasting may provide helpful information. For example, if prices of materials and labor have varied in the past, this information can be included in the statistical cost function. Then, the effect of expected future changes in these prices on costs can be determined. In a firm that operates several plants or branches, all producing and selling the same product, statistical cost analysis may prove useful in forecasting the costs of *operating* a new plant or branch. Statistical analysis is not as likely to be useful in determining the cost of constructing a new plant. Several illustrations of cost forecasting are given below.

Turning to the banking example, suppose a branch bank is operating three offices with an average of 3,250 demand deposit accounts per office. It is considering opening a new office that it expects to be able to attract 3,250 new demand deposit accounts having characteristics essentially similar to those of existing demand deposits. Management is concerned about the effect of this expansion on its costs of operation for demand deposits. The change in costs can be forecast by making appropriate changes in the statistical cost function shown in the cost equation below:

$$\log C_1 = \log C_0 + \alpha_1 (\log B_1 - \log B_0)$$
$$= 5.53860 + 1.0150 (.60206 - .47712)$$
$$= 5.53860 + .12681$$
$$= 5.66541.$$

Total costs are $345,623 before the addition of the new branch and will be $462,820 afterwards, an increase of $117,197. Average unit cost before expansion is $35.45, but after expansion it will be $35.60. The $.15 increase in average unit cost reflects added costs of coordination associated with the operation of the new branch.

Suppose that this branch bank is not considering opening a new branch but expects the number of demand deposits handled by each branch to increase from 3,250 to 4,333. The change in costs that occurs when 1,083 new demand accounts are added to each of the three existing branches can be computed in the same manner as described above: 5.53860 + .9503 (3.63682 − 3.51188) = 5.65733. Total costs will be $454,289 and average cost per account will be $34.95, a decline of $.50 per account. In both of the cost forecasting examples given here, there will be 13,000 accounts and $27.3 million in deposits (assuming that average account size is $2,100). In one example, though, there are four offices while in the other there are only three. Having one more branch for the same number of accounts and the same amount of deposits causes a difference of $7,531 or nearly 2 percent in total operating costs.

Management can also forecast the effect of an increase in the average annual wage paid per employee. Suppose management expects wages to rise by 10 percent from $5,700 to $6,270. Total costs will be: 5.53860 + .4312 (3.79727 − 3.75587) = 5.55645 or $360,125. Average unit costs will be $36.94, an increase of $1.49 per account. The effects of other anticipated changes, in addition to those illustrated above, can be determined in the same way. In fact, the effects of all expected changes on total costs can be forecast simultaneously.

Any business firm able to construct its own cost function can use it to forecast the effects of changes in any or all of its variables. This procedure is legitimate so long as there is no significant change in the production-cost relationship.

Concluding Remarks

These uses of statistical cost analysis were demonstrated for commercial banks. However, any business enterprise which produces its products on a relatively regular and continuing basis and which maintains detailed records about output, resource prices, product characteristics, and costs can construct its own statistical cost function and use it for product costing, incremental costing, or cost forecasting. Thus, a host of business enterprises have the potential to use some kind of management-oriented statistical cost analysis.

If the production-cost relationship is more complex than that presumed in break-even analysis or variable budgeting, statistical cost analysis may provide useful supplemental information that these more conventional cost accounting techniques are incapable of providing. It is not suggested that information derived from employing statistical techniques should supplant other types of information; rather, it is urged that statistical cost information be used in conjunction with other cost accounting information to help *improve* decision making.

REFERENCES

1. BELL, FREDERICK W. and NEIL B. MURPHY, *Costs in Commercial Banking: A Quantitative Analysis of Bank Behavior and Its Relation to Bank Regulation,* Research Report No. 41, Federal Reserve Bank of Boston, April, 1968.
2. LONGBRAKE, WILLIAM A., "Productive Efficiency in Commercial Banking: The Impact of Bank Organization Structure and Bank Size on the Cost of Demand Deposit Services," Federal Deposit Insurance Corporation, Working Paper No. 72-10.

Estimating the Cost of
Your Bank's Funds

Ronald D. Watson

16

By the time Franklin National Bank finally succumbed in 1974, it had been assured an honored spot in modern banking theory as the texbook example of how *not* to run a bank. One of Franklin's weaknesses was the incorrect method its management used to estimate the cost of the bank's funds.[1] During a period of high interest rates, the bank consistently underestimated the cost of raising money. In fact, the cost of the money that Franklin borrowed to invest was higher than the return on the investments it was making.

Most bankers are far more sensitive to this problem than Franklin's management was, but being aware of how important it is to know the cost of money and being able to make an accurate estimate of that cost are two very different things. Making good cost estimates takes time and requires a thorough understanding of how investors make their decisions. Further, these estimates must reflect current conditions in the money markets instead of being based on costs in the past; and they must take account of the effect that the bank's choice of a capital structure may have on its cost of funds. Getting an accurate estimate of the cost of funds poses some tough computational problems, but there isn't any other way to find out what rate of return is required to make a profit.

Reprinted, with deletions, from *Business Review,* May/June 1978, pp. 3–11, by permission of the Federal Reserve Bank of Philadelphia and the author.

[1]Sanford Rose, "What Really Went Wrong at Franklin National," *Fortune,* October 1974, p. 118.

The Old Way: Historical Average Costs

In the past, the most common method of estimating the cost of a bank's funds was to add together all the net expenses (interest, reserve requirements, and other expenses less service charge income) of borrowing current funds and divide the total by the amount being borrowed. This gave an historical estimate of the average return that had to be earned on assets acquired with these funds for the bank to break even in its investment activities. If the shareholders were to receive a return on the funds they supplied, a profit margin had to be added to this basic historical cost of funds estimate. . . .

But historical costs can be extremely unreliable as a pricing guide if conditions are changing over time. When interest rates are rising, the average cost of funds already obtained will be below the cost of replacing those funds by new borrowing, and the bank may accept new investments it should reject. When rates are dropping, the historical cost of funds will be higher than replacement costs, and the bank may be led to set too high a standard for new investments, passing up opportunities to make profits. Historical estimates can be unreliable also when a bank's capital structure is changing. If a bank's debt is increasing faster than its equity, for example, it may come to be regarded as a riskier operation, and this perception of added risk may raise the cost of the bank's funds from all sources. It's because of drawbacks such as these that bankers have turned from historical cost estimates to some basic economic principles for generating cost estimates.

The New Way: A Bit of Theory

The theory behind this new cost estimating method starts from a reasonable premise—that bank managers should make investment decisions which make the bank more profitable. This theory rationalizes the rules of thumb that many bankers actually use when they look at profitability—rules such as adding in a desired long-term profit margin as they try to gauge the expected cost of funds over time.

Matching Added Costs with Added Revenues

To obtain the largest profit available, a bank should compare the expected return from an investment with the current cost of obtaining the money needed to finance that investment. If the return (in the long run) from a new loan or security doesn't exceed the probable cost of financing that asset while the bank owns it, the bank would do better not to acquire it.[2] The added amount that would be brought in by

---

[2]Statement of the $MC = MR$ principle is intentionally very general, so that complications such as tied-product returns and discounted future benefits can be accommodated within the definition.

lending one more unit of money to a borrower is the *marginal revenue*. The added amount that would be paid out to procure one more unit of loanable funds is the *marginal cost*.

The use of current information in making the cost of funds estimates is extremely important. The cost of a bank's funds normally will change as market interest rates move. Some cost changes, as for CDs and Federal funds, will be highly visible, while others, as for demand deposits and savings accounts, will not be so obvious. The banker must keep abreast of both. As interest rates rise, a banker will find that other financial institutions will compete more vigorously for these funds, and the depositors themselves will make an effort to shift into the more lucrative investments. To attract and hold these monies a bank may have to step up its advertising, resort to premiums, and expand its menu of depositor services. The result will be a higher cost to the bank for funds from these sources.

Less obvious will be the rising cost of equity funds—the bank's common stock. The target rate that a bank's management sets for returns to shareholders should be adjusted to reflect any changes in yields on other long-term investments. Investors who have the alternative of investing in long-term bonds at 8 or 9 percent with little risk must expect to receive more than that from an investment in common stock, or they will stay with the safer security. When long-term interest rates rise 1 or 2 percentage points, the return to common shareholders must move by a similar amount. In a competitive money market, the bank's shareholders always will have investment options that offer the current market rates. Even though a bank may not be selling a brand new stock issue in this high-rate environment, it still must aim to earn the competitive rate for its current owners. If it doesn't, the owners would be better off to instruct management to pay the maximum dividend possible. The stockholders then could use the extra dividends to make investments elsewhere at the higher prevailing rates.

When New Costs Don't Match Old

The decision on a new investment should be made on the basis of the cost of new money. Even if a bank were lucky enough to obtain a large pool of funds at rates that are below current market levels, shareholders, who bear the risk of loss, should be the beneficiaries of this good fortune. If historical costs are used to set current loan rates, the benefits of having these relatively cheap funds will be transferred to the borrowers rather than being retained for the common stockholders. If circumstances were reversed, it's unlikely that borrowers would be willing to pay high interest rates on loans from a bank which had unusually *high* average costs. The fact that the bank had the misfortune of being stuck with large amounts of funds acquired when rates were very high wouldn't matter if cheaper sources were available elsewhere. Regardless of costs or the effect on profits available for stockholders, bankers can't charge borrowers a rate that is much higher than rates available elsewhere. So historical costs should not be considered in making today's investment decisions. Rather, the cost of an additional dollar of funds should be compared with the return that will be realized when that additional dollar is invested. So much for the theory.

But how should an estimate of the marginal cost of funds be made? Although averaging historical costs is relatively easy, figuring out the full cost of a new dollar of funds is another matter—especially if it's necessary to estimate the impact that using various sources of funds will have on the cost of other sources.

Marginal Cost Estimation Methods

Two basic options are available to the banker who is trying to make a marginal cost estimate. One is to identify the source of funds that the bank currently is using to raise new money. Once this source is identified, an estimate might be made of the cost of raising another block of these funds. This estimate of the marginal cost of a single source will serve as the *hurdle rate*—the minimum required rate of return—for any new investment of average riskiness. The other strategy is to estimate the marginal cost of each of the sources being employed within the bank. By weighting the cost of new dollars drawn from each source by the amount to be raised from that source, bankers can construct a weighted average of marginal costs. The second method sounds more complex, but it has some advantages over the first that make it worth considering.

The Marginal Cost of a Single Source

The most straightforward approach is to determine which source of funds the bank wants to use, compute its marginal cost, and use that estimate as the hurdle rate. Presumably, the source selected will be the cheapest one available to the bank. For example, if CDs are the source a banker turns to, the cost of additional dollars borrowed in that market is the relevant marginal cost. The interest rate on CDs is easy enough to determine, but this rate is only part of the real marginal cost of these funds.

Suppose a bank—for example, the hypothetical Ninth National Bank—wants to borrow $1 million for expansion. If it turns to the CD market and pays 7 percent, that interest rate is the base for the bank's cost calculations. But the job of estimating the marginal cost of this source is just beginning. The bank will incur a small cost in acquiring and repaying this money, and that cost should be included in the estimate. Also, there will be a reserve requirement against this source of funds (currently 1 percent to 6 percent, depending on term to maturity);[3] any obligation to keep a portion of the borrowed money in the form of idle cash raises the effective

---

[3]See "Member Bank Reserve Requirements," Federal Reserve *Bulletin,* August 1977, p. A9.

cost of the funds. These adjustments to the basic interest cost are relatively easy to make.

A much more difficult adjustment to the cost is the one required to compensate suppliers of other sources of funds for the added risk created by this new borrowing. Ninth National's leverage—its ratio of debt to equity—will be increased by the addition of more CD funds. Since higher leverage produces more risk for the bank, other creditors and shareholders may not be as willing to continue supplying Ninth National with funds at the same interest rates as before. Depositors whose funds are covered by deposit insurance probably won't care. But the holders of big deposits

---

The Single Marginal Source Calculation

Suppose the management of Ninth National is looking for another $100 and wants to raise the money by issuing CDs. It will be obliged to pay the going market interest rate for funds (say, 7 percent). It must then add to this amount several surcharges which raise the effective rate. The cost of reserve requirements on the CD funds might, for example, be 3 percent (annualized), the cost to acquire such funds 0.5 percent (annualized), and the cost of servicing the funds 0.3 percent (annualized). Using the formula

$$\text{Costs of Funds} = \frac{(\text{Interest Rate} + \text{Servicing Costs} + \text{Acquisition Costs} + \text{Insurance})}{(1 - \text{Reserve Requirement})}$$

the explicit cost of the CD funds is found to be 0.0804 or about 8 percent.

This is only part of the job. Since the bank now is being more heavily financed with short-term borrowed funds, the risk is greater. Both the other suppliers of borrowed funds and the shareholders may wish to raise the cost of future funds they provide for this bank. This additional indirect cost must be added to the explicit cost estimate. Suppose that raising $100 of new CD funds created $.20 in added costs for other sources of funds. The *real* marginal cost of the CD funds would be estimated as their explicit cost plus the risk spillover cost:

$$\text{Marginal Cost} = 8.04 \text{ percent} + 0.2 \text{ percent} = 8.24 \text{ percent.}$$

Failure to include all of these costs other than interest in the estimate will lead to a hurdle rate for new investments that understates the real cost of new funds.

and CDs might, because they are not fully insured, and their concern could cause them to shift their funds to another bank or demand a higher return from Ninth National. In either case, the bank's cost to attract and hold such deposits is likely to rise.

The same thing will occur with the capital note holders and the common stockholders. When they sense that risks are increasing, they'll seek a higher return on their investments. The ones that presently own these securities can't automatically start charging the bank a higher rate for funds that already have been committed, but investors will demand a higher return for any new invested funds. The bank will be obliged to increase its earnings and ultimately its dividends to stockholders in order to compensate them for their higher risk. If it doesn't, the interests of the current shareholders will be harmed, and that would be inconsistent with management's obligation to run the bank in a way which enhances the shareholders' wealth (see "The Single Marginal Source Calculation").

In any event, it should be clear that the impact which heavy use of one source of funding has on the cost of other sources should be included in any analysis of the cost of marginal funds. This risk spillover cost is very difficult to measure, but it must be included in the calculation. Accordingly, the cost of new CD money can be found only after considering the direct interest cost, any acquisition and servicing costs, reserve requirements, and risk spillover costs.[4]

The same principles apply to estimating the cost of demand and time deposits (handling, acquisition, reserve requirement, and deposit insurance costs are likely to be higher than for CDs) or capital notes (risk spillover may raise the cost of the bank's CDs and uninsured deposits as well as the cost of its common stock). Similarly, the nominal, before-tax cost of new common stock may overstate its real cost because it will have the effect of reducing overall risk and is likely to lower the net cost of other debt sources.

Averaging All Marginal Costs

The other approach to calculating a bank's marginal cost is to presume that the institution will be financed during the next few months in pretty much the same way as it's being financed now. Checking and savings accounts will open and close and the bank will experience deposits and withdrawals. But as long as advertising doesn't diminish and services don't deteriorate, total dollars from each retail source will change only gradually. The bank will wind up paying the going rate to hold funds from each of these sources. Similarly, market rates (plus associated costs) will be paid for any CDs sold even if they are simply replacements for maturing issues. Finally, the bank will have to pay competitive returns for capital if it expects to keep

---

[4]A more technical explanation of this calculation can be found in Ronald D. Watson, "The Marginal Cost of Funds Concept in Banking," Federal Reserve Bank of Philadelphia, Research Paper No. 19, January 1977; reprinted with revisions in the *Journal of Bank Research* Vol. 8 (Autumn 1977), pp. 136–47.

access to these sources of funds. In short, the mix of sources doesn't change and the bank must pay current rates for each source used (see "The Average of Marginal Costs Calculation").

The Average of Marginal Costs Calculation

Since figuring out the risk spillover costs is very difficult, the banker might prefer to calculate his explicit marginal costs for each source of funds and average those estimates to find out what the entire pool of funds presently is costing. Suppose that the bank is structured as follows:

	Added Dollars	Explicit Cost*	
Demand deposits	$30	.05	$1.50
Time deposits	40	.07	2.80
CDs	10	.08	.80
Capital notes	10	.09	.90
Common stock	10	.22	2.20
	$100		$8.20

Then Ninth National's estimate would be: marginal cost $= \dfrac{\$8.20}{\$100.00}$ $= 0.082 = 8.2$ percent.

*With acquisition, servicing, and reserve costs included.

If Ninth National is trying to calculate the overall cost of this pool of funds, it will need an estimate of the marginal cost of each source employed. That estimate must include any explicit interest payments, acquisition and servicing costs, deposit insurance, and reserve requirements. Such a calculation will be straightforward for CDs and capital notes but very difficult for demand and time deposits (even if the bank has a reliable cost accounting system). Estimating the percentage of the advertising budget that goes to keeping demand deposit levels steady or the additional advertising that would be required to increase time and savings deposits by a few percent is a very uncertain undertaking. At best it will involve a substantial amount of informed judgment.

When management is satisfied with these marginal cost estimates, an overall average can be calculated by multiplying each estimate by the fraction of the bank's funds that will be raised from this source in the near future. The weighted average will indicate the cost to the bank of buying the funds that will be used for investments or loans made during that time and it will serve as a minimum target rate of return for a new investment of average risk.

For all its complexity, this estimate has an advantage over the single-source cost estimate. With the weighted average approach there is no need to try to calculate the impact that risk spillovers have on the cost of other sources. The present level of the bank's leverage risk already is reflected in the prices of its liabilities and equity securities. If the composition of the pool of funds doesn't change, the risks aren't going to change significantly. The risk spillover that each source of funds creates for the other sources is neutralized in this pooling process and need not be estimated separately. As a result, estimates of the current marginal cost of each source, averaged across all sources, will provide a correct estimate of the bank's pool of funds without further risk adjustments.

Choose Your Poison

Both of the cost estimation methods just described have pitfalls. Calculating the marginal cost of a single source such as CDs looks easy. The interest rate is known and the reserve and handling costs are measurable. But estimating the size of the risk spillover adjustment that should be added to the other costs to get the real marginal cost is very difficult.

In addition, one of the basic principles of economic theory is that businesses should tap each source of funds until the cost of the next dollar raised from that source is the same as the cost of a dollar from each other available source. That's the way to maximize profit, since it keeps money costs as low as possible. If a bank concentrates its attention on the cost of just one source, it may lose sight of the availability of funds from other sources that are cheaper.

Computing a weighted average of marginal costs keeps a banker looking at all of his costs simultaneously. Estimating the marginal cost of the bank's demand and time deposits remains a sticky problem, but the uncertainties of calculating risk spillover adjustments are avoided. This method will not provide the manager with the information needed to balance the marginal cost of one source against the marginal cost of another. For that he needs a marginal cost estimate that includes the risk spillover adjustment for each type of funds used. But the banker doesn't have to worry abour risk spillover adjustments when he uses this method. He may not be getting the cheapest mix of funds, especially if he has overlooked a relatively cheap source; but he will be getting an accurate estimate of the cost of the pool of funds he's using. In this he has an advantage over his counterpart who computes the marginal cost of a single source but then continues to raise funds from all of the available sources. If the real marginal costs of each source are not really equal, use of the single-source technique will produce a faulty estimate.

A Sensible Procedure

Both processes produce the right answer when used correctly. And both are difficult to use correctly. The best approach is to remember that both methods *can* give the right answer. Calculate the bank's cost of funds both ways. Use a sharp pencil. Analyze the cost estimates employed. Think about the effect that leverage risk has on the cost of various sources of funds. Analyze what you're really paying for demand deposits.

If both methods can give a correct answer, the calculations you make should give the *same answer*. If they do, you have a cost of funds estimate. If they don't, you had better try to figure out why. Do you need better data about your costs? Is the bank being financed with too expensive a mix of sources? Are the institution's costs under both calculations higher than previously thought? Has the bank been adding new business at a loss rather than a profit?

The exercise may be frustrating. It may be disturbing. But a sharp banker has to go through it if he's to do a first-rate job of managing profits.

Income Tax of Commercial Banks

Margaret E. Bedford

17

Commercial banks are subject to a variety of taxes, including income or profits taxes, property taxes, taxes on the ownership of bank shares or capital, franchise taxes, and an assortment of other miscellaneous taxes. Of these, income taxes are clearly the most important. In 1974, the most recent date for which figures are available, income taxes amounted to $1.8 billion and are estimated to account for three-fourths of all taxes paid by commercial banks. Federal income taxes comprised 77 percent of this amount, and state and local income taxes comprised 23 percent.

In view of the importance of income taxation to commercial banks, this article examines the extent to which the income tax burden of banks has changed in recent years. Attention is given to the impact of tax code modifications on the tax burden and the various approaches commercial banks have taken to minimize their tax burdens. Also examined is the differential burden imposed by Federal income taxes and state and local income taxes on banks in the nation, the Tenth Federal Reserve District, and on banks of varying deposit sizes.

Federal Income Taxation of Banks

Federal income taxes for banks are computed by first determining net taxable income. In general, the base for taxable income represents income from operating

Reprinted, with deletions, from the Federal Reserve Bank of Kansas City, *Monthly Review*, July-August 1975, pp. 3-11, by permission of the publisher and the author.

transactions, such as interest on loans and securities (excluding interest on municipal securities), trust department income, service charges, etc., less allowable operating expenses, including wages, interest paid on deposits and borrowed money, occupancy expense of bank premises, etc. This figure is then adjusted to make allowance for net loan losses or recoveries, net securities gains or losses, and for a variety of other modifications to income.

Federal Tax Burden

The average tax burden for commercial banks has fallen significantly between 1961 and 1974.[1] Table 1 indicates that the ratio of Federal income taxes to net income for all insured commercial banks over this period moved from 34.8 percent to 14.5 percent, a drop of 20.3 percentage points. Similarly, the effective tax rate at Tenth District banks declined 17.7 percentage points to 18.6 percent over the same interval.

Banks of all sizes generally experienced a reduced tax burden between 1961 and 1974. The sharpest declines, however, were experienced by the largest banks. The effective tax rate for banks with deposits under $10 million dropped by only one-fifth or 5.2 percentage points, but banks with deposits over $100 million cut their effective tax rates by two-thirds or 23.3 percentage points. As a result, the effective tax rate in 1974 generally declined as bank size increased, giving the overall tax structure the appearance of regressivity. U.S. banks with deposits under $10 million, for example, paid Federal taxes equal to 23.4 percent of net income, compared with 16.3 percent for banks with deposits between $10 and $100 million and 13.0 percent for larger

---

[1]Throughout this article the tax burden, or effective tax rate, of commercial banks is measured by dividing "provision for income taxes" by net income or profits. Provision for income taxes, as reported annually to the FDIC, includes estimated income taxes related to the current year's operations but does not reflect adjustments (refunds or additional taxes paid) for previous years. Net income as used in measuring the tax burden is equivalent to gross profits before taxes. It is not taxable income, but rather total income less normal operating expenses. More specifically, net income includes such items as interest earned on state and local government securities, net long-term capital gains, etc.

This ratio is, of course, potentially subject to certain distortions. For example, a bank's provision for income taxes in a given year may differ significantly from the bank's actual income tax liability. A systematic bias in the figures for all banks though is unlikely. No adjustment has been made for the fact that the interest yield on tax-exempt securities is generally less than on taxable issues, thus imposing an implicit tax burden on investors in tax-exempts. Also net income could be biased by the timing of realizing loan losses and long-term capital gains or losses as well as changes in depreciation methods, etc. The importance of most of these possible biases cannot be determined, but none is likely to result in a regular distortion over time.

Since bank reporting procedures were modified in 1969, the figures have been adjusted to maintain comparability over the 1961-74 period. Some slight variations, however, still exist. A complete description of the 1969 changes in reporting procedures appeared in the *Federal Reserve Bulletin*, July 1970, pp. 564-72. For the 1961-68 period, net profits and recoveries (or net losses and charge-offs) on loans, securities, and other transactions were added to (subtracted from) net current operating earnings to obtain the pretax net income figures used in this article. For the 1969-74 period, interest paid on capital notes and debentures, which was reported by banks as an operating expense in the latest period but included with dividends on preferred stock in the 1961-68 period, was added to the FDIC figures for income before taxes and securities gains or losses. In addition, gross securities gains (losses) and gross extraordinary credits (charges) were added to (deducted from) net operating income to obtain the 1969-74 net income figures.

Table 1. Federal Tax Burdens at Insured Commercial Banks, United States and Tenth District (in percent)

	Ratio of Federal Income Taxes Paid to Net Income				Changes in Effective Tax Rates
	1961	1965	1969	1974	1961–74
All banks:					
United States	34.8	23.5	20.4	14.5	− 20.3
Tenth District	36.3	27.0	25.7	18.6	− 17.7
By deposit size:					
Less than $10 million					
United States	28.6	21.5	19.7	23.4	− 5.2
Tenth District	30.1	22.5	21.9	23.6	−6.5
$10 to $100 million					
United States	33.6	25.7	22.2	16.3	− 17.3
Tenth District	36.3	27.1	24.3	18.2	− 18.1
$100 million and over					
United States	36.3	23.0	19.7	13.0	− 23.3
Tenth District	41.6	30.8	30.3	16.0	− 25.6

Source: Reports of Income, Federal Deposit Insurance Corporation.
Note: Data for 1961-68 are not strictly comparable with data for 1969-74.

banks. Effective tax rates for banks of different sizes in the Tenth District were somewhat greater than the national averages, but exhibited the same general trends.

The shifts in effective tax rates reflect both modifications in tax laws and bank efficiency in exercising legal tax shelters. Federal income tax rates applicable to commercial banks generally fell from 1961 to 1965, but tended to rise thereafter. Specifically, between 1961 and 1965 the tax rate on the first $25,000 of taxable income was reduced from 30 percent to 22 percent and on income over $25,000 from 52 percent to 48 percent. In 1969 and the first quarter of 1970, a 10 percent surtax was imposed on all taxable income. Also, in 1969 banks were required for the first time to treat net long-term capital gains on securities as ordinary income. The tax rate for long-term capital gains on securities taken during a transitional period after 1969 and the tax rate on other long-term gains were raised. These tax law modifications suggest that reductions in tax rates contributed importantly to the sharp drop in the Federal tax burden experienced by commercial banks between 1961 and 1965. The remainder of the drop during this period, however, and that which has occurred since then is primarily attributable to bank utilization of tax shelters.

Tax Shelters

A number of provisions in the tax laws permit banks to reduce their tax liabilities. Two of these options are investing in state and local government obligations, the interest from which is wholly tax-exempt at the Federal level, and transferring funds to bad debt reserves to allow for future losses on loans. Tax benefits are also realized by banks engaged in lease financing and foreign operations. Banks leasing equipment are able to realize tax savings from the investment tax credit and from deductions for depreciation. Banks with foreign operations are permitted deductions for most taxes paid to foreign governments, or, alternatively, foreign income taxes may be claimed as a tax credit rather than a deduction. During the 1960s, the differential treatment of long-term capital gains and losses on securities also served to reduce the tax burden of commercial banks.

Each of these tax code features will be discussed in detail subsequently, but their relative importance for commercial banks in 1972 has been estimated in Table 2.[2] As can be seen, sizable tax benefits were realized from the interest exemption on state and local government securities and the net transfers to bad debt reserves. Gross depreciation also resulted in a sizable tax saving, but the significance of this figure must be heavily discounted. Available data do not permit the segregation of depreciation on leased assets from that on assets used directly in bank operations. Depreciation on regular plant and equipment is an expense of doing business, while depreciation benefits realized through leasing operations reflect, at least in part, a tax shelter.[3] Finally, the investment and foreign tax credits resulted in small, but noteworthy, tax savings. On balance, if these features had all been eliminated, the tax

[2]The figures in the first column of Table 2 are for 1972, the most recent year for which comprehensive figures are available, and were supplied by the Internal Revenue Service and the Federal Deposit Insurance Corporation. While the magnitude of individual entries has almost certainly changed since 1972, tax regulations have not experienced any major revisions, suggesting that the relative importance of the individual entries is probably the same.

In examining the figures, a number of data limitations must be remembered. The calculation of tax benefits assumes a marginal tax rate of 48 percent applicable to all banks. Insofar as some banks would have been subject to lower tax rates, the tax benefits shown in the table would be overestimates. Also, as explained in the text, the inability to isolate depreciation and the tax credit associated with leasing operations results in an overstatement of the tax benefits. On the other hand, data are not available for estimating the tax saving involved on long-term capital gains on securities. Banks realizing such gains on securities acquired prior to July 11, 1969, would have received a tax benefit. In addition, foreign taxes taken as a deduction from income rather than as a tax credit are not shown. In this sense, the table underestimates possible tax savings. Unfortunately it is impossible with present data to determine the extent of these potential biases.

[3]The tax benefits realized by banks engaged in leasing operations vary with the nature of the lease and the degree to which these tax benefits may be passed on to renters. Regulations governing bank holding companies require that leases must be the functional equivalent of loans and that the holding company must recover both the full acquisition cost of the equipment and the estimated cost of financing the property during the period covered by the lease. These costs may be realized through a combination of rental payments, estimated tax benefits (investment tax credit, gain from tax deferral from accelerated depreciation, and other tax benefits with a similar effect), and estimated residual values of the property at the time the lease expires. Banks generally follow these same rules, and similar regulations have recently been proposed for national banks.

The potential benefits from leasing can be seen from an example. If a bank makes a loan for the purchase of equipment, the borrower is able to deduct interest paid on the loan and depreciation on the equipment as expenses in computing taxable income; the bank receives no special tax advantage. However, if the bank were to lease the equipment to the customer, the customer is able to deduct rental payments to the bank which are equivalent to interest on the loan plus the repayment of principal (less any scrap value of the equipment). The bank is able to deduct depreciation on the equipment and may utilize the investment tax credit. In effect, therefore, the bank is allowed a deduction or tax credit for the functional equivalent of the principal of a loan. If the bank uses an accelerated depreciation schedule, additional benefits would be received through tax deferrals. Normal lease arrangements permit both the lessee and lessor to realize a portion of these tax savings but which of the two receives the majority of the tax benefit cannot be determined.

Table 2. Selected Tax Advantages of All Insured Commercial Banks, 1972

Description of Tax Advantage	Income Deduction on Tax Credit Claimed in 1972	Estimated Tax Benefit	Percentage Increase in Total Tax if No Benefit
	(In Millions of Dollars)		
Interest on state and local obligations	3,489	1,675	129.9
Net transfers to bad debt reserves deduction	485	233	18.1
Gross depreciation deduction*	1,389	667	51.7
Investment tax credit†	90	90	7.0
Foreign tax credit†	221	221	17.1
Federal income taxes paid	1,289	2,886	223.9

*Depreciation deductions cannot be separated between depreciation for ordinary bank assets and depreciation for leased assets. In addition, the depreciation deduction figure includes the deduction taken by noninsured commercial banks and mutual savings banks.
†Tax credits include those taken by noninsured commercial banks and mutual savings banks.

liability of commercial banks in 1972 would have more than doubled. These tax shelters have clearly been very important to the profitability of commercial banks.

Bank Investment in Municipal Securities The largest single tax saving for commercial banks, as shown above, is derived from investing in state and local government securities. While bank holdings of state and local obligations have a slight tendency to fluctuate inversely with the demand for loans, Figure 1 indicates that the relative importance of these securities in banks' earning asset portfolios has increased for all groups of banks since 1961. The largest rise, however, has been experienced by banks with deposits over $10 million. Banks with deposits under $10 million had only a slight increase in the fraction of earning assets invested in municipals. Figure 1 also shows that in recent years Tenth District banks have had a slightly higher proportion of their portfolios invested in municipals than all U.S. banks generally.[4]

The different behavior of large and small banks regarding holdings of municipals probably is due to the fact that the tax advantages of municipals are considerably greater for banks with larger net taxable incomes. A bank in the 22 percent tax bracket would receive a higher return from investing in taxable securities if the pretax yield on these securities is more than 1.28 times the return on tax-exempts. Similarly, a bank in the 48 percent tax bracket would require a minimum return on a taxable security of 1.92 times the return on a tax-exempt issue to benefit from

[4]Although Tenth District banks have a higher ratio of municipal securities to earning assets than U.S. banks, the District tax burden is higher. This reflects, in part, the greater use of other tax shelters by U.S. banks than by Tenth District banks and other factors affecting bank taxes and earnings which are not explicitly discussed here.

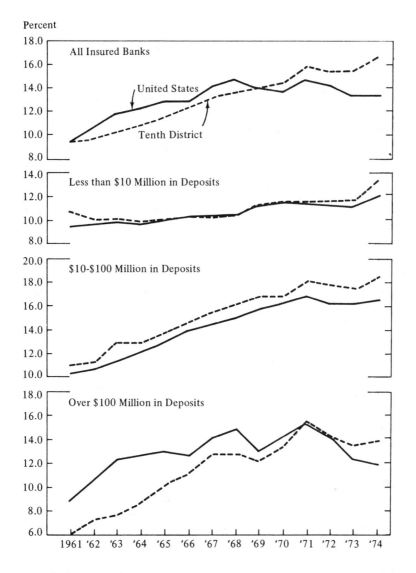

Percent

FIGURE 1. State and local government security holdings as a percent of earning assets.

investing in a taxable security.[5] A comparison of interest rates on intermediate-term U.S. Government issues with the rates on state and local Aaa securities during 1961-74 reveals that banks in the 48 percent tax bracket were always ahead to invest in tax-exempts. Banks in the lower tax bracket, on the other hand, were often able to earn the highest aftertax return by selecting taxable issues.[6] Smaller banks, which must rely mainly on their security holdings for a liquidity reserve, may also have been deterred from acquiring large amounts of municipals from a concern about their marketability during periods of strong loan demand.

Transfers to Bad Debt Reserves   Tax regulations permit banks to use one of two methods in handling loan losses. Under the direct charge-off method, recoveries or losses would be an addition to or deduction from taxable income in the year they occurred. Under the reserve method, a bank is allowed to build up a reserve for anticipated loan losses. Actual recoveries or losses during the year are charged to the reserve rather than to income. For tax purposes, however, allowable transfers to bad debt reserves are treated as an operating expense and thus serve to reduce net income subject to taxes.

The tax treatment of bad debt reserves has been modified over time.[7] From 1954 to 1964, banks were permitted to base tax-free reserves on an average experience factor derived from any 20 consecutive years after 1927. This period, however, included the Depression years of the 1930s when loan losses were unusually high. Consequently, many banks were able to transfer substantially larger amounts to bad debt reserves than were needed to cover current losses. Banks not in existence during the 1930s, though, were at a disadvantage in using this method. To equalize the deductions among banks, the rules for computing bad debt reserves were modified in 1965. Under the change banks were allowed to build up reserves totaling 2.4 percent of eligible loans outstanding at the close of the taxable year. Or, they were given the alternative of basing reserves on a probable experience method derived from the ratio of net bad debts during the most current 6 years to the sum of loans outstanding at the close of those years.

Under the 1969 Tax Reform Act, banks were further limited in the size of additions to bad debt reserves. The law provided an 18-year transitional period during which banks could claim additions to reserves by the greater of a percentage method or an experience method. The experience method is similar to the procedure used during the 1965-69 period. Until 1976, the percentage method allows a tax-free reserve up to 1.8 percent of eligible loans outstanding at the end of the taxable year.

---

[5]For a taxable security to be more profitable than a tax-exempt security, the following must hold true: (yield on taxable security) $(1 - \text{tax rate}) >$ (yield on tax-exempt security) or (yield on taxable security)/ (yield on tax-exempt security) $> 1/(1 - \text{tax rate})$. Assuming a yield of 8 percent on a taxable security and a rate of 6 percent on a tax-exempt security, investment in the taxable security will be more profitable for a bank in the 22 percent tax bracket since: $8\%/6\% = 1.33 > 1/(1 - .22) = 1.28$. A bank in the 48 percent bracket will benefit more by investing in the tax-exempt security since: $8\%/6\% = 1.33 < 1/(1 - .48) = 1.92$.

[6]This analysis assumes that the bank is making the purchase for the interest return only and does not take into consideration the tax effect of a capital gain or loss.

[7]To prevent banks from concentrating transfers to bad debt reserves in years of extremely high income, certain limitations are placed on the amount that can be added to the reserve in any one year.

This percentage will be further reduced to 1.2 percent from 1976 to 1981 and to 0.6 percent from 1982 to 1987. Beginning in 1988, the average actual loss experience will be the only allowable method for computing bad debt reserves.

Although the allowable percentage of loans that may be held as tax-free bad debt reserves has been reduced in recent years, the dollar volume of reserves has continued to grow with loan volume and additions to these reserves in some years have been quite large. For example, in 1974, U.S. banks had net transfers to bad debt reserves of 9.4 percent of pretax net income. Moreover, the ratio of bad debt reserves to loans outstanding at U.S. banks tends to rise as bank size increases. This is a partial reflection of the fact that larger banks mainly tend to utilize the reserve method of accounting for loan losses, whereas smaller banks frequently charge off loan losses only when realized and, consequently, have no bad debt reserve. Thus, bad debt reserve deductions result in a greater tax reduction for larger banks. In 1974, had there been no allowable tax free transfers to bad debt reserves, the total effective tax rate[8] would have been 3.1 percent higher for U.S. banks with more than $100 million in deposits, 2.2 percent greater for banks with deposits of $10 to $100 million, and only 1.2 percent greater for banks with deposits under $10 million.

Security Swaps   Prior to 1969, commercial banks were able to obtain important tax savings by controlling the timing of realizing capital gains and losses on securities. Rules in effect at the time required that banks first offset any long-term capital losses with long-term gains. Beyond that, however, net losses could be deducted from regular income without limit, producing roughly a 50 percent tax absorption of any loss for banks in the highest tax bracket. Long-term gains, on the other hand, were taxed at a maximum rate of 25 percent. Under these circumstances, banks could realize the greatest tax benefit by taking capital losses one year and capital gains another. If gains and losses of the same magnitude were both realized in the same year, no tax saving would occur. But if the capital loss were taken one year and gain in another, the bank would realize a tax saving of about 25 percent of the loss. One justification for the preferential capital loss treatment was that banks were often forced to sell bonds at capital losses during business cycle expansions to acquire funds to meet loan demands.

The Tax Reform Act of 1969 modified the tax treatment of capital gains by requiring banks to treat gains or losses on securities acquired after July 11, 1969, as ordinary income. The change considerably reduced the advantage to banks of alternating years of gains and losses, but did not remove all incentive for undertaking security swaps. If a bank realizes a loss on the sale of a security and subsequently invests in a higher-yielding bond, the bank would experience increased interest income. In addition, the bank could benefit by reduced taxes in the year of the loss and the postponement of the potential capital gains tax on the new securities until future

---

[8]The effect of these transfers could not be separated between the effect on Federal income tax burdens and the effect on state and local income tax burdens. Thus, figures for the effect on the total income tax burden are given.

years.[9] In any event, security swaps have been utilized by banks to moderate fluctuations in net income. Banks have tended to take large security losses in years of sharply rising incomes and to boost income by realizing gains during periods of declining profitability. The 1969 revisions did not alter this tendency.

Investment and Foreign Tax Credits Although the dollar impact has been comparatively small, both the investment tax credit and the foreign tax credit have reduced the domestic tax payments of commercial banks. A tax credit, of course, reduces the dollar amount of taxes paid by the amount of the credit. The investment tax credit was initiated in 1962 to spur economic growth and allowed a deduction from taxes up to 7 percent of the cost of a qualified investment in new or used property for the first year that the property is placed in service. The credit has remained in effect except for two brief periods of suspension from October 1966 to March 1967 and from April 1969 to December 1970. Just recently, moreover, the investment tax credit was raised to 10 percent for the period from January 22, 1975, through December 31, 1976.

Commercial banks have been able to utilize the investment tax credit on purchases such as computers used by the banks themselves and on purchases made for their lease financing operations. Normal depreciation on bank leased assets further serves to reduce tax payments.[10] Finally, if the equipment is ultimately sold for more than its depreciated value, additional tax savings are experienced. In bank leasing operations, tax benefits are often passed along to customers in the form of lower leasing costs. However, since banks are able to realize significant tax benefits which would not be possible if a loan had been made to purchase the equipment, leasing operations have frequently been viewed as a major tax shelter for commercial banks. These tax savings are undoubtedly responsible in large measure for the substantial growth in leasing operations by both banks and bank holding companies. Nonetheless, it should be recognized that, in periods of strong inflation, these benefits are inadequate to allow for full replacement costs. Some observers feel these tax features should be further liberalized to reduce the potential real capital shortage the country may face over the coming decade.

The foreign tax credit has also been called a tax shelter, but this observation is not fully justified. The credit was introduced to limit double taxation of income by both the United States and foreign countries. Before 1962, banks paid taxes on foreign income only when it was repatriated to U.S. shareholders through dividend distributions. However, since the Revenue Act of 1962 was passed, domestic corporations have been taxed according to their share of income from foreign subsidiaries. Banks have had the options of either deducting foreign taxes from net income, or claiming a credit for foreign income taxes paid or accrued during the taxable year. The latter

[9]For a description of the potential benefits, see Paul S. Nadler, "Are Tax Swaps Dead?" *Bankers Monthly,* August 15, 1972, pp. 15-16.

[10]See footnote 3.

method usually yields the greatest tax advantage, but the former is easier to compute.[11]

The sharp rise in foreign operations of large banks since the mid-1960s and the temporary suspensions of the investment tax credit are jointly responsible for the more rapid growth of foreign tax credits than investment tax credits. As might be expected, though, the investment tax credit has been more important for smaller banks and the foreign tax credit more important for larger banks. Large banks initiated a significant expansion of their foreign operations in the mid-1960s when the Voluntary Foreign Credit Restraint (VFCR) program restricted loans to foreigners. By lending through foreign branches which were not subject to VFCR guidelines, these banks were able to meet the growing credit needs of multinational corporations whose overseas operations were expanding.

Minimum Tax on Tax Preference Items   One feature of the Tax Reform Act of 1969 which has resulted in greater equalization of tax burdens between large and small banks is the Minimum Tax on Tax Preference Items. A preference item is essentially a provision in the tax codes which allows a bank to reduce its tax liability. The "minimum tax" imposes an additional 10 percent tax on some items of preference after an exemption of $30,000 and applicable Federal income taxes. Preference items of major interest to banks are contributions to bad debt reserves in excess of experience, accelerated depreciation on certain assets, and long-term capital gains. In general only the largest banks pay this tax. If this tax were eliminated, the disparity between the tax burdens of large and small banks would be even greater.

State and Local Income Taxation of Banks

While states govern the types of taxes imposed on state-chartered banks, the states must follow Federal statutes regarding taxation of nationally chartered banks. Until recent years, states were quite restricted in imposing taxes on national banks; states could tax bank shares, the dividends of owners, or the bank's net income. Interest received on U.S. Government obligations was not taxable under a direct income tax, but net income from all sources could be taxed under an excise or franchise tax. Only one of these methods of taxation could be used, and a state could only tax national banks if the head office was within the state. In addition, states or localities were permitted to levy real property taxes on national banks. Although states were free to

---

[11]The foreign tax credit is subject to a "per country" limitation or to an "overall" limitation. Under the per country limitation, the credit as a proportion of the U.S. tax cannot exceed the ratio of taxable income from the foreign country to total taxable income. Under the overall limitation, the proportion of all foreign taxes paid to the U.S. tax cannot exceed the ratio of the bank's taxable income from all foreign sources to all taxable income. Certain carryover and carryback provisions also apply to the use of the two limitation methods to adjust for variations in tax years between the United States and other countries and differences in the timing of including income or deductions in calculating the tax base. Also, the 1963 law provides for "grossing up" income from developed countries by the amount of the taxes paid when a tax credit is claimed.

impose any tax on state-chartered banks, competition between national and state-chartered banks and equity considerations prompted most states to treat the two groups of banks equally.

In December 1969, Congress liberalized the laws regarding state taxation of banks. States were allowed to levy any tax, except an intangible personal property tax, on a national bank having its main office in the state. States also were allowed to impose sales or use taxes, real property or occupancy taxes, documentary taxes, tangible personal property taxes, and license, registration, transfer, or other taxes on a national bank not having its main office in the state if those types of taxes were generally imposed on a nondiscriminatory basis. Subsequently a permanent amendment, passed in 1973, allowed states to treat national banks as state banks for tax purposes. The amendment further permitted the imposition of intangible taxes but retained limits on state taxation of nondomiciliary banks' income.

Tax Burden

Income taxes are the most important single tax levied by state and local governments.[12] Between 1961 and 1974, the burden of state and local income taxes nearly

Table 3. State and Local Income Tax Burdens of Banks,
United States and Tenth District (in percent)

	Ratio of State and Local Income Taxes Paid to Net Income				Changes in Effective Tax Rates
	1961	1965	1969	1974	1961–74
All banks:					
United States	2.3	2.6	3.4	4.3	+ 2.0
Tenth District	2.3	2.4	2.9	2.6	+ 0.3
By deposit size:					
Less than $10 million					
United States	1.4	1.7	1.7	2.5	+ 1.1
Tenth District	1.6	2.2	2.1	2.5	+ 0.9
$10 to $100 million					
United States	1.5	1.5	1.9	2.4	+ 0.9
Tenth District	2.2	2.7	2.8	2.8	+ 0.6
$100 million and over					
United States	2.8	3.1	4.3	5.3	+ 2.5
Tenth District	3.1	2.2	3.5	2.5	− 0.6

Source: Reports of Income, Federal Deposit Insurance Corporation.
Note: Data for 1961-68 are not strictly comparable with data for 1969-74.

[12]Banks also pay property taxes, sales taxes, documentary taxes, and other miscellaneous taxes to state and local governments. Although current data on the volume of these taxes are unavailable, a 1969 study by the Board of Governors of the Federal Reserve System revealed that these taxes accounted for 62 percent of all taxes paid to state and local governments while income taxes accounted for 38 percent.

doubled at all U.S. banks, rising from 2.3 percent of net income to 4.3 percent. (See Table 3.) This rise reflects both the upward movement of tax rates over the period and the imposition of income taxes in some states which had previously not taxed bank profits. By comparison, the average burden of state income taxes for Tenth District banks rose only slightly over the period from 2.3 to 2.6 percent. The lower effective tax rate for Tenth District banks than for banks in the nation reflects the smaller tax burden of District banks with deposits of $100 million and over. These banks had a tax burden of 2.5 percent in 1974, compared with 5.3 percent for U.S. banks of similar size. On the other hand, Tenth District[13] banks with deposits under $100 million had effective tax rates equal to or above the national averages. . . .

Concluding Remarks

Between 1961 and 1974 the effective Federal tax burden on commercial banks dropped about 60 percent, with large banks generally realizing the sharpest declines. Reductions in tax rates account for a portion of the decline, but the largest share has resulted from bank utilization of legal tax shelters. The more important of these include investments in state and local government securities, creation of reserves for bad debts substantially in excess of actual losses, and the development of equipment leasing operations. Banks in the Tenth Federal Reserve District generally experienced similar trends, but over the period were subject to an effective Federal tax burden above the national average.

[13]Colorado, Kansas, Nebraska, Wyoming, 43 western Missouri counties, northern New Mexico, and most of Oklahoma.

Cost and Profitability
of Bank Functions

Paul S. Anderson

As lenders to business, commercial banks have to be able to judge the operating efficiency of their borrowers in order to insure as far as possible the safety of their
loans. Banks have acquired the reputation of being coldly efficient in making these
judgments. In this article the tables are turned and the operating efficiency of banks
is investigated, using data compiled in the Functional Cost Analysis of the Federal
Reserve Banks. According to this analysis, some banking functions are persistently
much more profitable than others, while some actually entail losses year after year.
These variations in profitability and their persistence seem to contradict the cold efficiency of banks. The relative costs and profitability of the various functions are
relevant to public policy because many banking laws and regulations impinge on the
operations of banks.

The Functional Cost Analysis

About 20 years ago, the Federal Reserve Bank of Boston undertook an annual cost
survey among its member banks of the costs of various bank functions. This survey
was an outgrowth of less elaborate bank cost analyses which were being made by the

Reprinted, with deletions, from *New England Economic Review*, March/April 1979, pp. 43–61, by
permission of the Federal Reserve Bank of Boston and the author.

Federal Reserve Banks of Boston and New York. The functions which were first covered included demand and time deposits, capital funds, loans, securities, safe deposit boxes and trust administration. Since then, credit card, computer services to customers and the computer department functions have been added. Providing the data for this analysis requires quite a bit of bank time and effort but this was the only feasible way for smaller and medium-sized banks to obtain usable cost data. Later other Federal Reserve banks joined in the survey so that it is now nationwide.

The Functional Cost Analysis is an exceptionally useful management tool for participating banks. They can compare their costs for each function from year to year with averages of banks of similar size and deposit structure. Such comparisons with the actual operating results of like businesses are not available or even possible in most industries.

Each reporting bank presents, at the minimum, the total amount of direct labor costs per function. Because some employees work at several functions, banks carry out periodic time studies of such employees to establish a basis for allocating their wages. Tellers' wage costs for example, while largely assigned to demand deposits, also apply partly to savings deposits and various loan categories.

The difficulty in cost accounting is how to apportion the remaining costs among functions. Some of these other costs, supplies, for example, could be allocated directly if detailed records were kept of usage, but that is often not feasible particularly for smaller banks. Most other costs, like the president's salary, are true overhead costs and no direct method of allocation is possible. In the Functional Cost Analysis, all costs that are not allocated directly are distributed on the basis of a continuously analyzed relation of such costs to direct wage and salary costs per function.

While any method of allocation of indirect, overhead costs is a matter of judgment and thus could be challenged, there is a double check on accuracy in total functional costing. Since all overhead costs have to be assigned to some function, too much in one means that another has too little, so any misallocation shows up in at least two functions. Each year the methods of allocation are reviewed and revised if evidence warrants it.

Similar to the problem of distributing indirect or joint costs is that of evaluating the cost of interrelated functions. A clear example of interrelation is the close connection between business demand deposits and business loans. These two functions (as well as others) are treated as a package in dealings with business customers. It might contribute to overall bank profitability, for example, to provide more favorable lending terms in order to attract business deposits which are above average in profitability. Because of such interrelations, the cost results for each function must be viewed from an overall bank perspective.

The distribution of all costs provides a total cost for each function. This total is then divided by the size of each function to yield a percentage cost which is useful for comparative analysis. As an example, in 1977 the total cost of the demand deposit function of reporting banks averaged near 3.5 percent while that of time deposits was just over 6 percent.

For the demand deposit, time deposit and consumer installment loan functions, the total costs are also divided among the activities or processes involved in each function. Demand deposits, for example, involve receiving deposits, processing incoming and outgoing checks (home debits and transit items), cashing checks and maintaining the account. The relative time spent on each of these activities is estimated from time studies so that each type of activity can be measured in terms of "weight units." The cost per weight unit is obtained by dividing the total cost of the demand deposit function by the total number of such weight units. This cost per unit times the number of units involved in a single processing operation gives its cost. The average cost of cashing a check in 1977, for example, averaged just over 20 cents at the largest reporting banks. Costs of specific processes in the time deposit function are obtained in a similar manner while in the consumer installment loan function, costs are derived for making each loan and for collecting each payment.

Once all costs are distributed, the primary goal of the Functional Cost Analysis has been reached. But a further refinement is made, that of calculating the profit-

Table 1. Summary of Functional Costs and Incomes, 1977
(Average of Small, Medium, and Large Reporting Banks)

Funds-Providing Functions	Total Expenses	Less Service Charges, Fees, etc.	Net Expenses	Earnings on Funds	Net Earnings
	(Percent of Funds Provided)				
Demand Deposits	3.52	.88	2.63	5.66	3.03
Time Deposits	6.18	.01	6.17	7.07	.90
Capital and Borrowed Funds	4.07	.10	3.97	7.44	3.47

Funds-Using Functions	Gross Yield	Expenses	Net Yield	Cost of Funds	Net Earnings
	(Percent of Funds Used)				
Real Estate Mortgage Loans	8.72	.92	7.80	4.84	2.96
Installment Loans (Mainly Consumer)	11.33	3.59	7.74	4.82	2.92
Credit Card Loans	19.81	13.49	6.33	4.79	1.54
Commercial and Other Loans	8.59	1.78	6.81	4.82	1.99
Securities (Taxable Basis)	7.77	.16	7.60	4.82	2.78

Nonfunds Departments	Income	Expenses	Net Earnings
	(Average Department)		
Safe Deposit	$60,000	$103,000	− $43,000
Trust Services	$561,000	$675,000	− $114,000
Computer Services	$307,000	$366,000	− $59,000
Other (Largely International)	$1,478,000	$1,326,000	$152,000

Source: *Functional Cost Analysis* based on data furnished by 846 banks in 12 Federal Reserve Districts.

ability of each function by cross-allocating costs and incomes. Those functions which are funds sources, like demand and time deposits, involve costs but practically no income. But the funds-using functions, investments and loans, are the opposite; they generate practically all the income but have relatively little direct costs. To impute income to the funds-providing functions like deposits, it is assumed that their investible funds (total funds minus cash and reserve requirements) are invested proportionately among all loans and investments and thus receive the overall average rate of return. The loan and investment functions are assumed to get their funds from the source functions at the overall average cost. Thus the cross-allocation of costs and incomes uses the pool-of-funds rule rather than a procedure of trying to match specific sources with specific uses, for example, savings deposits with real estate mortgage loans.

The functions which do not involve the funds of the banks, namely, safe deposit, trust and computer services, generate their own incomes. Their costs are allocated in the cost distribution and their profitability can be computed directly.

Shown in Table 1 is a brief overall summary view of the results provided by the Functional Cost Survey. Incomes and net earnings are presented for each function. The most notable result in the funds-providing section is the wide disparity in the net expenses among these functions. Net time deposit expenses were 6.17 percent in 1977 while net demand deposit expenses were less than half as much at 2.63 percent. This difference has persisted since 1966 so it is not a temporary and abnormal result. The cost of capital and borrowed funds combined is low but this is because no "profits cost" is imputed to capital funds.

In the funds-using, or earning assets, group gross yields vary considerably, ranging from 7 ¾ percent for securities (on a taxable equivalent basis) to almost 20 percent for credit cards. But associated investment expenses have a similar range so that net yields vary much less. Even so, the net earnings rate on credit cards is only a little over half that of most other earning assets.

The nonfunds group such as safe deposits and trust services has the most surprising results. All operated at losses except the "other" category which is a miscellaneous collection of activities but is dominated by the international departments of the large banks. All these nonfund functions with losses in 1977 also have had losses in practically every year since this survey began so these 1977 results are not due to temporary aberrations in the data.

The cost and profit results for each of the functions are discussed in detail in subsequent sections. Then some of the broader implications of the survey are considered.

Demand Deposits

The demand deposit function is by far the largest banking function as measured by the number of employees. But since the early 1960s, it has ranked second at most banks to time deposits in terms of either dollar volume of funds involved or total costs. But demand deposits still contribute most to overall bank profitability because they are the lowest cost source of funds.

Interest payments on demand deposits have been illegal since 1933, so the only cost of acquiring them has been the handling expenses. In the Functional Cost Analysis, these handling or processing activities have been divided into the following four major operations:

- Home debits—processing checks drawn on account.
- Deposits—handling currency and checks deposited in account.
- Transit checks—handling and sending out for collection checks drawn on other banks which were received for deposit or for cashing.
- Account maintenance—statement preparation and mailing.

The average costs of these operations, which are calculated by use of weight units as described earlier, are as follows for 1977:

Each home debit	10 cents
Each deposit	20 cents
Handling and sending out each transit check	5 cents
Account maintenance per month	$2.70

A simple measure of the costs of checking accounts is the total cost per check written. In 1977, expenses totaled around $7.00 per account per month while an average of 22 checks were written, yielding a total handling cost of just over 30 cents per check.

Over time, total handling costs per check are subject to the same two influences as the unit costs of other goods and services, namely, changes in wage rates and changes in productivity. Bank wages have been rising over the postwar period, like all other wages, and the rise has accelerated during the past ten years. Productivity rises in check handling have about offset the increase in wage rates since the late 1950s so that the total cost per check is now about where it was then, around 30 cents. But the productivity changes have been uneven, spurting in the early 1960s so that the total cost per check declined to 20 cents in 1966 but rising very little since then. The total handling cost per check is now back to just over 30 cents and is still rising.

The sharp decline in check processing costs in the early 1960s evidently reflected for the most part the widespread introduction of combination bookkeeping-adding machines called "tronics" which automated account bookkeeping substantially. Except for adding machines, these tronic machines were really the only clear advance in check processing technology since the beginning of banking. Until they were introduced, checks had been entered into accounts by hand just as Tiny Tim's father did in Scrooge's counting house.

The bookkeeping clerk simply inserted the account statement into the tronic machine and then entered the transaction amount. The machine would post the transaction and the new balance into the account. These tronic machines were essentially limited-program computers where the magnetic back of the statement sheet was the memory. They were much cheaper than regular computers, however, and evidently were much less error-prone than computers have proven to be up to now.

Tronic technology began to be replaced during the latter 1960s by computer processing of magnetically encoded checks which can be read by machine. The new technology has increased productivity only modestly, at least up to the present, as reflected in the comparative rises in wages and in processing costs. Wage levels in check processing rose about 92 percent at reporting banks over the past 11 years while total check processing costs per check written rose almost as much, about 85 percent.

The advent of computer processing has affected the costs of the four main demand deposit processing operations quite differently, as shown in the following table:

Table 2. Average Item Costs of Reporting Banks

	1966	1977	Percentage Rise
	(Cents)		
Home Debit	6.6	9.6	45
Deposit	9.2	19.7	114
Transit Check	2.4	5.3	120
Account Maintenance (per Month)	145.0	268.0	85

Source: Same as Table 1.

Processing costs of deposits and transit checks actually increased more than wages while the cost of each home debit increased only half as much as wages. The explanation for most of the divergence in cost trends is the impact of magnetic ink encoding on various operations.

Banks have to encode the amount on every check which is received for deposit or for cashing. Encoding actually requires more handling than entering a deposit or check on a tronics machine. Thus computer processing provided very little saving of processing time in these two operations. The rise in item costs in excess of the wage rise probably was largely due to the allocation of the rather expensive computer cost. But in the case of home debits, over half on average are initially deposited or cashed at another bank which encodes them. Thus the home bank saves the encoding expense on those on-us checks which are transit items at another bank.

While computer processing did little to reduce costs initially, it does provide the capacity to process a large volume of transactions without having to increase the number of employees. It also makes available data which were previously not obtainable without great effort. For example, the computer performs "account analysis" for the determination of service charges.

Individual and Commercial
Checking Accounts

Demand deposits can be divided into two major categories, individual and all other, mainly commercial. These two categories differ substantially in average size, activity, costs and profitability, as seen in the following average 1977 figures for those Functional Cost reporting banks which provided separate data for the two groups:

Table 3.   Comparison of Individual and Commercial Demand Deposits,
1977 Functional Cost Reporting Banks

	Individual Demand Deposits	Commercial Demand Deposits
Average Size	$921	$8,850
Checks Written per Month	15	43
Total Cost per Month	$ 5.05	$ 12.90
Gross Investment Earnings on Account Balances per Month	4.24	40.91
Service Charges and Fees per Month	1.23	2.03
Net Earnings after Costs per Month	.42	30.04
Total Cost per Year, Percent of Average Balance	6.6%	1.7%
Net Earnings per Year, Percent of Average Balance	0.5%	4.1%

Source: Same as Table 1.

Commercial accounts are typically a lot more active than personal accounts and their handling costs are two and a half times larger. But because their average balance is nearly ten times that of personal accounts, their expenses, on an annual basis, amount to only 1.7 percent of average balances as compared to 6.6 percent for personal accounts.

The investment earnings rate on balances is assumed to be the same for both accounts under the pool of investment funds concept used in the analysis. Income from service charges and fees adds significantly to the gross earnings of personal accounts but relatively little to the much larger commercial account. But because the expense ratio of the average personal account is so high, its net earnings are only ½ of 1 percent as compared to 4 percent for the average commercial account. Quite clearly the overall profitability of demand deposits arises from the commercial category while personal accounts do little more than break even. Most banks offer special checking accounts for individuals which have somewhat higher service charges (about $1.70 per month) than do regular personal accounts ($1.23 per month). But usually no minimum balance is required and these special checking accounts have average balances of just over $400. The additional service charges are not sufficient to offset the low investment income from the small average balance, so that these accounts were even less profitable on average in 1977 than regular personal accounts, losing about 30 cents per account per month while regular accounts made an average profit of 40 cents per month.

New England banks that offered NOW checking accounts which paid 5 percent interest had large balances in these accounts, averaging $2,500. But this large average size was not sufficient to offset the 5 percent interest expense so that these accounts entailed an average monthly loss of about 5 cents. Furthermore, since most of these NOW accounts had formerly been profitable regular checking accounts due to their large size, the banks essentially also lost the 5 percent interest which they previously did not pay. This amounts to around $10 a month per account. In effect, a previous regular checking account averaging $2,500 which earned the bank about $10 a month was converted to a NOW account which lost 5 cents a month. With current levels of costs and earnings rates on loans and investments, a bank cannot both pay 5 percent and offer free checking on NOW accounts with average balances of less than about $3,000 and still make a profit.

Savings and Time Deposits

Handling expenses of savings and time deposits are low because these accounts have little activity, around three to five deposits and withdrawals per year. Consequently their expense ratios are also low, just over 1 percent for regular savings accounts, about ¼ of 1 percent for special notice time accounts and only 1/10 of 1 percent for time certificates of deposit. These expense percentages mainly reflect the average sizes and handling required of these three categories; savings account balances run just below $2,000 while special notice accounts and certificates of deposit are near $7,000. The certificate of deposit average is lower than might be expected because Functional Cost reporting banks include few of the billion dollar size banks, the bulk of whose certificates average well over $100,000 in size. The expense ratio of such giant accounts would be essentially zero, of course.

With these low expense ratios, the cost of savings and time deposits then depends primarily on the interest rate which is paid. These rates are limited by legal interest rate ceilings (so-called Regulation Q ceilings) on all but certificates of deposit of $100,000 or larger. Thus when earnings rates on assets are high, as in 1974, the profitability of these accounts is naturally higher than when earnings rates are lower, as in 1976 and 1977. In 1977, these accounts had average net earnings of just over 1 percent which made them more profitable than personal checking accounts but much less profitable than commercial checking accounts.

An interesting minor category in the time deposit department are the Christmas (and some other) club accounts. These are savings plans in which savers sign up to deposit a small amount regularly, typically $5 weekly. The deposits are withdrawable several weeks before Christmas (or some other date). Most banks pay interest on these accounts with a 4 percent rate being common. Usually the plan provides for no interest payment if the deposit is withdrawn before completion of the planned period. Some banks pay no interest at all and, as a result, the overall average interest cost for this category is just over 3 percent.

The weekly deposits make for quite a bit of handling. This, together with opening and closing expenses, brings the annual cost of servicing the account to over $7. Since the balance averages only about $110 over the year, servicing costs amount to over 6 percent of average outstanding balances. This is less than banks earn from these balances so these accounts are slightly unprofitable even before the interest cost is considered.

Capital and Borrowed Funds

Equity accounts provide about 8 percent of total funds at Functional Cost banks. In the cost calculations, their expenses are very small, less than 1 percent, because they exclude net income which is traditionally considered the cost of equity funds. The expenses assigned to equity are such minor items as handling expenses of dividend checks, unallocated directors' fees and outside examinations.

Various forms of borrowing account for only 2 percent of total funds at the smallest Functional Cost banks but over 10 percent at the largest. The large banks are usually net buyers (borrowers) of Federal funds, the chief source of borrowed funds, while the small banks are usually net sellers. Credit conditions were rather easy throughout 1977 and the average cost of borrowings was fairly low, around 6 percent, approximately the same as the total average cost, including handling expenses, of time and savings deposits.

Consumer Loans

Like deposits, bank loans vary in their characteristics, differing substantially as to type of borrowers, average size, maturity, security, loss rate, and costs of making and servicing. At one extreme are loans to prime business borrowers who already have an approved line of credit that cost very little to make and service. They are also very large so their percentage cost is practically zero. At the other extreme, credit card loans to customers involve quite a lot of processing and are very small, on average around $25 for each credit card sale, and their handling cost is around 12 percent

The most detailed Functional Cost lending analysis has been made of consumer installment loans. The average outstanding balance on these loans is near $2,000. Since at any given time an installment loan held by a bank is one-half paid off, the average initial size of these loans is about $4,000, a rather large size reflecting the fact that the majority of these loans are made for the purchase of new automobiles. Also included in this category are relatively small amounts of mobile home loans and inventory, or "floor plan," loans to auto dealers, which are much larger, as well as home appliance and check credit loans which are on average much smaller.

The average cost of extending a consumer installment loan is about $45. This is roughly equal to one average day's pay per bank employee (including officers), meaning that it takes one person-day in total to extend a consumer loan. This includes time spent in helping the applicant fill out an application, making the credit check, typing all the forms and finally extending the actual loan. Considering all the operations involved, banks are quite efficient in extending these loans. But Functional Cost banks now process about 10 percent fewer loans on average per worker than they did in 1966. By contrast, in the demand deposit function, they handle over 20 percent more check volume per worker than in 1966. One reason cited by bankers for this drop in installment loans processed per worker is that regulations, especially those concerned with "truth in lending," have slowed down the processing of these loans.

The cost of collecting each payment is about $3, or $45 for the 15-month life of the average loan. This is equal to the costs of making the loan and thus seems quite high. By comparison, the cost of recording a deposit to a checking account was only about 20 cents, as noted earlier, so the $3.00 cost of collecting a payment seems excessive. The explanation is that all costs subsequent to the making of the loan are included in payment costs, whereas in costing checking accounts, the cost of maintaining the account is separated from the costs of handling checks written and deposits made. Since the cost of maintaining a checking account is approximately $2.70 per month, the payment collection cost of $3.00 monthly is reasonable.

Other costs involved in lending are losses and the cost of funds. Following are these costs for 1977, together with the gross income on consumer loans and the net earnings (in percent):

Income

Gross interest income	10.8
Other income (minimum fees, penalties, etc.)	0.5
Total income	11.3

Costs

Making loans	1.8
Collecting payments	1.4
Loan losses	0.4
Cost of funds	4.8
Total Costs	8.4
Net Earnings	2.9

Loan losses on consumer loans are relatively low, reflecting the fact that banks impose fairly high credit standards on borrowers. Loss rates on loans at consumer, or small, loan companies are roughly four times higher, which is a consequence of their lower standards. Small loan companies have to charge higher rates, of course, as a result.

Credit Cards

Credit card loans are a recent innovation in banking. They were widely introduced during the 1960s and many thought they would result in a largely cashless society.

But their impact has been much less than anticipated. Initially banks granted credit cards rather indiscriminately and many holders used them fraudulently by stealing cards or submitting fictitious names on applications or else simply neglected to pay amounts owed. As a result, losses were far above those experienced on other loan types. Even after losses were reduced by more prudent issuance, handling expenses were so large that most banks had operating losses. With the decline in the cost of funds from 1974 to 1977, more than half of the banks reporting on their credit card operations in the Functional Cost survey have finally been able to make profits on this function, although for all reporting banks combined the profit rate is significantly below the average for other loans.

Gross income earned on credit cards is high, near 20 percent. It is composed of two parts, merchant discount and interest earned on balances which are outstanding beyond the non-interest period, which usually extends for some 25 days after the first billing. Merchant discounts are the amounts banks charge retail stores for handling their credit card sales; these discounts average around 2.3 percent for reporting banks. Thus, on the average $25 credit card purchase, a bank pays about $24.40 to the retail store submitting the charges but bills the customer for the full $25, resulting in a gain of 60 cents per sales slip.

On average, about 40 days elapse from the time the bank pays the retail store until it begins charging interest to the customer. This free credit period is an outright loss to the bank because costs are accruing on the funds it has tied up in these free credit balances. If the customer does not pay the balance within the free credit period, the bank begins earning interest at a rate which is generally 18 percent on the first $500 and 12 percent on amounts above $500.

The smallest size group of Functional Cost reporting banks, those with deposits up to $50 million, had losses of 0.3 percent on their credit card operations in 1977. The two larger groups, with $50–$200 million and over $200 million in deposits, had net earnings of 1.6 and 3.0 percent respectively. A comparison of these differing profit experiences brings out the major factors affecting profitability.

The small banks were actually more efficient in operations than were the two larger size groups. On average, each small-bank employee in the credit card function processed about 650 sales slips per week as compared to 400 and 580, respectively, in the two larger size groups. Also, total expenses per employee were about $28,000 per year at the smallest banks and $31,000 and $33,000, respectively, at the larger banks. Thus, in the two areas over which banks had direct control, the smallest banks were above average in efficiency.

But in areas which were largely beyond the bank's control, the larger banks had more favorable experiences. The average sizes of their sales slips were some 50 percent larger, about $27 versus only $19 at the smallest banks. As a result, the smallest banks processed $630,000 worth of sales slips per year per employee, only a little more than the medium banks' $580,000, despite the fact that the smallest banks processed over 50 percent more sales slips per employee. The largest banks processed $730,000 per employee per year. This dollar volume generates the merchant discount income at the rate of about 2.3 percent.

In addition, around 38 percent of the sales charges at the larger banks remained unpaid after the free credit period and thus began earning interest, while only 33 percent of sales charges at the smallest banks lasted long enough to earn interest. Consequently, annual interest income per employee at the biggest banks was $42,000, at the medium-size banks $28,000, and at the smallest banks only $22,000.

Losses on credit card charges were about 1.3 percent in 1977, down substantially from earlier rates. But even the 1.3 level is still significantly higher than the loss rate on regular consumer instalment loans, real estate mortgage loans or business loans. (Fraud losses are not included in these bad debt losses because they are considered nonrecurring rather than ordinary operating expenses.)

Mortgage and Business Loans and Securities

Costs of making and collecting real estate and commercial (including agricultural) loans are substantially higher than those of consumer installment loans. The annual operating costs of mortgage loans in 1977 were around $170 per loan outstanding while those of commercial loans were about $250, both well over double the $72 expense of handling consumer loans. But because mortgage and commercial loans are roughly ten times larger on average than consumer loans ($18,000–$22,000 versus $2,000), handling costs are lower, only 0.8 percent for real estate and 1.4 percent for commercial loans.

The costs of making a real estate mortgage loan amount to around $500, far above the average $45 cost of making a consumer loan, but because mortgage loans have average lives of over five years, the annual cost is below $100. Receiving and processing applications and performing credit checks and property appraisals involve a lot more time for mortgage loans than for consumer installment loans. This is particularly the case with commercial mortgage loans which are an appreciable share of the loans made by most commercial banks. Collection costs on real estate loans are probably somewhat higher than on consumer installment loans because the bank usually also collects payments for real estate taxes and these must be transferred periodically to the local governmental unit.

Commercial and agricultural loans are quite a bit more varied than are real estate loans. Included are such types as conventional single-payment loans, accounts receivable loans, leased equipment loans and term loans with floating rates. Costs of making these loans likewise vary greatly. A single payment loan to a prime borrower with a line of credit involves very little cost, while a leased equipment loan would involve a lot of advance investigation and preparation and much subsequent supervision.

The average size of loan in the commercial, agricultural and other category is a relatively small $18,000. This is smaller than might be expected because business loans are usually thought to be quite large, certainly larger than home mortgage loans. Furthermore, the average Functional Cost reporting bank can make loans as large as $2 million, which is one-tenth of average capital accounts of $20 million.

While these banks do make some maximum size loans, they make many more small loans to businesses which brings the average below that of real estate loans.

Loan losses have risen on both mortgage and commercial loans over the past ten years. In the mid-1960s, these losses were practically zero, and they are still less than 0.1 percent on real estate loans and around 0.4 percent on commercial loans. Unlike the largest banks in the country, most Functional Cost reporting banks had not financed real estate investment trusts to any extent, nor had they made many construction and development loans. These are the real estate loan types that in many cases have turned sour since 1973.

The costs of acquiring investments—including U.S. government securities, tax-exempt securities, and Federal funds sold—are low, below 0.2 percent. Investments have been somewhat more profitable than loans on average over the past ten years, as market interest rates have risen faster than the cost of funds. Before the mid-1960s, investments had significantly lower net earnings than loans.

Nonfunds Departments

As noted earlier, the distinguishing feature of the nonfunds department operations is that all except the foreign department had losses which have persisted since the beginning of Functional Cost analysis. While banks have raised their fees and charges over time for safe deposit boxes, trust functions, computer services and other miscellaneous activities, costs have kept pace so that losses continue. Why banks tolerate the protracted deficits in these operations will be discussed later, along with marketing and pricing operations concerning all bank functions.

The persistent losses of trust departments in the Functional Cost survey contrasts with profits often recorded in summaries of trust department operations compiled by several Federal Reserve banks at the request of the participating trust departments in their districts. The major reason for the different results is that the trust expenses reported in the special trust surveys generally include significantly less overhead costs than the Functional Cost analysis allocates to trust deparments. The allocations of overhead expenses in the special surveys are made by the trust officers submitting the reports, usually without an outside check. Overhead allocation in the Functional Cost analysis is subject to check in that the respective amounts to the various functions and departments allow comparisons for reasonableness. This aspect is, of course, one of the chief strengths of the Functional Cost procedures.

Possible Operating Adjustments in the Future

Banking has the reputation of being a stable industry, doing business in traditional ways year in and year out. Bankers are reluctant to make changes, especially those that involve eliminating services to customers or raising charges sharply.

But developments might occur which would reduce bank profitability substantially and force banks to make offsetting operating adjustments. One possible development that would reduce profitability, but would actually be very desirable for other reasons, is a return to price stability which would almost certainly lead to a reduction in interest rates to more normal levels.

A reduction in interest rates to levels prevailing in the early 1960s, for example, would cut the income of banks almost in half. Average yields on earning assets, net of lending expenses, were about 7.5 percent at Functional Cost banks in 1977, while from 1960 to 1965, average yields were only around 4 percent. Although interest costs of banks would also decline with a reduction in rates, these costs amount to only about half the interest income of banks. As a result, a given percentage point drop in both interest income and interest costs would reduce revenues twice as much as costs.

Another possible development which could cut bank profits by up to 50 percent is the removal of the prohibition of interest on all demand deposits. The legalization of NOW accounts (checkable savings accounts) in New England has already had an impact on bank earnings.[1]

The authorization of automatic transfers from savings to checking accounts throughout the Nation is also predicted to reduce earnings as individual demand deposits are pared down as a result. But these NOW accounts and automatic transfers apply only to individuals whose accounts make up only about a third of demand deposits. If interest payments on all demand deposits were allowed and competition led to average payments, net after service charges, of 3 to 4 percent, earnings of the typical Functional Cost bank would be reduced by nearly 50 percent.

What adjustments could banks make to offset a general fall in interest rates, or the payment of interest on demand deposits? One frequently mentioned in debates over bank costs is adjusting bank loan rates—raising them above current levels to cover interest on demand deposits or reducing them less than other interest rates if the general level of interest rates falls. But such interest rate adjustments are not really possible for banks because the general level of loan rates is set by demand and supply conditions in the market. Business loan rates tend to follow rates on commercial paper and negotiable certificates of deposit. Mortgage loan rates tend to follow bond rates and, in addition, are strongly influenced by thrift institutions. Consumer loan rates tend to remain quite stable and even though banks are the most important consumer lenders, they can hardly raise their rates above prevailing levels without losing market shares.

A second possible adjustment which, however, would not likely be successful either is to reduce interest rates on savings and time deposits. Banks would lose deposits to competing thrift institutions if they were to lower rates paid significantly. While a lowering of the rate ceilings under Regulation Q would accomplish the purpose of reducing bank costs, these ceilings have never been lowered, except for some minor adjustments, since they were imposed on commercial banks in 1935.

[1]See Ralph C. Kimball, "Impacts of NOW Accounts and Thrift Institution Competition on Selected Small Commercial Banks in Massachusetts and New Hampshire, 1974–75," *New England Economic Review,* January/February 1977, pp. 22–38.

If banks are not able to offset reduced earnings by raising interest rates on earning assets or reducing interest costs on sources of funds, the only remaining avenues open are to reduce operating expenses or else to impose or raise charges for banking services provided. The opportunities for reducing operating expenses are probably fairly limited because banks presumably are already striving to hold them down. Expenses could be reduced by eliminating some functions entirely but this is hardly acceptable if banks wish to retain their image as full service institutions. One area in which banks have retrenched is in branching. Branching has been mainly aimed at attracting individual accounts, but, as noted earlier, these have declined in profitability over the past 15 years or so.

The focus of possible future operating adjustments will have to be on the pricing of services. These prices, or charges, would, of course, be related to the cost of the services. The following tabulation shows the average distribution of noninterest operating expenses of Functional Cost banks among the various functions:

Table 4. Distribution of Noninterest Operating Expenses, 1977

Function	Percent of Total Noninterest Expenses
Demand Deposits	37
Time Deposits	12
Installment Loans	15
Commercial Loans	14
Real Estate Loans	6
Credit Card Loans	4
Securities	2
Trust Department	6
Safe Deposit Boxes	1
All Other (Excluding International)	3
Total	100

Source: Same as Table 1.

Some of these functions are much more easily priced explicitly than others due to the inherent nature of the function or the competitive situation. . . .

Summary

The Functional Cost survey conducted by the Federal Reserve banks in cooperation with nearly a thousand member commercial banks is a valuable cost analysis which is unique in comprehensiveness and detail among business cost surveys. Its prime purpose is to provide participating banks with comparative cost data covering the standard banking functions. This information enables banks to identify those operating areas which appear to be below standard in efficiency so that improvements can be undertaken.

The broader interest in the survey arises from the insight it gives on banking operations. Overall, demand deposits are by far the cheapest, and therefore the most profitable, source of funds because they have no interest cost. But within the demand deposit category large commercial accounts are very profitable but individual accounts are barely above the break-even point. NOW accounts paying 5 percent interest are actually slightly unprofitable at most banks even though their average size is three times that of regular individual checking accounts.

Among earning assets, real estate and consumer installment loans were the most profitable in 1977 while credit card loans were the least. While the rates charged on credit cards are high, typically 18 percent on the first $500 and 12 percent on amounts above, credit card processing costs are also high, reducing net yields. While the credit card function is a loss operation at some banks, its profitability has improved on average since it was introduced.

Commercial loans were somewhat below average in profitability in 1977 but that was largely due to the fact that market interest rates were at their lowest level in recent years. Yields on commercial loans fluctuate more than does the average cost of funds because the latter includes the cost of zero-interest demand deposits. When the general level of market rates is high, as in 1974, commercial loans are much more profitable than real estate or consumer loans whose average yields fluctuate less than the cost of funds.

A surprising result of the cost survey was that all three major service departments—safe deposit, trust and customer computer service—have been unprofitable over the entire period that these data have been compiled. Even though most banks are now aware of these losses, most have not succeeded in taking corrective steps. A number of banks have phased out customer computer services but such action is not possible in the safe deposit and trust functions. The latter two departments are standard, traditional and often legally contracted services of banks, as well as involving a heavy fixed investment, so they can hardly be discontinued. Improving their profitability will require substantial adjustments in fee schedules.

Among the interesting findings of the survey were the costs of various detailed activities. Following are examples of handling costs: a check drawn by a depositor, almost 10 cents; deposit to a checking account, 20 cents; a (transit) check drawn on another bank, 5 cents; withdrawal from a savings account, 80 cents; posting interest to a savings account, $1.55; making a consumer installment loan, $45; collecting a payment on a consumer loan, $3.

Profits have been quite good overall during the postwar period so banks have not been under special pressure to increase operating margins. But some possible developments in the future could affect bank profits substantially. The two that loom as most important are allowing interest to be paid on demand deposits and a reduction in the general level of interest rates to more normal levels. Either of these developments could cut net operating income of the average bank by as much as one-half unless offsetting actions were taken.

To counter reductions in income, banks would probably not be successful in raising interest rates on their loans nor in reducing interest paid on time and savings deposits. Competition is quite active in both these areas and if banks move loan rates up or deposit rates down unilaterally, competitors such as thrift institutions, insurance, commercial and consumer loan companies would cut in on the banks' share of the savings and lending markets.

The remaining options for banks are to reduce noninterest operating expenses and to charge for services performed. They probably do not have much leeway for reducing expenses if they are to continue providing their standard services. Thus they will have to consider raising those charges which they have already installed and to impose charges on services which they now provide free. Among services for which charges could be imposed or raised are the following: checking activity, deposits and withdrawals from savings accounts, making consumer loans, collecting payments on consumer loans and posting credit card charges.

New Directions in
Financial Competition

Perhaps the most revolutionary development in financial institutions in the 1980s will be electronic funds transfer systems (EFTS). No area of banking innovation has aroused more attention in the popular press. These systems will restructure many aspects of financial markets; in particular, EFTS, together with legislation enabling thrift institutions to offer noninterest-bearing accounts that are virtually checking accounts as well as to broaden their lending powers, will intensify competition among financial institutions. The implications for public policy, including monetary policy, will be far-reaching.

The four articles in this section address these issues. Selection 19 by William C. Niblack describes the various EFT systems, presents evidence of their impact in reducing bank costs, and scans competitive questions raised by their development. The next reading by Jean M. Lovati shows how EFTS together with legislation enabling thrift institutions to compete more effectively with commercial banks has changed our financial system. Essay 21 by James F. Dingle present a probable scenario for the impact of EFTS on private individuals, non-financial corporations, financial institutions, and government in terms of both their behavior and likely public policy responses. The final article in this Section by Edward J. Kane investigates the implication of EFTS for monetary policy.

Development of Electronic Funds Transfer Systems

William C. Niblack

19

Faster than any but the most optimistic thought possible, electronic banking is sweeping the country—overwhelming the laws that govern banks and other financial institutions, changing dramatically the banking and savings habits of millions of Americans. Ultimately, electronic banking will revolutionize the very concept of money itself and will probably force a profound change in how the Federal Reserve regulates the nation's money supply. Certainly it will touch off a flurry of competition for the nation's financial business unlike anything seen before.[1]

Developments in electronic funds transfer systems (EFTS) have long been a popular topic of discussion in banking circles, but as the above quotation from a national business magazine indicates, the subject now enjoys even wider currency. Although it does not appear likely that we are on the threshold of "the checkless-cashless society," recent developments have been so rapid that predictions of future developments and effects of EFTS often seem foolhardy at best.

The diversity of views on the subject of EFTS reflects the broad scope of current developments. Many bankers see EFTS as providing an opportunity for initiating new services and reducing costs, thus increasing profitability. Others, especially those representing small banks, view EFTS as being prohibitively costly; they fear that they would not be able to compete with the larger banks which could afford the

Reprinted from *Monthly Review*, September 1976, pp. 10–18, by permission of the Federal Reserve Bank of St. Louis and the author.

[1]"Bank Cards Take Over the Country," *Business Week*, August 4, 1975, p. 44.

necessary computer equipment and, as a result, would be forced out of the market. Thrift institutions view EFTS as a means of obtaining deposits for which only commercial banks have heretofore been permitted to compete and have thus been in the forefront of EFTS developments

Government will probably play a large role in the evolution of EFTS. Court interpretations of existing laws have already shaped the direction of some EFTS developments. New legislation and regulations will almost certainly be adopted, but as yet no clear trend in the nature of these changes is discernible. Some of these changes may be dependent on the findings of the National Commission on Electronic Funds Transfers.[2]

EFTS and the Payments Mechanism

To speak of *the* electronic funds transfer system is an oversimplification. In fact, EFT developments are proceeding in several directions, with a number of different systems in various phases of development or use. The common factor in these systems is that they speed the transfer of funds by communicating information relating to payments by electronic means rather than by use of paper instruments as is predominant today. Thus, EFT systems are designed to replace manual processes with electronic data processing and to speed the flow of funds through high speed data transmission.

Although EFTS is often considered a revolutionary development with far-reaching effects, EFT developments can be viewed as just another step in the evolution of the payments mechanism—the system by which resources are transferred from one economic unit to another. This evolution reflects the continuing effort to improve the efficiency of trading. Money, which is simply a device which facilitates trade, represented an improvement over barter in that it reduced transactions costs and thus freed resources for use in the production of other goods and services. Checks came into widespread usage because they offered considerable advantages over cash; they were easily transported in any amount, easily transferred between individuals, involved much less danger of loss or theft than cash, and served as proof of payment. Checks thus reduced the transactions costs involved in making many types of money payments. Still, considerable transaction costs are associated with the processing of these paper documents.

Furthermore, because of the indirect nature of the check clearing process, there is often a delay in the availability of "good funds" for the payee. These delays can be costly, especially when large sums are involved. The development of wire transfers, through which banks can effect funds transfers by sending electronic messages rather than paper documents, represented a major improvement in the payments mechanism. One of the large wire transfer networks is operated by the Federal Reserve System, which transfers large volumes of funds for member banks and their

---

[2]"EFT Commission Rebuffs Mitchell's Plea for Comment on Proposed Changes to Reg. J," *American Banker,* March 15, 1976, p. 1.

customers through its computerized communications system. The dollar volume of funds transferred by the Federal Reserve Communications System in 1975 was almost seven times as large as the amount handled by the Fed's check clearing system.[3] The average transfer is quite large—about $1.8 million in 1975—but the number of wire transfers is only a small fraction of the number of checks handled.

To the extent that wire transfers reduce transaction costs and processing time they can be said to improve the efficiency of the payments mechanism. However, the use of wire transfers has not significantly reduced the vast flow of paper through the payments system. A major reduction in paper volume would require implementation of electronic systems designed to be utilized for smaller retail-oriented payments, such as the systems described below.

Description of Some EFT Systems

For the sake of clarity and simplicity, EFT systems can be grouped into three categories: teller machines, point-of-sale systems, and automated clearing houses. These systems differ in types of payments handled and in means of processing.

Teller Machines

Machines through which an individual may conduct various routine banking services can be grouped under the heading of teller machines. Much of the recent EFTS development has involved these machines, which are called customer-bank communication terminals (CBCTs) by the Comptroller of the Currency and remote service units (RSUs) by the Federal Home Loan Bank Board. In principle, these machines can be located either on a bank's premises or elsewhere, conceivably at great distances from the bank. They may be manned or automatic and vary greatly in complexity, ranging from simple communications terminals to more complicated automated teller machines (ATMs). Services which ATMs can typically perform include receiving deposits, dispensing funds from checking or savings accounts, transferring funds between accounts, making credit card advances, and receiving payments. The less complicated manned terminals handle the communications between the customer and his bank while the receipt or disbursing of funds is physically accomplished by the clerk who operates the terminal.

Teller machines are usually accessed by a combination of a magnetic stripe card (on which account information is encoded) and a personal identification number which, for security reasons, is known only to the customer. If the device is connected "on-line" to the bank's computer, the customer's account is updated immediately; otherwise, a record maintained in the machine is periodically delivered to the bank for processing.

[3]*Annual Report of the Board of Governors of the Federal Reserve System* (1975), p. 379.

Point-of-Sale Systems

On-line systems which allow customers to transfer funds to merchants in order to make purchases are usually called point-of-sale (POS) systems. Systems of this type may be used for check authorizations and credit card transactions, as well as for so-called "debit card" transactions in which funds are immediately transferred from the purchaser's account to the merchant's account. Conceivably, they could also be used for instantaneously transferring funds between businesses and/or individuals, using terminals or pushbutton telephones.

Large-scale POS systems generally operate in the following manner. On-line terminals are located at check-out counters or other points of sale. When making a purchase, a customer's card is inserted into a terminal which "reads" the data encoded on it. Other data concerning the transaction are entered manually by the clerk or through an electronic cash register or products code reader. If the customer's bank is different from the store's bank, a switching and processing center (SPC) connects the computers of the two banks. The computer at the customer's bank verifies that the card and identification code are valid and that the customer's account has sufficient funds. The customer's account is debited for the amount of the purchase while the store's account is credited for the same amount. Both parties to the transaction receive a printed statement at the time of the transaction, and the customer's regular bank statement contains a descriptive listing, much like those which many credit cards presently use. Since some 30 percent of personal checks are written to grocery or other retail stores,[4] this type of system would allow automation of a substantial portion of check payments as well as many payments presently made by cash or credit card.

Automated Clearing Houses

Another type of EFT system, which is conceptually different from the two systems described above, is the automated clearing house (ACH). As the name suggests, an ACH is analogous to a traditional clearing house, in that it represents a system for the interbank clearing of debits and credits. The main difference between automated and conventional clearing houses is that the debit and credit items in an ACH exist in the form of electronic signals, whereas they are paper items in a conventional clearinghouse operation. An ACH is thus *not* a system for automating the handling and clearing of paper checks. The payment items must enter the system in the form of electronic data, usually computer-generated magnetic tape.

To illustrate how an ACH works, consider how a payroll payment could be made directly to an employee's checking or savings account through an ACH. The em-

---

[4]This estimate is based on surveys reported in *Research on Improvements of the Payments Mechanism: The Final Report on Phase I, An Analysis of Payments Transactions and Phase II, Payments Flow Data,* Vol. 1 of 3 (Atlanta: Georgia Tech Research Institute, 1971), p. 30.

ployee authorizes his employer to make such direct payments, eliminating the need for a check to pass through the employee's hands, be endorsed, cashed or deposited, and sent through the check clearing process to the employer's bank. The employer prepares the payroll data on computer tape and sends it to the company's bank. The bank directly credits the employee's account if he is a customer and combines the data for the remaining payees with those from other employers on a magnetic tape. This consolidated tape is delivered or transmitted to the ACH, where a computer processes all the data for a day in a single run, sorting out all payees for each participating bank. Each bank then receives a computer tape (or paper advice if it is not equipped to handle tape) which lists the payees and the amount to be credited to each account. The employer's accounts are debited by the originating banks. Net settlement among the banks is accomplished in the same manner as with paper checks.

ACHs are especially suited for handling recurring payments, such as payroll, social security, or pension payments, or recurring payments made by individuals. Payors would authorize their banks to pay a specified amount to a payee (mortgage lender, insurance company, etc.) on a specified date. Parties to these types of payments would receive a descriptive statement documenting the payment.

Many types of payments—those where the payee and amount vary—are not amenable to this type of preauthorization. The case of regularly recurring bills of varying amounts, such as utility bills, represents a middle ground between the extremes of identical recurring payments and more or less random payments. The customer could, for example, authorize his bank to pay the amount billed by a specified creditor.[5] Since many people are reluctant to give such broad power to their banks, a system called Bill Check has been developed.[6] This type of payment allows the customer to control the amount and timing of payments to creditors but still achieves some of the benefits of ACHs.

An ACH thus differs considerably from teller machines and POS systems. The ACH is essentially a "batch" processing system used for the interbank settlement of recurring credits and debits, whereas many of the other systems allow instantaneous transfers of funds between the customer and his bank or from the customer to third parties.

---

[5]American Express has initiated such a service for credit card customers in California. Based on a preauthorization, the full amount of a credit card bill would be paid from the customer's bank account to American Express, unless the customer objected within a specified period after receiving the bill. See "American Express Will Begin Testing Preauthorized Payments through CACHA," *Payment Systems Newsletter*, February 1975, p. 6.

[6]The Bill Check itself is a portion of the bill on which the customer indicates the amount to be paid and signs his name, and then returns to the creditor. This completed form authorizes a debit from the customer's account to pay the bill. The creditor transfers the data to computer tape and sends the tape to the ACH for processing. The paper Bill Check is retained by the creditor for its records. See Atlanta Payments Project, *Automated Clearing Houses: An In-Depth Analysis* (Atlanta: Committee on Paperless Entries, 1974), pp. 35–39.

Costs of Funds Transfers

Costs of the Check-Based Payments System

Knowledge of the number of checks written in a year and the cost of processing them is imprecise. However, it is estimated that in 1975 between 25 and 30 billion checks were written[7] involving total processing costs of around $6 billion.[8]

When a payee cashes or deposits a check through a teller line, lock box, or other arrangement, the first bank receiving the check must encode the amount of the check in magnetic ink character recognition (MICR) readable symbols. This completes the encoding of the check (the bank's routing number and payor's account number are already encoded on the check), so most of the remaining processing can be conducted by machines capable of reading the MICR characters. The transit items (those drawn on other banks) are sent to the bank on which they are drawn, either directly or through a clearing house, correspondent bank, or the Federal Reserve's check collection facilities. When the check returns to the bank against which it is drawn, the writer's account is debited, and the cancelled check is returned to the writer with the periodic statement. Altogether, the average check is handled some ten times and passes through two and one-third banks.[9]

Much of the processing described above is now automated. Machines read and sort the encoded check according to destination and perform most of the accounting functions. However, a number of the processing functions have not been amenable to automation. Many checks are still handled by tellers, the encoding process requires human handling, and the checks must still be physically transported through the banking system and back to the payor.

These manual processes appear to be among the most expensive in the check processing function. The average costs of these various processes were estimated by the Atlanta Payments Project through surveys of Atlanta banks.[10] The estimated cost of receiving an item through a branch was 7.4 cents and the cost of proof and encoding an item was 1.3 cents. Together, these accounted for nearly 60 percent of the 13.9 cents cost of processing an "on-us" item (a check deposited in the bank on which it was drawn) and more than 80 percent of the 10.6 cents costs of a transit item.[11]

[7]According to one estimate more than 24 billion checks were processed in 1974, with the number increasing at a 7.3 percent annual rate between 1971 and 1974. See R. William Powers, "A Survey of Bank Check Volumes," *Journal of Bank Research,* Winter 1976, pp. 245–56.

[8]The latest estimates of average check processing costs of commercial banks are in the 16–21-cent range. To these costs must also be added the indirect costs borne by writers and receivers of checks, as well as Federal Reserve expenses for check clearing. See Arthur D. Little, Inc., *The Consequences of Electronic Funds Transfers,* prepared for the National Science Foundation (1975), p. 51.

[9]Mark J. Flannery and Dwight M. Jaffee, *The Economic Implications of an Electronic Monetary Transfer System* (Lexington, Mass.: D. C. Heath and Company, 1973), p. 41.

[10]Atlanta Payments Project, *Automated Clearing Houses: An In-Depth Analysis,* pp. 218–19.

[11]An interesting sidelight of this study is that much of the cost of processing a check is borne by the bank of first deposit rather than the bank on which the check is drawn. Of course, the cashing bank frequently receives new deposits in the process which can compensate it for the costs it bears.

Given this situation, the prospects of lowering the average cost of check processing materially below its present levels do not appear to be good. Economies of scale in check processing may well be nearly exhausted. As labor and other costs rise, the average cost of check clearing is also likely to rise.

These factors have led many to believe that radical changes in the payments mechanism are necessary if costs are to be kept at present levels or be reduced. If the paper document which carries the payments data can be replaced by an electronic signal, manual handling can be significantly reduced and the flow of payments data accelerated by high speed data transmission.

Cost Characteristics of EFTS

Although few cost data are available because of the limited experience with EFTS, some dated but representative cost estimates are available. Most EFT systems involve large total cost, much of which is associated with the expensive computer hardware necessary to operate these systems: computers, terminals, and communication links. Even teller machines, which are among the less expensive types of systems, involve purchase costs that may exceed $40,000 per ATM, depending on features.

More complicated systems involve higher total costs. An on-line POS system would involve high costs not only for the banks' computers, the terminals in stores, and the communications links joining them, but also for the SPC which interconnects the computers of the different banks. In one study, published four years ago, the Atlanta Payments Project estimated total costs for a proposed POS system linking the banks in that city.[12] These included about $650,000 for SPC processing equipment and $655,000 for SPC development costs, about $1,200 for each terminal and associated communications equipment, and about $54,000 for bank communications interface equipment.

Competitive Questions Surrounding EFTS

EFTS has such a significant potential for changing costs and providing new services that it will likely have far-reaching effects on the structure of and competition within the financial industry. In turn, these competitive forces will doubtless influence the course of EFTS implementation, reflecting developments within the financial industry and concerns of legislators and regulatory agencies.

Many people expect that in the years to come EFTS will be one of the principal areas of competition among banks. The changing cost

---

[12]Atlanta Payments Project, *Research on Improvements of the Payments Mechanism: Phase III General Systems Design and Analysis of An Electronic Funds Transfer System,* Volume 3 of *Systems Design and Analysis-Point of Sale System,* 6 vols. (Atlanta: Georgia Tech Research Institute, 1972), Chap. 8.

structure associated with new ways of making payments also has considerable implications for the competition between commercial banks and thrift institutions.

COMPETITION AND REGULATION

Competition between firms and industries is generally considered a good thing, since it forces the sellers to pass the benefits of technological change on to the consumer in the form of lower prices and/or improved service. From the standpoint of the whole economy, competition also leads to an efficient allocation of resources.

In competitive markets, it is a normal form of adjustment for inefficient firms to incur losses and eventually drop out of the market. However, because of the widely held belief that considerable social costs are involved in bank failures, the depository financial institutions have been subjected to regulation which in general limits competition. Although there have been some recent regulatory efforts toward encouraging (or allowing) more competition, there is a distinct possibility that some limits will be placed on competition through EFTS, especially if increased bank failures or pressures on thrift institutions are expected to result from such competition. Thus, some efficiency gains which might result from EFTS probably will be foregone in order to avoid increased failures.

EFFECT ON STRUCTURE

Many observers expect that EFTS will lead to major changes in the structure of the banking industry. Since teller machines can provide many routine banking services and are much less expensive than traditional "brick and mortar" branches, many observers believe they will be the "branches" of the future. If so, there would be considerable competition as banks attempt to gain customers by installing these machines in convenient locations. It has been argued that big banks, through EFT machines, will enter the market areas of smaller banks all across the country and, because of the huge initial costs of EFT systems, the smaller banks will not be able to compete.

It is not clear, however, that smaller banks would be at a disadvantage in operating these machines. For example, relatively small banks might find that prudent deployment of these machines would enable them to expand their market areas at a much lower cost than with a conventional branch. These machines could thus prove *relatively* more beneficial to the smaller banks than to the larger ones which have the capability to operate a large number of conventional branches.

A major regulatory question is involved here: are teller machines branches within the meaning of the McFadden Act, which subjects branching by national banks to state branching laws, or simply communications devices? If the former is ruled to be the case, deployment of the teller machines would be subject to state branching restrictions and regulatory controls; if the latter is accepted their deployment might be relatively unfettered. All but one of the court decisions rendered to date have found the machines to be branches under the McFadden Act. Since this Act defines a branch to include "any branch place of business . . . at which deposits are received, or checks paid, or money lent," banks affected by the rulings have been forced to cease these functions at their remote teller machines which are not located in a permissible branch. Savings and loan associations are not subject to the McFadden Act and hence have not been subject to the same limitations as banks. Partly as a result of this apparent regulatory inequality, legislation which would exempt bank teller machines from these branching limitations has been enacted in some states and is pending in others.

OWNERSHIP OF EFT SYSTEMS

The question of ownership of EFT systems has frequently been raised. Some individuals and groups argue that operation of competing EFT systems would be uneconomical and could thus lead to increased bank failures. This argument is based, at least in part, on the belief that EFT systems are "natural monopolies," much like local public utilities.

The essential characteristic of the economic concept of natural monopoly is that economies of scale are so pervasive that average costs decline over the entire extent of demand in the market. One seller of the product could produce a given volume at minimum average cost, whereas two or more sellers would each be inefficiently small, necessitating higher prices.

The issue of ownership of EFT systems thus turns on the empirical question of whether there are extensive economies of scale in such systems. Although there is as yet little evidence on which to make a judgment, some generalizations can perhaps be made. There do appear to be economies of scale in such systems, but it is not at all clear that these economies of scale are so extensive that only one firm could operate a large-scale EFT system efficiently. For example, both major bank credit card concerns (which have large networks of participating banks and merchants as well as extensive computer systems for authorization of transactions and interchange of charge items among the banks) are presently developing POS systems, as are some larger correspondent banks and various other organizations. A retail store could utilize more than one competing system through a single dial-up type terminal and existing telephone lines.

The ownership question is applicable to ACHs as well. ACHs have developed similarly to conventional clearinghouses, with only one ACH serving a geographical area. All but two operating or planned ACHs are operated by the regional Federal Reserve Banks, the principal justification being that these ACH services are basically extensions of the present check clearing function of the Fed.

As in the case of POS systems, there is the question of whether competing ACHs would be feasible. The Justice Department, apparently believing that competition could develop in the provision of automated clearing services, has questioned whether the Federal Reserve System or other governmental agencies should directly operate the ACHs:

> The greatest danger is that a Federal EFT system—especially one that is artificially low-priced—could deter private competitors from deploying private EFT systems, and inflict severe injury on those who have already begun to operate them . . . Many private entities stand ready to supply the same sort of facilities and services that Reserve Banks offer to financial institutions . . . The Board [of Governors should] . . . play the role of overseer, and leave the practical day-to-day operations of the ACH to the private sector with the marketplace acting as the "regulator."[1]

ROLE OF THRIFT INSTITUTIONS

The role of thrift institutions in EFT systems is currently much at issue. These nonbank institutions have been in the forefront of some EFT developments, notably in teller machines and POS systems. This is partly because EFTS provides the thrifts an entry into the payments mechanism which legislation has largely denied to them, and partly because some laws and regulations have been less restrictive of EFTS development by thrifts than by banks.

The involvement of thrift institutions is currently at issue in many ACHs. Utilization of ACHs has usually been opened to all banks in an area, but thrift institutions have frequently been denied access, at least on an equal footing with banks.

Originally thrift institutions were required to use a "pass through" arrangement in which transfers to and from the thrift institutions were made through a bank which had direct access to the ACH. Of course, this involved additional costs and some delays for the thrifts. Interim guidelines adopted by the Board of Governors allow thrifts to receive direct delivery of credit or debit items from Fed-operated ACHs if the institutions have sufficient volume to warrant it and are on an existing

---

[1]Comments of the United States Department of Justice in the Matter of Regulation J, reprinted in *American Banker,* June 15, 1976, pp. 4 ff.

courier route. The guidelines also allow any institution which is a member of an automated clearing house association to send items to the ACHs. Previously only those institutions with demand deposit authority were allowed to originate these items. The thrifts believe that these guidelines still discriminate against many of them and leave them at a competitive disadvantage relative to the banks with more direct access.

It is a long-standing principle of antitrust law that where there is a unique resource such as a clearinghouse, all competing firms should have access to it.[2] At present there are legal distinctions between banks and thrifts, a major one being the ability to offer accounts from which customers can make payments to third parties. Demand deposit powers have traditionally been limited to commercial banks, but thrift institutions have long sought third party payment powers, primarily as a source of deposits. Although thrifts have developed some close substitutes for checks (notably NOW accounts) they apparently hope to bypass the cumbersome and expensive check-based payments system and to enter the payments mechanism directly through EFTS.

Many of the services already offered by thrifts serve as close substitutes for third party payment powers. For example, the First Federal-Hinky Dinky TMS system in Nebraska allows customers to deposit or withdraw funds through transfers from or to the supermarket's First Federal account. This is tantamount to a third party POS system. Introduction of services like these has forced banks to offer competing services. The distinction between savings accounts at thrift institutions and demand deposits at banks is being blurred, and with it the distinction between banks and thrifts themselves.

Greater competition among types of financial institutions can be expected to result from development of EFTS. A blurring of the distinctions between financial institutions and a lowering in price of services (and an increased return on deposits) could be expected, in the absence of restrictive regulation. Consumers stand to benefit as financial institutions compete in offering incentives to customers to shift from checking to EFT services. The economy as a whole could also benefit through a more efficient payments mechanism.

The Federal Reserve Bank of Cleveland has estimated total costs of operating a larger POS system, which would link 39 banks in the Fourth Federal Reserve District.[13] Assuming that the system would capture 6–7 percent of total retail trans-

[2]Donald I. Baker, "Antitrust and Automated Banking," *Banking Law Journal*, September 1973, p. 703–18.

[13]Arthur D. Little, Inc., *The Consequences of Electronic Funds Transfer*, pp. 196–98.

Table 1. Estimated ACH Operating Costs

Monthly Transaction Volume	Monthly Costs	Cost Per Transaction (cents)
20,000	$2,150	10.8
152,500	2,650	03.3
285,000	3,150	01.8
417,000	3,650	01.1
550,000	4,160	00.8

Note: These estimates are for the Atlanta ACH. The program used requires about one hour of processing time for any daily volume up to 25,000. Thus, some costs will be relatively fixed up to the monthly volume of 550,000 shown in the table. The Project anticipates that software changes could expand the hourly volume to 75-100,000; operating costs would remain about the same, and the average cost of a transaction would drop to about 0.2 cents.

Source: Atlanta Payments Project, *Automated Clearing Houses: An In-Depth Analysis,* Chap. 10.

actions, in the tenth year the average costs of operating the SPCs alone would be an estimated $3.8 million. Costs of participating banks in the tenth year would be another $13.9 million, it was estimated. Total costs for the first ten years of operation would exceed $100 million.

Many of the costs which are associated with EFT systems do not vary with the number of transactions and thus can be considered as fixed costs. An example is the depreciation of the computers, terminals, and other equipment used in the system which would be the same regardless of the level of usage. Some other costs probably do not vary significantly with the level of usage either. The costs of operating a computer used solely for an EFT system would probably be little higher at relatively high levels of transactions than at low.

There are other costs which do vary with the level of output or usage. For example, labor costs associated with operating a manned terminal may be greater at higher levels of usage than at low. The cost of computer time necessary to process teller machine or POS transactions would also depend on the number of transactions. One study estimated the cost of the infinitesimal amount of computer time necessary to process a POS transaction to be about 1 cent per transaction.[14]

To date, ACHs have utilized an existing computer (in most cases at a Federal Reserve Bank), since a computer run processing a whole day's accumulated items usually takes an hour or less. The processing time and labor costs do not appear to vary greatly with the number of transactions processed. Estimated costs of operating the Atlanta ACH at various levels of output are shown in Table 1.

A characteristic of the costs of many EFT systems is evident in this table: the average cost of a transaction declines significantly as the number of transactions in-

[14]Atlanta Payments Project, *Research on Improvements of the Payments Mechanism: Phase III,* Vol. 3 of 6, p. 166.

Table 2. Federal Reserve Payments Mechanism Expenses, 1975

Conventional Check Processing			Automated Clearing House Processing		
Checks Processed (Thousands)	Total Expense	Cost Per Check*	"Check Images" Processed (Thousands)	Total Expense	Cost Per "Image"
11,411,337	$120,559,005	0.995 cents	5,941	$431,883	7.27 cents

* This item excludes postage and expressage on items handled by others, which were included in the "Total Expense" category.

Source: Board of Governors of the Federal Reserve System, Functional Expense Report, 1975 Annual Report.

creases. This is caused by the predominance of relatively fixed costs in most EFT systems. From the standpoint of the Federal Reserve System, which operates most ACHs, a high level of output would have to be reached before the average cost of a transaction would fall below the Fed's average cost of clearing a check, which is about 1 cent. The data on Federal Reserve check processing and ACH costs presented in Table 2 indicate that, at current volumes, processing an ACH item is much more expensive to the Fed than processing a check. Of course, this means that ACHs are presently operating at far less than efficient volumes. Furthermore, potential cost savings to participating banks from making electronic payments through an ACH rather than using checks should also be considered. Data from the Atlanta Payments Project suggest that monthly volumes of more than 160,000 transactions at the Atlanta ACH would result in the average cost of an ACH transaction falling below the average cost of a check.[15]

Estimates of average costs of POS transactions also suggest that if sufficiently large volume is attained, the average cost of a POS transaction can fall below the average cost of a check. In the Cleveland Fed study, referred to above, the average cost per transaction over a three-year period was estimated to be 11.3 cents; this would be reduced to 7.1 cents by the tenth year because of expected economies of scale in operation of the system.[16]

Another cost concept should be considered. This is marginal cost, which is simply the change in total cost which results from increasing output by one unit. Marginal cost is thus not affected by fixed cost but only by variable costs. In the case of EFT systems, the marginal cost would be the change in cost that resulted from conducting one additional transaction. The considerations described above suggest that the marginal cost of an EFT transaction is likely to be very low. In most cases, little or no additional labor is involved, and only an infinitesimal amount of computer time is used. Thus, an additional transaction should add very little to the cost of the

[15]Atlanta Payments Project, *Automated Clearing Houses: An In-Depth Analysis,* p. 229. This estimate assumes no bank marketing costs associated with the ACH operation.

[16]Arthur D. Little, Inc., *The Consequences of Electronic Funds Transfer,* pp. 195–98. The Cleveland Fed Study estimates that the POS system would generate cost savings such that the annual savings would exceed annual costs by the seventh year and cumulative savings exceed cumulative costs by the tenth year. This estimate did not include savings experienced by merchants as a result of using the POS system.

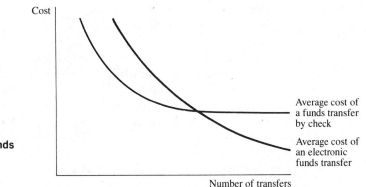

Hypothetical Costs of Funds Transfers

Cost

Average cost of a funds transfer by check

Average cost of an electronic funds transfer

Number of transfers

system. In comparison, the marginal cost of a check is probably relatively high because of the labor intensiveness of check processing.[17]

In summary, many EFT systems will involve large fixed costs but relatively small variable costs. Because of this predominance of fixed costs, average costs of EFT transactions will probably decline over a fairly large range of output. The hypothetical cost curves presented in the accompanying figure show the average cost of an electronic funds transfer to be greater than the average cost of a check at relatively low volumes. Beyond some point, however, the average cost of checks levels off while that of electronic funds transfers continues to fall. The average cost of electronic transfers is less than that of checks for relatively large volumes. Although these cost relationships are hypothetical, they demonstrate the general relationship between the costs of check systems and EFTS.

Customer Acceptance of EFTS

If the potentially lower unit costs of EFTS are to be realized, a substantial proportion of present payments must be switched to electronic means. Otherwise, banks may find themselves with the worst of both worlds: a large, slow, expensive check handling system, plus a very expensive underutilized EFT network. Thus, failure to consider customer acceptance of EFTS could have exactly the opposite effects from those hoped for.

At present, there seems to be little incentive for customers to change their payments practices from using checks to EFT systems. Surveys have found that individuals are generally satisfied with the present payments system. Using checks provides many benefits, including unquestioned proof of payment. The surveys also indicate that many individuals, especially those in lower income groups, have a negative attitude toward many aspects of EFT systems.[18] Customers tend to fear a

---

[17]One study estimated the marginal cost to be 14 cents, not much below the average cost estimated in the same study. Flannery and Jaffee, *The Economic Implications of an Electronic Monetary Transfer System,* p. 42, n. 10.

[18]See Arthur D. Little, Inc., *The Consequences of Electronic Funds Transfer,* pp. 43–46, 253–63.

"loss of control" over their finances which would result from preauthorized deposits or withdrawals, as well as possible losses of privacy, costly errors, and lack of proof of payment. Thus, in many cases, it may take considerable incentive to induce individuals to shift their payments from checks to electronic means.

Such an incentive could be provided if the cost savings which would result from a fully utilized EFT system were passed on to the customer. However, current regulations reduce the likelihood of banks providing such incentives. For example, since banks are prohibited by Regulation Q from paying an explicit return on demand deposits, they usually pay an implicit return by subsidizing the checking costs of their customers, either totally or in part.[19] Thus, the cost to the individual of writing an additional check is usually less than the marginal cost to society of processing the check. As a result, "too many" checks are written, and a greater than optimal quantity of resources is allocated to check processing. As long as banks are prohibited from explicitly paying interest on demand deposits, it does not seem likely that they will charge fees for checking services which approximate the marginal costs of the checks. As a result, the prospects of banks providing sufficient incentives for customers to switch from checking to the lower-marginal-cost electronic funds transfer services are reduced.

The underutilization of EFT systems which would stem from the prohibition of interest on demand deposits could be worsened if customers receive additional disincentives to use EFT systems. Such disincentives could take the form of high initial prices for EFT services which banks may charge, predicated on the notion of recovering the large fixed costs of the EFT systems relatively quickly.

Summary

Many of the questions surrounding EFTS cannot yet be answered definitely, since they depend on costs, regulations, and other factors for which there are few or no data. However, it is reasonable to expect marginal costs of making a transfer through EFTS to be less than through the check system; average costs of transfers could also be lower, if a sufficiently large volume is achieved. Such possibilities for reducing costs, other things equal, would encourage banks and other producers to increase their supply of these services relative to checking services. However, such factors as the prohibition against paying interest on demand deposits appear to reduce the incentive for customers to use EFT systems, thus slowing their development.

[19] "'Yields' on Checking Accounts Rise in Recent Years," Federal Reserve Bank of Philadelphia, *Business Review,* March 1975, pp. 14–15.

The Growing Similarity among Financial Institutions

Jean M. Lovati

Depository financial institutions are able to exist because of certain efficiencies which allow them to provide credit to borrowers at lower rates and higher net returns to depositors than would be available without such intermediaries.[1] These efficiencies, combined with nationally mandated priorities concerning the roles of these institutions in society, have produced institutions which are specialized in scope. Despite some efforts to maintain this specialization, financial institutions are forming a new framework within which to operate. By creating and reacting to competitive challenges, financial institutions are breaking away from their specialized roles and successfully altering traditional distinctions.

Changes in Asset Competition

Response of Thrifts to Rising Interest Rates

Most depository financial institutions are subject to regulatory ceilings on the rates they are allowed to offer to attract funds. In general, these ceilings pose few prob-

Reprinted, with deletions, from *Review*, October 1977, pp. 2-11, by permission of the Federal Reserve Bank of St. Louis and the author.
[1]This article focuses only on commercial banks, savings and loan associations, mutual savings banks, and credit unions.

Table 1. Distribution of Assets

	1960 ($ Millions)	1970 ($ Millions)	1976 ($ Millions)	Annual Rates of Change 1960–1970	Annual Rates of Change 1970–1976
Commercial Banks[1]					
Business Loans	$43,132	$112,215	$177,128	10.0%	7.9%
Mortgages	28,694	73,053	149,276	9.8	12.7
Consumer Loans	26,377	66,006	118,051	9.6	10.2
U.S. Treasury and Agency Securities	60,423	61,617	136,729	0.2	14.2
State and Local Securities	17,337	69,390	104,374	14.9	7.0
Other Assets	80,360	194,070	318,462	9.2	8.6
Total	256,323	576,351	1,004,020	8.4	9.7
Savings and Loan Associations					
Mortgages	$60,070	$150,331	$323,130	9.6%	13.6%
Investment Securities[2]	4,595	13,020	35,660	11.0	18.3
Other Assets	6,811	12,832	33,209	6.5	17.2
Total	71,476	176,183	391,999	9.4	14.3
Mutual Savings Banks					
Mortgages	$26,702	$ 57,775	$ 81,630	8.0%	5.9%
U.S. Government Securities	6,243	3,151	5,840	− 6.6	10.8
State and Local Securities	672	197	2,417	− 11.6	51.9
Corporate and Other Securities	5,076	12,876	33,793	9.8	17.5
Other Assets	1,878	4,996	11,131	10.3	14.3
Total	40,571	78,995	134,811	6.9	9.3
Credit Unions					
Loans Outstanding	$ 4,402	$ 14,152	$ 34,293	12.4%	15.9%
Other Assets	1,257	3,798	10,542	11.7	18.6
Total	5,659	17,950	44,835	12.2	16.5

[1] Insured banks.
[2] Includes cash.
Sources: *Banking and Monetary Statistics*, 1941–1970; Federal Reserve *Bulletins*.

lems to the institutions as long as the ceiling rates remain competitive with market rates. However, during periods of rising interest rates, short-term money market rates rise above the interest rate ceilings imposed on these institutions.

Because of their more diverse and more stable source of funds, commercial banks are not as seriously affected as "thrifts" by such an imbalance in relative interest rates;[2] being very specialized institutions, thrifts suffer more acutely from deposit outflows, called disintermediation, as market rates rise. When other short-term interest rates become more attractive than those which can be earned at the thrifts, depositors transfer their funds out of savings accounts and into other instruments. Twice during the last eight years, once in the second half of 1969 and again in 1974, disintermediation put severe financial strain on the operations of thrifts.

[2]Thrifts here include saving and loan associations and mutual savings banks.

To complicate matters, thrifts further suffer from problems relating to short-term financing of long-term assets (mortgages). Since only a fraction of thrifts' mortgage portfolios are replaced in any one year, the average return on mortgages (the major earning asset of the institutions) typically does not rise fast enough to match increases in short-term rates. At such times, thrifts are caught in an earnings squeeze.

As these situations arise, thrift institutions increasingly are being pressured to stabilize their deposit sources of funds. Thrifts, taking advantage of the current level of technology, are attempting this stabilization by offering new deposit services (which are discussed in a following section).

At the same time, when high and variable interest rates have forced many institutions to examine the structure of their assets, thrifts are emphasizing shorter-term assets in their portfolios.

Such assets typically have shorter maturities than mortgages, yet still are within regulatory bounds. Investments, such as U.S. government and agency securities and state and local government securities, are growing in importance. Investment securities at savings and loan associations (S&Ls) rose $23 billion between 1970 and 1976, or at an 18 percent annual rate, compared to an 11 percent rate between 1960 and 1970 (Table 1). These securities increased to 9 percent of assets in 1976 from 7 percent in 1970. Investment in corporate and other securities by mutual savings banks (MSBs) increased at a 17 percent rate over the six-year period, compared to a 10 percent rate in the 1960–70 period, and rose from 16 to 25 percent of total assets between 1970 and 1976.

To shorten the average maturity of other assets, some thrifts are emphasizing the development of consumer loans, often forging new regulatory powers. Mutual savings banks and state-chartered S&Ls in Connecticut, Maine, and New York state have been authorized to expand the type of consumer loans they make, which includes overdraft checking. Credit card services also have been accorded increased importance by thrifts. In 1974, Visa U.S.A. Inc. altered its bylaws to permit membership for MSBs, and in May 1976, membership was extended to S&Ls. As of August 1977, 124 of the nation's 469 savings banks were offering bank credit card services.[3]

One of the most publicized changes in thrifts' asset structure is the variable rate home mortgage (VRM), which is being successfully marketed by some state-chartered S&Ls in California and the Midwest.[4] The interest rate on a variable rate mortgage is tied to a cost of funds index such that the mortgage rate adjusts, within certain bounds, to changes in short-term market rates. With variable rate mortgages, the returns to the thrifts on their mortgage portfolios adjust more rapidly to changes in the level of interest rates than with traditional mortgages.

---

[3]*Savings Bank Journal,* August 1977, p. 40.

[4]In 1976, five California S&Ls together made about $6.4 billion in new mortgage loans. Of this amount, $4 billion, or 63 percent, were VRMs. These five associations represent approximately 30 percent of the S&L industry in California. *American Banker,* May 23, 1977.

Increased Competition from Credit Unions

In addition to pressures from high and variable interest rates, thrift institutions will be faced with increased competition for mortgages from credit unions (CUs). In the past, length of loan maturity at credit unions was restricted to not more than 10 years, effectively excluding CUs from the mortgage market. Although state laws often permitted more latitude to credit unions with respect to real estate loans, mortgage holdings of state-chartered CUs typically have been small.

This is likely to change as a result of legislation recently passed by Congress which enables CUs to supply mortgage loans within expanded size and maturity ranges. As a result of legislation which was formally passed in April 1977, CUs are able to make mortgages with maturities up to 30 years and home improvement or mobile home loans with maturities up to 15 years.

Consumer Loan Market

While credit unions are recent competitive additions to the mortgage market, they are mature and effective competitors with commercial banks in the consumer loan market.[5] Credit unions, with $34 billion in consumer loans in 1976, represent the third consumer instalment lender in the country and hold over 16 percent of the 1976 dollar volume of consumer instalment loans outstanding. Over 76 percent of credit union assets is devoted to consumer loans. Commercial banks, with $118 billion devoted to consumer loans, hold 48 percent of the total outstanding consumer instalment debt.

From 1960 to 1970, consumer loans at CUs increased strongly at a 12 percent annual rate. Since 1970, growth has been even more rapid; CU loans have more than doubled between 1970 and 1976, increasing at an average annual rate of 16 percent. The consumer loan business at commercial banks has not grown as fast. Between 1960 and 1970, these loans grew at an annual rate of 9.6 percent, slightly slower, on average, than in the subsequent six years.

The growth of CU loans, and therefore their assets, has been aided by favorable loan rates compared to those of commercial banks and other lending institutions. . . . Credit unions are able to profitably offer lower instalment loan rates because they experience lower fixed costs on loans. Several factors contribute to lower fixed costs, including lower costs in assembling information on loan applicants and collecting payments. Regulations governing CUs require a common bond among members before organization of a credit union is permitted. This common bond often provides an established source of information on members and facilitates the payment of the loan through payroll deductions, for example.

---

[5]Commercial banks, finance companies, and credit unions comprise the three largest sources of consumer loans. As mentioned above, S&Ls and MSBs are not yet strong competitors in this market.

Moreover, because of the subsidies granted them, credit unions often realize free office space and clerical help, pay no Federal taxes and generally pay little state tax, thus escaping many expenses other institutions face.[6]

During December 1974, for example, direct loans on new cars carried an interest rate of 11.62 percent at commercial banks, while at credit unions such loans carried a rate of 10.34 percent. Personal loans at commercial banks were made at an interest rate of 13.60 percent at that time; at CUs they were made at an 11.56 percent rate.[7] . . . Since credit union rates already include such factors as the cost of credit life insurance, the basic rates would be even lower than those indicated here.

Although the difference in rates charged has not been so great since 1974, it is nevertheless noteworthy. During 1976, interest rates for new auto loans at CUs varied between 15 and 53 basis points below those at commercial banks. Personal loans at credit unions fluctuated between 157 and 198 basis points below personal loan rates at commercial banks.

As a result, credit unions are advancing their position in the consumer loan market. Based on instalment credit outstanding, CUs held 13 percent of the total credit outstanding in 1972 (15 percent of automobile credit). In 1976, they held about 17 percent of total credit outstanding (23 percent of automobile credit). Commercial banks, on the other hand, have held a fairly constant share of instalment credit, averaging about 48 percent of the total. The share of automobile credit held by commercial banks declined from 62 percent in 1972 to 58 percent in 1976.

Thus, CUs have found themselves in a favored position relative to commercial banks in the consumer loan market. This advantage, combined with favorable interest rates at a time when the public has become increasingly interest-rate conscious in the face of inflation, has propelled the growth of CUs. As a result, credit unions are providing commercial banks with intensifying competition for consumer loans. Moreover, as S&Ls and MSBs continue to move to shorten the maturity of their asset portfolios, thrifts will become more effective competitors in this market as well.

Future competition in this market is likely to focus on credit card services. Membership rules of Visa U.S.A. Inc. were extended in 1976 to include credit unions. Recently, Visa approved 32 credit unions as card-issuing members, 22 of which participate in a pilot program sponsored by Credit Union National Association. As CUs are given endorsement to apply for Visa credit, they undoubtedly will improve their competitive position. Federal credit unions are limited by regulation to charging no more than one percent per month on the unpaid balance of a loan. Under present conditions, this regulation would limit interest rates on credit card services to 12 percent per year, while many banks typically are charging 18 percent annually.

[6]Peggy Brockschmidt, "Credit Union Growth in Perspective," Federal Reserve Bank of Kansas City, *Monthly Review,* February 1977, pp. 3–13.

[7]Interest rates for credit unions are from the National Credit Union Administration and are centered three-month moving averages of weighted interest rates; those for commercial banks are from the Board of Governors of the Federal Reserve System.

Changes in Liability Competition

Deposit liabilities of financial institutions are also undergoing change, primarily surrounding the distinction between demand and savings deposits. Important institutional changes have occurred since 1970 which have allowed more vigorous competition for deposits among institutions. . . . Combined with various maximum rates of interest allowed financial institutions, these changes will likely translate into new positions in the competition for deposits. . . .

Some thrifts were permitted in 1970 to make preauthorized nonnegotiable transfers from savings accounts for household-related expenditures. However, the major impetus for change occurred in 1972 when MSBs in Connecticut and New Hampshire began to offer Negotiable Order of Withdrawal (NOW) accounts. These accounts are essentially interest-bearing savings accounts on which checks can be written. While, at first, introduction of NOW accounts was limited to these two states, authorization for NOW accounts was expanded in 1976 to include MSBs, S&Ls, and commercial banks in all New England states.[8] . . . Moreover, expanded authority for NOW accounts is currently being proposed to include all states.[9]

At credit unions, similar services are called "share draft accounts." Introduced at five credit unions in 1974, share drafts are now available at more than 940 CUs in 46 states.[10] These accounts, offered through a Credit Union National Association program, permit payable-through drafts which are drawn on the members' interest-bearing share accounts. Share drafts are processed through the credit union's account at a commercial bank.

In addition to NOW accounts, savings and loan associations have also initiated several services which allow them to compete for demand deposit business that has gone, traditionally, to commercial banks. Primarily through the use of electronic services, these thrifts have access to another source of deposits, one which they may be able to more successfully retain than other sources during business cycle fluctuations. At the same time, these services allow thrift depositors to use their savings accounts more like the transaction accounts of demand deposits.

Through electronic terminals, called remote service units (RSUs), depositors of thrift institutions are able to perform within seconds many of the transactions formerly conducted through demand deposit accounts, such as withdrawing cash, making charge account and loan payments, and transferring funds from one account to another.[11] One basic advantage of these units is that they frequently are located in such convenient places as supermarkets, airports, and factories. More-

---

[8]On January 1, 1974, total NOW account balances in Massachusetts amounted to $138 million. Three years later, in January 1977, NOW balances totalled $1.47 billion. During the same time perod, NOWs in New Hampshire increased from $5 million to $186 million.

[9]Some institutions, mainly state-chartered thrifts, have surpassed the initial offering of NOW accounts. Savings banks in New England and five other states are authorized to offer demand deposit accounts.

[10]About 200,000 CU members wrote approximately $800 million in share drafts during 1976.

[11]Between January 1974 and December 1976, 112 applications for remote service units have been approved by the Federal Home Loan Bank Board. Federal Home Loan Bank Board *Journal,* April 1977, p. 39.

over, S&Ls as well as MSBs have introduced telephone transfers to third parties and automatic payment services which allow their customers to more easily utilize their savings accounts for transactions purposes.[12]

As far as customers are concerned, the new deposit services at nonbank institutions are little different from demand deposit accounts of commercial banks, except in one important respect: typically, nonbank deposit services explicitly pay interest, whereas those of commercial banks do not.[13] Commercial banks have been prohibited since 1933 from explicitly paying interest on demand deposits. Savings deposit accounts at S&Ls and MSBs, on the other hand, are permitted by law to bear interest which is one-quarter of one percent higher than similar accounts at commercial banks.[14] Thus, not only have thrifts begun to compete with commercial banks for demand deposits, but by servicing their "demand deposits" from savings accounts, thrifts generally seem to be making the most of their interest rate advantage.

Credit unions are in an even better competitive position. The maximum rate permitted members' savings accounts at CUs is 7 percent. Although not all CUs pay the highest rate, about 50 percent paid between 6 and 7 percent in 1975, significantly higher than the ceiling rates at other institutions. This favorable rate differential for CUs not only appeals to current and potential members, but also allows credit unions to retain funds when other institutions are suffering from disintermediation.

By increasing the convenience of the services which compete with demand deposits, nonbank institutions effectively have decreased the transactions cost to customers of their accounts. Coupled with the higher maximum interest rates allowed these institutions, their deposit growth rates generally have been stronger than those of commercial banks. Since 1970, savings of credit union members have increased at a 17 percent annual rate, and in the last two years, have grown at about a 19 percent rate. . . . Total deposits of commercial banks, on the other hand, grew at nearly a 10 percent rate in the period between 1970 and 1976, up from the 8 percent rate which prevailed between 1960 and 1970. Savings capital of S&Ls and deposits of MSBs grew at annual rates of 9 and 7 percent, respectively, between 1960 and 1970. The latter institutions maintained deposit growth rates of 15 and 9 percent, respectively, since 1970.

While many new demand deposit services began in 1974, data on such services tend to be incomplete, making comparisons difficult. However, NOW account data are the most complete, and available across institutions. These data indicate that the dollar volume of NOW accounts . . . increased from $65 million in 1974 to $1.3 billion by the end of 1976. NOWs at S&Ls and MSBs have also shown intense growth, though not as strong as at commercial banks. Between 1974 and 1976, NOWs at thrift institutions increased $146 and $367 million, respectively. . . . In the

[12]Fourteen savings banks in New York, Connecticut, Maine, New Jersey, Pennsylvania, and Washington offer pay-by-phone services. . . .

[13]In a few areas, nonbank deposit accounts called Non-Interest Negotiable Order of Withdrawal accounts, (NINOWs) do not bear interest.

[14]Current ceilings on passbook accounts at commercial banks and thrifts are 5 and $5^{1}/_{4}$ percent, respectively.

same two-year period, share draft balances at CUs grew from $375,000 to $803 million.

In an era of rising prices, people have become more aware of the cost of holding money. More money holders are seeking methods of reducing noninterest-bearing claims in favor of highly liquid earning assets that can either be easily transformed into payments media or used indirectly for payments. The above figures tend to indicate the extent to which these preferences are influencing relative rates of deposit growth.

Impact

In certain areas, new competition has prompted commercial banks to retaliate in order to maintain or regain their competitive position. In some cases, commercial banks have been successful in initiating telephone transfers and automatic payment services similar to those at nonbank institutions.[15] Perhaps the best example of a situation in which commercial banks have been able to equalize competition is the case of NOW accounts in New England. Initiating NOW accounts in 1974, two years after their introduction by MSBs, commercial banks have surpassed savings banks in NOW balances and have about equalled the number of savings banks offering the accounts.[16] . . .

In other cases, commercial banks have been less successful. For example, although national banks have initiated electronic terminals, called Customer Bank Communication Terminals (CBCTs), placement of them has been limited and certainly more restrictive than that of the similar Remote Service Units of savings and loan associations. The courts have judged that CBCTs are branches as defined in the McFadden Act of 1928, a severe competitive blow to commercial banks. This ruling subjects placement of CBCTs to state laws prohibiting or limiting branch banking by commercial banks. S&Ls are not subject to any comparable ruling.

Moreover, as more institutions pay interest on their "checking accounts," more pressure is placed on commercial banks to pay interest on comparable accounts. Legislation has been proposed which would allow all financial institutions in the nation to offer NOWs, with an identical ceiling rate.[17] Legislation of this sort would eliminate the interest rate differential on passbook/NOW accounts among institutions.

[15]One area in which commercial banks have been successful in attaining an equal footing with S&Ls is for Individual Retirement Accounts (IRAs) and Keogh plans. S&Ls offer these accounts to savers at a 7.75 percent interest rate, while commercial banks offered comparable accounts at a maximum rate of 7.5 percent. Effective July 6, 1977, commercial banks which are members of the Federal Reserve System can introduce a new category of time deposit accounts which are available for use as IRAs and Keogh plans and pay a maximum rate of 7.75 percent.

[16]See Ralph C. Kimball, "Recent Developments in the NOW Account Experiment in New England" and Donald Basch, "The Diffusion of NOW Accounts in Massachusetts," Federal Reserve Bank of Boston, *New England Economic Review,* November/December 1976, pp. 3-19 and pp. 20-30, respectively.

[17]Credit unions have been included among such legislative packages for share drafts.

With one uniform interest rate, it is a short step to complete elimination of all interest rate differentials. Moreover, if nonbank institutions have formal access to other sources of funds, regulators may argue that the institutions no longer "require" the advantage of the interest rate differential to maintain deposit flows.

Whether or not such proposals pass, the innovations which have occurred already have increased the number of alternative services available to consumers. Consumers are now able to obtain larger mortgages at CUs, a wider range of consumer services at MSBs, and closer substitutes for checking accounts at S&Ls. Moreover, the quantity and variety of services offered at each type of financial institution will probably continue to increase in the future.

Such changes are altering the focus of most financial organizations. Having begun as basically specialized institutions, they are now taking on a more diverse character. The distinction between the asset and liability powers of bank and nonbank institutions is becoming blurred, and with it, the distinction between the institutions themselves.

Conclusion

Commercial banks, savings and loan associations, mutual savings banks, and credit unions perform many similar functions. They accept the savings of economic units and allocate them to borrowers. Since 1970, these institutions have been becoming similar in more specific ways. Nonbank institutions are diversifying and broadening the scope of their assets. S&Ls are including shorter-term assets in their portfolios; MSBs and CUs are devoting more assets to various types of consumer loans. In terms of liabilities, demand deposit accounts are no longer the exclusive domain of commercial banks. All types of thrift institutions are permitted some type of demand deposit services.

Thus, competition is intensifying among the institutions and will likely provide them with incentives to increase efficiency and reduce costs to customers in the future. As a result, consumers have more alternatives for "banking" services from which to choose. In the process, asset and liability powers of the institutions have yielded to equalizing forces. Regulations and incentives for specialization, which maintained the distinction among institutions, are being broken down.

The traditional roles of nonbank financial institutions are changing; their domain, once narrow, is now much more extensive and similar to that of commercial banks. However, there is likely to be some limit to this process of financial institutions becoming more similar. Given current trends, the extent of specialization of the institutions is likely to be determined by competitive forces as well as by public policy to channel credit to specific uses.

The Public Policy
Implications of EFTS

James F. Dingle

21

The Public Policy Implications of EFTS

There is a growing understanding of the extent to which electronic systems for financial transactions (commonly but imprecisely known as EFTS) will restructure many aspects of financial markets during the next few decades. This article is intended to serve as a guide showing probable developments based on the gradual extension of the use of electronic systems in various financial contexts. It points out the ways in which public policy, particularly monetary policy, is most likely to evolve as a result of this trend.

The method used in the paper entails two steps. A probable future scenario is prepared for four sectors of the economy—private individuals, nonfinancial corporations, financial intermediaries and the government. These scenarios take into account the currently available technology of computers and communication devices as well as the ways in which financial institutions plan to apply this technology. Special attention is given to the extent and speed with which customers in these four sectors will react to such flow of market information as prices, interest rates and exchange rates. The second step is a consideration of how stabilization policy might be conducted, given the outlined scenario. In order to identify potential problems, the

Reprinted from *Journal of Bank Research,* Spring 1976, pp. 30–36, by permission of the Bank Administration Institute and the author.

logic of policy formation is traced—from its objectives, through the various policy instruments to their lagged impact on the economy. Summary tables of the analyses are also included.

In very broad terms, the results suggest a strong need for the financial community to react much more rapidly to short-run market trends occurring in all countries. In response, public policy will have to rely increasingly on computerized information systems and preprogrammed control routines. The technology is consequently biased toward dirigisme.

Table 1. Changes in Behavior Likely to be Caused by Electronic Systems for Financial Transactions

Sector:	Activity				
	Regular Payments	Borrowing	Lending	Foreign Exchange	Nonlegal
Private Individuals	Money cards partially displace bank notes and coin. Expenditure constrained by credit lines, not by budgets. Preauthorization of mortgage, insurance items.	Instant credit. Automated credit authorization systems, eventually linked internationally.	Wages automatically deposited with, also invested by banks. Access to financial intermediaries by telephone and by retail store terminals.	By banks, with exchange rates set more frequently.	Counterfeiting becomes card theft, wire tapping. "Bounced" checks become automatic overdraft loans.
Nonfinancial Corporations	Wages deposited directly in banks. Terminals used instead of checks for cash management.	Money markets used for one-hour loans. All countries become sources of immediate funds. Overdraft loans replace float.	Minimized cash balances. One-hour term deposits. Delegation by small firms of cash management to banks.	By banks, SWIFT. Exchange rate developments influence hourly cash management.	Check "kiting" eliminated by a zero settlement lag. Weekend investment duplications will grow until a universal settlement lag is established. Instant "payoffs."
Financial Intermediaries	Automated settlements and deposit accounting by banks. Service charges pro rata. Nonbanks negotiate access to automated clearings. Provisions of accounting, portfolio services.	Demand deposits bear interest or decline radically. Time deposits defined with hourly maturities. Savings instruments designed for automatic wage deposit flows.	By money cards and preestablished credit lines. Prime lending rate sensitive to world money market rate. Overdraft loans large if settlement lag zero.	Correspondent balances decline radically. Hourly management of the net foreign assets. Westward cash flow at the close of day's business.	The derivation of information from clients' settlements.
Government	Social Security and interest transfers deposited directly. Tax revenues withheld automatically. Income tax return calculations centralized, using computer data banks.	A paperless personal savings instrument evolves. Special short-term debt issues for nonresidents. Government bonds reside in automated securities depositories; development of purely book-entry debt.	Lender-of-last-resort function will be performed in a zero-lag money market. Continuous adjustment of bank reserves, as open market purchases clear immediately.	Speed and scope of exchange market intervention greatly enlarged.	Legality of electronic payments may be long in question. Probable invasions of privacy by misuse of data banks.

A Probable Scenario

Private Individuals   Money cards used in a similar way as credit cards by individuals shopping in retail stores will cause bank deposits to be transferred electronically and with very little delay to the accounts of the vendors. The demand for bank notes and coin will thus gradually decline. The computer terminals located in the retail outlets will also be able to provide the individual with instant bank credit in accordance with prearranged credit lines. Consequently instead of "bounced" checks there will be immediate overdraft loans. Consumer expenditure will thus be determined to a certain extent by the size of these credit lines. Private individuals will authorize regular electronic transfer of their wages or salaries directly from their employers to personal bank accounts and preauthorize such regular payments as mortgage interest and insurance premiums to third parties. The distinction between such credit transfers and payments for retail purchases will not be significant due to a shortened clearing lag. Counterfeiting will give way to card theft and wiretapping. Large currency payments will become increasingly rare and therefore suspect. Moreover, payments made nationally and internationally for illegal activities could become relatively less anonymous due to the ease with which electronic transactions can be audited.

Nonfinancial Corporations   The typical corporate treasurer will utilize a computer terminal rather than checks or drafts for an increasing proportion of company payments. The direct depositing of employees' wages mentioned earlier provides an example. The same terminal will provide reports on the cash balances of the corporation at the completion of each clearing period, which may be shortened from the current one day to one-half or one-quarter day. As a result, the management of the corporation's cash position will become increasingly sensitive to changing money market conditions and exchange rates. The ability to borrow by overdraft loans with negligible lag and at market rates will compensate for the fact that float—the payment items in the process of settlement—will be drastically reduced. Semilegal transactions, such as "check kiting" and the duplication of financial investments in two countries over the weekend, will therefore become increasingly difficult. In short, the demand-for-money function of corporations will probably decline, and simultaneously become more responsive to short-term yields around the world.

Financial Intermediaries   Banks will continue to computerize the settlement of payment orders as well as the related deposit accounting operations. Banks will gradually extend the use of banking terminals located in retail stores. One result of this development will be a further reduction of float, because the accounts of both payers and payees will be adjusted at the same time. A widening range of services will be offered to clients, including cash and financial portfolio management. The charges for these services and for normal payments processing may tend to be closely related to the costs involved. Conversely, banks might restrict the access of near-banks to electronic systems or charge them exorbitant rates for services as a means of limiting the competition from such financial intermediaries. Moreover, banks could utilize the computers of clearing systems to derive useful information concerning the transactions of private individuals and corporations. Internationally, the correspondent balances of banks will be increasingly tightly managed as the facilities provided by SWIFT expand.[1] The reduced lags in the settlement processes within and between nations may be sufficient to permit working balances to be passed on to time zones farther west as business closing hours lengthen correspondingly. At the very least a world short-term money market interest rate will evolve analogous to the deposit and loan rates prevailing in the Eurodollar market. An increasingly large portion of domestic banking operations will become sensitive to this international rate.

To remain competitive with banks, the near-banks or nonbank intermediaries will either share directly in the establishment of the automated payments system or negotiate access to it. In addition, they will extend the range of financial services that they provide to the public. Consequently, the distinction between near-banks and banks may fade, subject to legal constraints. In financial markets such as those for stocks and bonds the gradual development of depositories using computers to record the changing ownership of securities will be observed. Market trends will be influenced by the widening use of rapid information services carrying the current price developments, as well as by purchases and sales made on the advice of computer-assisted portfolio management counselors.

Government   Social Security benefits, interest payments, pensions and government salaries will be deposited directly in the bank accounts of recipients by electronic transfers. The withholding of income taxes and the collection of sales taxes are likely to be integrated with the payments system. Even the yearly calculation of individual tax returns may be done automatically by governments, since increasing proportions of the relevant information will be held in public-sector data storage devices. The management of the public debt will probably entail the development of a paperless personal savings instrument based on the automatic withholding of an agreed proportion of regular income payments. The payments associated with central bank intervention in the securities and exchange markets will be effected by computer terminals.

Public Policy Issues

While the objectives of public policy are unlikely to change significantly over the next few decades, the evolving financial structure of the economy will necessitate certain governmental responses. A primary issue concerns the information upon which policy is based. The flow of regularly reported information from which policy agencies derive current measurements of the state of the economy is now of such scale and such urgency that the operations of collation, summarization and analysis can only be performed by computer. Yet ironically, automating the generation of

---

[1]See William Hall, "SWIFT, the Revolution Around the Corner," *The Banker,* June 1973, pp. 633–39, for a description of the Society for Worldwide Interbank Financial Telecommunications.

Table 2.   Public Policy Responses to Changed Financial Behavior

Sector:	Policy Aspect:					
	Objectives	Economic Structure	Response Lags	Instruments	Information Base	Constraints
Private Individuals	Full employment. Price stability. Distribution of income.	Consumption function includes credit lines. Declining demand for currency. Savings allocation choices made by banks homogeneously.	Shorter lags due to instant cash and credit.	Variable credit lines. Income tax withholding at more easily varied rates.	Monitor outstanding credit and unused lines. Monitor payments to generate National Accounts consumption flows.	Privacy questions posed by centralized and international credit authorization systems. Effects on bank profits. Appearance of directly controlling consumption.
Nonfinancial Corporations	Price and wage formation. Degree of concentration. Degree of foreign control. Quality of life.	Continuous and internationally managed cash positions. Demand for cash falls and becomes highly interest sensitive. Delegation of cash management to banks.	Responses to rate changes occur in a few minutes within countries. Somewhat longer lags internationally due to working hours and time zones.	Cost and availability of bank credit. Continuous influence by money market and exchange rates. Choice of the optimal settlement lag.	Monitor stocks and flows of corporate bank balances. Monitor inventory investment for National Accounts.	Political acceptability. Legal structures.
Banks	General acceptability of money. Security against bank collapse. Control of monetary aggregates. Degree of concentration. Degree of foreign control.	Demand for excess bank reserves drops to zero. Interbank reserve markets evolve. Greater use of a world short-term rate. Discrimination in automated settlements.	Transactions clear immediately. Lags virtually zero for the sum of managed accounts. Credits extended immediately under automated systems.	Continuous control of the reserve supply. Open-market purchases by terminal, with immediate effect. Possible directives in terms of industries' or regions' credit.	Refined monetary aggregates. New definitions to match new types of deposits. Greater sectoral detail. Better velocity measures.	Saturation point reached on financial information. Computerized monetary policy poses political problems.
Nonbank Financial Intermediaries and Markets	Security against collapse. Degree of concentration. Degree of foreign control. Market stability.	Spread of bank-like services. Velocity rises. Control by banks in the form of shared service routines such as those for portfolio management. Homogeneity and "rationality" rise.	Lags virtually zero for the items under computer control. Transactions clear immediately.	Extension of reserve requirements to near-banks.	Monitor near-banks in a manner consistent with bank reporting.	Differing legislation for various types of near-bank.
Nonresidents	Balance of payments. Speed of exchange rate movements. Control of excessive speculation.	Short-term capital movements respond immediately to news. High degrees of market integration across borders.	Lags very short, though constrained by working hours and time zones.	Exchange market intervention capacity and speed increase. Possible use of computers to scale and time the interventions.	Exchange market monitors by automated settlements. Detailed data on nonresident transactions.	The requirements to finance and to neutralize the effects of exchange intervention.

these reports by many respondents has rendered the flow of information significantly less reliable in the short run. Worse still, the ability to alter quickly the detail contained in the reports to understand a particular current economic problem has often been reduced rather than increased by the use of computers. Nevertheless, these losses can be compensated for by the opportunity to derive fully up-to-date and highly detailed data on the current economic scene from a new and computerized payments system, and to plan for the swift processing of this flow of information in a manner that facilitates policy decision-making. A second and equally important issue for public policy is the need to revise the various control instruments in the light of the changed relationships and response speeds within the financial world. These two issues are examined here, sector by sector.

Private Individuals   The objectives of governmental policy are full employment, price stability and an equitable distribution of income. The instruments used to achieve these objectives include changes in tax rates and tax structure, combined with changes in the cost and the availability of credit. The basic character of these instruments, nevertheless, may change only slightly over time. Automated payments and instant credit will, however, greatly increase the importance of consumer credit lines and automated credit authorization devices. The control over the availability of credit to individuals could be tightened if it were possible to vary the credit lines in a countercyclical manner. Such a new policy instrument might indeed prove necessary to offset the destabilizing effects of the much shorter lags in consumer reactions. In a period of hyperinflation, for example, the instant availability of all personal deposits would greatly facilitate the hoarding of goods. In more usual periods, the pre-authorized depositing of wages and salaries with financial intermediaries will imply a new character for the choice as to how personal savings are allocated, because it tends to place these decisions in the hands of portfolio guidance services of financial intermediaries. Depending on the similarity of the computer programs used in this regard, savings behavior could become significantly more homogeneous. Finally, the flow of information concerning households that is used in policy formation could be broadened and accelerated by the use of automated payments data to generate the consumption statistics for the National Accounts.

Nonfinancial Corporations   The objectives of public policy in this case include those stated in the preceding section, since the inflationary aspects of price and wage formation are to be minimized while maintaining the level of employment. In addition, a desire often exists to control the degree of concentration within various industrial sectors, e.g., foreign ownership and the performance of corporations with respect to broader social objectives such as reducing pollution and easing congestion. The instruments of policy are and will continue to be variations in taxes, tariffs and credit conditions, the last being controlled principally by influencing the growth of commercial banking operations. As corporate financial behavior evolves in terms of internationally and closely managed cash positions, the fundamental relationships between national income, interest rates and monetary aggregates will gradually shift. It will thus be essential to extend the range of information reported on these items to follow the evolution. For example, the foreign cash holdings of domestic corporations are of major importance. Conceivably small and medium-sized corporations will allow their banks to manage their cash positions on a regular basis. Such a tendency could lead to a significant increase in the homogeneity of financial behavior, which implies de facto concentration. The degree of homogeneity will also rise as a result of shorter reaction lags. Not only will the information on interest levels and exchange rates move through the markets more swiftly in the future, but the use of computers to aid in financial decision-making, combined with the swifter settlement of transactions, will tend to increase the pace and the scale of daily financial market developments. In response, the policy agencies will, of necessity, speed up the incoming flow of information and very likely increase the degree of detail to develop more sensitive indicators of corporate behavior. Agencies will rely increasingly on the computer as an aid in setting the levels of the various policy instruments. Central banks in several industrial countries including the U.S. are already quite advanced in the techniques of control econometrics, although applications are just beginning to be reported.

Banks   Policy objectives within this context include ensuring the security of the institutions against financial collapse, and controlling the degree of concentration in banking (or the degree of discrimination against near-banks) and the degree of foreign control. Bank deposits must be a generally acceptable means of payment: Easy and inexpensive to use and secure against fraud. The instruments of policy vary widely from country to country, combining deposit reserve requirements, the management of the supply of reserves, open-market operations in securities and foreign exchange control or market intervention. In the next decade, the central banks must ensure that money transferred by electronic means continues to be a reliable, convenient, secure and legal aspect of society. The regularly used techniques of monetary policy for stabilization purposes must evolve in step with their financial contexts. For example, the continous control of the supply of bank reserves during the day may become necessary. In such a case, a computer terminal linking the central bank to the automated payments system would be needed for the settlements arising from securities and exchange market intervention. The central banks must also monitor the process of computerizing the payments system to prevent this extremely costly mechanism from being used to heighten barriers to entry into banking or into financial intermediation in general. National contexts in which a concentrated private banking sector has by law the control over the payments system demand particularly subtle policies. Regarding on-going stabilization policy, the monitoring of electronic transactions could be used to develop refined measures of monetary velocity as well as greater detail in the National Accounts, to be available after a brief processing lag. Without the assistance of computers, however, this new information would quickly saturate the policy-makers and have an adverse effect on the quality of the decisions made. The inclination to use control-theoretic models of the economy will gradually mount. Consequently the political and social implications of model usage should be considered.

Nonbank Financial Intermediaries   Within this context the objectives of public policy include ensuring the security against institutional collapse and influencing the degree of concentration, the extent of foreign control and the responsiveness to monetary policy. The instruments of policy are relatively few in number, reliance being placed on adjustments in commercial bank activity that are passed along to near-banks by the normal stimulus of financial market conditions. The ability of individuals and corporations to move their cash balances swiftly to near-banks in response to interest rate changes will increase monetary velocity, heighten competition between banks and near-banks and accentuate the interest cost as opposed to the credit availability impact of monetary policy. Extending uniform reserve requirements to the deposits of near-banks could thus be justified on the grounds of both efficiency and equity. Information reported by near-banks could be standardized and made consistent with bank reporting. The extension of the information base would be constrained in the short run, however, by differing legislation covering the various types of financial intermediary.

Nonresidents   The maintenance of a viable balance of payments, which may be seen as an objective of policy, frequently amounts to the control or neutralization of destabilizing short-term capital movements. The instruments of policy include the use of bank reserve management and open-market operations to influence relative interest rates, direct intervention to guide the price of the domestic currency on the exchange markets, directives concerning banking-sector foreign positions and the administrative control of certain transactions with nonresidents. In the future, as the speed and scale of short-run capital movements grow under the influence of world-wide cash management and electronic systems for international payments, exchange market intervention by central banks may eventually be backed up by high-speed information systems based on the flow of automated payments, combined with computer routines that translate the strategies of the monetary authorities into the volume, pricing and timing tactics of market intervention. The constraints to finance or neutralize these intervention payments in the domestic context may lead to the development of special short-term government debt instruments designed specifically for non-residents.

The Overall Impression

The combined impact of swifter reaction speed and more homogeneous behavior in the context of electronic systems for many transactions may well render the financial system less stable because the dampening effect of slow and varying reactions in different institutions and countries will gradually be lost. The response of public policy seems likely to involve a greater reliance on mechanized high-speed information systems generating economic indicators and on computer aids to decision-making. The latter aspect will force the quantification of the various policy objectives mentioned above. The choice of specific targets for the rates of inflation and employment, for example, is rightly considered a political decision due to the implications of the two numbers for the distibution of income between sectors of the economy. But politicians will be noticeably reluctant to make such precise choices because of possible adverse reactions by their constituents. Consequently technicians within policy-making groups will be tempted to specify the goals of policy themselves and to set the instruments of policy accordingly. Such a development appears undesirable.

Finally, the new technology of electronic transactions would appear to be biased towards dirigisme. This results from the gradual diminution of the human element in the decisions being taken in all sectors of the economy. Markets exist only when people trade. But portfolio yield-maximizing computer routines interacting electronically no more form a market than do the state planners who allocate resources in a fully controlled economy. Consequently care must be taken to ensure that the long-run impact of the new financial technology corresponds broadly to the national philosophy.

EFT and Monetary Policy

Edward J. Kane

National monetary policies have two dimensions:

1. **Framework Policy**, which imposes a particular set of control instruments and a particular decision process on day-to-day policymakers;
2. **Levels Policy,** which tunes the framework controls to settings or levels appropriate to achieve macroeconomic or regulatory goals.

In the United States, problems raised by electronic funds transfer (EFT) for monetary policymakers are mainly framework problems with substantial regulatory implications. They are predominantly *transitional* problems, aggravated in this instance because regulation-induced innovation is drastically shortening the time frame of EFT development. EFT innovations are not just a case of a superior new technology replacing old ways of doing things. Some of the attractiveness of EFT comes from its ability to make a number of burdensome regulations obsolete, too.

Chief among the affected regulations are those governing commercial bank deposit interest rates, reserve requirements, and branch offices. To alleviate the burden of these regulations, commercial banks develop with the help of EFT services substitute arrangements for: (1) traditional deposits, designed to be exempt from (or less heavily taxed by) reserve requirements and deposit-rate ceilings, and (2)

Reprinted, with deletions, from *Journal of Contemporary Business,* Spring 1978, pp. 29–50, by permission of the author and publisher.

traditional banking offices, designed to be exempt from existing restrictions on the number and location of bank branches. Simultaneously, EFT changes the macroeconomic meaning of various monetary aggregates and the sensitivity of sectoral spending plans to market and institutional interest rates.

Regulation induced innovation reduces institutional costs and/or increases customer benefits relative to a preexisting regulatory environment, but not necessarily more than an optimal relaxation of the irritant regulations would. . . .

EFT and the Fed's Macroeconomic Control Framework

Three Alternative Conceptions of Monetary Policy Process

How one envisions EFT's impact on the macroeconomic control framework depends in part on how one perceives the process through which monetary policy affects aggregate demand. In the economic literature, one can discern three alternative conceptions of monetary stabilization:[1]

1. the monetarist view,
2. the interest sensitivity view,
3. the bank credit view.

The three views differ principally in how they perceive the channels of monetary policy for periods as short as business cycle upswings or recessions. Each view derives its name from the variable it casts as the prime mover in transmitting central-bank policy impulses to household and business spending units.

The Monetarist View

The monetarist view identifies something called the *money supply, M*, as its focal variable. Increases and decreases in M are said to impact directly on household consumption and business investment decisions. Conceptually, these impacts occur as the consequences of *multiplier coefficients, m* or m_i operating on initiating changes in M. The predicted changes in spending are supposed to ensue whether or not interest rates move appreciably and whether or not bank credit is affected. The monetarist view maintains that new money "burns a hole" in society's collective pockets and, obversely that removing money from circulation makes spending units trim their preexisting expenditure plans.

The Interest Sensitivity View

The interest sensitivity view focuses instead on spending units' reaction to changes in borrowing and lending *interest rates, i.* Lower interest rates reduce the cost of ac-

---

[1] William I. Silber, "Monetary Channels and the Relative Importance of Money Supply and Bank Portfolios." *Journal of Finance,* March 1969, p. 81–87.

quiring assets whose benefits are strung out in time. Obversely, higher interest rates raise the cost of acquiring such assets. This implies that business demand for investment goods and household demand for consumer durables (including housing) will be inversely related to interest rates. Under this view, monetary policy works by effecting targeted changes in interest rates, which in turn cause changes in spending plans. Changes in *i* translate into changes in *interest sensitive spending*, recognizing of course that different components of spending may react at different speeds and in different degrees. It should not matter whether large or small changes in *M* or bank credit are required to bring about the spending only *indirectly* through their impact on interest rates.

The Bank Credit View

The bank credit view portrays commercial bank loans (particularly loans to businesses), L_B, as the principal vehicle through which changes in the most volatile components of aggregate spending are initially effected. As compared to open market financings, bank loan arrangements are easy to negotiate and to prepay on short notice as changing economic conditions call forth adjustments in spending plans. Under this view, sharp changes in bank credit are required to facilitate sharp changes in GNP. Disturbances in *M* or *i* may well be the force behind spending units' desire to adjust their spending plans, but bank credit is the medium through which changes in spending plans reach fruition. During the past decade, the combination of high open market interest rates and relatively inflexible deposit rate ceilings has spawned numerous close nonbanking substitutes for straightforward bank loans. These regulation-induced innovations have put the bank credit view of monetary policy increasingly into eclipse.

When applied to the United States, all three views presume that the central bank affects their respective focal variables primarily through open market operations. By buying or selling government securities, the Federal Reserve alters both the vector of relative yields quoted in the market place and total member bank reserves. Changes in member bank reserves reinforce the yield effects of open market operations and lead via appropriate multipliers to changes in *M* and bank credit. Nonmember banks and thrift institutions not subject to Federal Reserve reserve requirements take offsetting actions that undo part of the effects on *M, I,* and L_B worked through member banks. On the other hand, restrictions imposed by state laws and by other federal regulators (principally the FDIC and FHLBB) as well as the dictates of good banking practice limit the extent to which these institutions can engage in offsetting behavior. Nevertheless, this partial slippage may slightly retard the development of intended policy impacts and redounds on balance to the benefit of nonmember institutions. In effect, the Federal Reserve uses member banks as a fulcrum for applying pressure to the generalized financial system. As a fulcrum, member banks tend to bear a heavier portion of the burden imposed by monetary restraint. This differential burden contributes mightily to what the Fed calls its "membership problem": the continuing decline in the percentage of eligible banks (and bank assets) that belong to the Federal Reserve System.

How EFT Changes Tasks of Central Banking

Developments in EFT produce new instruments and revised institutional arrangements that must be melded into each view of the monetary policy process. Adherents of the monetarist view must expand their conception of the assets that potentially enter the contemporary money supply. Adherents of the interest sensitivity view (I will call them "interists") must enlarge the set of interest rates that monetary authorities must set their sights on. Finally, adherents of the bank credit view (to whom I refer as "creditists") must expand their conception of what constitutes a bank. . . .

Effects of EFT on Monetary Policy Process

The Expanded Monetary Perspective

In monetarist analysis, the concept of money extends far beyond that of a mere medium of exchange. In principle, an individual's money stock consists of whatever set of assets in which he customarily holds funds earmarked for imminent disbursement. In Friedman's famous phrase, "money is a temporary abode of purchasing power" between receipt and disbursement.

Innovations in EFT offer businesses and households new ways to execute transactions. These newly developing transactions vehicles allow spenders to economize on their holdings of traditional moneys such as currency or balances in demand deposit accounts. Emerging money substitutes change in an evolutionary (and imperfectly predictable) way the operational definition of what assets constitute the United States money stock.

To track the changing patterns of asset substitutability for money, or "moneyness," over time, it is necessary to conceive of money as a *weighted aggregate*. For any time and place, M is found by summing across assets the *fraction* of each holding that functions as money. The average fractional weight, $W(t)$, that applies to asset j varies with time, t. It expresses the average money qualities that asset j has for its owners at time t.[2] Although efforts are made to avoid double counting and to exclude balances owed among monetary institutions, conventional definitions of the money stock reported by the Federal Reserve otherwise take all weights as either zero or one. M_1 is the sum of designated currency and demand-deposit components: M_2 is the sum of M_1 and net time and savings deposits at commercial banks: similarly for M_3, M_4, ad infinitum.

Allowing weights to take on values between zero and one provides a conceptual framework by which monetarist analysis can incorporate the effects of EFT. In this extended monetarist view, during times of monetary restraint nonmember institutions have greater ability to offset Federal Reserve leverage on member banks. Not only can they expand the amounts of their outstanding liabilities, they can undertake

---

[2]See Kane, 1964, and the literature cited in Moroney and Wilbratte, 1976.

innovations designed to increase the degree of moneyness that these instruments offer to business and household owners.

Because changes in individual assets' money characteristics are not directly observable, the monetarist view of monetary policy loses its vaunted concreteness in times of rapid innovation. Then, even over relatively short periods, policymakers must take into account the behavior of money substitutes. For policy to be made on a monetarist basis would require that more and more institutions regularly report balance sheet changes directly to the central bank. But even if reporting requirements were universal, supplementary survey techniques for estimating individual assets' money characteristics weights do not yet exist. Without contemporary data on the changing pattern of asset weights, varied movements in traditional and nontraditional moneys cannot be reduced to a single interpretable aggregate.

It is ironic that the Federal Reserve's tentative moves (dating from 1970) toward a "monetary aggregates strategy" of policy control have coincided with developments in EFT that make such a strategy harder than ever to implement. Moreover, federal efforts to limit interinstitutional interest rate competition contribute greatly to the problem. Maintaining ceilings on deposit interest rates below free market levels in booms forces financial institutions to look all the harder for alternative ways of competing. The rapid spread of EFT technology, especially among nonbank institutions, is in large part regulation induced.[3]

In the monetarist view, EFT is important because it is systematically invalidating traditional concepts of money and dramatically expanding the set of institutions capable of producing money. One of the great attractions of monetarist control strategies is the freedom it gives policymakers to ignore detailed developments in individual markets. EFT is making it increasingly clear that in the near future this freedom will temporarily be more apparent then real.

Credit Perspective

In principle, the problem of controlling bank credit is much like that of controlling bank liabilities. Policymakers need to collect information on bank balance sheets and to take actions that influence total bank assets. However, "creditists" want authorities to concern themselves also with influencing the relative attractiveness of bank loans and other bank investments.

Parallel to the issues raised for monetarists, institutional changes occurring over the last 15 years require "creditists" to extend their concept of what institutions are engaged in the banking business. Political and economic pressures have been steadily obliterating traditional differences in the products offered household customers by banks and thrift institutions. Moreover, traditional differences between deposit instruments and competing investment vehicles have diminished as well. Whenever

---

[3]Edward J. Kane, "Institutional Implications of the Changing Regulatory and Technological Framework of S&L Competition," prepared for Second Annual Conference of the Federal Home Loan Bank of San Francisco. *Changes in the Savings and Loan Industry,* December 9-10, 1976.

market interest rates rise substantially above ceiling rates on household savings deposits,   business borrowers and nontraditional intermediaries (such as money-market funds and real estate investment trusts) increasingly borrow directly from the household sector.

These developments make many other institutions' credits (e.g., cash advances from credit card companies) functionally equivalent to old-fashioned bank loans. Although one might develop a weighted-aggregate approach to credit to parallel that just sketched for money, no such analytical tradition has yet emerged. Although the Federal Reserve tends to give banks' commercial and industrial loans special attention, neither the Fed nor academic analysts currently center their theories of monetary policy on this variable.

Institutionally, the major effects of EFT on credit markets will be microeconomic and distributional ones.[4] *First,* EFT opens up a regulatory loophole through which thrift institutions can offer checking account substitutes. Deployment of well-located electronic terminals should expand thrifts' share of local deposit markets, with deposits at all institutions tending to rise relative to currency holdings. *Second,* EFT—and especially its incorporations into on-line POS (point-of-sale) systems—should greatly expand the role played by overdraft credit in deposit institution portfolios. *Third,* keen interinstitutional competition for households' deposit and overdraft business in local markets should lower effective interest rates on consumer loans. These developments are going to trim profit margins for consumer finance companies.

Interest Perspectives

Interest advocating policymakers ("interists") must perceive interest rates broadly —as the sum of explicit and implicit (i.e., inflation adjusted) after-tax rates of return. In the interest perspective, the policymakers' first task is to ascertain which real world interest rates most directly affect the spending plans of each economic sector. Their second task is to identify policy instruments that are linked reliably to these crucial interest rates. Finally, authorities must manipulate these instruments to push the designated interest rates to their target levels.

EFT promises to complicate all of these tasks, principally with respect to retail financial markets. For households, EFT is expanding the number of institutional sources and of contractual vehicles for borrowing and lending. For conscientious policymakers, each new arrangement defines an additional interest rate to monitor, to link to an instrument, and potentially to influence. Additional channels of control must be regularly identified and explored.

Because income tax rates differ across the population and because implicit returns and inflation expectations are difficult to monitor, interest advocates ("interists") do not deal with directly observable magnitudes, either. Still, since nominal interest rates are directly observable and EFT seems to be rationalizing the nonprice elements of financial arrangements, the problems EFT raises here are conceptually

---

[4]Kane, 1976; Eisenbeis, Tucker.

straightforward. With efficient capital markets, the traditional instruments of monetary policy (open market operations, reserve requirements, and central bank discount policy) will affect the new interest rates in qualitatively predictable ways. As structural problems emerge, they can be identified econometrically and appropriate structural adjustments made.

Unlike the other two views, the interest perspective highlights structural problems. With interinstitutional competition the driving force behind the rapid spread of EFT, structural maladjustments are bound to develop. To minimize such difficulties, authorities must not distort institutional incentives. Within boundaries set by political constraint, detailed interference with market processes should be kept to a minimum. This will be determined by political constraints.

EFT Implications for the Structure of Monetary Institutions

Because it confronts rather than finesses structural issues, "interestism" provides the most congenial perspective from which to address the policy issues raised by the ongoing transition to EFT. One might suppose that it would be useful to distinguish between the microeconomic problems of regulating the EFT industry and the macroeconomic problem of providing the central bank with sufficient policy instruments to execute a countercyclical monetary policy. To the extent that it is distinct from regulatory difficulties, the second issue is not a problem. Open market operations give the Fed sufficient control on interest rates, at least as long as it is recognized that the Fed could in principle buy and sell assets in any markets officials found it appropriate or necessary to influence quickly. The issue is not the adequacy of Fed controls but their structural implications, particularly those associated with Fed reserve requirements.[5]

Regulatory Problems with EFT

The final sections of this paper focus on three connected regulatory problems raised or aggravated by EFT:

1. Reserve requirements;
2. Ceilings on deposit interest rates;
3. Policies toward electronic terminals.

Decisions made on these matters are going to determine the future shape of depository institutions.

[5]When posed in a monetarist fashion, the false issue concerns an alleged need to extend Federal Reserve regulatory dominion to nonmember banks and nonbank thrifts to maintain the Fed's capacity to engage in effective monetary stabilization. Extending reserve requirements to all EFT institutions would ease some distributional inequities and might reduce policy lags, but it is by no means necessary for effective control.

Reserve Requirements

Reserve requirements may be interpreted as an excise tax on deposits or as a confiscatory tax on selected forms of income. Requirements in excess of what an institution would voluntarily hold constitute a 100 percent tax levied on the income that would have been earned on funds put aside to meet the requirements.[6] The existence of Federal Reserve requirements creates an incentive for commercial banks to withdraw or to refrain from joining the Federal Reserve System. This incentive is especially strong for small banks, for whom the benefits of system membership have traditionally been small.

For all banks, the incentive varies inversely with the opportunity, cost and quality of correspondent services offered to members by the Fed, and directly with the onerousness of reserve requirements applicable to comparable nonmember banks in the same home state and with the same level of interest rates on earning assets. Increases in interest rates heighten the cost advantage enjoyed by nonmember banks and nonbank institutions. Although it could do so, the Fed has not yet stabilized this incentive by setting a variable rate of interest on member bank reserves.[7] Differences in the level of reserve requirements on different types of liabilities, including the absence of reserve requirement on innovative liabilities, lead member banks to promote the expansion of their less heavily taxed sources of funds.

Inasmuch as EFT allows thrift institutions to make deep inroads into traditional banking markets, it aggravates the Fed's so-called membership problem. To stop the erosion in system membership, Fed officials have long recommended universal reserve requirements for commercial banks. Although states'-rights forces in Congress have stymied this proposal, events have now passed it by. With EFT destroying distinctions between depository institutions, even uniform reserve requirements for all banks would leave the burden of monetary stabilization centered inequitably on one class of competing institution. In such circumstances, the less-regulated sector inevitably tends to grow at the expense of the regulated one.

Three Options to Halt the Decline
in Fed Membership

To prevent itself from presiding over a smaller and smaller segment of the monetary industry, the Fed has three (partly complementary) options. *First*, it could ask Congress to impose a uniform structure of reserve requirements on all depository institutions. This strategy runs afoul of intense counterpressures from the thrift institution and nonmember bank lobbies. To be adopted, the schedule of uniform requirements would have to be much lower than the Fed's current schedule. Moreover, if high requirements were extended to nonmember institutions, it would merely shift the

[6]Edward J. Kane, "All for the Best: The Federal Reserve Board's 60th Annual Report." *American Economic Review,* December 1974, p. 835-50.

[7]Stephen H. Axilrod, et al., "The Impact of the Payment of Interest on Demand Deposits." Staff Study (Washington: Federal Reserve Board, Jan. 31, 1977) (mimeo).

margin of the unregulated sector to credit card firms, money market mutual funds, and large retailers. *Second,* the Fed could pay interest on reserve balances. It could do this in two basic ways: (1) by allowing some fraction of a member bank's reserve to be held in interest bearing securities; or (2) by paying interest on reserve balances at some fraction to 100 percent of the discount rate, thereby upgrading the discount rate as a policy instrument. Alternatively, the reserve rate could be distinguished from the discount rate and based on a market-determined interest rate such as the Federal funds rate.

Although this strategy would lower the opportunity costs of reserve requirements, the administrative problem of finding appropriate fractions (values whose associated windfall burdens or subsidies would be small in magnitude) could become a source of intense controversy. Of course, explicit costing of the services the Fed performs for its member banks should accompany any scheme for paying interest on reserves. *Third,* the Fed might lower its reserve requirements to align them with liquidity needs and the opportunity costs of the compensating balances imposed by correspondent banks on nonmember banks that clear and settle their transactions for them. It would not be difficult to monitor these needs and costs broadly and to adjust future reserve requirements accordingly. The single most useful step would be to eliminate, or at least to reduce to 1 percent, reserve requirements against time and savings deposits.[8] Though themselves small in magnitude, these requirements are very burdensome. In a sense, this approach is a natural extension of the Fed's decision to adopt graduated reserve ratios, which have lowered effective reserve ratios for smaller banks to reduce these institutions' net costs of membership.

Although the second and third strategies may look suspiciously like giveaway programs for banks, tax revenues to replace the Treasury's previous interest free use of banks' substantial reserve deposits at the Fed could be generated both more fairly and more efficiently by narrowing a few of the many income tax loopholes that render average *explicit* federal tax rates on commercial bank incomes scandalously low. The principal benefit of either strategy would be to lessen the role played by arbitrary regulatory differentials in shaping the institutional fabric of the United States monetary sector. In the competitive environment generated by EFT, resulting improvements in resource allocation should accrue predominantly to depository institution customers.

Implications of EFT Ceilings on Deposit Interest Rates

Demand Deposits

Prohibition of explicit interest on demand deposits has had two principal effects. *First,* it has promoted nonprice competition by banks for these funds. Banks have

---

[8]Especially if the prohibition of interest on demand deposits were retained, widening reserve requirement differentials would further stimulate the use of savings accounts for transactions purposes. Monetarist policy targets would have to take the resulting changes in moneyness into account.

paid implicit interest in the form of services provided account holders for charges well below the cost to the banks of performing them. *Second,* the prohibition has led nonbank institutions to seek to invade these markets by designing interest-bearing instruments of their own that function in one or more ways like checking accounts. The litany of checking account substitutes runs from NOW accounts and drafts payable against money market mutual funds, through written and telephonic thrift institution payment orders, to providing access to savings account at off-premises electronic terminals.

Although the interest prohibition was intended to preclude destructive competition for demand deposits among banks, it has merely shifted the focus of the competitive thrust to nonprice terms and to nonbank institutions. For example, the push for EFT among many savings and loan associations (S&Ls) comes from the perception that they can use EFT to gain an unshakeable foothold in the market for payment services. Many believe this would facilitate their becoming "full service financial centers for households." Similarly, the money–market mutual fund industry was able to maintain its size during 1974–76 in the face of falling interest rates by expanding the percentage of firms that permit customers to redeem their holdings via bank drafts. On-line POS systems will tempt credit card issuers and large retailers to pay interest on customers' credit balances. Similarly, variations in interest charged on overdraft balances will affect customers' demand for checking balances.

Through automated repurchase agreements and telephone transfers between time and demand accounts, many commercial banks are already paying substantial interest rates on what are essentially demand funds. However, these schemes are less efficient than explicit interest on checking accounts would be. These arrangements expend bank and customer time and effort that would be spared if checking account interest could be paid. To rationalize the pricing of EFT services and to prevent retail deposit markets from experiencing further wasteful invasion by high-cost competitors, the prohibition of demand deposit interest should be eliminated as soon as possible.

Time and Savings Deposits

So-called Regulation Q ceilings restrict interest payable on time and savings accounts, but only for accumulations smaller than $100,000. These ceilings, which are intended to help thrift institutions' profit balances during sharp increases in interest rates, have two features. *First,* they prevent savings deposit rates from following open market interest rates upward in booms and—by destroying industry patterns of price leadership—essentially prevent these rates from declining when interest rates ease. This noncyclical pattern means that savings deposit rates transmit cyclical impulses to household savers, encouraging them to spend more of their incomes in booms and to save more in recessions.

Given the differentially high transactions costs imposed on small investments by dealers in the wholesale capital markets, these ceilings discriminate throughout the interest rate cycle against small savers. Individuals with substantial savings can and do move their funds out of depository institutions to high-yielding instruments when market rates rise, returning them if market rates fall back through the inflexible ceilings. The resulting waves of disintermediation and reintermediation influence depository institutions (particularly S&Ls) to adopt more cautious investment policies.

The Savings Differential

These ceilings' *second* main feature is the so-called "differential," which allows thrift institutions to pay a slightly higher rate than commercial banks for time and savings funds. This differential is intended to shelter S&Ls (and to a lesser extent mutual savings banks) from the full weight of commercial bank competition.

During the last few years, institutions and instruments exempt from Reg. Q ceilings have made major inroads into traditional depository-institution markets. Among these institutions are credit unions, money–market mutual funds, and real estate investment trusts. Among the substitute instruments are share drafts, check redemption privileges at money market mutual funds, NOW accounts, telephone and electronic access to commercial bank savings deposits, repurchase agreements, floating-rate notes, and interest on public utility credit balances. Through regulation-induced innovation, financial markets punish the very institutions the ceilings were installed to protect.

To minimize the erosion of their deposit markets, S&Ls have turned increasingly to new types of deposit arrangements: longer term certificates of deposit, mortgage-backed bonds and (assisted by EFT) third-party payment services. These innovations are rapidly changing the nature of the S&L business. In particular, S&L managers are beginning to see EFT as a way to offset the deleterious long-run effects of operating under Reg. Q ceilings.

Politically, for the foreseeable future, Reg. Q ceilings seem invulnerable. They are supported by cohesive lobbies that can strongly articulate the transition costs to them of removing the ceilings and opposed by academics and consumerists who can point only to small and hard-to-quantify benefits for the average customer. While considerations of equity and efficiency cry out for the abandonment of Reg. Q, it is a politically treacherous issue on which the EFT Commission must be careful about expending its goodwill. . . .

The Branch Office Issue

Electronic terminals may be regarded as limited service branches of financial institutions. Two straightforward regulatory implications flow from this analogy. *First,* because depository-institution branches have traditionally been regulated, electronic terminals might also be regulated. *Second,* because the terminals perform only a few of the services available at a "brick-and-mortar" branch, regulation of terminals should in any case be relatively less restrictive.

In practice, the question of whether to regulate terminals never arose. In fact, the courts have ruled that under the McFadden Act remote terminals established by national banks are indistinguishable for regulatory purposes from brick-and-mortar branches. In many states, these rulings leave national banks disadvantaged vis-à-vis competing thrift institutions and state-chartered banks. For national banks in states that allow conventional or electronic branches, the United States Comptroller of the Currency (who regulates national banks) has established abbreviated branch-application procedures for CDMs and ATMs. Although these new procedures cut red tape, state restrictions on capitalization and on the number and location of branches must be met. In states that prohibit branches but allow electronic terminals, these requirements prevent national banks from engaging in EFT competition with federal S&Ls and state chartered banks and S&Ls. This situation cries out for speedy legislative remedy.

EFT technology has made federal and state regulatory concepts and formulas outmoded. A CDM is more like a telephone delivery system than a brick-and-mortar branch. An ATM substitutes for routine teller services; it cannot arrange loans, open accounts, answer procedural questions, or even make small change. The principal reasons for regulating these machines are primarily that they are expensive (and therefore a drain on bank capital) and secondarily to guard against "overbanking" in local markets.

The harder one looks, the more decisions about the deployment of electronic terminals seem insufficiently different from decisions about personnel deployment to justify substantial regulatory oversight. Any provision for increased customer services (e.g., hiring more or faster tellers or equipping them differently) has similar effects. At the margin, the new services shift demand from other institutions and generate costs which could be capitalized and viewed as a charge against the firm's net worth. As technological developments and competition bring down the costs of CDMs and ATMs, their asymmetric regulatory treatment is going to be harder and harder to defend.

What is needed now are loose and flexible regulatory formulas whose capitalization and locational requirements will not prevent depository firms from combining labor and capital in a cost-effective manner. Congress and state legislatures would be well advised to exempt terminals from regulation under broad conditions. They might insist, for example, that deposit insurance agencies or state banking commissioners be informed in advance of planned EFT investments. But they might empower these regulators to intervene only in cases of undercapitalized firms and/or overbanked markets, where these disabling conditions would have to be proved by objective tests.

Restraints that regulatory policies impose on the deployment of particular resources tend to raise the cost and/or reduce the quality of the services ultimately performed. Inflexible formulas designed to protect competitors from overinvesting in equipment perpetuate inefficient ways of doing things and deny customers the benefits of competition. Inflexible regulation encourages unregulated higher cost firms in other industries to enter the regulatees' markets to alleviate this situation. In turn, incursions by unregulated firms add new levels of complexity to the regulators' basic tasks. . . .

Summary

It is striking how many of the institutional problems that have emerged with the onset of EFT arise directly from the pattern of government regulation of deposit interest rates, reserve requirements, and branch bank establishment. Although completely unintended, these problems are the predictable consequences of policies that try to override—rather than adapt to—the logic of the marketplace.

To forestall unintended difficulties of even greater magnitude, it seems wise now to relax some of these existing restrictions and to avoid imposing new ones on emerging instruments and institutions until both the need for them has been clearly established and the EFT system has attained greater maturity. Whatever difficulties it may generate in the process, the market can find more efficient ways to install EFT than bureaucrats can.

Perhaps EFT's greatest threat is to the survival of small banks and small thrift institutions. If, in the face of substantial scale economies, small institutions are going to survive without ongoing government protection, opportunities for sharing inter-institutional EFT facilities will have to be identified and nurtured carefully.

BIBLIOGRAPHY

BAKER, DONALD J. "Does Antitrust Law Preclude the Need for Geographic Constraints on Banking?" *Banking Law Journal* 93 (October 1976), pp. 1005–19.

The Economics of a National Electronic Funds Transfer System. Boston: Federal Reserve Boston Conference Series No. 13, 1974.

EISENBEIS, ROBERT A. "The Competitive Implications Associated With the Use of Electronic Terminals." Washington: Federal Reserve Board, Oct. 18, 1976. Mimeographed.

FLANNERY, MARK J., and DWIGHT M. JAFFEE. *The Economics of an Electronic Monetary Transfer System.* Lexington, Mass.: Lexington Books, 1973.

KANE, EDWARD J. "Money As A Weighted Aggregate." *Zeitschrift für Nationalökonomie* 24 (1964), pp. 221–43.

MANDELL, LEWIS. "EFTS and Competition in National Banks," pp. 21–30. Chicago: Federal Reserve Bank.

MORONEY, JOHN R., and BARRY J. WILBRATTE. "Money and Money Substitutes: A Time-Series Analysis of Household Portfolios." *Journal of Money, Credit, and Banking* 8 (May 1976), pp. 181–98.

National Commission on Electronic Funds Transfer. "Electronic Funds Transfer and Monetary Policy." Washington, August 18, 1976. Mimeographed.

NIBLACK, WILLIAM C. "Development of Electronic Fund Transfer Systems." *Federal Reserve Bank of St. Louis Review* 58 (September 1976), pp. 10–18.

PHILLIPS, ALMARIN. "Competitive Policy for Depository Institutions." In Phillips, ed., *Promoting Competition in Regulated Markets,* pp. 329–366. Washington: The Brookings Institution, 1975.

STARLEAF, DENNIS. "Nonmember Banks and Monetary Control." *Journal of Finance* 30 (September 1975), pp. 955–75.

STEVENS, EDWARD J. "EFT and Monetary Policy: What's the Problem?" Cleveland: Federal Reserve Bank, Sept. 10, 1976. Mimeographed.

TUCKER, DONALD P. "Monetary Policy and Credit Availability Effects of Electronic Funds Transfer." Washington: Federal Reserve Board. Nov. 2, 1976. Mimeographed.

WALKER, DAVID A. "An Analysis of EFTS Activity Levels, Costs, and Structure in the United States." *Proceedings of 1976 Conference on Bank Structure and Competition,* pp. 1–20. Chicago: Federal Reserve Bank, 1976.

International Banking

VI

Over the past two decades—and at a much accelerated pace in the 1970s—U.S. banks have substantially increased their activities overseas. From only 8 banks with 131 branches holding $3.5 billion in assets in 1960, these operations expanded to include 130 banks with 738 branches and over $250 billion in assets by 1977. In a similar, though somewhat less dramatic fashion, foreign banks have in recent years expanded their operations in the U.S. market, increasing total assets of their branches in this country from $24 billion in 1972 to over $60 billion in 1976. Articles 23 and 24 in this section, by Allen B. Frankel and Joseph G. Kvasnicka, review these trends and the factors responsible for this internationalization of commercial banking.

As noted in these articles, the pattern of expansion of U.S. banking overseas has been strongly influenced by regulatory constraints on permissible activities of head offices located in this country. One aspect of these constraints has been the restrictions placed on lending to foreign borrowers from offices in the United States. Recently there have been suggestions to liberalize regulations to permit the establishment of "offshore branches" in the United States that could conduct international business on a basis comparable with that in other international financial centers. The possibility of such activities of "foreign windows" of U.S. banks has raised questions about both the equity of current regulations and the potential impact of such operations on domestic monetary policy. A view of the regulatory and monetary policy issues raised by these issues in international banking is provided in Reading 25 by Charles Freedman about some of the proposals of the FINE Study.

The vast expansion of the overseas operations of U.S. banks has raised questions about the risks incurred by these banks in this heretofore unfamiliar environment. These questions have been made all the more relevant by the increased exposure of banks in the developing world. Articles 26 and 27, by Janice M. Westerfield and Nicholas P. Sargen, address these issues, the former examining the several problems of risk evaluation for international lending and the latter concentrating more specifically on the experience of bank lending to LDCs.

International Banking:
The Activities of U.S. Banks Abroad

Allen B. Frankel

Expansion of Branch Networks: 1965-70

The position of the U.S. dollar in international finance, the continued expansion of international activities of U.S. corporations, the rapid growth of world trade, and the increasing internationalization of the world's capital and money markets presented the U.S. banking industry with new opportunities. However, the existing regulatory environment largely shaped the channels through which U.S. banks could respond. A set of programs restraining the outflow of funds from the United States, introduced by the U.S. government in 1964–65 in an effort to shore up the country's balance-of-payments position, exerted a strong influence on the international activities of U.S. banks.

The federal government's capital control program consisted of the Foreign Direct Investment Program (FDIP), the Interest Equalization Tax (IET), and the Voluntary Foreign Credit Restraint (VFCR) program. Under FDIP, initiated as a voluntary program in 1964 and made mandatory in 1968, U.S. corporations were limited in the amount of funds that they could transfer to their corporate affiliates overseas. At the same time the foreign affiliates were constrained as to the amount of locally generated earnings they could retain for reinvestment purposes. The IET, by impos-

Reprinted, with deletions, from *Business Conditions*, September 1975, pp. 3–9, by permission of the Federal Reserve Bank of Chicago and the author.

ing a tax on yields of securities of foreign origin, lowered the effective yield of such securities, making them less attractive to U.S. residents—and thus making it more difficult for foreigners (including the foreign affiliates of U.S. corporations) to finance their capital requirements in the U.S. market. Under the VFCR program,

Overseas Branches of U.S. Member Banks, 1965-75 (as of January 1)

Country of Location	1965	1966	1967	1968	1969	1970	1971	1972	1973	1974	1975
Belgium-Luxembourg	2	4	6	8	9	11	11	8	8	15	15
France	4	4	4	6	7	11	12	15	17	15	17
Germany	3	6	8	9	14	17	21	22	27	30	30
Greece	1	1	1	2	5	8	9	13	14	16	18
Italy	1	1	1	2	2	3	4	6	7	8	10
The Netherlands	3	3	3	3	5	7	7	7	6	6	6
Switzerland	1	1	2	3	3	6	7	8	8	9	9
United Kingdom	17	21	21	24	32	37	41	45	49	52	55
Total Europe[1]	32	43	48	59	80	103	116	128	142	157	167
Bahamas	2	3	3	3	8	32	60	73	94	91	80
Cayman Islands	—	—	—	—	—	—	—	—	2	32	44
Total Caribbean[2]	5	9	9	10	22	53	89	107	131	164	164
Argentina	16	17	17	25	33	38	38	38	38	38	37
Brazil	15	15	15	15	15	15	16	19	21	21	19
Colombia	5	6	6	8	17	23	26	28	28	32	36
Panama	10	12	15	19	21	26	29	29	32	33	33
Total Latin America[3]	72	79	93	123	155	182	191	195	190	195	198
Taiwan	—	2	2	2	2	2	2	2	3	5	7
Hong Kong	6	6	8	10	12	13	13	15	19	23	24
India	5	6	8	8	11	11	11	11	11	11	11
Indonesia	—	—	—	—	4	6	6	6	6	6	6
Japan	13	14	14	14	14	15	15	17	21	25	31
Lebanon	3	3	3	3	3	3	3	3	3	3	3
Persian Gulf[4]	2	2	3	3	3	3	8	11	10	10	11
Singapore	—	8	8	8	8	9	11	11	11	14	18
Total Asia[5]	45	55	63	69	78	83	91	98	112	126	143
Total Africa[6]	3	2	2	3	3	1	2	2	2	2	5
Overseas Areas of U.S.	23	23	29	31	35	38	43	47	50	55	55
Grand Total	180	211	244	295	373	460	532	577	627	699	732
U.S. Member Banks with Overseas Branches	11	13	13	15	26	53	79	91	107	125	125

[1] Also includes Austria, Ireland, Monaco, and Romania.
[2] Also includes Barbados, Haiti, Jamaica, Netherlands Antilles, Trinidad-Tobago, British Virgin Islands, and other West Indies.
[3] Also includes Bolivia, Chile,* Dominican Republic, Ecuador, El Salvador, Guatemala, Guyana, Honduras, Mexico, Nicaragua, Paraguay, Peru, Uruguay, and Venezuela.
[4] Includes Bahrain, Qatar, Saudi Arabia, and United Arab Emirates.
[5] Also includes Brunei, Fiji Islands, Israel, Jordan, Korea, Malaysia, Pakistan, Philippines, Thailand, and Vietnam.
[6] Includes Liberia, Kenya, Mauritius, and Nigeria.*
* No resident U.S. branches as of January 1, 1975.

administered by the Federal Reserve Board, the head offices of U.S. banks were requested to limit their foreign lending to ceilings that reflected their historical foreign credit levels.[1] The program severely curtailed the capacity of home offices of U.S. banks to meet the overseas needs of their large corporate customers.

As a result of these restrictions U.S. corporations had to rely on external sources of funds to finance their growing investments abroad. To accommodate their corporate customers, U.S. banks established networks of foreign branches for purposes of tapping foreign sources of funds and setting up loan placement and service facilities. Given the nature of the impetus, the need and desire to expand abroad was not limited to the banks that traditionally engaged in an international banking business. Up to the early sixties only U.S. banks located in the coastal centers—primarily New York City, with some representation by Boston and San Francisco—operated overseas branches. What was especially notable about the rapid buildup of networks of foreign branches of U.S. banks in the period 1965–70 was that banks headquartered in such cities as Chicago, Pittsburgh, Detroit, and other regional money centers entered foreign markets aggressively.

Regulation Q

The government's capital restraint program was not the only factor that induced U.S. banks to establish and expand their foreign branch networks. Another regulatory barrier to the activities of U.S. banks in their home environment played an equally important role in inducing U.S. banks to establish a presence abroad.

The Federal Reserve System's Regulation Q places a limit on the rate of interest U.S. banks are allowed to pay on deposits received at their offices in the United States. In 1966 and again in 1969–70 as the level of U.S. interest rates rose due to the combined impact of a booming economy and an increasingly tight monetary policy, U.S. banks were restrained by Regulation Q ceilings from paying domestic depositors interest rates that could compete with the interest return from alternative financial instruments, such as U.S. government Treasury bills and short-term unsecured promissory notes issued by large U.S. corporations (commercial paper). Banks experienced a run-off in deposits at domestic offices because of their inability to compete effectively for domestic funds. To supplement their traditional sources of funds, U.S. banks found it expedient to turn to their foreign branches that were not subject to interest rate ceilings and, thus, were free to compete for funds. Deposits taken in at overseas branches were transferred back to the United States for use by the domestic offices.

London branches, in particular, developed considerable capabilities in attracting U.S. dollar-denominated deposits (so-called Eurodollars)[2] because of the ad-

---

[1] In November 1971 banks were provided with the option of adopting a ceiling related to their size.

[2] Eurodollars are U.S. dollar-denominated deposits at a non-U.S. resident bank such as, for example, a London branch of a U.S. bank.

vantages these international money-center establishments offered corporate as well as foreign governmental clients. The overlap in business hours between London and the Continent allowed readier access to dollar deposits located in London than at U.S. head offices. The vigorous competitive environment and the absence of reserve requirements resulted in London branches paying higher interest rates on dollar deposits than domestic U.S. offices or European banks paid on local currency deposits. Also, the branches could pay interest on dollar deposits with maturities less than 30 days—a practice prohibited to domestic offices under Regulation Q.

In addition, in 1966 the London branch of a New York bank introduced the negotiable Eurodollar certificate of deposit, a technique soon adopted by London branches of other U.S. banks. The introduction of negotiable Eurodollar certificates of deposit and the subsequent development of a secondary market for them is a classic example of a successful transfer of "financial technology" developed earlier by U.S. banks to meet the challenges of the domestic environment.

The bottom line result of the combined impact of the regulatory environment and of the internationalization of U.S. business activities was that the number of U.S. banks with foreign branches went from 11 in 1965 to 79 in 1970, and the number of foreign branches of U.S. banks rose dramatically from 180 to 532. The number of such branches in Continental Europe increased from 15 in 1965 to 66 in 1970. For the most part these branches were "downstream" facilities from London money-center branches, set up as loan placement and service facilities for large corporate customers. But branches also accepted deposits in the local currencies, thereby acquiring the funds needed for financing the local requirements of the affiliates of U.S. corporations.

Head Office Borrowing Declines

By mid-1970 the incentive to establish overseas branches for the purpose of securing a deposit-taking facility not subject to Regulation Q was greatly diminished by two changes in the regulatory environment. First, effective September 1969, the Federal Reserve Board placed a 10 percent reserve requirement on any increase in the net liabilities of U.S. offices of member banks to their overseas branches. Second, effective June 1970, the Federal Reserve Board suspended Regulation Q ceilings on interest rates payable on large denomination certificates of deposits with maturities of 30 through 89 days.[3] In the wake of these changes U.S. banks did not show the same degree of interest in borrowing from their branches that they did in 1969—despite the reoccurrence of tight money conditions in 1973 and 1974. The effect of this diminished borrowing was that the considerable deposit-generating capabilities of the overseas branches, particularly those located in London, were now available to fund the lending activities of the branches. This change is put in dramatic perspective by the following numbers. At the end of 1969 about 40 percent of the $33.7

---

[3]In May 1973 interest rate ceilings on large CDs maturing in 90 days or more were suspended.

billion in net assets (i.e., total assets less interbranch claims) of overseas branches represented claims on U.S. head offices. By contrast, in August 1974, the time of peak utilization of borrowings from branches by U.S. head offices during the period of domestic monetary tightness of 1973-74, only 5.7 percent of the net assets of overseas branches, totaling $122 billion, were in the form of claims on head offices.

Adaptation: 1970-73

Beginning in 1970, the overseas branch networks of U.S. banks found themselves in a situation where their own funding capability, and the diminished requirements of their head offices, allowed them the leeway to initiate a more aggressive credit extension program. In part, their aggressiveness took the form of a willingness to accept a diminished net return on their loans. In part, the new aggressiveness took the form of innovations in lending techniques—for example, floating rate Eurocredits[4] and cash flow financing.[5]

The 1970-73 period also was one of considerable geographic diversification for U.S. banks with multibranch networks. The diversification created additional "one-stop" facilities for clients with either local currency needs or external currency needs. The advantage of the branch network in meeting the external currency requirements of clients of an individual branch can be described as follows: any branch in the network would be willing to provide funds to any other branch in the network at a preferred rate because it would not have to take into account the possibility of default. Besides allowing participation in additional banking markets, the geographical diversification of branch locations enhanced the network's ability to generate commission income from financial advisory services—e.g., investment advisory services to multinational corporations, either United States or third-country based.

The number of U.S. bank branches located in Europe (outside the United Kingdom) increased from 66 to 105 in the 1970-73 period. In Asia, U.S. banks added 55 branches to the 83 that were in operation at the beginning of the period. The geographical dispersion of the additions to the branch networks is suggestive of a

---

[4]The floating rate Eurocredit refers to the lending technique which involves tying the interest rate to an interbank deposit rate, e.g., the six-month London interbank offered rate. Depending upon the borrower's creditworthiness and other terms of the credit, a premium (or spread) is added to the interbank rate. In the 1970-73 period the maturity of the Eurocredit lengthened appreciably from a "normal" period of three to seven years to a "normal" period of ten to 12 years with at least one sizable Eurocredit being for 17 years. In addition, there was a considerable narrowing of the spread charged over the interbank rate. For prime borrowers in the developed countries, this meant a reduction from above 1 percent to a range between $3/_8$ percent and $5/_8$ percent. For prime borrowers in the less developed countries, this meant a reduction from a spread near 2 percent to a range between $3/_4$ percent and 1 percent.

[5]The use of cash flow financing represented a departure from the standard practice of asset-protection lending—i.e., the reliance on collateral security. For a discussion of cash-flow lending by U.S. banks overseas see George H. Perry, "Lending to Foreign Local Companies" in *Offshore Lending by U.S. Commercial Banks,* ed. F. John Mathis (Bankers' Association for Foreign Trade and Robert Morris Associates, 1975), pp. 133-50.

continuing effort at enhancing the downstream capabilities of the networks. In a related development U.S. banks sought special relationships with selected foreign banks, either via participation in jointly owned consortia banks or by the acquisition of shares in the foreign banks themselves. In a large number of cases the acquired interest was in a banking institution with a geographic expertise that the U.S. bank desired in order to complement its own capability.

The expansion in the number of U.S. banks with overseas branches in the period 1970-73 was made possible by the Federal Reserve Board allowing a special type of foreign branch that became known as the "shell" branch.[6] The shell branch permitted smaller U.S. banks to establish a foreign domicile for the international portion of their corporate activities. This proved advantageous to the banks during the VFCR period. Following the termination of the VFCR program, the favorable tax treatment and the absence of reserve assessments against deposits booked at the shell branch continues to make this form of branching attractive. At the end of 1974, of the 125 U.S. banks with overseas branches, 76 had but single branches located in the Caribbean, either in Nassau or the Cayman Islands. For these branches the credit activities of the shell are directed at interbank money market placements and purchases of small shares of syndicated loans.

Establishment of shell branches was not limited to small banks. Large banks also acquired shell branches. When the shell is a part of an extensive worldwide banking organization, credit activities of the shell are directed not only at interbank placements and purchases of loan shares but also at funding credits originated within the network.

Expansion in Head Office Activities: First Half, 1974

The termination of the VFCR program in January 1974 made possible a sharp increase in the level of foreign credits placed directly by U.S. bank offices (including U.S. offices of foreign banks). A large proportion of the $11 billion placed in the first half of 1974—a 42 percent increase over the level of outstanding credits at the end of 1973—apparently took place in response to increased credit demand from the banks and/or trading companies of such oil-importing nations as Japan, Brazil, Mexico, and—to a lesser extent—some Western European countries. As banks of these countries drew on credit lines outstanding with U.S. banks, they chose domestic offices rather than overseas branches because of the slightly lower costs available in U.S. markets. Thus, the increase in loans to foreign banks during the first half of 1974 may have been a "one-shot" affair. In the nine months following June 30, 1974, loans to foreign banks fell by about $2 billion despite a continuing positive

---

[6]The special nature of shell branches derives from a provision in the letter from the Federal Reserve Board to a bank conveying approval of such a branch stating ". . . that there is to be no contact with the local public at the branch, and that its quarters, staff, and bookkeeping may, at least in part, be supplied under contract by another party."

differential between Eurodollar interest rates and domestic U.S. interest rates. Also, of the $11 billion increase in bank claims against foreigners, $3.4 billion represented bankers' acceptances[7] made for the account of foreigners; mainly acceptance credits created to finance Japanese trade with countries other than the United States. However, purchases by U.S. accepting banks of their own acceptances for their loan portfolios amounted to only $700 million during the period. This suggests that U.S. banks, in a period of strong domestic loan demand, were prepared to provide their banks' names in return for the acceptance fee (usually 1 ½ percent of the face value), but were unwilling to commit their funds.

Despite the termination of the VFCR program and the slight continuing incentive to move funds from the United States to the Eurodollar market in the first half of 1974, the overseas branches of U.S. banks improved their net creditor position vis-à-vis their head offices by $500 million. There is evidence of a two-way flow with the monies coming in being short term and the increase in claims of head offices against branches being somewhat longer term—these being used to finance branch positions in the very active Eurocredit market in the first half of 1974. Overall, branches increased their claims against foreigners, excluding banks, by about $9 billion in the first half of 1974, with about $1 billion of this in loans to foreign governments, presumably related to financing of oil-related deficits.

In assessing the developments in the first part of 1974, it appears clear that the removal of the VFCR guidelines combined with favorable credit demand conditions had considerable impact on the international activities of U.S. banks. Both head offices and branches of U.S. banks expanded their foreign credit activities rapidly. However, the head offices did not make use of the placement capacity that their branches had built up during the VFCR period.

Consolidation: Second Half, 1974, through First Half, 1975

By mid-1974 conditions in international banking markets were strained in the wake of revelations of foreign exchange losses by several European banks and the actual failure of the I. D. Herstatt Bank in Germany. The uncertainties flowing from these developments caused some depositors to become distrustful of placements with Eurodollar banks, including the branches of U.S. banks. The considerable differential between Eurodollar interest rates and domestic U.S. rates that appeared in the third quarter of 1974 could be characterized as the premium that depositors required for the placement of funds in the Eurodollar market. (The interest rate differential was over 200 basis points on instruments with a three-month maturity.) This made it extremely attractive for U.S. banks to shift funds from head offices to branches to support loan activity.

---

[7]Bankers' acceptances are negotiable drafts drawn to finance U.S. exports, U.S. imports, or trade between other countries and are termed "accepted" when a bank guarantees payment at maturity.

**Head Offices Became Net Creditors of Their
Overseas Branches in 1974**

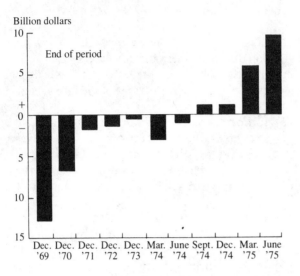

Head offices of U.S. banks became net creditors of their overseas branches in the third quarter of 1974, reversing a debtor-creditor relationship that had persisted since the initiation of the VFCR program in 1965. The experience of this period proved beyond doubt that when a wide differential exists between Eurodollar and domestic U.S. interest rates, head offices of U.S. banks, unrestrained by the VFCR program, would supply the funds required by the lending activities of their overseas branches.

In the last quarter of 1974 and the first quarter of 1975 there was a narrowing of the interest rate differential between the Eurodollar market and the U.S. market, but no full-scale return to the "normal" differential established in the first half of 1974. The narrowing was attributable largely to official statements in the third quarter that lender-of-last-resort assistance would be available under appropriate circumstances to Euromarket participants. As domestic loan demand weakened late in 1974, U.S. banks, recognizing the continuing differential between Eurodollar and U.S. interest rates, tended to make money market placements with foreign banks. In addition, U.S. banks so increased their rate of purchase of their own bankers' acceptances and those of other banks, that total investments in acceptances increased by $950 million in the fourth quarter of 1974.

In the first quarter of 1975 there was a notable revival in medium-term Eurocredit markets as domestic bank loan outstandings dropped rapidly in the United States. The revival in activity in the Eurocredit market continued through the second quarter with developing countries, including certain oil-exporting countries—such as Algeria and Indonesia—reentering the market as borrowers, and with U.S. head

**Intra-Network Claims of Overseas Branches
Increased Dramatically in the Seventies**

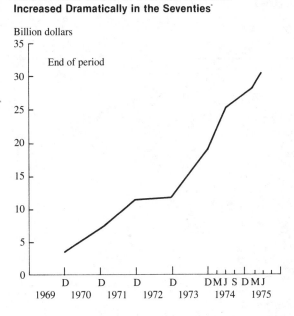

Billion dollars

offices increasing net claims against overseas branches by almost $5 billion through the first quarter and nearly $4 billion in the second quarter. Branches in the Caribbean and United Kingdom—really, the money management centers for the U.S. bank branch networks—were the initial recipients of the funds made available by the U.S. head offices. These branches, in turn, booked loans to borrowers in Eurocredit markets either by entering into syndicated loan arrangements or by making funds available to downstream branches.

It appears that the U.S. recession with its accompanying reduction in demand for domestic credit has been a prime stimulant to the integration by U.S. banks of their head offices and overseas branch networks.

International Banking: Foreign Banking Activities in the United States

Joseph G. Kvasnicka

The Dynamics of Growth

. . . The growth of foreign banking in the United States has been a complex
phenomenon that does not lend itself readily to generalizations. The motives that
prompted foreign banks to establish presences in the United States have varied over
time, as well as between individual banks within a given period of time. Yet several
factors related to the changing role of the U.S. economy and the U.S. dollar in the
world economy provide a base for a rough identification of three major phases of
growth. In the first phase, dating from the early nineteenth century, the major rationale for foreign banks to establish banking facilities in the United States was to
facilitate trade and flow of long-term investment between the United States and the
home country. The second phase began following World War II with the emergence
of the U.S. dollar as the world's major currency and of the United States as the
world's money and capital market. The third phase, beginning roughly in the mid-
sixties, can be characterized as the worldwide response of the banking industry to
the multinationalization of major manufacturing corporations.

Reprinted, with deletions, from *Business Conditions,* March 1976, pp. 3–8, by permission of the
Federal Reserve Bank of Chicago and the author.

Phase I: Financing International Trade and Investment

The financing of international trade is one of the traditional functions of banks. The provision of banking services in financing international trade has been typically based on the correspondent relationship between unaffiliated banks located in different countries. However, in many instances banks found that it is more efficient—and profitable—if the foreign "correspondent" was an office of the parent institution. Thus, as international trade expanded during the nineteenth century, a number of British, French, and Dutch banks proceeded to establish foreign branches, particularly in the raw materials-producing countries of Latin America, Asia, and Africa. Similarly, as the flows of investment capital between the "Old World" and the newly developing regions increased, foreign offices of major European banks became the conduits, overseers, and points for servicing of the underlying indebtedness.

Several foreign banks, motivated by these considerations, established offices in the United States in the nineteenth century. But it was not until after World War I that the emerging importance of the United States as a trading and capital-producing nation began attracting significant foreign banking presence. The 1920s witnessed a considerable influx of foreign banks, including Japanese and European, in the United States. However, the worldwide depression of the thirties and the war-affected forties stunted further growth.

U.S. Offices of European Banks Increase Their Share of the U.S. Market (As Measured by Total Assets)

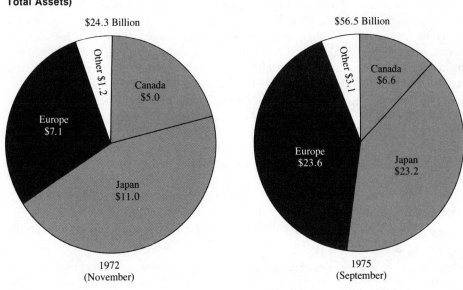

With the gradual resumption of world trade following World War II, the traditional motives for multinational expansion of banking became again relevant. Moreover, additional incentives for foreign banks to establish facilities in the United States were created by the emergence of the dollar as the major world currency.

Phase II: Financing Dollar Transactions

The emergence of the dollar as the major world currency following World War II was largely predicated on the dominant position of the U.S. economy. The dollar represented a unique purchasing power—the means of acquiring a great variety of goods not available elsewhere. At the international monetary conference at Bretton Woods, it was installed as the kingpin of the postwar international monetary system. It became a standard for defining the value of virtually all world currencies, and was widely used as a currency of denomination and settlement of international transactions. As such, the dollar became sought by prospective buyers in the world markets. Sellers in international markets became willing and eager to accept dollars in payment for goods because dollar balances could be, exchange regulations permitting, lent profitably to prospective buyers. Foreign banks, as well as the foreign branches of U.S. banks, gradually became the intermediaries in the overseas trading in dollar balances, accepting dollar deposits and making dollar loans. Their role was enhanced by certain U.S. regulatory restrictions that made holdings of dollar balances on deposit with banks in the United States less attractive to foreign owners.[1] This overseas market in U.S. dollars became known as the Eurodollar market. It grew rapidly into a multi-billion dollar enterprise.

The mechanics of the trading in dollars among banks abroad and their customers, however, placed new demands on the foreign banks. By accepting dollar deposits they incurred dollar-denominated liabilities; while such liabilities were "backed up" by claims on those to whom banks extended dollar loans, the transactions nevertheless opened the banks to the possibility of having to meet dollar deposit withdrawals without always being able to synchronize such withdrawals with the maturity of their dollar-denominated loans. The inter-bank trading in dollar balances that enabled foreign banks to borrow dollars from other foreign banks, and the possibility of converting domestic currency into dollars (regulations permitting), provided the first lines of defense against a liquidity squeeze for any bank confronted with sudden withdrawals. Yet the possibility existed that the inter-bank dollar market as well as the conversion possibilities could dry up in the wake of unsettlements in foreign exchange markets. The banks realized that a banking office in the United States provided an added protection against such possibility: the office could obtain needed funds in the "natural habitat" of the dollar—the U.S. money market. Thus, the desire to establish a banking office within the United States

---

[1]Regulation Q of the Federal Reserve's Rules and Regulations prohibits U.S. banks from paying interest on deposits with maturity of less than 30 days and places restrictions on the rates of interest that banks may pay on deposits of longer maturities.

became an integral part of the involvement of major world banks in the Eurodollar market.

In addition to serving this particular function, the U.S. office of a foreign bank could serve a more general function related to the use of the dollar as an international medium of exchange. The U.S. office of a foreign bank could utilize the dollar funds it received as deposits or that it purchased in the U.S. money markets to provide loans to customers of the parent bank or to sister branches located in foreign countries. This accommodation has been particularly important where local authorities restricted residents from obtaining dollars by conversion of their domestic currency into dollars.

As the dollar became more freely convertible into foreign currencies, other considerations provided a motivation for foreign banks to open banking operations in the United States. A banking office in the U.S. money market provided the parent foreign bank an outlet through which it could invest (after conversion) surplus liquid funds accumulated in its own currency when interest rates in the U.S. money mar-

---

Clearing International Transactions

"Clearing," in general, refers to the process by which a financial transaction between two parties involving intermediation of commercial banks is "settled." For example, John Doe writes a check on his account at Bank A to make a payment to Joe Smith who deposits it in his bank, Bank B. Bank B sends the check to the Federal Reserve or to a Clearing House (a corporation set up for this specific purpose) where it receives credit to the account the bank maintains there. Simultaneously, the Federal Reserve or the Clearing House debits the account of Bank A and sends the check to it. Essentially the same process takes place when a German importer instructs his bank to make a dollar payment to a Japanese exporter. The all-important thing that must be kept in mind is the fact that a dollar payment involving foreign banks, undertaken any place in the world, invariably entails *transfer of balances in the U.S. banking system.* If the two foreign banks involved in the transaction on behalf of their customers do not maintain offices in the United States, they would rely on their correspondent U.S. banks to affect the transaction. The German bank that maintains correspondent balances at Bank A in Chicago would draw on its balances and instruct Bank A by cable to transfer the appropriate dollar amount to the account the Japanese bank maintains with its correspondent Bank B in Chicago; Bank A would issue a "check" in favor of Bank B that would be cleared in the same way as the transaction between Doe and Smith. In those instances when a foreign bank would maintain an office in the United States, that office would then assume the role of the correspondent.

kets were higher than at home. This opportunity has been particularly valuable for banks from countries where the short-term money market has not been as well-developed as in the United States and where opportunities for short-term investment have been limited. Similarly, a U.S. office of a foreign bank could be used to supplement the liquidity needs of the parent in its own currency. The branch could tap the U.S. money market on short notice and cable the dollars to the parent bank. After conversion into domestic currency, the bank could use the funds to meets its liquidity needs.[2]

Another factor closely related to the uniqueness of the U.S. money and capital market that motivated foreign banks to establish a presence in the United States was the desire of foreign banks to engage in the business of underwriting and trading in securities. Unlike U.S. banks, banks in many foreign countries are permitted (and typically, are heavily involved in) the securities brokerage and underwriting. For many of them it has become a logical extension of their domestic activities to establish a presence in the world's largest capital market through establishment of brokerage operations.

Finally, a banking facility in the United States provided foreign banks an opportunity to participate directly—and thus more efficiently and profitably—in the process of "clearing" dollar transactions undertaken by themselves and their customers outside of the United States. (See box.) Such transactions have expanded tremendously as the dollar increasingly became the medium of exchange in international transactions, as the Eurodollar market and its underlying transfer of dollar balances grew, and as foreign exchange transactions involving conversion of foreign currencies into dollars (and vice-versa) increased in volume. Currently, it has been estimated that the debits and credits in the accounts of U.S. banks involving transfers of balances at instructions from abroad exceed $40 billion daily.

These, as well as other considerations derived from the prominent role of the U.S. economy and its currency, led to a large influx of foreign banks in the postwar period. By the end of 1965 there were 41 foreign banks conducting banking business in the United States, with assets totaling $7 billion. Ten of these banks were Japanese, 18 European, five Canadian, and eight from developing countries. In the latter part of the sixties the emergence of new modes of operation of large manufacturing corporations throughout the world provided additional reasons for banks to come to the United States.

Phase III: Corporate Multinationalization

Establishing manufacturing facilities abroad, in close proximity to foreign markets and sources of cheap labor and raw materials, became a new trend in expansion of

---

[2]A good example of these types of functions performed by the U.S. offices of foreign banks can be found in operations of Canadian banks in the United States. For many years these offices have been employing large amounts of surplus liquid balances accumulated by the parent banks to make call loans to U.S. securities dealers and brokers.

major world corporations. U.S. corporate giants pioneered such moves early in the sixties, followed by major foreign corporations. Since the United States represented a major market for many foreign corporations, inflow of foreign direct investment into the United States eventually became quite sizable. The book value of the foreign direct investment in the United States rose from $5.6 billion at the end of 1965 to almost $22 billion at the end of 1974. The foreign banks followed their corporate customers into the United States, and in some instances preceded them, in order to continue to provide them with financial services as an extension of long-established relationships.[3]

The impetus of the influx of foreign banks into the United States in that period has not come solely from the multinationalization of their own domestic corporations, however. The U.S. corporate expansion abroad also created conditions that provided incentives for foreign banks to come to the United States. As affiliates of U.S. corporations abroad established relationships with major local banks, these banks found it expedient to extend the relationship to the corporate headquarters of U.S. corporations by establishing offices in the United States. Such relationships have revolved around financing shipments of parts and semifinished products between the corporate headquarters in the United States and the affiliated suppliers in the foreign countries. Also, through their presence in the United States, foreign banks have often been able to provide for specialized financing of exports of U.S. corporations. For example, certain European banks with extensive foreign branch networks dating back to their colonial trade relationships were able to offer U.S. companies easier entry into new markets.

The "customization" of banking services by U.S. branches of foreign banks during this phase of expansion has not been limited to wholesale banking. Some foreign banks have found it profitable to expand into retail banking, with particular focus on their ethnic groups in the United States. For some foreign banks catering to nationals or descendants of nationals became the major reason for establishing their presence in the United States. Many foreign banks have made great efforts to expand the scope of their activities geographically, have entered into close relationships with the U.S. customers, and, in general, have endeavored to become an integral part of the U.S. banking scene.

In many respects Phase III of the foreign bank expansion in the United States can be characterized as an acclimatization and blending of foreign banks' operations with the operations typically carried on by the indigenous U.S. banks—a true multinationalization of banking in which national origin almost vanishes as a differentiating characteristic. The numbers reflecting the growth of foreign banks in the United States in the postwar period are quite impressive. By the end of 1975 there were close to 80 foreign banks with 184 banking offices located in the United States. Total assets of these offices as of the end of September 1975 amounted to $56.5 billion. About 42 percent, or some $23.6 billion, of the total assets were held by

---

[3]See "International banking: Part I," *Business Conditions,* December 1975, for a discussion of how the activities of multinational U.S. corporations influence U.S. banks to expand into foreign markets.

European banks; a similar proportion, totaling $23.2 billion, was held by Japanese banks while 12 percent, or $6.6 billion, were held by Canadian banks. The remaining $3.2 billion in assets were distributed among the banks of other nationalities. . . .

The FINE Proposals on
Foreign Banks in the United States
and American Banks Abroad

Charles Freedman

Introduction

The FINE study is the first major study of the financial system to pay serious attention to the role of foreign banks in the United States and American banks abroad.
This interest is clearly the result of the rapid growth of international banking (in
both forms) in the last ten years. The FINE study . . . offers a wealth of factual information and analysis on various facets of international banking. The analysis of
foreign banks in the United States can be readily divided into two categories—macroeconomic aspects and microeconomic aspects. The former includes the impact of
foreign banks in the United States on the efficacy of U.S. monetary policy and on
the U.S. balance of payments. The latter includes a wide variety of topics that relate
mainly to the fact that the restrictions on foreign banks operating in the United
States differ from those generally applying to domestic banks. As we shall see, these
differences can be dealt with on the level of both allocative efficiency and equity. In
the analysis of the operations of U.S. banks abroad, the study raises questions about
capital adequacy, supervision, and riskiness of portfolios. . . .

Macroeconomic Considerations

Although the major focus of the FINE recommendations and of the staff study (prepared by Jane D'Arista) is on inequities in the treatment of U.S. domestic banks vis-à-vis banking institutions owned by foreign banks, a substantial amount of attention is paid to the monetary policy and balance-of-payments effects of activities of the foreign-owned banks operating in the United States. Unfortunately, much of the argument is confused and many of the effects attributed to foreign-owned banks are exaggerated.

What are the implications for U.S. monetary policy of the existence and behavior of foreign-owned banks? Will the proposed changes aid controllability? The answers to these questions depend crucially, first, on whether the Federal Reserve is trying to control bank liabilities or bank assets, and also which subset of liabilities or assets and, second, what mechanism of control the Federal Reserve uses. Suppose, initially, that the authorities are attempting to control some measure of the money supply such as M_1 or M_2 and that they use monetary base control to implement their policy. The proposal to require foreign branches to hold reserves upon their Eurodollar borrowing would in no way increase the controllability of M_1 or M_2, since these aggregates do not include Eurodollar borrowings. Nor would prohibiting foreign branches from accepting nonbank deposits aid in the control of the monetary aggregates. Foreign-owned branches are, in principle, in precisely the same position as U.S. banks in having to hold reserves against nonbank deposits.[1] Basically, the question at issue is the stability of the money multiplier in terms of the appropriate aggregate and there is no reason to believe that either of these recommendations would increase stability. Furthermore, if as is currently the case, the Federal Reserve attempts to control the monetary aggregates via movements in interest rates (especially the Federal funds rate) then the two recommendations regarding reserves on Eurodollar borrowing and prohibition of nonbank deposits have even less merit from the point of view of controllability. For by adjusting interest rates the Federal Reserve is moving holders of money along their demand curves. It does not matter where these deposits are held. Nor, in this approach to the implementation of policy, does it matter whether banks are required to hold reserves against deposits.[2]

Suppose the authorities tried to control the assets of the banking system (in particular some measure of credit to the nonbank sector) on the basis of a belief in the existence of credit rationing. Note that, in the United States today, such a belief is

---

[1]There is the difference that most branches come under state regulation and are not members of the Federal Reserve System. Hence, the reserves that they are required to hold are those imposed by state law on nonmember banks. The difference therefore arises as part of the problem of the existence of nonmember banks and is not specific to foreign-owned banks.

[2]Although there is no valid argument from the point of view of controllability for the recommendation that the same reserve requirements be imposed on foreign borrowings of foreign-owned banks as on domestic banks, such an argument can be made on grounds of efficiency and equity. See section 4. Also, if the authorities use the manipulation of free reserves to control interest rates this would have to be taken into account in establishing the regulatory setting.

not generally accepted and does not underlie the policies of the Federal Reserve. One might then argue that the foreign-owned banks would indeed be responsible for the increased difficulty the authorities would have in controlling their target. At a time of increased tightness in the United States, foreign-owned banks will increase their borrowing abroad, particularly from their parent and affiliated banks, and utilize the funds to make loans to corporate and industrial borrowers either directly, or indirectly via loans to domestic banks. However, this ability to mobilize funds abroad is not unique to foreign-owned banks. Domestic banks, especially those with foreign branches, are even more active in borrowing funds abroad at times of domestic stringency. Nor will the proposed changes in regulation prevent these flows from occurring unless the reserve requirements imposed on borrowing from abroad raise the cost of this borrowing to a point that makes it unprofitable. Furthermore, it is not obvious that even such measures would effectively insulate U.S. borrowers from foreign lenders. As the experience of both Germany and the United States in attempting to control capital flows makes clear, it is extremely difficult to reduce flows between countries [1]. If banks in the United States were prevented from intermediating between U.S. borrowers and European lenders, European banks including foreign branches of U.S. banks could accomplish the same result by inducing the borrowers to book their loans outside the United States. Admittedly, small corporations might be unable to take advantage of this form of borrowing but over time their ability would likely grow as institutions adapted to the regulatory constraints. In any event a large proportion of current international intermediation could still be carried out in other ways.

The basic point is that the difficulties caused for monetary policy are a result of increased financial integration. This process is sufficiently widespread that no single institution or group of institutions can be held to be mainly responsible. If the authorities wish to control the total assets of banks via some form of base control, then it is appropriate to impose the same reserve requirements on foreign banks as those imposed on domestic banks. But given the degree of international integration, this type of control will not result in much greater insulation of the United States from the rest of the world.

A similar argument can be made with respect to balance-of-payments effects of actions of foreign-owned banks and the proposals for imposing reserve requirements on foreign-owned banks in order to lessen the impact of such flows. Increased elasticities of capital flows with respect to interest rate changes have led to increased volatility of international reserves under a fixed exchange rate system in response to shifts in interest rate differentials. But banks are only one of a number of channels through which funds flow. Any attempt to prevent such flows, short of complete exchange controls, is apt to lead to the opening of other channels. There is probably relatively little that can be done to prevent short-term capital flows, and the existence of these flows is not itself a valid argument for the proposed changes in reserve requirements governing foreign-owned banks in the United States.

We conclude that the existence of foreign banks has probably not hindered the authorities from controlling monetary aggregates, the avowed target of monetary policy. If the authorities should decide to control the asset side of the banking system via some form of base control, then as mentioned it would probably be helpful to have the same type of reserve requirements on foreign borrowings of foreign banks as on those of domestic banks. In neither type of situation does the prohibition of foreign banks from accepting domestic nonbank deposits aid in controllability. . . .

U.S. Banks Abroad

The FINE recommendations regarding the operations of U.S. banks abroad derive from concerns about the riskiness of the foreign operations of U.S. banks and about the competitive advantages of large U.S. banks over small ones. There are three recommendations that flow from the concern about riskiness. First, the authorities would have the right to impose special capital requirements on banks with foreign operations in order to ensure capital adequacy. Second, U.S. banks would be allowed to establish branches only in those countries that permit examination of the branch and access to its records by the U.S. authorities. Third, advance approval by U.S. authorities would be required for U.S. banks investing abroad in a joint banking venture, establishing a foreign subsidiary, or acquiring an interest in a bank operating abroad.[3] In order to encourage smaller banks to enter international banking and to reduce the competitive advantage of large banks, the report recommends that U.S. banks be authorized to establish overseas departments in their domestic offices that would be allowed to engage in the same activities as foreign branches of U.S. banks. The final recommendation of the FINE report is that discount privileges be extended only on domestic paper.

Obviously, the basic concern underlying the recommendations regarding capital adequacy, branch examination, and prior approval of further expansion abroad is that the operations of U.S. banks abroad increase the risk of failure of the parent bank. The conclusion drawn is that increased regulation of these operations is required. As recent bank failures and losses of banks operating in the Eurodollar market have shown, there is certainly reason to be concerned about some aspects of bank operations abroad. The staff study on which the recommendations are based focuses on three elements of risk—loans to nonbanks, interbank deposits, and foreign exchange transactions.

Before turning to an examination of these three elements, it is worth pointing out that at virtually every stage of the analysis in the staff study, there appears to be a problem of insufficiency of data. Whether it is a question of the exposure of banks in their loans to nonbank borrowers or the maturity structure of bank assets or foreign exchange position there are not enough data to determine whether a problem

---

[3]There are also antitrust aspects to this recommendation in that joint ventures would be governed by U.S. antitrust law.

exists or not. It is thus clear that increased data collection on the foreign operations of the banks is absolutely essential, both as an early warning signal of potential problems and as a prerequisite to sensible regulation. Such information would clearly benefit the banks themselves if it helped give a clearer idea of the final destination of the funds entering into the Eurodollar market.

The main risk connected with loans to nonbanks is, of course, the risk of default of the borrower. An individual bank making an unsecured loan to a country or corporation will often have incomplete information about the size of loans made by other banks to the same borrower and hence will have difficulty in assessing the riskiness of the loan and assigning the appropriate risk premium. In addition to direct loans to a borrower the bank may be making indirect loans to the same borrower via interbank deposits in other banks. Hence the bank's exposure may be greater than the loan on its own books. Despite this, it appears from the evidence of numerous witnesses at the hearings that until now loss experience on foreign loans has been better than that on loans in the domestic market. This, of course, could change in the future.

The second major risk that is cited involves the large amount of interbank deposits in the Euromarkets. The basic concern here is an extension of the domino principle, i.e., the failure of a single large bank could have massive repercussions throughout the entire system. The third element of risk is based on the gross size of contracts between banks for the sale and purchase of foreign exchange (both spot and forward). Again it is argued that the inability of a single large bank to meet its commitments could have major repercussions on all the banks with which it has contracts outstanding.

The FINE recommendations would act to reduce the risk arising from the behavior of an individual bank but would have little effect on the risk arising from the interdependence of banks. The proposals to ensure capital adequacy and to require prior approval of expansion abroad could be helpful in preventing situations in which the bank increases its own risk excessively by being undercapitalized or by entering into unduly risky arrangements. In addition, improved supervision would draw attention to problems of internal control by the head office over branches of the sort that have been the cause of some recent bank problems. Thus these recommendations do reduce the probability of the failure of an individual bank, but they do little to reduce the risk that the failure of a large bank will cause major repercussions throughout the entire system. The recent discussions among monetary and regulatory authorities aimed at fostering greater harmonization of regulation and cooperation in supervision in the sphere of international banking are much more important in dealing with this problem.

The recommendation that U.S. banks be permitted to establish branches only in those countries where U.S. authorities are allowed to conduct complete examination would force U.S. branches in certain jurisdictions to be closed. This seems an unduly strong measure to deal with a problem that seems amenable to other solutions involving cooperation among the regulatory authorities. For example, the Federal

Reserve considers that the arrangements it has made with the Swiss authorities provide sufficient scope for proper supervision. . . .

REFERENCE

1.   HEWSON, JOHN, and EISUKE SAKAKIBARA. *The Eurocurrency Markets and Their Implications: A "New" View of International Monetary Problems and Monetary Reform.* Lexington, Mass.: D. C. Heath, 1975.

A Primer on the Risks of · International Lending and How To Evaluate Them

Janice M. Westerfield

Among recent changes on the U.S. banking scene, surely one of the most dramatic has been the surge in international lending. Loans to foreign governments, firms, and individuals have grown both in volume and in earnings, and some aggressive international bankers have found that their foreign earnings actually exceed their domestic ones.

The steep upward trend in international involvement, which is tied in with overall trade expansion and new opportunities for profit, has brought different kinds of risks as well as substantial returns. The lender who makes loans in foreign countries has all the risks that he would have at home. But, beyond these, he has to consider risks which derive from the unique political, social, and economic conditions of the country in which the loan is placed.

These risks obviously are important to bankers because banking is a profitmaking industry and risk affects profit. Now that international lending has become such a high-volume business, the possibility that foreign loan losses might have an adverse impact on the American banking industry as a whole has become a matter of concern to government and to the public.

Even the most careful risk management won't obviate all the hazards of lending in foreign countries. But bankers are working hard to identify, evaluate, and reduce

Reprinted from *Business Review*, July/August 1978, pp. 19–29, by permission of the Federal Reserve Bank of Philadelphia and the author.

**Short-Term and Long-Term Claims on
Foreigners Reported by Banks in the
United States**

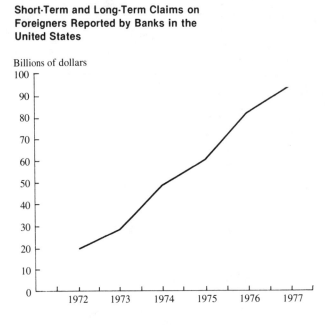

Billions of dollars

the risks that go with foreign lending. And those who succeed in reducing their risks, through geographical diversification of their loans, or by other means, stand a good chance of receiving returns that repay their efforts abroad.

U. S. Banks Go International

Since the beginning of the decade, U.S. banks have moved decisively into international finance, increasing their foreign claims and their earnings from foreign assets.

Growth

The statistics tell most of the international lending story.

Foreign claims of banks in the U.S. have grown from about $21 billion in 1972 to over $92 billion in 1977—a compound annual growth rate of 30 percent. And foreign branches of U.S. banks now have about double that volume of claims on foreigners. Earnings of foreign assets also are up sharply, especially in relation to domestic earnings. A Salomon Brothers study of thirteen large bank holding companies found that, from 1970 to 1976, their foreign earnings rose by about $700 million while earnings at home grew by less than $40 million.[1] Thus 95 percent of the

---

[1]Thomas Hanley, *U.S. Multinational Banking: Current and Prospective Strategies* (Salomon Brothers, 1976).

increase in their total earnings came from international operations. By 1976, foreign earnings accounted for more than half of total earnings for six of these bank holding companies. For the whole group, foreign earnings averaged 43 percent of total earnings.

And Its Causes

The growth of international banking operations is related to a number of developments, especially the overall expansion of U.S. trade with other countries. Also important have been the spread of multinational corporations, the effect of government regulation on domestic profit opportunities, and the impetus for financing trade deficits that changes in petroleum prices have generated in some foreign countries.

U.S. trade has increased. American merchandise exports rose from $50 billion in 1972 to $115 billion in 1976, and imports showed similar growth. Much of this growth in dollar value—part of it real, part of it caused by inflation—was financed by U.S. banks, through letters of credit and banker's acceptances and through other instruments. To take a simple illustration: An exporter may ship goods in July and desire payment immediately, but the importer probably won't have the funds to pay until he receives the goods in October. Under circumstances such as these, both parties may agree to have a bank forward payment to the exporter and lend money to the importer through creation of a banker's acceptance during the time the goods are in transit. Once the importer receives and processes his shipment, he reimburses the bank for the amount of the acceptance (including applicable interest). *Trade financing* of this sort has become commonplace for U.S. banks.

Many firms that first incorporated in the United States now operate through subsidiaries in other countries and have a significant percentage of their assets and employment positioned abroad. As these firms have expanded into foreign countries, they have brought their bankers with them. In Europe alone, for example, *U.S. multinationals,* with substantial financing by U.S. banks, have upped their direct foreign investment to over $56 billion.

This investment has paid off. Over the period 1966–75, sales by American affiliates in Europe rose by about 9 percent per year in real terms. And although reduced earnings prodded U.S. businesses to cut their foreign subsidiaries somewhat in 1976 and 1977, there remains a significant amount of multinational activity in Europe, and in other parts of the world, for U.S. banks to finance.

Interest in foreign banking operations probably has been encouraged by the regulatory environment at home. It's certain that *domestic banking regulations* helped to shape the responses of U.S. banks to changes in trading patterns. In the 1960's, the federal government imposed controls on outflows of U.S. financial capital. These controls encouraged American corporations to finance their foreign investments with foreign funds. But in order to accommodate their corporate customers, U.S. banks set up foreign branches that tapped foreign capital sources. For this reason and others, branches of U.S. banks became more firmly established abroad. And this result was abetted by Regulation Q, which, by limiting the interest rates paid on domestic deposits, further induced U.S. banks to set up foreign branches to supplement their traditional sources of funds. The number of overseas branches increased from 180 in 1965 to 732 in 1975.

Thus regulation, along with the internationalization of U.S. corporate activities, helped spur the growth of overseas branches. And despite some regulatory changes, there remain considerable incentives for setting up overseas offices to service multinational corporate customers.

Finally, *balance-of-payments deficits* in other countries have played an important role in the growth of U.S. bank claims on foreigners. Especially since the quadrupling of oil prices in 1973, many third-world countries have been unable to generate enough export earnings to pay their oil import bills without outside help. Among these countries, the poorest have had little access to credit markets; but others have found help in the form of medium-term loans from U.S. commercial banks. Substantial credits have been extended directly to foreign governments or their dependencies rather than to businesses or individuals.

Thus American banks have been responsive to large-scale developments in world trade as well as to regulation at home and payments shortfalls in other countries. And they are striving to consolidate the gains they have made so far as well as to explore new foreign profit opportunities. But their foreign operations have brought new kinds of risks—risks which deserve close scrutiny.

Identifying Foreign Loan Risks

The primary principles for foreign lending are the same as for domestic—define and assess risk exposure and then reduce the risk that borrowers will default. But when a prudent banker makes a loan abroad, whether the borrower is an individual, a firm, or a government, he'll be thinking about not only these principles but also country risk.

Basic Risks

The chances that a loan will be repaid in full are affected by many characteristics of the borrower. The less sound the borrower is financially, the greater the risk that part of the interest or principal of the loan will not be repaid. Thus an understanding of the financial condition of the borrower is important for domestic and foreign loans alike.

Besides the amount of repayment, the time of repayment also affects risk. Just as his domestic counterpart, the international lender must consider what he needs to preserve the overall liquidity of his portfolio. Liquidity—the ability to meet day-to-day obligations—may be impaired by having too much money tied up in long-term investments. Loans maturing in, say, five years cannot be used to pay liabilities due in six months. Thus the lender has to know not only how much of a return he can expect on his loan but also when he can expect to get it. And there are circumstances which could make a lender less confident of his expectations when he deals with foreign borrowers than when he deals with domestic ones.

Country Risk

There are certain risks that can attach to a loan just because it is placed in a foreign country. One kind of country risk is *sovereign risk,* which derives from the unique mix of political, social, and economic institutions that characterizes a sovereign state. Another kind is *currency risk*—the risk that a loss will be caused by currency restrictions or trade barriers.

Default occurs whenever a borrower fails to repay either the principal or the interest on a loan. Sometimes a borrower may want to reschedule debt—to stretch out payments because they can't be met out of current resources. When a loan is rescheduled, the borrower usually must pay an interest penalty to compensate the lender for the higher risk of eventual loss. But the lender still may lose out on part of his return; and even if he doesn't, his liquidity may be reduced by having his money tied up longer than expected. A foreign government that can offer assurances against default and rescheduling of loans to private borrowers and autonomous government agencies will make such loans more attractive to international lenders.

Sovereign risk is closely tied to political developments, particularly the attitudes of the government authorities towards foreign loans or investments. Some countries attempt to smooth the way for foreign funds, whether those funds are flowing to public or private borrowers. But others make it very difficult to establish and maintain profitable lending operations. Minor obstacles can appear in the form of wage-price controls, profit controls, tax and legal restrictions, and so on. These forms of government interference generally raise the costs of doing business and sometimes reduce the chances that the lender will be fullly reimbursed. Further, they may be signs that the borrower should face up to the possibility of nationalization of an investment, expropriation of assets, of prohibition of foreign loan repayment—any of which could change the risk picture.[2] Although the chance of expropriation may be small, the loss associated with it is so complete that it cannot be ignored. Sometimes partial compensation is offered, but even this may be delayed for long periods while host governments negotiate with foreign investors or lenders.

Currency risk, which can occur by itself or in combination with sovereign risk, has to do with currency value changes and exchange controls. Some loans are denominated in foreign currency rather than in dollars, and if the currency in which the loan is made loses value against the dollar during the course of the loan, the repayment will be worth fewer dollars when the loan comes due (though the asset loss may be offset by liabilities in the same currency). Because not all foreign currency markets are well developed, international loans sometimes cannot be hedged to reduce this kind of currency risk. Credits that are denominated in dollars, as most

---

[2]There are few recorded cases of large-scale nationalization by a foreign government. Chile and Cuba appear to be two examples.

are, also may be subject to currency risk. Exchange controls, which are relatively common in developing countries, may limit the cross-border movement of funds or restrict a currency's convertibility into dollars for repayment. Or exchange rate changes may affect the borrower's capacity to generate sufficient earnings to pay off dollar loans.

All in all, the lender who wants the returns that go with foreign operations must be prepared to make an extra effort to identify his risks. But that's only the beginning. Once it's known what *can* happen, the lender has to evaluate the likelihood that it *will* happen. And that takes information.

Risk Evaluation

Lenders have different ways to evaluate risk. In some cases they use in-depth studies of foreign countries. In others they use statistics that indicate a borrower's financial condition or checklists that pull together economic, social, and political data.

In-depth studies usually are based on both statistics and other information about a country's economic and financial management. Depending upon the extent of a bank's international operations, its evaluations may be quite comprehensive. Besides background information on basic economic trends in the foreign economy, these evaluations often contain careful analyses of inflation, fiscal policies, trade and capital flows, debt accumulation, political stability, and other variables.[3] Since some circumstances that affect country risk cannot be captured in statistics, it is inevitable that practical judgment and experience also come into play. And lenders who maintain branches or representative offices abroad may rely on their staffs not only to generate business but also to help them keep up with local developments that aren't reflected in a timely way by indicators and checklists. So the overall in-depth evaluation of a country is likely to come from many sources.

When bankers find it too costly or time consuming to get in-depth analyses, they may turn to on-site reports, checklists, and statistical indicators—separately or in combination—for assessing the debt-servicing capabilities of prospective borrowers. These aids may not be long on theory, but they do provide ways to get a grip on the information that a loan officer has to grapple with.

Some of the statistical indicators are designed to measure foreign exchange earnings entering a country against outgoing expenditures for debt servicing. The debt-service ratio was the first such indicator to be used extensively. This ratio states a country's interest and amortization payments as a percentage of its export earnings

---

[3]The way country risk is assessed will depend somewhat upon the purpose for which the assessment is to be used. Bankers are interested primarily in avoiding debt-servicing difficulties and in making profitable loans. International institutions such as the International Monetary Fund want country studies as background information for annual consultations or for approving drawings from one of the Fund's facilities. The World Bank does its country evaluation studies for the purpose of deciding how much to loan and what kind of technical assistance to provide to its various members.

Statistical Indicators

Several indicators are used by international lenders to gauge country risk. These indicators, and the techniques of using them, do not have a high degree of reliability as predictors of debt-servicing difficulties. But they still may provide useful information to lenders.

The *debt-service ratio,* which probably is the most commonly used statistical indicator, measures foreign exchange earnings challenged into debt servicing against total exchange earnings from (current account) exports.

The ratio of the current account deficit to export earnings from goods and services—the *current deficit-export ratio*—measures temporary balance-of-payments difficulties and may fluctuate considerably from year to year. When combined with the *cumulative deficit-export ratio* over, say, a three-year period, the current deficit-export ratio can give a longer term picture of the amount and rate of growth of a country's debt burden.

The *interest-reserve ratio* measures net interest payments on external debt against international reserves in the most recent period. The interest payments reflect the debt interest burden for all debt accumulated. (Amortization data, which is not comprehensive in any case, is excluded.) This ratio measures the short-run ability of a country to meet its interest payments—out of international reserves, if necessary. The focus is on reserves as a last source of funds to service debt.

A variant of this ratio which also uses net interest payments is the *interest-export ratio.* This measures the debt interest burden against average annual export receipts and is a proxy for the debt-export ratio.

Indicators such as these focus on a country's ability to repay its external debt out of current account export earnings. But a reduction in these earnings needn't lead to debt-servicing difficulties or attempts to cut back imports, since grant aid, capital inflows, and international reserves may be used along with export earnings to service debt. Thus a country may have more flexibility than is suggested by external debt indicators.

Other indicators, which chart both internal and external economic conditions, are used for overall ranking purposes as well as for in-depth country studies. Some measures suggested by the literature include economic growth rates of gross domestic product and money supply as well as export earnings stability and level of economic development.

from goods and services. Other indicators, such as the current account deficit, net interest payments, and growth rate of real GNP, have been developed to supplement the debt-service ratio. And sometimes, because any of these individual indicators used alone may be misleading, several of them will be combined to construct composite indicators for more reliable identification of problem borrowers (see Statistical Indicators).

Somewhat similar are the checklists of economic, social, and political variables that some bankers use along with their statistical indicators. These checklists are designed to yield supplementary information about a country's economic and financial management. The checklists are not standard from bank to bank, but they usually include variables about GNP, money supply growth, foreign trade, debt accumulation, and so on. The checklist items generally are not ratios, as the statistical indicators are, but they can be assigned numerical ratings and aggregated into a total score for each country.

Neither the checklists nor the statistical indicators are reliable predictors of debt-servicing difficulties. Often they signal false alarms. Most of the indicators and checklists describe conditions as they were a year or two ago. Even when current, they describe the situation only as it now is; they do not tell how the picture will change in the future. And predicting debt-servicing difficulties is essentially peeking into the future. Nevertheless, these indicators may serve as warning signals that a prospective foreign borrower ought to be examined more closely.

Thus the lender has to decide how much information he needs to negotiate a loan with a prospective borrower, and then he has to go out and get it. If the information simply is not available, or if it indicates too high a risk for the expected rate of return, the loan applicant may be turned down. But even if the decision is made to go ahead with the loan, the prudent banker will want to reduce the risk of loss.

Methods of Reducing Risk

Bankers have several ways to cut risk. They can seek third-party support in the form of loan guarantees or management assistance for borrowers; they can share risk exposure with several lenders; or, most important, they can diversify their loans among several borrowers or areas. And the regulatory authorities may be able to assist international lenders in holding down their country risk exposure.

Third-Party Help

One way for a banker to reduce the risk on a loan is to get a third party to agree to pay back both principal and interest if the borrower defaults. Foreign governments and central banks sometimes act in this capacity. But the guarantee is good only so long as the backer is solvent and adheres to the contract. And if the same government or central bank guarantees several loans, there's a chance that its ability to supply the required funds might be strained if more than one of these loans were to require funds at the same time.

An alternative to the foreign government guarantee is the external guarantee by a parent company or outside institution. The Overseas Private Investment Corporation, for example, offers programs to insure bank loans against the risks of war, expropriation, and inconvertibility, as well as to finance loans directly. Also, the U.S. Export-Import Bank (Eximbank) guarantees medium-term loans made by commercial banks against both political and credit risk. And the Foreign Credit Insurance Association, acting as agent for member insurance companies and the Eximbank, offers insurance against these risks.

Another form of third-party help that many bankers find reassuring is the presence of institutions such as the International Monetary Fund. The IMF does not assist the lender directly. It does not, for example, provide commercial bankers with its country reports. But it can put the lender's mind more at ease by fostering conditions in a borrower country that increase the likelihood of loan repayment.

In the course of determining whether a country that has balance-of-payments difficulties is eligible to draw from its funding facilities, for instance, the IMF examines the prospective borrower's current condition and economic policies. And it negotiates measures that the borrower must take to qualify for eligibility. A country's adherence to these measures, which the IMF monitors, can increase the probability that the borrower will be able to repay without difficulty. Thus the international banker benefits indirectly but importantly from having the IMF on site.

Risk Pooling

When third-party assistance isn't available, bankers still can cut the risk for any one institution by making a participation loan. Under this kind of arrangement, several banks combine their funds to reduce exposure directly for individual banks. This type of effort may include a sharing of expertise among the participants, but generally each bank wants and is expected to make its own assessment. Since participation loans sometimes are large and involve big-name banks, the country that gets them probably will feel that its access to credit markets will be served best by prompt repayment.

While third-party presence may reduce default risk and pooling may lessen the exposure of individual banks, there is another strategy that deserves consideration. Instead of focusing on each loan prospect in isolation as it comes along, the banker can examine each one for its effect on risk to the total loan portfolio.

Diversification

The portfolio approach to managing assets is important to bankers because they want to maintain a steady stream of returns over time. The typical lender does not want to put all his eggs in one basket, where they all can be broken simultaneously.

And, in any case, he is prevented from doing so by legal restrictions. Instead, he diversifies the portfolio by investing in a variety of loans, so that, in case one borrower defaults, the earnings from other investments will minimize the effect of the loan loss on the bank's total earnings.

But whether diversification reduces risk for a given portfolio depends on how the returns on individual loans are correlated with one another—to what extent they are affected in similar ways by common conditions or events. Diversification will be a source of potential risk reduction if returns on individual loans are *not* perfectly correlated.[4] Thus of two loans with the same rate of return and riskiness, the one that is less perfectly correlated with the rest of the portfolio will be the more attractive; and it may even happen that a loan with a relatively low rate of return will be a useful addition to a portfolio because it's imperfectly correlated with the rest of the portfolio's contents (see Appendix).

Portfolio diversification can be pursued in several ways, of which geographical dispersion may be the most obvious. When loans to a foreign recipient are under consideration, it's usually the country-specific aspects of the loan that are first considered. That is, everything else being held constant—the maturity, loan guarantee, characteristics of the firm and industry, and so on—it's the sovereign state that makes the difference. This element in the choice among countries is what is identified most commonly as country risk.

But the choice among countries may ignore another source of country exposure, and that is loan concentration. A bank develops expertise in certain countries and cultivates sources yielding first-hand information, which is essential to sound decisionmaking. Furthermore, detailed knowledge of the borrower is required in order to form opinions about probabilities of repayment. The argument can be made that expertise built up in a country over a long period is hard to beat. But if several loans have already been generated in, say, Country A, an additional loan in Country A may actually be more risky than a first loan in, say, Country B. Why? Because risks of excessive concentration may not be fully offset by first-hand information.

The risks of undue concentration stem from the possibility that a common factor may have an adverse effect on all the loans in a given country. This is because the economic and political management of a country influences all its economic units. If some adverse development should occur, many units within the country would be similarly affected. Take the case of a country that depends on two or three export products for its foreign exchange earnings. Although foreign exchange may also be obtained from other sources such as capital inflows or reserves, many countries derive foreign currency supplies primarily from export earnings. When the export market for a country's products deteriorates and foreign exchange earnings fall

---

[4]Citicorp states this point in its 1976 annual report (p. 25) as follows: "Overseas earnings, which contributed over 70 percent of the total earnings in 1976, are derived from doing business in more than 100 countries. Citicorp's worldwide policy of broad diversification of both assets and liabilities helps maintain earnings stability and reduces the risk of excessive concentration in any one particular country, currency, or industry."

short, the government, its agencies, and many businesses all may have insufficient earnings to repay debts on schedule.[5]

Besides the effects of sovereignty and concentration on country exposure, interaction effects between foreign and domestic loans are important for diversification. Thus a bank's portfolio ought to be considered in its entirety and not analyzed in separate foreign and domestic sections. Risk to the overall portfolio probably can be reduced when some foreign loans are added to a predominantly domestic portfolio. The reason is that the business cycles of most other countries differ in timing and magnitude from those of the U.S., and so foreign borrowers and domestic borrowers are unlikely to suffer from overall economic declines at the same time. Thus diversification can be construed broadly over country, currency, industry, maturity, and so on.

Reducing portfolio risk for the same expected return (or else increasing the return for the same risk level) is the benefit the banker hopes to get through diversification.

Supervision and Country Risk

The growth of U.S. bank claims on foreigners and the increase of other capital flows are major developments requiring assessment by the U.S. monetary authorities. Because information about happenings in the rest of the world often is incomplete, this task is a difficult one. The first step may be to gather information about the magnitude and geographical distribution of foreign exposure. The Federal Reserve, the Office of the Comptroller of the Currency, and the Federal Deposit Insurance Corporation are doing just that in a semiannual country exposure report of more than 400 banks, their overseas branches, and subsidiaries. The detailed information on borrowers and maturities is designed to assist these agencies in judging the risks that banks face in their international lending.

Several policy proposals are being discussed now, such as guidelines that would guard against excessive loan concentration in one country in relation to a bank's total capital. Others involve closer monitoring of bank internal procedures. Further, last January the Comptroller of the Currency issued a ruling on loan concentration designed to clarify the interpretation of banking law which limits national bank loans to individual borrowers to 10 percent of total bank capital. This ruling attempts to define the conditions under which governments, their instrumentalities, and their agencies can be considered separate borrowers.

---

[5]A few countries rely mainly on earnings from just one export to repay their debts. A fall in the price of this export can produce debt-servicing difficulties and consequent debt rescheduling.

It follows that international lenders have a lot to gain by diversifying their loan portfolios. Spreading out their loans to achieve a relatively constant return is the best hedge against crippling loan losses. Even though there may be great advantages to specializing in one country and becoming thoroughly acquainted with conditions there, bankers ought to be willing to sacrifice some information advantage for the security of diversification.

How Regulators Can Help

The agencies that regulate American banking have watched international developments more and more closely as the volume of lending has grown. They recognize that geographical expansion has brought a new kind of risk, and they are interested in assuring the soundness of U.S. banking efforts abroad.

The regulator's position is a delicate one. Mere acceptance of international lending guidelines that banks set for themselves may not provide an effective level of monitoring. But imposition of uniform limits on the volume of a bank's foreign loans, for example, could operate to restrict foreign profit opportunities severely, with consequent harmful effects on the overall health of the American banking system (see "Supervision and Country Risk").

The answer appears to lie in helping banks improve their information on foreign borrowers and avoid unusually large concentrations of credit in a single country. At present, the agencies with the heaviest involvement in international lending—the Federal Reserve System, the Comptroller of the Currency, and the Federal Deposit Insurance Corporation—are moving deliberately forward with such an approach. They are developing a data collection system that will help banks track their foreign exposure by recording the volume and maturity of loans in a given country, whether the loans have external guarantees, and whether they are denominated in local or nonlocal currency (usually dollars). This approach provides an analysis of loan concentration by country with respect to a bank's overall financial capital. With this information in front of them, bank managers and examiners are in a position to evaluate lending procedures and portfolio risk.[6]

Summing Up

Lending to foreigners involves country risk exposure and requires an assessment of risks of government policies and risks of currency or trade restrictions. Commercial bankers perceive that the profitability of their foreign operations and thus a substantial portion of their earnings vary directly with how well they evaluate foreign risks. Government authorities, as well, stress the importance of a careful analysis of country risk to ensure sound banking practices.

[6]See "A New Supervisory Approach to Foreign Lending," Federal Reserve Bank of New York, *Quarterly Review,* Spring 1978, pp. 1-6.

Because of the problems associated with incomplete information, bankers, regulators, and other concerned parties have developed a mix of qualitative and quantitative methods to evaluate risks associated with foreign claims. Yet, in the past, these measures have tended to focus on a single country and its political, economic, and social fabric. While these indicators are useful, they generally ignore how a single event might adversely affect a whole country. Nor do they recognize how countries depend on one another in the trading, financial, political, and other spheres.

Since these common relations are reflected in returns on loans, appreciable gains may be made from examining how an individual claim fits into the overall portfolio. Diversification of loans is essential if risk to the total portfolio is to be kept at an acceptable level. And imperfect correlation of returns is the key to successful diversification. As international operations continue to grow, bankers can be expected increasingly to explore the benefits that diversification could bring to the world of foreign lending.

Appendix:
Diversification Can Reduce Risk

Suppose that a U.S. bank has decided to allocate $1 million of its funds to foreign loans in Country A or Country B. The bank feels it has developed some expertise in Country A, and it already has made several loans to public or private borrowers there. It has no loans outstanding in Country B. The maturities of the loans will be the same in whichever country they're placed.

The bank's international experts know the rate of return over the maturity of each loan and the probability of default. Using these basic data, they can calculate both the expected return and the variance of return. (Variance of return measures risk and is a function of the probability of obtaining a return that differs from the expected return.)

The loan to Country A would have a yield to maturity of 10 percent and a default risk of 2 percent. The calculation for the loan's expected return then is:

$$E(R_A) = 0.98(0.10) + 0.02(0) = 0.098.$$

The calculation for its variance is:

$$\text{var}(R_A) = 0.98[0.10 - E(R_A)]^2 + 0.02\,[0 - E(R_A)]^2 = 0.00033.$$

Note that a 2-percent default risk means that the bank has a 2-percent chance of receiving no payment on its loan and a 98-percent chance of receiving the full 10-percent yield.

The loan to Country B would have a yield to maturity of 10.2 percent and a default risk of 4 percent. Calculations will show that the loan to Country B would have the same expected return as Country A's—0.098—but a higher variance—0.00040. Thus the whole picture would be as follows:

	Yield to Maturity	Default Risk	Expected Return	Variance of Return
Country A	10.0%	2%	0.098	0.00033
Country B	10.2%	4%	0.098	0.00040

Assume, however, that the bank wants to diversify by splitting the $1 million 50–50 between the two countries instead of lending the full amount to the country with the lower variance—Country A. Further, assume that the returns on the loans to Country A and Country B move together somewhat and have a correlation coefficient c = 0.4. Finally, assume that the portfolio has an expected return that is equal to the expected return on the loan to Country A while the variance is less than it would be if the full amount were loaned to Country A:

$$\text{var}(R_p) = X_A^2 \, \text{var}(R_A) + X_B^2 \, \text{var}(R_B) + 2c_{AB}X_AX_B\sigma_A\sigma_B$$

$$= 0.00026.$$

The loan to Country B has the same expected return as, and a higher variance than, the loan to Country A. But when Country B is added to the portfolio, the variance of the portfolio as a whole is less than the variance of either individual loan. Thus the variance of return on the individual loans has been offset by the less than perfect correlation among the returns. Diversification has reduced portfolio risk for the same expected return.

If the bank desires to find out what percentage allocation to Country A would *minimize* the variance of the portfolio return, this percentage (X_A^*) can be computed as well.[†] The minimum-variance portfolio turns out to have 58 percent loaned to Country A and 42 percent loaned to Country B. Again, diversification reduces portfolio risk for the same expected return, although the variance—$\text{var}(R_p^*)$ = 0.00025—is only marginally less than that of the 50–50 portfolio.

[†]$X_A^* = [\text{var}(R_B) - c_{BA}\,\sigma_B\sigma_A]/\text{var}(R_A) + \text{var}(R_B) - 2c_{BA}\sigma_B\sigma_A$

$= 0.58.$

$X_B^* = 1 - X_A^* = 0.42.$

Commercial Bank Lending to Developing Countries

Nicholas P. Sargen

. . . The recent debate over commercial bank lending to developing countries has focused attention on the alleged high risks entailed in LDC loans. Economic theory, however, leads one to expect that commercial banks will require added compensation if they perceive defaults or reschedulings on LDC loans to be greater than those on loans to developed countries. Hence, commercial banks will not necessarily be vulnerable to LDC external-debt problems, provided their perception of LDC lending risk is generally accurate. On the other hand, if commercial banks systematically understate the risks involved in lending to developing countries, the added revenues they receive on LDC loans will not be sufficient to cover the added costs incurred, and their profit and liquidity positions will be squeezed by LDC defaults or reschedulings. In examining developing country lending risk, therefore, it is important to separate two issues: (1) On what basis do commercial banks form their perception of LDC lending risks, and to what extent are they compensated for the added perceived risk? (2) Is the market perception of LDC lending risk "correct"—i.e. is the compensation sufficient to cover added costs?

To answer these questions, we have analyzed data compiled by the World Bank on publicized Eurocurrency credits completed between the third quarter of 1974 and the third quarter of 1975—altogether, 67 loans to developed countries, totaling $3.8

Reprinted, with deletions, from *Economic Review*, Spring 1976, pp. 20–30, by permission of the Federal Reserve Bank of San Francisco and the author.

billion, and 177 loans to developing countries amounting to $10.0 billion. Information in each case included the borrower and borrowing country; the leading creditor institutions; the month of the loan agreement; the amount of the credit; the commitment period; and the spread over the London Inter-Bank Offer Rate (LIBOR).

Average Premium on Loans to LDCs

First, we were interested in the premium investors receive on credits to developing countries compared with their credits to developed countries. This involves an analysis of the most typical form of Eurocredit, a revolving credit at a floating interest rate. Funds are drawn as a short-term advance, usually renewable at the end of three-month or six-month periods (called the "renewal period" or "rollover period") for a designated term (called the "commitment period"). Rates to borrowers are quoted on the basis of the three-month or six-month LIBOR rate plus the "spread." The latter covers overhead cost, profit, and risk, and is determined on the basis of the borrower's creditworthiness and competitiveness of the market when the commitment is made.

Table 1.   Regression Results: Variations in Spreads on Eurocredits, 1974.3–1975.3[a]
(*t*-Statistics in Parentheses)

(i) Developed (DC) and Developing Country Loans[b]

Spread =	Constant	Average Reduction for Developed Countries	Average 1975 Increase	Maturity[d]
R² = .48	1.41	−.25	.40	−.017
D.W. = 1.58	(18.3)	(6.70)	(10.4)	(1.78)
S.E.E. = .25				
D.F. = 240				

(ii) Developing Countries Only[c]

Spread =	Constant	Income "Effect"	Mexico "Effect"	Debt[d] Service Ratio	Inflation[d] Rate	Average 1975 Increase	Maturity[d]
R² = .54	1.46	.10	−.27	.006	.005	.26	−.04
D.W. = 1.86	(15.9)	(2.80)	(4.40)	(2.35)	(3.80)	(5.58)	(3.96)
S.E.E. = .21							
D.F. = 170							

[a] Data Source: World Bank, *Borrowing in International Capital Markets*, November 1974–November 1975.

[b] Regression equation is of form: Spread $= a_0 + a_1 \begin{Bmatrix} LDC = 0 \\ DC = 1 \end{Bmatrix} + a_2 \begin{Bmatrix} 1974 = 0 \\ 1975 = 1 \end{Bmatrix} = a_3 \cdot$ (Maturity). Hence, the constant term can be interpreted as the average 1974 LDC spread, unadjusted for maturity.

[c] LDC Spread $= b_0 + b_1 \begin{Bmatrix} \text{High Inc.} = 0 \\ \text{Other} = 1 \end{Bmatrix} + b_2 \begin{Bmatrix} \text{Other} = 0 \\ \text{Mex.} = 1 \end{Bmatrix} + b_3 \cdot$ (Debt Ser.) $+ b_4 \cdot$ (Inf.) $+ b_5 \begin{Bmatrix} 1974 = 0 \\ 1975 = 1 \end{Bmatrix}$ $+ b_6 \cdot$ (Mat.)
Hence, the constant term can be interpreted as the average 1974 spread for higher-income LDCs, unadjusted for maturity, debt-service ratio, and the inflation rate.

[d] Coefficient must be multiplied by the value of the variable. Maturities are usually 5–8 years; debt- service ratios are generally between 10–20 percent; inflation rates are usually in the 15–30 percent range.

The first regression equation in Table 1 illustrates how the spread varied depending (1) on the recipient of the Eurocredit, whether developed or developing country, (2) on the date of commitment, whether 1974 or 1975, and (3) on the length of the commitment period. Each of the variables is statistically significant, although the maturity of the loan has a relatively small coefficient and small t-statistic. The latter finding is not surprising, however, in view of the variable interest rates on Eurocredits. The regression results show that borrowers from developing countries paid an average spread of about 140 basis points in 1974, whereas developed country borrowers paid about 25 basis points less on average, reflecting the lower perceived lending risks. In 1975, although the spread was about 40 basis points higher for each of the two groups, the LDC-DC differential did not change significantly. Expressed as a percentage of borrowing costs (LIBOR + spread), the developing-country premium translated into an additional 2 to 3 percent rate of return on investment over that on developed-country loans.

Variation in Spreads

Further analysis takes into consideration the fact that there are variations within the group of developing countries. Typically, they are separated into prime and non-prime categories, based in part on each country's per capita income. The second regression in Table 1 takes this into account by distinguishing between higher-income countries and lower- or middle-income countries (using World Bank definitions). In addition, we have included a separate dummy variable for Mexico, in view of that country's long experience as a borrower in international capital markets.

The choice of other variables is less clear-cut. For example, banks differentiate between government and private borrowers, but that distinction is not very meaningful if a loan to a private borrower carries a government guarantee, or if the institution is quasi-official. The data also indicate that project risk is less important than country risk in setting spreads—but there is no generally accepted framework for assessing country default risk. In the absence of such a framework, analysts have tended to use those economic indicators which reflect a country's capacity to service its debt, although there is no general agreement as to which indicators are important in this regard. Despite the large number of possible measures, we have limited ourselves to two of the most commonly used; first, the inflation rate, and second, the debt-service ratio, i.e., the proportion of foreign-exchange earnings on current account absorbed by public-debt service.

All the variables included in the regression are statistically significant and have the anticipated signs. The coefficients of the inflation variable and the debt-service variable are quite small, however, so that each adds only about 10 basis points to the spread on average, assuming a 20 percent inflation rate and 15 percent debt-service ratio. Lower- and middle-income countries paid only about 10 basis points more than higher-income countries, whereas Mexico paid about 25 basis points less than other higher-income countries and about 35 basis points less than lower-middle

income countries. In sum, no single factor appears to dominate in explaining variations in LDC spreads, although Mexico clearly is in a separate category from other
developing countries.

It is also instructive to note how commercial banks responded to the large LDC
trade deficits. The regression indicates that developing country spreads increased
about 25 basis points on average between the second half of 1974 and the first three
quarters of 1975. Increases in spreads for major Eurocurrency borrowers other than
Mexico, however, were well above the developing country average. The spread
which Brazil paid, for example, increased from ¾ of one percent on 12-year loans in
late 1974 to 1¾ percent for 5-year loans in 1975, while the spread for Spain increased from 1 percent on 8-year loans to 1¾ percent on 5-year loans. Hence, the
relatively small difference in spreads between higher-income countries and lower-
middle income countries reflects, in part, bankers' revised perceptions of lending
risks to heavy borrowers. Countries which incurred debt problems generally paid the
highest spreads, in addition to experiencing sharp reductions in new lending flows.

Comparisons with Earlier Periods

Comparisons of Eurocurrency loan premiums over longer time periods are difficult
to make, since calculations for earlier periods are based on bond flotations rather
than bank loans. The evidence, however, strongly suggests that the premium attached to portfolio investment in developing countries today may well be at an all-
time low. The yield premium between developed and developing country bond issues
is much lower today than in 1958–65, when the average LDC yield was nearly one-
half to two-thirds higher than that of high-grade U.S. domestic corporate bonds,
and between one-third and one-half higher than that on Canadian issues. Differential yields in the 1920s were somewhat smaller (40 percent over U.S. corporate bonds
and 25 percent over Canadian public issues in the U.S.), but still well above the differential developing countries pay today.

The narrowing LDC premium in part reflects the increasingly impressive economic performance of the higher-income developing countries. While these countries have been adversely affected by the events of the last several years, their prospects today are still considerably brighter than they were fifteen or twenty years ago.
In addition, the banking system has developed various risk-reducing mechanisms,
such as variable interest rates, for example, or syndicated bank loans, which provide
a means of spreading country risks that are borne by individual banks.

Finally, attitudes towards default have changed considerably since the 1930s and
1940s, when there were massive LDC defaults on bond issues. At that time, developing countries which encountered foreign-exchange crises had little incentive or option to avoid default.

> Prior to the Great Depression, external long-term debt consisted primarily of bond issues
> floated abroad. Only rarely could a refunding be arranged prior to actual default. Then

some agreement had to be reached by the debtor and the bondholders, often represented by committees, which could not bind the bondholders but could merely recommend acceptance of the proposal. In some instances the debtor made a unilateral offer to the private creditors, which they could accept as the alternative to not being repaid at all. The governments of the creditors were not parties to the agreements, though they could use diplomatic means to protect their nationals.

The differences in the post-war period are striking. Since the late 1950s there have been at least 25 instances, involving 15 different countries, where debt arrearages have had to be negotiated. Governments of creditor and debtor nations were parties to the negotiations, and the outcome in each case was a rescheduling of a country's debt, rather than outright default. Given present institutional arrangements for handling debt problems, the likelihood of a developing country repudiating its debt is now perceived to be quite low.

Past experience suggests that the market's perception of LDC risk has not systematically understated the costs involved. The relevant issue today, though, is whether the developing country debt situation will be the same in the future as in the past. There are few signs to indicate a hardening attitude in creditor government attitudes, although governments of some developing countries have urged a moratorium on foreign debt-service payments. The more likely development is that future reschedulings will involve both official and commercial-bank credits. One can only speculate, however, as to how often countries will have to reschedule, whether bank credits will be rescheduled in proportion to their share of external debt-service payments, and whether credits will be rescheduled at market interest rates. The debt negotiations in Argentina, Chile, and Zaire are significant because they provide the first test cases of reschedulings in countries where commercial-bank credits comprise a sizable portion of the external debt service. As these negotiations are concluded, it is possible that the market's perception of LDC risk could be altered.

Banking Structure

VII

For many years the only major competitors of commercial banks were commercial banks. However, the recent banking revolution has broadened the product line of banks. Relaxed restrictions on branching in some states, on electronic banking facilities, and on holding company acquisitions have brought banks into increased geographic competition with one another and have expanded nonbanking product lines. Finally, thrift institutions, weakened by their dependence on two products—savings accounts and mortgages—during a period when market rates of interest exceeded the rates legally payable on deposits, have sought to diversify into markets dominated by commercial banks. Through the introduction of interest-bearing negotiable order of withdrawal (NOW) accounts and consumer lending, as well as through electronic banking experimentation (described by the readings in Section V), thrift institutions have become more competitive with commercial banks.

Under these conditions the whole concept of the structure of banking markets deserves careful examination. The three readings in this section provide the foundation for such an examination.

In Essay 28 Alfred Broaddus develops an overview of these problems, paying particular regard to the *geographic* market for banking services. Next, Joel M. Yesley provides a comprehensive survey of the theoretical and empirical studies on the *product* market in commercial banking. George J. Benston's article is an outstanding analysis of the literature on bank cost functions, bank concentration, bank mergers, and market entry. Benston's analysis provides insight into the costs and benefits to the public from changes in the banking structure.

The Banking Structure: What It Means and Why It Matters

Alfred Broaddus

Nearly anyone who customarily reads business and financial publications has encountered the phrase "the banking structure." Most readers are aware that the phrase refers to certain characteristics of the banking industry such as the number of banks in particular localities and the size and relative market power of specific banking institutions. But many readers would probably like the answers to three basic questions. First, precisely what is meant by the structure of the banking industry and how is it measured? Second, what factors determine the banking structure and which of these factors can bank regulatory agencies control or influence? Third, what is the operational significance of the banking structure? That is, how does the banking structure affect bank performance? This article will discuss each of these questions in turn. In doing so, the goal of the article is to provide the reader with the means to evaluate critically published material concerning the banking structure.

I. What Is the Banking Structure?

Economists use the word "structure" to refer to the number and size distribution of buyers and sellers making up a particular economic market. The key word in the

Reprinted from the Federal Reserve Bank of Richmond, *Monthly Review,* November 1971, pp. 2-7, 10, by permission of the publisher and the author.

preceding sentence is market, for one cannot determine the structure of a market until the market under consideration is carefully defined and delineated. It will be useful to discuss the market definition problem generally and subsequently apply this discussion to the definition of banking markets.

General Problems in Market Specification

Speaking broadly, the market for any good or service consists of the individuals, business firms, and government agencies buying or selling the item in question. In practice, however, it may be quite difficult to designate precisely which buyers and sellers constitute a particular market. In defining a market, two especially vexing problems arise: (1) specification of the product or products exchanged in the market and (2) delineation of the geographic area covered by the market.

PRODUCT DEFINITION

Two distinct conceptual difficulties exist with respect to market classification according to product. First, some nonidentical goods (such as coffee and tea) are substitutes in the eyes of the consuming public. Second, some goods (such as bread and butter) complement one another when consumed jointly.

(1) Substitutable Products   Prior to the 1930s, economists traditionally considered a market to encompass the exchange of a narrowly specified good at a uniform price. The work of Edward Chamberlin and others, however, suggested that it is useful for many analytical purposes to study market activity in terms of groups of nonidentical but substitutable goods.[1] This approach raised an immediate question: How broadly should one define the group of substitutable goods traded in a particular market? Unfortunately, economic theory does not offer a precise criterion. For the purposes of practical market analysis, an eclectic approach is taken: Markets are defined both narrowly and broadly with respect to product groups, the choice in any particular case depending on the goals of the study at hand. To give a simple illustration, an analyst might consider the market for all passenger automobiles. Or, he might prefer to analyze more narrowly defined markets for automobiles having particular mechanical or stylistic characteristics such as sport cars or station wagons.

(2) Complementary Products   The product specification problem posed by the existence of complementary goods is particularly relevant to service industries. Specifically, what particular products constitute an integrated service product? For example, hospitals provide a wide variety of specific medical services. Does a separate market exist for each of these services? Or is there a broadly defined market for the composite group of "hospital services"?

THE GEOGRAPHIC DELINEATION OF MARKET AREAS

Designating the geographic area covered by a market presents an additional set of conceptual difficulties. Speaking generally, the geographic area covered by a specific

[1]See reference [5] in the bibliography accompanying this article.

market is the region within which a particular group of consumers and producers customarily exchange a product among themselves. The geographic segmentation of markets results from barriers to the transfer of goods and services over distance. The character and strength of these barriers vary greatly from one product or group of products to another. For bulky or highly perishable physical goods, the barrier is high transport costs. For certain legal and financial services, the barrier is the unfamiliarity of individuals and firms in one locality with individuals and firms in another locality. In contrast, the markets for certain financial instruments exhibit relatively weak spatial barriers. For example, the market for U.S. government securities extends over much of the world. In attempting to define the geographic region covered by a particular market, the principal difficulty lies in determining precisely what barriers to interlocational trade exist, the strength of these barriers, and the market boundaries to which they give rise.[2]

The Definition of Banking Markets

This general discussion of markets and market definition can now be related to banking (see Figure 1).

The *product specification problem* for banking markets is complicated by both product substitutability and product complementarity. With respect to complementarity, the essential question concerns the degree to which the wide variety of services

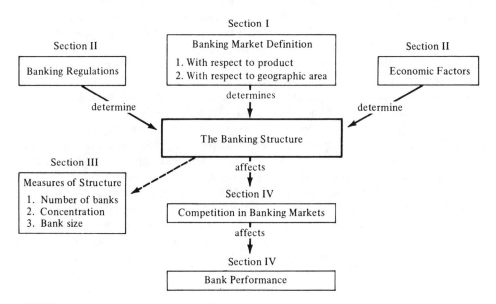

FIGURE 1. A schematic guide to the discussion.

[2]For a classic discussion of the geographic characteristics of markets, see Marshall [19, pp. 323-330].

banks provide are related. Banks make loans, accept deposits, process checks, and provide trust services. In addition to these traditional services, banks have expanded their activities in recent years to include the provision of such diverse services as investment consultation and the leasing of computer facilities. Do all of these services so complement one another that it is reasonable to speak of a market for "banking services"?[3] Or, at the other extreme, does each of the individual services provided by banks constitute a distinct product for purposes of market definition?

Whether one views banking services as a composite product or as a group of distinct products, it is clear that nonbank financial institutions provide a variety of services similar to and, in varying degrees, substitutable for the services offered by commercial banks. Hence, in defining markets for banking services, one must determine which nonbank institutions should be included as sellers in these markets. This is the problem posed by product substitutability for the definition of banking markets.

Determination of the *geographic pattern of banking markets* is directly related to product specification. If a distinct market exists for each bank service, it seems reasonable to speculate that the geographic extent of these markets varies considerably from one service to another. For example, while markets for loans to small business firms appear to be local in character, the market for large loans to prime corporate borrowers is probably national in scope. Yet even where the decision is made to differentiate the markets for particular bank services extensively, the geographic area covered by the market for a specific service is often unclear. For example, do markets for loans to small business firms in urban areas include the entire metropolitan region or only some portion of the region? At the other extreme, if the aggregate group of bank services is considered a composite product for purposes of market definition, it becomes quite difficult to specify criteria for geographic market delineation.

One additional issue regarding the geographic specification of banking markets should be noted. In the United States, legal restrictions on bank branching differ from one state to another. Other factors aside, the market area for a given bank service may depend to some degree on the stringency of branching restrictions. Branching regulations are especially relevant to the designation of market areas in metropolitan regions. In cities where branching is permitted, each bank can, with the approval of the proper bank regulatory agencies, enter any neighborhood in the city through the establishment of a branch office. Where branching is prohibited (that is, where "unit" banking prevails), each bank must confine its facilities to a single office in a particular neighborhood or financial district. On these grounds, it has been argued that markets for such bank services as checking deposits cover the entire metropolitan area where branching is permitted, but that these markets are segmented in cities where branching is prohibited.[4]

---

[3]The banking industry itself has vigorously promoted the idea that individual banking services are interrelated with its "full service bank" advertising slogan.

[4]See Shull and Horvitz [23, pp. 328-330].

The Measurement of Banking Market Structure

As stated earlier, the structure of a specific market refers to the number and size distribution of buyers and sellers transacting business in that market. Often, the term is more restrictively employed to designate the number and size distribution of *sellers* in a given market. Throughout the remainder of this study, the phrase "banking structure" will be used in this more limited sense; that is, the term will refer to the number and size distribution of *banks* in particular banking markets.

Certain statistics are commonly employed to specify the structure of banking markets. These statistics include: (1) the number of banks in the market, (2) the number of bank offices in the market, (3) the ratio of banks or bank offices to the population of the market area, (4) "concentration ratios," which indicate the percentage of total deposits held by the largest banks in the market, and (5) the absolute size of individual banks in the market as measured by total deposits or total assets.

In evaluating such data, the essential point is that each statistic, if it is to provide useful structural information, must be appropriately applied to a particular market defined with respect both to product and geographic area. To take an extreme example, the number of banks in the United States or the percentage of total domestic deposits held by the three largest banks in the nation tells one little about the structure of local markets for small business loans or checking accounts. In practice, the difficulty encountered in developing useful data on the structure of banking markets arises at a considerably finer level of detail. In states where branching is permitted, for example, should the geographic market area for a particular bank service be defined to include the entire state, local regions, or portions of local regions? What groups of bank services constitute integrated banking service markets in given areas, and which nonbank financial institutions compete with banks in these markets? In short, the problem encountered in developing and evaluating information concerning the structure of banking markets amounts largely to the problem of defining banking markets.

This discussion began by asking what constitutes the banking structure. As we have seen, no definitive answer can be given to this question until some ultimate consensus is reached regarding the pattern of banking markets. No such consensus is likely to be achieved. Moreover, no agreement would be permanent if it were attained, since the pattern of banking markets is in a continual state of evolution. For purposes of practical analysis, however, the situation is not as bleak as it might appear at first glance. Economists have devoted considerable effort to the analysis of banking markets, and some fundamental results have been achieved.[5] Most economists agree that banking services form a group of related but distinguishable products rather than a composite product. Further, it is generally recognized that geographic market areas vary in extent from one service product to another. Finally,

---

[5]For two examples of recent detailed banking market studies see Gelder and Budzeika [10, pp. 258-266] and Luttrell and Pettigrew [18, pp. 9-12].

most students of financial markets agree that both bank and nonbank institutions compete in integrated markets for certain types of financial services.

The Banking Structure and the
Organization of Banking Institutions

The banking structure was defined above as the number and size distribution of banks in given banking markets. A full understanding of the structure and functioning of banking markets, however, requires additional information regarding the organization of banking institutions. For example, it is important to know whether banks in a given market are unit banks or whether they belong to branch bank or bank holding company systems. The existence of such systems can directly affect the structure of banking markets. As indicated earlier, the proper geographic delineation of a given banking market may depend on branching regulations affecting banks in the market. Moreover, some banking analysts have argued that markets are characterized by fewer banks and greater concentration of bank resources where branching is permitted than where unit banking prevails.[6]

A particularly important organizational phenomenon during the past decade has been the extensive growth of bank holding companies.[7] The structural significance of bank holding companies is twofold. First, the holding company device can be used to bring two or more banks under common corporate control. Second, the device can be employed to bring one or more banks and one or more nonbank institutions under common corporate control. Therefore, bank holding company expansion can directly affect the number of independent banks operating in a market and the concentration of financial resources in the market. In addition, the linking of bank and nonbank activities by bank holding companies may broaden the market (with respect both to service product and geographic area) within which a given subsidiary bank operates.

II. What Determines the Banking Structure?

Since the banking structure refers to the number and size distribution of banks operating in particular banking markets, it follows that the factors which determine the structure of a specific market are the factors which affect the number and size distribution of banks operating in the market. In this section, these factors are identified and briefly discussed.

Economic Factors

A basic tenet of general market theory is that demand and supply conditions characterizing a given market effectively determine the number and size distribution of

---

[6]For evidence on this point, see Shull and Horvitz [23, pp. 312-339].

[7]Briefly defined, a bank holding company is a company which controls one or more banks in addition to whatever institutions it owns.

firms serving the market. Other things equal, the strength of demand in a market determines how many firms can operate profitably in the market. On the supply side, two especially important determinants of market structure are the technical characteristics of production and the relative ease with which new suppliers can enter the market. Regarding these latter two factors, it is well known that firms in certain industries enjoy economies of large-scale production: that is, decreasing average or "unit" costs up to a certain level of output. If, in a given market, the output volume at which unit costs begin to rise is high in relation to total market demand, small firms will be driven from the market and new entry will be discouraged. Under these conditions, the market is likely to be characterized by a small number of large firms and a high degree of resource concentration.

Which of these economic determinants of market structure play active roles in shaping the structure of banking markets? The demand for banking services clearly influences the number of banks operating in particular areas. Moreover, demand conditions directly affect bank size. With respect to supply conditions, much attention has been given to the possibility that scale economies exist in the production of banking services. While statistical evidence suggests the presence of such economies, there is little agreement regarding their quantitative significance or their precise impact on the structure of banking markets.

Legal and Institutional Factors

Economic factors, such as those just outlined, only partially determine market structure. Of great importance is the regulatory environment within which a market functions. In the United States, market structure has been directly and extensively affected by the application of antitrust statutes to particular industries. Moreover, entry into several strategic industries is restricted by law or by regulatory authority.

It is quite clear that a principal determinant of the structure and organization of American banking markets is the complex "dual" system of federal and state banking regulations. Two categories of banking regulations directly affect the banking structure: (1) restrictions on the formation of new banks and (2) regulations which affect structure through their impact on bank organization.

Restrictions on bank formation are embodied in the chartering authority of federal and state regulatory agencies. Federal law and most state laws contain criteria to guide these authorities in approving or disapproving specific applications to establish new banks. These criteria include capital adequacy, the general character of proposed management, and probable effects on the convenience and needs of the community to be served. Because these guidelines are quite broad, regulatory agencies exercise, in effect, discretionary control over bank formation. Through the exercise of this authority, agency decisions directly influence the number of banks and the distribution of bank resources in specific markets.[8]

We have already discussed the impact of bank organization on the structure of

---

[8]For a detailed analysis of the regulation of bank formation, see Motter [20, pp. 299-349].

banking markets. In the United States, bank organization is shaped by federal and state laws affecting branching, bank mergers, and acquisitions by bank holding companies. Branching across state lines is prohibited. State laws variously permit statewide branching, permit limited branching (usually within local areas), or prohibit branching altogether. Where branching is permitted, federal and state regulatory agencies rule on applications to establish new branches and on applications to merge two or more banks. Agency decisions in specific cases directly influence the number of banks and the distribution of bank resources in particular markets. Further, the authority of the Board of Governors of the Federal Reserve System to approve or disapprove bank holding company acquisitions permits the Board to influence the number of independently controlled banks and the pattern of resource ownership in particular banking markets.

III. What is the Significance of the Banking Structure?

Some Theoretical Considerations

Perhaps the most significant hypothesis generated by general market theory concerns the relationship between the structure of a market and the efficiency with which the market allocates economic resources. Specifically, the theory asserts that the structure of a market determines the degree of competition in the market and that the degree of competition, in turn, affects the performance of producers with respect to the quantity of goods or services produced, efficiency in production, and prices charged in the market. Speaking generally, the theory draws the following conclusions. First, greater competition exists in markets characterized by large numbers of producers where no producer controls a significant share of the market. Second, given market demand, more competitive markets lead to greater output at lower prices. Hence, according to the theory, the aggregate welfare of the consuming public is improved by markets having numerous competitive producers.

With respect to banking, these theoretical propositions imply that the significance of the banking structure lies in its impact upon the performance of the banking industry in providing bank services to the public. Further, the theory seems to imply that markets with numerous competitive banks are preferable to markets exhibiting other structural characteristics.

The validity of market theory, however, depends critically on several highly restrictive preliminary assumptions regarding the nature of particular industries or markets to which the theory is applied. Where these preliminary assumptions do not correspond to reality, one cannot conclude that a competitive market structure is optimal.

Two of these assumptions are especially relevant to banking. First, the theory assumes that the rapid exit of relatively inefficient firms from competitive markets will not, in and of itself, detrimentally affect the functioning of the market. By eroding public confidence, however, bank failures may disrupt the operation of banking markets. It is true that deposit insurance mitigates some of the harmful effects of bank failures. Nonetheless, the fact that bank failures produce effects external to the failing banks themselves raises serious doubts regarding the desirability of unrestrained competition between banks.

Second, the theory assumes that the technically efficient level of an individual firm's total output is small in relation to aggregate market demand for the product in question. This condition is not met by firms engaged in productive activities characterized by significant economies of scale. Where scale economies exist, highly competitive market structures may be undesirable, since the numerous firms producing in such markets may be forced to operate at suboptimal output levels. As indicated above, several empirical studies have suggested the existence of scale economies in banking. The results of these studies are controversial and by no means conclusive. Nonetheless, they raise additional doubts regarding the desirability of competitive bank markets.

The Banking Competition Controversy

These considerations lie at the heart of what has become known as the "banking competition controversy." Essentially, this debate focuses on a single question: What is the optimal structure of the banking industry? The controversy has a long history and is reflected in the development of bank regulation during the past several decades.

During the 1920s and early 1930s, the highly unsettling effect of widespread bank failures stimulated an equally widespread distrust of unrestricted bank competition.[9] As a result, the Banking Acts of 1933 and 1935 included provisions designed to reduce competition among banks. In particular, the 1935 Act established standards for chartering national banks which tightened restrictions on bank formation. At the same time, state governments imposed a variety of additional restrictions.

In conjunction with the introduction of deposit insurance, these regulations have reduced the rate of bank failure significantly. Within this regulatory environment, however, structural changes of a different sort have appeared during the past two decades. Specifically, the number of independent banks has declined during these years as a result of numerous mergers and bank holding company acquisitions. Consequently, many observers of bank activity have become convinced that too little rather than too much competition exists in banking markets, causing harmful effects on the consumers of bank services. This attitude received its principal practical manifestation when, in 1963, the United States Supreme Court held that a proposed

---

[9]Significantly, use of the term "overbanked" to refer to markets containing an excessive number of (consequently weak) banks originated during these years.

merger of The Philadelphia National Bank with The Girard Trust Company Exchange Bank violated Section 7 of the Clayton Antitrust Act.[10]

Statistical Evidence

In its present form, the banking competition controversy is essentially a debate concerning the effects of the apparent decline in banking competition on bank performance. To enlighten the debate, a number of studies have attempted to measure statistically the relationship between the banking structure on the one hand and bank performance with respect to the quality and pricing of bank services on the other. As indicated earlier, market theory suggests that producers in more competitively structured markets supply greater output at lower prices.

In order to test the validity of this hypothesis for banking markets, the studies just mentioned have employed two sets of variables designed to measure (1) the structure of banking markets and (2) the market performance of banks. Structural variables include the number of banks serving a market, the concentration of banking resources in the market (usually measured by the proportion of total market deposits held by the largest banks serving the market), and bank size. Performance variables include (1) price variables such as interest charged for various types of bank loans and interest paid on time and savings deposits and (2) quantity (i.e., "output") variables such as the ratio of loan volume to total deposits.[11] Market theory suggests that, where other market characteristics are identical, banks will charge lower interest rates on loans, pay higher interest rates on time and savings deposits, and maintain higher loan-deposit ratios in markets having larger numbers of independent banks, larger numbers of competing nonbank financial institutions, and less concentration of banking resources.

The statistical studies referred to above have attempted to test these hypotheses. They have also analyzed other relationships between structure and performance and have attempted to determine whether or not economies of scale exist in the production of bank services. For the reader's convenience, these studies are listed in the accompanying bibliography. Their major findings are briefly summarized in the following paragraphs.

(1) Several studies [14, 15, 22] attempted to determine whether or not the number of banks and nonbank financial institutions competing in particular markets affected bank performance in these markets. While some of the results tend to confirm the above hypotheses, other results either contradict these hypotheses or suggest that no systematic relationship exists.

(2) Conclusions regarding the effects of banking resource concentration were also mixed. A number of studies [7, 8, 15, 21], however, found that less concentrated

---

[10]*U.S.* v. *The Philadelphia National Bank* et al., 374 U. S. 321 (1963).

[11]Use of the loan-deposit ratio as a measure of bank "output" arises from the preeminence of lending among bank activities. While the issues raised by this choice are beyond the scope of this article, it should be noted that many students of banking object to the procedure on theoretical grounds.

markets generally exhibited lower interest rates on loans and higher interest rates on time and savings deposits, results which support the theoretical hypotheses.

(3) The results of several studies [4, 8, 14, 16, 22] appear to suggest that, on balance, the performance of large banks is superior to the performance of small banks with respect to both interest rates and the proportion of total bank resources devoted to lending. This finding must be approached very cautiously, however, since large and small banks serve characteristically different types of customers.

(4) Test results were generally inconclusive regarding the performance effects of the organization of banks into branch and bank holding company systems. Four studies [8, 16, 17, 22], however, found that banks belonging to branch and holding company systems maintained higher loan-deposit ratios than banks not associated with such systems.

(5) Economies of scale appear to exist in the production of many banking services. While some studies [1, 11, 12, 13, 22] found these economies to be quantitatively significant, two recent tests [2, 3] concluded that they are relatively small.

While the findings of particular studies were often contradictory or inconclusive, this summary has indicated that, in some cases, several studies (usually employing quite different data) reached similar conclusions. One must be extremely careful, however, in generalizing on the basis of these results. Statistical tests of the sort employed in these studies are subject to inherent limitations. Moreover, the conclusions reached in several of the studies reflect the manner in which market areas comprising study samples were delineated. The earlier discussion of the problems encountered in defining banking markets, therefore, raises additional doubts regarding the validity of test results. In short, the findings summarized here can only be considered suggestive.

IV. Conclusions

This article has attempted to clarify the meaning of the banking structure, to specify its determinants, and to suggest how it might affect individual bank behavior. Section I listed several common measures of banking market structure and indicated the critical problem posed by accurate market definition in applying and evaluating these measures. Section II described the combination of economic conditions and regulatory practices which determines the structures of actual banking markets. Finally, section III outlined several theories of the relationship between banking market structure and bank performance and summarized related statistical evidence. It is hoped that this discussion has illuminated some of the issues surrounding the banking structure and related questions regarding bank competiton.

BIBLIOGRAPHY

1. ALHADEFF, D. A. *Monopoly and Competition in Banking.* Berkeley, California: University of California Press, 1954.
2. BELL, F. W. and N. B. MURPHY. *Costs in Commercial Banking: A Quantitative Analysis of*

Bank Behavior and IB Relation to Bank Regulation. Boston: Federal Reserve Bank of Boston, 1968.

3. BENSTON, G. J. "Economies of Scale and Marginal Costs in Banking Operations," *The National Banking Review,* 2 (June 1965), 507-49.

4. CARSON, D. and P. H. COOTNER. "The Structure of Competition in Commercial Banking in the United States," *Private Financial Institutions.* Englewood Cliffs, New Jersey: Prentice-Hall, Inc., 1963, pp. 55-155.

5. CHAMBERLIN, E. H. *The Theory of Monopolistic Competition.* Cambridge, Massachusetts: Harvard University Press, 1933.

6. COHEN, K. J. and S. R. REID. "Effects of Regulation, Branching, and Mergers on Banking Structure and Performance," *Southern Economic Journal,* 34 (October 1967), 231-49.

7. EDWARDS, F. R. *Concentration and Competition in Commercial Banking: A Statistical Study.* Boston: Federal Reserve Bank of Boston, 1964.

8. EDWARDS, F. R. "The Banking Competition Controversy," *The National Banking Review,* 3 (September 1965), 1-34.

9. FLECHSIG, T. G. *Banking Market Structure and Performance in Metropolitan Areas.* Washington, D.C.: Board of Governors of the Federal Reserve System, 1965.

10. GELDER, R. H. and G. BUDZEIKA. "Banking Market Determination: The Case of Central Nassau County," *Federal Reserve Bank of New York Monthly Review,* 52 (November 1970), 258-66.

11. GRAMLEY, L. E. *A Study of Scale Economies in Banking.* Kansas City: Federal Reserve Bank of Kansas City, 1962.

12. GREENBAUM, S. I. "Banking Structure and Costs: A Statistical Study of the Cost-Output Relationship in Commercial Banking," Unpublished Ph.D. dissertation, Johns Hopkins University, 1964.

13. HORVITZ, P. M. "Economies of Scale in Banking," *Private Financial Institutions.* Englewood Cliffs, New Jersey: Prentice-Hall, Inc., 1963, pp. 1-54.

14. HORVITZ, P. M. and B. SHULL. "The Impact of Branch Banking on Bank Performance," *The National Banking Review,* 2 (December 1964), 143-88.

15. KAUFMAN, G. G. "Bank Market Structure and Performance: The Evidence from Iowa," *Southern Economic Journal,* 32 (April 1966), 429-39.

16. KOHN, E. *Branch Banking, Bank Mergers and The Public Interest.* New York: New York State Banking Department, 1964.

17. LAWRENCE, R. J. *The Performance of Bank Holding Companies.* Washington, D.C.: Board of Governors of the Federal Reserve System, 1966.

18. LUTTRELL, C. B. and W. E. PETTIGREW. "Banking Markets for Business Firms," *Federal Reserve Bank of St. Louis Review,* 48 (September 1966), 9-12.

19. MARSHALL, A. *Principles of Economics.* 9th ed. New York: The Macmillan Co., 1961.

20. MOTTER, D. C. "Bank Formation and the Public Interest," *The National Banking Review,* 2 (March 1965), 299-349.

21. PHILLIPS, A. "Evidence on Concentration in Banking Markets and Interest Rates," *Federal Reserve Bulletin,* 53 (June 1967), 916-26.

22. SCHWEIGER, I. and J. S. MCGEE. "Chicago Banking," *Journal of Business,* 34 (July 1961), 255-63.

23. SHULL, B. and P. M. HORVITZ. "Branch Banking and the Structure of Competition," *The National Banking Review,* 1 (March 1964), 301-41.

24. WALLACE, R. S. "Banking Structure and Bank Performance: A Case Study of Three Small Market Areas," Unpublished Ph.D. dissertation, University of Virginia, 1965.

Defining the Product Market in Commercial Banking

Joel M. Yesley

The similarity of financial services provided by nonbank financial institutions and by commercial banks has stimulated a considerable amount of controversy among economists, bankers, administrators of banking regulations, and courts regarding the institutional scope of the product markets in which banks operate. Most are of the opinion that the similarities among the individual services provided by these two general types of institutions—with only a few exceptions such as checking accounts—place them in direct competition with each other. Others, however, hold a considerably narrower view of the scope of the product market in commercial banking. This group contends that banks sell their services in "packages" rather than individually and, in effect, produce a single composite product that cannot be duplicated by other types of institutions. Futhermore, in this view, customers are limited to banks if they wish to satisfy all their financial needs at one institution. Therefore, nonbank financial institutions, which generally provide only one or two basic deposit or loan products, are not able to compete effectively with banks.

The definition of the product market is a central issue in determining the competitive significance of structural changes in banking markets caused by the entry of new institutions and mergers of existing ones. Those who regard banks as multiple-product firms that compete in several product markets attach less significance to the loss

Reprinted, with deletions, from the Federal Reserve Bank of Cleveland, *Economic Review*, June–July 1972, pp. 17–31, by permission of the publisher.

of an independent bank in a specific geographic market because of a merger than adherents of the narrow product market concept. The latter group, by excluding the products of nonbank financial institutions from consideration, would regard a bank merger as contributing to a greater concentration of financial resources in a given market area.

The report of the Hunt Commission, which was made public in December 1971,[1] has generated considerable interest and discussion regarding the degree of competition among the various types of depository financial institutions (commercial banks, savings and loan associations, mutual savings banks, and credit unions). The Commission recommended that these financial institutions be permitted to provide a wider range of financial services and that all depository institutions be subject to the same reserve requirements, tax treatment, and interest rate regulations. The primary aim of the Report is to improve the efficiency of the financial system by eliminating differences in regulations that may have inhibited open competition among depository institutions. Implementation of these recommendations would pave the way for a considerably more homogeneous financial structure and significantly enlarge the institutional scope of the product market in commercial banking.

This article reviews the development of the controversy concerning the product market in commercial banking in both economic literature and in the courts. In the absence of a universally accepted body of economic theory on this vital issue, courts have been left to define the business of banking. As will be illustrated in this article, decisions between the lower courts and the Supreme Court have frequently differed. A number of recent empirical studies that have analyzed the significance of various influences on the demands for the assets of depository institutions are also briefly reviewed. The article concludes with a discussion of possible areas for futher research that should be useful in appraising changes in banking structure.

Nature and Recent Growth of Financial Institutions

Nature   Financial intermediaries channel funds from savers to borrowers by purchasing primary securities (debt or equity instruments of nonfinancial institutions) with funds obtained from depositors. These intermediaries can be divided into two broad classifications: commercial banks and nonbank financial institutions. The latter category includes depository institutions such as savings and loan associations, mutual savings banks, and credit unions, as well as life insurance companies, investment companies, and finance companies. The major difference between these two types of intermediaries is in the form of debt that each creates. Commercial banks substitute money (deposits and currency) for primary securities, whereas nonbank financial institutions create various forms of nonmonetary claims on themselves, such

---

[1]Hunt Commission, *The Report of the President's Commission on Financial Structure and Regulation* (Washington, D.C.: Government Printing Office, 1971).

as savings deposits, shares, equities, and other assets. In addition, commercial banks administer the national payments mechanism by transferring deposit credits among spending units.

The assets and liabilities of commercial banks are, in general, considerably broader than those of nonbank financial institutions. Commercial banks generally receive short- and intermediate-term deposits (ranging from balances in checking accounts payable on demand up to certificates of deposit with wide-ranging maturities) from individuals and all forms of governmental and business organizations, and they supply funds of varying maturities to an equally diverse group of borrowers in a number of forms (e.g., rediscounts, term loans, installment loans). In addition, banks provide a number of specialized services, such as trust facilities and safe deposit boxes.

Other types of depository institutions, however, receive the bulk of their funds from households. The purchases made by nonbank financial institutions, including those that do not accept deposits, are usually concentrated in one type of liquid asset. Credit unions, which concentrate their assets in consumer loans to members, and investment companies (e.g., mutual funds), which concentrate in corporate equities, are the most specialized types of nonbank intermediaries. Savings and loan associations, which accept funds that may generally be withdrawn without notice, are the next most specialized institutions because of legal restrictions limiting them to the financing of residential structures. As of year-end 1970, savings and loan associations had allocated just over 85 percent of their total assets to mortgage loans and accounted for one-third of the total credit extended to the mortgage markets. Mutual savings banks, which are nonprofit thrift organizations operated solely for the benefit of depositors, also allocate most of their total assets (73 percent as of year-end 1970) to residential mortgages.

Specialization of assets is least pronounced for finance and life insurance companies. There are two types of finance companies: sales finance and consumer finance or small loan companies. Sales finance companies make loans, generally on a short- or intermediate-term basis, for the purchase of durable and capital goods by individuals and businesses. Consumer finance companies lend only to individuals for a wide range of purposes, including the purchase of goods and services. Both types of finance companies acquire funds by issuing commercial paper and long-term bonds and by borrowing short-term from banks. Life insurance companies accumulate funds from premium payments and issuing stock, and they invest primarily in corporate and government bonds.

Growth   The total assets of all financial intermediaries have increased fivefold since World War II. Commercial banks, however, have shared considerably less in this growth than other types of financial intermediaries. For example, between 1950 and 1960, the assets of commercial banks grew at an average annual rate of 4.4 percent, which is well below the growth rate of other types of financial institutions. Over the past decade, the growth of commercial bank assets accelerated to an 8.4 percent annual rate, the average growth rate for all financial institutions over this period. Most nonbank financial institutions, however, still grew at significantly faster rates. In 1950, about 54 percent of the total assets of financial intermediaries was accounted for by commercial banks. By 1960, this share had declined to 41 percent and has remained fairly stable since then. A substantial part of the decline was caused by the growth of other financial intermediaries, particularly savings and loan associations and life insurance companies. Regulatory restrictions on commercial banks and a shift in public preferences away from demand deposits and business loans toward interest-bearing liquid assets and consumer and mortgage loans have been cited as the major causes of this uneven growth.[2]

Economic Theory and Banking Markets

The question of what constitutes the product market in commercial banking has received a considerable amount of attention in the literature on banking structure.[3] Economists generally agree that nonbank financial institutions are collectively able to produce close substitutes for the individual financial services provided by commercial banks, with the major exception of checking accounts. However, the concept of the bank as a multiple-product firm competing in several markets with various nonbank institutions is not universally accepted.

The Bank as a Single-Product Firm   Donald Hodgman is the major advocate of the single-product market concept of commercial banking. His theoretical model of the banking firm emphasizes relationships of complementarity or interdependency among financial services provided by commercial banks.[4] Individual banks encourage deposit retention by assuring deposit customers of immediate loan accommodation and favorable terms. Hodgman uses the term "customer relationship" to describe the high degree of complementarity between deposits, loans, and other

---

[2]Jules Backman and Arnold W. Sametz, "Workable Competition in Banking," *The Bulletin of the C. J. Devine Institute of Finance,* New York University, No. 22 (November 1962), p. 30.

[3]This question also has important implications in the area of monetary policy. John G. Gurley and Edward S. Shaw assert that control over the stock of money as narrowly defined (currency in circulation plus demand deposits at commercial banks) is not sufficient to stabilize the economy since consumer expenditures are determined by the total stock of liquid assets including those held at nonbank intermediaries. Since they regard these institutions as direct competitors of banks, they question the effectiveness of monetary policy, especially in inflationary times when depositors at commercial banks are likely to shift funds into nonbank financial institutions for higher returns. This increases the lending ability of those institutions at a time when monetary policy is attempting to restrict bank loans. See Gurley and Shaw, "Financial Intermediaries and the Saving-Investment Process," *Journal of Finance,* May 1956, and *Money in Theory of Finance* (Washington, D.C.: The Brookings Institution, 1960). On the other hand, Milton Friedman has adopted a considerably narrower view of the product market in commercial banking, asserting that neither mutual savings bank deposits nor savings and loan shares are very close substitutes for time deposits at commercial banks. This conclusion is based mainly on observations of patterns in the growth rates of these types of deposits from 1954 to 1958. See Milton Friedman and Anna Jacobson Schwartz, *A Monetary History of the United States, 1867-1960* (Princeton: Princeton University Press, 1963).

[4]Donald R. Hodgman, *Commercial Bank Loan and Investment Policy* (Champaign, Illinois: University of Illinois, 1963).

financial services, such as trust administration, payroll preparation, account collection, and investment counsel.

He asserts that the prevailing concept of the relevant product market in literature pertaining to bank regulation is developed primarily around the lending and investing activities of commercial banks, rather than the input or deposit market. Hodgman argues that this popular conception of the bank as an institutional investor, maximizing the interest return available from a wide range of lending and investing alternatives carrying acceptable risks, is misleading. In Hodgman's opinion, this view, which supports the multiple-product concept, ignores the dependence of deposits and loans upon the provision of banking services.

He refers to two widespread practices in banking that cannot be explained by the prevailing concept. One is nonprice credit rationing, which is frequently adopted by banks in periods of credit restraint. Banks usually cite a responsibility to long-term deposit customers when declining loan requests from nondepositors instead of quoting unrealistically high rates. This preference for depositors is based on the contribution of service income to long-run bank profits rather than a maximization of interest returns on loans. Hodgman asserts that a bank can charge a lower contract rate on a loan to a depositor than to a nondepositor and still earn a higher effective rate of return because of charges for complementary services. Furthermore, a loan to a depositor constitutes a smaller drain on a bank's lending capacity than an identical loan to a nondepositor. The other practice that does not support the concept of banks as institutional investors is the tendency of bankers to sell government securities at a capital loss to accommodate prime borrowers in times of tight money.

In view of the close relationship between deposits and loans, Hodgman bases his definition of the product market on the totality of services provided by banks. He does not believe that commercial banks compete significantly with other types of financial intermediaries since the latter are not individually capable of duplicating the basic product of commercial banks—the safeguarding and transfer of money—or the wide range of services that comprise the "customer relationship."

The customer relationship hypothesis was confirmed in a study of 30 Massachusetts municipalities that borrowed in anticipation of tax revenue.[5] The tax anticipation notes issued by Massachusetts towns are generally purchased by commercial banks that also hold deposits of these towns. This group of bank borrowers was considered ideal for testing the hypothesis, since their notes were homogeneous, the nonprice terms of the loan were standardized, and no lines of credit were in effect.

This study indicated that interest rates charged by banks were the lowest where the purchasing bank handled all of a town's business instead of merely holding the proceeds of a note issue as they were being spent. Furthermore, concessions on loan rates tended to be greater as the loan size increased, a practice attributed to bankers' expectations of larger and more profitable deposit accounts. It was concluded that

---

[5]Neil B. Murphy, *A Test of the Deposit Relationship Hypothesis*, Staff Economic Study No. 38 (Washington, D. C.: Board of Governors of the Federal Reserve System, 1970).

"nonprice terms and deposit relationships are of sufficient importance in explaining the determinants of commercial bank pricing behavior to warrant further, more comprehensive investigation."[6]

The Bank as a Multiple-Product Firm   Economists who view banks as multiple product firms generally make a distinction between the business and nonbusiness customers of a bank in analyzing the strength of product interdependencies. David Alhadeff, a leading spokesman for the broad market concept, maintains that

> The available evidence suggests that package sales are typically made compulsory only for business borrowers (and not to all of them) in the form of a compensating balance requirement. Significantly, the tie-in sales are restricted to those services (business loans and transactions deposits) for which banks are the dominant or sole suppliers whereas bank services that nonbanks also supply (such as home mortgage loans, consumer loans, and savings accounts) can usually be negotiated separately.[7]

He views commercial banks as department stores of finance, producing a number of distinct services. He has divided these services into five categories: loans, safekeeping facilities (e.g., deposit accounts and safety boxes), investment outlets for the public in the form of time and savings accounts, checking facilities in the form of demand deposit accounts, and miscellaneous specialized services such as trust facilities.

Alhadeff, along with Clifton Kreps, believes that competition between banks and other types of financial institutions is more significant in credit product markets than in the deposit markets, partly because their deposit services tend to be more homogeneous than their lending services.[8] Both economists have focused their analyses on the consumer, mortgage, and business loan markets. They assert that commercial banks compete with a wide range of other institutions, including finance companies, credit unions, savings and loan associations, mutual savings banks, life insurance companies, and a number of Federal agencies in the consumer and morgage loan markets. Alhadeff and Kreps agree that banks are generally isolated from significant competition in the business loan market, especially in the small loan segment. Alhadeff notes that, other than commercial finance companies, nonbank financial institutions are not very active in this market. However, he does not regard finance companies as effective competitors since they specialize in serving marginal risk borrowers, who would likely have difficulty obtaining loans from commercial banks.

Alhadeff has also asserted that some nonbank financial institutions compete with commercial banks for demand deposits, even though the former institutions do not

[6]*Ibid.,* p. 59.

[7]David A. Alhadeff, "Monopolistic Competition and Banking Markets," in *Monopolistic Competition Theory: Studies in Impact,* ed. by Robert C. Kuenne (New York: John Wiley & Sons, Inc., 1967), pp. 364–365.

[8]David A. Alhadeff, "A Reconsideration of Restrictions on Bank Entry," *The Quarterly Journal of Economics,* May 1962, and Clifton H. Kreps, Jr., "Characteristics of Local Banking Competition," *Banking and Monetary Studies* (Homewood, Illinois: Richard D. Irwin, Inc., 1963).

offer third-party payment facilities. He divides demand deposits into two categories: those held for transactions purposes and those held as liquid reserves to serve as buffers against unexpected expenditures. Although commerical banks are unique in satisfying the transactions needs of the demand depositor, Alhadeff contends that credit unions, savings and loan associations, and mutual savings banks provide highly liquid interest-bearing deposit substitutes for demand deposits held as a liquid reserve. A more generalized form of his hypothesis was originally proposed by James Tobin and William J. Baumol, who maintained that the volume of idle transactions balances increases at a slower rate than total transactions and income and is inversely related to the level of interest rates available on alternative assets.[9]

Judicial Interpretation of the Product Market in Commercial Banking

The Federal laws that were designed to promote competition in the banking industry have not attempted to define the product market in commercial banking.[10] The three Federal bank regulatory agencies—Federal Deposit Insurance Corporation (FDIC), the Comptroller of the Currency, and the Board of Governors of the Federal Reserve System—have therefore had a more or less free hand in determining the competitive significance of nonbank financial institutions in ruling on bank mergers. The decisions of these agencies, however, are subject to review for possible violation of antitrust laws by the Department of Justice. If the decisions are challenged, the cases are initially tried in the U.S. District Courts and may come before the Supreme Court if an appeal is made.

The first case in which the Supreme Court treated the product market as a major issue in evaluating bank competition involved a proposed merger between the second and third largest banks in Philadelphia.[11] The lower court accepted the narrow product market concept, stressing the unique scope of commercial banking services and the high degree of interdependency among them. The action to enjoin the merger, however, was dismissed on the basis of a finding of no violation of the antitrust laws.

The Supreme Court reversed the decision of the lower court, primarily because of a difference of opinion regarding the geographic market. However, the higher court agreed with the district court's product market definition, mainly because of the uniqueness and significance of the demand deposit.

---

[9]William J. Baumol, "The Transactions Demand for Cash: An Inventory Theoretic Approach," *Quarterly Journal of Economics,* November 1952, and James Tobin, "The Interest-Elasticity of Transactions Demand for Cash," *Review of Economics and Statistics,* August 1956.

[10]For a discussion of these laws see "Federal Laws Regulating Bank Mergers and the Acquisition of Banks by Registered Bank Holding Companies," *Economic Review,* Federal Reserve Bank of Cleveland, January 1971.

[11]*United States* v. *Philadelphia National Bank* et al., 210 Supp. 348 (1962); 83 S. Ct. 1715 (1963).

(T)hey [commercial banks] alone are permitted by law to accept demand deposits. This distinctive power to accept demand deposits . . . makes banks the intermediaries in most financial transactions (since transfers of substantial moneys are almost always by check rather than by cash) and, concomitantly, the repositories of very substantial individual and corporate funds.[12]

The court further reasoned that the dominance of highly liquid demand deposits in the deposit portfolios of banks made them the most important source of short-term business credit. Moreover, it found that other bank services are not subject to competition from nonbank financial institutions, even though the services are similar. The court mentioned consumer loans and savings deposits as examples, arguing that banks can obtain funds more cheaply than finance companies and therefore lend at lower rates, and also that savings deposits of commercial banks enjoyed a "settled consumer preference" over those of other institutions.

In the Lexington Bank Case (1964),[13] the Supreme Court reaffirmed its narrow concept of the product market in commercial banking, emphasizing once again both the uniqueness of the checking account and the wide scope of banking services, specifically mentioning deposit boxes, Christmas Club accounts, correspondent bank facilities, collection services, and trust department services.

The first major merger case to come before a district court under the *Bank Merger Act of 1966* (see below) was the Crocker-Anglo Citizens Bank Case (1967), which involved the fifth and seventh largest banks in California.[14] The district court adopted a considerably broader concept of the product market than the Supreme Court had in previous decisions. This lower court ruled that savings and loan associations, commercial finance companies, government lending agencies, credit unions, and life insurance companies provided reasonable substitutes for many of the financial services offered by banks. The court also noted that the combined share of the deposits and loans of all financial institutions in California accounted for by the two banks proposing to merge would be only one-half the comparable percentage based only on commercial bank resources. This difference of product market perspective was an important factor inducing the judge to rule against the Department of Justice, which did not appeal the decision.

Competitive Implications of the Bank Merger Act of 1966

The primary purpose of the *Bank Merger Act of 1966*, which amended the *Bank Merger Act of 1960*, is to clarify the application of antitrust laws to bank mergers. It permits some acquisitions that would have been illegal under a strict application of the competitive standard established in the *Clayton Act*, providing any anticompetitive effects

---

[12]*Ibid.*, p. 326 (footnote omitted).
[13]*United States* v. *First National Bank and Trust Company of Lexington* et al., 208 Supp. 457 (1962); 84 S. Ct. 1033 (1964).
[14]*United States* v. *Crocker-Anglo National Bank* et al., 263 Supp. 125 (1966); 277 Supp. 133 (1967).

> were clearly outweighed by increased public benefits. The language of Section 7 of the *Clayton Act,* which prohibits acquisitions of business concerns that would substantially lessen competition in any line of commerce in any section of the country, was incorporated in the 1966 Merger Act with only one change, the exclusion of the phrase "in any line of commerce."
>
> The Supreme Court has not attached any significance to the omission and continues to regard bank services in total as the relevant line of commerce or product market of commercial banking. The defendant banks in merger cases, however, have argued that Congress intended that the competitive implications of mergers be judged on a multiple-product basis, which would permit the consideration of nonbank financial institutions as competitors of banks. The determination of a merger's legality would, therefore, require some judgment as to the community's need for each of the bank's services.[15]

The Provident Bank Case[16] was the first merger case to reach the Supreme Court under the *Bank Merger Act of 1966* in which the definition of the product market became a major issue. After the case was remanded to the district court for further consideration on procedural grounds, the district court reversed its original decision and ruled the proposed merger between the fifth and seventh largest banks in the four-country Philadelphia market was in violation of the law. The court, however, rejected the narrow concept of the product market held by the Department of Justice on grounds that by omitting the phrase "in any line of commerce" in the *Bank Merger Act of 1966,* Congress had intended a test of the overall competitive impact of a merger in a number of individual product markets.

The lower court alluded to the uniqueness of demand deposits and the interdependency of commercial bank services, especially for corporate customers. However, the interrelationships of these services were not strong enough to preclude direct competition from other types of financial institutions, which the court limited to mutual savings banks and savings and loan associations on the basis that "they alone offer direct and meaningful competition to commercial banks. . . ."[17] In stressing competition for savings deposits, the lower court denied that commercial banks enjoyed a "settled consumer preference," as the Supreme Court had asserted in the Philadelphia Bank Case. The increasing importance of this competition in recent years was noted, as illustrated by the decline in the proportion of demand to time deposits at all national banks from 70 to 30 percent in 1960 to a rough equivalency as of the end of 1967.

[15]Franklin R. Edwards asserts that the courts were directed to ascertain the overall competitive impacts of mergers on the basis of a weighing of the effects on the separate product lines, including "commercial banking" as a distinct product. See "Bank Mergers and the Public Interest: A Legal and Economic Analysis of the 1966 Bank Merger Act," *The Banking Law Journal,* September 1968.

[16]*United States* v. *Provident National Bank* et al., 262 Supp. 297 (1966); 87 S. Ct. 1088 (1967).

[17]*United States* v. *Provident National Bank* et al., District Court Opinion (1968), p. 40.

The Supreme Court's most recent affirmation of the narrow concept of the product market occurred in the Phillipsburg National Bank Case (1970).[18] The proposed merger was between the third and fifth largest banks located in the two-city area of Phillipsburg, New Jersey, and Easton, Pennsylvania. Finding that banking as a whole was not the relevant line of commerce, the lower court analyzed competition in terms of individual product lines. Competition between the banks involved in the merger and other types of financial institutions, such as savings and loan associations, credit unions, insurance and finance companies, was emphasized. The lower court also noted that the banks involved in the merger were operated more in the manner of savings institutions than larger commercial banks.

The Supreme Court took issue with the lower court regarding the appropriateness of analyzing competition between commercial banks on a submarket or separate-product basis. It asserted that the use of submarkets should be confined to cases involving mergers between commercial banks and other types of financial institutions. The Court emphasized customers' desires to satisfy all their financial needs at a single institution, making nonbank financial institutions less attractive than banks. It also appeared to accept Hodgman's notion of the customer relationship in referring to interdependencies among the services provided by banks:

> For some customers, full service banking makes possible access to certain products or services that would otherwise be unavailable to them; the customer without significant collateral, for example, who has patronized a particular bank for a variety of financial products and services is more likely to be able to obtain a loan from that bank than from a specialty financial institution to which he turns simply to borrow money. In short, the cluster of products and services termed commercial banking has economic significance well beyond the various products and services involved.[19]

The Court distinguished between small and large banks in applying this version of the "customer relationship" hypothesis, since this was the first merger case involving two relatively small (less than $30 million in total deposits) banks to come before it. The Court asserted that customers who would tend to hold relatively small accounts would be likely to have their checking and savings accounts in the same local bank, even when higher savings interest rates were available elsewhere. This general banking relationship would prevail because the convenience factor and the advantages of a good relationship with the local banker would be more important for small depositors and borrowers, who would have less access to a variety of financial institutions than larger customers.

In summary, the district courts have generally accepted a somewhat broader concept of the product market in commercial banking than the Supreme Court. The Supreme Court has emphasized both the uniqueness of some of the individual services provided by commercial banks and the high degree of interdependence among

---

[18]*United States* v. *Phillipsburg National Bank and Trust Company*, et al., 306 Supp. 645 (1969); 90 S. Ct. 2035 (1970).

[19]"U.S. Supreme Court Disallows Bank Merger," *The Banking Law Journal*, April 1971, p. 353.

them. The Court attributed this interdependence to the desire of bankers to handle all the banking business of their customers and the preference of the public for one-stop banking and the ready accommodation of borrowing needs. On the other hand, the district courts have maintained that the specialized nature of nonbank financial institutions has not significantly hindered their ability to compare with commercial banks, especially in the markets for savings deposits and home mortgage loans.

Statistical Evidence

While the controversies in economic theory and in the courts over the relevant product market have been unresolved, the statistical evidence strongly supports the broad market concept. This section reviews five recent statistical studies on the substitutability of time deposits among different types of depository institutions and one study that directly tested the theory of a bank as a single-product firm. Four of the five studies on substitutability and the other study support the broad product market concept. An implicit assumption of the studies on deposit substitutability is that the supply curves of deposits are infinitely or highly elastic with respect to their "own" rate of interest (see Figure 1).[20] One analyst, who has extensively reviewed empirical studies estimating the substitutability relationships among financial assets, has accepted the validity of this implicit assumption "because the regulation of the savings deposit market by Federal Agencies and state commissions, as well as the stickiness

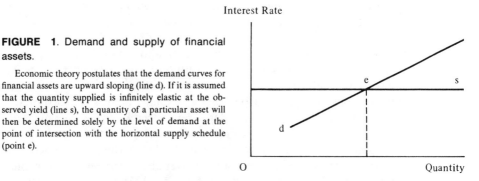

FIGURE 1. Demand and supply of financial assets.

Economic theory postulates that the demand curves for financial assets are upward sloping (line d). If it is assumed that the quantity supplied is infinitely elastic at the observed yield (line s), the quantity of a particular asset will then be determined solely by the level of demand at the point of intersection with the horizontal supply schedule (point e).

[20]Least squares multiple regression techniques were generally used in these studies to describe how a dependent variable (to be explained) is related to a number of independent or explanatory variables. A demand equation is estimated to fit the actual observations of the dependent variable in such a way that the sum of the squared deviations between these observations and those predicted by the estimated equation is minimized. The independent variables have generally included an income or wealth constraint on deposit holders, the "own" rate of interest of an asset, the yields on substitute assets, and sometimes a variable to measure the transactions or convenience costs associated with the acquisition of assets. These studies have hypothesized that the income and "own" price or yield elasticities are positive (i.e., more of a particular asset will be demanded as its yield of the income of the asset holder increase) and that an increase in the yield of an alternative asset will depress the demand for the asset whose relative yield declined (i.e., the assets are substitutes).

of the rates set by deposit-type intermediaries, make it reasonable to assume that individual savings institutions determine a yield and accept deposits at that set rate."[21]

The first study to employ multiple regression techniques utilizing observations across geographic areas and over time in exploring the product market was by Edgar Feige.[22] He concluded on the basis of the pooled data (observations from all states for the 1949–1959 period) that demand deposits were either weak substitutes or independent of savings and loan associations shares and mutual savings bank deposits in demand. He also concluded that time deposits at commercial banks and savings and loan shares were independent of each other and that time deposits and mutual savings bank deposits were either weak substitutes or independent. Finally, Feige did not find any strong substitutability or complementary relationship between savings and loan association shares and mutual savings bank deposits.

A different conclusion emerged from the work of Cohen and Kaufman, who found that time deposits at commercial banks and "near-bank" deposits were close substitutes for each other because time deposit growth was related positively and in a significant degree to the ratio of interest paid on these deposits by banks to that paid on near-bank deposits, whereas near-bank deposit growth was negatively related to this ratio by an even higher degree.[23] Their estimated demand equations for annual changes in total deposits, demand deposits, and time deposits were based on pooled data for all states for 1951–1961. They found that almost 30 percent of the variance in percent change in time deposits and 27 percent of the variance in near-bank deposits were explained by the independent variables.

Jerry L. Jordan also found a strong substitutability between time deposits at commercial banks and savings and loan shares, based on a significantly negative relationship between the demand for time deposits and the ratio of the yield on savings and loan shares to the yield on time deposits.[24] His regression results, based on state data from 1956 through 1966, also indicated that both mutual savings bank deposits and savings and loan shares are close substitutes for time deposits on the basis of convenience cost, and, to a smaller extent, the relative yield. More than half of the variation among the states in per capita holdings of these three types of assets was consistently explained by the independent variables in his demand equations.

A variation of Milton Friedman's permanent income formulation of the demand for money was developed by Tong Hun Lee, who attempted to determine by regression analysis the most significant interest rate variable affecting the demand for money.[25] Lee began by fitting data for 1951–1965 to his demand for money equa-

---

[21]George K. Kardouche, *The Competition for Savings*, Studies in Business Economics No. 107 (New York: National Industrial Conference Board, 1969).

[22]Edgar L. Feige, *The Demand for Liquid Assets: A Temporal Cross-Section Analysis* (Englewood Cliffs, N.J.: Prentice-Hall, Inc., 1964).

[23]Bruce C. Cohen and George G. Kaufman, "Factors Determining Bank Deposit Growth by State: An Empirical Analysis," *Journal of Finance,* March 1965.

[24]Jerry L. Jordan, "The Market for Deposit-Type Financial Assets," *Project for Basic Monetary Studies, Working Paper No. 8,* Federal Reserve Bank of St. Louis, March 1969.

[25]Tong Hun Lee, "Alternative Interest Rates and The Demand for Money: The Empirical Evidence," *American Economic Review,* December 1967.

tions, using one interest rate differential on an alternative asset (e.g., the difference between the yield on savings and loan shares and the yield on money) at a time as an independent variable in each equation. Lee also computed regression equations using varying combinations of the difference between the yields of savings and loan shares and money and the difference between the yields of another alternative asset and money as independent variables, finally including all the yield differences in one equation. In all of these regressions, the negative coefficients of the yield on savings and loan shares remained highly significant, while those of the yield on time deposits were progressively less significant as more variables were introduced.

Lee concluded on the basis of his tests that savings and loan shares were the closest substitutes for money among time deposits, short-term paper, long-term bonds, and equities. Lee also noted that these empirical results were consistent with the substitution hypothesis of Gurley and Shaw and the Baumol-Tobin hypothesis, which emphasized the influence of opportunity cost (i.e., interest foregone by not purchasing alternative assets) in the holding of demand deposits.

Using a different approach, V. Karuppan Chetty conluded that time deposits were the closest substitutes for money, followed by mutual savings bank deposits and, finally, savings and loan shares.[26] He estimated the elasticity of substitution between money and other liquid assets by using a utility function approach to generate a number of indifference curves between money and other assets.[27]

The validity of the single market concept in commercial banking was directly tested by Alan McCall.[28] He hypothesized that a bank's loan and demand deposit service prices would be higher and the rates on time and savings deposits lower than those of another bank in a more competitive market, other things being equal. McCall employed conventional multiple regression techniques to isolate the influence of competitive market structure on pricing performance from that of noncompetitive factors such as bank deposit size, local economic activity, and type of market (e.g., city, county). All the banks in his sample group had less than $50 million in deposits and were located in the Ohio-Kentucky region of the Fourth Federal Reserve District. The regression equations indicated that only the service charge rate on demand deposits was related to competitive structure, thereby implying that banks compete with varying degrees of intensity in different product markets. McCall concluded that

> Such inconsistent pricing results clearly support rejection of the single line of commerce hypothesis for small- and medium-sized banks. . . .Specifically, small- and medium-sized banks have multiple lines of commerce and geographic markets. . . .[29]

[26]V. Karuppan Chetty, "On Measuring the Nearness of Near-Moneys," *American Economic Review,* June 1969.

[27]A utility function approach relates the level of enjoyment or appreciation of a good to the rate of consumption. The indifference curves represent the various combinations of two goods that will yield the same total satisfaction.

[28]Alan S. McCall, *A Statistical Investigation of Commercial Banking as a Single Line of Commerce,* Working Paper No. 69-10 (Washington, D.C.: Federal Deposit Insurance Corporation, 1970).

[29]*Ibid.,* pp. 9-11.

Relatively little statistical work has been done on the degree of loan substitutability between banks and other types of financial institutions. However, evidence of significant shifts in the share of credit extended by commercial banks in some of these markets, especially the consumer loan and business loan markets, is an indication of interinstitutional competition (see Tables 1 and 2). Proponents of the narrow product market approach have sometimes argued that commercial banks have a competitive advantage over other institutions offering credit in these markets, since finance companies must rely on banks for a substantial portion of their funds. However, data collected by Raymond Goldsmith indicate that business finance companies, personal finance companies, and sales finance companies acquired only 24 percent, 20 percent, and 12 percent, respectively, of their funds from commercial banks in 1965.[30] Competition between commercial banks and finance companies is concen-

Table 1. Sources of Short-term Funds for Nonfinancial Corporations, Selected Years (percent distribution)

Source	1963	1967	1971p
Open market paper	n.a.	12.5%	10.3%
Short-term bank loans	29.9%	30.0	20.7
Finance company loans	7.5	n.a.	17.2
Other sources	62.7	57.5	51.7

Source: Bankers Trust Company, New York.
p—Projected.

Table 2. Percent Distribution of Selected Financial Assets by Type of Institution, Selected Years

Institution	1963	1967	1971p
Consumer Credit			
Commercial banks	45.5%	39.1%	48.9%
Nonbank financial corporations*	28.6	13.0	10.9
Credit unions	9.1	15.2	16.3
Others	16.9	32.6	23.9
Mortgage Loans on Single-Family Dwelling Units			
Commercial banks	13.7	14.9	15.1
Savings and loan associations	43.4	43.8	44.8
Mutual savings banks	13.6	14.2	13.4
Life insurance companies	15.0	12.6	9.5
U.S. agencies	3.4	4.5	7.6
Individuals and others	11.0	10.0	9.6

Source: Bankers Trust Company and Federal Home Loan Bank Board.
p—Projected or preliminary.
*Includes finance companies, factors, mortgage companies, and real estate investment trusts.

[30]Raymond W. Goldsmith, *Financial Institutions* (New York: Random House, 1968).

trated in the consumer loan market in which finance companies devote about two-thirds of their total funds.

With regard to competition in mortgage loan markets, one study concluded that the rates charged by savings and loan associations are very responsive to competitve pressures from commercial banks.[31] Another investigator found that increased competition between commercial banks and savings and loan associations in the Chicago area over the 1960 to 1965 period, as a result of a liberalization of regulations on commercial banks, almost completely eliminated rate differences at these institutions.[32]

Conclusion

The Supreme Court has consistently accepted the narrow product market concept of commercial banking, although the multiple-product concept of the banking firm has received more support from economists. The latter concept has been indirectly verified by statistical studies that have revealed a close substitutability between deposits provided by commercial banks and those of other more specialized depository institutions. Few investigators, however, have attempted to estimate directly the strength of interrelationships among the services provided by commercial banks. The use of tie-in arrangements, whereby the seller attempts to condition the availability of some of the goods or services he provides upon the acceptance by the customer of others, has generally been outlawed in banking. Nevertheless, banks can legally grant more favorable terms on loans to customers who agree to accept, or have accepted, other services. Hodgman's theory of the customer relationship appears plausible for business or corporate customers, who are likely to maintain large demand deposit balances at banks where they expect to borrow. However, the compensating balance requirement, which is at the core of Hodgman's theory of the customer relationship, does not generally apply to the average loan customer who may be interested in a consumer or mortgage loan.

The willingness of the typical personal demand deposit customer of a commercial bank to satisfy his other major financial needs at other banks or nonbank financial institutions would probably depend to a large extent upon the importance of the convenience of one-stop banking to him. He is likely to find a similar degree of accommodation of particular needs at both types of institutions. The use of customer surveys would provide more direct evidence than statistical studies as to how the public evaluates comparable services provided by banks and other financial institutions and the importance of one-stop banking.

[31]Phoebus J. Dhrymes and Paul J. Taubman, "The Savings and Loan Business: An Empirical Survey," *Savings and Residential Financing: 1969 Conference Proceedings,* Donald O. Jacobs and Richard T. Pratt, coeditors (Chicago: United States Savings and Loan League, 1969).

[32]Allen F. Jung, "Terms on Conventional Mortgage Loans—1965 vs. 1960," *National Banking Review,* Vol. 3, No. 3, March 1966.

The improved understanding of the product market in commercial banking result-ing from such surveys would permit more uniformity in the analyses of competitive effects of bank acquisitions that are conducted by the regulatory agencies, the De-partment of Justice, and the courts. Ideally, a weighting scheme that would reflect the ability of nonbank financial institutions to compete with banks would be devised for each major product market in which banks operate. Factors such as legal con-straints (e.g., maximum interest rates payable on savings deposits) as well as the lending policies of nonbank financial institutions (e.g., maximum acceptable credit risks) would be considered in the analysis of competitive strength. This approach would be an improvement over the sole criterion of size that is currently used in the analysis of competitive effects of structural changes in banking markets.

The Optimal Banking Structure:
Theory and Evidence

George J. Benston*

The Optimal Banking Structure and the
Public Interest

The consuming public, in contrast to producers and the government, is served best by organizations that determine, meet, and anticipate the public's demands at the least cost for a given level of quality. For consumers, the banking structure is optimal where financial institutions have the desire and ability to serve them and are rewarded accordingly. In general, this situation prevails when firms are wealth-maximizing competitors that are neither subsidized, penalized, or regulated by the government and where entry into and exit from the market is not constrained. Firms in such a market seek to produce goods and services according to the demands of consumers as expressed by the consumers' willingness to exchange their resources (money) for services.[1] The level of output is that which, at the margin, balances the cost of

Reprinted from *Journal of Bank Research* 3, no. 4 (Winter 1973): 220-37, by permission of the Bank Administration Institute and the author.

* Support for this paper was provided by Lincoln First Banks, Inc., who did not direct it in any way (other than suggesting the subject) and who are not responsible for the contents or conclusions. Helpful comments and suggestions were made by Ken Stewart, Sue Beis, Douglas Rupert, Steven Waite, and members of the Workshop in Applied Economics at the University of Rochester.

[1]Specific consumer demand depends on the distribution of wealth among individuals. Fiscal measures are preferable to the control of market prices and institutions to correct (according to some ethical standard) a maldistribution of wealth.

resources used by the firm with the amount of resources consumers are willing to exchange for the output.[2]

In producing goods and services, firms try to combine resources optimally, so that a given level and mix of outputs is produced with the most efficient combination and amounts of inputs. This optimal use of resources occurs not because producers wish to conserve society's wealth but because they wish to maximize their own wealth and/or position in the industry. Thus the labor services of tellers, bookkeepers, managers, and others are combined with computers, adding machines and other equipment, supplies, buildings, etc., to produce at the least cost the services demanded by businessmen, housewives, and others.

In contrast to competitive markets, however, consider the situation where there is only one bank (or a cartel). The bank's owners could gain a higher return by charging consumers higher prices and/or providing fewer services, even though less output was purchased, than in a competitive market. While government regulation might be invoked to reduce the prices charged (as is done in public utility regulation), it is unlikely that the regulated prices would be set at the optimal level, as they are by competition.

Government regulation, even when imposed for the benefit of the consumer, is not as effective as competition because regulators generally cannot know as much as the banks' managers about the demands of consumers and the ways in which resources can be combined to fulfill these demands. Nor are government regulations always designed and enforced solely to benefit the consuming public. Regulations often are imposed to create cartels, reduce competitive pressures, or benefit a particular supplier or group of firms. Regulators, in direct contact with those whom they regulate rather than with consumers, tend to identify more with suppliers and their problems than with the general public and its problems. In contrast, competition among suppliers regulates more effectively the prices charged and quality of service rendered.

Also, competitive markets provide suppliers with the motivation to serve the public and use resources efficiently. If one bank does not provide services to meet the needs of customers, another bank can prosper by doing so. If a bank operates inefficiently, its owners and managers forfeit the resources wasted.

For competitive banking markets to operate optimally, four important conditions must exist. First, entry into the market must be unrestricted. If such is not the case, a poorly run bank or one that finds itself in a monopoly position can continue to offer higher-priced and/or inadequate services to the public to the extent that people lack alternatives. Obviously, it would be preferable for suppliers to find those people whose demands are poorly met. Second, exit, either by merger or failure, must be possible. If such is not the case, the structure of the industry may not change to meet changing circumstances (which may be internal or external to the bank). Both of these conditions are under the control of governmental authorities who often (incorrectly) do not apply them to the banking industry.

---

[2]A rigorous description of resource allocation in competitive markets is available in most price theory textbooks.

Third, banks must not collude to form a cartel or monopoly. The possibility of monopoly is meaningful because the owners of banks can increase their wealth if they can create a cartel. However, where entry into the market is not restricted, a monopoly would be subverted by the same desire of people to increase their wealth since sharing, at least in part, the extraordinary profits of monopolies is a lure for new entrants. But since such entry may take time, during which period the public is ill served, and since new entrants may join the cartel, thus reinstating the monopoly, governmental authorities cannot rely entirely on market forces to cure monopolies.

Fourth, economies of scale that result in "natural" monopolies must not exist. If the most efficient bank size is the largest bank possible, then a competitive market will result in the survival of one bank. Although its ability to take advantage of its monopoly position would be limited by the possibility that new competitors could enter the market (even if for a limited time), it still would be the sole seller of banking services.

To summarize, then, the operation of market forces that would allocate resources and serve the public optimally depends on 1) unrestricted entry and exit from the industry and 2) the absence of collusive or natural monopolies. Evidence from the United States on the extent to which these considerations presently apply to the banking industry or are likely to apply in the future is discussed next. The possibility of natural monopoly and the presence of economies of scale are considered first because the policies adopted by the banking authorities cannot change the situation but rather must adapt to it.

Economies of Scale in Banking

The Effects of Economies, Diseconomies, and No Economies of Scale

If the banking industry is characterized by significant and continuous economies of large-scale operations, eventually only one bank would survive under free competition. Then the banking authorities would be faced with a dilemma. An efficient banking industry is desirable because the public (customers and bank owners) benefits from bank services being produced at the least cost. However, the resulting monopoly is undesirable to consumers because they will not participate fully in the economies of scale and, perhaps more important, they will have few alternatives to the services provided by the monopoly bank. Should new competitors be unable to enter the market, the authorities might have to restrict the size to which a bank can grow or regulate the prices it charges the public.

If banking is characterized by diseconomies of scale, a large number of smaller banks could operate side by side. In this event, the authorities might view attempts of banks to merge as organizational changes motivated more by a desire to eliminate competiton than by a desire to achieve operating economies.

If banks are not subject to important economies or diseconomies of scale, the optimal size and number of banks will be determined by the market that is served, the particular talents of bank managers, and anticompetitive mergers. The considerable demands for bank services by the large number of customers in cities, for example, would result in many more banks, both in number and kind,than would exist in rural areas. Also the particular talents of banking managers play an important role in the form the bank may take; e.g., some may specialize in retail services and others in wholesale services. Changes in the talents of managers (and their ability to adapt to changing markets and technology) also can affect the way in which the bank is run, and the rate of growth experienced. Were it not for the final factor, anticompetitive mergers, the optimal policy of government authorities in this situation would be to allow changes in the number of banks via new entrants and mergers (assuming for the moment that free entry and exit do not create other problems).

Evidence on Economies of Scale

Let us consider, then, the existing evidence on economies of scale. Several studies have been published that provide a fairly good, though not sufficiently complete, picture of the cost structure of commercial banks. The most useful of these studies are by Benston [June 1965] and Bell and Murphy [1968], which use data gathered by the Federal Reserve in its functional cost analysis program.[3] These researchers defined the output of banks as the average number of deposit accounts and loans processed per year, holding constant variations in the size and activity of accounts and loans. Number of deposit and loan accounts is preferable to dollars as a measure of output because banks process these accounts and they generate operating costs. In addition, comparing costs per dollar of deposits of banks that deal with both large- and small-balance customers is like comparing costs per dollar of sales of a wholesaler to those of a retailer. Such a comparison might lead to the erroneous conclusion that wholesalers (or large banks with fewer but larger accounts) are more efficient than retailers (or small banks with relatively more customers), *cet. par.*

Separate analyses were made of the direct costs of processing demand deposits, time deposits, installment loans, mortgage loans, business and other loans, securities, and collateral services (trust and safe deposit). In addition to output, the studies accounted for effects of type, average balances and activity of accounts, wage levels in the area, number of branches operated, and other factors, by including these as independent variables in multiple regressions. Overhead (administration, business development, and occupancy) was analyzed separately.

Benston analyzed data for 1959, 1960, and 1961 from 80 to 83 banks, of which the largest had $55 million in assets. Bell and Murphy analyzed data for 1963, 1964, and 1965 from 210 to 283 banks, of which the largest had $800 million in assets. For most banking services, the elasticities—average percentage change in operating costs asso-

---

[3]Other published studies include Alhadeff [1954], Gramley [1962], Greenbaum [1967], Horvitz [1965], Powers [1969], and Schweiger and McGee [1961]. These studies are critically reviewed and rejected because of the methodology used. See Benston [May 1972] for this analysis.

ciated with a unit percentage change in output (the number of accounts served)—are less than one, indicating economies of scale. However, the economies due to large-scale operations are not great (none is less than .85) and, for all except demand deposit and real estate loan services, are not significantly less than 1.00 on a consistent basis.

Although the differing elasticities for different banking services indicate that a bank cannot be represented completely by a single cost function, an overall average elasticity can be constructed by calculating the effect on costs of a 10 percent increase in each banking service measured at the average level of activity for the banks sampled (which, in effect, provides a weighted average). Bell and Murphy [1968, pp. 68–9] determined that total operating costs increase by 9.3 percent when weighted overall output increases by 10 percent (holding all other variables constant at their geometric mean values). Figure 1 was constructed using this overall measure of economies of scale. The "base" bank charted has an output of 10 and average operating (unit) costs of 100. A bank with an output of 50 has unit costs of 89.4 and one ten times larger than the base bank, with an output of 100, has unit costs of 85.1. Higher-output banks have less than proportionately lower unit costs: A bank with output of 500 has unit costs equal to 76.1 and a 1000 unit output bank's costs are 72.5 compared to 100.0 for the base bank, although they are 50 and 100 times larger. Thus, as Figure 1 shows, the operating cost advantages of larger size diminish rather quickly.

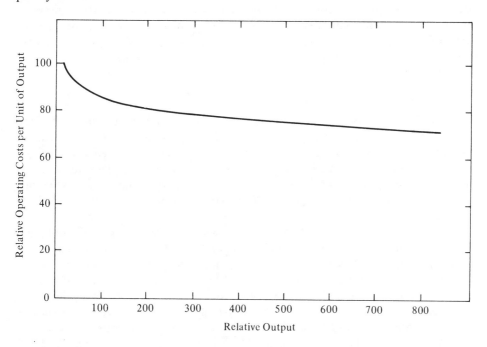

FIGURE 1. Relationship between cost and output based on an overall elasticity of .93.

Two additional aspects of the relationship between the size of banks (as measured by output in terms of numbers of accounts and loans) and costs should be considered. Figure 1 was constructed by assuming that larger banks have the same types of output (demand deposits, installment loans, etc.) and organization as do smaller banks. This assumption is useful with respect to types of output, because the type of output (measured by the number of deposit and loan accounts) need not be a function of bank size measured by total deposits or assets. But usually a bank cannot grow large (in terms of the number of customers it serves) unless it establishes branch offices. Therefore the costs of branching must be considered explicitly.

The studies reported above show that operating costs of banks with branches are higher than those of unit banks with the same rate of output, *cet. par.* The relationship between additional branching cost and savings from larger-scale operations was examined by Benston [May 1965] and Bell and Murphy [1968], who found that one offset the other. In their sample, Bell and Murphy found that the average (large) branch bank had the same costs per unit of output as the average (small) unit bank, even though the branch bank operated multiple outlets [p. 67, table IV-6]. Thus branch banks can offer customers the convenience of many offices without incurring greater net operating costs.

A similar study of the costs of savings and loan associations (which are only authorized to service savings deposits and mortgage loans) was made by Benston [1969]. Data from most U.S. associations (3,159) for each of five years (1962 through 1966) were analyzed. Consistent elasticities that average .92 over the entire range of the data were found—virtually the same as those found in the other studies for comparable outputs of commercial banks. The major difference was considerably higher branching costs for the specialized savings and loan associations.

Limitations of the Evidence

Before the implications of the data on regulation are explored, four limitations of the commercial bank studies should be mentioned. First, the latest year of the data is 1965. Since that date, changes in computer technology may have altered the production function for some of the banking services examined. Second, the studies do not specify well the effect of branch banking. Third, the "giant" banks are not represented; the largest bank included has 57,000 demand deposit accounts (assets of $801 million).

These three shortcomings are alleviated somewhat by a recent, as yet unpublished, study of demand deposit costs by Daniel, Longbrake, and Murphy [1971]. They used 1968 functional cost data that included 956 banks, the largest of which had more than 100,000 demand deposit accounts, about twice the number of accounts of the largest bank in the Bell and Murphy [1968] studies. For the 610 banks which had computers for more than a year, their analysis shows slightly lower economies of scale (.929 with a standard error of .014) than those previously measured; insignificant economies of scale for the 78 banks which had computers less than a year (.987 with a standard error of .046); and small but significant diseconomies of scale for the

268 banks with no computers (1.043 with a standard error of .021). This further research thus indicates that once computer technology is adopted, banks with a higher level of output have a somewhat smaller operating advantage over small banks than previously measured, but banks without computers (which generally are small) have a considerably greater operating disadvantage, at least with respect to demand deposits.

The fouth limitation of the cost studies is that they exclude some possibly important aspects of economies of scale. A bank that receives deposits and makes loans over a heterogeneous geographical economic area can reduce its discretionary assets (lower-yielding reserves and investments) because offsets from different areas reduce the variability of its cash flows. A large bank also can more readily capture gains from innovations than can a small bank, especially considering that innovations in service industries, such as banking, are readily copied and expropriated by others. On the other hand, small banks have the advantage of direct motivation and control of employees and the ability to innovate and change without going through a bureaucratic structure. Nor are differences in the quality of output, which might be associated with size, measured completely. To the extent that these advantages and disadvantages of size are reflected in earnings rather than in costs, they will not be included in cost studies of economies of scale.

Policy Implications of the Evidence

Given the limitatons of the data (particularly the absence of very large banks from the samples), the primary policy implication that may be drawn from the studies reviewed above is that the authorities need not be overly concerned about the existence of a natural monopoly in banking were banks allowed to grow in size (*de novo* or by merger). Very small banks, however, may not be economically viable in the absence of regulatory protection. But this fact, by itself, does not justify such protection.

However, the conclusion about small banks must be tempered by a caveat and by the findings of other studies. Advances in computer technology, particularly off-premises computers and, to some extent, time sharing, are making the newer methods available to small banks.[4] The belief that well-run small banks probably can adopt this new technology and otherwise compete successfully with large banks is supported by studies by Kohn [1966], Kohn and Carlo [1969], and Chandross [1971], which are reviewed below. The experience of state-wide branching in California also reinforces the belief that small banks can exist side by side with large, branch banks. As Table 1 shows, the largest bank, Bank of America, does not seem to have had an overwhelming advantage over smaller banks.

---

[4]Daniel et al. [1971] found that banks who used off-premises computers had lower operating costs per demand deposit account than banks who used in-house computers. The value of time sharing for small banks, however, is questioned in an article by Bower and Downes [1971] that reports on studies made for the FDIC.

Table 1. Percentage of Total Commercial Bank Deposits Held by California Banks

| | (As of December 31) | | | |
	1940	1950	1960	1970
Largest Bank	34.4%	43.6%	42.3%	37.8%
Next Largest Three	24.6	23.1	32.7	31.8
Largest Four	59.0	66.7	75.0	69.6
Next Largest Four			13.4	16.1
Largest Eight	41.0	33.3	89.6	85.7
All Other Banks			10.4	14.3
	100.0	100.0	100.0	100.0

Sources: 1940 and 1950, Alhadeff [1954]. Table 8, p. 42. 1960 and 1970, FDIC.

Hence, the conclusion of this section is that the banking authorities should have few fears that unrestricted competition would result in one or a few surviving banks as a result of natural monopoly. Rather, while large branch banks have some operational cost advantages over small banks, on average, it appears that these advantages are not great enough to overcome specific managerial or other advantages that individual banks may have. Therefore, it is concluded that a wide range of medium-sized and large banks can exist, although very small banks would have to be extremely well run or in protected positions to survive were the market for bank services free from restraints.

Competitive Behavior and the Number and Concentration of Banks in a Market

The data on economies of scale indicate that, were it not for the possibility of anti-competitive collusion, the banking authorities could allow all except perhaps the largest banks to merge and otherwise change their form of organization without fear that a natural monopoly would exist. The data also indicate that the operating costs of a large bank (one with, say, 60,000 demand deposit accounts or $800 million in assets) are 7 percent (or less) lower than those of a bank half as large. Consequently, unless a merger reduces meaningful competition, it should not be prevented. Otherwise, operating and other inefficiencies may be continued, desirable change stifled, and owners of resources prevented from using their property as they wish. A possible additional exception is the merger of very small banks in rural areas. The data indicate that considerable economies of scale might result, but competition also would be reduced and possibly eliminated. Therefore, in order to determine the relative advantage to the public of mergers, the authorities should have evidence that mergers which reduce the number of competitors actually measurably reduce the benefits the public derives from banking services. This evidence is examined next.

In general, it would appear that the greater the number of competing firms, the more likely it is that effective competition will occur, and the less likely it is that collusive arrangements will be entered into, or, if agreed to, maintained, *cet. par.* However, it is not obvious how many banks are required for active competition or what is the optimal size or spatial distribution of banks in a market. Four banks may seem preferable to three, but three actively competing may in fact be preferable to two well-run banks and two poorly run banks. Similarly, four banks with assets of $100 million each may be preferable to one bank with assets of $300 million and ten with assets of $10 million. It may also be true that for some customers the former is preferable and for others the latter distribution is better. To further complicate matters, banks produce many different products for which the market varies, even assuming that one can measure the market for demand deposits, time deposits, the various types of loans, etc.

Evidence on Concentration and Prices

Despite the difficulties involved, a number of researchers have attempted to measure the relationship between the number or concentration of banks in a market and their competitive behavior. Most of these studies have serious conceptual and statistical shortcomings that result in findings of limited, if any, value. Few of the studies included many of the obviously important variables (such as type, risk, and cost of handling loans) that might explain differences in interest rates charged. Concentration and definition of markets is crudely measured; generally the percentage of deposits or assets held by the largest two or three banks in a county or SMSA (standard metropolitan statistical area) is used. The effect on prices of having more than two or three competitors in an area is rarely measured. Nevertheless, the brief review of the studies that follows can provide some insight and conclusions for policy making.[5]

The effect on gross interest rates on business loans of the number and/or concentration of banks in a market, generally defined as a city or standard metropolitan statistical area (SMSA), was studied by Edwards [1965], Kaufman [1966], Meyer [1967], Holland [1964], Brucker [1970], Schweiger and McGee [1961], Edwards [1964], Flechsig [1965], Phillips [1967], and Jacobs [1971]. These studies are summarized very briefly in Table 2. All of these studies (except Flechsig's and a Federal Reserve study reported by Holland) indicate that the greater the concentration ratio (the percentage of assets or deposits held by the largest two or three banks) in a market and/or the smaller the number of banks, the higher the average rate charged on loans. However, this finding, while it may be correct, is limited by the measurement problems encountered by most of the researchers.

In several of the studies [Edwards 1965, Kaufman, and Meyer], interest rates on loans were measured as the gross rate received on all loans at a bank without accounting for even major differences in risk and types of loans held by the banks (such

---

[5]Also see the historical survey and review of studies on the banking structure given in Fischer [1968] and Guttentag and Herman [1967].

Table 2. Summary of Studies on the Effect of Concentrations of Bank Performance

Study	Data and Measure of Performance	Method	Measure of Concentration	Shortcomings	Findings
A. Interest Rates on Business Loans					
Brucker [1970]	Balance sheets and income statements of banks by state economic areas; ratios of gross income to total loans	Regression	Percentage of total assets held by largest three banks	Same as Edwards [1965]; also variables used are poorly out of date	Somewhat higher rates, but findings are not meaningful
Edwards [1964]	FRB loan surveys; total business interest paid divided by total loans	Regression	Percentage of deposits held by three largest banks in SMSA	Not clear yet whether difference in yields is due to differences in risk and regional supply and demand	Slightly higher rates, but findings are not meaningful
Edwards [1965]	Balance sheets and income statements of 1,400 banks in 36 areas; ratio of gross income to total loans	Tables and regressions	Percentage of deposits held by three largest banks in SMSA	Interest rates measured as total earnings on all loans—risk and type	Slightly higher rates, but findings are not meaningful
Flechsig [1965]	Same as Edwards [1964]	Regression	Same as Edwards [1964] but excludes MSB deposits	"Corrects" Edwards' work by using regional variables	No significant differences
Holland [1964]	Balance sheet, income statement ratios	Regression	One-, two- and three-bank towns	Only short summary of findings given; no data	No difference
Jacobs [1971]	Survey of loans made to 8,500 customers by 160 banks who returned questionnaires of 600 polled	Regression	Percentage of deposits held by offices of the largest three banks in SMSA	Few; only study that includes considerations of deposits held by borrowers	Slightly higher rates due to concentration; somewhat higher for small businesses due to branching restrictions
Kaufman [1966]	Balance sheet and income statements of Iowa banks; ratios of gross income to total loans	Regression	Number of banks of market share of largest bank in country	Same as Edwards [1965]. In addition, differences in costs were not even crudely measured	Higher rates, but findings are not meaningful
Meyer [1967]	Same as Edwards [1964] excluding state-wide branching areas	Regression	Same as Edwards [1964]	Same as Edwards [1964] and Edwards [1965]	Slightly higher rates, but findings are not meaningful
Phillips [1967]	Four FRB surveys of short-term business loans in 19 cities; rates weighted by size of loans	Regression	Percentage of deposits held by largest three banks in city	Other services received by borrowers and implicit payment for deposits not accounted for	Slightly higher rates

Table 2. *(continued)*

Study	Data and Measure of Performance	Method	Measure of Concentration	Shortcomings	Findings
Schweiger and McGee [1961]	Comparative shopping for standardized consumer loans	Tables and averages	3-unit vs. 8 multiple-office cities and number of banks in towns in 6 Illinois counties	Limited coverage; no statistics given to determine significance of differences	Somewhat higher rates
B. Interest Rates on Mortgage Loans					
Aspinwall [1970]	Interest rates on conventional single residence mortgages by SMSA, size of bank, loan value ratio	Regression	Percentage of time deposits held by largest three institutions and number of institutions	Risk and regional differences not fully accounted for; lending by mortgage and insurance companies ignored	Slightly higher rates where fewer institutions
C. Deposit Services					
Bell and Murphy [1969]	Functional cost and savings data for 14 cities	Regression	Percentages of eight classifications of deposits held by three largest banks	None	Higher service charge
Edwards [1965]	As above; average rates on time and savings deposits	As above	As above	Only percentage change in population used to specify demand	Lower rates
Kaufman [1966]	As above	As above	As above	As above	Lower rates paid
Weiss [1969]	Survey of all commercial banks in New England on adoption of no-charge checking accounts	Tables	Percentage of demand deposits under $10,000 held by largest three banks in SMSA and Herfindahl index	Concentration only factor accounted for	No-charge checking accounts introduced where concentration lower

as installment, mortgage, and commercial). Brucker accounted for these differences very crudely by including in his regressions the percentage of various types of loans to total loans. However, like the others, he did not account for the reduction in interest rates charged businesses for their noninterest-bearing deposits or other services purchased.[6]

Holland simply reports the findings of a Federal Reserve study but does not give the actual estimates made. Schweiger and McGee used data gathered by comparative shoppers for standard automobile loans; however, they did not provide adequate statistics to determine whether differences detected are other than random.

Edwards [1964], Flechsig, and Phillips used data from Federal Reserve Board

---

[6]Many other criticisms of these studies could be made. See Benston [June 1972] and Murphy and Weiss [1969].

surveys of business loans made at a large sample of banks. Edwards found a statistically significant (but economically small) positive relationship between rates charged on loans and percentage of deposits held by the largest three banks in an SMSA. Flechsig reran the data used by Edwards and found that the relationship could be due to regional differences. In both of these studies, there was no accounting for the size of loans. Since larger loans generally have lower gross interest rates than smaller loans, a correlation between their average size in more or less concentrated areas would confound the results. Phillips corrected this error by computing separate regressions for interest rates on each of four sizes of loans granted by banks in 19 cities in each of four periods. Thus he presents replicated, disaggregated data. Phillips found a statistically significant (but economically slight)[7] positive relationship between loan rates and concentration.

Jacobs' study is the best of this group. He studied the determinants of the rates charged on loans for 8,000 customers at 160 banks, accounting for the deposits held by the borrowers, the size of their loans, collateral, length of borrowing relationship, other demand variables, concentration measured by the deposits held by the offices of the three largest banks in the SMSA, and the extent of branching regulations. He found a statistically significant (but economically slight)[8] positive relationship between loan rates and concentration. Jacobs also found a statistically significant negative relationship that was economically more important[9] between loan rates and restrictions on branching for small companies (assets under $5 million) only.

Aspinwall [1970] studied the relationship between rates charged on conventional mortgages on single-family dwellings and the number or concentration of commercial banks, savings and loan associations, and mutual savings banks in SMSAs. He adjusted for the effects of differences among the SMSAs in loan-to-value ratios, deposit size of commercial banks, change in the number of households, and median family income. The regressions computed reveal that the greater the number of banking institutions, the lower are average interest rates. However, as found in the other studies reviewed above, the magnitude of the relationship is small.[10] Moreover, Aspinwall did not include such important mortgage lenders as mortgage, finance, and insurance companies. Their absence may account for his findings.

Researchers also have studied the effect of concentration on interest rates paid on time and savings deposits [Kaufman 1965 and Edwards 1965] and the fees charged for checking accounts [Bell and Murphy 1969 and Weiss 1969]. These studies also are summarized in Table 2. The former studies found that time and savings account interest rates were lower in areas with high concentration ratios. Since savings accounts are more homogeneous than commercial loans, this finding is less subject to the criticisms mentioned above relating to gross interest on commercial loans.

---

[7]A 10 percent increase in concentration was associated with a 6 basis point increase in loan rates.

[8]A 10 percent increase in concentration is associated with an increase in loan rates of 5 basis points.

[9]A movement from unit banking to restricted branching might lower loan rates by 18 basis points and from restricted branching to state-wide branching another 18 basis points.

[10]An area with 20 instead of 10 institutions has interest rates on mortgages that are 3 basis points lower; for an area with four instead of three institutions, the average rate is 1 basis point lower.

The papers on demand deposit service fees are well done. Bell and Murphy adjusted for the effects of differences in the cost of servicing regular checking accounts in 14 New England market areas, and used as measures of concentration the share of deposit accounts (measured in eight alternative ways) held by the largest three banks. Whether measured by dollars or numbers, all revealed that service charges, net of operating costs, were significantly higher in areas that were characterized by greater concentration of deposit accounts of all sizes. Weiss studied the offering of "no service charge" (NSC) checking accounts by New England banks and found that ". . . where NSC checking was introduced early, there is generally a large number of commercial bank competitors and the retail banking markets are relatively less concentrated" [Weiss, pp. 17–18].

Thus, it appears that banks are somewhat more competitive and serve the public better where there are a greater number of institutions. However, there is little available evidence that shows how many more than two or three banks are desirable for the existence of meaningful competition that benefits the public. Nor do the studies on business loan interest rates reveal more than the slightest relationship between rates charged and concentration. Nevertheless, it seems reasonable to conclude that regulatory authorities should be wary of approving mergers between banks (particularly large ones) that serve the same market. And they should consider Jacobs' finding that unrestricted branching is more beneficial for small businesses than is decreased concentration.

Regulatory Policy Toward Mergers and Acquisitions

It is now established in U.S. law that mergers that significantly lessen competition should be approved only when one or more banks may fail because the market cannot support as many banks as presently exist. In deciding whether a merger "may 'substantially' lessen competition, or tend toward monopoly,"[11] the banking authorities face two problems: 1) Whether the larger, postmerger bank provides net competitive benefits to the public through greater competition in some banking markets and reduced competition in others; and 2) whether the merger will foreclose future potential competition. To provide a context in which these problems can be discussed, and perhaps solved, let us consider first the reasons for which banks wish to merge with or acquire other banks.

Motivations for Mergers and Acquisitions

Three possible motivations for bank mergers may be delineated: 1) Bankers believe that normal and perhaps extraordinary profits can be made by entering new markets, but they are prevented by state laws from establishing branches *de novo;* 2) bank

---

[11]*Brown Shoe Company* v. *The United States*, 370 U.S. 294, 321 (1962).

managers believe that stockholders' wealth will be maximized[12]; or 3) top management wants the bank to grow to increase their power, prestige and/or salary.[13] Let us examine these three points in greater detail.

1) **Mergers because *De Novo* Branching is Prohibited**   Where state laws restrict branching, banks wishing to expand into a given area must acquire existing banks by merger or through purchase by a holding company. In these states, regulations may actually cause increased concentration.

2) **Wealth Maximization, Cost Economies, and Capital Flow Facilitation**   A merger might increase the wealth of the owners of an acquired bank through operating and cash management economies from joint operations, profits from increased and/or improved services (such as a larger branch network), solution of management succession and estate tax problems, increased marketability of shares of a closely held bank, etc. The acquiring bank's owners may benefit for many of the same reasons and also may find it preferable (in the capital budgeting sense) to buy an operating bank than to start a branch *de novo;* in effect, the "premium" (amount over book value) paid for an acquired bank represents the present value of the expenses of establishing a new branch, expenses that are not capitalized in the accounting records of the acquired bank. If the acquiring and acquired banks are not substantial competitors and if there are no restrictions on entry into the market, the possibility of monopoly profits cannot be part of these calculations.

But what evidence is there that mergers result in operating or other economies? The data presented above on economies of scale indicate that operating economies would result from mergers of small banks into branch systems but that mergers of large banks probably would not give rise to important savings in operating costs (especially when one considers the cost of merging). Studies have been made of postmerger operations of merged and purchased banks that provide additional data on this question.

The postacquisition performance of banks acquired by holding companies was examined in several studies. Lawrence [1967] studied the performance of 43 banks acquired by holding companies during the period 1954-63 and compared their pre- and postacquisition data with data from 55 independent but similar banks. He found that the acquired banks increased their loans (especially installment loans) and increased service charges on demand deposit accounts, but otherwise, ". . . differences in performance between acquired banks and other banks were minimal" [Lawrence, p. 24]. Talley [1971] replicated Lawrence's study with data from 82 banks acquired by holding companies between 1966 and 1969. His results paralleled those reported by Lawrence, with the exception that the banks in Talley's study did not increase their demand deposit service charges. A comparable study of holding company acquisition in three northern states by McLeary [1968] presented similar findings, as did an analysis of postacquisition operations of New England banks by Weiss [1971]

---

[12]This hypothesis is argued strongly by Federal Revenue Board Governor George W. Mitchell [1965].
[13]This hypothesis is presented by Cohen and Reed [1967] and, the authors believe, demonstrated. While they may be correct, their data cannot support this conclusion.

and of Ohio banks by Ware [1971]. Finally, Piper and Weiss [1971] summarize a further analysis of data derived from Piper's [1971] study of 102 holding company acquisitions and conclude that the "operating revenues of the acquired banks generally increased significantly after acquisition, often largely as a result of expansion in consumer lending (reflecting a change in product mix rather than higher prices). However, revenue increases were typically matched by correspondingly large increases in operating costs" [Piper and Weiss, p. 5].

With respect to holding company acquisitions, then, the published studies do not indicate that operating economies or significantly improved services to the public, other than expanded consumer lending, resulted, or that poor banks were prevented from failing. But as Weiss [1971] concludes, "The available evidence suggests that holding company acquisitions have not led to . . . anticompetitive results and that postacquisition price changes [to consumers] are relatively minor" [p. 10].

No studies are available on whether true mergers (an acquired bank being integrated into the whole as a branch) resulted in reduced operating costs. However, Cohen and Reid's [1967] comparison of stock prices of banks that merged with those that didn't indicates little net advantage to stockholders. In addition, Rotwein's [1965] study of bank mergers in California between 1947 and 1960 indicates that, in these mergers, there was little possibility of improvement in operating costs since the banks acquired were well run and were probably acquired for this reason. Smith [1969] studied 139 mergers between 1960-1967 in the Fourth Federal Reserve District. He compared the profitability, asset, and liability distribution of acquiring and acquired banks with a matched sample of nonmerging banks and reached conclusions similar to Rotwein's. (Neither of these studies considered the effect of mergers on performance.) Thus there is reason to believe that mergers were not undertaken for and did not result in operating costs savings.

However, there is not sufficient data available for acceptable conclusions to be reached. In particular, it is important to emphasize that savings in operating costs are not the only (or most important) economy that may be derived from mergers. An important operating factor (particularly relevant to banking) is facilitation of capital flows from one part of a state to another. Investors' wealth can be increased by shifting capital from a declining to an expanding area, as population and business shift or are expected to shift, throwing expected rates of return from banking out of equilibrium.[14] Because stockholders pay income taxes on dividends but not on earnings retained by corporations, it is preferable for stockholders that their bank invests directly in areas with higher rates of return. Therefore, such investments can best be made by mergers with banks in expanding areas. The opportunity to invest in other banks is especially important for U.S. banks because they cannot make equity investments in other businesses (unless they form bank holding companies) or in banks outside of their own states. In addition, investment in banks is usually preferable for stockholders because bank managements have a natural advantage in evaluating and operating in their own area rather than nonbanking activities. Thus, while it is true

---

[14]I am indebted to William Meckling for insights into this question.

that capital can (and does) flow directly to banks in higher rate of return areas in form of direct equity and debt investments (until the expected risk-adjusted marginal rate of return is equalized in all investments), the flow is increased and the total social value of resources within a state is maximized if mergers are possible.

In addition, studies on the postmerger performance of banks acquired as branches by Kohn [1964], Horvitz and Shull [1964], Bacon [1967], and Kaufman [1969] indicate that the public has benefited from mergers. Kohn's is the most careful study of those reviewed. He compared the premerger loan ratio, services charges, rates paid on savings deposits, lending activity, etc., of the banks acquired with their postmerger behavior as branches. New York State bank mergers between 1951 and 1961 inclusive were studied by means of a questionnaire (80 percent replies were received). He concludes that the merged banks generally increased lending to their communities and, with respect to prices and services, "the great majority of bank mergers in New York State during the period 1951 through 1961 have been, on balance, beneficial to the interests of the public both in terms of their immediate and longer-range effects . . ." [Kohn, p. 187]. Horvitz and Shull replicated Kohn's study for all 1962 mergers nation-wide. Except for increases in service charges on checking accounts, their results parallel Kohn's findings.[15]

Bacon studied the merger of 15 of the 21 banks in Marion County, Indiana. He reports that most of the banks merged were small, poorly managed institutions, ill-equipped to serve their customers. Kaufman reports the results of surveys of customers before and after a merger of two of the three banks in Elkhart, Indiana. He found that, "Only a small proportion of the customers viewed the decline in the number of banks as having an unfavorable effect on either the quality of banking services or the number of competitors" [Kaufman, p. 7]. Thus, a merger that results in a branch does appear to benefit or at least not damage the public.

3) **Bank Size or Growth Maximization**   There is evidence that this motivation for merger is of some importance. Piper's [1971] study of holding company acquisitions and Smith's [1969] study of mergers reveal that the acquiring banks more often than not paid premiums to the stockholders of the acquired bank that do not seem economically justified. The premium paid may be a function of state laws that prohibit *de novo* branching. However, there is reason to believe that the desire of bank management for growth as such is a motivating factor for many mergers. Nevertheless top management's desire for growth need not be contrary to the stockholders' interest. For one thing, growth may be a good proxy for expected profits. For another, allowing top management to pursue their desire for growth may be an excellent way of motivating and compensating those managers.

If we assume, for argument's sake, that the management of a given bank consummates a merger that does not benefit the bank's stockholders, it follows that the merged bank will not be as profitable as other banks, stockholders will lose, and,

---

[15]This finding may be related to the greater proportion of time to total deposits and rate of interest paid on time deposits by branch banks. Lower charges on demand deposits are implicit interest payments on these deposits. Branch banks may prefer explicit interest payments and charges for service.

eventually, management will be replaced. But even if one assumes that stockholders are unable to get rid of inept or unsuccessful management, still the public will not be harmed. Management may attempt to offset the adverse effects of its diseconomic merger by raising prices or reducing services. But the public can always switch to other banks and, assuming that entry is not restricted, other financial institutions, lured by the new profit potential, might step into the ill-served market, thus forcing the offending institution to serve the public better or leave the market. Finally, while it is true that investors may be harmed, it is not the banking authorities' function to protect stockholders from inept management except in situations of fraud.

In conclusion, reason and evidence support the policy of not restricting mergers regardless of the motivations involved, except in situations where collusion among banks results in monopoly practices. This also assumes that entry into banking is unrestricted. But before the question of entry is considered (in section V), the two regulatory problems raised in the first part of this section are discussed.

Effects of Mergers on Competition in Different Markets

The first problem faced by the banking authorities is whether or not a merger will reduce competition more than it is increased. In this regard, the greatest consideration must be given to that portion of the public for whom there are relatively few alternative sources of banking services. Specifically, the demands of local customers—small businessmen and individuals—generally should be favored over the demands of large businesses which can borrow in many cities. Arguments that a merger is necessary to increase the loan limits of a bank usually are without basis since banks can, and do, participate with other banks in making large loans.

But to apply this criterion the authorities must measure, among those banks that wish to merge, the specific business of specific groups of customers. This requires operational definitions of the relevant markets. As the controversy over the 1963 Philadelphia-Girard merger decision illustrated, the relevant market is difficult to define because banks produce many products that may be purchased by customers in widely differing areas.[16] Some recent research on the problem by Gelder and Budzeika [1970] and Eisenbeis [1971] shows that the market for banking services may be quite wide and is not coextensive with standard legal or geographic boundaries. While it may be easy to measure the effect on competition of the merger of two of the three banks in an isolated town, it is difficult in a town served by, say, six medium-sized banks to assess the impact of the merger of two of them. It appears, then, that unless a merger will "substantially lessen competition," a liberal policy on mergers together with a less restrictive policy on entry will provide the best protection to the public against possible collusion.

---

[16]See the papers originally published in the *National Banking Review*, reprinted in Administrator of National Banks, *Studies in Banking Competition and the Banking Structure* [1966].

Potential Competition

The second problem faced by banking authorities is whether or not to prevent mergers of banks that do not presently compete on the theory that such mergers will foreclose future competition between them. This doctrine of potential competition has been followed in New York State (and is being emphasized by the FDIC). According to a study by Kohn and Carlo [1969], it appears to have been successful in increasing the number of competitors in some markets. Between 1961 and 1963, the New York State Banking Department denied 10 of 13 cases in the belief that major institutions would otherwise enter the market of the mergee. As a result, potential competition became actual competition. Still, it is difficult, as Kohn and Carlo point out, to determine whether potential competition actually will occur. And there is a further problem, where entry has occurred, in determining whether the new competitors did in fact provide better service than a merged instition would have provided.[17] Finally, by denying mergers in instances other than those where competition clearly will benefit a significant part of the public, the authorities may stifle needed change in the banking structure and certainly are denying the owners of banks the right to dispose of their property as they see fit.

Aside from these limitations, it should be noted that validity of the potential competition doctrine is based on two assumptions: 1) That the market in which entrance is desired is monopolized; and 2) that the supply of potential competitors is limited.

With respect to the first assumption, if the market does not offer an opportunity for at least ordinary returns (net of the cost of entry), new entrants will not appear, monopoly or no. In a market characterized by monopoly profits, the immediate question is, "Why have other banks not entered the market?" One answer may be that entry was restricted by banking laws, in which event concern with the elimination of potential competition is misplaced. Another is that profit potential might be less than the cost of establishing a new bank or branches. As a result, *de novo* entry would not be economical. In this event, infusion of additional capital via merger may be the only way to increase the resources available to consumers in such a market as discussed above.

The assumption that there is a limited supply of entrants in turn assumes that: 1) The market for banking services within the state cannot support many banks; 2) the resources available from existing banks or new entrants are insufficient for expansion into the market; and/or 3) bankers lack the desire to enter new markets even though there are potential net profits to be gained. Under the first limitation, the merger of two banks will eliminate one of them as a possible competitor and, if there are few competitors operating in the state, this reduction may "substantially lessen competition and tend towards monopoly." For small states, this possibility requires the

---

[17]Often, the fact that a city of SMSA is served by four or fewer commercial banks is believed to be evidence of oligopoly practices. However, the evidence on concentration and performance reviewed above provides no support for this belief.

authorities to decide whether possible improvements (and, for small banks, economies of larger scale) outweigh the possible anticompetitive effects of merger.

An assumption that existing banks lack resources for expansion into new markets and/or that there are an insufficient number of effective competitors within a state depends on the exclusion of banks from other states, because there are few, if any, nonlegal barriers. The limitation is an artificial and arbitrary one imposed by the bank regulatory authorities (as discussed in section V). Were interstate banking permitted, the resource limitation could be eliminated by entrance of "foreign" banks, and branch offices and/or out-of-state holding companies could offer their services to the public.[18]

It is possible that where bankers lack the motivation or ability to enter a new market *de novo,* it is because they learned their banking in a period when such possibilities were prevented by restrictive regulations. Consequently, when such bankers do attempt to expand into new markets by merger, they may do so without first carefully considering the alternative costs and benefits of establishing *de novo* branches. Adequate evidence that this situation exists might prompt banking authorities to educate bankers and/or delay approval of merger applications until the applicants show that they have fully considered *de novo* alternatives. However, since it is doubtful that many bankers would fail to adapt to new regulations within a few years, a delay/education policy should be temporary, automatically terminating after a set period of time.

The conclusion, then, is that continuing restriction of mergers based on the potential competition doctrine is not well founded in theory for any but small states, if those. Even where the number of potential instate entrants is limited, it would be preferable to allow out-of-state banks to establish offices. The potential competition doctrine is justified, if at all, by the behavioral assumption that banks previously restricted need to be forced to consider *de novo* entry. Thus the doctrine has only short-run, temporary value for large states and is not an optimal policy even for small states.

Conclusion

In summary, the evidence reviewed on bankers' motivations for mergers indicates that savings in operating costs do not appear to have been a strong motivation for or result of holding company acquisitions, although such savings may have been obtained in "true" mergers, where the acquired bank became a branch of the acquiring bank. More important motivations may have been avoidance of state restrictions on *de novo* branching and facilitation of capital flows between declining and expanding

---

[18]Federal law prohibits national and Federal Reserve member banks from establishing branches outside of the states in which they are chartered. Most states have similar restrictions on the banks they charter and on out-of-state banks. The Federal Reserve may permit holding companies to purchase or establish banks in states other than the one in which they are chartered only if this is expressly permitted by state law.

areas of a state. Management's desire for growth and large size also may have been important in merger decisions. Whatever the motivation, the data show that mergers result in better services, lower prices, and higher rates on savings for the consuming public.

Thus, it appears that when mergers do not substantially eliminate competition they are in the public interest. True, in some markets mergers will eliminate competition for some customers and in others enhance it. But, considering the difficulty of defining those markets in which banks actually compete, it is preferable to control possible monopoly practices by following a liberal merger policy together with relatively unrestricted entry (by new banks, branches, and extended powers of other financial institutions). An analysis of the potential competition doctrine reveals that it is based on the belief that the supply of potential competitors is limited and/or that bankers desire to expand via merger without first adequately considering the benefits of *de novo* expansion. To the extent that they hold true, both of these conditions are the result of laws that restrict entry. Therefore, the rationale for restricting entry into banking markets is considered next.

Entry

As discussed in section I, unrestricted entry of firms into markets is sufficient for competitive behavior that benefits the public. But entry into U.S. banking markets is restricted. Only institutions chartered as commercial banks can offer some of the most essential banking services (particularly demand deposits). Commercial bank charters must be applied for and often are denied. The establishment of branches frequently is prohibited or restricted by state law. Given the (to economists) obvious value of unrestricted entry for eliminating or reducing the antisocial effects of monopolies and poor management, why is it difficult to enter the banking business?

Barriers to Entry

Two types of barriers to entry may be distinguished: 1) Economic barriers and 2) regulatory barriers. Each is considered in turn.

In his comprehensive study, *Barriers to New Competition* [1956], Bain groups economic barriers to entry into four classifications: Economies of scale, product differentiation, absolute-cost, and capital requirements. None of these is an important barrier to entry into banking.

To begin with, economies of scale (discussed previously) are not great above a quite low level of output. And, although economies of scale for giant banks have not been studied rigorously, the fact that Bank of America and other very large banks in New York City and Chicago have not overwhelmed other banks argues against great scale as a barrier to competition (see Table 1). Furthermore, Kohn [1966] has shown that small banks can compete effectively with large banks.

Product differentiation is difficult to achieve in banking because money is one of the most standard of goods. Quality and innovative packaging of services are used to compete for greater share of market, but these can be copied easily. In addition, bank examination and FDIC insurance have reduced if not eliminated most differences in the risk characteristics of banks.

Absolute-cost advantage refers to control over raw materials, patents, etc., by established firms, which bars new entrants from efficient production processes or forces them to incur higher costs. There are few such situations in banking. Labor, materials, equipment, and money are available from competitive markets and do not give one bank or another an advantage in acquisition (except where government rules intervene, such as Regulation Q, which limits the rate of interest banks can pay on deposits).

The last possible economic barrier, capital requirements, is lower for banking than for most other industries.[19] Thus, there are few, if any, economic barriers to entry into banking.

Government regulations, on the other hand, are an important barrier restricting entry and competition. Banks are chartered by the Comptroller of the Currency or by the individual states. Branching is controlled by state laws. Before passage of the Banking Act of 1935, entry into commercial banking essentially was unrestricted. In most states it usually was not difficult to get the state banking commission to grant a state charter if a national bank charter was denied by the Comptroller, and vice versa.[20] But the Banking Act of 1935 required that the Federal agencies (Comptroller of the Currency, Federal Reserve, and FDIC) consider "the financial history and condition of the bank, the adequacy of its capital structure, its future earnings prospects, the needs of the community to be served by the bank. . ."[21] before deposit insurance is granted. Peltzman [1965] analyzed the effect of the Act on new bank formation and estimated that "the net result of these restrictions has been the loss of competition from about 2,200 new banks which would have formed in the absence of entry controls. There appears to be no noticeable offsetting gain to this loss" [p. 174].

Rationale for Government Restrictions

Restrictive control over entry was established because legislators and the public believed that "overbanking" and destructive competition were responsible for the U.S. bank failures of the 1920s and, in large part, for the collapse of the banking system in the 1930s. There is some evidence to support the belief that bank failures in

---

[19]National bank and state Federal Reserve member charters require a minimum capital and surplus of $120,000 to $240,000 (depending on the size of the community). New York State (as an example) requires capital of from $50,000 to $100,000. However, the chartering authorities usually require more than the minimum amount. If the requirements are greater than the amount that is optimal for an investment, they can be an economic barrier or, at least, an obstruction.

[20]See Federal Reserve System Committee on Branch, Chain, and Group Banking, Vol. 10 [1932].

[21]Section 101 (12 U.S.C. 1814(b), 1815, 1816).

the 1920s were a function of "overbanking." In a study of the causes of bank failures in this period, Benston [1971] finds that the data suggest, though do not demonstrate, a positive relationship between increased chartering and subsequent increased failures [pp. 17-20]. However, there is also reason to believe that the economic gains from expansion in banking facilities were greater than the losses due to bank failures. The great wave of failures in the 1930s, in any event, was due primarily to the restrictive monetary policy followed by the Federal Reserve that reduced the liquidity available to banks and resulted in great capital losses, particularly in bond holdings. For this period, prior chartering of banks bore little relationship to failures.

There have been relatively few bank suspensions in the postdepression period. Only 131 banks were suspended from 1943 through 1969, an average per year of .03 per 100 banks operating. Most of these failures were due to embezzlement and financial irregularities by officers and employees; very few were due to poor management and none to "destructive competition" [Benston, 1971]. Thus, it appears that fears of overbanking are not revelant today.

In any event, prevention of bank failures should be given much less attention. Many of the original reasons for preventing such failures are no longer relevant.[22] Among these no longer valid reasons are maintenance of the currency, prevention of bank runs, protection of small depositors, and disruption of communities and the economy in general. The first reason is obsolete since commercial banks no longer issue currency. Federal deposit insurance has prevented bank runs and completely protects most depositors. So long as there is more than one bank in a community or permissible branch banking, the failure of a bank causes most people only an inconvenience and is less disruptive that the failure of most large businesses. Generally, research on the great depression (and on depressions in general) has shown that bank failures were not a primary causal factor and, in any event, resulted in a decline in the money supply and credit that could have been readily offset by the Federal Reserve [Warburton 1966, particularly p. 2].

Nor should there be concern over "destructive competition" generally. Aside from absence of any theory that supports this concept, there is no evidence that the phenomenon ever occurred,[23] particularly in banking markets. The findings of several studies support this conclusion. Benston [1964] and Cox [1966] independently examined the hypothesis that banks' payment of interest on demand deposits (which was prohibited by the Banking Act of 1933) resulted in their taking greater risks than they otherwise would have and failing. The evidence shows conclusively that such was not the case. Motter and Carson [1964] very carefully studied the effects of removal of restrictions against New York City banks from opening branches in

---

[22]See Benston [1971] for a more complete discussion.

[23]The Standard Oil case is the standard example of destructive competition. While folklore has it that Rockefeller forced out his competition by undercutting their prices in order to create the Standard Oil monopoly, an excellent study by John S. McGee shows that this did not happen. Rockefeller, being very smart, did not engage in destructive competition. Rather he bought out his competitors, sharing with them the monopoly profits he expected to gain [McGee, 1958].

adjoining Nassau County in 1960. They report that the existing banks were not made unprofitable or unsafe; rather, "there can be no doubt that Nassau consumers benefited from the expansion of banking facilities" [Motter and Carson, p. 152] in the form of added convenience, lower rates on loans, and higher rates on savings deposits. In an analysis of the effects of the some 100 *de novo* branches opened in New York State between July 1, 1960, and December 31, 1964, Kohn [1969] also found that the profitability of competing banks was not significantly adversely affected, although their deposit growth rate did slow down. He concludes that ". . . the evidence does not support the view that most unit banks are unable to adjust successfully to a new competitive force in the community" [p. 22].

The effect of new bank entry was studied by Chandross [1971] and Fraser and Rose [1972]. Chandross analyzed the effect of new bank entry into 98 formerly one-bank towns during 1950-61. He compared the ratios of net operating income to assets, net profits to capital, and capital to risk assets. While there is evidence that the banks took greater risks, these risks were no greater than those accepted by comparable, nonmonopoly banks. Fraser and Rose conducted a similar study of the effects of a new bank on existing banks in isolated one-, two-, and three-bank towns in the Eleventh Federal Reserve District (southwest) during 1962-64. They found the new banks ". . . brought about significant changes in the nature of the banking services offered to the local communities by the established banks. Loan-asset ratios increased, greater emphasis was placed on business and consumer loans, while the prices for key banking services . . . did not appear to rise relative to the norm. Also, established banks in the new entry communities were spurred into entering the competition for time deposits. These benefits to the public occurred without an adverse impact upon bank profitability or growth" [Fraser and Rose, pp. 76-77].

Restrictions on branching stem from concerns that are almost contrary to the fear of bank failures. From 1921 through 1931, only seven of the 8,816 U.S. banks suspended were branch banks with more than 10 branches, of which only three operated branches outside their main office city. This record reflects the fact that unit banks, especially small ones, cannot diversify their portfolios or personnel and so suffer greatly when a local economic depression or errors in judgment occur. [Federal Reserve Committee, Vol. 10, 1932, p. 60]. California, with state-wide branching, had relatively few failures even among unit banks, and Canada, which permits country-wide branching, had only one failure (in 1923).

Fear of concentration of resources in a few large banks is a major reason for opposition to branch banking. However, Horvitz and Shull [1964], who researched this question very carefully, compared unit banking states with states that permit branch banking and found that, after taking account of population and geographic region, the number of competing banks is greater in towns not a part of metropolitan areas, about the same in smaller standard metropolitan statistical areas (SMSAs), though fewer in larger SMSAs. Thus, for consumers in smaller communities, who have fewer alternatives, branch banking results in a greater choice as well as greater convenience. Similarly, Jacobs [1971] found that small businesses were charged lower commercial loan rates in branch banking than in restricted branching and unit branching SMSAs.

The benefits to the public of new entrants into a market has been fairly well documented. Studies by Kohn [1964] and Horvitz and Shull [1964] comparing the pre- with the postmerger behavior of unit banks merged with branch banks show no reduction in loans to the local community and a general increase in interest rates paid on savings deposits. Weiss [1969] reports that new banks were pioneers and early adopters of "no service charge checking." Motter [1965], who studied the performance of banks chartered in 1962, concludes that ". . . the operating results to date have been favorable for most of the 1962 class. Bank customers have enjoyed substantial benefits from this class" [p. 369]. The effect of new banks in reducing monopoly profits is shown in the study by Chandross [1971], reviewed above.

The conclusion of the reasoning and evidence must be that greatly reduced governmental restrictions on entry would be in the public interest. Possible bank failures can be controlled by requiring new banks to have adequate capital and to be managed by responsible and experienced bankers. But, these considerations should not be overemphasized, as they have been since 1935. Given both FDIC insurance and bank examination by the FDIC, state and federal banking authorities can be much more liberal in granting new charters than they have been. This liberality also will allow them similar liberality in permitting mergers.

It is important to note that entry can take several forms, in addition to new charters. The authorities can be much less fearful of managerial errors by banks which establish branches, since a branch can be unprofitable generally without seriously affecting the parent bank. Another important source of new entrants is expansion of the powers of other financial institutions. Were U.S. thrift institutions, in particular, given the power to make unsecured consumer installment and business loans and to provide checking account services, they would constitute actual or potential entrants in many banking markets. Thus, for most states, the supply of new entrants probably would be sufficient to present existing banks with actual and potential competition. There are almost no economic barriers to entry. Only regulatory barriers are important. These should be reduced almost to the point of removal.

BIBLIOGRAPHY

Administrator of National Banks, *Studies in Banking Competition and the Banking Structure,* articles reprinted from *The National Banking Review,* Washington, D.C., January, 1966.

ALHADEFF, D. A., *Monopoly and Competition in Banking,* Berkeley: University of California Press, 1954.

ASPINWALL, RICHARD C., "Market Structure and Commercial Bank Mortgage Interest Rates," *Southern Economic Journal,* XXXVI, April 1970, 376-84.

BACON, PETER W., "Bank Mergers: A Study of Marion County, Indiana," *Business Conditions,* Federal Reserve Bank of Chicago, December 1967, 11-16.

BAIN, JOE S., *Barriers to New Competition,* Cambridge, Harvard University Press, 1956.

BELL, FREDERICK W. and NEIL B. MURPHY, "The Impact of Market Structure on the Price of a Commercial Bank Service," *Review of Economics and Statistics,* LI, May 1969, 210-13.

BENSTON, GEORGE J., "Interest Payments on Demand Deposits and Bank Investment Behavior," *Journal of Political Economy,* LXXII, October 1964, 431-49.

———, "Branch Banking and Economies of Scale," *The Journal of Finance,* XX, May 1965, 312-31.

———, "Economies of Scale and Marginal Costs in Banking Operations," *The National Banking Review,* 2, June 1965, 507-49.

———, "Cost of Operations and Economies of Scale in Savings and Loan Associations," *Study of the Savings and Loan Industry,* directed by Irwin Friend, Federal Home Loan Bank Board, Washington, D.C., July 1969, 677-761.

———, "Savings Banking and the Public Interest," *Journal of Money Credit and Banking,* IV, Part II, February 1972, 133-226.

———, "Economies of Scale of Financial Institutions," *Journal of Money Credit and Banking,* IV, May 1972, 312-41.

———, "Bank Examination," study prepared for the President's Commission on Financial Structure and Regulation, 1971 (forthcoming in *The Bulletin,* New York University).

BOWER, RICHARD S. and DAVID H. DOWNES, "The Time-Sharing Decision in Banking," *Journal of Bank Research,* 2, Autumn 1971, 9-12.

BRUCKER, ERIC, "A Microeconomic Approach to Banking Competition, *The Journal of Finance,* XXV, December 1970, 1133-41.

CHANDROSS, ROBERT H., "The Impact of New Bank Entry on Unit Banks in One Bank Towns," *Journal of Bank Research,* 2, Autumn 1971, 22-30.

COHEN, K. J. and S. R. REID, "Effects of Regulation, Branching, and Mergers on Banking Structure and Performance," *Southern Economic Journal,* 34, October 1967, 231-49.

COX, ALBERT H., *Regulation of Interest Rates on Bank Deposits,* Ann Arbor, Bureau of Business Research, Graduate School of Business Administration, University of Michigan, 1966.

DANIEL, DONNIE L., WILLIAM A. LONGBRAKE and NEIL B. MURPHY, "The Effect of Technology on Bank Economies of Scale for Demand Deposits," *Journal of Finance,* forthcoming.

EDWARDS, F. R., *Concentration and Competition in Commercial Banking: A Statistical Study,* Boston; Federal Reserve Bank of Boston: 1964.

———, "The Banking Competition Controversy," *The National Banking Review,* 3, September 1965, 1-34.

EISENBEIS, ROBERT A., "Local Banking Markets for Business Loans," *Journal of Bank Research,* 2, Summer 1971, 30-9.

Federal Reserve System Committee on Branch, Chain, and Group Banking, *The Dual Banking System in the United States,* unpublished unofficial study, 1932.

———, *Summary,* Vol. 10, unpublished unofficial study, 1932.

FISCHER, GERALD C., *American Banking Structure,* New York; Columbia University Press, 1968.

FLECHSIG, T. G., *Banking Market Structure and Performance In Metropolitan Areas,* Washington, D.C.: Board of Governors of the Federal Reserve System, 1965.

FRASER, DONALD R. and PETER S. ROSE, "Bank Entry and Bank Performance," *The Journal of Finance,* XXVII, March 1972, 65-78.

GELDER, RALPH H. and GEORGE BUDZEIKA, "Banking Market Determination—The Case of Central Nassau County," *Monthly Review,* Federal Reserve Bank of New York, November 1970, 258-66.

GRAMLEY, L. E., *A Study of Scale Economies in Banking,* Kansas City, Missouri: Federal Reserve Bank of Kansas City, 1962.

GREENBAUM, S. I., "A Study of Bank Costs," *The National Banking Review,* 4, June 1967, 415-34.

GUTTENTAG, JACK M. and EDWARD S. HERMAN, *Banking Structure and Performance,* New York University Graduate School of Business Administration, *The Bulletin,* No. 41/43, 1967.

HOLLAND, ROBERT, "Research into Banking Structure and Competition," *Federal Reserve Bulletin,* 50, November 1964, 1383-99.

HORVITZ, P. M., "Economies of Scale in Banking," in *Private Financial Institutions,* Englewood Cliffs, New Jersey: Prentice-Hall, 1965, 1-54.

HORVITZ, P. M. and B. SHULL, "The Impact of Branch Banking on Performance," *The National Banking Review,* 2, December 1964, 143-88.

JACOBS, DONALD P., *Business Loan Costs and Bank Market Structure,* Occasional Paper 115, National Bureau of Economic Research: New York, 1971.

KAUFMAN, G. G., "Bank Market Structure and Performance: The Evidence from Iowa," Southern Economic Journal, 32, April 1966, 429-39.

———, "Customers View a Bank Merger—Before and After Surveys," *Business Conditions,* Federal Reserve Bank of Chicago, July 1969, 5-8.

KOHN, ERNEST, *Branch Banking, Bank Mergers and the Public Interest,* New York: New York State Banking Department, 1964.

———, *The Future of Small Banks,* New York: New York State Banking Department, 1966.

KOHN, ERNEST and CARMEN J. CARLO, *The Competitive Impact of New Branches,* New York: New York State Banking Department, 1969.

LAWRENCE, ROBERT J., *The Performance of Bank Holding Companies,* Board of Governors of the Federal Reserve System, 1967.

MCGEE, JOHN S., "Predatory Price Cutting: The Standard Oil (N.J.) Case," *The Journal of Law and Economics,* I, October 1958, 137-69.

MCLEARY, J. W., "Bank Holding Companies: Their Growth and Performance," *Monthly Review,* Federal Reserve Bank of Atlanta, October 1968, 131-8.

MEYER, PAUL A., "Price Discrimination, Regional Loan Rates, and the Structure of the Banking Industry," *The Journal of Finance,* XXII, March 1967, 37-48.

MITCHELL, GEORGE W., "Mergers Among Commercial Banks," in *Perspectives on Antitrust Policy,* Almarin Phillips, Editor; Princeton, New Jersey: Princeton University Press, 1965.

MOTTER, D. C., "Bank Formation and the Public Interest," *The National Banking Review,* 2, March 1965, 299-349.

MOTTER, DAVID C. and DEANE CARSON, "Bank Entry and the Public Interest: A Case Study," *National Banking Review,* 1, June 1964, 469-512.

MURPHY, NEIL B. and STEVEN J. WEISS, "The Effect of Concentration on Performance: Evaluating Statistical Studies," *Bank Administration,* November 1969, 34ff.

PELTZMAN, SAM, "Bank Entry Regulation: Its Impact and Purpose," *National Bank Review,* 3, December 1965, 163-77.

PHILLIPS, A., "Evidence on Concentration in Banking Markets and Interest Rates," *Federal Reserve Bulletin,* 53, June 1967, 916-26.

PIPER, THOMAS R., *The Economics of Bank Acquisitions by Registered Bank Holding Companies,* Research Report No. 48, Federal Reserve Bank of Boston, March 1971.

PIPER, THOMAS R. and STEVEN J. WEISS, "The Profitability of Bank Acquisitions by Multi-Bank Holding Companies," *New England Economic Review,* Federal Reserve Bank of Boston, September/October 1971, 2-12.

POWERS J. A., "Branch Versus Unit Banking: Bank Output and Cost Economies," *The Southern Economic Journal,* XXXVI, October 1969, 153-64.

ROTWEIN, EUGENE, "Bank Mergers and Bank Concentration in California in the Postwar Period," a paper prepared for the Federal Reserve Bank of San Francisco, reprinted in Hearing before the Subcommittee on Banking and Currency, House of Representatives, "To Amend the Bank Merger Act of 1960," 89th Congress, 1st Session, 1965; 130-7.

SCHWEIGER, I. and J. S. MCGEE, "Chicago Banking: The Structure and Performance at Banks and Related Financial Institutions in Chicago and Other Areas," *The Journal of Business,* XXXIV, July 1961, 201-366.

SCOTT, KENNETH E. and THOMAS MAYER, "Risk and Regulation in Banking: Some Proposals for Federal Deposit Insurance Reform," *The Stanford Law Review,* 23, May 1971, 857-902.

SMITH, DAVID L., *Characteristics of Merging Banks,* Staff Economic Study No. 49, Board of Governors of the Federal Reserve System, 1969 (Summary also printed in *The Federal Reserve Bulletin, 55,* July 1969, 579-80).

TALLEY, SAMUEL H., "The Effect of Holding Company Acquisitions on Bank Performance," *Staff Economic Studies,* No. 69, 1971, Board of Governors of the Federal Reserve System.

WARBURTON, CLARK, *Depression, Inflation and Monetary Policy, Selected Papers 1954-1953,* Baltimore, Maryland, The Johns Hopkins Press, 1966.

WARE, ROBERT F., "Characteristics of Banks Acquired by Multiple Bank Holding Companies in Ohio," *Economic Review,* Federal Reserve Bank of Cleveland, August 1971, 19-27.

WEISS, STEVEN J., "Bank Holding Companies and Public Policy," *New England Economic Review,* Federal Reserve Bank of Boston, September/October 1971, 2-12.

———, "Commercial Bank Price Competition: The Case of 'Free' Checking Accounts," *New England Economic Review,* Federal Reserve Bank of Boston, September/October 1969, 3-22.

Holding Companies, Mergers, Branching, and Chartering

Having desire and ability to attract new customers but faced with legal constraints on traditional banking activities and a relaxation, by the Comptroller of the Currency, of constraints on nonbanking activity, banks were prompted to expand into nonbanking activities under the holding company form. Currently the Federal Reserve Board and Congress are attempting to determine how they should regulate bank holding companies. Which activities should be permitted? Should nonbank affiliates be examined and regulated in the same ways as commercial banks, or should regulators not guarantee their solvency and concentrate only on protecting commercial bank affiliates? The first two articles in this section come to grips with the considerations that underlie these questions by examining the potential cost and benefits of the holding company form of organization. Article 31 by Norman N. Bowsher focuses mostly on the issues surrounding the effect of holding companies on *banking* concentration and competition. He concludes that while commercial banking has changed only moderately as a result of these activities, the net effects have been favorable for the public. Article 32 by Dale S. Drum surveys the issues surrounding bank entry into *nonbanking* activities, concluding that insufficient evidence is available to draw any implications on this important question.

Next Donald I. Baker, after outlining arguments used to rationalize banking regulation, considers some key policy alternatives for the future regulation of branching and chartering by commercial bank businesses.

Have Multibank Holding Companies Affected Commercial Bank Performance?

Norman N. Bowsher

Since the late 1960s there has been a rapid expansion of multibank holding companies which has had far-reaching impacts on the structure of banking in the nation. These multibank holding companies (MBHCs) were established as alternatives to branching systems in a number of states where branch banking was prohibited or severely limited.[1] The holding company device for controlling and managing banks is not new—having been used since about the turn of the century—but its importance has increased dramatically in the last decade. MBHCs' control of commercial bank deposits increased from 8 percent at the end of 1965, to 16 percent at the end of 1970, and to 34 percent at yearend 1976.

The rapid expansion of MBHCs in recent years and the changes in banking structures and practices brought about by this development have generated much controversy regarding the merits and desirability of holding companies. This article reviews evidence on some major issues raised by the emergence of MBHCs.

Reprinted from *Review,* April 1978, pp. 8–15, by permission of the Federal Reserve Bank of St. Louis and the author.

[1]MBHCs have been established in various branch banking states. Organization as an MBHC can have advantages over that of a branch banking system. For instance, a holding company system can often maintain lower aggregate reserves than the same-sized branch network.

Competition and Concentration

There has been a longstanding public concern in this country over the possibilities for excessive concentration in banking. Many have feared that increased concentration would place resource allocation in the hands of a relatively small number of banking organizations in the financial centers. Reflecting these attitudes and policies based on them, the structure of American banking has been unique in the world, with its numerous independent banking institutions. At the same time, because of limits on bank entry and branching, maximum interest rates on deposits, and other regulations, competition has been limited and individual banks, particularly in some smaller communities, have attained some degree of monopoly power.

A chief issue which has emerged with MBHC development has been the effects that these holding companies have had on concentration and competition in banking. With entry into banking limited by prevailing government regulations, acquisitions by holding companies could increase concentration by reducing or eliminating competition, and permit the remaining firms in the market to obtain monopolistic profits by raising prices and lowering services. Since there are no widely agreed upon measures of concentration and competition, and since in some ways increased concentration could be consistent with more, not less, competition, evaluations have not been uniform.[2]

Concentration Nationally

From a review of banking developments since the mid-1960s, it does not appear that national concentration has been a crucial problem. Although numerous acquisitions did affect concentration from what it would likely have been otherwise, given all other factors, concentration has changed only slightly during the period of rapid holding company expansion.

Concentration, as measured by total domestic deposits held by the 100 largest banking organizations in the country, changed little in the period 1957 to 1968 when holding company activity was relatively dormant. From a level of 48.2 percent in 1957, concentration rose slightly to 49 percent in 1968. However, despite an acceleration in holding company acquisitions after 1968, many of which were made by the 100 largest banking organizations, nationwide concentration by these firms decreased from 49 percent of domestic deposits to 47 percent in 1973.[3]

---

[2]Evidence has been advanced which supports both the hypothesis that increased market concentration results from efficiency of large organizations and the hypothesis that increased concentration facilitates collusion among firms. The relationship between efficiency and concentration, by itself, implies that customers gain as a result of higher concentration, but the relationship between collusion and concentration, holding companies are associated with higher concentration, there are both potential benefits and costs for bank customers from such lessened restrictions. Gerald P. Dwyer, Jr. and William C. Niblack, "Branching, Holding Companies, and Banking Concentration in the Eighth District," this *Review* (July 1974), pp. 11–18.

[3]Samuel H. Talley, "The Impact of Holding Company Acquisitions on Aggregate Concentration in Banking," Board of Governors of the Federal Reserve System, *Staff Economic Studies* (80), 1974.

More recent calculations find that between 1963 and mid-1977 the 10 largest banking organizations' share of domestic deposits declined from 20.4 to 18.3 percent while the share of the top 25 dropped from 31.9 to 28 percent. The 100 largest organizations' share declined from 49.7 to 45 percent over this period.[4]

The apparent reason for this somewhat surprising result is that growth of domestic deposits (as distinct from foreign) was slower at the larger banking offices during the 1968–77 period than deposit growth at smaller banking offices. Also, there was a constraining influence on the larger organizations from antitrust laws and policies. Although over one-half of the 100 largest bank holding companies acquired other banks through the holding company device, a large portion of those acquired were *de novo* or small "foothold" acquisitions.

Nevertheless, acquisitions by the 100 largest banking organizations between 1968 and 1973 did maintain nationwide concentration of domestic deposits above what otherwise would have prevailed. If the quantitative impact of these acquisitions is subtracted from the 1973 actual ratio of concentration, the resultant *adjusted* nationwide concentration ratio for 1973 would have been 44.7 percent. Since the actual ratio was 47 percent, holding company acquisitions in the 1968–73 period, everything else equal, increased concentration by 2.3 percentage points above the level that would have existed in the absence of such acquisitions. Thus, the pronounced increase in the share of total deposits of banks in MBHCs, mentioned in the introduction, reflected primarily the largest banks in the nation forming MBHCs and not acquisitions by the large banking organizations.

Concentration Statewide

There is justification for measuring concentration in an area smaller than the nation since the market for most banks is considerably less than the entire country. Since the state is the largest area within which banks can legally branch and form holding companies, and hence attempt to gain monopoly power, some feel that states are the relevant areas for measuring concentration.[5] Also, interbank rivalry may be dependent not only on local market concentration, but also on the degree to which a few large banking organizations in a state, each of which has banking offices in several

[4]Statement by Phillip E. Coldwell, member of the Board of Governors of the Federal Reserve System, before the Committee on Banking, Housing and Urban Affairs, United States Senate, March 7, 1978.

[5]It might be noted, however, that the Justice Department has failed to win a banking case on the grounds of statewide concentration alone or the closely related grounds of potential competition statewide. See Aubrey B. Willacy and Hazel M. Willacy, "Conglomerate Bank Mergers and Clayton 7: Is Potential Competition the Answer?" *Banking Law Journal,* February 1976, pp. 148–95. Nevertheless, the legal issue of whether states are appropriate areas for administering antitrust policies is not settled since legislatures in a few states prohibit expansion by merger or acquisition beyond some statewide concentration level. See Katharine Gibson and Steven J. Weiss, "State-Imposed Limitations on Multibank Holding Company Growth," Federal Reserve Bank of Chicago, *Proceedings of a Conference on Bank Structure and Competition,* 1976, pp. 208–209. Also, Senate Bill S72, the "Competition in Banking Act of 1977," would prohibit bank mergers or holding company acquisitions if the resulting banking institution would control more than 20 percent of the banking assets within the state.

common local markets, agree not to engage in competitive behavior in any such local markets.[6]

Available evidence indicates that trends in statewide concentration in banking have varied markedly from state to state, with average changes remaining small. Between 1960 and 1976, there was no overall trend toward increased concentration of the three largest banking organizations in each state. Calculations of averages of changes indicate that states which allowed statewide branching experienced a very small increase in the proportion of domestic deposits held by the three largest banking organizations: 0.2 percentage point. Limited branching states and unit banking states experienced average decreases of 1.7 and 2.9 percentage points, respectively. Among statewide branching states, those with the highest concentration in 1960 exhibited the greatest decline in concentration, while those with the lowest concentration exhibited the greatest increase.[7]

Among the five largest banking institutions in each state, an increase in concentration occurred in 28 states, a decline in 22 states, with one unchanged in the 1968–73 period (the District of Columbia was treated as a state). The median increase for all states was only 0.7 percentage point. In the 38 states permitting MBHCs, concentration tended to increase during the period, while in the 13 states which prohibited them, concentration tended to decline. Nevertheless, the impact of MBHC acquisitions on statewide concentration was limited almost entirely to states with low or moderate concentration.[8]

It might have been expected that holding company activity would have its greatest impact on concentration at the state level, since holding companies are prohibited from operating in broader regions and since legal actions designed to prevent monopolistic formations are usually focused on smaller banking markets. Yet, what would appear to represent a significant increase in aggregate concentration in some states sometimes does not, in fact, represent any meaningful change in structure. The increases in concentration often involved acquisitions of banks which had formerly operated as members of a banking group unified through common owners and directors and interlocking management.[9]

Concentration in Local Markets

Concentration in local markets is more crucial from a competitive point of view than is concentration nationally or statewide.[10] In a local market, banks and their

---

[6]See Elinor Harris Solomon, "Bank Merger Policy and Problems: A Linkage Theory of Oligopoly," *Journal of Money, Credit and Banking,* August 1970, pp. 323–36.

[7]Statement by Philip E. Coldwell, member of Board of Governors of the Federal Reserve System, before the Committee on Banking, Housing and Urban Affairs, United States Senate, March 7, 1978. See also Manfred O. Peterson, "Aggregate Bank Concentration and the Competition in Banking Act of 1975," *Issues in Bank Regulation* (Park Ridge, Ill.: Bank Administration Institute, 1977), pp. 37–41.

[8]Talley, "The Impact of Holding Company Acquisitions on Aggregate Concentration in Banking," Board of Governors of the Federal Reserve System, *Staff Economic Studies* (80), 1974.

[9]See Nancy M. Goodman, "Holding Company Developments in Michigan," Federal Reserve Bank of Chicago, *Business Conditions,* October 1975, pp. 10–15.

[10]This view has been adopted by the U.S. Supreme Court in evaluating competition. See *U.S. v. Philadelphia National Bank* in 1963; and *U.S. v. Marine Bancorporation* in 1974.

customers are in sufficiently close proximity for competitive interaction to occur, and both information and transaction costs tend to rise for many types of services as the distance between the bank and customer increases, reducing the threat of effective outside competition.[11] Local markets characterized by a structure with relatively few firms and high barriers to entry will facilitate pricing conduct that is aimed at achieving joint profit maximization through collusion, price leadership, or other tacit pricing arrangements.[12] Nevertheless, greater publicity is given to trends in concentration in the nation or at the state level than at the local level. This probably reflects the difficulty of defining a local market, but also reflects a popular misconception that "bigness" alone is a measure of monopoly power.

It appears that concentration has remained unchanged or has decreased in most local banking markets during the period of rapid holding company acquisitions. A study of 213 metropolitan areas and 233 country banking markets over the 1966–75 period concluded that most banking markets became less concentrated in that period. Also, the procompetitive changes in banking market concentration occurred with greatest frequencies and in the largest magnitudes in those markets which had a relatively high concentration ratio in 1966.[13] In addition, local areas experiencing MBHC activity generally had lower initial concentration than areas where no MBHC acquisitions occurred.[14] Also, MBHCs tend to acquire banks in markets characterized by relatively fast growth in terms of banking offices, and relatively favorable ratios of deposits per banking office.[15]

One positive influence on local competition may be stringent standards for approval of holding company acquisitions by the Board of Governors of the Federal Reserve System. Before approval is given to a holding company to acquire a bank, the Board analyzes the effects of the proposal on competition in the local banking markets. An application is denied if its effects would be to reduce materially competition in a local market, unless there are other strong mitigating factors.[16] Managements of relatively large holding companies generally assume that proposed

[11]One study concluded that distance dominates all other factors in determining the selection of a banking office. Lorman L. Lundstein and Lewis Mandell, "Consumer Selection of Banking Office—Effects of Distance, Services and Interest Rate Differentials," Federal Reserve Bank of Chicago, *Proceedings of a Conference on Bank Structure and Competition,* April 1977, pp. 260–86.

[12]See Stephen A. Rhoades, "Structure-Performance Studies in Banking: A Summary and Evaluation," Board of Governors of the Federal Reserve System, *Staff Economic Studies* (92), 1977.

[13]Samuel H. Talley, "Recent Trends in Local Banking Market Structure," Board of Governors of the Federal Reserve System, *Staff Economic Studies* (89), 1977.

[14]Jack S. Light, "Bank Holding Companies—Concentration Levels in Three District States," Federal Reserve Bank of Chicago, *Business Conditions,* June 1975, pp. 10–15. See also, Stephen A. Rhoades, "Characteristics of Banking Markets Entered by Foothold Acquisition," *Journal of Monetary Economics,* July 1976, pp. 399–408, which concluded that the procompetitive effects of holding companies are less than they might otherwise be.

[15]Gregory E. Boczar, "Market Characteristics and Multibank Holding Company Acquisitions," *Journal of Finance,* March 1977, pp. 131–46.

[16]In administering the Bank Holding Company Act, the Board of Governors of the Federal Reserve System has been adamant not only in denying applications by holding companies to acquire existing banks with which they compete, but in addition, the Board has stood ready to deny applications on the basis of potential competition and probable future competition. See Harvey Rosenblum, "Bank Holding Companies—Part II," Federal Reserve Bank of Chicago, *Business Conditions,* April 1975, pp. 13–15.

acquisitions of relatively large independent banks in an area where the MBHC has a subsidiary would be denied, and few such applications are even submitted.

In analyzing the growth of MBHC subsidiaries after acquisitions, no significant effects in the market share of affiliated banks vis-à-vis banks remaining independent were found in four studies.[17] This probably reflects offsetting effects of MBHC affiliation. On the one hand, subsidiaries of MBHCs enjoy greater financial strength and ability to offer a wider range of services. On the other hand, the independent banks, on balance, can probably give more personalized service and adapt more quickly to changing local conditions. Indeed, the independent bank's response to MBHCs in their area has probably intensified competition.

Bank Services

A related issue raised by the MBHC development is the effect of holding company affiliation on the availability and cost of bank services. The evidence available on bank performance is mostly indirect, such as changes in bank operating ratios; hence, most conclusions are tentative.

It has been argued that holding companies are able to offer more and better banking services to the customers of their affiliates than are independents because of their larger size and superior management. This assertion cannot be tested directly, but a reasonable proxy variable for the general quality of banking services is the rate of growth of a bank's deposits. Presumably, banks providing more and better services grow faster than other banks. However, as noted in the previous section, growth of affiliates has not been significantly different on average than growth of competing independent institutions.

Federal Reserve System application of the Holding Company Act probably has some influence on fostering better and broadened service by MBHC affiliates. To promote public interest, the Federal Reserve System evaluates the effects of a bank holding company acquisition on the basis of convenience and needs of the community to be served.[18] Every MBHC application to acquire a bank must include a description of changes, if any, the holding company plans to initiate in either availability or prices of services and how these changes will benefit the public. Proposals frequently include establishment of a trust or foreign banking service, raising interest rates on time and savings deposits to Regulation Q maxima, reducing rates on

---

[17]Lawrence G. Goldberg, "Bank Holding Company Acquisitions and Their Impact on Market Shares," *Journal of Money, Credit and Banking,* February 1976, pp. 127–30; Stuart Hoffman, "The Impact of Holding Company Affiliation on Bank Performance: A Case Study of Two Florida Multibank Holding Companies," Federal Reserve Bank of Atlanta, *Working Paper Series,* January 1976; David D. Whitehead and B. Frank King, "Multibank Holding Companies and Local Market Concentration," Federal Reserve Bank of Atlanta, *Monthly Review,* April 1976, pp. 34–43; and Jerome C. Darnell and Howard Keen, Jr., "Small Bank Survival: Is the Wolf at the Door?" Federal Reserve Bank of Philadelphia, *Busines Review,* November 1974, pp. 16–23.

[18]U.S.C., title 12, section 1843, as amended by Acts of July 1, 1966 (80 Stat. 238) and December 31, 1970 (84 Stat. 1763).

credit insurance premiums, providing data processing services, expanding certain types of loans, and providing more customer facilities, such as parking lots. Convenience and needs factors alone are seldom the decisive factor in ruling on a case but these pledges can be crucial in determining whether the proposal is approved when it appears that other factors are marginal.[19] In one study in which stated intentions of MBHC applications were compared with actual implementation, no instances were found in which promised actions were not subsequently taken. In a number of cases, however, intentions were not fully realized.[20]

Even though many MBHCs have implemented promised services and/or reduced prices, the differences between services offered by MBHC banks and other banks have been marginal. Statistical analyses show that bank branching and size are stronger determinants of most bank behavior ratios than MBHC affiliation.[21] Affiliated banks tend to reduce cash and low-risk securities and increase loans, suggesting greater credit availability by MBHCs.[22] Much of the gain, however, reflects the acquisition of a number of formerly ultra-conservative banks. The ratio of time and savings deposit interest to total time and savings deposits at MBHC affiliates increased relative to those of independent banks, but the change was not statistically significant.[23] The ratio of trust revenue to total revenue tends to be higher for affiliates than for independents, from which some analysts conclude that MBHCs offer more trust services. However, empirical evidence indicates that trust revenue of banks in counties in which one or more banks are affiliated with holding companies was neither higher nor lower than in other counties, holding other factors constant.[24]

In short, most MBHC banks resemble non-MBHC banks.[25] The impact of MBHC management upon the behavior of affiliated banks is best analyzed on an individual bank basis. MBHC acquisition of a "problem bank" or an ultra-conservative bank could serve the public interest, whereas an MBHC acquisition of a well-managed independent bank would apparently offer few public benefits.

A study of the effects of 43 acquisitions of rural community banks in Ohio com-

---

[19]See Michael A. Jessee and Steven A. Seelig, "An Analysis of the Public Benefits Test of the Bank Holding Company Act," Federal Reserve Bank of New York, *Monthly Review,* June 1974, pp. 157–67.

[20]Joseph E. Rossman and B. Frank King, "Multibank Holding Companies: Convenience and Needs," Federal Reserve Bank of Atlanta, *Economic Review,* July/August 1977, pp. 83–91. This study, however, had basic limitations. For example, the results were based primarily on a survey of MBHCs, taking the company's word for what was done.

[21]William Jackson, "Multibank Holding Companies and Bank Behavior," Federal Reserve Bank of Richmond, *Working Paper* 75-1, July 1975.

[22]See Lucille S. Mayne, "A Comparative Study of Bank Holding Company Affiliates and Independent Banks, 1969–1972," *Journal of Finance,* March 1977, pp. 147–58. Another study, however, found that within county changes in bank structure in Ohio by holding company acquisition did not materially alter the supply of credit. Richard L. Gady, "Performance of Rural Banks and Changes in Bank Structure in Ohio," Federal Reserve Bank of Cleveland, *Economic Review,* November/December 1971, pp. 3–14.

[23]Samuel H. Talley, "The Effect of Holding Company Acquisitions on Bank Performance," Board of Governors of the Federal Reserve System, *Staff Economic Studies* (69), 1972.

[24]R. Alton Gilbert, "Trust Revenue of Commercial Banks: The Influence of Bank Holding Companies," Federal Reserve Bank of St. Louis, *Review,* June 1974, pp. 8–15.

[25]See Robert F. Ware, "Characteristics of Banks Acquired by Multibank Holding Companies in Ohio," Federal Reserve Bank of Cleveland, *Economic Review,* August 1971, pp. 19–27.

pared with 101 comparable independent banks in the same communities found several interesting impacts of the MBHCs. The affiliates showed a greater preference for consumer lending, but some lack of interest in real estate and farm lending. Affiliate banks charged higher rates of interest on loans, but they required somewhat lower downpayments and extended credit over slightly longer periods. Independent banks generally provided more auxiliary services with special emphasis on farm management consulting and general tax and financial advice. Holding companies introduced a number of services for the acquired banks, such as data processing, marketing, and loan participation arrangements. Some independent banks responded by joining consortia and relying heavily on correspondents in order to obtain comparable services.[26]

The available evidence suggests that MBHC affiliation has produced a slight enlargement in the availability of banking services. Holding companies have had only a slight net effect on prices of affiliated banks relative to those of the remaining independents. In short, as one might expect in a competitive environment, availability and prices of services have been little different at banks, regardless of corporate form.

Operating Efficiency and Profitability

Although it has frequently been contended that one advantage of joining an MBHC is improved operating efficiency for the acquired bank, empirical evidence does not indicate any such clear improvement of efficiency of affiliates over independents. The impact of affiliation on operating efficiency and profits is difficult to assess from financial statements since MBHCs may attempt to shift reported profits to the consolidated holding company rather than report them for each affiliate. This may be particularly true where the holding company does not completely own the affiliate. One study found no significant change in operating costs when an MBHC acquired a unit bank and an increase in such costs when it acquired a bank with branches.[27]

MBHC affiliates, as components of banking organizations larger than most independent banks, probably experience some economies of scale.[28] MBHCs are able to consolidate risks by generally having a larger asset base and serving a wider geographical area than most independent banks, reducing cash and capital re-

[26]Warren F. Lee and Alan K. Reichert, "Effects of Multibank Holding Company Acquisitions of Rural Community Banks," Federal Reserve Bank of Chicago, *Proceedings of a Conference on Bank Structure and Competition,* May 1–2, 1975, pp. 217–25.

[27]Donald J. Mullineaux, "Branch versus Unit Banking: An Analysis of Relative Costs," *Changing Pennsylvania's Branching Laws: An Economic Analysis,* Federal Reserve Bank of Philadelphia, Technical Paper, 1973, pp. 175–227.

[28]See Ernst Baltensperger, "Economies of Scale, Firm Size, and Concentration in Banking," *Journal of Money, Credit and Banking,* August 1972, pp. 467–88; and Ernst Baltensperger, "Costs of Banking Activities—Interactions Between Risks and Operating Costs," *Journal of Money, Credit and Banking,* August 1972, pp. 595–611.

quirements. Other operating efficiencies for affiliates include better access to capital markets,[29] advertising, data processing, specialized lending, and trust and foreign banking services.

Although ratios of total revenues to total assets have been higher for affiliates than for independent banks, total operating expenses to total assets have also been higher.[30] In particular, MBHCs incur larger employee benefit costs and greater "other expenses" than independent banks.[31] Because MBHCs are usually the larger banking organizations, one would intuitively expect them to have employee benefit plans which would tend to be extended to subsidiaries. The "other expenses" category includes many diverse bank expenses, and the actual reasons for the higher "other expenses" for holding company banks are not known. One could speculate that costs relating to the holding company structure and included in this category, such as management or legal fees, could conceivably drain some "profits" from the subsidiary banks.

Nevertheless, holding company acquisitions have probably had only moderate effects on prices, expenses, profitability, or performance of acquired banks.[32] Since MBHCs have slightly higher operating costs than independent banks, it has been contended that affiliation with a holding company entails net *diseconomies* of scale rather than economies.[33] Using a different line of reasoning, a study of Alabama banks over the period 1968 to 1973 found that, on balance, technical and operational efficiency improved for both independent and affiliate banks. Since this was a period in which the dominant change in the state's banking industry was the emergence of an aggressive MBHC movement, the findings were tentatively attributed to that activity.[34]

Since there are significant differences between individual holding companies, it is probably misleading to group them in some average. Many of the performance mea-

[29]Cost of raising capital tends to be lower for large firms than for smaller enterprise. See Roger D. Blair and Yoram Peles, "The Advantage of Size in the Capital Market: Empirical Evidence and Policy Implications," Center for the Study of American Business, *Working Paper* 24, Washington University, St. Louis, December 1977.

[30]See Rodney D. Johnson and David R. Meinster, "The Performance of Bank Holding Company Acquisitions: A Multivariate Analysis," *Journal of Business,* April 1975, pp. 204–12; and Robert J. Lawrence, Board of Governors of the Federal Reserve System, *The Performance of Bank Holding Companies,* 1967.

[31]Jack S. Light, "Effects of Holding Company Affiliation on De Novo Banks," Federal Reserve Bank of Chicago, *Proceedings of a Conference on Bank Structure and Competition,* 1976, pp. 83–106.

[32]Samuel H. Talley, "The Effect of Holding Company Acquisition on Bank Performance," Board of Governors of the Federal Reserve System, *Staff Economic Studies* (69), 1972. Also, Lucille S. Mayne, "Management Policies of Bank Holding Companies and Bank Performance," *Journal of Bank Research,* Spring 1976, pp. 37–48.

[33]Dale S. Drum, "MBHCs: Evidence After Two Decades of Regulation," Federal Reserve Bank of Chicago, *Business Conditions,* December 1976, pp. 3–15. See also, George J. Benston and Gerald A. Hanweck, "A Summary Report on Bank Holding Company Affiliation and Economies of Scale," Federal Reserve Bank of Chicago, *Conference on Bank Structure and Competition,* April 1977, pp. 158–68.

[34]Terrence F. Martell and Donald L. Hooks, "Holding Company Affiliation and Economies of Scale," *Journal of the Midwest Finance Association,* 1975, pp. 59–71.

sures indicate that operations of banks affiliated with particular holding companies differed significantly from both independent banks and banks affiliated with other holding companies. It was possible in a number of instances to reject the hypothesis that holding-company-affiliated banks can be treated as elements of a single group as far as performance is concerned.[35]

Examining the profitability of MBHC banks compared with independent banks through the use of performance ratios has not produced uniform results. In one study, MBHC affiliation was found to have a negative impact on the ratios of net income to total assets and on net income to equity.[36] Another inquiry found no significant difference in holding company performance on net income to equity from that of independent banks.[37]

Two studies by John Mingo, taken together, hint at a third view of the profitability of MBHC affiliates. The first study found that holding companies tend to purchase banks with earnings to capital ratos below those of other banks.[38] The second found that holding company banks, after acquisition, tend to have higher net earnings to capital ratios than do independent banks.[39] A conclusion that MBHCs improved the profitability of acquired banks, however, may not be warranted in view of the changed samples.

The evidence on the profitability of MBHC affiliates is mixed, and the issue is not likely to be settled soon. In a number of cases, subsidiaries have been less profitable than independents of similar size in the same general area. However, the holding company may be attempting to maximize profits of the system rather than for each subsidiary. Also, many acquisitions have been of banks with below average profitability, and it may take more time to get a fair evaluation of their performance within the holding company. To date, only a few MBHC affiliates have been liquidated, sold, or spun off, indicating that any drag on the system's profitability has not been intolerable.

Bank Soundness

Holding companies claim that they strengthen acquired banks in a number of ways. At times, they provide additional capital, personnel training, or skilled management. They diversify risks and lower the costs of providing certain specialized services. Resources of the entire system can be mobilized to solve a local bank's prob-

[35]Arthur G. Fraas, "The Performance of Individual Bank Holding Companies," Board of Governors of the Federal Reserve System, *Staff Economic Study* (84), 1974.

[36]Jack S. Light, "Effects of Holding Company Affiliation on De Novo Banks," Federal Reserve Bank of Chicago, *Proceedings of a Conference on Bank Structure and Competition,* May 1976, pp. 83–106.

[37]William Jackson, "Multibank Holding Companies and Bank Behavior," Federal Reserve Bank of Richmond, *Working Paper* 75-1, July 1975.

[38]John J. Mingo, "Capital Management and Profitability of Prospective Holding Company Banks," *Journal of Financial and Quantitative Analysis,* June 1975, pp. 191–203.

[39]John J. Mingo, "Managerial Motives, Market Structure and the Performance of Holding Company Banks," *Economic Inquiry,* September 1976, pp. 411–24.

lems. Yet, most analyses have indicated that the alleged benefits of MBHCs on bank soundness are exaggerated. It is still not clear whether the holding company movement has, on balance, increased or reduced the soundness of banks.

The Board of Governors of the Federal Reserve System denies applications of proposed holding company acquisitions if the payments necessary to retire debt incurred in buying the bank's stock would be likely to drain its retained earnings. In addition, capital has been supplied by the parent holding companies to a number of subsidiaries. Nevertheless, the capital positions of a number of acquired banks have been relatively low. The average ratio of capital to total assets or deposits is generally lower for affiliated banks than for independent counterparts.[40] However, it has been found that holding company affiliation caused only a small decline in the capital to deposits ratio, one which was not statistically significant.[41]

MBHC banks, on average, are leveraged to a greater extent than independent banks (as measured by lower capital/asset ratios), and hold greater proportions of higher-yielding (presumably more risky) assets than do comparable independents. Also, as market concentration increases, capital to asset ratios rise for independent banks as a class but decline for holding company banks. Such observations suggest that independent banks take most benefits of greater market power in the form of reduced risk, while MBHC banks are less risk-averse.[42] Although affiliation tends to increase the payout ratio (dividends to net income) for affiliated banks,[43] the funds may still be retained within the MBHC organization.

Through the use of the holding company, some organizations have engaged in "double leveraging"—that is, raising funds through parent debt issues and "downstreaming" equity capital to bank subsidiaries. This practice allows the subsidiaries to increase reported capital ratios, while increasing the leverage of the holding company as a whole.[44]

A conclusion that affiliated companies hold less capital to assets or deposits than their independent counterparts does not necessarily indicate that they are undercapitalized or less stable.[45] The risks of banking are usually more diversified by having a larger asset base, by engaging in more activities and by operating over a wider region in an MBHC arrangement than for an individual bank. Since such diversification reduces the lead bank's risk, the MBHC might assume a somewhat greater

[40]See Arthur G. Fraas, "The Performance of Individual Bank Holding Companies," Board of Governors of the Federal Reserve System, *Staff Economic Study* (84), 1974, and William Jackson, "Multibank Holding Companies and Bank Behavior," Federal Reserve Bank of Richmond, *Working Paper* 75-1, July 1975.

[41]Samuel H. Talley, "The Effect of Holding Company Acquisitions on Bank Performance," Board of Governors of the Federal Reserve System, *Staff Economic Studies* (69), 1972.

[42]John J. Mingo, "Managerial Motives, Market Structures, and the Performance of Holding Company Banks," *Economic Inquiry,* September 1976, pp. 411-24.

[43]William Jackson, "Multibank Holding Companies and Bank Behavior," Federal Reserve Bank of Richmond, *Working Paper* 75-1, July 1975.

[44]See Federal Reserve *Bulletin,* February 1976, p. 115.

[45]See "Bank Holding Company Financial Developments in 1976," Board of Governors of the Federal Reserve System, Federal Reserve *Bulletin,* April 1977, pp. 337-40.

risk in each of its subsidiaries than otherwise without increasing the exposure of the system.[46] Hence, even though an individual affiliate has less capital cushion, this might be matched by help it could reasonably expect from its parent should adversity arise.[47]

Summary and Conclusions

Despite a tremendous expansion of MBHCs during the last decade, commercial banking has changed only moderately as a result of these activities.[48] Recognizing that it is too early to appraise adequately all the ramifications, the weight of the evidence so far seems to indicate that the net effects of the holding company movement have been favorable for the general public. The fear that commercial banking would become less competitive if holding companies were permitted has not been substantiated. In many local markets, affiliates of MBHCs have increased competition, and the independent bank's response to the introduction of a holding company competitor has frequently also been to intensify competition.

On balance, MBHCs have offered a slightly wider range of banking services and have increased credit extended to consumers and small businesses over what otherwise would have been likely. As a result, revenues of affiliates have been higher than at independent banks, but costs have also been greater.

Affiliates of MBHCs are not as well capitalized as their independent counterparts, but risk is reduced through greater diversification. Independent banks do not seem to have been harmed by the introduction of a holding company operation in their market area, having grown at roughly the same rate as similar-sized MBHC affiliates. Evidence on profitability of affiliates versus independent banks is still mixed.

[46]Leverage was found to be statistically significant in explaining market risk premium on long-term debt when bank issues alone were examined, but was statistically insignificant when issues of bank holding companies alone were analyzed. Anne S. Weaver and Chayim Herzig-Marx, "A Comparative Study of the Effect of Leverage on Risk Premiums for Debt Issues of Banks and Bank Holding Companies," Federal Reserve Bank of Chicago, Staff Memoranda, 1978.

[47]Nevertheless, the potential benefit from diversification in MBHC organizations has been found to be limited due to the relatively homogeneous nature of holding company acquisitions of banks. See Peter S. Rose, "The Pattern of Bank Holding Company Acquisitions," *Journal of Bank Research,* Autumn 1976, pp. 236–40.

[48]See Stephen A. Rhoades, "Structure and Performance Studies in Banking: A Summary and Evaluation," Board of Governors of the Federal Reserve System, *Staff Economic Studies* (92), December 1977, p. 45. Based on a review of 39 studies of market structure and performance published since 1959, it was concluded that the changed market structure has had only a small quantitative effect on price or profit performance in banking.

Nonbanking Activities of Bank Holding Companies

Dale S. Drum

Although bank holding companies (BHCs) have existed for over three-quarters of a century, their impact on the banking and financial sectors has become significant only in the past decade.[1] Prior to 1971 BHCs were divided into two basic types, multibank and one-bank holding companies. Multibank holding companies (MBHCs) were defined as corporate entities controlling at least 25 percent of the ownership of two or more banks and since 1956 have been required to register with the Board of Governors of the Federal Reserve System. Historically, MBHCs have been used largely to circumvent intrastate and interstate branch banking prohibitions, but in recent years, they have been expanding into nonbanking areas.

One-bank holding companies (OBHCs), on the other hand, have had a more varied history. Originally, OBHCs were organized by families or individuals to control small banks while at the same time gaining certain tax advantages offered by incorporation. In other instances large nonfinancial holding companies would acquire a bank to facilitate the availability of banking services for their customers and

Reprinted from *Economic Perspectives*, March/April 1977, pp. 12–21, by permission of the Federal Reserve Bank of Chicago and the author.

Note: Numbers in brackets [ ] refer to the numerically listed bibliography. Citations are either to studies the results of which are described in this article or to scholarly elaborations of topics discussed.

[1]The historical and legal development of bank holding companies has been traced in several articles in *Business Conditions* [22, 29, 30]. The banking aspects of multibank holding companies were surveyed in the December 1976 issue [9].

employees. This latter type was frequently referred to as a "conglomerate" bank holding company [22, 25, 29].

About a decade ago, however, a distinct change occurred in the rationale behind the formation of OBHCs. This marked phenomenon was the bank-originated OBHC, whereby the holding company was formed at the initiative of the bank itself. By so doing, the bank holding company could diversify both the range of financial activities it could perform and the geographic area it served. Prior to the 1970 amendments to the Bank Holding Company Act of 1956, OBHCs were neither required to register with the Board nor were they subject to the act's restrictions. Many of the activities performed by OBHCs, though financial in nature, were activities prohibited both to banks per se and to registered (multibank) holding companies. The term "congeneric" has frequently been applied to this form of BHC [22, 25, 29].

The rapid growth of OBHCs and their tendency to acquire nonbanking business enterprises raised the spectre of the *Zaibatsu* (large multi-industry combinations common in Japan) dominating the American economy and threatening the traditional separation of banking from commerce. The logic of allowing banks to perform functions indirectly which they could not perform directly was questioned. In addition, the combination of banking with related nonbanking activities could produce anticompetitive effects. These concerns precipitated the inclusion of OBHCs into the act via the 1970 amendments, which restricted OBHCs to the same range of activities permitted MBHCs and also liberalized the criteria for determining the permissibility of new activities.

This article presents, in light of economic analysis and empirical evidence, the issues surrounding BHC entry into nonbanking activities. These issues include the permissible nonbanking activities, diversification, risk and the soundness of BHCs and the banking system, concentration and competition, operating efficiency, and pricing and profitability. Unfortunately, however, the empirical evidence available to decide the issues is scanty because (1) nearly all attention heretofore has been focused on the banking aspects of MBHCs; (2) the gathering and analyzing of data from affiliated nonbanking subsidiaries is extremely costly; and (3) data from nonbanking nonaffiliated firms operating in nonbanking activities are very limited, thus making meaningful comparisons difficult.

Permissible Activities

The list of permissible nonbanking activities for BHCs (see table) has increased only slightly during the last two years[2]—one new activity was approved, while five proposed activities were denied and two were placed "under consideration." There are apparently three reasons for the slackening. To begin with, the Board has adopted a "go slow" policy toward all BHC expansion, including both new activities and the

---

[2]The regulatory status of nonbank activities as of February 1975 is given in [30, pt. 1, pp. 3–6].

Status of Bank Holding Company Nonbanking Activities under Section 4(c)(8)
(as of March 11, 1977)

Activities Approved by the Board	Activities Denied by the Board
1. Dealer in bankers' acceptances[2]	1. Equity funding (combined sale of mutual funds & insurance)
2. Mortgage banking[2]	2. Underwriting general life insurance
3. Finance companies[2]	3. Real estate brokerage[2]
a. consumer	4. Land development
b. sales	5. Real estate syndication
c. commercial	6. General management consulting
4. Credit card issuance[2]	7. Property management
5. Factoring company[2]	8. Nonfull-payout leasing[1]
6. Industrial banking	9. Commodity trading[1]
7. Servicing loans[2]	10. Issuance and sale of short-term debt obligations ("thrift notes")[1]
8. Trust company[2]	11. Travel agency[1,2]
9. Investment advising[2]	12. Savings and loan associations[1]
10. General economic information[2]	
11. Portfolio investment advice[2]	**Activities Pending Before the Board**
12. Full payout leasing[2]	
a. personal property	1. Armored car services[2]
b. real property	2. Underwriting mortgage guarantee insurance[3]
13. Community welfare investments[2]	3. Underwriting & dealing in U.S. Government and certain municipal securities[2,3]
14. Bookkeeping & data processing services[2]	4. Underwriting the deductible part of bankers' blanket bond insurance (withdrawn)[1]
15. Insurance agent or broker—credit extensions[2]	5. Management consulting to nonaffiliated, depository type, financial institutions[1,2]
16. Underwriting credit life & credit accident & health insurance	
17. Courier service[2]	
18. Management consulting to nonaffiliate banks[2]	
19. Issuance of travelers checks[2]	
20. Bullion broker[2]	
21. Land escrow services[1,2]	
22. Issuing money orders and variable denominated payment instruments[1,2,4]	

[1] Added to list since January 1, 1975.

[2] Activities permissible to national banks.

[3] These were found to be "closely related to banking" but the proposed acquisitions were denied by the Board of Governors as part of its "go slow" policy.

[4] To be decided on a case-by-case basis.

acquiring of nonbanking firms engaged in activities already permissible. For example, the Board has denied applications to acquire mortgage guarantee insurance companies and firms underwriting and dealing in U.S. Government and certain municipal securities. Although all of these meet the criteria of being "closely related to banking" (see below), the Board apparently did not believe the time and circumstances were "right" for BHC entry.

In addition, it is conceivable that the list of permissible activities is close to being exhausted. To be exempt from prohibition, nonbanking activities must meet a two-part test. First, each activity must be "closely related to banking or managing or controlling banks." To qualify for exemption, one of the following connections must be made:

1. that banks generally have in fact provided the proposed service;
2. that banks generally provide services that are operationally or functionally so similar to the proposed services as to equip them particularly well to provide the proposed services;
3. that banks generally provide services that are so integrally related to the proposed services as to require their provision in a specialized form.[3]

Second, the activity must be "a proper incident" to banking and must pass a "net public benefits" test, requiring that the possible benefits to the public—greater convenience, increased competition, or efficiency gains accruing from the acquisition—outweigh possible adverse effects—increased concentration, decreased competition, or unsound banking practices. Since many of the activities clearly meeting both these criteria have already been approved by the Board, the number of future additions to the list of permissible activities is likely to be small. In February the Board determined that the ownership of savings and loan associations by BHCs is not a permissible activity. Although considered "closely related to banking," in the Board's view the potential adverse effects of affiliation with banking outweigh the potential benefits.

Lastly, the adverse economic conditions during the 1973–75 period caused serious financial problems for some BHCs resulting in the fall of BHC stock prices and contributing to the Board's "go slow" policy. Many BHCs have been reluctant to push for either new activities or new acquisitions, which has been reflected by a considerable reduction in BHC applications of both types being submitted to the Board in recent years. However, as economic conditions improve, this trend is likely to be reversed [26].

The Board has been criticized by some for being too permissive with respect to the activities BHCs are allowed to perform, while it has been criticized by others for being too restrictive. Clearly, both criticisms cannot simultaneously be correct, and they serve to highlight certain problems faced by the Board in ruling on proposed activities.

First, the words "closely related to banking" in Section 4(c)(8) of the act are extremely vague. Essentially, the interpretation was left up to the Board, subject to judicial review. To some degree the Board may feel constrained by what it believes the courts will accept.

Second, it appears that the Board, in making its determinations on activities, considers those activities which are permissible for national banks. With a few exceptions the permissible activities for bank holding companies and national banks are

---

[3]*Federal Reserve Bulletin,* February 1976, p. 149.

nearly identical (see table). Thus the range of activities BHCs may perform is not very different from that of many banks.

Two other facets of the controversy over the nonbanking activities of BHCs should be noted. While the list of permissible activities is impressive, BHC entry by acquisition has been predominantly limited to three areas: consumer and commercial finance, mortgage banking, and insurance (underwriting and broker or agency) [26]. De novo entry has, by and large, been limited to these three plus leasing and advisory services. Intuitively, these activities seem to afford the greatest opportunity for the application of banking expertise.

Given the controversy surrounding the importance and range of nonbanking activities, one would expect that these activities constitute a relatively significant proportion of the BHC organization. Quite the contrary is true, however. Currently, nonbanking subsidiaries account for less than 5 percent of the total consolidated assets of BHCs [8, 32] and about 3 percent of the assets of the largest 50 BHCs [33].

Risk, Soundness, and BHCs

Perhaps the most important and controversial current issue regarding entry of BHCs into nonbank activities has been the impact of such expansion and diversification upon the integrity and soundness of affiliate banks, the holding company, and the banking system. Although BHCs entered nonbanking areas en masse following the 1970 amendments, entry into these activities has subsided while the controversy has continued.

Proponents of BHC expansion argue that through acquisition of nonbank subsidiaries, the overall level of risk for a given level of return can be lowered, thereby strengthening the BHC and, consequently, the banking system. Performance of nonbank activities allows a BHC to diversify both by activity and by geographic market area, especially since nonbank activities may be performed across state lines. Ever since the advent of multiproduct and multimarket firms, the logic of diversification has been employed by firms in nonregulated industries to stabilize the profitability of the total organization by insulating it from seasonal or cyclical variations affecting the organization's component divisions.

Opponents of BHC expansion question whether entry into nonbank activities has actually stabilized the banking industry by reducing risk per dollar of investment. They also raise issues regarding permissible types of risks for BHCs.

The spectrum of alternatives ranges from permitting BHCs to engage in no activity riskier than traditional banking services to allowing BHCs to undertake activities considered much riskier than the basic functions of banking. The Board's position on BHC activities appears to be about midway between these two extremes.

The assessment of risks differs among depositors, managers, owners, and regulators. The Board, however, must view the riskiness of nonbank activities within the context of safety for the entire banking system, a constraint not imposed by the other groups. That is, the Board must consider the riskiness of each activity with respect to the bank affiliate and ultimately upon the banking system, whereas the other groups view the bank affiliate as one of several activities to be performed by the enterprise.

Economists and financial analysts disagree over methods for quantifying risk, giving rise to many views regarding the identification and objective measurement of various risks. Consequently, the relationship between diversification and risk and the resultant impacts on the soundness of individual BHCs and the entire banking system is difficult to assess.

Risk is essentially the lack of perfect knowledge in making decisions. A relevant measure of BHC performance is the mean, or average, rate of return either on assets or equity capital. A frequently used, but not universally accepted, statistical measure of risk is the standard deviation (or variance) of the rate of return, which shows the dispersion (variation) of the profit rate about its average value.

Two principal views exist regarding the relationship of risk, diversification, and permissible BHC activities. One view holds that risk, measured by the standard deviation or variance of the rate of return alone, is a sufficient criterion for determining the desirability of entering nonbank activities. Any activity having a greater variance in its rate of return than banking is defined as being riskier than banking, and some analysts extend this to say these should not be permissible activities. A second view holds that variance alone is not a sufficient criterion. Rather, the proper criterion in evaluating activities should be risk relative to the expected, or average, return, although some upper limit to the amount of risk appropriate for BHCs to assume is probably implicit.

In combining two activities, risk becomes a function not only of the individual variances, but also of the degree of correlation between the profit rates of the activities. If the profit rate of two activities exhibits negative correlation, the variance of the combined profit rate, and thus the risk, will be lower than each activity taken alone. If the activities are positively correlated, the advantages of diversification may still exist. Combining activities having positive correlation between the rates of return may possibly increase the total risk but reduce the risk relative to the total level of production. The return to the BHC, as with any investment portfolio, is likely to be more stable the wider the range of activities (industry securities) held. In general, firms in the same industry are more likely to do poorly at the same time than are firms in unrelated industries.

An interesting situation arises regarding those activities that pass the "closely related to banking" test of Section 4(c)(8) of the act. The more closely related the nonbank activity is to banking, the more likely there will be a positive correlation between the profits of that activity and banking, and the smaller the advantages arising from the diversification principles. BHCs can, therefore, reduce their relative risk exposure most by expanding into the nonbank areas most remote from banking (unless earnings variances are a great deal higher than in banking). From 1956–70 only one activity—banking—was explicitly permitted bank holding companies by the act, and little exercise of the diversification motive was open to BHCs.

The justification for diversification is not solely restricted to the expected reduction in the variation of profits. Diversification also helps mitigate uncertainty; in particular, by lessening a BHC's dependence on one activity, it reduces the potential losses if that activity were to become obsolete or unnecessary.

Before we can make any assessment of the impact diversification has had upon the soundness of the banking system, we must know the risk levels associated with each of the nonbanking activities BHCs are likely to enter, as well as the degree of correlation between their profits and profits in banking.[4]

Because nonbanking activities are required to be "closely related to banking," one might expect the correlation between the profits of banking and several of the nonbanking activities to be positive since they would be subject to common influences. While limited empirical evidence exists on this issue, one study indicates that the profits of several permissible nonbank activities are *negatively* correlated with bank profits, suggesting that it is possible to significantly reduce a BHC's level of overall risk by diversifying into these activities [14]. For example, the returns in insurance and real estate financing tend to be high when returns in banking are low. On the other hand, the profitability of other nonbank activities—such as business credit, consumer credit, and loan servicing—exhibits a positive correlation with bank profits. The different leasing functions have mixed correlations. These correlations are based upon the profits of each industry and are predicated on the activities being performed independently. Once banking is combined with another activity under the same corporate umbrella, these correlations may no longer hold.

With respect to measuring the degree of risk in various activities, the evidence is somewhat contradictory. One study, measuring risk by the coefficient of variation of industry profit rates (the standard deviation of the profit rate divided by the average profit rate), found banking to be one of the most risky activities that BHCs are allowed to perform [14]. Another study, measuring risk by the standard deviation in the monthly rate of return on the common stock of firms in various industries over the 1961–68 period, found banking to be the least risky of the activities considered [11]. While both studies have shortcomings, the latter was characterized by a very small sample size (e.g., only 19 banks, two mortgage banking firms, one insurance company). Moreover, the return (and standard deviation) was computed on a monthly basis, which would seem to be meaningful only from the viewpoint of the small investor. The actual annual profits of the firm—an item of major interest to managers, controlling owners, and regulators in assessing risk—were ignored in the study.

Thus, empirical evidence currently is not sufficient to judge which nonbanking activities, taken in isolation, are more risky than banking and which are less risky; nor is it adequate to identify those activities having the greatest stabilizing effect on holding company profits.

While the variation in and correlation of profits are important concerns in dealing with soundness, they are not the only concerns, Another is the problem of capital-

---

[4]Industrial firms practicing diversification have not enjoyed unequivocal success. Diversification *per se* may not have been the cause of this lack of success, however, since too rapid growth and expansion, undercapitalization, and adverse economic conditions may also have contributed to their lackluster performance.

ization, both of the BHC and of the nonbank affiliate. The question has been raised whether parent holding companies tend to be undercapitalized [5, 21, 34], and there is some evidence to indicate that they are [21]. Also, some evidence suggests that BHC nonbank affiliates in consumer finance and mortgage banking have lower equity capital-to-total asset ratios than the respective industry standards [35] (referred to as leverage, but this is only one of several possible definitions in use). Whether BHC nonbank subsidiaries in other activities are more highly leveraged than their nonaffiliated competitors is not known. Furthermore, the statistical methodology is somewhat faulty in that no effort was made to measure each firm's leverage ratio prior to acquisition. It is conceivable that the preacquisition leverage was also higher than the industry standards.

In the final analysis, however, a more preferable method of evaluating the soundness of the banking system might be to simultaneously examine the mean and variance of earnings *and* the capital structure [36]. While this approach seems intuitively appealing, most studies have focused on one or the other.

Other factors play important roles in determining the soundness of the banking and financial sectors. For example, the soundness of any business entity depends upon the degree to which it is legally insulated from the other bank or nonbank companies with which it is affiliated. Soundness also depends upon the degree to which BHCs provide their affiliates with financial and managerial resources, thereby strengthening the affiliates. By instituting more aggressiveness and risk into the operating policies of affiliates or introducing intersubsidiary transactions having the eventual effect of weakening the bank or other affiliates, BHCs could significantly weaken themselves and the banking and financial sectors. These considerations are important, but at the present time we have little knowledge of their extent and impact.

In sum, it appears at this time that we are a long way from having any definite knowledge of the impact of the nonbank activities of BHCs upon the soundness of the banking and financial sectors. The partial evidence which is available provides tenuous answers at best. As a final thought, it should be noted that even if entry into the nonbank activities were to reduce the risk of failure for the BHC, the external social cost of failure will very likely rise because as the organization becomes larger, the absolute cost of failure both to the organization and to the financial system also becomes greater [5]. Therefore, the net effect depends on what happens to the "expected cost" of failure, obtained by multiplying the increased cost of failure by the reduced probability of occurrence.

But, to the extent that nonbank expansion is a substitute, rather than a complement, to bank expansion, the overall size of BHCs need not increase.

Concentration and Competition

After the 1970 amendments were passed, BHCs moved rapidly into many of the permissible nonbanking areas, creating concern about the impact this expansion would have upon the concentration of economic resources.[5] One of the primary factors the Board is required to consider under Section 4(c)(8) of the act is the prevention of "an undue concentration of resources." Typically, concentration is discussed at three levels: aggregate or nationwide concentration, statewide concentration, and local or market concentration. Unfortunately, comment on the effects of nonbanking activities upon statewide concentration is not possible at this time because no work has been done in the area.

Aggregate Concentration Since BHCs participate in banking as well as nonbanking (but closely related to banking) activities, the phrase "concentration of resources" must refer to financial resources. Between 1966 and 1973 the share of total financial assets held by the largest 100 BHCs increased from 16 percent to 29 percent [33].[6] While this increase is substantial, it is questionable whether a 29 percent share accounted for by the largest 100 firms constitutes undue concentration by the standards of most U.S. "industries." It should be kept in mind, however, that BHC entry into the nonbanking areas has not been uniform across activities.

On the other hand, it does not appear that BHC entry into nonbanking activities, per se, has been a major contributor to this increase in aggregate concentration. The Board has limited entry into these activities largely to either de novo or foothold entry; as a result, nonbank assets account for less than 5 percent of consolidated holding company assets for all U.S. BHCs and only 3 percent for the largest 50 BHCs. While the amount of assets held in nonbank activities has been growing, it does not explain the 13 percentage point increase in the share of financial assets held by the 100 largest BHCs. Rather, this change appears to be more likely a result of the increased use by large banks of nondeposit sources of funds to finance asset growth.

Local (Market) Concentration Market concentration is, by far, the most important measure of concentration because it is most closely associated with the degree of competition in a local area [9]. While there is no direct evidence on this issue with respect to nonbank activities, it may be possible to get some insight into the future by looking at the Board's policies related to permissible forms of entry into nonbank activities.

The Board seems to be following a two-part policy regarding BHC entry into the nonbanking areas. First, the acquisition of large firms (i.e., firms having a large share of the market) is discouraged [17]. Second, entry into new markets by either de novo or foothold means is encouraged. In particular, the Board has made de novo entry administratively much simpler than the acquisition of a going concern. De novo entry has been emphasized because it adds a new decision maker to the market and increases the number of competing firms, thereby raising the likelihood that BHC entry will have a procompetitive effect. De novo entry would probably be less prevalent in the absence of the act and the Board's enforcement policies.

With regard to credit services it is possible that BHC activity has improved the

---

[5]For a fuller conceptual discussion of concentration and competition, see [9].
[6]Excluding foreign branch assets, however, the figures are 15 percent and 24 percent, respectively. The largest relative increase has thus been in this category.

allocation of financial resources. Being able to expand geographically, especially interstate, has allowed BHCs to compete over a wider area, and thereby offer credit in locations where the demand is greatest.

At the same time, however, the magnitude of mortgage lending has apparently not been affected by BHC affiliation. Preliminary evidence indicates affiliated mortgage banks grow no faster than nonaffiliated mortgage banks, while commercial banks neither increase nor decrease their mortgage lending activity upon affiliation with a mortgage bank [27].

Operating Efficiency

Improved operating efficiency for nonbank firms is a commonly cited benefit of affiliation with a bank holding company. That is, through affiliation, the nonbank firm can potentially achieve some cost reductions through the parent holding company's ability to generate new business for the nonbank affiliate, thus increasing the affiliate's level of output. If the affiliate is operating on the downward sloping portion of its average cost curve, this increase in output could then be translated into lower unit cost. The public would benefit if and when this lower unit cost is passed on in the form of lower charges. Even if they are not passed on, lower operating costs would increase the profitability of the bank holding company, thus enhancing the strength of the banking and financial systems.

A second source of potential cost savings arises from economies of affiliation, which could result if some of the functions previously performed by the independent firm were centralized at the BHC level or if the purchase of some inputs was centralized. For example, since the parent company may have greater access to the capital market, it may be able to acquire capital funds for the affiliate at a lower rate than an independent firm of equal size could obtain.

While these arguments have intuitive appeal, at the present time there is no evidence to support them. No systematic effort has been made to study empirically the impact of BHC affiliation upon the operating costs of nonbanking firms. On the other hand, studies examining the impact of affiliation upon banking firms indicate that affiliated banks, for some reasons, have higher costs than independent banks [9]. While the exact causes of this phenomenon have not been determined, one possible reason is that affiliate banks are subject to higher charges from the nonbank subsidiaries or the parent holding company [9]. A definitive judgment cannot be made at this time as to the impact of affiliation upon the operating efficiency of firms engaged in nonbanking activities; more work needs to be done in this area.

Pricing and Profitability

Pricing In the eyes of the Board public benefits arise from BHC performance of nonbank activities when affiliates charge lower prices for any given service than their nonaffiliated competitors. Empirical evidence on this issue is sparse and provides little insight. The only nonbanking activity about which there is any evidence is insurance underwriting. Regulation Y stipulates that BHCs cannot underwrite credit life, accident, or health insurance unless the premiums charged are less than the ceiling rates established by the state. According to a recent study analyzing the results of this policy, rates charged by BHC affiliates in 1974 resulted in approximately a 13 percent savings in premiums [28].

Profitability   Because of the lack of information concerning either the operating efficiency or pricing of nonbank affiliates, the impact of affiliation on the profitability of nonbank companies cannot be predicted. However, a recent study covering 1973 and 1974 indicates that the rates of return on invested capital in two of the more popular nonbank activities—mortgage banking and consumer finance—are considerably lower for BHC affiliates than for each respective industry as a whole [35]. There are at least three reasons for this occurrence. First, because of their comparatively recent entry into these activities, BHC affiliates could be charging lower prices in an effort to attract customers from their longer-established competitors; second, affiliates could be incurring higher costs; or third, affiliates could be carrying higher levels of invested capital than the average firm in the industry (which contradicts Talley's study). Some combination of the three is also possible. At the present time, however, which influences may predominate is not ascertainable. Additionally, because the profitability of these firms prior to affiliation is not known, their lower rates of return may not be due to affiliation.

Summary

Nonbanking activities of BHCs are a hotly contested issue which will become even more heated in the future. To draw any definitive conclusions, based on evidence available at this time, about the efficacy of BHC entry into the nonbanking areas and the resultant impact on the financial system would be overstepping the bounds of credibility. Evidence to support any conclusions is lacking both in quantity and quality, and unfortunately, if historical experience is a guide, probably half a decade will pass before we are in a position to make a more definitive declaration.

REFERENCES

1. BAKER, DONALD. "An Antitrust Look at the One-Bank Holding Company." In Federal Reserve Bank of Chicago. *Proceedings of a Conference on Bank Structure and Competition . . . 1969,* pp. 125–31. Chicago, 1969.
2. BUNTING, JOHN R. "One-Bank Holding Companies: A Banker's View." *Harvard Business Review* XLVIII (May/June, 1969), pp. 99–106.
3. CHASE, SAMUEL B., JR. "Bank Holding Companies, the Profit Motive and the Public Interest." In Federal Reserve Bank of Minneapolis. *Banking Organizations and Their Regulation: Proceedings of a Conference . . . 1973,* pp. 15–21. Minneapolis, 1974.

4. CHASE, SAMUEL B., JR. "The Bank Holding Company as a Device for Sheltering Banks from Risk." In Federal Reserve Bank of Chicago. *Proceedings of a Conference on Bank Structure and Competition . . . 1971,* pp. 38–54. Chicago, 1971.

5. CHASE, SAMUEL B., JR. and MINGO, JOHN J. "The Regulation of Bank Holding Companies." *Journal of Finance* XXX (May 1975), pp. 281–92.

6. CHILDS, BRADLEY D. "Bank Holding Company Acquisitions: The Role of Non-Banking Financial Activities." *Bank Administration* LI (August 1975), pp. 30–33.

7. COLDWELL, PHILLIP E. "Ten C's of Holding Company Regulation." Remarks before the Fall meeting of the Association of Bank Holding Companies, Phoenix, Arizona, November 1976.

8. COLDWELL, PHILLIP E. "Statement before the Subcommittee on Financial Institutions Supervision, Regulation, and Insurance of the Committee on Banking, Currency, and Housing, U.S. House of Representatives." *Federal Reserve Bulletin* LXII (February 1976), pp. 113–19.

9. DRUM, DALE S. "MBHCs: Evidence After Two Decades." Federal Reserve Bank of Chicago. *Business Conditions,* December 1976, pp. 3–15.

10. EDWARDS, FRANKLIN R. "Tie-In Sales in Banking and One-Bank Holding Companies." *Antitrust Bulletin* XIV (Fall 1969), pp. 587–605.

11. EISEMANN, PETER C. "Diversification and the Congeneric Bank Holding Company." *Journal of Bank Research* VII (Spring 1976), pp. 68–77.

12. FISCHER, GERALD. "Market Extension by Bank Holding Companies: History, Economic Implications, and Current Issues." In Federal Reserve Bank of Chicago. *Proceedings of a Conference on Bank Structure and Competition . . . 1969,* pp. 43–72. Chicago, 1969.

13. HALL, GEORGE. "Some Impacts of One-Bank Holding Companies." In Federal Reserve Bank of Chicago. *Proceedings of a Conference on Bank Structure and Competition . . . 1969,* pp. 73–94. Chicago, 1969.

14. HEGGESTAD, ARNOLD A. "Riskiness of Investments in Nonbank Activities by Bank Holding Companies." *Journal of Economics and Business* XLVII (Spring, 1975), pp. 219–23.

15. HOLLAND, ROBERT C. "Bank Holding Companies and Financial Stability." *Journal of Financial & Quantitative Analysis* X (November, 1975), pp. 577–87.

16. JESSEE, MICHAEL A. "An Analysis of Risk-Taking Behavior in Bank Holding Companies." Ph.D. Dissertation. University of Pennsylvania, 1976.

17. JESSEE, MICHAEL A., and SEELIG, STEVEN A. "An Analysis of the Public Benefits Test of the Bank Holding Company Act." Federal Reserve Bank of New York. *Monthly Review,* June 1974, pp. 151–62.

18. JOHNSON, RICHARD B., ed. *The Bank Holding Company, 1973.* Dallas: Southern Methodist University Press, 1973.

19. LAWRENCE, ROBERT J., and SAMUEL H. TALLEY. "An Assessment of Bank Holding Companies." *Federal Reserve Bulletin* LXII (January 1976), pp. 15–21.

20. LERNER, E. M. "Three Financial Problems Facing Bank Holding Companies." *Journal of Money, Credit and Banking* IV (May 1972), pp. 445–55.

21. MINGO, JOHN J., RHOADES, STEPHEN A., and WOLKOWITZ, BENJAMIN. "Risk and Its Implications for the Banking System." *Bank Administration,* LII, Pt. I (February 1976), pp. 52–58; Pt. II (March 1976), pp. 47–51.

22. MOTE, LARRY R. "The One-Bank Holding Company—History, Issues, and Pending Legislation." Federal Reserve Bank of Chicago. *Business Conditions,* July 1970, pp. 2–16.

23. NADER, RALPH, and JONATHAN BROWN. "Disclosure and Bank Soundness: Non Bank Activities of Bank Holding Companies." Washington, Public Interest Research Group, June 30, 1976.

24. NADLER, PAUL S. "One-Bank Holding Companies: The Public Interest." *Harvard Business Review* XLVII (May/June 1969), pp. 107–13.

25. "One-Bank Holding Companies before the 1970 Amendments." *Federal Reserve Bulletin* LVII (December 1972), pp. 999–1008.

26. RHOADES, STEPHEN A. "Changes in the Structure of Bank Holding Companies since 1970." *Bank Administration* LII (October 1976), pp. 64–69.

27. RHOADES, S. A. "The Effect of Bank-Holding Company Acquisitions of Mortgage Bankers on Mortgage Lending Activity." *Journal of Business* XLVIII (July 1975), pp. 344–48.

28. ROSENBLUM, HARVEY. "A Cost-Benefit Analysis of the Bank Holding Company Act of 1956." Unpublished paper presented at the Western Economic Association Conference, San Francisco, California, June 1976.

29. ROSENBLUM, HARVEY. "Bank Holding Companies: An Overview." Federal Reserve Bank of Chicago. *Business Conditions,* August 1973, pp. 3–13.

30. ROSENBLUM, HARVEY. "Bank Holding Company Review, 1973/74." Federal Reserve Bank of Chicago. *Business Conditions,* Pt. I (February 1975), pp. 3–10; Pt. II (April 1975), pp. 13–15.

31. SALLEY, CHARLES D. "1970 Bank Holding Company Amendments: What is 'Closely Related to Banking'?" Federal Reserve Bank of Atlanta. *Monthly Review,* June 1971, pp. 98–106.

32. SCHOTLAND, ROY A. "Bank Holding Companies and Public Policy Today." In U.S. Congress. House. Committee on Banking, Currency and Housing. FINE, *Financial Institutions and the Nation's Economy.* Book I, pp. 233–83. Committee Print. 94th Congress, 2d session, 1976.

33. SEELIG, STEVEN A. "Aggregate Concentration and the Bank Holding Company Movement." Unpublished paper. Fordham University, 1976.

34. SILVERBERG, STANLEY C. "Bank Holding Companies and Capital Adequacy." *Journal of Bank Research* VI (Autumn 1975), pp. 202–207.

35. TALLEY, SAMUEL H. "Bank Holding Company Performance in Consumer Finance and Mortgage Banking." *Banking Administration* LII (July 1976), pp. 42–44.

36. WOLKOWITZ, BENJAMIN. "Measuring Bank Soundness." In Federal Reserve Bank of Chicago. *Proceedings of a Conference on Bank Structure and Competition . . . 1975,* pp. 73–84. Chicago, 1975.

Chartering, Branching, and the Concentration Problem

Donald I. Baker

... In approaching the broad issue of market structure, the Hunt Commission does not seem to come to grips openly with the underlying questions in any detail. I believe that these questions are at least two in number: First, *why* do we directly regulate market structure in banking? And, secondly, *how* should we regulate bank structure—which is a matter of both agency structure and substantive legal standards?

There seems to me to be a great tendency, not only in banking but in other regulated industries, to muddle through on fundamental questions like these. To do so is to make regulation seem obscure and highly technical—much loved by the inside experts, but rather poorly understood by the public at large. So, therefore, let's ask the questions.

Why do we regulate bank structure? One can imagine a variety of arguments, of varying degrees of persuasiveness and plausibility, as to why bank structure is regulated. These include the following:

1. To protect banks, depositors, and communities from bank failures;

2. To protect banks from possible "destructive competition";

3. To protect small banks from the competition of large banks;

Reprinted, with deletions, from *Policies for a More Competitive Financial System,* June 1972, pp. 21-39, by permission of the Federal Reserve Bank of Boston.

4. To assure bank shareholders of an adequate rate of return on their capital;

5. To protect bank managements from their own follies; and

6. To deal with the actual or imagined evils of "concentration."

. . . *How should we regulate structure?* At issue here is the broad question—addressed at least in part by the Commission—of dual regulation as between state and federal agencies and the question of the legal standards to govern the regulator's conduct.

Competitive regulation—and that's what it is—is a phenomenon largely unique to banking. It is a useful tool (although some would say a cosmetic) if our overriding goal is to keep down the level of effective public regulation. This is important because there is a natural tendency for regulators to favor enterprises subject to their regulation, over the needs of third parties or the public generally.[1] Dual regulation of bank entry works against this protectionist tendency since one or the other chartering authority may let a new entrant in.[2] The Hunt Commission recognizes this practical truth in supporting dual regulation. A single agency, it says, "may become overzealous in protecting existing firms, with the result that entry by new firms is effectively foreclosed."[3]

On the other hand, in the bank merger area, competitive regulation has often served us poorly. Chairman Frank Wille at the FDIC made this point clearly in an excellent speech in early 1971.[4] There is a continuing threat of competition in regulatory permissiveness on mergers. The Comptroller of the Currency has approved virtually every merger application filed with him for a long period of time, while the other two agencies have applied stricter standards. This might have led to an extensive switch to national charter, but for strong antitrust enforcement by the Department of Justice. The latter has in fact tended to equalize the "regulatory advantage" enjoyed by national banks in the merger area—and thereby avoid something which could be likened to a Gresham's Law of bad regulation driving out good. At the

---

[1]See LeDuc, "The FCC v. CATC, et al., A Theory of Regulators' Reflex Action," 23 FCC B.J. 93 (1969); Scherer, *Industrial Market Structure and Economic Performance* (1970), 538-540; *Hush-A-Phone Corporation* v. *United States*, 238 F. 2d 266 (D.C. Cir. 1956). In the area of banking, Dr. Paul Horvitz has discussed these regulatory issues in a provocative article. Horvitz, "Stimulating Bank Competition Through Regulatory Action," *The Journal of Finance* (March 1965), 9-10. See also Almarin Phillips, "Competition, Confusion, and Commercial Banking," *Journal of Finance*, 19 (March 1964), 39-41; Ross M. Robertson, "The Rationale of Banking Regulation," *Proceedings of a Conference of Bank Structure and Competition* (Federal Reserve Bank of Chicago, 1970), 118-120.

[2]We had a rather interesting illustration of this point in connection with the pending Supreme Court case, *United States* v. *First National Bancorporation*. This is a potential competition case. In the trial court, the defendants offered evidence as to the prospects for new entry. The Comptroller's regional representative testified that he would not recommend and could not foresee a new national bank charter in Greeley. The state superintendent of banking was unwilling to take a position at trial, and within a matter of months authorized the formation of a new state bank by another Colorado holding company. See *American Banker*, June 2, 1972, p. 1.

[3]*The Report of the President's Commission on Financial Structure and Regulation*, 1971, p. 60.

[4]The Bank Merger Act Revisited," Washington, D.C. March 26, 1971.

same time, the subject deserves further study not given it by the Hunt Commission; and, in particular, Chairman Wille's proposal for centralized regulatory authority in the merger area deserves study.[5]

The Hunt Commission really did not face these underlying questions of policy in a detailed, analytic way. Nevertheless, they should be kept in mind as we discuss the specific questions of entry, mergers, and concentration in banking.

The Entry Question—Chartering and Branching

It is trite but true that the conditions of entry are a key factor in industry performance.[6] It is equally true that entry into banking and into local banking markets has generally been held at a level below that which marketplace forces would have dictated.

The Hunt Commission would ease up on the restrictions to entry in two ways: First, the Commission would relax the degree of product specialization among banks and other depositary institutions; and, secondly, it would eliminate some of the existing geographic barriers. I am basically only considering the latter here.

The existing geographic barriers are extensive. Federal law prevents a bank or a bank holding company from operating bank offices in more than one state (12 U.S.C. 36; 12 U.S.C. 1842(d));[7] it gives the states a veto over bank holding company activities (12 U.S.C. 1846); and in the McFadden Act, it binds national banks to the same branching standard as the state banks in a particular state (12 U.S.C. 36).[8] Taken as a whole, this package represents a substantial deference to the states on the whole issue of entry. It is important because state law is very restrictive in many states. Fifteen prohibit branch banking altogether, while 16 others limit branch banking to local markets. Still others provide "home office" protection to existing banks, and a few even protect branch offices in the same way. Finally, 11 states prohibit multiple bank holding companies by statute, and 5 others restrict them in lesser ways. As a result of these various limitations, only 12 states remain with both state-wide *de novo* branching and freedom of holding company entry.

The Hunt Commission favors state-wide banking. It recommends that "by state

---

[5]"The Bank Merger Act Revisited," *supra.*

[6]See Scherer, *supra,* 10, 216-218, 376-377; Phillips, *op. cit.,* 41; Bernard Shull and Paul M. Horvitz, "Branch Banking and the Structure of Competition," *Studies in Banking Competition and the Banking Structure* (The Administrator of National Banks: January 1966), 108-110.

[7]Of course, a very limited number of banks operated banking offices in more than one state at the time these restrictions came into force, and these operations were "grandfathered." In addition, a number of bank holding companies have "grandfathered" subsidiaries in more than one state; while additional acquisitions by the holding company are prohibited, the existing subsidiaries may branch or merge with other banks to the extent permitted by state law.

[8]The concomitant federal restrictions on savings and loan associations result from a combination of statute law and regulatory policy. Savings and loan holding companies are prohibited by statute from acquiring associations in more than one state (12 U.S.C. 1730a(c)(3)). Specific restrictions on branching are enunciated in regulations issued by the Federal Home Loan Bank Board.

laws, the power of commercial banks to branch, both *de novo* and by merger, be extended to a statewide basis, and that all statutory restrictions on branch or home office location based on geographic or population factors or on proximity to other banks or branches thereof be eliminated" (Recommendation 6, pp. 61-62).

Needless to say, I embrace this recommendation with some enthusiasm. It is quite similar to what the Department of Justice recommended last year to the Council of State Governments—namely, that the states be urged to revise and liberalize existing restrictions on branching and holding company activity.[9]

The Commission does not discuss the underlying basis for its recommendation in great detail—but a strong case exists for it. The legislative limitations which the Commission and the Department were criticizing stem largely from a widespread fear of overbanking prevalent following the bank holiday of 1933. As I have indicated, those conditions are entirely different from those which pertain today. The case for reform is clearly stated by former Superintendent William Dentzer of New York. Talking about the situation in New York, he notes that "the most telling argument in favor of some modifications of existing law is that it offers the hope of increasing competition and the range of consumer choice for banking services in a number of communities throughout the State."[10] Moreover, "without major changes, new competition cannot readily be introduced into many markets. Such competition would provide bank managements with more challenges than they now face, the likely result being that the public would be better served." In criticizing his state's home office protection law, he notes the "anomalous situation" that, while designed primarily to protect small banks in local communities, it serves also to protect some of the largest upstate banks with deposits in the billion dollar range.

I think Mr. Dentzer hits just the right tone. The concern of public policy should be to stimulate banking performance in the local markets, to provide the spur of competition. I fear that too often deliberations on law and structure have focused more on the interests of small banks than on the needs of small bank customers. Moreover, Mr. Dentzer's department has sponsored some interesting studies on the effect of large bank entry into markets they were formerly barred from. "These studies indicated that the profitability of small independent banks is not adversely affected either when large institutions entered the small bank's community by merging with one of the other small banks there or when new branches or larger institutions open near the home office community of these small banks. In both situations, to be sure, the rate of deposit growth of the small banks slowed down, although rarely was there any absolute decline in deposits."[11]

[9]Research Paper and Policy Statement of the United States Department of Justice Regarding State Legislation Affecting the Structure of Banking Markets (submitted under the Suggested State Legislation Program to the Council of State Governments, 1971).

[10]"Banking Structure in New York State: A Thinking Man's Guide to the Issues," Rochester, New York, October 15, 1970.

[11]*Ibid.* He is referring to studies entitled: Ernest Kohn, *The Future of Small Banks,* The New York State Banking Department, December 1966, 12-19; Kohn and Carlo, *The Competitive Impact of New Branches,* The New York State Banking Department, December 1969, 8-9.

Leaving Branching Policy to the States

One feature of the Hunt Commission proposal that has attracted criticism is that the Commission would continue to leave branching policy, and holding company entry, in the hands of the states. Some would-be practitioners of practical politics say that there is very little opportunity for getting the necessary changes enacted at the state level, and that therefore the Commission should have opted for some form of federal preemption in this area. From a legal standpoint, this could be done—since Congress, by repealing the McFadden Act limitations on national banks, could easily have forced the states to follow suit. From a practical standpoint, however, I think such a course would be unwise. In some states, and I suspect Illinois is an example, there seems to be a strong and rather broadly held belief that big banks represent an evil that should be curbed. The spirit of William Jennings Bryan lives on. These are feelings that transcend notions of efficiency, and transcend the normal desire of banks to be protected from increased competition. The people in such a state should, in my view, be allowed to make the choice whether to have unit banking or not, even if the decision itself may seem to have a "horse and buggy" quality in the age of high-speed computers and communications. Retail banking is most affected by these historic limitations, and at the same time retail banking is a largely local business; if local citizens want to make a local choice to stay with the past, and to possibly pay more for it, this is the choice they should be allowed to make. To summarize, I strongly endorse the Hunt Commission's proposals for liberalized bank entry into new geographic markets within a state, and I endorse the thought that it would be better done at the state level. In any event, repeal of the McFadden Act seems even less likely than reform at state level in many states—a point which is underscored by recent liberalizations of state law in New York and New Jersey.

Interstate Banking

The Hunt Commission never really faced up to the interstate banking issue. The report simply says in passing that: "Although the Commission rejected proposals to permit interstate branching or metropolitan area banking by federal legislation, it urges states to be progressive in changing their laws" (p. 62). I think this is a significant subject worthy of a great deal more consideration. On the broad question of interstate banking, I really have not seen enough evidence one way or another to convince me whether the existing prohibitions are wise or not. In the end, economics will probably not provide us with any final answers. Certainly the proven economies of scale in banking[12] are not such as to lead one to believe that wide open or even limited interstate banking is likely to substantially change cost performance in the

---

[12]*Cf.* F. W. Bell and N. B. Murphy, *Costs in Commercial Banking: A Quantitative Analysis of Bank Behavior and its Relation to Bank Regulation* (Boston: Federal Reserve Bank of Boston, 1968).

industry. In the end, the case against wide open interstate banking may well turn out to be more political than economic—resting on the desire to avoid concentrations of political power and generally the type of banking structure found in England or Canada, where a handful of institutions dominate commercial banking in the country.[13] (I say this is a political issue more than an economic one because I think that, even with interstate banking, the antitrust laws would be more than adequate to prevent the type of narrow concentration found in some of these foreign countries.)

Metropolitan Area Banking

I also believe that the idea of "metropolitan area banking" deserves more careful attention than the Commission apparently gave it. Geographic barriers can be highly arbitrary, especially when erected by circumstances centuries ago. Take, for example, the Washington Metropolitan Area, which includes the District of Columbia and parts of Maryland and Virginia. Banks and holding companies are basically confined to one of the three sectors. The boundaries that divide them date back to some seventeenth century grants by English kings, to the creation of the original District of Columbia at the end of the eighteenth century, and to the return of half the District of Columbia to Virginia in the mid-nineteenth century. Yet it is a common area, from the standpoint of business, media, traffic flow, and so forth. In such circumstances, one can ask whether banking organizations should not be permitted—perhaps by the holding company route—to operate and compete throughout the whole metropolitan area. The question deserves serious study. I suspect that such a metropolitan approach would make for better banking competition in downtown Washington, as well as in the Virginia and Maryland suburbs. Somewhat similar situations exist in New York and Philadelphia, as well as in a few other metropolitan areas, mostly in the East and Middle West. I wish the Hunt Commission had given more study to this problem.

Standards for Authorizing New Branches and Charters

The Hunt Commission really did not detail the exact substantive standards which regulators should apply in authorizing new branches and charters. This is too bad, as the area deserves a great deal more careful thought. The FDIC has recently indicated that competitive policy is an important consideration in branching cases[14]—a

---

[13]That large banks already have substantial political power is an obvious reality—rather strikingly illustrated by the success of Manufacturers Hanover in obtaining special legislation (P.L. 89-356) to exempt it from the adverse antitrust decision in *United States* v. *Manufacturers Hanover Trust Co.,* 240 F. Supp. 867 (S.D.N.Y. 1965).

[14]FDIC Order Denying Application of Citizens and Southern Emory Bank to Establish a Branch, dated October 15, 1971.

position I agree with—but the statutes are less than specific on the point. Even amended Section 4(c)(8) of the Bank Holding Company Act, providing standards for the Federal Reserve Board to authorize banking entry into financially related activities, is much more specific in telling the regulator what to consider. Specifically, the statute requires the Federal Reserve Board to consider whether performance of a particular activity by bank holding companies ". . . can reasonably be expected to produce benefits to the public, such as greater convenience, increased competition, or gains in efficiency, that outweigh possible adverse effects, such as undue concentration of resources, decreased or unfair competition, conflicts of interest, or unsound banking practices."[15] You will note that the stress here is on benefits to the public, not on protecting competitors. This is important, and it is the kind of thinking that the Hunt Commission should have given its consideration to.

My own view is that the legal standards governing the granting of bank branches and bank charters should be more specific than most of these presently are; and, as with the amended Bank Holding Company Act, the focus should be on benefits to the public in the form of new services and so forth. I would favor more liberalized entry—at least in circumstances where no bank failures were threatening. Outside of the potential failure situation, I would do far more to leave it to the management as to whether the community is "overbanked" or not.

I would also consider writing into bank entry statutes a provision requiring the regulator to give preference to banks not already in a market in handing out branches and charters. This is contrary to the law or policy in some states (where the preference runs the other way),[16] but it seems to me to make considerable sense. Local banking markets are in most cases quite oligopolistic. Such oligopoly positions can to some extent be eroded if the leading firms in the local market are encouraged by law to go elsewhere for expansion and other banks are encouraged to expand within the market. The community with four banking offices, which is capable of supporting a fifth, is likely to be more competitive if the fifth office is awarded to a strong competitor not already in the market.

Preemptive Branching

This last point is related to the problem of preemptive branching. An existing bank branch or charter really has two elements: First, it is a franchise doing business in the particular local market, and, secondly, it is a means of excluding others from the market. Thus, a leading organization already in a banking market can on occasion foreclose new entry by applying first for all the new banking opportunities—even if this involves running uneconomic offices for a period. This difficult problem has been raised by the Federal Reserve Board in several cases involving the creation of new *de novo* subsidiaries by leading holding companies already in a local market. . . . The

---

[15]P.L. 91-607, amending 12 U.S.C. 1843(c).
[16]See Purdon's *Penn. Statutes Annotated,* Title 7, Section 905(b).

problem of preemption is even worse where the bank involved has secured some sort of exclusive right—typically in a shopping center or industrial park.[17]

The Hunt Commission does not really deal with this preemptive branching problem. Nor is there any clean straightforward solution. Regulators simply should be required to apply sound antitrust principles in passing on branch and charter applications—and antitrust law would prevent the truly dominant firm from acquiring new business opportunities before they become viable in order to foreclose them from others.[18] In addition, direct antitrust enforcement is a possibility, at least where the preempting enterprises enjoy some contractual type of exclusive right which restrains competition.

To summarize, the Hunt Commission's recommendations relating to bank entry are generally sound. I certainly endorse the Commission's proposals for eliminating geographic barriers and home office protection within the state. I also concur in the Commission's observation that dual control over entry is less likely to lead to protectionism of existing enterprises (see p. 60). At the same time, considerably more thought is needed on the whole issue of substantive standards which regulators should be required to apply in authorizing entry. The existing statutes are often too vague, and frequently fail to make clear that the overriding concern in this field is the needs and convenience *of the public* for banking services, rather than the convenience of the banks themselves. Competition is an important consideration, and this should be spelled out.

The Concentration Question—And Merger Policy Generally

The Hunt Commission did not seem to put great weight on "concentration" in its deliberations. This is perhaps just as well, since the concept of "concentration" is often subject to a great deal of loose usage—especially among us noneconomists—in discussing bank structure questions. The concept is used at at least three levels— local market concentration, state-wide concentration, and national concentration. At the price of parading my ignorance, let me give you my views on each of these concepts.

"Local" concentration in banking seems to me to be the most important. It is the economist's classic sort of market concentration: It is a means of measuring market

---

[17]See complaint in *United States* v. *Wachovia Bank and Trust Co.*, Civ. C-135-WS-71, filed June 22, 1971 (involving an exclusive right to a night depository in a shopping center mall); and First National Bancorporation, Inc., 57 FED. RES. BULL. 47 (1971) (involving an apparently exclusive right in an industrial park).

[18]See *United States* v. *Aluminum Company of America*, 148 F. 2d 416 (2nd Cir., 1945).

position of competitors in the local service market in which they all operate. In banking, local concentration is generally quite high.

"State-wide" concentration will in most instances represent an aggregation of local competitive retail market positions. The results of such state-wide aggregation vary greatly: In a few states, such as Oregon and Rhode Island, we can see that two banks dominate the state entirely, while in some other states a reasonable degree of diversity and choice exists even among the larger banking organizations.[19] In addition, state-wide concentration may be an appropriate *market* measure of certain whole-sale-type services offered on a state-wide basis (such as correspondent banking or perhaps factoring).

"National concentration" is almost pure aggregation of local market positions. Of course, on a national scale, banking is a quite "unconcentrated" industry, with over 13,000 banks. Taking total bank deposits as a universe, one finds that the largest institutions in the country—although very large indeed—do not dominate the country. Thus, by my calculations based on December 1971 figures on domestic deposits, the nation's top five banks (with deposits of $67 billion) account for about 12 percent of national deposits; the top 10 (with deposits of $99 billion) account for 18 percent; and the top 25 (with deposits of $146 billion) account for 27 percent; and the top 100 (with deposits of $228 billion) account for 42 percent. Thus, the top 183 banks account for exactly half of all domestic deposits. In addition, there are a few national wholesale markets for large commercial borrowers and customers in which national concentration figures would be appropriate.[20]

The concentration question is important at at least two levels. One concerns the broad policy questions of structure—including state-wide banking and indeed even interstate banking. The other concerns merger policy, and particularly antitrust enforcement in the merger area.

I have already generally discussed the legislative issue. I would note, however, that most of the use of concentration in this area is concerned with state-wide or even national concentration. When the opponents of branch banking or holding companies scream out about "concentration," they are not talking about local markets— but rather are expressing concern about domination of a state or indeed the nation by the large money center banks.

On the other hand, merger policy in general, and antitrust merger policy in particular, have been primarily concerned with competition and concentration at the local level. Banking is always a local business, and for larger banks it may often be a regional or national business. The antitrust laws and enforcement have stressed local markets because convenience is a vital factor for retail customers and local business; and effective choices are the most limited at the local level. Economic performance in local markets has often been quite poor, with the "quiet life" the order of the day. . . .

[19]See "Recent Changes in the Structure of Commercial Banking," 56 FED. RES. BULL. 195-210 (1970).

[20]See *United States* v. *Manufacturers Trust Company,* 240 F. Supp. 867, 901-922 (S.D.N.Y. 1965).

Antitrust Enforcement

The Justice Department's often controversial enforcement efforts are directed to this challenge. We have been actively concerned about anticompetitive local bank mergers, and have brought 26 cases against such transactions since 1966. (We have also been concerned over the years with anticompetitive arrangements between local bank competitors: These include price-fixing, cross-ownership arrangements, director interlocks, and "understandings" among the local bankers against poaching on each others' customers.) Our enforcement with respect to such local mergers has two elements: First, to prevent elimination of viable competitive alternatives, and secondly, to preserve the opportunities for new entry. The two policies are necessarily related in a state such as New Jersey where a "home office protection" statute prevents *de novo* entry, and hence new entry by a "virulent competitor" can only come by acquisition.[21]

Ever since the *Philadelphia National Bank* decision in 1963,[22] antitrust enforcement in banking has stressed concentration in local markets. Section 7 of the Clayton Act represents a strong Congressional mandate that increases in market concentration which are created by merger are generally not to be tolerated. The Department of Justice and the Supreme Court have vigorously applied this policy of preventing local concentration. This policy applies in smaller markets which are usually more concentrated than large metropolitan ones. The Supreme Court was very clear on the point in its 1970 *Phillipsburg* decision: "Mergers of directly competing small commercial banks in small communities, are subject to scrutiny under these [antitrust] standards. Indeed, competitive commercial banks, with their cluster of products and services, play a particularly significant role in a small community unable to support a large variety of financial institutions."[23] The alternative, said the Court, "would be likely to deny customers of small banks—and thus residents of many small towns— the antitrust protection to which they are no less entitled than customers of large city banks. Indeed, the need for that protection may be greater in a small town. . ." where the alternative institutions are more limited.[24]

So much for local concentration. The antitrust rules add up to a strict test. As Chairman Wille of the FDIC said in a speech last year, "It is unlikely that many mergers of viable banks already competing in the same market can be justified" under the *Phillipsburg* standard.[25]

The Hunt Commission did not really deal with this problem of local concentration in any detail. Nor, as I see it, are there any real reasons for them to have done so, for so far as mergers are concerned, the situation is under reasonable control. What is

---

[21]In states where holding companies are permitted, it may be possible to enter "closed" markets through *de novo* bank charters.

[22]374 U.S. 321 (1963).

[23]*United States* v. *Phillipsburg National Bank,* 399 U.S. at 358 (1970).

[24]399 U.S. at 361–2 (1970).

[25]"The Bank Merger Act Revisited," *supra* n. 6.

required—and what we may continue to expect—is continuing vigorous enforcement by the Department of Justice in this area.

Concentration—or more accurately dominance—at the state-wide level is something that has been a matter of growing concern to the Department of Justice. Here, however, we are not talking about concentration in a real market sense so much as the elimination of potential competition into local banking markets within a state. The state boundaries are of course significant to competitive analysis in banking, because they delineate the widest area from which potential competitors can be drawn. I am therefore concerned when I see a trend in a state in which the leading banking organizations move on to a position of state-wide dominance by acquiring the leaders in local banking markets throughout the state. In most of the states where the Department has brought suit, there were only a handful of banks, or holding companies which could enter a market *de novo* or by a small "toe hold" acquisition, and from the outset be a competitive force to be reckoned with in that market. Any time one of these few significant potential entrants enters a concentrated local market through acquisition with the local market leader, then that loss of potential competition is likely to occur. Therefore, the Government argues that a Section 7 violation can be found in a bank merger case if the Government proves that (1) the acquiring defendant is one of but a fairly small number of capable potential entrants legally eligible to enter a market; (2) the acquired bank is a leader in a concentrated local market; and (3) the acquiring defendant has an alternative means of entry (e.g., either the market is growing fast enough to support additional banking facilities *de novo* now or in the future or a small competitor is present in the market as an entry vehicle).

I think that this approach is particularly appropriate in commercial banking. There are several considerations here. First, the availability of potential entrants is limited by law: No bank or holding company can enter a state from the outside. This necessarily limits the number of significant potential entrants and makes potential competition even more important. Secondly, all potential entrants are not equal in banking: The large, strong bank has a higher legal lending limit than the smaller bank, and therefore can compete for a broader range of customers; it may offer a wider range of services and may have other advantages as well. This gives it a better chance than a smaller potential entrant to challenge, as a *de novo* or foothold entrant, the leaders in the local banking market. Thirdly, the barriers to entry and full competition imposed by law and regulation make it more important—not less important—to preserve the opportunities for future competition. If a few large, strong banks come to entirely dominate banking throughout a state—as in Oregon—no relief from the outside is available except in the very, very long term, and perhaps not even then. One does not suddenly establish a new billion dollar bank as if it were a hot-strip mill or a Caribbean resort complex. In these circumstances, the strongest banks in a state (if relatively few in number) should be preserved as challengers to local market leaders—rather than being permitted to accumulate a position of overall dominance through piecemeal acquisition of local leaders. . . .

There has also been a certain tendency among defendants and commentators to mix up concentration at national and local levels in order to justify mergers. This is a real case of apples and oranges. The argument runs that we have "too many" banks in this country, and therefore we ought to be hospitable to some consolidation by merger. This argument is fine so far as it goes, but it ignores the fact that, even if we have "too many" banks on a national basis, we have too few banks in most local markets. What I am suggesting is this: There is no reason not to have some rationalization of banking structure so long as one does not eliminate significant local alternatives—in other words, so long as the mergers involve parties in different markets, while avoiding any threat of state-wide (or national) dominance.

To summarize, I think that concentration in banking is a matter of serious concern at the local level because it is here that market choices are limited. On the state-wide level, there should be concern, because state-wide "concentration" can lead to important reductions in potential competition. On the other hand, "concentration" on a national basis is really not at this time a pressing policy problem. . . .

Perspectives on the
Financial System

IX

No contemporary study of banking is complete without a critical examination of the recommendations of the Hunt Commission—the
President's Commission on Financial Structure and Regulation. In
1975 the Ford administration proposed the Financial Institutions Act,
which would have enacted many of the recommendations of the Hunt
Commission. Was this a step in the right direction? Did it go too far or
not far enough? Of the scores of articles available on this issue, this
section features three excellent, representative readings.

The introductory paper by Clifton B. Luttrell effectively airs the
view that the Hunt Commission proposals, while attuned to the benefits of increased private competition in financial markets, failed to go
far enough in liberating the free market from the yoke of government
interference. The reading by Lester C. Thurow disagrees, arguing
cogently for increased government action to bring credit allocations
effected by the market mechanism into line with social priorities. This
article is followed by an incisive critique of Thurow's analysis by Edward J. Kane.

In the late 1970s, hearings were held by the U.S. House of Representatives Committee on Banking, Currency and Housing on proposals for restructuring the nation's financial institutions to promote
efficiency and competition. The "Discussion Principles" that were

generated by that committee's Financial Institutions and the Nation's Economy (FINE) study evoked such turmoil in the financial community that none of the resulting legislation was enacted by Congress. James L. Pierce was the director of the FINE study. In Article 37 he explains why the Discussion Principles were drafted and analyzes why they failed to be enacted.

The Hunt Commission Report —
An Economic View

Clifton B. Luttrell*

The Hunt Commission, appointed by President Nixon to study the structure and regulations of the nation's financial institutions, was composed of ten executives of financial agencies, six executives of other firms, two academic economists, one labor union leader, and an attorney-politician. The professional staff which apparently exercised a major influence in formulating both the objectives and final recommendations of the report consisted largely of economists. Chief staff roles were played by the Co-Directors Donald Jacobs of Northwestern University and Almarin Phillips of the University of Pennsylvania.

The President issued the Commission a mandate to "review and study the structure, operation, and regulation of the private financial institutions in the United States, for the purpose of formulating recommendations that would improve the functioning of the private financial system."[1]

The Commission's intermediate objective in carrying out this mandate was "to

Reprinted from the Federal Reserve Bank of St, Louis, *Review,* June 1972, pp. 8-12, by permission of the publisher.

*This presentation was given before a group who had some prior knowledge of the contents of *The Report of the President's Commission on Financial Structure & Regulation,* commonly known as the Hunt Commission Report. Interested readers may find it helpful to consult the *Report* for more complete information on the points discussed.

[1]*The Report of the President's Commission on Financial Structure & Regulation* (December 1971), p. 1.

move as far as possible toward freedom of financial markets and equip all institutions with the powers necessary to compete in such markets."[2]

The Commission recognized that most of the problems of our financial system are the result of legislation enacted in response to financial crises, such as that of the early 1930s. The Commission recognized that the resulting overly protected financial system is not suited to efficiently meet the nation's current demands for financial services and outlined a series of proposals to make it more competitive and flexible. From an economic view the proposals generally elicit favorable comment.

In consequence, my discussion consists largely of providing theoretical background for some of the recommendations which lacked such a foundation and offering some criticism of minor features of the proposals which appear to be the result of compromises between the occupational interests of some Commission members and the Commission's overall objectives.

Competition in the Private Enterprise System

An economist views a competitive private enterprise system as an elaborate mechanism that unconsciously coordinates the production of goods and services through competitive prices and markets. Each good and service, including the different kinds of human labor, has a price. Although the true price of a commodity is the amount of all other goods and services foregone, it is convenient to express prices in money units. Everyone receives money for what he sells and uses the money to purchase what he desires. If people want more automobiles they will bid up the price and the higher-priced automobiles will provide incentive for increased automobile production.

The competitive price mechanism thus brings into equality production and consumption of each good and service. Such a mechanism assures that producers will produce at the lowest possible cost since, if they fail to economize on labor or other resources, competitors can undersell them and attract their customers. Higher profits are awarded to the most efficient producers and reduced profits or losses are incurred by the less efficient. In the absence of external effects of production, such as pollution, the free competitive system works most efficiently with a minimum of legal interference.

Financial institutions, which constitute a major sector of our private enterprise system, are subject to the same competitive forces as other firms. Commercial banks purchase time and savings deposits, attract demand deposits, make loans, sell investment funds and trust services, and perform numerous other services incidental to banking. Other financial firms also purchase and sell financial claims and services.

Those firms that can buy, service, and sell most efficiently will tend to grow the fastest and make the greatest profits. They will tend to innovate more readily, have

---

[2]*Ibid.*, p. 9.

greater flexibility, and contribute more to community prosperity and growth than the less efficient firms. With these objectives in view, the Hunt Commission proposed that the legal restrictions on financial institutions be loosened somewhat to permit greater competition among firms. It believed that the present excessive legal restraints have both retarded the growth of the more efficient financial firms and slowed general economic development.

During the course of my discussion, I do not take the recommendations one by one, but group them into broad classes having common characteristics relative to the functioning of financial markets.

Proposals for Relaxing Interest Rate Restrictions

First, I shall comment on the Commission's proposals for removing restrictions with respect to interest rates. These recommendations call for phasing out interest rate ceilings on time and savings deposits and dividend restrictions on savings and loan association shares, providing for market rates on FHA and VA loans, and removing statutory rate ceilings on mortgage loans.

Interest rate ceilings were authorized at the Federal level during the early 1930s to prevent so-called "cutthroat" competition. The large number of bank failures at that time were believed by some observers to be the result of "excessively risky loans" which banks were forced to make in order to maintain competitive interest rates on deposits. Thus, a mass of New Deal legislation was enacted to reduce such competition. Banks were prohibited from paying interest on demand deposits, and regulatory authorities were given a responsibility to set ceiling rates on time and savings deposits. A cursory examination of banking since then gives the appearance that the program has been highly successful. Bank failures have indeed declined to a very low rate.

The reduced rate of bank failures, however, cannot be traced to the interest rate ceilings. The rate of failures since the Great Depression of the 1930s has been no greater in those years when market rates were paid on time and savings deposits than when Regulation Q restrictions prevented the payment of market rates. For example, since 1945 there have been seven years when Treasury bill rates were generally above the maximum ceiling rates on savings deposits, thus preventing banks from paying the market rate for savings. During these years an average of 5.29 banks failed per year. Almost the same rate, 5.17, failed per year during the eighteen years when Treasury bills were well below the ceiling rates on time and savings deposits.[3]

The modest proposals of the Commission for reducing such restrictions were certainly in the right direction, but they were made with the apparent fear of treading

---

[3]For a comprehensive analysis of the impact of interest rate regulation see Albert H. Cox, Jr., *Regulation of Interest Rates on Bank Deposits* (Ann Arbor: University of Michigan, 1966), and George J. Benston, "Interest Payments on Demand Deposits and Bank Investment Behavior," *Journal of Political Economy* (October 1964), pp. 431–449.

on quicksand when in fact the foundation was solid. As indicated earlier, during most of the period since the Great Depression the ceilings on time and savings deposit rates have been sufficiently high to be ineffective. Nevertheless, few failures have occurred.

Hazardous situations for bank survival have occurred only in periods following sharp variations in money growth from the trend rate, as in the years since 1965. During this period of rapid money growth, spending and prices rose sharply and inflationary expectations were reflected in higher interest rates. The market rates rose above the ceilings and financial intermediaries were prohibited from paying competitive rates. The inflow of savings declined as savers found other types of investments that yielded higher returns. The restrictions were thus probably more damaging than helpful to the survival of financial intermediaries.

The Commission wisely recommended that the rate restrictions on FHA and VA loans be removed. Prior to limiting the points that could legally be charged borrowers under the FHA and VA programs, the point spread between the face amount of the mortgage and the amount of funds actually disbursed accounted for the difference between the legal and market rates. Once the points that could be paid by purchasers were limited by law, sellers were forced to make up the difference between legal and market rates by raising their selling price on homes, thus creating an additional problem in real estate sales. The proposal that such mortgages be made at market rates would involve fewer calculations and less effort in shopping for and transacting real estate business.

Although the recommendation that states remove the statutory ceilings on mortgage loan rates is another move toward market-determined rates, I see no reason why the recommendation was limited to mortgage loan rates. All loan rate limitations channel funds into less risky loans and deny borrowers who have limited assets the right to pay higher rates to cover such risks. Since lenders make only the less risky loans when rates are actually restricted, the restrictions in effect deny higher-risk borrowers access to credit markets. Competition among lenders will assure a market rate to borrowers in the same manner that commodity and other prices are determined in competitive markets.

The Commission pointed out the problems involved in enforcing the prohibition of interest payments on demand deposits. Among the numerous substitutes and subterfuges used to escape the regulation are provisions for "free" services, lower loan rates to those having large deposits, and third party payments by savings and loan associations. A firm or business selects the bank that will provide the package of banking services with the greatest return at the least cost. Thus, if legal restrictions prohibit the payment of the market price for one type of service, the impact of such restrictions will likely be offset by price or service concessions elsewhere.

Despite the use of numerous substitute payments, money is the more efficient means of payment. Other forms of payment lead to poor allocation of resources, since money is the only means whereby all can maximize their returns on deposits at the margin. Nevertheless, the Commission concluded that the undesirable effects of the immediate abolition of the prohibition of interest payments on demand deposits would be greater than the costs imposed by its continuation.

Relaxing Operational Restrictions on Financial Institutions

The proposals that structural and operational restrictions on financial institutions be relaxed should lead to lower-cost financial services. The removal of restrictions, such as limitations on branch banking, and the relaxation of loan and investment restrictions on savings and loan associations (S&Ls) and mutual savings banks should increase the ability of these firms to compete in all markets. Permitting S&Ls and mutual savings banks to accept checking accounts and all the depository institutions to sell and manage mutual funds should likewise lead to greater competition in both banking and the mutual fund business.

The proposals would permit S&Ls and mutual savings banks to compete with commercial banks in servicing checking accounts and convert to commercial banks if they so desire. If they want to become commercial banks, I see no reason why their access to the banking field should be prohibited. Furthermore, I see no reason for the continuation of limited entry into banking as long as the participants can provide assurance of reliability.

It has been argued that banking is a special type of industry into which entry should be limited to protect vital public interests. For example, it is argued that medicine, steamfitting, plumbing, law, and the clergy require special licensing by the state or some association to assure the safety of the public. To such arguments I would reply that the restrictions to entry have always been passed with a grandfather clause; that is, those who were then in the occupation could remain.

If public safety were the major factor, the unqualified should be removed at the time entry is restricted. In addition, if public safety were foremost in view, regular examinations would be required to see that those in the occupation remained qualified. New techniques often result in old methods becoming obsolete. Instead of such assurance that current practitioners remain qualified once a license is obtained, license holders generally have a right to a lifetime practice without further qualification. I thus conclude that most licensing and chartering restrictions are used primarily to restrict entry and provide an element of monopoly power to those already in the business and are in fact not in the public interest.

The conversion proposals, along with others which provide for additional chartering powers, tend to loosen the restrictions on entry into banking. With more agencies having power to charter banks or depository institutions which have free conversion privileges among themselves, we may again approach free entry into the finance business. With free entry we can remove most bank holding company and merger restrictions. Such restrictions will then be obsolete since monopoly is almost impossible given the relatively small efficiencies of scale among financial institutions, except for the very small firms.

The Commission recognized the fact that branching can increase competition in many bank markets.[4] Nevertheless, it failed to recommend Federal legislation on this subject. For example, it could have proposed that the National Banking Act be amended to permit state-wide branching by national banks. Instead, it recommended that state laws be changed to permit state-wide branching. This recommendation provides for little optimism that changes in bank structure will be forthcoming, given the deliberation with which most states move, when they move at all, to improve banking services. One can only conclude that a significant amount of compromising among the Commission members led to such a recommendation.

Public Welfare Goals

Throughout the report there is considerable discussion about housing goals. The Commission, however, logically refused to make recommendations for special financial agency regulations designed to increase credit flows into the housing market.[5] It apparently could not resist completely the pressure for so-called socially desirable credit, however, since it did recommend special tax credits to investors in residential mortgages. However, as pointed out by two dissenters, such credits would mean heavier taxes elsewhere and fewer financial resources in the nonhousing sector of the economy.

Insurance on Bank Deposits and S&L Shares

In view of the proposal that savings and loan associations and mutual savings banks be permitted to function more like commercial banks, the Commission's recommendation that all depository insurance corporations be combined into the Federal Deposit Guarantee Administration is appropriate. Nevertheless, the Commission rejected any change in the current method of assessing premiums at a fixed percent of deposits, despite substantial variations in portfolio risks among banks. In addition, the proposals, if implemented, may further widen the variation of risks among firms. For example, if S&Ls and mutual savings banks are permitted to invest in equities up to 10 percent of their assets, their portfolios will carry greater risks than under current operating practices. Similarly, commercial bank risks will increase if some banks invest in the proposed special-purpose equities such as community rehabilitation projects.

The increased competition within the financial system provided in the proposals should warrant the establishment of deposit insurance rates in some relationship to risk. Even under current supervisory regulations, deposit insurance assessments could be used instead of moral suasion to achieve desired objectives, such as capital

---

[4]*The Report of the President's Commission on Financial Structure & Regulation*, p. 45.
[5]*Ibid.*, pp. 84-85.

to asset ratios consistent with risks in individual firms and minimum insurance premiums consistent with a reasonably competitive financial system.

There are significant reasons why the deposit insurance assessments should be made on the basis of risks. First, if all financial firms pay the same rate of assessment on deposits, those with higher risk assets are being subsidized to the extent that such banks are a heavier expense to the insuring agency. Thus, there is some incentive to increase risks given the current inflexible system of assessments. With the increased competition in prospect, the incentive to take greater risks may be increased.

More to the point, however, equity capital in any organization is designed to be the chief risk taker. Since the FDIC has assumed much of the banking risks, it has replaced part of the risk-bearing function of equity capital. Banks have thus found it profitable to permit their capital to asset ratios to drift downward since there is little incentive for high ratio maintenance. With a higher assessment on banks with low capital ratios, they will have greater incentive for building up capital and reducing deposit insurance costs.

Reserve Requirements

The Commission's recommendations that all institutions holding demand deposits be required to become members of the Federal Reserve System would place them all under similar competitive rules. Likewise, the proposals for eliminating reserves on time and savings deposits, equal reserve requirements for all banks, and the gradual reduction of reserve requirements over time are moves intended to achieve greater equity among financial firms.

Chartering, Regulations, and Supervisory Recommendations

The recommendations for granting federal charters to stock savings and loan companies, mutual savings banks, and mutual commercial banks will tend to increase competition. As pointed out in the report, when a particular type of financial institution can be chartered by only one administrative agency, the agency tends to become overzealous in protecting existing firms and forecloses entry by new firms. It is much easier to appease existing firms with a charter denial and confuse the public with the comment that the area is becoming "overbanked" than to serve the public interest by granting charters freely.

As pointed out earlier, I can see no reason why free entry will cause overbanking, overfarming, or an excess of participants in any industry. As long as there is sufficient incentive in an occupation to attract new entrants with their labor and capital, any legislative or administrative action to limit entry reduces efficiency in the production of goods and services.

The proposal that any depository institution has the right to change its charter to that of another type of depository institution should help to assure that overly protective chartering will not occur. If any of the numerous chartering agencies will freely grant charters, there should be relatively free entry into each type of financial activity.

Most of the proposals for restructuring the regulatory and supervisory agencies apparently have little economic content. The new office of Administrator of State Banks would be an independent agency taking over most of the bank supervisory functions of the Federal Reserve System and the FDIC. The Comptroller of the Currency's function would be removed from the Treasury Department and made an independent agency. The Commission felt that these moves would tidy up the administrative functions and leave the Federal Reserve System free to concentrate its attention and resources on economic stabilization policy.[6] I have some reservations, however, in concurring with the view that the additional concentration on stabilization objectives will provide much improvement in stabilization actions. Nevertheless, there may be some specialization gains.

Single Tax Formula

The proposals for enactment of a single tax formula for all financial agencies which hold demand deposits and an eventual uniform tax formula for all depository institutions offering third party payment services are consistent with maximum efficiency. The Commission urged Congress to enact a tax system that would provide for uniform tax treatment for such firms whether organized on a stock or mutual basis. Currently, firms organized on a mutual basis generally receive more favorable tax treatment. There is little justification for different tax rates for firms just because they happen to be organized differently. If one type of financial intermediary pays less tax, it is in effect being subsidized by those paying more. Under such an unequal tax system there is no means of determining whether a firm can operate competitively. If it cannot operate in a competitive market without subsidies, it should not be in existence since it is wasting valuable resources.

Summary

In summation, the Commission's recommendations are generally consistent with the goal of increasing competition in a private enterprise economy. Its proposals for broadening the activities of financial firms and reducing their structural rigidities are all consistent with greater efficiency. The proposals for tax equality and greater uniformity of operating rules, such as reserve requirements and portfolio holdings, tend to provide greater equality of opportunity for profitable operation. The most

---

[6]*Ibid.*, p. 91

efficient firms survive and prosper under such conditions and the less efficient tend to drop out and are taken over by the survivors. Relatively free entry and exit are typical of competitive firms. Such a system meets our demands for goods and services at the lowest per unit cost. The Commission's proposals would move our financial system a long step toward greater competition.

My major complaints with the proposals are the timidity shown in certain recommendations, such as the ten-year interval for removing interest rate controls on time and savings deposits, the hesitancy in recommending freedom for banks to purchase demand deposits, the useless recommendation that states permit state-wide bank branching, and the lack of analysis with respect to deposit insurance assessments. These failures, however, can probably be attributed to compromises which were necessary to reach the major agreements in the report. Thus, the recommendations were probably the best obtainable given the occupational interests of the Commission members.

Proposals for Rechanneling Funds to Meet Social Priorities

Lester C. Thurow

I support the primary and secondary thrusts of the recommendations of the President's Commission on Financial Structure and Regulation. The primary thrust of these recommendations is that each financial institution should decide for itself where its comparative advantage lies within the domain of financial intermediaries and that institutions that are doing the same things should be subject to the same regulations. The secondary thrust is that the amount of regulations should be substantially reduced. While it is easy to quibble about details and timing I think the Commission should be given the benefit of the doubt on these matters. They result from a balancing of objectives that no outsider can make and that no insider with vested interests should be allowed to make.

I do this despite my interest in channeling funds toward social priorities. First, the present institutions and regulations have not channeled funds toward social priorities in sufficient quantities to be worth the inequities that they have produced. The present arrangements are simply not worth preserving as a vehicle for meeting social objectives. Second, the present arrangements assume that you can compartmentalize financial intermediaries so that institutions that are under different regulatory handicaps do not compete with each other. This assumption has simply proven to be untrue. Moreover, there probably is no set of regulations that could stop poaching on

Reprinted from the Federal Reserve Bank of Boston, *Policies for a More Competitive Financial System,* June 1972, pp. 179-89, by permission of the publisher and the author.

the other guy's turf. As a result, all regulations should be across-the-board regulations on all intermediaries.

I also admit that all social priorities could be met with budgetary expenditures and/or tax credits (tax expenditures). I am convinced that in a perfectly functioning world most social priorities *should* be met with budgetary expenditures. Both complex tax incentives and financial regulations are apt to end up doing more for some intermediary than they do to promote the ultimate social objective. (Tax deductibility for state and local government bonds is probably the best current example of such a result.) The financial community is perfectly right in saying that in a perfectly functioning world, social priorities *ought* to be someone else's problem.

The recommendations of the President's Commission essentially spring from a vision of perfectly competitive capital markets. Each saver sends his savings into the capital markets and is paid a competitive (equal) rate of interest by the financial intermediaries. Financial intermediaries in turn allocate the savings to those lenders who are willing to pay the highest rate of interest. With the exception of allowing for differences in risk and the costs of making loans (economies of scale in handling large borrowers), all borrowers pay at the same rate of interest. Differences between lending rates and borrowing rates reflect the financial intermediaries' costs (including a necessary profit) of making loans. The level of the competitive interest rate insures that the demand for savings equals the supply of savings. In such a world no one cares to whom he lends or from whom he borrows. The same conditions are available everywhere. In such a world, social priorities are quite properly left in the government budget.

The question then becomes one of whether the real world is close enough to a perfectly functioning world so that we can afford to operate on the premise that the real world functions perfectly. Alternatively we could ask what changes would be necessary to bring the real world close enough to a perfectly functioning world to make the assumption valid.

Discrepancies

While a host of deviations between such a model and the real world could be noted, there are three major facts of life that are not in accordance with the ideal world. First, not all savings are allocated in the capital markets. In the ideal world they should be. Second, credit rationing is a pervasive fact of the real world. In the ideal world it does not and cannot exist. Third, customer relationships are thought to be important. In the ideal world the whole concept of a regular and valued customer does not exist. To some extent these are not three independent deviations. The latter two spring principally from the first.

Corporate retained earnings are the major source of unallocated savings within the capital markets. They enjoy special tax and legal advantages. They are subject to neither the allocation procedures of the capital marketplace or to the allocation desires of their owners (the individual shareholders). From the point of view of the arguments used to justify deregulation for financial institutions, all earnings (including depreciation charges) should be paid out as dividends and then brought back into the firm in the form of borrowings or equity issues. Corporate taxation could be abolished, but all dividends and depreciation allowances above the initial investment would be taxed as personal income. As a result, corporations would be forced to compete for all of their capital needs. Unless this is done, corporations have two major advantages in the country's capital markets. First, they have tied savings for which they do not have to compete. Second, their tied savings (cash flow) can be used as collateral to obtain extra funds in the capital markets. Conversely, the supply of savings for which others must compete is smaller than it should be.

Our actual financial markets are marked by credit rationing and by preferences for large regular corporate customers over small, irregular, noncorporate customers. Why? The answer lies in imperfect knowledge and in the tied savings of the corporate sector. Profit-maximizing financial intermediaries obviously want to cultivate the business of corporations with large flows of tied savings (cash flows). In our real world of oliogopoly relationships, such a connection is the best method for maximizing long-run profits. Yet such long-run profit maximization will result in too few funds being allocated to the infrequent noncorporate borrower from the point of view of economic efficiency.

Logically all of the assumptions that lead to the actual recommendations of the Commission lead to the abolition of retained earnings. Single economic efficiency considerations demand it, yet the Commission did not recommend it. Politically, I understand why such a recommendation was not made, but its absence leads to a report which at best must be described as self-serving. Given this large imperfection in favor of corporate borrowers, there are *only* two options. Create equal preferences within the financial markets for noncorporate borrowers or stop the preferences for corporate borrowers. I am willing to stop the special preferences for corporate borrowers, but I suspect that realistically we must focus on equal preferences for noncorporate borrowers. Without such preferences, credit rationing will allocate too many funds to the corporate sector and too few funds to the noncorporate sector. The question is how such a bias can be corrected in a manner that will not violate the primary and secondary thrusts of the Commission's recommendations. This is not a question of equity but of efficiency.

An Examination of Special Cases

Before examining the possible countervailing preferences that could be created for small, irregular, noncorporate borrowers, it is necessary to examine the special cases that are advanced for special financial regulations for special sectors. The areas usually cited include housing, state and local governments, agriculture, exports, and small businesses. In addition to its absolute merits, however, each case needs to be examined with an eye to alternative solutions. Are special financial regulations or institutions the best way to solve the problem?

A. State and Local Governments

The basic problem of state and local government finance is not one of borrowing power, but one of taxing power. The relevant question is not "How do we borrow more?" but "How do we raise more tax revenue?" Revenue sharing and more use of the personal income tax completely dominate special borrowing provisions as a method of solving the financial problems of state and local governments. States are large institutions that can compete in the credit markets and they can easily establish financial intermediaries to obtain borrowing economies of scale for small local governments in their jurisdictions. If the taxation problem were solved, the borrowing problem would not exist. Unless the tax problem is solved, there is no way to solve the borrowing problem.

B. Exports

Exports are a peculiar case in that arguments for special aid revolve around what is given in other countries. The operative problem then becomes one of countering these provisions with equal and offsetting preferences or by devaluations which take these incentives into account. From an efficiency standpoint it is clear that setting exchange rates in such a manner as to offset these special provisions is preferable. If this is not done, however, there remains a case for special financial provisions for exports.

C. Agriculture and Small Business

Agriculture and small business would benefit from any general program to insure equitable treatment for the small, irregular, noncorporate borrower, but the case for special provisions over and beyond this must rest on the argument that small independent entrepreneurs contribute something to the country over and beyond their economic output. This may be true (it is a question of value judgments), but I think that I would agree with the President's Commission that the noneconomic benefits different sectors produce should be rewarded in government budgets and not in regulations of the financial system. There simply is no method of regulation that yields everyone a gain equal to his noneconomic benefits. In addition the whole society, not just savers, should be forced to compensate for such noneconomic benefits.

D. Housing

If housing generates positive or negative externalities, private money markets will provide too little or too much housing since all of the benefits or costs of housing are not considered in each individual investment decision. Housing is probably subject to two types of externalities. First, a whole set of sociological externalities may flow from housing. These are popularly thought to include crime, alienation, and other factors. As a result, when social benefits are included, too little is invested in housing. Second, housing is subject to financial externalities through the neighbor's house. Knowing this, each individual in the neighborhood has an incentive to undermaintain his own home since doing so will have little effect on its value as long as all of the other homes in the neighborhood are well maintained. Conversely, it does little good to maintain your own home if others are not maintaining theirs. The result of individual economic rationality, however, is collective irrationality. Too little is invested in housing maintenance and housing (and commercial properties) deteriorate much faster than economic rationality would warrant.

Social costs and benefits are also created by the seasonality of construction in northern climates. Each person wishes to build his home in the good weather period when construction costs are lowest; each person legitimately ignores the social costs of idle resources during periods of bad weather. Some of these costs are absorbed by the factors of production in the industry, but many are absorbed by society through unemployment compensation, inflation, and restrictive work rules. Rational social policies may call for much more bad weather construction than will ever occur as a result of individual decision making.

As a result, even in a world of perfect markets, some government program would be necessary to stop such collective irrationality from taking place. Individual housing decisions will lead to too little being invested in housing. Some form of incentive is needed to inject the sociological benefits of housing into the private economic calculus and to prevent the social costs of seasonality and neighborhood deterioration.

In addition, when a society decides upon its optimum distribution of private money incomes through its tax policies, society is de facto deciding on its optimum distribution of marketable economic goods. There may be goods, however, that society wishes to distribute in a different manner. Such goods are "merit wants" and the usual preference is to distribute them more equally than the general basket of goods and services. There is no method for doing this through the private market mechanism, however, since there can only be one distribution of money incomes. Consequently, these goods are furnished through government policies even though they do not meet the classical tests of pure public goods. The most common such merit wants are education, housing, and health care. In each of these cases society seems to have indicated that it wants these particular goods to be more equally distributed than other marketable economic goods. If you like, we are more communistic with respect to some goods than others.

Thus the question arises as to how housing can be more equally distributed than the distribution of money income. Private market mechanisms will never bring about such a distribution without government interference of some sort.

As a result, a strong case can be made that private market mechanisms will not lead to an optimum (from an efficiency or equity viewpoint) investment in housing or to an optimum distribution of this investment across the population even if the current preferences for corporate borrowers were eliminated. I agree with the President's Commission that the merit want, seasonality, and sociological externalities aspects of this question should most properly be handled through the government budget. They reflect social benefits. But what about the neighborhood financial externalities? Too little will be invested in housing simply from the point of view of private economic efficiency. Given this situation, I think that it would be completely in accordance with the Commission's desires to improve markets if one were to establish special provisions for housing. Internalizing economic externalities is a completely legitimate and necessary role for government regulation of financial markets. According to the economic theory to which the Commission subscribes, these externalities *should not* be reflected in government budgets.

As a result, I would argue that the Commission's own vision of perfectly functioning private capital markets should have lead it to recommend the creation of a general preference for small, irregular, noncorporate borrowers (or the elimination of retained earnings and depreciation allowances) and a special provision for housing to internalize the private economic externalities.

The Second Best

Considerations of the second best might also have lead the Commission to reflect a bit more on how society should engender the social benefits (as opposed to private benefits) that flow from some of these areas. Theoretically, it is clear that such incentives should reside in government budgets. This is the correct place to spread the burdens of paying for them. In a perfect world, taxing savers (by imposing special financial regulations) to pay for social benefits is unfair. In a less than perfect world, taxing savers may be a "better" (more progressive, fewer horizontal inequities, etc.) tax than the actual income tax. Perfect taxes are better taxes than perfect regulations, but actual regulations may be better taxes than actual taxes. To me it is not obvious that a general tax on savers would be more "unfair" than the current structure of taxes. A general tax certainly would be more progressive and have fewer horizontal inequities than the current tax structure. (Bad regulations may of course be worse than bad taxes.) In any case, the Commission has completely forgotten to think about what role financial regulation may play in our complete structure of taxes. It is a better tax or a worse tax than our current structure of taxes.

Tax reform (the Commission's recommendations are in fact a form of tax reform) is a perfectly appropriate consideration, but unfortunately it is impossible to recommend that a tax be eliminated without proving that the replacement taxes are better than the tax they are replacing. Financial regulations are not the world's best tax, but they may be better than most of the world's actual taxes.

Policy Options

Given the Commission's primary and secondary goals of letting each institution determine its own actions while equalizing and reducing regulations, there are essentially two policy options. One is based on fiscal powers and the other is based on regulatory powers.

The fiscal option is the one recommended by the Commission. The government is simply told that it must raise taxes, capture some fraction of savings, and lend this money to those borrowers whom society decides to aid. Unfortunately, once again the Commission does not follow its own logic and spell out the tax implications. To the extent that the aid was designed to compensate for noneconomic social benefits, taxes should be raised in accordance with the general structure of taxes. (If society started with an optimum tax system, an across-the-board surtax would be appropriate.) To the extent that the aid was designed to offset deviations in the financial markets from an economic optimum, across-the-board tax increases are not appropriate. To the extent that the fiscal mechanism is correcting for the preferences given to large corporate borrowers in the marketplace, the necessary taxes should be placed on corporate cash flows and corporate borrowings. The resulting revenue would then be lent to small, irregular, noncorporate customers. The taxes necessary to compensate for the financial externalities of property investments should properly be placed on existing property owners. Property taxes should be levied and the revenue lent to those maintaining or improving existing properties and those building new properties.

These special taxes are appropriate since they are the only taxes that will bring capital markets into conformity with perfect capital markets. The existence of large, tied corporate cash flows means that too much savings go to corporations. The fiscal mechanism for correcting this is taxes on corporate savings and lending that stop this excessive flow. Similarly, property owners should pay for the financial externalities of housing investments since they are going to reap the financial gains if property is well maintained, improved, and well built. This is the appropriate fiscal mechanism. In neither case is the appropriate mechanism a general tax increase.

Alternatively there is the asset reserve requirement. Under a system of asset reserve requirements, the government places a 100 percent reserve requirement of some fraction of each financial institution's assets unless this fraction is invested in the desired sectors. If national goals called for investing 25 percent of national savings in housing and other preferred sectors, each financial institution would have a 100 percent reserve requirement on that fraction of its assets. As long as it invested 25 percent of its assets in housing, however, it would not have to leave any reserves with the government. If it had only invested 20 percent of its assets in housing, 5 percent of its assets would have to be held with the government as required reserves. If it invested nothing, 25 percent of its assets would be held as reserves. Thus, financial institutions are essentially given the option of making interest-paying loans in the housing field or making an interest-free loan to the government. Different asset reserve requirements are essentially different tax rates.

The asset reserve requirement has several advantages over the present system for aiding housing. First, it works. It can insure that housing gets whatever fraction of total funds policy makers think housing should get. Credit crunches have no effect on its effectiveness. Funds cannot flow away from housing since there are no financial institutions that can avoid housing investment. Every financial institution is required to be a housing institution to some degree. (This does not mean, however, that every financial institution must operate in the housing field at the retail level. Specialized housing institutions could issue bonds for those institutions with no expertise in housing and no desire to get into this business.) Second, it is a simple straightforward regulation that does not require the cumbersome and complex set of regulations necessary to maintain the present system. Third, it does not discriminate between the small saver and the big saver. Each can receive the same interest returns. Fourth, institutions are not locked out of other areas. If a savings and loan society has a good industrial lending opportunity, it can make such a loan. Fifth, the government does not have to raise the taxes necessary to finance the fiscal alternative and does not need to build a bureaucracy large enough to manage a large direct involvement in the housing field. In sum, it is consistent with the equal regulation goals of the Commission.

To the extent that asset reserve requirements are used to correct the two capital market imperfections on which I have been focusing, they are regulations called for by simple economic efficiency. No equity considerations emerge. To the extent that asset reserve requirements were used to stimulate noneconomic social benefits, there is an equity issue. It is fair to force savers to invest part of their funds for social, as opposed to private, goals. Once again this comes back to the previous second-best question as to whether an asset reserve requirement is a better or worse tax than other taxes that might be used to obtain the same goal.

The answer to this question is obviously a matter of value judgment that I have not been elected to make. Relative equity, however, is often easier to determine. Let me venture the hypothesis that a system of general asset reserve requirements that shifted into these sectors by the present system of regulations would be more equitable than the present system of rules and regulations. Horizontal inequities among savers would certainly be eliminated. Given the progressivity of savings rates, such a regulatory tax on savings would certainly be a progressive tax.

Finally, it must be noted that asset reserve requirements (formal or informal) are used in many developed countries. Based on two studies conducted by myself and some colleagues at M.I.T. for the U.S. House Banking and Currency Committee, they seem to be the only effective regulatory mechanism for moving funds into priority areas.[1] This does not eliminate the need to choose between the fiscal and regulatory approach, however, since the fiscal approach can also work. Nor would adoption of the asset reserve requirement allow the elimination of all budgetary expenditures for the same areas. Asset reserve requirements can move funds into particular areas, but they really cannot be used to move funds to particular individuals. If the goal is low-income housing, as opposed to just housing, for example,

---

[1]For the discussion of how various foreign countries attempt to aid sectors of social priority see *Activities by Various Central Banks to Promote Economic and Social Welfare Programs*. A Staff report of the Committee on Banking and Currency, U.S. House of Representatives, Dec. 1970; *Foreign Experiences with Monetary Policies to Promote Economic and Social Welfare Programs*. A Staff report of the Committee on Banking and Currency, U.S. House of Representatives, 1972.

expenditure programs and asset reserve requirements would need to be coordinated. Without programs to move the necessary funds into the desired areas, however, distributional policies simply cannot work. If there are no funds to build houses, new houses cannot be distributed.

Conclusions

Thus the country faces three choices—maintain the present complex, cumbersome, and ineffective regulations for aiding social priorities; nationalize social lending; or adopt general across-the-board asset reserve requirements. As an economist, I would opt for the nationalization of social lending with the appropriate surtaxes (i.e., taxes on corporate savings and borrowings, and taxes upon property owners). It is the most efficient economic solution. As a political economist, I would opt for general asset reserve requirements.

I do this because I think it is politically naive to believe in the possibility of abolishing all regulations designed to aid sectors of social priority without real compensation—i.e., a better system than the present one. In our political system the decisions to abolish financial regulations and substitute budgetary expenditures and taxes are not made by the same people at the same time and in the same place. Who would allow his favorable financial regulations to be abolished in exchange for a vague statement urging someone else to do something? The nationalization of social lending and the abolition of special financial regulations simply cannot be tied together to be voted up or down together. If they could, they might be a viable package. As it is, they are not. On the other hand, the elimination of the present regulations and the substitution of general asset reserve requirements can be considered as one package. The two sets of regulations are in the same domain, made by the same people at the same time and in the same place.

Discussion

Edward J. Kane*

If a discussant's job is to foment controversy, there is a heaven for discussants and Lester Thurow's paper has brought me to its gates. I cannot imagine laying my hands on a professional-quality paper with whose analysis and policy recommendations I could disagree more. First, I dispute Professor Thurow's analysis of why large corporations receive advantaged access to credit in tight money. I trace this phenomenon primarily to the prohibition of interest on demand deposits, the maintenance of which is presumably one of the "details" of the Hunt Commission program on which Thurow urges us "outsiders" to give the Commission the benefit of the doubt. Although I will concede him his views on agriculture and exports, I further reject both his diagnosis of what constitutes the nation's fundamental housing problem and the specific reform which he proposes as a remedy. Finally, I find the empirical evidence on the success of asset reserve requirements abroad that he cites with such assurance to be thin and unconvincing. It consists ultimately of a casual review of data covering a handful of years in a single country whose continuing housing shortage is among the worst in the world (Sweden) and ignores a long record of U.S. experience with detailed intervention in capital markets under the Federal Reserve System. This latter record is so unremittingly dismal that, even if the success of the Swedish

Reprinted from the Federal Reserve Bank of Boston, *Policies for a More Competitive Financial System,* June 1972, pp. 190-98, by permission of the publisher and the author.

*The author wishes to thank Charles C. Brown, Kenneth A. Lewis, and Parker B. Willis for helpful comments on an earlier draft of this comment.

experiment were to be established scientifically, it is hard to see how or why a serious reformer would want to hand the Fed yet another selective control.

I. Corporations' Capital-Market Advantages

Professor Thurow attributes the favored treatment that large corporate customers receive in intermediary loan markets to the existence of sizable tied savings in the form of undistributed corporate profits that do not flow explicitly through capital markets. Ignoring the concept of opportunity cost, he suggests that corporations planning capital investments do not have to compete for these tied savings. Surely corporate managements must weigh expected returns on such investments against those available from other uses. Stock market pressures and competition in the market for corporate executives should see to it that managers who ignore opportunity costs are replaced.

I am also puzzled that Thurow would think that financial intermediaries would be dazzled by tied savings *per se*. What matters is not the *savings* flow, but the transactions flow and the deposit balances a firm must hold to facilitate its transactions. Whether profits are eventually distributed to stockholders or invested in new plant and equipment, additional funds accumulate between major disbursements. These temporary accumulations and regular transactions balances are what lead financial intermediaries "to cultivate the business of corporations." Moreover, with price competition ruled out for demand deposits and greatly restricted for time deposits, it is only natural that large depositors exact compensation in other ways.

This transferral of pressure from the demand deposit market to the loan market illustrates the well-known principle that restrictions on competition in one market create pressure counter to the restriction in whatever related but unregulated markets happen to exist. It is akin to the way that squeezing one end of a balloon forces air to rush into the other or "unregulated" part of the balloon and to place it under strain.

Because banks are forbidden to pay explicit interest on demand deposits, they compete for profitable accounts through offers of *implicit* interest instead. This implicit interest takes the form of price and service concessions to valued demand deposit customers in other areas of bank activity. As a kind of tied-sale agreement, a bank stands ready to perform special or routine accounting and financial services for valued customers at charges well below marginal costs. A bank is also expected to grant loans at favorable interest rates and/or to commit itself to furnish loan funds to these customers, no matter how tight the bank's current financial condition may be.

With these as its origins, it is plain that the favored treatment of large depositors would not be abolished by forcing corporations to pay out all profits in dividends. Nor do "economic-efficiency conditions demand it [this abolition]." Except for complications due to the preferentially lower tax rate on stockholders' capital gains, the direct investment of retained earnings is analogous to a farmer's reservation demand for his produce. Holding back enough product to meet his seed and consumption needs saves a farmer trucking and marketing costs. If invested according to marginal principles, retained profit constitutes a similar market by-pass, one that reduces a corporation's capital market transactions costs (including lender information costs). This saves resources, and the savings are greater the less competitive capital markets prove to be.

II. The Housing Problem

In view of the federal government's immense and longstanding efforts to assist would-be homeowners, mortgage lenders, and the construction industry, Thurow's preoccupation with providing an abstract welfare theory justification for singling out housing for special tax transfer or capital market assistance seems terribly out of focus. The operative policy problem is to determine in what specific ways current federal programs are failing and to design reforms to remedy these failures. To substitute for this question an abstruse welfare economics exercise burlesques the very role of an advising economist.

Most observers (including the Kaiser Committee in 1968) hold that the overriding housing problem facing the United States today concerns how to provide more and better low-income homes. This requires increasing the production and rehabilitation of decent housing and somehow distributing it to persons who have traditionally been red-lined out of our nation's subsidized mortgage markets. The goal is to make available some income in kind and then (to avoid slips between the cup and the lip) to force-feed it to the poor. In this process, financing is only one obstacle. It looms as a large obstacle primarily because of red-lining, a practice that makes subsidizing the mortgage market an ineffective way of getting at the problem.

What we want are both: (1) incentives to improve the quality of new and existing housing; ways to lessen the alienation the poor feel toward current and replacement homes so that these will be adequately maintained or even improved, and (2) incentives to undertake appropriate new construction; ways to give low-income persons sufficient income to divert resources to meeting their housing needs, backed up by methods for insuring that the prospective income will in fact be spent on improved housing. Although Thurow neglects the first problem altogether, progress on the second problem should help to alleviate the first. Environmental alienation would be lessened by giving low-income persons tangible opportunities to link up with "visible" owners and to become owners themselves. Anyone who has been both a homeowner and a renter knows how differently one regards—and makes one's children regard—a dwelling unit that is one's own. For most individuals, an owned home becomes a veritable extension of oneself. Anyone who has done much renting also knows how differently one feels about a rental unit that is owned by an absentee landlord as against one whose owner lives nearby and takes an active interest in the condition of the place. Moreover, a move to resident ownership should increase the competition for occupants in low-income areas, competition that should in part take the form of product improvement. Replacing slumlords with owner-occupants should therefore be high on the social agenda. The greater the extent to which low-income apartment buildings can be made owner-occupied, the more fully we can tap individual incentives to maintain and improve the low-income housing stock.

Better urban and rural environments require a better distribution of income: nothing more nor less than sizable transfers of wealth. It is wishful thinking to suggest—with or without coordination with expenditure programs . . .—that the problem can be approached with nearly equal efficiency by forcing financial institutions to hold more mortgages. The federal government has been subsidizing mortgages in this way for years. The evidence on the distributional effects of this policy is very dismal.[1] Low-income persons who wish to be either homeowners or resident owners of apartment buildings are consistently pushed out of the institutional mortgage markets by higher-income individuals of negligible default risk. Distributionally, it is bad enough that high-income persons get disproportionately more low-interest mortgages, ironically often to buy commercial property. But low mortgage rates also spell low returns for thrift institutions (currently constrained to specialize in mortgages) and for the low-income saver who has few alternative outlets for his savings. From the point of view of the average consumer, the great virtue of the Hunt Commission *Report* is that it recognizes the harm caused by placing this system of constraints on lenders and seeks to eliminate it.

Besides these distributional problems, mortgage reserve proposals suffer from the fatal flaw that the mere use of real estate collateral and a mortgage instrument in no way guarantees that the funds being borrowed are used to finance a real estate venture of any sort. Even when they are, the funds may simply be marked-up by the borrower and passed along to higher-risk borrowers. In many cases, to become a resident owner of a low-income apartment building, an individual is forced to pay an inflated purchase price and usurious interest rate to a high-income seller who is his only realistic source of finance. With the building's rental income determining the terms of the sale and finance agreements, any advantage the lender might get by borrowing on real estate collateral in subsidized markets is unlikely to be passed on to his low-income mark.

Financial markets can contribute to solving our low-income housing problems most effectively by lessening their tendency to discriminate against low-income persons. This requires relaxing existing restraints on the payment of interest on deposits of all sorts.

Discrimination against households in the market for commercial bank loans is rooted in the prohibition against paying interest on demand deposits; the obvious first step is to repeal this prohibition. This would allow banks to compete openly rather than covertly for profitable demand deposit accounts and should shift the competitive focus of banks and business customers away from the loan market. The second step is of course to free savings deposit rates at all depositary institutions,

---

[1]See the patterns of asset-holding and real estate debt by income class tabled in my "Short-Changing the Small Saver: Federal Government Discrimination Against Small Savers During the Vietnam War," *Journal of Money, Credit and Banking, II* (Nov. 1970), pp. 513-22.

both so that low-income savers who have few other accumulation opportunities can earn the opportunity cost of their funds and so that the specialized mortgage-lending industry can compete freely for funds and mortgages.

In contrast, introducing additional portfolio restrictions on mortgage lenders may well worsen the discrimination against low-income savers and borrowers. This possibility serves as the principal focus for the rest of my comments.

III. Second-Best Solutions

Professor Thurow's remedies for commercial banks' tendency to favor corporate customers and for the housing problem involve introducing new portfolio restrictions: prohibitive taxes or marginal reserve requirements designed to force a particular response from the firms subject to the restriction. It seems to be an article of faith among social activists that any and all shortfalls in policy performance derive from society's not yet having seen the wisdom of giving government authorities still another set of controls. They seldom bother to investigate whether the policy difficulties can be traced to structural defects or excesses in the controls authorities already have: to an instrumental keyboard that is too big rather than too small. Interventionists typically act as if the contrapositive of the LeChatelier Principle holds in public administration: that one can improve processes of social and economic adjustment more by adding a new policy restraint than by relaxing a preexisting one.

Relying on the LeChatelier Principle, I believe that Thurow's reforms would make capital markets even less efficient and socially effective than they are now. What we need is not more interference with capital market mechanisms but *less*. We need to wipe out corporations' privileged "relationships" with commercial banks at their source by abolishing the prohibition against paying competitive interest on demand deposits. Introducing price competition into the market for demand deposits would break the incestuous link between a bank's willingness to accommodate a customer's loan request in tight money and the deposits that the customer brings to the bank. This reform would increase the attractiveness of mortgages to banks at such times. Given the size of bank portfolios, even a small increase in banks' propensity to acquire mortgages in tight money would greatly ameliorate the cyclical instability of mortgage flows.

I regret having to harp on a single theme. I do so because demand deposit interest was rejected by the Hunt Commission and its distributional and allocational effects so poorly analyzed in the Commission *Report* that apparently even well-trained and socially conscious economists fail to grasp just how this reform would improve competition for bank loan funds between the corporate and the noncorporate sectors.

IV. Asset Reserve Requirements

I have no quarrel with asking the Federal Reserve to concern itself with the distributional impact of monetary policy. This impact can and should be bettered. I take issue instead with two naive presumptions: (1) that introducing new restrictions on the detailed operations of U.S. capital markets is any way to improve this impact, and (2) that the nation could rely on the "independent" Federal Reserve System to administer the new controls effectively.

On the contrary, it can be shown: (1) that much of the unequal impact of tight money on various sectors grows out of current restrictions on various institutions' ability to compete for deposit funds, especially on commercial banks' freedom to compete for profitable demand deposit accounts; and (2) that (whatever its success in stabilizing the national economy) in its fifty-odd years of operation, the Federal Reserve System has proved spectacularly unsuccessful in its attempts to intervene in *specific markets.* Its efforts at detailed intervention—such as the real bills discounting policy, the almost identical February 2, 1929, and September 1, 1966, letters to member banks, and Regulations V, W, X, and (most recently) Q—have gone sour time and time again. Counting upon the Fed to regulate the flow of credit among competing sectors is like counting upon a major league Washington baseball team to finish in first place. When the Capital's erstwhile Nats last became strong enough to vie for a pennant, they were bid away to Minnesota and replaced with a much weaker team. Then last autumn even this weaker team became valuable enough to be auctioned off to Texas. So too with the staff of the Federal Reserve. Before the Fed could assemble a team of administrators strong enough to handle the job Thurow seeks to thrust upon them, these able administrators would be bid away to richer positions in the private economy.

The Fed's staff is simply no match for the market economy. Consider how the Federal Reserve's efforts to enforce Regulation Q led to a veritable epidemic of controls, with each stopgap policy action begetting several others until the control system partially broke down (on large CDs) and the underlying problem passed away of its own accord. To plug leaks, new restrictions were introduced in markets for Eurodollars, Federal Funds, commercial paper, and Treasury bills; the U.S. savings bond program was allowed to run down and its market invaded by bank minibonds and participation certificates, and threatened by Sears Roebuck and AT&T; mortgage markets required huge injections of federal money even to operate at very low levels. When open-market rates fell below Regulation Q ceilings, new problems were revealed. The industry's former pattern of mortgage rate and depositary savings rate price leadership had been destroyed, and with the backlog of mortgage demand, it proved almost as hard to get these rates to move down with open-market rates as it was to hold them down when open-market rates were rising.

No matter what bureaucratic obstacle the Fed placed in the market's way, survival demanded that firms locate a reliable loophole. With apologies to the exceptionally able and dedicated public servants gathered here today, loopholes were found because on balance private firms recruit better talent, train and motivate this talent more carefully, and when the going gets tough, can drive their staffs far harder. Employees and managers of private firms outnumber and have personally much more at stake than their counterparts at the Fed.

However, the economic case against the asset reserve proposals goes beyond the Federal Reserve's institutional weakness and can be summarized in a few sentences. First, no one knows enough either about social priorities or about how credit, goods, and factor markets interact to use financial markets as an effective vehicle for allocating funds among competing sectors in accord with social priorities. Such programs as the tax-exemption of interest income on state and local securities and federal government interventions in the mortgage markets have on balance reduced the effective progressivity of our tax system and generally helped the rich at the expense of the poor. Second, besides having a miserable track record in administering selective controls, the Federal Reserve has allocated precious little research effort to the important task of learning from its individual past mistakes. Third and most importantly, specific restrictions tied to the amount borrowed or the size, purpose, or location of the borrower as envisaged in asset reserve proposals are based on partial-equilibrium thinking: They can be justified only by ignoring affected parties' natural inclination to take actions directed at getting around the legislated restrictions. In particular, such controls can be largely and easily offset by bank and borrower adjustments in related markets, adjustments that lead frustrated regulators to extend the range of their controls to more and more loan instruments and lender activities. To this list of economic counterarguments, realistic political economists ought to add a fourth: New selective controls inevitably introduce windfall gains and losses, with these being shaped by legislative and administrative decisions closely influenced by the unsatisfactory current distribution of political and economic power whose correction is being sought.

The case for greater Federal Reserve intervention in loan markets has no firm economic foundation. Growing Congressional pressure on our "independent" Federal Reserve System to do something about the distributional problems tearing at our society grows out of popular pressures focusing increasingly on Congress. The problems are fundamentally *political* ones and best handled by honest reform of our tax and welfare systems. Everyone should recognize that to assign these unsolved problems to the Fed is to compromise and politicize this institution to a degreee that not only is inconsistent with its basic charter but even threatens its future viability.

V. Summary

I have argued that allowing freer competition among depositary institutions for all types of deposit funds is a far more promising way of reducing inequalities in sectoral access to funds than introducing still another set of restraints on institutional portfolio allocation. I recognize that any movement to free interest rates at depositary institutions will be resisted by financial trade associations that pack considerable political muscle. But what is the alternative? Can anyone claim that the Fed would know how to manipulate asset reserve requirements so as to allocate funds and resources in accord with the social priorities, even assuming that these priorities were clearly established? Can the Fed conscientiously count upon Congress to inform it as

to social needs? I think not. In fact, I view Congressional interest in imposing responsibility for distributional problems on the Federal Reserve System as a cynical political gambit designed to buy time and reelection without having to confront the sear-
ing political problems of our time. The Fed cannot itself make the hard choices
necessary to effect sizable changes in the distribution of income and opportunity. It
can only consent to serve as a scapegoat for particular Congressmen and for the
powerful banking, defense, oil, and other lobbies that influence their decisions. Congressmen want to be able to assure their constituents that *something* is being done to
improve the distribution of income and opportunity. At the same time, the lobbies
wish to forestall any real change. The Fed's dismal record in administering selective
controls in the past makes it a candidate that can meet both objectives, combining
the appearance of action with little probability of success. In view of the electorate's
lack of economic sophistication, the Fed's public acceptance of this new responsibility could carry Congress and the lobbies through another business cycle without
open conflict.

If there were reason to believe that Congress would use this period of grace to
develop a new workable consensus on national priorities, the game might be worth
the candle. But as matters stand, I would recommend lighting a flame somewhere
else.

The FINE Study

James L. Pierce

Financial markets in the United States have undergone fundamental change since the 1930s. We now live in a world of highly integrated money and capital markets that bring ultimate borrowers and lenders together in many efficient and elegant ways. Unfortunately, the federal statutes and regulations that specify the rules of the game for the participants in financial markets have not kept pace with the financial revolution. These legal and regulatory constraints are still grounded in the New Deal legislation of the 1930s.

Although some of these laws and regulations are still desirable today, many are not. Laws that regulate the activities of savings and loan associations (S&Ls) are mind boggling in their complexity and prevent S&Ls from competing in financial markets by severely limiting their depository and investment powers. These restrictions have failed in their intended purpose of smoothing the flow of funds into housing finance while they have deprived small depositors of a market return on their savings. Federal bank regulation is also in need of revamping. The regulatory agencies operate under vague and overlapping authority. The bank regulators have demonstrated that they are not equipped to deal with banking of the 1970s with its numerous methods of liability management, large-scale international operations,

Reprinted, with deletions, from *Journal of Money, Credit and Banking,* November 1977, pp. 605–18, by permission of the Ohio State University Press and the author.

This article is part of a symposium on the FINE Study, commissioned by the editor of the *Journal of Money, Credit, and Banking.*

and complex holding company activities. The Federal Reserve System is an anachronistic institution—neither private nor entirely public. Over the last forty years the Fed has evolved from a banker's bank to the prime vehicle for conducting economic stabilization policy, yet its policies are made in secret and it is answerable to no one for them.

Because many federal constraints have become archaic, there has been mounting pressure in recent years for financial reform. This paper describes the latest and perhaps the most ambitious recommendations for financial reform: The FINE (Financial Institutions and the Nation's Economy) Study commissioned by the House Committee on Banking, Currency and Housing. . . .

The FINE study sought to analyze the various parts of the financial system as interconnected elements in an overall structure. A unified approach was used in order to produce an internally consistent set of recommendations that would avoid the pitfalls of a piecemeal approach. Individual studies were undertaken to supply background for specific recommendations [12]. The object of the studies was to distill from the work of previous commissions, such as the Hunt commission, the Heller commission, and the Commission on Money and Credit, or from individual studies in the economics, finance, and law literature, materials needed to make recommendations with respect to financial reform in five interrelated areas.

The five areas are: (1) the depository and investment powers of nonbank depository institutions and the relationship between commercial banks and other depository institutions, with particular emphasis on the implications for housing finance of liberalizing powers of the nonbank depository institutions; (2) the regulation, supervision, and examination of depository institutions; (3) the structure and operations of the Federal Reserve System; (4) international banking: the activities of U.S. banks abroad and of foreign banks in the United States; (5) the activities of bank holding companies.

Many of the ideas and concepts put forth in the Discussion Principles were hardly new; some have been around for a long time, although, perhaps, not quite in the form proposed by FINE. Many of the recommendations simply recognized the inevitable evolution of the financial system and sought to remove artificial constraints on this natural process.

The Depository Institutions

It was proposed in the Discussion Principles that all federally chartered institutions—S&Ls, credit unions, and newly established federal mutual savings banks (MSBs)—be allowed to function with full powers for asset and liability diversification. In essence they could engage in any activity allowed of a commercial bank except direct commercial lending. They could, however, purchase corporate debt on the open market.[1] If S&Ls or MSBs desired to get into the business of direct com-

---

[1]This dichotomy was imposed in order to avoid building in a conflict of interest between indirect and direct commercial lending.

mercial lending, they would be allowed easy conversion to commercial bank status. Regulation Q and the prohibition against paying interest on demand deposits would be eliminated with a transition period, but without final review. The prohibition against interstate branching would also be relaxed.[2] All depository institutions would receive equal treatment under the tax codes, and would receive equal treatment with respect to reserve requirements and access to Federal Reserve facilities.

The basic thrust of these proposals is to depend as much as possible on freely selected specialization by depository institutions. Some of these firms would choose to be heavily committed to housing finance, others to consumer finance, others to wholesale activities, and still others would diversify fairly evenly across activities. Market forces should determine specialization, not the government.

But what would become of mortgage finance if the reforms were implemented? If savings and loans and other thrift institutions become more like commercial banks, might they also act more like these banks and allocate a relatively small proportion of their resources to mortgage lending? This development may or may not occur. With their new powers, the thrift institutions might be able to expand relative to commercial banks and other competitors, and they might continue to put a relatively large share of their funds into mortgage loans. If this occurred, the mortgage market would not suffer. This is the scenario upon which the conclusions of the Hunt commission and FIA rely. However, it is very difficult to predict the outcome of the proposed reforms for mortgage finance. Past experience with the behavior of thrift institutions is not a very useful guide for predicting their behavior under a regime of greatly increased investment and depository powers. . . .

It appeared that the key to reform of thrift institutions lay in recognizing and appreciating the links between the nation's specialized depository institutions (S&Ls and MSBs) and national programs to finance housing. Although one can criticize these housing programs as being ineffective and costly, it is important to recognize the extent to which the desire to channel funds into housing has conditioned the structure of thrift institutions. It became abundantly clear during the drafting of the Discussion Principles that significant enhancement of the depository and loan powers of the thrifts would be politically feasible only if one could offer assurances that housing finance would not suffer in the process. If the assurances were not viewed as sufficient, Congress would not be willing to abandon the notion of using the thrifts as conduits for housing finance.

It appeared prudent, therefore, to design programs that would induce *all* depository institutions (including commercial banks and credit unions) to provide an "acceptable" flow of funds into housing. For that reason the Discussion Principles proposed a special housing finance program that was designed to complement the increased powers of the thrifts in such a way that one could be confident that housing finance would not suffer in the process of effecting financial reform. . . .

The program outlined in the Discussion Principles rejects the use of legislative

---

[2]The bank on interstate branching would only be lifted in large metropolitan areas. Political concern over opposition of the thousands of rural banks prevented a total lifting of the ban from being proposed.

portfolio restrictions and proposes that depository institutions be allowed to select their own degree of specialization in housing finance. Instead, special financial inducements to all depository institutions would be provided. Three inducements to invest in mortgage loans are outlined in the Principles: a mortgage interest tax credit, a special FHLBB long-term loan program, and a credit to required reserves based on an institution's holdings of mortgage loans. A scheme for providing insurance against unexpected shifts in the term structure of interest rates was added later as a fourth inducement [7].

With the exception of term-structure insurance, the inducements would be available only for mortgage loans used to finance housing (owned or rented) for "low or moderate income" households.[3] Restrictions of this kind pose obvious administrative problems and expenses, but they were deemed necessary to avoid proposing federal subsidies for the rich. . . .

Although these inducements were intended to influence portfolio allocation by making mortgage lending more attractive than it otherwise would be, the program was designed to appeal equally to all types of depository institutions.

Recommendations for variable rate, or variable payment, mortgage loans were not included in the Discussion Principles for two reasons. First, there is nothing in federal law to prevent depository institutions from granting variable rate conventional mortgage loans now. Federal S&Ls are currently prevented, under FHLBB regulations, from granting such loans. But, if S&Ls were granted the greatly increased powers envisioned in the Discussion Principles, the pressure to retain this regulation would surely disappear. Banks, state-chartered S&Ls, and other institutions that are able to grant such mortgage loans have had some success with them. Second, the subject of these instruments had become a politically explosive one and there seemed to be little to be gained by raising the issue at that time.

What distinguishes the proposals in the Discussion Principles from the classic treatment of S&Ls (which is retained in diluted form in the Hunt commission proposals and in FIA) is that no one is being *forced* to do anything. The proposals say that if Congress is unhappy with the amount of mortgage lending that comes from a more freely competitive financial system, then the system should be *induced,* through market incentives, to devote more of its resources to "deserving" borrowers. To the greatest extent possible the program should be designed to allow an assessment of their cost.

Regulation of Depository Institutions

The regulation of depository institutions is a frustrating and difficult topic to study. It is difficult to evaluate current regulatory practices because it is virtually impossible to determine what the various regulators are attempting to accomplish. Further-

---

[3]The term "low or moderate income" was not defined in the Discussion Principles. In FRA, low or moderate income was approximated by limiting qualifying mortgage loans to 150 percent of the median house price in a given geographical area or to 150 percent of the median rental price in the area.

more, it is difficult to assess regulators' actions because many of their actions are taken in secret. About the only record one has is provided by congressional hearings following some sensational bank failure. It is by no means clear that evidence obtained in these hearings provides a good indication of the activities of regulators under more normal conditions.

In an effort to gather background information on the objectives and procedures of bank regulators, an extensive questionnaire was submitted to the three federal bank regulatory agencies: the comptroller of the currency, the Federal Reserve, and the FDIC.[4] Relevant portions of the questionnaire were also sent to the SEC and the Justice Department. Unfortunately, the FDIC never did bother to respond and the comptroller and the Fed did not respond in time to have all their responses included in the formulation of the Discussion Principles. . . .

It seems fair to say that the statutory authority and activities of the bank regulatory agencies have changed little since the 1930s. Yet the behavior and activities of the banks they regulate—particularly large banks—has changed fundamentally. The 1960s marked the start of a revolution in banking. Banks, or at least large banks, moved from passively accepting deposits to actively determining their own size through liability management. They now issue negotiable CDs, buy Federal funds, issue Eurodollars and foreign denominated liabilities, and issue subordinated debt. Their holding companies sell commercial paper and floating rate notes, and issue long-term debt. The proceeds from all these activities are invested in a staggering array of assets ranging from ordinary commercial loans, to oil tankers and jumbo jets, to a wide variety of foreign loans. U.S. banks are interlocked with each other and with foreign banks through joint ventures and consortia. Smaller banks have been able to get into the action through participation agreements with their larger cousins. There seems to be no end in sight to the new markets and activities that U.S. banks will enter either directly or indirectly. The efficiency and market power of the large banks appears to give them an advantage in a seemingly endless variety of activities.

These developments are impressive and in many respects probably beneficial, but the regulators have not changed their procedures or activities in the face of the banking revolution that has faced them. If bank regulations and regulatory procedures were adequate and appropriate in the 1950s and early 1960s, they must be inadequate and inappropriate today. The little that one can learn from available information supports the contention that current regulatory procedures are inadequate. There is little evidence that the regulators have reduced risk taking below what it otherwise would be and some evidence that current regulatory practices have actually encouraged risk taking.

There is a limited amount that legislation can do to improve regulation. There is no way of guaranteeing that the regulator will do a good job. About all that can be

---

[4]Because the Discussion Principles would allow S&Ls to have roughly the same powers as commercial banks, it did not appear relevant to attempt an evaluation of the current regulation of S&Ls but rather to focus on bank regulation. Furthermore, a fair amount is known about the regulation of S&Ls. See the papers by Herman, Block, and Bartell in [3].

done is to create a framework in which the regulator's job is made as manageable as possible and to provide guidelines indicating what the regulators should seek to accomplish.

It was proposed in the Discussion Principles that the regulation, supervision, and examination of all federally chartered depository institutions be consolidated into a single Federal Depository Institutions Commission.[5] This "Carteresque" consolidation would merge the activities of five separate agencies—the comptroller of the currency, the FDIC, the Federal Reserve (its regulatory and supervisory functions only), the Federal Home Loan Bank Board and the National Credit Union Administration—into a single agency. Consolidation would remove the overlapping jurisdictions, the potentially conflicting regulations, and the competition for constituents that characterizes the current regulatory framework.[6]

The changes in the powers of thrifts proposed in the Discussion Principles would blur the distinctions between banks and other depository institutions. If thrift institutions become more like banks, but the regulatory agencies were left unchanged, regulation in effect would become even more diffused and fragmented than it is today. Unless the regulatory agencies are combined, institutions that provide roughly the same services would be regulated by any one of five different federal agencies. This situation would be impossible.

Since a move to equalizing the powers of depository institutions calls for a revamping of the regulatory structure, it seemed appropriate to recommend a total consolidation. There appeared to be no compelling reasons for dividing the institutions among two or three agencies because to do so would immediately raise potential jurisdictional problems.[7]

The proposals in the Discussion Principles would allow for different treatment of state and national banks. A single federal agency need not stifle the incentive and innovations of state-chartered banks. A single agency would allow a rational evaluation of what the differences should be in the supervision and regulation of state and national banks. Contrary to the statements of some critics, the purpose of consolidation as outlined in the Discussion Principles was to obtain some order and sense in federal agencies, and not to encroach on state agencies. Recent experience with NOW accounts and variable rate mortgages serves to highlight the importance of retaining a viable system of state banks and state supervisors.

There is no guarantee that reorganization and consolidation would improve the quality of regulation. Although organizational changes can facilitate improvements, true reform ultimately depends upon improving the approaches and attitudes that the regulators take to their jobs.

Several themes emerged in the papers prepared for the FINE study concerning regulation of depository institutions (see the papers by Chase, Hester, Silber and

[5]For a discussion of current regulatory structure and practices and of the issues involved in consolidation see [1].

[6]For a succinct discussion of the deficiencies of the current regulatory structure see the testimony by former Vice Chairman of the Federal Reserve Board J. L. Robertson [15, pp. 420–23].

[7]Several states have successfully combined regulation of depository institutions under one agency. These single agencies appear to be functioning quite well.

Garbade, and Schotland in [12, pp. 145–283]). First, there is no discernible regulatory philosophy. Second, the regulators have managed to retard competition and innovation while at the same time allowing banks to increase their vulnerability to risk. Third, the regulators have retarded the development of normal market pressures as a means of disciplining bank behavior. Fourth, the steps that the regulators have taken to correct even their admitted shortcomings have been hesitant and slow.

The Federal Reserve System

The next major area of reform is in the structure and operations of the Federal Reserve System.[8] The Federal Reserve System is currently engaged in three different activities: it executes montary policy; it supervises and regulates state member banks and bank holding companies; and it performs services for member banks such as check clearing, transferring funds among member banks, and even coin wrapping. The effective execution of monetary policy is not compatible with the regulatory and service functions provided by the Fed. These other functions are time-consuming and they divert attention away from monetary policy considerations. Perhaps equally important, they put the authorities responsible for monetary policy in constant contact with technical banking questions. This contact cannot help but affect the Fed's attitudes toward banking relative to other elements in the economy. General monetary policy should be no more concerned about banks than it is about other participants in financial markets or about firms and consumers in the non-financial sectors of the economy. Yet, the Federal Reserve is preoccupied with the performance of the banking industry.

Congressional and public involvement in monetary policy decisions has been peripheral at best and easily ignored. In contrast with fiscal policy, monetary policy is shaped largely in secret. The removal of monetary policy from public pressure is both a virtue and a vice; it allows monetary policy to be flexible in a way that is virtually impossible for spending and taxation policy and it exempts monetary policy from narrow political considerations. But the balance between independence and public accountability has been tipped too far in one direction. The Federal Reserve has become almost a fourth branch of government, exempt from the system of checks and balances written into the Constitution for other areas of public policy.

The recommendations in the Discussion Principles are designed to cut the cord between monetary policy and other Federal Reserve activities, to bring the Federal Reserve more into the public realm, and to be more responsive to the needs of all major elements of society. At the same time, the Federal Reserve would retain the scope for flexibility in policy, and a measure of independence great enough to insulate policy from transitory political considerations.

---

[8]For a detailed discussion of the issues involved see [6]. Also see the testimony of Friedman, Modigliani and Tobin [14, pp. 2162–65; pp. 194–98; pp. 2368–73].

In the recommendations of the Discussion Principles, all the Fed's regulatory and supervisory duties would be transferred to the new Federal Depository Institutions Commission and the ultimate authority for the execution of monetary policy would rest in the hands of a five-member board of governors. The board would, in turn, be advised by presidentially appointed presidents of the regional reserve banks and by regional advisory committees.

The Federal Reserve Board would be placed explicitly under the Employment Act of 1946 and required to present reports to Congress indicating the next year's monetary policy objectives and how it intends to achieve its goals. These reports would explain the basic monetary policy plans for the coming year and how the board conditioned its plans on expected fiscal policy. The report would provide the board's economic forecast for the coming year and explain how its policies would help achieve the expected results. The board would have to explain how it resolved conflicting goals or objectives and how it evaluated policy alternatives.

The regional reserve banks would lose their quasiprivate status and become full-fledged government institutions. The presidents of the reserve banks would receive presidential appointments and Senate confirmations. The stock in the reserve banks, which is currently owned by member banks, would be retired. The reserve banks would continue to perform their current service functions for all depository institutions, not just member banks. There would no longer be any designation of member bank. Any depository institution that accepts deposits that are subject to reserve requirements[9]—and this would include S&Ls, MSBs, and credit unions, as well as all insured commercial banks—could take advantage of the Fed's facilities. No regulation or supervision would go with receipt of these services.

Although these recommendations go too far for some observers[10] and not far enough for others, they do appear to meet the objectve of correcting the current imbalance between flexibility and independence on the one hand and greater public accountability on the other. The recommendations are also consistent with the regulatory and depository institution reforms described above.

Holding Companies

The holding company recommendations are designed, in part, to solve some of the problems that have developed recently in holding company operations. The most notable problems involve the purchase of questionable loans by banks from non-

---

[9]The payment of interest on these reserve balances was not included in the Discussion Principles. Along with the more obvious benefits, if interest were paid on reserves, it would be possible to consider either having the Fed charge for the services it performs or returning many of the service functions to private markets. In the hearings on FINE and FRA, a great deal of support was offered for the payment of interest on reserves.

[10]The authors of the Discussion Principles were not fully prepared for the vehement response and opposition of the Federal Reserve, the banking community, and elements in the financial press to the proposed reforms. In light of this experience it is easy to understand why the Hunt commission had limited provisions dealing with the Federal Reserve System.

banking subsidiaries in their holding companies or from institutions advised by some element of the holding companies. Such transactions can, and have in the past, weakened banks in a holding company. These situations could become even more acute than they already are, and would surely increase in number, as nonbank depository institutions enter the holding company movement. Thus, the Federal Depository Institutions Commission would be required to determine that transactions between a depository institution and its holding company or transactions between the depository institution and nonfinancial subsidiaries would not weaken the the depository institution itself. Depository institutions in a holding company also could not have transactions with any company it manages or advises. This reform is particularly directed toward the REIT debacle.

These restrictions are necessary in order to keep risk-taking under control. Because the government feels obligated to protect the soundness of banks it is important that this protection not be carried over to nonbanking subsidiaries or the parent company itself. There is a danger that if transactions are not restricted, the regulators will feel compelled to take the nonbanking elements of the holding company under their wing, in order to protect the bank(s), and thus to protect these companies and their holding companies themselves instead of the bank alone.[11] Although it is not feasible to isolate depository institutions totally from the activities of other elements in their holding companies without removing all rationale for these institutions to be in holding companies, it is possible to restrict the amount of risk that they can assume from other subsidiaries. Limitations on transactions would reduce this risk exposure.

These restrictions, combined with the proposal in the Discussion Principles for interstate branching, should reduce the incentive to spin off certain activities, such as consumer credit and loan origination, from the depository institution. Lending activities of these kinds have been separated from banks as a method of circumventing restrictions on interstate branching. These activities could be monitored more easily by the regulatory authorities, by the public, and by the institutions themselves, if they were part of the depository institution rather than separate corporate entities within the holding company. Thus, the proposal to allow interstate branching would not only increase competition among depository institutions (to be assured by the strong department within the new commission), it would also serve to bring the holding company movement under closer control and inspection.[12]

The remaining recommendations concerning holding companies involve public disclosure of activities of the holding company—particularly as they relate to transactions with depository institutions and the activities of officers of these institutions, such as fees earned through transactions—and the requirement that the holding company have a minimum number of independent, unaffiliated directors. These

---

[11]An example of the danger of protecting the holding company is provided by the common practice of a holding company issuing debt and using the proceeds to increase the capital of the bank(s) in the holding company. This is an empty gesture if the regulators protect the holding company from failure.

[12]For a discussion of the tendency of depository institutions to circumvent regulations see [10].

reforms should act to induce holding companies and their subsidiaries to perform more in the interests of stockholders and less in the interests of insiders than has heretofore been the case. Recent cases of unseemly insider transactions within banks and other affiliates revealed in the press serve to highlight the need for these reforms (see [4, 9]).

International Banking

The recommendations concerning international banking—the activities of U.S. banks abroad and of foreign banks in thc United States—represent a recognition that large banks today are really multinational corporations with rather loose affection for their parent countries.[13] Yet the activities of these banks have important implications for the stability, competitiveness, and responsiveness of the American financial system. In order to make the activities of the U.S. banks operating abroad more consistent with the national interest, the Federal Depository Institutions Commission would have authority to impose capital requirements on U.S. banks operating abroad through branches, subsidiaries or joint ventures upon a finding that these foreign activities threaten the soundness of the parent bank. Furthermore, U.S. banks would be allowed to operate branches abroad only in those countries that will allow full and periodic examination of the records and activities of the branch. A branch is a branch whether located domestically or abroad and its records must be available to examiners in order that possible fraudulent activities can be detected and the soundness of the bank can be evaluated.

Moreover, the soundness of the operations of foreign branches of U.S. banks has important implications for the Federal Reserve System as the nation's lender of last resort. The Fed's responsibility in this regard is to provide liquidity within the context of the U.S. economy. Thus the Federal Reserve's discount privileges should be extended only on domestic paper. With this proposed restriction, foreign subsidiaries of U.S. banks could not sell their (foreign) paper to the parent bank who could in turn offer the assets as collateral at the discount window. To allow the use of foreign paper at the discount window opens the door for the Federal Reserve to be lender of last resort in all countries.

Foreign bank subsidiaries chartered in the United States are part of the domestic banking system and should be treated like any other bank, including being subject to reserve requirements and having access to the Fed's discount window for their domestic (U.S.) paper. But branches and agencies of banks chartered outside of the United States are part of the parent bank's overseas network and as such are not, and should not be, considered as part of the American banking system. For this reason, these institutions should not be allowed to accept domestic (U.S.) deposits or to have access to the discount window. To allow these institutions to accept

---

[13]For a detailed discussion of the international activities of banks see [2].

domestic deposits opens the door for protection of these banks in the same manner as U.S.-chartered banks are protected, but without enabling the United States to regulate and supervise the activities of the parent bank because it is located overseas. If a foreign bank wished to accept domestic deposits it would have to become a U.S.-chartered subsidiary.

Why Does Financial Reform Fail?

The Discussion Principles caused a great turmoil within the financial community because they were viewed as revolutionary and anti-everybody. The only strong support for the recommendations was heard from academic economists and a few consumer groups; most consumer groups were apathetic. Banks, S&Ls, MSBs, the regulators of these institutions, the home-builders, the labor unions, and the administration were opposed. It was made abundantly clear that a bill incorporating all the recommendations of the Discussion Principles had no chance of passage.

In response to this opposition, the House Banking Committee drafted the Financial Reform Act of 1976. This proposed act diluted many of the FINE proposals and eliminated others. Despite the efforts to compromise, FRA met vehement opposition and all efforts to achieve financial reform were abandoned.

There appears to be a fundamental reason why financial reform is so difficult to achieve. Several groups in the economy believe they would be made significantly worse off as a result of financial reform and so they understandably oppose attempts at reform. Most thrift institutions believe they would be injured if Regulation Q were removed. Most banks want to keep Regulation Q, but get rid of the differential that favors the thrifts. The thrifts in turn view the differential as crucial to their survival. Few institutions welcome the prospect of greater competition and few banks want to lose either their monopoly over demand deposits or the prohibition against paying explicit interest on these accounts.

The depository institutions have learned to deal with the existing regulatory structure and are made uncomfortable by the prospect of a new and unknown regulatory apparatus. The regulators themselves resent the criticism they have received lately and have no intention of giving up their bureaucratic preserves without an intense fight. The Federal Reserve especially is a politically powerful and entrenched institution that will fight to the finish to retain its current powers and autonomy. Bank holding companies[14] and international bankers see little to gain from greater regulation and supervision over their activities and potentially a great deal to lose.

Many institutions are cautious about trading the current financial environment for one they have no experience with. Understandably, these institutions feel uncomfortable with the uncertainties of how they might fare in a different environment. Many S&Ls, for example, fear the implications of giving up their current pro-

---

[14]The concern of bank holding companies was heightened by replacing the more balanced proposals in FINE with a set of restrictive provisions—such as the requirement that Congress approve any new holding company activities in FRA.

tected status in return for an uncertain world of greater flexibility and increased competition. The homebuilders and building-trade unions fear that increasing competition among depository institutions and eliminating forced specialization might reduce production and employment in the housing industry.

Although the special interests have no difficulty in perceiving their penalties, either real or imagined, the public at large apparently has difficulty in assessing the benefits of reform. The potential aggregate benefits to households of removing Regulation Q are substantial (see [5]) but they probably do not seem very important to most individual households. It must be difficult for the public to perceive the benefits of increased competition among institutions. Because of the cloak of secrecy that covers monetary policy and bank regulation and because of the complexity of the issues, it must be even more difficult for the public to appreciate the implications of reform in these areas. The benefits of reform are diffused both over time and over many economic units; the general public apparently does not feel the benefits with sufficient intensity to mount an effective campaign to counter the efforts of various special interests. As a result, financial reform is very difficult to accomplish in a meaningful, comprehensive form.

Perhaps it will be necessary to wait for market pressures to force a liberalization of powers for thrift institutions. Developments in several states suggest that it is just a matter of time before changes in state law force changes in federal law. Reform of the regulatory structure and of the Federal Reserve must await better public education and a commitment to appoint responsible and responsive individuals to regulatory and monetary policy posts.

REFERENCES

1. CHASE, SAMUEL. "The Structure of Federal Regulation of Depository Institutions." In *FINE—Financial Institutions and the Nation's Economy—Compendium of Papers Prepared for the FINE Study*. Book 1, pp. 145–71. U.S. House of Representatives. Committee on Banking, Currency and Housing. 94th Cong., 2d sess., June 1976.

2. D'ARISTA, JANE. "Foreign Bank Activities in the United States," and "U.S. Banks Abroad." In *FINE—Financial Institutions and the Nation's Economy—Compendium of Papers Prepared for the FINE Study*. Book 2, pp. 717–800 and 803–935. U.S. House of Representatives. Committee on Banking, Currency and Housing. 94th Cong., 2d sess., June 1976.

3. FRIEND, IRWIN, ed. *The Study of the Savings and Loan Industry*. Washington, D.C.: Federal Home Loan Bank Board, 1969.

4. HESTER, DONALD. "Opportunity and Responsibility in a Financial Institution." In *FINE—Financial Institutions and the Nation's Economy—Compendium of Papers Prepared for the FINE Study*. Book 1, pp. 173–91. U.S. House of Representatives. Committee on Banking, Currency and Housing. 94th Cong., 2d sess., June 1976.

5. KANE, EDWARD. "Short-Changing the Small Saver: Federal Government Discrimination against Small Savers during the Vietnam War." *Journal of Money, Credit, and Banking* 2 (November 1970), pp. 513–22.

6. MAYER, THOMAS. "The Structure and Operations of the Federal Reserve System: Some Needed Reforms." In *FINE—Financial Institutions and the Nation's Economy—Compendium of Papers Prepared for the FINE Study:* Book 2, pp. 669–725. U.S. House of Representatives. Committee on Banking, Currency and Housing, 94th Cong., 2d sess., June 1976.

7. PIERCE, JAMES. "A Program to Protect Mortgage Lenders against Interest Rate Increases." In *FINE—Financial Institutions and the Nation's Economy—Compendium of Papers Prepared for the FINE Study.* Book 1, pp. 93–99. U.S. House of Representatives. Committee on Banking, Currency and Housing. 94th Cong., 2d sess., June 1976.

8. *The Report of the President's Commission on Financial Structure and Regulation.* Washington, D.C.: U.S. Government Printing Office, 1971.

9. SCHOTLAND, ROY. "Bank Holding Companies and Public Policy Today." In *FINE—Financial Institutions and the Nation's Economy—Compendium of Papers Prepared for the FINE Study.* Book 1, pp. 233–93. U.S. House of Representatives. Committee on Banking, Currency and Housing. 94th Cong., 2d sess., June 1976.

10. SILBER, WILLIAM, and KENNETH GARBADE. "Financial Innovation and EFTS: Implications of Regulation." In *FINE—Financial Institutions and the Nation's Economy—Compendium of Papers Prepared for the FINE Study.* Book 1, pp. 193–208. U.S. House of Representatives. Committee on Banking, Currency and Housing. 94th Cong., 2d sess., June 1976.

11. SWAN, CRAIG. "Housing and Financial Reform." In *FINE—Financial Institutions and the Nation's Economy—Compendium of Papers Prepared for the FINE Study.* Book 1, pp. 27–92. U.S. House of Representatives. Committee on Banking, Currency and Housing. 94th Cong., 2d sess., June 1976.

12. U.S. Congress. House. Committee on Banking, Currency and Housing. *FINE—Financial Institutions and the Nation's Economy—Compendium of Papers Prepared for the FINE Study.* Books 1 and 2. 94th Cong., 2d sess., June 1976.

13. ———. *Financial Institutions and the Nation's Economy (FINE) Discussion Principles.* 94th Cong., 1st sess., 1975.

14. U.S. Congress. House. Subcommittee on Financial Institutions Supervision, Regulation and Insurance of the Committee on Banking, Currency and Housing. *Financial Institutions and the Nation's Economy (FINE) "Discussion Principles": Hearings.* 94th Cong., 1st sess., December 1975.

15. ———. *The Financial Reform Act of 1976: Hearings.* 94th Cong., 2d sess., March 1976.

The Role of Bank Regulatory Institutions

As the banking industry undergoes tremendous change, so too does the role of the bank regulator. In the1970s several bills were put before Congress to consolidate all bank regulatory activity into a single agency. The first three articles of this section deal with this issue. In Essay 38 J. L. Robertson presents a strong case for a single regulatory agency.

The bank regulation bills, together with a host of other reform legislation failed to be enacted. (See the article by Pierce in Section IX for an analysis of the total reform package and why it failed to pass.) Nevertheless, the Federal Reserve, the FDIC, and the Comptroller of the Currency have recently taken a step in the direction of reform by adopting a uniform supervisory system for rating banks. Article 39 by George R. Juncker outlines this system. This article should be read in conjunction with the readings in Section III on bank capital adequacy.

In the 1970s there were several notable bank failures related to ostensibly risky new banking practices discussed in readings throughout this book. (See for example, the articles by Schweitzer in Section II, Watson in Section III, and Bowsher in Section VIII.) Reading 40 by Chayim Herzig-Marx reviews some of the vital statistics regarding bank failures. Should banks be allowed to fail? Which banks? Selection 41 by Thomas Mayer could have been entitled "The

Optimal Number and Size Distribution of Bank Failures.'' Some of the most important research in the area of bank failures has been carried out by Joseph F. Sinkey, and in Essay 42 Sinkey summarizes his research and views on the problem of failed banks, bank examinations, and early warning systems.

Since the late 1970s a controversial issue in banking regulation is the erosion of membership in the Federal Reserve System. Many, especially central bankers, argue that membership in the Federal Reserve should be mandatory for all banks; others contend that the level of reserve requirements should be lowered to make Fed membership attractive; and yet others insist that if the Fed were to pay interest on member bank reserves (and sell its services to member banks) Fed membership would improve, as would the efficiency of financial markets. Article 43 by George Benston provides a penetrating, capsulated summary of the issues surrounding Federal Reserve membership and offers recommendations. These recommendations are Benston's alone, but they represent an excellent example of the debate in this area.

The Case for a Single Bank Regulatory Agency

J. L. Robertson

. . . Supervision must be based on frequent reports submitted by the banks, recorded on a computer and spot-checked by examiners, instead of on lengthy on-the-scene examinations. Virtually all large banks are technically capable of submitting whatever information is demanded by a supervisor on a daily or a weekly basis. Many middle-sized banks have a similar capacity. Small banks will probably have to be examined in the traditional way for the time being. The reallocation of manpower inherent in this change would create a large pool of examiners who would be available to respond instantaneously and comprehensively at the incipient stages of any bank's problem. It would enhance the quality and effectiveness of bank supervision without any concomitant increase in personnel or facilities.

The proposed system would enable a supervisor to determine at a glance the status of a bank—its capital, liquidity, asset, and liability position—and compare that present status with the standards of the regulatory agency. If a bank fails to meet those standards, examiners can be dispatched immediately to ascertain the causes and institute necessary changes—long before the brink has been reached. This may entail a greater use of the Cease and Desist authority, but that is the purpose Congress had in mind when it vested that authority in the federal supervisors.

Excerpts from a letter to Senator William Proxmire, December 23, 1974. Reprinted, with deletions, from U.S. Congress, Senate, Committee on Banking, Housing, and Urban Affairs, *Compendium of Major Issues in Bank Regulation*, 94th Cong., 1st sess., Committee Print No. 2, August 1975, pp. 903-09, by permission of the author.

In my view, this kind of updated supervision cannot be achieved soon enough—if ever—so long as federal bank supervision is divided among several federal agencies—each jealous of its prerogatives, each determined to maintain its own carefully constructed empire. It would take years—and I mean years—of negotiation before an agreement could be reached within the existing system concerning the kind of information needed to provide an accurate picture of each bank, let alone devise appropriate standards by which banks should be judged, and without which it would be impossible to achieve anything like uniformity of supervision and competitive equality.

For this type of supervision to be effective, it would be necessary to attract to the supervisory force highly qualified analysts who could design and effectuate sound standards, examiners who could pinpoint the trouble spots, and obtain correction speedily, and supervisors willing and able to enforce those standards and applicable laws with complete impartiality. Since this cannot be done under our outmoded system of divided authority, I suggest it is time for Congress to reconsider a merger of the bank supervisory functions which are now divided among three agencies. This is a surprisingly manageable task; it is not nearly as difficult as it would appear at first glance.

I suggest that the *bank supervisory functions* of the Federal Reserve System, and all the functions of the Comptroller of the Currency and the Federal Deposit Insurance Corporation, be merged into a Federal Bank Commission, leaving all monetary policy functions in the Federal Reserve System where they now reside. The Federal Bank Commission, as I conceive it, would be created by Congress. It would have five members, appointed by the President and confirmed by the Senate, who would serve ten-year terms—one term expiring every two years. The Commission would formulate all regulatory policies and be responsible for all administrative actions and decisions, but its supervisory work would be carried on under the direction of a single head. Its insurance function would be in a separate division. It might be desirable to have a third division devoted to holding company supervision. The bank supervision staffs of the three existing agencies would be consolidated in the Commission. The expenses of the Commission would be paid out of the deposit insurance assessment fund, so that the banking system would continue to bear the cost of its supervision.

Perhaps it is unnecessary to spell out the plan in more detail because it has received Congressional consideration previously. Bills which would effectuate it were introduced in the Congress during the past decade, and hearings were held by the House Banking and Currency Committee in 1963 and 1965. The records of those hearings are, of course, available to your staff. However, I might note here that while I have always felt that it would be better to merge the agencies into a new Federal Bank Commission, which could start fresh, free from the traditional positions of any existing agency, some people who favor a merger think the supervisory powers of all the agencies should be vested in one of the existing agencies. The overriding point to bear in mind is that there should be only one federal bank supervisory agency rather than *three* federal agencies with overlapping authority[1] and sometimes inconsistent points of view, where the result is a race of laxity—each agency striving to see that the banks it supervises are not disadvantaged by a more lenient attitude or ruling of one of the other agencies. Banks are now free to switch from one supervisory authority to another, seeking the most lenient supervisor. Recently a bank in a southern state switched to the jurisdiction of a particular supervisor which it thought would approve a proposed merger, and then, the merger having been approved, returned to its original supervisory authority where the merged operation could be conducted on a more economical basis for the bank.

In the sixties I believed that the greatest benefit of a single federal bank supervisory authority would be the establishment of a single set of rules and standards, applicable to all banks, which would eliminate competitive inequalities. Also, in addition to increased efficiency resulting from the elimination of a crazy-quilt pattern of overlapping authority in the federal supervision of banks, it was my belief that the concentration of supervision in a single agency would facilitate the maintenance of a strong banking system, which is so essential to our national well-being. I felt that the importance and prestige of the Commission would enable it to attract and hold the highest caliber of men; needless to say, this is of the utmost importance.

The reasons underlying the proposals of a decade ago are more valid now than they were then. Because of an unprecedented quest for growth and expansion, there are today many banks whose loan to deposit ratio is dangerously high and whose capital to asset ratio is drastically low; whose escape from any crisis is heavily dependent upon individual banker's abilities to acquire volatile short-term funds; and whose liquidity is almost nonexistent. The need for reform in bank supervision is imperative and immediate. It would not take many replicas of United States National Bank of San Diego and Franklin National Bank to shatter public confidence and the whole banking system.

Finally, and in light of recent suggestions by others, I should make clear that in my opinion, based on forty years experience in the field of federal bank supervision, including twenty-one years as a Governor and seven years as Vice Chairman of the Federal Reserve Board, the merged supervisory function should not be vested in the Federal Reserve System. The function of formulating and implementing monetary policy and the equally important and coordinate function of supervising banks and

---

[1] . . . This hodgepodge supervisory overlap is not getting better. For example, in connection with its proposal for legislation designed to control foreign banking in the United States, the Federal Reserve's press release of December 3, 1974, states: "The Comptroller of the Currency would issue licenses for all foreign banking facilities in the United States upon approval of the Secretary of the Treasury. The Comptroller would also supervise foreign-owned national banks and federally insured branches of foreign banks. The Federal Reserve would exercise supervisory authority under the Federal Reserve Act and the Bank Holding Company Act. The Federal Deposit Insurance Corporation would be required to submit proposals to extend its deposit insurance, now covering subsidiaries of foreign banks, to banks, to branches, and agencies."

bank holding companies cannot be performed by one agency without seriously compromising the effectiveness of each function. Furthermore there should never be a possibility of utilizing the supervisory function to enforce a given monetary policy today and an opposite one tomorrow, to look at bank loan portfolios through rose-colored glasses today and black ones tomorrow. . . .

A New Supervisory System
for Rating Banks*

George R. Juncker

The commercial banking system which serves the United States is a very diverse one. Its nearly 14,500 banks range from single-office institutions, with less than $1 million in assets and serving a limited market area, to the international banking giants with hundreds of offices located in the world's financial centers and with assets which total many billions of dollars. Federal supervision of such a diverse banking system is necessarily a complex and demanding task for the three agencies that share responsibility for seeing that the banking system is safe and sound and serves the financial needs of the nation. While all three federal agencies have approached the analysis of bank condition in a somewhat similar way, past differences in bank rating procedures and techniques used by the agencies had complicated the task of evaluating the condition of the banking system as a whole. In May, the Federal Reserve System, the Office of the Comptroller of the Currency, and the Federal Deposit Insurance Corporation (FDIC) announced adoption of a uniform system for rating the condition of the nation's commercial banks.

The new rating system gives senior officials at the supervisory agencies a capsule summary of the condition of individual banks as well as an indication of the health of groups of banks or the overall banking system. The ratings are intended as a tool to focus attention on real and potential problems and to permit the effective

Reprinted from Federal Reserve Bank of New York, *Quarterly Review*, Vol. 3, No. 2 (Summer 1978), pp. 47–50, by permission of the author and publisher.
*Editor's Note: This article is closely related to the readings in Section III on bank capital adequacy.

allocation of supervisory resources among the banks. Federal law gives primary supervisory responsibility for the nation's 4,700 national banks to the Office of the Comptroller of the Currency. The Federal Reserve System exercises direct supervisory authority over about 1,000 banks that are chartered by state banking authorities and that are members of the Federal Reserve System. The FDIC provides federal supervision over more than 8,700 insured, state-chartered commercial banks that are not members of the Federal Reserve System. In addition, the Federal Reserve System is charged with primary responsibilities for supervising the more than 2,000 bank holding companies in the United States with one or more commercial bank subsidiaries.

The new Uniform Interagency Bank Rating System will help ensure consistency in the way the Federal bank supervisors view individual banks within the banking system. The new rating system has two main elements:

1. An assessment by federal bank examiners or analysts of five critical aspects of a bank's operations and condition. These are adequacy of the bank's capital, the quality of the bank's assets (primarily its loans and investments), the ability of the bank's management and administration, the quantity and quality of the bank's earnings, and the level of its liquidity.

2. An overall judgment incorporating these basic factors and other factors considered significant by the examiners or analysts, expressed as a single composite rating of the bank's condition and soundness. Banks will be placed in one of five groups, ranging from banks that are sound in almost every respect to those with excessive weaknesses requiring urgent aid.

The new rating system builds upon the foundation of earlier systems used by the three agencies. These rating systems date back to at least as early as 1926 when the Federal Reserve Bank of New York used a simple system to categorize over 900 member banks then in the Second District.[1] Each of the three federal banking supervisors adopted its own rating system in the mid-1930s after extensive interagency discussion. These systems tended to be very complex and attempted to combine subjective judgments and quantitative standards.[2] Probably because of their rigidity and complexity, coupled with improvements in the strength and stability of the nation's economy and banking system, these rating systems began to fall into disfavor in the 1940s as simplified approaches were sought. In 1952, the

---

[1]This rating system went by the name of MERIT. Based heavily upon management and asset quality in relation to capital, a rating of M was assigned for banks in good condition, E for satisfactory condition, R for fair, I for unsatisfactory, and T for serious.

[2]One system "scored" six characteristics—management, loans, securities, capital account, deposit growth, and earnings—and combined these numeric scores with a series of weighting factors. Judgmental inputs on factors not specifically measured were not permitted, making the resulting score difficult to interpret either as an absolute measure of condition or even in its relationship to other scores.

[3]The Federal Reserve and the Comptroller of the Currency have used what is essentially this rating system almost continuously since it was originally adopted. The specific definitions used in that system were included in former Governor Robert Holland's testimony before the Committee on Banking, Housing, and Urban Affairs, United States Senate (February 6, 1976).

Federal Reserve System and the Office of the Comptroller of the Currency agreed on the basic structure of a rating system. That system, like the new uniform system, provided for separate ratings for capital adequacy, asset quality, and management and included an overall judgment of the bank's condition.[3]

The Federal Reserve's responsibility for supervising the activities of the nation's registered bank holding companies created particular interest in the design of an improved system for rating banks which could be used by all three federal bank regulatory agencies. . . .

Under the new system, each performance characteristic and the composite is rated on a scale from one to five, which indicates the extent of the bank's strength or weakness. A rating of "1" indicates strength; "5" indicates a degree of weakness requiring urgent corrective actions. Thus, the strongest possible rating for a bank would be:

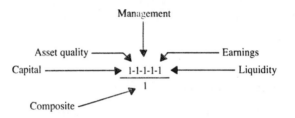

On the other hand, a rating of $\dfrac{4\text{-}5\text{-}4\text{-}5\text{-}3}{4}$ would indicate a bank with critical problems with asset quality and earnings and an overall condition that is less than satisfactory. Close supervisory attention and financial monitoring would be indicated by such a rating.

The examiner-analyst in using the new system evaluates each of the five elements of a bank's condition and the composite rating independently according to specifically defined standards. (See box for the definitions of each composite rating and the description of each performance zone as agreed upon by the three agencies.) While the five performance dimensions are somewhat interdependent, each is rated separately. Similarly, the composite is not determined by calculating an average of the separate components but rather is based on an independent judgment of the overall condition of the bank. Other factors, such as local economic conditions and prospects, trends in financial performance, and affiliation with a bank holding company, are evaluated by the examiner-analyst and incorporated into his overall assessment of the bank's condition.

Arriving at a six-number representation of a bank's condition is an exercise which requires sound analytical judgment. It is admittedly an attempt to reduce to quantified terms a very complex judgmental evaluation process. A single ratio or group of ratios cannot fully or accurately describe all the underlying factors that influence a bank's past, present, or future performance. Thus, consistency in the new system depends not, for example, on rigid definitions of what constitutes adequate earnings but rather on an appreciation by the examiner-analyst of the several roles earnings play in making a bank sound and the matching of the bank's particular and peculiar situation to the agreed-upon definitions.

The first of the five performance dimensions—*capital adequacy*—gives recognition to the role that capital plays as the foundation supporting business risks within the bank. The greater the risks faced by a bank, the greater is its need for a strong capital base. In appraising these risks, the Federal supervisors review the risk "mix" of the asset portfolio as well as the skill with which management plans ahead and minimizes risks. The vitality of a bank's market area is also included in the analysis. The examiner-analyst also reviews the bank's capital-to-risk assets relationship, its trend, and a comparison of the bank's ratio with other banks of similar size and doing similar types of business.

An appraisal of the quality and collectibility of a bank's loans and investments has traditionally been one of the key parts of a federal supervisory examination. The *asset quality* performance rating is largely based upon data on the overall quality of

I. Composite Rating

The five composite ratings are defined as follows:

COMPOSITE 1
Banks in this group are sound institutions in almost every respect; any critical findings are basically of a minor nature and can be handled in a routine manner. Such banks are resistant to external economic and financial disturbances and capable of withstanding the vagaries of the business cycle more ably than banks with lower composite ratings.

COMPOSITE 2
Banks in this group are also fundamentally sound institutions but may reflect modest weaknesses correctable in the normal course of business. Such banks are stable and also able to withstand business fluctuations well; however, areas of weakness could develop into conditions of greater concern. To the extent that the minor adjustments are handled in the normal course of business, the supervisory response is limited.

COMPOSITE 3
Banks in this group exhibit a combination of weaknesses ranging from moderately severe to unsatisfactory. Such banks are only nominally resistant to the onset of adverse business conditions and could easily deteriorate if concerted action is not effective in correcting the areas of weakness. Consequently, such banks are vulnerable and require

more than normal supervision. Overall strength and financial capacity, however, are still such as to make failure only a remote possibility.

COMPOSITE 4

Banks in this group have an immoderate volume of asset weaknesses, or a combination of other conditions that are less than satisfactory. Unless prompt action is taken to correct these conditions, they could reasonably develop into a situation that could impair future viability. A potential for failure is present but is not pronounced. Banks in this category require close supervisory attention and monitoring of financial condition.

COMPOSITE 5

This category is reserved for banks whose conditions are worse than those defined under Composite 4. The intensity and nature of weaknesses are such as to require urgent aid from the shareholders or other sources. Such banks require immediate corrective action and constant supervisory attention. The probability of failure is high for these banks.

II. Performance Evaluation

The five key performance dimensions—capital adequacy, asset quality, management-administration, earnings, and liquidity—are evaluated on a scale of one to five defined as follows:

Rating No. 1 indicates *strong performance*. It is the highest rating and is indicative of performance that is significantly higher than average.

Rating No. 2 reflects *satisfactory* performance. It reflects performance that is average or above; it includes performance that adequately provides for the safe and sound operation of the bank.

Rating No. 3 represents performance that is flawed to some degree; as such, is considered *fair*. It is neither satisfactory nor marginal but is characterized by performance of below-average quality.

Rating No. 4 represents *marginal* performance which is significantly below average; if left unchecked, such performance might evolve into weaknesses or conditions that could threaten the viability of the institution.

Rating No. 5 is considered *unsatisfactory*. It is the lowest rating and is indicative of performance that is critically deficient and in need of immediate remedial attention. Such performance by itself, or in combination with other weaknesses, could threaten the viability of the institution.

the assets held by the bank as developed during a supervisory examination. The new system, like earlier ones, relies heavily upon the classification of the bank's credits into loss, doubtful, and substandard categories according to the likelihood of the bank's actually absorbing a loss on a credit.[4] Loan and investment policies, the adequacy of valuation reserves, and management's demonstrated ability to collect problem credits would also be considered by the examiner-analyst in coming to a judgment regarding overall asset quality.

The third element in the rating evaluates the quality of a bank's corporate *management* including its board of directors. Management's technical competence, leadership, and administrative ability are evaluated along with the internal controls and operating procedures that have been installed. The bank's compliance with banking laws and regulations is another factor in the appraisal, as are the provisions for management succession. Judgments regarding management's willingness and ability to serve the legitimate banking needs of the community are also considered.

The strength of the bank's *earnings* is the fourth element in the performance rating. Here, a judgment is rendered on the adequacy of earnings to provide a sufficient return to the bank's stockholders, to generate sufficient cash flows for the normal needs of borrowers, and to provide for the future needs through the development of capital. The "quality" of earnings is also analyzed, with particular attention paid to the adequacy of the bank's additions to valuation reserves and to the tax effects on net income. Peer-group comparisons and trends in earnings provide additional quantitative evidence for the rating.

The *liquidity* rating is based upon the bank's ability to manage its assets and liabilities in such a way as to ensure that it can meet the demands of both depositors and borrowers without undue strain. Among the factors considered in evaluating liquidity are the availability of assets readily convertible into cash, the bank's formal and informal commitments for future lending or investment, the structure and volatility of deposits, the reliance on interest-sensitive funds including money market instruments and other sources of borrowing, and the ability to adjust rates on loans when rates on interest-sensitive sources of funds fluctuate. The examiner-analyst will review the frequency and level of borrowings and include judgments of the bank's ability to sustain any level of borrowings over the business cycle or to attract new sources of funds. These judgments also include analyses of the bank's present and future access to traditional money market sources of funds and other domestic and foreign sources. The bank's average liquidity experience over a period of time, as well as its liquidity position on the examination date, would be considered. For Federal Reserve member banks, the use of the discount window is also reviewed to determine if borrowings are for other than seasonal or short-term adjustment purposes.

After analyzing the five key factors, the examiner-analyst arrives at a *composite*

---

[4]The usual rule of thumb used for interpreting these classifications is that all credits classified loss will indeed represent eventual losses. 50 percent of aggregate credits classified doubtful will be charged off, as well as 20 percent of substandard classifications. Of course, actual loss experiences vary from credit to credit and bank to bank depending upon a wide variety of circumstances.

rating which summarizes the agency's overall view of the bank's condition and reflects the level of continuing supervisory attention which the bank's condition seems to warrant. A composite "1" rated bank would receive little supervisory attention between examinations, while a composite "5" bank would be subject to constant monitoring and a corrective action program developed by the bank's management and directors and accepted by its Federal supervisors.

The new rating system provides a uniform structure for use by the three Federal supervisory agencies in evaluating the condition of the nation's commercial banks. This uniformity of approach is expected to lead to more consistent and even-handed supervisory treatment. It should also enable more informed judgments regarding trends in the condition of the banking system as a whole.

Bank Failures

Chayim Herzig-Marx

Public interest in bank failures has been renewed recently as a number of multimillion dollar banking firms have been declared insolvent. Legislators, who share the concern, have asserted that "the existing structure of regulation of banking institutions under Federal law . . . is incapable of insuring the safe and sound operation of the commercial banking system of the nation."[1] Regulators have responded with increased bank surveillance and with "early warning systems" to guard against further failures.

When banks fail, investors and sometimes depositors sustain losses; society bears some costs as well. However, the dollar magnitude of such losses is far less than one might expect, and the actual amount of losses sustained is to some extent dependent upon the manner in which regulatory authorities dispose of the failed bank. Yet the mechanics of handling bank failures remain a mystery to most people.

Historical background

Waves of bank failures have recurred throughout American history. During the panic of 1893 nearly 500 banks suspended operations, out of only 9,500 banks then

Reprinted, with deletions, from *Economic Perspectives*. March/April 1978, pp. 22, 24–31, by permission of the Federal Reserve Bank of Chicago and the author.
[1]U.S. Senate, A *Bill to Establish a Federal Bank Commission* . . . , S. 2298, 94th Cong., 1st sess., 1975, p. 2.

in existence. During the monetary crisis of 1913, 105 banks failed and in each of the next two years, over 150 banks failed.

In the 1920s an average of 588 banks failed each year.[2] Between 1930 and 1933, the last four years prior to the establishment of the Federal Deposit Insurance Corporation (FDIC), 9,100 banks suspended operations in this country—an average of 43 banks per week. During these four years depositors sustained losses of $1.3 *billion*. These failures prompted extensive legislation aimed at preventing a recurrence of such disastrous numbers of insolvencies. Banks were barred from paying interest on demand deposits and from engaging in certain activities, such as stock underwriting, on the grounds that these practices had proved excessively risky. While the wisdom and effectiveness of these restrictions has been questioned, the establishment of the Federal Deposit Insurance Corporation in 1933 did indeed bring about the long sought-after stability in the banking system. By guaranteeing the safety of depositors' funds, federal deposit insurance effectively put an end to banking panics. A potential insolvency at one bank no longer threatened deposits at other banks in the same economic region, putting an end to the domino effect which had always plagued American banking.

Federal deposit insurance, however, does not stand as the only bulwark against banking panics. Monetary and fiscal policies of the government are aimed at preventing economic depression, whether due to severe contractions of the money supply or to other causes. The ability and willingness of the Federal Reserve System to provide liquidity to the banking system also helps to insure that the public will not lose faith in bank deposits as a safe and sound means of holding money balances.

The effectiveness of federal deposit insurance in reducing numbers of bank failures is readily seen. During the first four years of FDIC experience, only 249 banks failed, of which 180 were insured. Losses to depositors of insured banks were only $717,000, while losses to depositors of uninsured banks were $6.7 million and losses to the FDIC were just under $9 million. The establishment of deposit insurance thus has had two effects. First, the number of failing banks has been reduced dramatically. Second, for banks with deposit insurance, the risk of financial loss has shifted from depositors to the FDIC's insurance fund, accumulated from premiums paid by insured banks. To understand how the FDIC shifts risk from depositors to itself, it is necessary to understand what happens when a bank fails. A discussion of general provisions governing bankruptcy proceedings will help to clarify the role of the FDIC.

Bankruptcy in General

Bankruptcy is a legal proceeding in which a financially distressed firm is placed under the supervision of a court. The court appoints one or more trustees to oversee

---

[2]Data on bank suspension prior to 1934 are not wholly comparable with data from later years. Some suspended banks subsequently reopened.

the operations of the firm during adjudication. Any creditor failing to receive timely repayment of amounts due him may sue to initiate bankruptcy proceedings against the debtor firm. Firms owing amounts in excess of their abilities to repay may themselves file for bankruptcy to obtain protection from their creditors pending resolution of their indebtedness. In a typical bankruptcy proceeding, creditors present their claims against the failed firm. If the creditors can agree to a debt restructuring, usually involving extended debt maturities as well as some debt "forgiveness," the firm may continue in operation. Otherwise, the assets of the firm are liquidated and the creditors are compensated from the proceeds.

The determination of how much each creditor is paid becomes crucial. Most creditors share in the liquidation proceeds in proportion to their financial claims on the firm. These are called "general creditors." Some creditors are able to establish a prior claim to the liquidation proceeds. Called "preferred creditors," they must be paid in full before any distribution can be made to the general creditors. The benefit of establishing a credit preference is evident (lawsuits over assertions of preferences are common), making the validation of preferences one of the most important aspects of bankruptcy proceedings.

Bankruptcy in Banking

Like any other business, a bank can voluntarily place itself in bankruptcy or can be sued by creditors who are refused repayment. These events rarely occur, however, because the banking industry is subject to extensive public regulation. In particular, a bank can be placed in receivership (the equivalent of bankruptcy) by a regulatory authority, but only by the authority issuing its charter.[3] This is an important distinction between banks and other commercial businesses since in banking the chartering agency, which represents neither the business itself nor creditors of that business, has the power to force the firm into bankruptcy proceedings.

Fairly wide latitude is granted to bank supervisors in determining whether a bank should be placed in receivership. If a bank is insolvent, if its capital is impaired, if it is engaging in practices that are likely to result in substantial financial loss to depositors, or if it is about to engage in such practices, the supervisor is justified in taking control of the bank and placing it in receivership. A bank is insolvent when its assets, even though liquidated in an orderly and prudent manner, would not suffice to pay off its noncapital liabilities. A bank's capital is "impaired" when charges against the capital account (e.g., to write off losses or uncollectable debt) exceed the sum of contingency reserves, undivided profit, and surplus. Because of supervisors' wide latitude, a bank is usually closed long before it actually defaults on its debts.

Once a bank is declared insolvent, it is taken over by regulatory authorities and closed to all business. The Comptroller of the Currency or state bank supervisor

---

[3]The Federal Reserve and the Federal Deposit Insurance Corporation, although they are both heavily involved in bank supervision and regulation, lack the legal power to close a financially distressed bank.

places the bank in the hands of a court with jurisdiction in such matters (usually a federal district court), The court appoints and oversees a receiver, whose job is to examine the books and accounts of the bank and to verify assets and liabilities. The receiver is also responsible for collecting interest and principal due on outstanding loans and investments. Public notice is given, usually for about three months, for all creditors of the failed bank to present proof of their claims. The receiver judges the validity of all claims presented.

A large body of case law exists dealing with preferences in bank failures.[4] Most transactions with a bank arise out of a debtor-creditor relationship. For example, one who deposits money with a bank is a creditor, and the bank stands as a debtor to him. In order to establish a preference in a bank failure case, one must demonstrate that his relationship with the bank was not simply that of a creditor, but rather that the relationship was one of principal and agent or that the bank was acting in a trust capacity. Banks often act as agents for municipal governments or other political subdivisions in the collection of taxes. The political units thereby achieve the preferred status of a principal with respect to the tax deposits rather than that of a creditor. Another situation establishing a preference occurs when money is deposited in a bank with the express stipulation that the funds are to be used to purchase certain securities. The bank then acts as the agent for the depositor, and his claim on the bank takes priority over that of other depositors. Pledging assets to secure deposits also establishes a preference. Depositors who are not preferred creditors are merely general creditors of failed banks. General creditors share pro rata in all liquidation proceeds, but only *after* preferred and secured creditors have been compensated.

At federally insured banks, the Federal Deposit Insurance Corporation relieves depositors of financial risk by entering into the bankruptcy proceedings. When an insured bank fails, the FDIC guarantees to each depositor the amount of his account, up to the current insurance limit (now generally $40,000). The FDIC then becomes subrogated to the rights of depositors to the extent of insurance payments; that is, each depositor's claim to liquidation proceeds passes to the FDIC for the amount by which the FDIC reimbursed the depositor. The FDIC then becomes a general creditor of the failed bank and shares in liquidation proceeds pro rata with other general creditors.

Claims of capital investors in failed banks rank below those of general creditors. There are three classes of capital investments: capital notes and debentures, preferred stock, and common stock. In order to be exempt from interest rate ceilings and reserve requirements, capital notes and debentures must be explicitly subor-

---

[4]Most state banking laws do not deal specifically with preferences. Among Seventh District states only Iowa makes explicit the order of payment of creditors of failed banks. Section 524.1312 of the Iowa Code specifies that, in the event that liquidation proceeds are not sufficient to pay off all creditors in full, the order of distribution is, first, all costs of the receiver; second, all preferred claims (in full or pro rata if proceeds are not sufficient to compensate all preferred creditors); third, depositors; fourth, all other general creditors; fifth, holders of capital notes and debentures. The Iowa code thus elevates depositors above other general creditors.

dinated to all deposits. They are also, therefore, subordinated to all creditors' claims that rank on a par with deposits. Thus, holders of capital notes of a failed bank will not receive any recovery on their investment until all preferred and general creditors recover the full amount of their investments.

If any funds remain after holders of capital notes have been paid off in full, stockholders may receive something. In cases in which the failed bank had both preferred and common stock outstanding, preferred stockholders have priority.

The Federal Deposit Insurance Corporation thus plays a key role in settling depositors' claims against failed banks. In fact, in the vast majority of failure cases, the Corporation is appointed receiver for the failed bank and for failed national banks must be appointed receiver. Regardless of the method of disposition chosen, substantial monetary outlays on the part of the FDIC will normally be required.

Disposing of Failed Banks

The FDIC has several options for disposing of failed banks. Unlike other business failures, which can be wound up only by a debt restructuring or by a liquidation, bank failures can be handled in five distinct ways: (1) by "purchase and assumption"; (2) by "deposit payoff"; (3) by chartering a Deposit Insurance National Bank; (4) by providing financial aid; (5) by reorganizing. Only reorganizing does not involve the FDIC.

Purchase and Assumption

The FDIC is empowered to dispose of failed banks by arranging a merger with a sound bank (which may be newly chartered for that express purpose). In a "purchase and assumption" negotiations are entered into between the FDIC and sound banks interested in acquiring the business of the failed bank. Acquiring banks must assume all deposit liabilities of the failed institution and may choose to assume other liabilities as well. In the typical case the assuming bank acquires all matured liabilities with the exception of long-term debt. Contingent liabilities are usually not assumed.[5]

The assuming bank will acquire some, but not all, assets of the failed bank. Many of the failed bank's assets will not be sound, making them undesirable for purchase. If the bank failed through defalcation, some assets may be fictitious. Undoubtedly, some loans will have been classified.[6] Typically, therefore, the assuming bank will

---

[5]For an exhaustive definition of contingent liabilities, see Glenn G. Munn, *Encyclopedia of Banking and Finance,* 7th ed. (1973), pp. 222–23. In general, contingent liabilities are obligations not expected to fall due. Some examples in banking are letters of credit, acceptances, accommodation endorsements, liabilities resulting from pending or possible litigation, and futures contracts to deliver foreign exchange. Matured liabilities are those whose incurrence is definite and accomplished, such as deposits, capital notes, and rental charges for space and equipment.

[6]Classified assets are those a bank examiner believes unlikely to repay all interest and principal.

acquire a smaller dollar amount of assets than liabilities. The difference is made up by a cash payment from the FDIC to the acquiring bank.

Potential assuming banks bid competitively for the opportunity to acquire the sound and ongoing business of the failed bank. Each competing bank submits a bid to the FDIC, which includes a promise to pay to the Corporation a specified sum of money, called a "premium," if the bid is accepted. Usually the FDIC will accept the bid that carries the highest premium. The premium is "paid" in the form of a lower cash advance from the FDIC. That is, the FDIC pays out to the winner of the bidding enough cash to make up the difference between liabilities assumed and assets taken plus premium. In this transaction the FDIC gains title to all the assets not specifically selected by the assuming bank (hence the term, "premium," in that the FDIC gains title to certain assets without any corresponding liabilities). The size of the premium and the FDIC's ability to collect interest and principal on the assets it receives govern the chances that the failed bank's stockholders will recover their investment.

In addition to administering the exchange of assets and liabilities and paying the cash advance, the Corporation sometimes makes long-term loans to beef up the assuming bank's capital position.

Deposit Payoff

The FDIC is seen most clearly in its role as guarantor of deposits when a bank failure is handled by the liquidation or "deposit payoff" method.

When a failed bank is paid off, the FDIC (assuming it has been appointed receiver) assesses the validity of depositors' claims against the failed bank. Secured or preferred depositors, such as political subdivisions, are paid first out of the failed bank's assets. Other depositors who have valid claims receive the value of their deposits from the FDIC, up to the insured maximum. Usually, the FDIC disburses funds in the form of deposits in another bank. If a depositor has received a loan from the failed bank, the amount of the loan may be offset against his deposit.

In exchange for paying depositors the value of their deposits, the FDIC acquires legal claims against the failed bank's assets and becomes a general creditor of the failed bank in the depositors' stead.

As the assets of the bank are liquidated, creditors are compensated from the proceeds. The FDIC shares pro rata with other general creditors, such as depositors whose accounts exceeded the insurance maximum, suppliers of business forms or office equipment, and similar other parties to whom the bank owes money.

Deposit Insurance National Bank

Infrequently, the FDIC sets up a new bank in place of the failed bank for a temporary time, normally two years. Chartered in effect by the Comptroller of the Currency, with no capital, the bank is titled Deposit Insurance National Bank (DINB) and is automatically granted deposit insurance. The bank makes no loans, holds only U.S. Treasury securities or other securities guaranteed as to principal and interest by the U.S. government or cash assets, and conducts basically a payments business only. All insured deposits in the failed bank are transferred to accounts in the Deposit Insurance National Bank.

Failures handled as DINBs are classified as deposit payoffs, since depositors can withdraw the amount of their deposits. This method is used only where no other banking facilities are available in a community, in the hope that local people will be encouraged to organize a permanent bank for themselves. The FDIC can, if it wishes, sell the business of the DINB by accepting bids to capitalize the bank.

Financial Aid

A bank may become insolvent before any actual default on obligations occurs. The FDIC is empowered to make long-term loans to a distressed bank if the FDIC and the chartering regulator agree that continuance of the insolvent bank is necessary to the economic well-being of the community or is desirable because the demise of the bank would bring about excessive concentration of banking resources. Such loans, coupled with close supervision and perhaps mandatory changes in operating personnel and procedures, can help restore a distressed bank to a sound condition. The most notable occurrence of this type of assistance involves the Bank of the Commonwealth of Detroit, which has received loans totaling $35.5 million from the FDIC.

Reorganization

State banking laws and the National Bank Act provide that a failed bank can be reorganized, presumably with reduced capital and other liabilities to reflect the reduced market value of its assets. Intervention by the FDIC is not required.

Reorganization is especially useful when liquidation of the bank will result in large losses for all classes of creditors. To invoke such a procedure, therefore, requires the concurrence of creditors holding claims to a large fraction of the bank's nonequity liabilities, typically 75 or 80 percent.

Of the five methods of disposing of failed banks, legal reorganization is used least frequently—virtually never. Financial aid is used more often to prevent actual failure than to dispose of a failed bank. Deposit Insurance National Banks are used infrequently and are really only an alternative means of paying off depositors. The great majority of failed banks are handled either by purchase and assumption or direct payoff.

The FDIC seemingly has gone through cycles in which it preferred first one method of dealing with failures and then another. From 1934 to 1944 both payoff and assumption methods were extensively used. Between 1945 and 1954, however, every bank failure was handled as a purchase and assumption transaction. Then, from 1955 through 1964, almost all failures were paid off. Since 1965 both payoffs and assumptions have been used.

Data on numbers of bank failures are understated, just as numbers of business bankruptcies are also understated. Besides the possibility of financial aid from the FDIC to keep a distressed bank afloat, emergency mergers are sometimes consummated before the acquired bank actually fails. Occasionally, the merger takes place with the blessings of the federal bank regulatory agencies but without any financial assistance. The most prominent example of this occurred in 1975, when the Security National Bank of Hempstead, New York, was acquired by Chemical Bank. Had the merger not taken place, Security, with deposits of $1.3 billion and assets of $1.7 billion, would have become the second largest bank failure in U.S. history.

In other cases, the FDIC has used direct financial assistance to facilitate mergers. In 1975 the FDIC assisted in the merging of a newly organized bank with the Palmer First National Bank and Trust Company of Sarasota, Florida, after receiving assurances that such assistance was necessary to bring about the acquisition and to avert the failure of Palmer First National. These are but two instances in which failures have been preempted by mergers. It is not known how many insolvencies have been prevented this way.

Normally, the FDIC chooses the method that minimizes the loss to the insurance fund. The distribution as well as the total amount of losses to creditors are strongly influenced by the method chosen by the FDIC. It is possible that one method— usually deposit payoff—may result in a somewhat smaller loss to the insurance fund while generating much larger losses to other creditors than any alternative method. However, when a large bank fails, the FDIC is under great pressure to handle the case by a purchase and assumption. Although possibly more costly to the insurance fund, a purchase and assumption guarantees that depositors, whether fully insured or not, will suffer no losses.

What Do Bank Failures Cost?

Regardless of the distribution of losses among creditors, bank failures impose costs upon society. Resources must be devoted to what is essentially the unproductive task of disposing of the failed bank, collecting interest and principal from the failed bank's assets, and compensating creditors of the failed bank—tasks performed by the receiver and by the FDIC as insurer. Labor and other resources may be idled if the bank's demise results in a lack of credit in the community. If the payoff route is chosen, deposits are not immediately available to depositors. Thus, there is an opportunity cost due to the temporary sterilization of working capital. This cost does not arise in purchase and assumption cases. Those resources that had been allocated to businesses that failed (i.e., to defaulting debtors of the failed bank) and that could have been channeled to more productive uses represent wealth that, aside from any liquidation value that may remain, is permanently lost to society. The potentially most important social cost of bank failures is that they might lead to a rapid contraction of the money supply, possibly inducing a period of economic depression. This is the cost that is the primary concern of bank regulation and deposit insurance. Finally, chronic failures might lead to a loss of faith in the payments mechanism. If people become disenchanted with "bank money," they will be induced to hold more currency. The fact that most money is presently held in the form of demand deposits at commercial banks indicates that people generally prefer this form of money. Thus, the occurrence of a situation in which people are driven by uncertainty to hold more currency and less demand deposits than usual would impose a social cost.

Even when bank failures do not result in net losses to society, they bring about transfers of wealth among individuals. Wealth has been transferred from creditors of banks—stockholders, other investors, and sometimes uninsured depositors—to debtors of banks—those whose failures to repay their borrowings brought about the insolvency. Under theoretically ideal conditions—accounting practices that correspond exactly with economic and financial theory and instantaneous liquidation of a failed business—the dollar amount of wealth transfers from bank creditors to bank debtors will exceed the overall cost to society. This is true because bank debtors receive a net benefit from the amounts they borrowed and never repaid. Under real-world conditions, the estimates will likely diverge even farther. The major creditors of failed insured banks, in dollar terms, are depositors, the FDIC, bondholders, and stockholders. Estimating losses to these creditors will give a good indication of the upper bound of the cost to society from bank failures.

Depositors

According to FDIC data 99.6 percent of the amount of deposits in banks failing from 1934 to 1976 has been paid or made available to depositors. Since in deposit assumption cases all deposits are immediately available, losses to depositors arise only in deposit payoff cases. The vast majority of deposits in paid-off banks has already been made available to deposits, mostly by direct payments from the FDIC (i.e., a demand deposit in another bank), but partly through offset against outstanding loans, through security or preference, or through the proceeds of asset liquidation. The FDIC expects eventually to repay about 96 percent of deposits in failed banks handled as deposit payoffs, leaving a loss of less than $20 million over the entire 1934–76 period. Thus, even though large deposits are not fully covered by deposit insurance, depositors of insured banks cannot be said to have sustained major losses from bank failures. On the other hand, losses in the form of opportunity costs (interest foregone while deposits are unavailable) may be quite large but are extremely difficult to calculate.

FDIC

The Federal Deposit Insurance Corporation estimates that, based upon all its activities undertaken to protect depositors of failed banks, its total loss from banks

---

[7]*Annual Report of the Federal Deposit Insurance Corporation, 1976,* tables 125 and 127.

failing between 1934 and 1976 will be just over $285 million. This loss covers not only disbursements in payoff and assumption cases but also amounts advanced to protect assets, net losses on purchases of assets from operating banks, defaulted principal on loans made to operating banks to avert failure, and other similar expenditures. Thus, it is obvious that federal deposit insurance operates to shift the burden of risk from depositors to the Federal Deposit Insurance Corporation's insurance fund.

Bondholders

Long-term capital notes and debentures are securities that have become relatively popular only in recent years. Thus, most losses to bondholders have occurred in the decade of the 1970s.

Stockholders

Recoveries by stockholders are infrequent. The FDIC last published a study of stockholder recoveries in its 1958 Annual Report. The overall finding was that in only 91 out of a total of 436 failures did stockholders recover any part of their investment.

The method used by the FDIC to dispose of the bank influences the likelihood of recoveries by stockholders. Stockholder recoveries are less likely in payoff cases because the class of general creditors is augmented by uninsured depositors. In purchase and assumption cases stockholders have on occasion received stock in the continuing bank, especially when two failing institutions were merged into a single sound bank or when a failing bank was merged into a newly chartered bank. In a few other scattered cases, stockholders of assumed banks also recovered a small fraction of their investment.

It would appear that everyone seems to come out at least as well off when the deposit assumption route is chosen as when the FDIC pays off depositors directly. If so, why does the FDIC ever use the payoff method?

There are several reasons. An assuming bank requires indemnification against legal actions that may arise as a result of the closing of a bank. In certain cases the uncertainty surrounding a bank failure may be so great that such indemnification could prove expensive in terms of legal and court costs. In unit banking states finding a suitable merger partner can be quite difficult since the failed bank cannot be operated as a branch. Thus, the assuming bank, if it were not newly chartered, would have to be quite close by. Then, too, the FDIC could estimate that the total cost of paying off depositors could be less than arranging a merger. Even in the assumption cases, the FDIC is saddled with some assets of the failed bank, normally the worst credit risks. Negotiation costs can be avoided if the FDIC takes over the entire portfolio. And all the purchase bids received by the Corporation could turn out to be negative numbers!

Basically, while the FDIC was instituted to protect depositors in case of bank failures, it has a responsibility to dispose of failed banks with minimum cost to itself.

Estimating Losses in the 1970s

Losses are incurred by depositors only in payoff cases. Some failures handled as payoffs in the 1970s have involved banks whose depositors were fully insured. In other payoff cases, the percentage recovery by general creditors (and therefore that of uninsured depositors) is known. In those payoff cases where the ultimate status of depositors' recoveries is not known, losses to depositors are estimated at 3½ percent of total deposits. This figure is slightly higher than historical average losses in payoff cases.

Losses to bondholders are estimated from information supplied by the Federal Deposit Insurance Corporation. The assumption is made that bondholders of failed banks will lose the entire principal amount of their investments. No component is included for lost interest.

Losses to the FDIC are the Corporation's estimates.

Losses to stockholders are the most difficult to estimate. The ratio of the market value of common stock to the book value of equity for banks and bank holding companies whose equities are widely traded can be formed and applied to the book value of equity for banks that failed. Applying the ratio to book value of equity two years before failure should correct for the large losses sustained by failing banks prior to their closing. The assumption is made that stockholders lose the entire amount of their investment in banks that fail. Data on stockholders' equity are taken from the December Report of Condition two years prior to failure.

Several banks failing in recent years have been owned by bank holding companies. Since the banks comprised the bulk of the holding companies' assets, in all probability those holding companies will also file for bankruptcy. Because some of

Table 1. Estimated Losses due to Bank Failures

Year	Number of Failures	Disposition: Deposit Payoff	Purchase and Assumption	Estimated Losses to Creditors Depositors	Debtholders	Stockholders	FDIC	Total
				(thousands)				
1970	7	4	3	$ 585	$ 0	$ 8,572	$ 825	$ 9,982
1971	6	5	1	3,541	0	31,124	1,215	35,880
1972	1	1	0	713	0	1,863	4,000	6,576
1973	6	3	3	0	15,000	56,097	150,269	221,366
1974	4	0	4	0	29,608	167,243	4,100	200,951
1975	13	3	10	1,138	2,600	49,103	35,045	87,886
1976	16	3	13	649	7,038	88,191	15,308	111,186
Total	53	19	34	$6,626	$54,246	$402,193	$210,762	$673,827

the holding companies themselves had long-term bonds outstanding, it is reasonable to assume that holders of those bonds will suffer losses. Since they are as yet unknown, these losses are not included in Table 1 but could easily exceed $100 million.

Losses to the four major categories of creditors of failed banks totaled over $673 million for the seven years, according to the estimates in Table 1. Of this sum 60 percent represents losses to stockholders and another 31 percent represents losses to the FDIC. Depositors' losses are less than 1 percent of the total amount lost. Thus, it appears that federal deposit insurance accomplishes its major goal: insulating depositors from loss in the case of bank failure.

Losses to debtholders, insignificant before 1973, are beginning to take on sizable proportions. This reflects both the increasing popularity of debt capital and the greater size of the banks that have failed in recent times. Since 1973 nearly 9 percent of total losses have been incurred by holders of capital notes and debentures. Franklin National Bank of New York had an especially large volume of capital notes outstanding, accounting for the large loss to bondholders in 1974.

Losses to the FDIC tend to be considerably larger than losses to depositors except in the years in which the deposit payoff technique was relied upon most heavily. Thus, in 1970 and 1971 losses to depositors exceeded losses to the FDIC. The FDIC's largest expected loss resulted from failures in 1973. Interestingly, the FDIC's losses expected from 1974 failures, including Franklin National Bank, should be quite small, while losses to stockholders will be extremely large.

Thus, despite public and legislative concern that an inordinately large number of banks have failed in recent years and that society has paid a heavy price in lost wealth, the evidence shows that bank failures are still relatively rare events and losses are borne, not by depositors, but by capital investors and the federal deposit insurance fund. Since insured banks themselves contribute insurance premiums out of their earnings, one can justifiably conclude that the banking system is fully capable of safeguarding the stock of bank money against all but the most drastic contingencies. Protecting against such extreme contingencies, however, is properly the province of monetary and fiscal policy.

Moreover, that losses in bankruptcies be borne by capital investors is fitting. Indeed, stockholders and bondholders should be fully aware of the risks they take in making investments in banks or in any other firm. Since they enjoy whatever return their investment brings, they should properly bear the risks.

Summary

Two important legal distinctions separate bank failures from other business failures. In banking, the chartering authority, which is neither a creditor of nor an investor in a bank, is empowered to declare the firm insolvent; in other businesses, only creditors or the firm itself can initiate bankruptcy proceedings. While but two means of resolving a bankruptcy proceeding are available for most businesses, five methods can be used in banking. The two most commonly used methods are deposit payoff (liquidation) and purchase and assumption (merger into a sound institution).

Deposit insurance operates to reduce the number of bank failures and to minimize the financial impact of failures on small depositors. The FDIC accomplishes this by inserting itself in the legal proceedings between depositors and the failed bank, substituting a guaranteed reimbursement of the insured amount of an account for an uncertain claim against the assets of the failed bank.

Because of its prominent role in disposing of a failed bank, the FDIC is typically appointed receiver. The Corporation then serves in two roles: as guarantor of deposits, the FDIC is potentially a general creditor of the failed bank; as receiver, the FDIC is responsible for evaluating assets and liabilities and validating claims and preferences.

Bank failures generate costs, part of which can be thought of as wealth transfers and part of which represent net wealth losses to society. Wealth is transferred from creditors of banks to debtors of banks.

Estimates of losses to creditors of banks that failed from 1970 to 1976 reveal that stockholders and the Federal Deposit Insurance Corporation bear the brunt of the costs, accounting for 91 percent of all losses sustained.

Preventing the Failures of Large Banks

Thomas Mayer

The question of whether large banks should be allowed to fail brings us face to face with a conflict between two social goals. On the one hand, the goal of optimal resource allocation suggests that even very large banks, like other firms, should be allowed to fail. On the other hand, the stabilization goal suggests that, given the present institutional structure, failures of large banks should be prevented lest they lead to runs on other banks, and to a significant reduction in the money stock. The solution suggested here for this conflict is small changes in the institutional structure. . . .

Bank Failures

There are two characteristics of banks which make the process of weeding out by failures less socially desirable than it is in other industries. One is the obvious point that since banks provide the bulk of our money supply, large-scale bank failures could cause a major depression. The second special characteristic of banking is that, in the absence of government regulation and insurance, bank deposit customers would operate with a high degree of ignorance. A free market system is efficient

Reprinted, with deletions, from U.S. Congress, Senate, Committee on Banking, Housing, and Urban Affairs, *Compendium of Major Issues in Bank Regulations,* 94th Cong., 1st sess., Committee Print No. 2, August 1975, pp. 865–82, by permission of the author.

because it allows buyers to determine the volume of production, and buyers are generally able to judge the desirability of a product or service better than anyone else is. But, in the absence of government regulation and insurance, this is not so for bank deposits. One of the critical characteristics of a bank deposit is its safety, and for most depositors the costs of ascertaining the safety of a bank are extremely high, if not prohibitive. This market failure argues for removing banking from the private sector into the public sector. But outright government ownership of banks creates its own inefficiencies.

Consequently, we have settled for a compromise solution, one which eliminates the danger of loss for most depositors, as well as the danger of a reduction in the circulating medium, while leaving banks still in the private sector, albeit subject to very heavy supervision. This compromise is to insure bank deposits, but to allow inefficient banks to fail.[1] By insuring deposits we cut the link between bank failures and a reduction in the money stock, and we also provide the depositor with a safe haven for his funds, something the private market alone cannot do. Although this is, in principle, an ingenious compromise, the actual arrangement falls short of the achievable potential. This is because we go beyond the insurance of deposits in several ways. One way we do this is to limit bank failures below their optimal level (probably substantially so) by limiting entry into banking, and also by imposing serious restrictions on bank portfolio choices. Another way is that in the case of very large banks we appear to have drifted into a policy of insuring, not the deposits, but the bank itself.

Another important way in which we depart from the compromise solution of insuring deposits rather than banks is that we do not insure all deposits, but only deposits up to $40,000. The reason for this is that large depositors are supposed to be able to evaluate a bank (presumably at fairly moderate cost), and should therefore be able to exercise a disciplining function over banks. In general, deposit insurance removes one incentive which banks have to manage their assets safely. This is that in the absence of deposit insurance depositors would avoid banks they consider to be unsafe. To some extent we compensate for the absence of this incentive toward sound banking by imposing government regulation over banks and examining them. If we had complete faith in these controls there would be no reason for not insuring all deposits. But we do not have this faith. It is difficult for bank examiners, who of necessity cannot be as familiar with the bank as its own management is, to second-guess it, and besides defalcations may readily escape notice.[2] Consequently, we back up the system of government regulations and examinations by giving large depositors an incentive to supervise banks on their own.

[1]Portfolio regulation of banks should be thought of as a way of protecting the FDIC's fund rather than as needed for any other reason such as the "strategic" nature of banks.

[2]Bank examinations are not audits. However, the FDIC could, in principle, conduct bank audits as well as examinations. Moreover, the FDIC's ability to control risk taking by banks could be increased by imposing very rigid and inflexible regulations on banks, e.g., a minimum capital/deposit ratio which every bank regardless of its special circumstances would have to meet. But such inflexibility would make for inefficiencies.

But although we rely on depositor supervision in principle, in practice we use it only to a very limited extent, if at all. There are three reasons for this. One is that most bank failures that have occurred have been failures of small banks which presumably had few deposits in excess of the insurance limit.[3] Second, in most cases of bank failure the FDIC has not closed the bank, but has merged it into another bank with the consequent de facto protection of all deposits. Third, in the case of *very* large banks, it is widely believed, and probably correctly so, that the government would not allow them to fail, in the sense of going into receivership. Hence, in practice we really make little use of depositor supervision. But there is evidence of *some* depositor supervision because the rate banks have to pay on large CDs seems to be affected not only by the bank's size, but also by its balance sheet ratios. Moreover, Peltzman has found that banks do substitute FDIC insurance for capital, which suggests that depositor supervision has an influence on a bank's capital ratio.[4]

How efficient is depositor supervision? Unfortunately the information needed to answer this question with a substantial degree of confidence is not available. It could—and should—be investigated by looking at two things. One is the extent to which the relative rates banks have to pay on large CDs are correlated with highly sophisticated, rather than naive, notions of what indicates bank safety. Second, it would be worthwhile looking at depositor behavior in failing banks prior to the public announcement of their failure. To what extent, if any, did large sophisticated investors withdraw deposits and to what extent were they aware that something was amiss?

In the absence of such studies there exists no hard evidence on the effectiveness of depositor supervision. But there are some plausible reasons for thinking that it is not very effective. One is that in the case of small banks, most failures appear to be due to fraud or defalcation, and such failures cannot be predicted by looking at the bank's balance sheet ratios. And even local depositors who know the bank's management personally are not likely to be able to predict it, human ability to dissemble being what it is. Second, in the case of *very* large banks depositor supervision is probably reduced by the widespread belief that the government would not allow such a bank to fail. Third, and probably most significantly, by handling most failures via the merger route the FDIC has, in effect, protected large depositors in most cases of failures so that even large depositors can feel safe now. It is not really correct to say that we do not insure deposits of over $40,000; it is more correct to say that we create some degree of uncertainty about the protection of deposits above $40,000.

[3]For small banks supervision by large depositors might be ineffective. Substantial depositors in a bank that does not issue large CDs are likely to be either local business firms that are borrowing from the bank, and hence reluctant to remove their deposits from it, or the proverbial "little old lady" who keeps a very large bank deposit because she thinks that only banks are safe.

[4]Sam Peltzman, "Capital Investment in Commercial Banking and its Relationship to Portfolio Regulation," *Journal of Political Economy,* vol. 78, January/February 1970, pp. 1-26.

Allowing Large Banks to Fail

Having seen that we protect depositors rather than banks as far as the general run of banks is concerned, let us ask whether we should do the same for large banks, say the top dozen or two dozen banks. It is worth noting, right at the outset, that were we to protect large banks themselves rather than just their depositors, while continuing to protect, at least de jure, only the depositors of small banks, this would generate two obvious disadvantages. One is that stockholders of large banks (as well as large depositors and nondeposit creditors of such banks) are given a significant advantage over their counterparts at other banks. This is not only inequitable, but also, by reducing the cost of equity capital, large deposits, and nondeposit funds to large banks, it provides them with a competitive advantage. This is contrary to public policy which usually tries to help small banks by such devices as lower reserve requirements.

Furthermore, the protection of large banks but not of other banks is likely to create considerable public uncertainty about exactly where the cutoff point is, and which banks are protected. Thus, someone might buy a large CD in a bank believing that it is in the charmed circle, and then find out the hard way that this is not so. To be sure, the government could issue a list of banks thus favored, but since there is no way one can defend drawing the line at one point rather than a bit further down the list of banks, the government is not likely to issue such a list, and draw upon itself the ire of stockholders (and uninsured creditors) of banks just below the cutoff point.

But there is a case to be made for protecting large banks. This case is that the failure of a large bank is much more likely to set off bank runs than is the failure of small banks. There are four reasons for this. The most obvious, but probably the weakest, is that the failure of a large bank is much more dramatic than even a series of failures of small banks. A more important reason is that the causes of failures are likely to be different for large and small banks. Failures of small banks are usually due to defalcation. Hence, when a small bank fails, depositors in other small banks can reasonably intepret this failure as being due to a condition peculiar to that particular bank, and as not relevant to the safety of their bank. But large banks are unlikely to be brought down by defalcation. If a large bank fails it is most probably the result of its having acquired unsound or illiquid assets. Since there is a *tendency* for large banks to hold similar assets (since banks face more or less similar cost and demand conditions), if one large bank fails creditors of other large banks may have good grounds to become suspicious about the safety of their bank. The extent to which this happens depends, of course, on the particular circumstances of the failure. Thus the failure of the Franklin National did not seem to have caused *serious* concern about the safety of other banks since it was known that the Franklin National, in trying to expand rapidly, had taken unusual risks. But suppose that a large bank is threatened with failure because a foreign government to which it, and other large banks, have made substantial loans has declared a debt moratorium. In this case the failure of one large bank would dramatize the problem faced by other large banks, and might start a run on them. Hence, the failure of a large bank is more likely to set off runs on similar banks than is the case for the failure of small banks.

Third, large banks have made much greater use of nondeposit funds than have small or medium-sized banks. Since nondeposit creditors do not have FDIC protection unless the FDIC follows its usual merger route, large banks are much more subject to "runs" than are small banks.[5] Given the great expansion of nondeposit borrowing by banks in recent years, we should broaden the concept of bank runs to include not only withdrawals by depositors, but also the inability of a bank to renew its short-term nondeposit borrowings as they run off.

Finally, presumably a larger proportion of deposits in large banks than in small or medium-sized banks is above the $40,000 insurance ceiling.[6] To be sure, in the past the FDIC has nearly always protected all deposits fully by arranging mergers rather than paying off depositors. But depositors cannot be sure that this will *necessarily* happen in the case of their bank, and hence, when a large bank is in danger of failing they are likely to withdraw large demand deposits or to refuse to renew their CDs.[7]

Thus one can make a cogent case that the failure of a large bank creates a much greater danger of a run on similar banks than is true for the failures of small banks. But at the same time there still exists a powerful case against protecting large banks from failure. The above discussed beneficial effects of failures (allowing resources to be drawn away from areas of low productivity) applies to large banks just as well as to small banks. And the disciplining function of the *fear* of failure is, if anything, even more important for large banks than for small banks. This is so because in the nature of things, if banks are to be protected from failure, the government must have the right as a last resort to step in and remove the bank's officers, or employ other serious sanctions against the bank if it takes too many risks. But a large bank with an extensive legal department, by threatening to involve the FDIC in a very expensive legal battle, might make the FDIC reluctant to seek sanctions against it. And to these two disadvantages of protecting large banks one must add the disadvantages of discriminating between large and small banks discussed above.

Thus we have a situation where we should try to prevent the consequences of failures of large banks, but at the same time also avoid giving complete protection to

[5]Such a deposit runoff is, however, limited by the fact that, aside from FDIC protection, many large depositors who are also borrowers have the protection of being able to offset their deposits against their outstanding loans.

[6]Unfortunately, information on the number of accounts above $40,000 by size of bank is not presently available. However, we do have data on the number of accounts over $20,000 and on the number of accounts of over $100,000. These data show that banks with assets of over $1 billion do have a larger proportion of their accounts in these two categories than is true for banks in general. (See FDIC, *Summary of Accounts and Deposits in all Commercial Banks—June 30, 1972*, p. 20.)

[7]It is worth noting that the danger is a run on just a few large banks. A run on all large banks simultaneously need not be dangerous. Large depositors are hardly likely to withdraw currency from a risky bank; they have little choice except to move their funds into another bank. Thus, if all large banks are run at the same time their deposit inflow should suffice to pay off those depositors who want to withdraw their accounts.

large banks. This suggests the desirability of a compromise solution. And two such compromises can readily be developed.

One compromise is to announce that when a large bank begins to fail it will be allowed to go under, but that once *it* has failed no other large bank will be allowed to fail for a period of, say, two years.[8] Such an announcement would prevent the failure of one bank from starting runs on other large banks, and would thereby safeguard the money stock. At the same time, it would not remove the incentive to safe management since no large bank would want to be the first to fail. To be sure, once the first large bank has failed, all other large banks would feel safe, but since their safety net would be there only for two years, while a reputation for riskiness could easily last beyond two years, they would not be likely to abuse this temporary protection.

An alternative solution would be to treat large banks the same way as small banks and protect only their depositors, while taking steps to reduce the danger of runs on other banks. Thanks to the FDIC there is no danger of runs by small depositors, so that one only has to worry about runs by (1) large depositors and (2) short-term nondeposit creditors of banks. If the deposit insurance ceiling were eliminated and all depositors were protected, a large bank *should* be able to withstand a run of its nondeposit creditors. It could bribe such nondeposit creditors to maintain their loans to it by offering a high enough interest rate to induce them to do so.[9] For large banks' liabilities other than deposits, capital and loss reserves on the average equal approximately two and a half times bank capital.[10] (Some of these liabilities are, of course, long-term and hence are no problem.) Suppose that a bank has to pay a 10 percent risk premium on all its borrowed funds. On the average for large banks the cost of doing so would equal per year 25 percent of its capital. This would therefore represent a serious loss to its stockholders, who would have to dilute their equity by raising new capital. But the bearing of risk is the function of stockholders, and stockholders in large banks should bear their risks like stockholders in other industries.

Hence, reducing the potential for bank runs by eliminating the deposit insurance ceiling would be a feasible way for handling the danger of runs on large banks. But if the insurance ceiling is eliminated for large banks, it should also be eliminated for small banks.[11]

---

[8] If this is done, "large banks" should be defined unequivocally. Unfortunately, as pointed out above, the government is likely to be reluctant to do this. Admittedly, if two or more large banks approach failure at the same time there is a problem because the government controls the timing of failure. Perhaps in such cases an independent commission could be charged with declaring the "victor" in the race to fail.

[9] In principle, the elimination of Regulation Q would allow banks to bribe small depositors, too, but to bribe all depositors might prove too costly.

[10] These calculations relate to "large commercial banks" defined as those banks that are included in the Federal Reserve's tabulation of "weekly reporting banks, assets and liabilities of large commercial banks," *Federal Reserve Bulletin,* vol. 60, August 1974, p. A.24.

[11] If the insurance ceiling is eliminated for banks it would probably be eliminated for savings and loan associations and mutual savings banks, too. This would help the competitive positions of these institutions vis-a-vis banks.

Such a policy would eliminate depositor supervision, and steps should be taken to make up for the resulting loss of control over bank risk taking, even though, as pointed out above, depositor supervision has probably only a limited effect. One possibility is to punish excessive risk taking by making the insurance premium dependent upon the riskiness of a bank's assets. Banks could then, in effect, purchase the right to take more or less risk. At present the FDIC does not possess sufficient weapons to deal with a bank that takes too many risks. As we well know from other fields, the threat of massive retaliation is not an effective weapon in every case. Banks can chip away at regulations by a sequence of small steps, and it may be difficult for the FDIC to call a halt at any one of these steps. It is therefore not surprising that, for example, the regulatory authorities seem to have little actual control over the average capital ratios of banks.[12] Giving the FDIC the much less drastic sanction of raising insurance premiums on particular banks should aid it materially. Moreover, insofar as a bank does fail because it took too many risks, the FDIC is compensated for its outlay by the higher insurance premiums it is collecting from other banks in that risk class.[13]

A second possible substitute for depositors' supervision would be to make bank failures more expensive both for bank managers and for the stockholders who are supposed to exercise control over the bank. Thus, the FDIC could adopt a rule of denying insurance to any bank which employs in an executive capacity someone who had been a senior executive of a bank that failed, or even a junior executive with some responsibility for the failure. This should provide bank managers with a powerful incentive to avoid failure. Indeed, there is a danger that such a regulation would inhibit risk taking too much. Furthermore, one could give a stockholder an additional incentive to prevent his bank from taking excessive risks by making bank stock assessable.

Another possibility would be to add a private enterprise component to the insurance system. The reason why we have governmental rather than private insurance of bank deposits is that no private firm is big enough to insure all deposits. Only the government, with its ability to "print money," can do so. But this does not mean that the government has to do all of it. Small bank failures—and these are certainly the typical failures—could be covered by private insurance. Thus a bank could be required to obtain deposit insurance for, say, the first $10 million or 5 percent of deposits from a private insurance company, and the FDIC would insure deposits for losses above that.[14] This would bring the vigilance which we usually associate with private enterprise to bear on the problem of bank safety. Private insurance companies, either by charging higher rates to risky banks, or by refusing insurance alto-

---

[12]See Samuel Peltzman, *loc. cit.*

[13]For a further discussion of this proposal see Kenneth Scott and Thomas Mayer, "Risk and Regulation in Banking: Some Proposals for Federal Deposit Insurance Reform," *Stanford Law Review,* vol. 23, May 1971, pp. 886-94, and the literature cited therein.

[14]The private insurance company should then be required to reinsure with the FDIC in case its resources might not be sufficient.

gether (which would in effect normally eliminate a bank), would give banks an incentive to avoid excessive risks.[15] Admittedly, this would mean that both a private insurance company and the FDIC would have to examine a bank which is insured by both, but the examinations could be jointly undertaken, or the information could be shared.

In summary then, both permitting—and preventing—the failure of large banks have serious disadvantages. Hence, some alternative policies should be considered. One is to allow the first large bank to fail, but to prevent runs on other large banks by protecting them for a limited period of time. The second is to limit bank runs by abolishing the FDIC insurance ceiling de jure as well as de facto. Since the FDIC usually protects all deposits already, the main effect of this change would be to eliminate the uncertainty which large depositors now face.

Loans at Below Market Rates

When the Federal Reserve kept the Franklin National afloat it did so by making it loans at rates substantially below market rates. Such a subsidy to inefficient banks is completely unwarranted. The rate charged on such loans should be equal to the rate the private market would charge on such loans. This does not mean charging the Federal Funds rate or the discount rate since a bank that is in danger of failing could not, in the absence of de facto Federal Reserve or FDIC underwriting, borrow at the Federal Funds rate, or the discount rate. Rather, the rate charged should reflect fully the risk that the loan will not be repaid. This might make the interest rate very high, but if a bank feels that it would be unwise for it to borrow at such a high rate, then presumably the productivity of the loan is less than its cost (i.e., the risk premium plus the "pure" interest rate) and the loan should therefore not be made. Rather, the bank should be allowed to fail.

One could even make a case for charging a rate greater than the risk premium plus the pure rate. If it is known that a large bank is in serious trouble it could have difficulty in borrowing from the private market (in the absence of de facto Federal Reserve or FDIC guarantees), and hence the Federal Reserve has some monopoly power in lending to it. Should the Federal Reserve exploit this monopoly power? One could argue that it should do so because this provides additional revenue to the Treasury. Since the raising of Treasury revenue via taxes imposes a deadweight burden on the economy, obtaining revenue from the exploitation of the Federal Reserve's monopoly power *may* be a relatively efficient way of gathering some revenue. However, one can make a strong case for the principle that the public should pay directly via taxes for government expenditures, and that the extremely indirect "tax" of lending at a punitive rate to banks in trouble should therefore be avoided. But certainly, a below-market rate is unjustified.

---

[15]There is, however, the danger that pressures would be brought to bear on Congress to provide mandatory insurance for small banks that could not obtain private insurance, and whose demise would leave a town without a single bank.

Problem and Failed Banks, Bank Examinations, and Early Warning Systems: A Summary

Joseph F. Sinkey, Jr.

The purpose of this paper is to summarize my research and views on problem and failed banks, bank examinations, and early warning systems. Although the focus is on early warning systems, some fundamental questions related to problem and failed banks and the bank examination process need to be considered. For example, what is a problem bank? Can bank failures be predicted? How do bank examiners identify problem and failing banks? This paper begins with a discussion of these questions. The main focus of the paper, an early warning system for identifying problem commercial banks, follows these remarks. The paper ends with a section entitled, "If I Were the Banking Czar."

Problem and Failed Banks

What Is a Problem Bank?

Banking agencies have interpreted their "safety-and-soundness" mandate as one of failure prevention.[1] By identifying banks with the highest failure risks, so-called

Reprinted, with deletions, from Edward I. Altman and Arnold W. Sametz, eds., *Financial Crises: Institutions and Markets in a Fragile Economy* (New York: John Wiley and Sons, 1977), pp. 24–41, by permission of the publisher, editors, and author.
[1] Congressional oversight and recent hearings on problem and failed banks have reinforced this interpretation.

problem banks, the banking agencies hope to achieve this goal. The FDIC's Division of Bank Supervision identifies three classes of problem banks, which are separated according to examiners' perceptions of failure (or insolvency) risks. Banks perceived as having at least a 50 percent chance of requiring FDIC financial assistance in the near future are classified as *potential payoffs* (PPOs). Banks that appear to be headed for PPO status unless drastic changes occur are referred to as *serious problems* (SPs). And finally, banks that have significant weaknesses, but a lesser degree of vulnerability than PPO or SP banks, are called *other problems* (OPs).

In a recent letter from former FDIC Chairman Frank Wille to Senator Proxmire, the FDIC's general guidelines for identifying SP and OP banks were described.[2]

Serious Problem. This category usually includes banks in which the nature and volume of weaknesses and the trends are such that correction is urgently needed. The net capital and reserves position of such banks (i.e., their book capital and reserves less supervisory adjustments for *all* adverse asset classifications, nonbook liabilities and shortages) is likely to be substantially negative. In addition, management is usually rated Unsatisfactory or Poor. Representing the greatest area of financial exposure to the Corporation, "Serious Problem" nonmember banks necessarily receive the most concentrated FDIC attention and supervision.

Other Problem. Generally, a bank may be designated an "Other Problem" bank if net capital and reserves are nominal or a negative figure. However, the adequacy of net capital is not the only criterion for the Other Problem designation. There will be some banks whose net capital and reserves are positive figures but which, nevertheless, belong in this problem bank category because of excessive loan delinquencies, a rapid rate of asset deterioration, significant violations of law or regulations, and unusually low "adjusted" capital position (i.e., book capital and reserves less all assets classified Loss and 50 percent of all assets classified Doubtful), an undesirable liquidity posture, pronounced management deficiencies or other adverse factors. Generally speaking, management has been rated Unsatisfactory, with a rating of Fair or Satisfactory the exception.

The FDIC's December 31, 1975, Problem Bank List

This list, which is maintained with the cooperation of the Comptroller of the Currency and the Board of Governors of the Federal Reserve System, consisted of 347 commercial banks with total deposits of $20.4 billion. The insured deposits of these 347 banks were estimated to be $9.9 billion, or 48.5 percent of their total deposits.[3]

---

[2]This letter was dated February 5, 1976 (copies are available from FDIC's information office). Regarding PPO banks (ones that could fail in the near future), the letter stated that no specific guidelines are used.

[3]As of June 30, 1975, the FDIC's deposit insurance fund contained $6.4 billion. Recent adverse publicity about problem and failed banks has caused some unwarranted concern about the size of the FDIC's insurance fund relative to its risk exposure. This should not cause undue concern because (1) the FDIC has special drawing rights with the U.S. Treasury in the case of an emergency; (2) not all of a failing bank's assets are "bad"; and (3) the prevention of widespread depression failures is the province of monetary and fiscal policy.

Sixty-nine of the 347 banks (19.9 percent) were members of the Federal Reserve system (52 of the 69 were national banks). These 69 banks, however, accounted for 65 percent of the total problem bank deposits and for 45 percent of the estimated insured problem bank deposits.

According to degree of problem status, the list consisted of 27 PPO banks (7.7 percent), 88 SP banks (25.4 percent), and 232 OP banks (66.9 percent). The average OP bank had total deposits of $65 million, with $28 million (43.1 percent) estimated to be insured. The average SP bank had total deposits of $54 million, with $33 million (61.1 percent) estimated to be insured. And finally, the average PPO bank had total deposits of $20 million, with $15 million (75 percent) estimated to be insured.

Since the holding company form of organization now dominates the commercial banking industry, it is important and interesting to look at the holding company affiliations of problem banks. (As of year end 1974, bank holding companies controlled 3462 commercial banks with $509 billion in deposits, accounting for 68.1 percent of all commercial bank deposits.)[4] Only 53 of the 347 problem banks (15.3 percent) were affiliated with multibank holding companies.[5] Sixteen of the 53 affiliated banks were lead banks of multibank holding companies, while 37 banks simply were affiliates of multibank holding companies. Lead banks accounted for 9.8 percent ($2 billion) of the total problem bank deposits and 14.2 percent ($1.4 billion) of the estimated insured problem bank deposits; the corresponding figures for affiliated nonlead banks were 7.6 percent ($1.6 billion) and 12.3 percent ($1.2 billion). The average lead problem bank had total deposits of $450 million (the median deposit size was only $84 million and the average, with one multibillion dollar outlier excluded, was $134 million). Estimated insured deposits at the average lead problem bank were $87 million (the median was $57 million). The average affiliated nonlead problem bank had total deposits of $42 million and estimated insured deposits of $33 million. The average independent (or one-bank holding company) problem bank had total deposits of $57 million and estimated insured deposits of $25 million.

Can Bank Failures Be Predicted?

On March 25, 1809, The Providence *Gazette* reported the failure of the Farmers Exchange Bank, Glocester, Rhode Island.[6] Farmers was the first American bank ever to fail. The *Gazette* stated that the directors and managers of the bank ". . . practiced a system of fraud beyond which the ingenuity and dishonesty of man cannot go." The Rhode Island legislative report of 1809 indicated that business at the Farmers Exchange was conducted ". . . as the perplexed and confused state of the books sufficiently evinces, negligently and unskillfully."

---

[4]Robert C. Holland, "Bank Holding Companies and Financial Stability," *Journal of Financial and Quantitative Analysis* (November 1975), pp. 577–87.

[5]One-bank holding companies are not included in these figures.

[6]Bray Hammond, *Banks and Politics in America* (Princeton: Princeton University Press, 1957), pp. 172–77.

Table 1. Ten Largest U.S. Bank Failures

Bank	Year Closed	Total Deposits (million $)
1. Franklin National Bank, New York, N.Y.	1974	1445
2. United States National Bank, San Diego, Calif.	1973	932
3. Hamilton National Bank of Chattanooga, Tenn.	1976	870
4. American City Bank & Trust, Milwaukee, Wis.	1975	145
5. American Bank & Trust, Orangeburg, S.C.	1974	113
6. Northern Ohio Bank, Cleveland, Ohio	1975	95
7. Public Bank, Detroit, Mich.	1966	93
8. Sharpstown State Bank, Sharpstown, Texas[a]	1971	67
9. State Bank of Clearing, Chicago, Ill.	1975	61
10. Birmingham-Bloomfield Bank, Birmingham, Mich.	1971	58

Source: Annual Report, FDIC (various issues).
[a] Indicates a deposit payoff, others are deposit assumptions.

For over 167 years, the major cause of bank failures, dishonest bank managers, basically has remained the same. The form of dishonesty (e.g., insider transactions, embezzlement, manipulation, etc.) has varied, but the driving force has not changed. For example, of the 84 banks that failed between 1960 and April 30, 1976, 45 of the failures were due to improper loans to officers, directors, or owners, or loans to out-of-territory borrowers (there was misuse of brokered funds in 22 of these cases); 25 of the cases could be traced to embezzlement or manipulation; and finally, 14 of the failures were due to managerial weaknesses in loan portfolio administration.[7] To summarize, nothing essentially is new in the causes of bank failures.

Something that is new in bank failures is the recent phenomenon of the large-bank failure.[8] Since the FDIC was established in 1934, 9 of the 10 largest U.S. bank failures have occurred since 1970 (see Table 1). Why have larger banks suddenly become failure-prone? I do not pretend to know the precise answer to this question. However, for the most part, the causes of these large-bank failures have not been much different from those of small-bank failure. For example, the failures of United States National, Northern Ohio, and Sharpstown State can be traced mainly to some form of dishonest managerial practice;[9] the collapses of Franklin National, Birmingham-Bloomfield, and Public were caused mainly by incompetent management rather than dishonest management; and finally, the failures of Hamilton National, American City, American, and State Bank of Clearing were associated with overextended real estate loan portfolios that were caught in the real estate and construction slump of the past few years. Generalizing from these causal factors, it ap-

[7]George W. Hill, *Why 67 Insured Banks Failed—1960–1974* (Washington, D.C.: Federal Deposit Insurance Corporation, 1975). Updated through 1976 using FDIC Division of Liquidation reports.
[8]Paul M. Horvitz, "Failures of Large Banks: Implications for Banking Supervision and Deposit Insurance," *Journal of Financial and Quantitative Analysis* (November 1975), pp. 589–601.
[9]C. Arnholt Smith's alleged manipulations with his California Westgate Corporation in the United States National case are the most notorious.

pears that the failure of larger banks can be traced more to incompetent management (and/or increased economic uncertainty) rather than to the dishonesty factor that has been so prevalent in the closing of smaller banks. Except for failures due to severe economic depression (such as those that occurred during the 1930s) or local economic problems, a bank's viability ultimately rests with the honesty and ability of its managers and board of directors. Managers who cannot or will not manage and directors who cannot or will not direct are the causes of bank failures. Can such managers and directors be identified through balance sheet and income expense data? In other words, can bank failures be predicted?

Meyer and Pifer concluded that ". . . even when failure frequently results from embezzlement and other financial irregularities, financial measures can evaluate the relative strengths of firms."[10] The firms in this case were 39 commercial banks that failed between 1948 and 1965. The fact that Meyer and Pifer's model was never implemented by the FDIC (where it was developed) could be interpreted as a lack of confidence in it. However, since changes in bank supervision or examination are difficult to implement, this may be an unfair criticism.

Given some of the difficulties encountered with problem prediction models (discussed below) and the lack of failure prediction studies in banking (except for Meyer and Pifer's), I have undertaken to reexamine the failure prediction question. Thirty-seven banks that failed between 1970 and 1975 will be analyzed in this forthcoming study.

The Bank-Examination Process

Bank Capital, Loan Evaluations, and Problem Banks

The banking agencies interpret their "safety-and-soundness" mandate as one of preventing bank failures. By identifying banks with the highest failure risks, so-called problem banks, banking authorities hope to achieve this goal. The problem bank identification procedure is rooted in the bank examination process. The purposes of a bank examination are:[11]

1. To determine asset quality.
2. To determine the nature of liabilities
3. To ascertain compliance with laws and regulations
4. To evaluate controls, procedures, accounting practices, and insurance
5. To evaluate management and its policies
6. To determine capital adequacy.

[10]Paul A. Meyer and Howard W. Pifer, "Prediction of Bank Failures," *Journal of Finance* (September 1970), pp. 853–68.

[11]Bank Examiners' Orientation Course, mimeographed notes, (FDIC, 1973). For additional information concerning bank examinations see George J. Benston, "Bank Examination," *The Bulletin,* Nos. 89–90 (May 1973), NYU Graduate School of Business.

It is shown later in this paper that the multidimensionality of this process can be reduced to a single ratio which combines the asset quality and capital adequacy factors, the FDIC's net capital ratio.

Although the banking agencies' manuals refer to benchmark measures of capital adequacy and the incorporation of other factors, in practice, the most important indicator (to banking authorities) of a bank's "safety and soundness" flows from the loan evaluation process, that is, the ratio that relates a bank's adversely classified assets to its capital and reserves. Regarding loan evaluations, the FDIC's *Manual of Examination Policies* states:

> One of the most important aspects of the examination process is the evaluation of loans, for, in large measure, it is the quality of a bank's loans which determines the risk to depositors. To a great extent, conclusions regarding the condition of the bank, the quality of its management, and its service to the community are weighted heavily by the examination's findings with regard to loans. (Section H, p. 1.)

Adversely classified assets (mainly low-quality loans) are listed as "loss," "doubtful," or "substandard" based upon an examiner's estimation of probable default. The classification of assets is an art and not a science; that is, an examiner's judgment is the primary determining factor.[12] According to the FDIC manual, the primary measure of a loan's riskiness is ". . . the willingness and ability of a debtor to perform as agreed . . ." (Section H, p. 1). The manual interprets this to mean that the borrower has the financial resources to meet his or her interest and principal payments as contracted.[13]

Alternative Weight Capital Ratios

The FDIC's Form 96 provides a statistical summary of a bank examiner's report. The information on this form is further condensed into a ratings vector consisting of two capital adequacy ratios, an earnings ratio, and a managerial rating.

The FDIC's Adjusted Capital Ratio

The adjusted capital ratio (ACR) is defined as:

$$ACR \equiv [K + R + N - L - 0.5D]/A, \tag{1}$$

---

[12]The FDIC manual states: "Loan evaluation is not an exact science. The broad scope of the lending function and changing patterns in banking preclude the use of a single formula in the appraisal of loans. Much depends on the Examiner's knowledge, judgment, perception, analytical technique, and the ability to reach sound conclusions; attributes which are developed through training and experience." (Section H, p. 1.)

[13]The manual adds, "[This] does not mean, however, that borrowers must at all times be in position to liquidate their loans for that would defeat the original purpose of extending credit" (Ibid.).

where K = total capital accounts
$\quad\quad R$ = valuation reserves
$\quad\quad N$ = nonbook sound banking values
$\quad\quad L$ = "loss" classifications
$\quad\quad D$ = "doubtful" classifications
$\quad\quad A$ = quarterly average of gross assets for the calendar year, where gross assets are defined as total balance sheet assets including reserves but excluding expense accounts and cash shortage accounts.

Equation (1) compares a bank's "loss" and 50 percent of its "doubtful" classifications to its capital and reserves (N is relatively small and can be ignored in this discussion). Equation (1) assigns a weight of 0 to the "substandard" classification.

The FDIC's Net Capital Ratio

The net capital ratio (NCR) is defined:

$$NCR \equiv [K + R + N - L - D - S]/A, \tag{2}$$

where S = "substandard" classifications. In Equation (2), all three adverse classification categories are assigned a weight of 1, that is, Equation (2) relates a bank's total classified assets to its capital and reserves. Ignoring N, Equation (2) can be written:

$$NCR \equiv [K + R - C]/A, \tag{2'}$$

where $C = L + D + S$.

The FDIC's justification for its conservative treatment of the "substandard" category is contained in its manual: ". . . it is the function of the Substandard classification to indicate those loans which are unduly risky and which may be a future hazard to the bank's solvency. No bank can safely hold a large amount of low quality loans, even though they are not presently subject to either a Doubtful or Loss classification" (Section H, p. 5).

It is shown below that NCR is the most important discriminator between problem and nonproblem banks. That is, a bank's volume of "substandard" assets relative to its capital and reserves is the most important factor in identifying a problem situation.

A Probability-Weighted Capital Ratio

Because of inappropriate and arbitrary weighting schemes, Equations (1) and (2) either understate or overstate, respectively, a bank's risk exposure to adversely classified assets. These two formulas should be discarded in favor of the following probability-weighted capital ratio (WCR):

$$WCR \equiv [K + R + N - \gamma_L L - \gamma_D D - \gamma_S S]/A, \tag{3}$$

where the γ coefficients are "prospective probabilities" ($1 \geq \gamma_L > \gamma_D > \gamma_S \geq 0$). One way to estimate these prospective probabilities is to examine historical charge-off rates for each of the classified asset categories. That is,

$$\hat{\gamma}_L = \frac{L^*}{L}$$

and

$$\hat{\gamma}_D = \frac{D^*}{D} \tag{4}$$

$$\hat{\gamma}_S = \frac{S^*}{S}$$

The variables with asterisks indicate the dollar amount of the particular classified asset category that was actually written off against bank capital; they are ex post measures. In contrast, the variables without asterisks are examiners' ex ante measures of loan quality. To estimate the γ coefficients would involve an extensive and detailed follow-up on individual classified assets. Moreover, since the coefficients may differ for different size banks and for different stages of the business cycle, these factors (and other ones deemed relevant) should be controlled for when estimating the γ coefficients. Given the resources available to the banking agencies and the need for a more relevant measure of a bank's risk exposure, such a study should be undertaken immediately.[14]

Empirical Findings

The discriminant analysis tests presented in this section show that the *NCR* is the most important variable separating problem banks from nonproblem banks. These tests are descriptive and not predictive. That is, examiner-determined problem and nonproblem banks are being reclassified statistically to clarify how examiners distinguish between such banks.

The problem banks analyzed were the 143 commercial banks on the FDIC's March 31, 1974 problem bank list.[15] These banks were compared with a random sample of 163 nonproblem banks, drawn from the 9060 banks (about 65 percent of the population) with examination reports for the year 1973 on file with the FDIC as of December 31, 1973. If a bank had more than one report on file for the year, the latest one was used. Although no deliberate pairing was made, there were no statistically significant differences between the two groups in terms of average size or average number of banking offices.

---

[14]I have recommended that the FDIC develop such a project. The banking agencies should develop a coordinated effort in this regard.

[15]The list consisted of 113 insured nonmember banks, 11 state member banks, and 19 national banks. The typical problem bank was a unit bank with total deposits of $9.4 million. Five of the problem banks had total deposits greater than $100 million but less than $1 billion. Originally, 175 banks were selected for the nonproblem group, however, 12 banks were eliminated because of incomplete data.

Table 2. Discriminant-Analysis Tests: 143 Problem Versus 163 Nonproblem Banks Using 1973 Examination Data

Test Number	Variables	Mean (%) (Standard Deviation) Problem	Nonproblem	Test of Equality of Group Means	Test of Dispersion Matrix Equality between Groups	Misclassification Rate (%) (306)	Type I Error (%) 143	Type II Error (%) 111
1	ACR	6.4 (2.6)	8.8 (2.5)	Reject ($F = 68.6$)	Reject ($F = 55.2$)	26.8	35.0	19.0
2	NCR	−2.3 (5.2)	7.6 (3.0)	Reject ($F = 428.8$)	Reject ($F = 42.6$)	4.6	4.9	4.0
3	NIA[b]	0.16 (1.21)	0.85 (0.53)	Reject ($F = 43.0$)	Reject ($F = 97.8$)	34.3	66.4	6.0
4	NCR NIA	(see above)		Reject ($F = 233.6$)	Reject ($F = 47.8$)	5.5	7.0	4.0
5	SUB[b]	11.6 (7.2)	1.9 (2.2)	Reject ($F = 268.9$)	Reject ($F = 182.1$)	12.4	19.6	6.0
6	TCL[b]	14.6 (8.2)	2.3 (2.5)	Reject ($F = 331.9$)	Reject ($F = 182.1$)	11.1	16.1	6.0
7	TCA[b]	10.1 (5.5)	1.4 (1.5)	Reject ($F = 370.4$)	Reject ($F = 218.5$)	9.8	14.0	6.0

[a] Classifications were made using (1) the Eisenbeis and Avery (1972) computer program MULDIS, (2) a quadratic discriminant function since the null hypothesis of dispersion matrix equality between groups was rejected, (3) the Lachenbruch "holdout" classification technique and (4) the sample proportions as a priori probabilities of group membership.

[b] NIA = Net income (after taxes and securities gains or losses) as a percentage of total assets; SUB = substandard loans as a percentage of total loans; TCL = total classified loans (i.e., substandard plus doubtful plus loss) as a percentage of total loans; TCA = total classified as (loans and securities) as a percentage of total assets. ACR and NCR, components of the ratings vector, are defined in the text.

[c] Additional multivariate tests, not reported here, could not improve upon the classification accuracy of NCR, even when NCR was included in the set.

The purposes of discriminant analysis are to test for group mean and dispersion matrix differences, to describe the overlap between groups, and to construct rules to classify observations into appropriate groups.[16] Based on 1973 examination data, these tests are reported in Table 2. A total of 21 examination variables was tested. The results for 6 of these variables and a bivariate combination are presented in Table 2. The 6 variables are the components of the ratings vector, except for the managerial rating which is a qualitative measure, and three ratios of classified loans (assets) to total loans (assets).[17]

The tests of equality of group means and equality of group dispersion matrices were rejected for all six variables, including a bivariate test of *NCR* and *NIA* [net income (after taxes and securities gains and losses) as a percentage of total assets].[18] The most significant variable and the most important discriminator between the groups (on either a univariate or multivariate basis) was the net capital ratio [*NCR*, see Equation (2)]. The *NCR* for the average problem bank was -2.3 (5.2) compared to 7.6 (3.0) for the average nonproblem bank. (Figures in parentheses are standard deviations.) The *NCR F* statistics were 428.8 for the group means (significant at the 0.29282 E-12 percent level) and 42.6 for the dispersion matrices (significant at the 0.67734 E-8 percent level). With use of the Lachenbruch "holdout" classification technique, 95.4 percent of the 306 banks were reclassified correctly.[19] The type I error was 4.9 percent (7 banks), while the type II error was 4.3 percent (7 banks). The classification rule used for reclassifying the 306 banks was:[20] Classify as a problem bank if *NCR* $\leq$ 2.74 percent.

To summarize, the *NCR* is the most important variable for distinguishing between problem and nonproblem banks. Recalling the construction of *ACR* and NCR [see Eqs. (1) and (2)], it is clear that a bank's volume of "substandard" loans relative to its capital and reserves is the kicker in the *NCR* formula. However, because of the conservative weight attached to the "substandard" category, banking agencies tend to overstate a bank's true risk exposure.[21]

---

[16]The foundations of discriminant analysis are described in Eisenbeis and Avery, *Discriminant Analysis and Classifications Procedures* (Lexington, Mass.: Lexington Books), 1972.

[17]The FDIC managerial ratings are good, satisfactory, fair, unsatisfactory, and poor. The most common rating for the problem-bank group was unsatisfactory (65 percent of the banks), while for the non-problem bank group it was satisfactory (71 percent).

[18]The test of dispersion matrix equality is important because, if this hypothesis is rejected, a quadratic classification equation rather than a linear one should be used. See Eisenbeis and Avery (1972), especially pp. 37–52.

[19]The Lachenbruch technique withholds the observation to be classified and computes the classification equation using $N - 1$ observations. The withheld observation then is classified. This procedure is repeated until all observations have been classified.

[20]This rule was derived from the following quadratic equation: $1.8195(NCR) - 0.071387(NCR)^2 - 4.4503 \leq 0$. If the value of the left-hand side of this equation is equal to or less than zero, the bank is classified as a problem bank.

[21]Regarding the usefulness of substandard loan data, Benston and Marlin concluded that ". . . the value of the loan-criticism function is not demonstrated and, thus, is questionable" (p. 42). "Bank Examiners' Evaluation of Credit," *Journal of Money, Credit and Banking* (February 1974), pp. 23–44.

An Early Warning System for Identifying Problem Commercial Banks

A Realistic Objective and Potential Advantages

The proposed early warning system is not designed to be a substitute for existing bank examination procedures and personnel, nor is it intended to be a replacement for the human skills and judgments needed in solving problems of bank supervision. The realistic and limited objecive of the system is to act as an aid in scheduling bank examinations. That is, potential problem banks would be examined more frequently and more intensely than nonproblem banks.

The major potential advantages of an effective early warning system are:

1. **Prevention of bank failures.** The safety-and-soundness mandate of bank regulation has focused upon the prevention of bank failure. Early identification of problem banks may result in fewer bank failures and smaller losses for the FDIC's deposit insurance fund. Moreover, large losses, such as the $150 million loss the FDIC incurred in United States National's failure, reduce the percentage rebate of the net insurance assessment income by the FDIC to insured banks. Clearly, an effective early warning system could have monetary benefits for bankers.

2. **More efficient allocation of banking agencies' resources.** Advance information regarding the condition of a bank should be an important factor in determining the order, scope, intensity, and frequency of a bank's examination. Such information should enable banking agencies to allocate resources more efficiently among problem and nonproblem banks.

3. **Increasing the usefulness of balance sheet and income data.** All three federal banking agencies regularly collect these data from the banks they supervise. These data are the primary inputs to the early warning system. The value of these preexamination data would be enhanced greatly by an effective problem bank detection mechanism.

4. **Making the identification of problem banks more objective.** Relative to a bank's capital position, "substandard" loans are perhaps the most important variable separating problem from nonproblem banks. Regulatory authorities admit that the procedure for uncovering these risky loans is an art and not a science. A more objective appraisal of a bank's potential riskiness would strengthen bank examination procedures.

5. **Supplying banking agencies with data to evaluate their examination and supervisory performances and the effectiveness of the early warning system.** Given a prediction of a bank's "safety and soundness," the agencies would be able to evaluate bank examiners' ratings and vice versa. Moreover, an early warning system should be an important pedagogical device for bank examiners and banking schools.

The Information Content of Balance Sheet and Income Expense Data

The basic concept (or null hypothesis) of any early warning system focuses upon the information content of the data being analyzed. In this particular case, the null hypothesis concerns the information content of balance sheet and income expense data relevant for identifying future problem banks. Having analyzed these data for about 3 years, there is no doubt in my mind that the information content is there. This means that information relevant for scheduling bank examinations and even for excluding certain banks from the traditional bank examination process is available. It does not meant that on-the-spot bank inspections would be eliminated entirely or that 100 percent accuracy in identifying problem banks would be achieved.

With regard to implementation of an early warning system, two critical problems remain. First, the information must be extracted in a timely and efficient manner. And second, supervisory and examination personnel must be convinced that the information is useful. The first problem can be resolved by having on-the-spot examinations begin after the data have been analyzed. For example, what is so sacred about starting examinations in January of each year? Why not start on-site examinations *after* year-end data have been analyzed? Based upon past experience, such examinations (for the entire population of insured banks) could begin in early May. In addition, since large banks present the greatest potential risk exposure to the FDIC insurance fund and the economy, they could be analyzed separately and therefore with increased timeliness. Moreover, with income expense data now being collected quarterly for the largest banks and semiannually for other banks, additional information for monitoring banks on a year-round basis will be available.

A Statistical Model

The basic statistical technique being used in the proposed early warning system is multiple discriminant analysis. The critical feature of this procedure is that it permits simultaneous consideration of several factors reflecting problem bank status. The specific model being used is a seven-variable one. It was developed to distinguish between, and reclassify, groups of examiner-determined problem and nonproblem banks. The seven variables used in the model are:

1. LRI = interest and fees on loans as a percentage of total operating income (measures revenue concentration)
2. $OEOI$ = total operating expense as a percentage of total operating income (measures operating efficiency)
3. USA = U.S. government securities as a percentage of total assets (measures liquidity and asset composition)
4. SLA = state and local securities as a percentage of total assets (measures asset composition)

Table 3. Problem-Nonproblem Data — Total Deposits ≥ $100 Million (December 31, 1975)

Variable	Mean	Standard Deviation
Group 1		
1	69.1586914	9.6096869
2	102.7339020	17.4362183
3	9.9596987	5.3950968
4	9.1377068	5.7388134
5	57.8825989	7.8070116
6	− 0.4411117	4.6645279
7	7.6206331	1.7653618
Group 2		
1	64.4605865	9.5528612
2	87.1609802	7.3002062
3	12.8995619	7.8169279
4	12.9021988	5.1964607
5	51.6375580	9.3493404
6	0.1067407	6.2188101
7	8.1263905	1.5832119

Table 4. Problem-Nonproblem Data — Total Deposits < $100 Million (December 31, 1975)

Variable	Mean	Standard Deviation
Group 1		
1	70.9135437	9.6027336
2	106.0741577	28.8503418
3	13.8828249	9.2217979
4	7.4121246	6.6670637
5	57.8737030	10.5903721
6	3.2493048	6.0943060
7	8.0725117	2.2649603
Group 2		
1	60.0428162	12.7342634
2	83.8326569	10.7402124
3	19.5872803	11.8564816
4	12.3208561	7.1627436
5	49.6287231	11.8667755
6	4.3126907	6.0482178
7	8.8678141	2.3825607

Table 5. Problem-Nonproblem Data — Number of Banks in Deposit Size Classes

Deposit Class	Group 1, Problem	Group 2, Nonproblem	Total
≥ $100 million	27	837	864
< $100 million	302	12,430	12,732
Total	329	13,267	13,596

5. LA = total loans as a percentage of total assets (measures loan volume)

6. NFA = net Federal funds (sales minus purchases) as a percentage of total assets (measures Federal funds activity and aggressiveness of liability management)

7. KRA = capital and reserves for bad debt losses on loans as a percentage of total assets (measures capital adequacy).

It should be emphasized that there is nothing magical about these *particular* seven variables. If certain dimensionalities are captured, the form that the individual variables take is relatively unimportant. Moreover, using only the loan revenue (*LRI*) and operating efficiency (*OEOI*) variables, the classification results were quite comparable to those using all seven variables. However, statistically speaking, we have more confidence in the seven-variable model. Using the seven-variable model, about 75 percent of the previously identified problem-nonproblem situations can be reclassified correctly.

Year-end 1975 data for these seven variables, stratified according to (1) problem (group 1) and nonproblem (group 2) status, and (2) total deposits greater than or equal to $100 million or less than $100 million, are presented in Tables 3 and 4. These data are for all banks that have passed data editing checks. The number of banks in each group is listed in Table 5.

Comparison of the means and standard deviations in Tables 3 and 4 (and of the variance-covariance matrices) indicates that there is substantial overlap between the problem and nonproblem groups. (Lack of separation between groups tends to reduce classification accuracy.) Not surprisingly, identification of banks with characteristics more similar to those of problem banks than those of nonproblem banks produces classification errors. This implies that there is no substitute for the judgment and analysis of the examination staff, particularly with respect to "close" cases. Thus the real usefulness of such early warning systems will not be as a substitute for bank examination, but rather as a means to direct examination talents to those areas where judgment and further analysis will result in the highest payoff.

An additional feature of the early warning system is the computation of three statistics indicating how similar each predicted problem bank is to all insured commercial banks in (1) the United States, (2) the bank's FDIC region, and (3) the bank's state. This feature indicates how similar a bank is to all other banks in its nation, region, and state.[22]

An Alternative Approach:
The Outlier Technique

Because of the high degree of overlap between examiner-determined problem and nonproblem banks (on the basis of balance sheet and income expense comparisons),

[22]The present computer early warning system is quite flexible. For example, it can handle different sets of variables and alternative comparisons across different classes of banks. In addition, the print routine enables flagged banks to be printed out by state or by FDIC region.

an early warning system based upon examiners' definitions and groups may not provide an appropriate foundation. An alternative approach is to abandon examiner-determined groups and work with peer groups (e.g., all banks with deposits greater than $100 million). In this peer group or outlier analysis, each bank in the group (which may include both problem and nonproblem banks) is compared with the average performance of the group. The Eisenbeis and Avery multiple discriminant analysis program (MULDIS) has been adapted to handle this one-group outlier technique. A chi-square score, which serves as a measure of resemblance between a particular bank and the group average, provides an approximation of the percentage of the population of peer group banks that can be expected to lie farther from the peer group's center (in either direction from the mean vector) than a particular bank.

Experiments with the proposed outlier technique in the cases of the failure of Franklin National and United States National and the emergency merger of the Security National Bank of Long Island have been conducted. . . . In addition, outlier tests using alternative peer groups have been performed. A simple but effective outlier (or ranking) variable is a bottom line or operating efficiency measure (such as *OEOI* described above). For example, Keefe Management Service of New York City attempted to evaluate the riskiness of the FDIC's largest banks. They came up with a 35-variable measure of riskiness and ranked the banks on this basis. The rank correlation coefficient between their 35-variable ranking and a 1-variable ranking [net operating income (before taxes and securities gains or losses) as a percentage of total assets] was 89.1 percent. After all, the bottom line is really what it is all about.

If I Were Banking Czar

If I were banking czar, I would issue the following guidelines to my Department of Supervision and Examination *and* to the public:

1. Problem and failed banks have existed for a long time and will continue to exist in the future. Our job is to keep such institutions, especially failed ones, at a level consistent with maintaining confidence in the banking system. Accordingly, the actual number of failures or problems during any period of time is not important, as long as the confidence factor is maintained. (We should anticipate inquiries from Congress and other interested parties regarding how we intend to measure the confidence factor and its critical level. In this regard, we should explore such potential measures as customer confidence surveys; monitoring of bank stock prices, deposit flows, large certificate of deposit rates and flows, Federal funds flows and rates, etc.).

2. Supervision and examination procedures will be directed toward preventing, monitoring, and eliminating the dishonest, incompetent, and inequitable elements in banking. Our supervision-and-examination arsenal will consist of two main weapons: (1) computerized early warning mechanisms and (2) on-site bank inspections. Alternative early warning models will be employed as screening devices to schedule on-the-spot bank inspections. With regard to the traditional bank examination and its focus on loan evaluations, the basic premise will be that such examinations for every bank in every year are not necessary. On-site bank inspections will not be eliminated. On the contrary, every bank will be inspected *at least* once a year to check for violations of laws and regulations, unfair lending practices (e.g., "redlining" and other forms of discrimination), and other irregular and anti-competitive banking practices. These mandatory inspections will of course require much less time and money than the traditional bank examination. Known problem banks and banks that have been flagged as being in need of special supervision or potentially in need of special supervision will be given more detailed and thorough bank inspections. These inspections will be designed to pinpoint problems and potential remedies. Peer group analyses (hence peer group pressure) will be used in explaining actual and potential problem areas. In some cases, even traditional loan evaluations will be made. However, loan evaluations and criticisms should be handled delicately so as not to encourage discriminatory lending practices. Although our inspection system will have a bottom line focus (banks are given monopoly power, in varying degrees of course depending upon their particular market, hence they should be able to generate a reasonable profit), we will not be myopic in this regard. For example, if a bank has low earnings because it is providing full service to *all* its customers, this will be given appropriate weight. In contrast, if a bank has low earnings because of self-serving and/or incompetent managers and/or directors, this will be given appropriate weight also, but with a negative sign. Moreover, in cases where banks have appeared to abuse their monopoly power, we will encourage greater competition. Clearly, our inspection system will require substantial human input and analysis; it will not be a machine-sans-human system. The major changes will include (1) increased computer analysis as a filtering mechanism for identifying banks with financial difficulties, and (2) reallocation of human resources (*a*) away from detailed loan evaluations and toward more productive areas and (*b*) away from safe-and-soundness banks and toward problem banks.

REFERENCES

SINKEY, JOSEPH F., JR. *Problem and Failed Institutions in the Commercial Banking Industry.* Greenwich, Conn.: Johnson Associates Inc., 1977.

SINKEY, JOSEPH F., JR. "The Bank-Examination Process and Major Issues in Banking: A Survey." *The Bankers Magazine,* forthcoming.

SINKEY, JOSEPH F., JR. "Can Bank Failures Be Predicted?" Research in progress.

SINKEY, JOSEPH F., JR. "Security National Bank of Long Island: A Balance-Sheet and Income-Expense Analysis of Our Largest Emergency Merger." Research in progress.

SINKEY, JOSEPH F., JR. "Bank Capital, Loan Evaluations, and "Problem" Banks." FDIC Working Paper No. 76–2.

SINKEY, JOSEPH F., JR. "Franklin National Bank of New York: A Portfolio and Performance Analysis of Our Largest Bank Failure." FDIC Working Paper No. 75-10. This paper has been revised slightly and is forthcoming in two parts: one in the *Journal of Financial and Quantitative Analysis* and the other in the *Journal of Bank Research.*

SINKEY, JOSEPH F., JR. "Early-Warning System: Some Preliminary Predictions of Problem Commercial Banks." *Proceedings of a Conference on Bank Structure and Competition.* May 1975, pp. 85-91.

SINKEY, JOSEPH F., JR. "A Multivariate Statistical Analysis of the Characteristics of Problem Banks." *Journal of Finance,* March 1975, pp. 21-36.

SINKEY, JOSEPH F., JR. "Adverse Publicity and Bank Deposit Flows: The Cases of Franklin National Bank of New York and United States National Bank of San Diego." *Journal of Bank Research,* Summer 1975, pp. 109-12.

SINKEY, JOSEPH F., JR. "The Failure of United States National Bank of San Diego: A Portfolio and Performance Analysis." *Journal of Bank Research,* Spring 1975, pp. 8-24.

SINKEY, JOSEPH F., JR. "The Way Problem Banks Perform." *The Bankers Magazine,* Autumn 1974, pp. 40-51.

SINKEY, JOSEPH F., JR. and ROBERT D. KURTZ. "Bank Disclosure Policy and Procedures, Adverse Publicity, and Bank Deposit Flows." *Journal of Bank Research,* Autumn 1973, pp. 177-84.

SINKEY, JOSEPH F., JR. and DAVID A. WALKER. "Problem Banks: Identification and Characteristics." *Journal of Bank Research,* Winter 1975, pp. 208-17.

Federal Reserve Membership*

George J. Benston

Equity and the Burdens of Membership

Analysis and data . . . show that the Federal Reserve could control the money supply, bank credit and interest rates with or without a change in the present system. But should the decline in membership accelerate and the proportion of deposits held by member banks decrease substantially, monetary control might become more difficult. Considering that the cost of membership is considerable and is likely to increase as the opportunity cost of reserves increases, this possibility should not be dismissed summarily.[1] In addition, the Federal Reserve has complicated its control over the money supply over the years, apparently to reduce the costs of membership to small banks. It would be preferable, therefore, to "solve" the problem in a manner that makes control over money more rather than less effective.

However, the rationale for a change in the present system of required, largely nonearning, reserves by member banks rests predominantly on equity considerations. It is clear from the analysis and data . . . that member banks are taxed

Reprinted from *Federal Reserve Membership: Consequences, Benefits, and Alternatives*, pp. 58–75, by permission of the Association of Reserve City Bankers and the author.

*The analysis and conclusions presented by the author are the result of independent research efforts and do not necessarily reflect the views of the members of the Association of Reserve City Bankers.

[1]However, if the Fed views monetary policy in terms of control over interest rate, the extent to which banks are members is not important.

rather heavily for the increasingly dubious privilege of membership. The incidence of the tax often is assumed to fall on member banks and a change in the present system often is supported by appeals for equitable treatment among competitive financial institutions. While it is true that the tax on nonearning reserves (net of membership benefits) falls initially on member banks, it actually is a tax on the users of bank money. Furthermore, the tax on bank customers also has resulted in a gain for the owners of nonmember banks.

As an aid to explicating these statements (that are not often made), consider a situation where all banks that offer the public demand deposit (bank-money) services are required to be Federal Reserve members and keep a given percentage of these deposits in noninterest bearing reserves. The banks' profits from this service are equal to the net earnings derived from the depositors' funds (which are reduced by the required reserves) plus fees charged less the cost of providing the service. This (expected) profit must be sufficient for the banks' owners to get a return on their investments at least equal to the return expected on the next best alternative investment available to them or they will refuse to invest in banking. Should a tax be imposed on demand deposit services (such as increased reserve requirements), present owners will bear capital losses, and new and shiftable resources will be invested elsewhere until the prices charged to users of bank-money rise sufficiently to provide the required returns to investors. Therefore, the net earnings that cannot be earned on required reserves less the benefits from Federal Reserve membership are paid for by the user of bank-money. The owners of the banks neither benefit nor lose from their banks' membership in the Fed, since all pass the net costs (or benefits) to their customers.

Now consider the present situation, where some banks are not required to be members. The price charged to bank money users still must be sufficient to enable investors to earn the competitive rate of return on their assets. Therefore, if member banks dominate the market for bank money services, they will set the price in conjunction with the demand function of consumers of these services. The nonmembers then can operate under their umbrella, to the benefit of their owners. Those nonmembers who tend to be inefficient (or who appear to be inefficient because they distribute dividends to their owner-managers in the form of higher salaries or perquisites) also can prosper under this price umbrella. However, investors' resources will tend to move into nonmember banks and away from member banks. This shift, though, is restrained by the difficulty of obtaining bank charters, the prohibition against providing deposit services unless an organization has a commercial bank charter, and the cost to members of leaving the System (discussed in the following paragraphs). As the statistics show, few newly chartered state banks elect to become members. But existing member banks must overcome the costs of switching status, including the cost of overcoming inertia.

Several aspects of the cost to banks of relinquishing membership in the Federal Reserve should be distinguished. National banks must bear the cost of obtaining state charters, since otherwise they must be members. They also must give up the prestige of being a national bank. The latter, while intangible, apparently has been a strong force for many bankers, perhaps because the larger, stronger banks tend to be national banks. Membership also is considered prestigious by many state chartered banks. For example, in Peter Rose's [1977] survey "prestige" was ranked as the principal advantage of membership by 6 percent of the banks that never were members. It also was considered to be "very important" or "important" by 79 percent of these banks. (Of the banks that withdraw from the System, though, only 26 percent deemed prestige "very important" or "important" and only 2 percent identified it as the principal advantage of membership.) Therefore, the cost of membership is offset somewhat by the benefits from prestige. However, as the costs increase and as more otherwise prestigious banks assume nonmember status, the benefits tend to exceed the costs of leaving the System.

Large member banks, in particular, may incur considerable costs by withdrawing from the System. For one thing, they are likely to engage the displeasure of a powerful regulatory agency. The Federal Reserve administers the Bank Holding Company Act, which gives it power over multi-bank and one-bank holding companies. Prior approval of the Board is required for purchase of more than 5 percent of the shares of any bank or nonbanking activity by a bank holding company. The Board's latitude in these decisions is rather wide. As they put it [Board of Governors, 1974, pp. 114-15]: "In determining whether to grant approval of the acquisition, the Board is required to consider competitive and other public interest factors" including "what effects, if any, the acquisition might have over the longer run on the solvency of the holding company banks." Former Chairman Burns [1977, p. 640] testified that "the Board is deeply concerned about the structural weakening of the Nation's banking system that is being caused by membership attrition. Nonmember banks do not, of course, have ready access to the Federal Reserve discount window; they must rely instead on correspondent banks to meet their urgent credit needs. However, banking history demonstrates that correspondent banks cannot fulfill the function of lender of last resort in periods of strong over-all credit demands." Therefore, a holding company bank that might want to withdraw, must consider that the Board is likely to view this action as one that might adversely affect its long run solvency and, consequently, deny its applications for additional acquisitions.

Banks that offer correspondent services also would bear large costs should they leave the System. These, generally large, banks use the no-charge check clearing and wire transfer facilities of the Fed to effect their operations, which makes membership almost a prerequisite to being a correspondent bank. In addition, member banks are not permitted to keep deposits in excess of 10 percent of their capital accounts with nonmembers. And, though Burns stated that "banking history demonstrates that correspondent banks cannot fulfill the function of lender of last resort in periods of strong credit demands," in fact they have and they do, in part by borrowing from the Federal Reserve. Therefore, though respondents need not be members, correspondents generally must.[2] This does not mean, however, that the

---

[2] Member banks held 96 percent of inter-bank deposits as of December 31, 1976.

benefits of membership accrue to the correspondent banks. As Knight's [1972, p. 9] survey reveals, the average small bank (deposits less than $5 million) maintains balances with 5 correspondents, while banks with $50 to $100 million in deposits have an average of 13 correspondents. Furthermore, Knight [1976] also finds a wide variety of levels and types of charges for correspondent services, which is evidence that correspondent banks do not collude to fix prices.[3] Therefore, it seems highly likely that competition among correspondents results in the benefits of Federal Reserve membership being passed on to respondents to the point where the correspondent banks earn a "normal" return on their shareholders' investments (including their investment in personnel who are effective in maintaining personal relationships with respondents). But should a bank that offers correspondent services leave the System, it would have to relinquish the benefits of the membership. It could not, though, raise its fees to (or increase the "due to" balances required of) its respondents, since its competitors would have incentives not to follow its lead. Its investments in correspondent banking activities, though, are fixed (at least in the short run) and are not transferable to others except at a relatively high discount. These investments include not only physical facilities but also personal relationships and goodwill developed over a long period. Therefore, should a correspondent bank relinquish membership, its shareholders would incur a capital loss on this investment.

Though most very large banks probably cannot benefit, on balance, from leaving the System, many fairly large banks and small banks generally can benefit. Two events are now occurring which may change this situation. First, as more banks leave the System, the dominance of deposit money markets by member banks tends to be lost. When member banks no longer dominate (and, to some extent, even before), it will be to some nonmember bank's advantage to "come out from under the umbrella" and lower its prices (or increase services) to obtain more business. After a while, it will be preferable for its competitors, member and nonmember, to reduce prices also. Both types of banks will suffer some capital losses, but the member banks will have to book reductions of income or even losses. At this point they may find that the cost of changing membership status is exceeded by the benefits.

The second event is the development of explicit payments of interest on demand deposits by means of NOW (negotiable order of withdrawal) accounts. While banks most probably are paying interest on demand deposits in the form of free services and reduced service charges based on the balance maintained, they may have been able to take advantage of the cost to small depositors of switching accounts or finding alternatives (such as investing in money funds). The offering of NOW accounts with their explicit payments of interest may have overcome this inertia and used up some of the banks' economic rent. Perhaps more important, though, is the fact that NOW accounts permit mutual savings banks and savings and loan associations to enter the market for bank money. As is the situation for any new

---

[3]The prohibition against interest payments on demand deposits imposed by the Banking Act of 1933 restricts correspondents to non-price competition for bankers' balances.

entrant to a market, the newcomers compete for the business serviced by existing firms by reducing prices and/or increasing services. The result is reduced profits for the existing firms. The situation in Massachusetts and New Hampshire during 1974–1975 was studied by Paulus [1976], who concluded that the result was a modest reduction in deposit market shares of commercial banks and reduced after tax earnings by an average of 2½-percent in 1974 and 9 percent in 1975.[4] The consequence of this reduction in profits appears to be an increased awareness of the cost of membership in the Federal Reserve that serves to overcome inertia. At least, that is the contention of former Federal Reserve Board Chairman Burns, who concluded from the withdrawal of New England banks from the System: "The influence of NOW accounts on the cost sensitivity of commercial banks is clearly visible in these statistics." [1977, p. 639] Whether or not Burns is correct, the present system clearly is inequitable and a change should be considered.

Proposed changes

Mandatory Membership and Uniform Reserves[5]

As . . . historical review . . . points out, required membership by all commercial banks was not proposed or instituted when the System was designed. Indeed, the capital requirements imposed by the Fed made it very difficult for many state banks to join. The enormous number of bank failures in the early 1930s changed that approach. The Banking Act of 1933 required state chartered banks to become members of the Federal Reserve by July 1936 as a condition of qualifying for deposit insurance. However, this requirement was repealed before that date. In 1961 mandatory membership for all insured commercial banks was proposed by the Commission on Money and Credit. Most recently, in 1971, the President's Commission on Financial Structure and Regulation went even further in recommending mandatory membership in the Federal Reserve System for all state chartered commercial banks and all thrift institutions that offer third party services.

Subjecting all insured banks to the Federal Reserve's reserve requirements without mandatory membership was proposed by the Fed in 1948. The Board of Governors' [1948, p. 6] justification for this legislation was very similar to the statement made today:

> It is inequitable to have member banks bear the entire burden of credit action undertaken in the public interest. . . . Member banks already carry higher effective reserve requirements than nonmembers, even where the required percentages are the same. . . . Nonmember banks, nevertheless, benefit by the strength which the very existence of the

[4]However, LeMaistre [1977, p. 15] reports that FDIC staff studies of the causes of the decline in bank profits show that though ". . . Massachusetts banks were especially hard hit by the 1974–75 recession . . . [the] magnitude of the earnings declines in Massachusetts from 1974 to 1976 does not appear to be related to the decision to offer NOW accounts."

[5]Knight [1974B] provides an excellent, concise history of these proposals.

Federal Reserve System gives to the entire credit structure of the country. Failure to apply national monetary measures to all insured banks seriously impairs the effectiveness of national monetary policy.

Uniform reserves were endorsed in 1950 by a Subcommittee headed by Senator Paul Douglas and in 1952 by Representative Wright Patman when the Board of Governors reiterated it. The American Bankers Association's paper for the Commission on Money and Credit favored uniform reserves on all demand deposits and no reserves on time deposits. In 1961 the Commission on Money and Credit endorsed the ABA proposal for a nongraduated uniform reserve against all demand deposits, whether held by reserve city or country commercial banks or by thrift institutions. The Commission also called for removal of reserves against time deposits. They argued, as have many economists, that since time deposits are not part of the money supply as usually defined, the reserves only complicated monetary control.[6] In 1963, the President's Committee on Financial Institutions made a similar recommendation. Following that, the Federal Reserve Board annually proposed that graduated reserve requirements be imposed on all insured banks, wherein the requirements would be lower for small banks regardless of their location. (This scheme was established for member banks in 1972.) In 1971, The President's Commission on Financial Structure and Regulation recommended uniform reserves for all financial institutions offering third party payments, with a five year phase-in period for present nonmember institutions.

The advent of NOW accounts has led to additional agitation by the Federal Reserve for some system of uniform reserves. In January 1974 the Board of Governors requested that Congress pass legislation that would enable the Board to impose reserve requirements similar to those imposed on member banks on all institutions who offer demand deposits or NOW accounts to the public. An exception would be made, however, for time and savings deposits and on the first $2 million of demand deposits. A proposal presently before the Congress would permit financial institutions to offer NOW or share draft accounts on condition that they would maintain reserves equivalent to those required of member banks.

These proposals obviously met with effective opposition for (including the recently proposed legislation) they were not adopted despite the impressive array of prestigious support. The 1933 requirement was repealed, further Congressional action came to naught, the American Bankers Association's President in 1973, Rex Morthland, reversed the ABA's stand and the Treasury would not endorse the President's Commission on Financial Structure and Regulation's recommendation. (They proposed that the Federal Reserve's requirements apply only to member banks and to members of the Federal Home Loan Bank.) Most recently, the Conference of State Bank Supervisors attacked uniform reserves and mandatory Federal Reserve membership vigorously (see pamphlets by Robertson and Phillips

---

[6]My paper (Benston [1969]) came to a similar conclusion, based on the empirical analysis discussed above.

[1974] and Kreider [1976]). The reasons for this opposition are not difficult to discern. State chartered banks fear the domination of the Federal Reserve, continuing a concern voiced strongly and repeatedly since before the System was established. Nonmember commercial banks and thrift institutions clearly do not want any non-interest bearing reserve requirements imposed on them, for this would subject their owners or managers to capital losses. Banks who offer correspondent banking services tend to be opposed because (as is discussed above) they fear a loss in their investments in this business since the Federal Reserve would supply some services without charge directly to their nonmember respondents. Member banks benefit from the Fed's concern about banks leaving the System, since this acts as a constraint on the Fed's imposition of restrictions and costs on its members. And as long as member banks dominate the market for demand deposit services, member bank owners get a competitive return on their investments. Though users of bank-money pay the cost of Federal Reserve membership and though the present system results in the inefficient use of resources, the costs are too diffusely imposed to make it worthwhile for users to mount an effective opposition to the status quo. Therefore, it seems likely that mandatory membership or uniform reserves will not be instituted so long as only nonmember institutions would lose and nobody else would clearly or significantly gain. But, as member banks leave the System and as thrift institutions obtain the right to offer third party payment services, the remaining member banks' owners will begin to bear the costs of membership. At this point, they may find it worthwhile to try to change the system.[7]

Lower or Zero Reserve Requirements

Some critics of the Federal Reserve's attempts to have membership or equivalent member bank reserves imposed on other financial institutions argue that the Fed rather should reduce the burdens of membership. One method proposed is to reduce reserve requirements on demand deposits while eliminating them for time and savings deposits. Another would reduce reserve requirements only for deposits under a given aggregate amount in the hope of stemming the attribution of small banks. However, . . . analysis of state reserve requirements . . . shows, the Federal Reserve cannot compete with the states unless it lowers its required reserves to the point where the requirements would equal the savings in due from correspondent balances that membership affords . . . required reserves would have to be reduced to about one and a half percent of total deposits for this policy to be effective on the average. But since this requirement still would be too high for some banks, particularly the small banks whose average collected due from correspondents balances are estimated to be less than one percent of total deposits; thus the change would neither be

---

[7]Reserves equal to 100 percent of deposits has been proposed by advocates of money supply control, most recently and forcefully by Friedman [1960]. This alternative is not discussed at length because it has not been even semi-seriously considered for some time.

equitable or effective. Furthermore, a reserve requirement of this low magnitude is not very different from no requirement at all.

Zero reserve requirements are not ridiculous as the Federal Reserve implies. The money supply can be controlled by the Fed through open market operations that affect the public's and the banks' currency holdings as well as with government securities. . . . Furthermore, as the studies of nonmember bank behavior . . . show, the existence of nonmember banks whose required reserves essentially are zero has not adversely affected the Fed's control over monetary aggregates. And, although member bank required reserve ratios have declined since the Second World War, Dewald's [1972] study shows that the predictability of changes in the money multiplier has remained high. However, it is conceptually clear that the lower is the reserve requirement, the less predictable is the effect on the money supply of an open market operation of a given magnitude simply because the money multiplier is an inverse function of the required or voluntary reserve ratio and because it is subject to some unpredictable changes. Therefore, Carson [1964], formerly a proponent of zero reserve requirements, has written that low uniform required reserves would be preferable to zero reserves [Carson, 1973]. I should emphasize, though, that the possibility of unpredicted changes does not necessarily mean that money supply control would be importantly affected, since the changes could be relatively small and/or offsetting.

Another form of zero reserve requirements would permit member banks to hold reserves in the form of interest bearing obligations, such as government bonds. The Federal Reserve Bank of San Francisco's [1977] survey shows that 91 percent of the banks favor this proposal (71 percent strongly). A similar proposal would permit banks to count balances with correspondents as part of required reserves. These changes, though, would have the same effect as eliminating all reserve requirements. Since banks would hold government securities and maintain balances with correspondents in any event, required reserves actually would be voluntary. It would be more efficient simply to eliminate reserve requirements altogether.

Interest Payments on Reserves

The payment of some interest on reserves is proposed in a recently submitted (1977), administration endorsed, bill (S.2055) for the stated purpose of stemming membership attrition. This legislation, if enacted, would give the Fed the authority to pay interest not exceeding 10 percent of the Federal Reserve's net earnings.

Though the proposal is new to the legislative process, it has been discussed in academic circles for some time, though not usually in terms of keeping banks from leaving the System. Tolley [1957], for example, suggested the payment of interest on reserves for other, and I think, better reasons. He argued that the tax on bank money (that non-interest bearing required reserves represents) distorts resource allocation. He pointed out that, since the resource cost of allowing someone to hold bank money is essentially zero, there is no reason to give people an incentive to use resources for conserving bank money to avoid paying the tax. Friedman [1960, pp. 71–75] endorsed Tolley's position and added that it is not equitable for the government to pay interest to holders of bonds but not to holders of bank money.[8]

Three objections have been raised against this proposal. The first, though only mentioned in the academic literature, deserves consideration. Mayer [1966] argued that since the liquidity value derived from demand deposits is not subject to personal income tax, it might be optimal to tax the deposits by not paying interest on reserves. While his point has merit, it applies (as he noted) only to personal deposit accounts (and, with equal merit, to non-taxed imputed income from any personally held asset that yields benefits, such as a car, house or art work). Therefore, while this objection is valid, it does not speak to the major resource misallocation, the activities of businesses to conserve bank money.

The second objection, more generally argued, is that banking markets are not competitive. Therefore, the owners of banks who receive the interest payments will simply be given capital gains. The available evidence, though, is contrary to this presumption. The studies reviewed in Benston [1973] are consistent with the belief that most banking markets are very competitive. The non-competitive markets tend to be small towns from which competitors are restricted from entering by unit banking or home office protection laws. These areas often are served by nonmember banks. Another major anti-competitive aspect of demand deposit services is that most states legally prohibit thrift institutions from offering checking accounts to the public. The only other significant impediment to competition among banks for the public's demand deposits is the prohibition of explicit interest payments on these accounts. These limitations of competition certainly do not benefit consumers and result in inefficiently conducted banking operations. Even so, there is little evidence that supports or reason to believe the hypothesis that banking markets are not highly competitive. Rather . . . it is more likely that the present system permits nonmember bank owners to reap extra gains.

The third objection is that the U.S. Treasury would lose revenues upon the payment of interest on reserves. Most of the Federal Reserve's net income, earnings on its portfolio less operating expense, are transferred to the Treasury. Hence, any interest paid to member banks would equivalently reduce these payments. Secretary of the Treasury Blumenthal, in his testimony on S.1664 on June 20, 1977, pointed out that the ceilings on the amount of interest payments proposed would result in a net "cost" to the Treasury of only $200 million a year, since the Treasury might otherwise lose between $200 and $300 million a year should banks (and their reserves at the Fed) continue to leave the System. This argument, while understandable from the point of view of a Treasury official who sees his responsibility as maximizing the revenue of his department, is not a valid tax argument on equity grounds. A tax on member bank reserves is not a tax on large banks or on their owners. Necessarily, it is passed along to the users of bank money (as per the discussion above). The final

---

[8]Friedman [1960] proposed payment of interest on reserves as part of a plan to require 100 percent reserves against deposits and, hence, allow the monetary authorities precise control over the money supply.

payers of the tax are the final consumers of bank money services or of the output of producers who use bank money. There is no way of knowing whether these are deserving or undeserving people. Therefore, while the Treasury may lose revenue should interest be paid on reserves, the users of bank money gain a reduction in taxes. The inequitable aspect of the present system is that owners of nonmember banks escape the tax.

Nevertheless, the appearance (if not the fact) of interest payments on reserves as a "rip off" by banks is difficult to overcome. For this reason (and others), determination of the specific interest rate to be applied to reserves might easily become a political matter. Therefore, the very imaginative proposal by the Board of Directors of the Federal Reserve Bank of Kansas City (FRBKC) [1977, pp. 35–36] is worthy of consideration. As an alternative to the direct payment of interest on reserves, they recommend:

> That member banks be allowed to invest a portion of their required reserve balances in any direct obligation of the United States Government held in the Federal Reserve portfolio. The maximum security holdings for reserve purposes would be the daily average amount of reserves eligible for investment. Member banks would be permitted to select the issues in which they wished to invest and would thereby receive the full interest return and any capital gain or loss experienced. All purchases and sales of securities for reserve purposes would be at prevailing market prices, and the securities would be retained in safekeeping at Reserve Banks. To prevent fluctuations in the market value of securities in safekeeping from altering the reserve base of the banking system, all securities held by banks to satisfy reserve requirements would be valued at purchase price.
>
> Banks owning reserve securities would be permitted to sell them at any time. However, to minimize the administrative burden, banks choosing to switch or liquidate securities would be ineligible to reinvest those funds for a predetermined period of time. This limitation would not apply to banks seeking to roll-over securities at maturity.

(Other technical considerations, such as the availability of a sufficient supply of Federal Reserve owned securities that are not pledged against Federal Reserve notes, are discussed and dealt with.)

The FRBKC would limit the amount of reserves that could be invested to a level commensurate with the estimated cost of membership. Since their analysis . . . indicated (incorrectly, as is shown) that the cost as a percentage of deposits was much higher for small than for large banks, they propose a schedule that allows marginally lower percentages of investable reserves as a bank's deposit size increases. Thus the allowable average percentage of total required reserves that could be invested in securities held at the Federal Reserve ranges from 55 percent for banks with less than $10 million in deposits to 15 percent for banks with $1 billion in deposits or more. Paulus [1977, Table 12, p. 36] similarly suggests a rate of interest on reserves that decreases marginally as the amount of reserves increases. He illustrates a schedule that would pay banks 5 percent on the first $1 million of required reserves at the Fed, 4 percent on the second million, 3 percent on the third million, 2 percent on additional reserves up to $30 million and 1 percent on all additional reserves. This schedule is designed to equalize the decreasing burden that he estimates is borne by larger banks. However, . . . the data do not show this pattern.

These proposals illustrate the difficulty of determining the "correct" (or what perhaps should more accurately be labeled, the "politically acceptable") rate of interest on required reserves (or level of reserves on which interest is paid that can be invested in securities at the Fed). Analyses of the costs of membership not only indicate different percentages of deposits at banks aggregated by deposit size; the costs for individual banks within each aggregate may not even be reasonably close (they obviously are not the same). One aspect of the net costs of membership about which analysis . . . was weak is the estimated value of the benefit members derive from Federal Reserve services. A proposed solution to this situation is outlined below.

Interest Payments on Third Party
Payments Balances

Related to the payment of interest on required reserves is the question of interest payments on depositors' balances. As the development of NOW accounts has caused bankers, regulators and Congress to reconsider the costs of Federal Reserve membership, so has it caused them to reconsider the prohibition of interest on demand deposits enacted in 1933. It is now generally known that the payment of interest on demand balances prior to 1933 did not cause banks to invest in risky assets and lead to failures [Benston, 1964, Cox, 1966]. More recently, the payment of interest on NOW accounts has not seriously weakened the affected banks. The former Chairman of the FDIC testified that "In the opinion of FDIC examiners, problems caused by NOW accounts are unlikely to be much greater than those encountered when 'free' checking accounts and consumer certificates of deposits were offered. . . . no institution has failed and none has been judged to be in an unsafe and unsound condition because of NOW accounts." [LeMaistre, 1977, p. 7]

Most regulators and bankers now admit that NOW accounts are but the latest competitive device with which banks avoid the Government imposed cartel arrangement that prohibits interest payments on demand deposits. Interest payments on balances with correspondent banks take the form of a wide range of services provided for fees that are offset by earnings credits on average collected balances [Knight, 1976]. Large commercial and individual depositors similarly are paid interest on their balances with a variety of services, such as payroll preparation, lower charges for transactions services, note collection, investment and business advice, credit arrangements and favorable interest on loans. Even individual demand depositors with relatively small balances are offered transfers to and from interest bearing savings accounts, free checking, and no-charge travelers checks. The latest of these developments is NOW accounts, which essentially are demand deposit accounts on which interest can be paid because they are called a form of savings account. The only distinction, though, between a NOW account and a checking account is that the NOW payments instrument is not quite as flexible as is the ordinary check.

The sometimes torturous arrangements to get around the prohibition of interest on demand deposits are recognized by Burns [1977, pp. 636–38]. He lists the ways in which interest is, in fact, paid on demand deposits, recognizes that NOW accounts are evidence that "The broad movement towards explicit interest on transactions balances has eroded the distinction between demand deposits and time or savings deposits" [p. 617] and concludes, "Simple prudence suggests that the movement toward explicit payment of interest on transactions balances ought to proceed more deliberately than it has to date." [p. 737] The former Chairman of the FDIC [LeMaistre, 1977, p. 4] would move quickly in permitting financial institutions to offer depositors explicit interest payments so that they may have ". . . the opportunity to determine for themselves how they wish to spend their portion of the income the bank earns on their deposits." As he explains, "If interest were paid, a depositor might choose to consume the same services that banks now offer in the course of competing with other institutions for his account or he might choose to forego such services and spend his interest income on different goods and services. . . . Free or below-actual-cost checking encourages inefficient use of resources because depositors have little or no incentive to economize on check writing, even though clearance costs are substantial" [p. 4]. Therefore, he would remove the Regulation Q ceiling on savings and time deposits and restrictions on NOW accounts.

Removal of prohibitions of and limitations on the payment of interest on deposit accounts is a corollary of the payment of interest on banks' required reserve balances because of concern that the interest revenue received by banks might not be passed to the users of bank money. While competitive forces probably would ensure that depositors would receive the benefits from the removal of the tax on reserves, there would seem to be no reason not to remove restrictions that would slow down, if not prevent, this process from occurring. Additional, related changes that would appear to be corollaries of the payment of interest on reserves is the removal of restrictions against thrift institutions from offering any form of third party payments (conditional on their having to maintain the same reserves as do other suppliers of bank money).

Explicit Charges for Federal Reserve Services

As financial intermediaries other than commercial banks enter and seek to enter the market for providing third party payments, they have asked that the facilities of the Federal Reserve be made available to them. Former Board Chairman Burns concurs. In his testimony before the Senate Subcommittee on Banking, Housing and Urban Affairs he said [1977, p. 641]:

We believe that open access to the System's check collection services is desirable, providing a means can be devised for effectively equalizing the terms of access by all depositary institutions. Equalization requires that all institutions bear the same level of costs for a given level of services. Member banks, in effect, already pay for payments services received through foregone income on reserves. The practicality of requiring equivalent balances from nonmembers is questionable in view of the apparent reluctance of the Congress to enact a system of uniform reserve requirements. Thus, unless the Congress moves in this direction, equalization presumably will have to be accomplished by means of a system of equitable charges and responsibilities applicable to all institutions.

But even were uniform reserves required of all financial institutions that offer third party payments and even were interest paid on required reserve balances, all institutions would not bear the same level of costs for a given level of services that Burns (correctly) states is required for "equalization." All banks do not use the same level of services nor is the level and type of services demanded necessarily related to their levels of required reserves. . . . Furthermore, as Hoskins [1975] ably points out, the Federal Reserve's (or anyone else's) production of services that are provided at no charge necessarily results in inefficiencies. First, there is likely to be overproduction of a resource that is distributed free of charge, for the simple reason that demand curves slope downward—the lower the price, the greater the demand. (However, it should be noted that the check encoding and batching required by the Fed does impose a significant cost on many banks, particularly small ones, which leads them to prefer paying for the services of correspondents.) Second, the no-price system does not provide the Fed with signals about which services users demand and how much innovation is optimal. As a consequence, the Fed may overinvest in sophisticated equipment whose costs exceed its value to users. Third, nonmembers cannot be prevented from using the Fed's facilities although they do not pay for them, with the consequence that the present system is not equitable.

Two objections might be raised to a charge-for-service system. One is that the Fed would find it difficult to determine the "correct" amount to charge for its services, since it is difficult to measure marginal costs and to estimate demand elasticities. However, as Knight's [1976] survey reveals, many banks that offer correspondent services are able to arrive at prices that apparently satisfy their customers. Furthermore, the general movement in banking is toward "unbundling," charging customers for individual services separately from crediting them with the value of funds deposited. And, a positive price is likely to be more accurate than the present zero price. The second objection relates to the effect of unbundling on the Federal Reserve. At present, the Federal Reserve's operations are not subjected directly to a market test. (However, the fact that the correspondent banking system provides banks with a large volume of the services offered at no explicit charge by the Fed indicates that the Fed does face indirect competition.) It is a rare manager, indeed, who prefers to face the risks of competition that explicit pricing would emphasize. Therefore, it would not be surprising to find the Fed objecting to a system that, in effect, would subject its operations to the rigors of the market.

Abolish Membership for All Banks

At the conclusion of his analysis for the Commission on Money and Credit, "Nonmember Banks and the Effectiveness of Monetary Policy," Warburton [1963] noted that an original purpose of the Federal Reserve, responsibility for the safety and soundness of individual banks, had been superseded by the creation of the FDIC. This function not only became redundant but interferes with the basic task of the Federal Reserve, monetary control, by diverting the attention and resources of its Board to regulatory matters. Therefore, Warburton recommended that membership in the Federal Reserve be abolished. In addition, since the benefits and burden of central banking should be equal for all providers of bank money, Warburton further recommended that the Banking Act of 1933, which requires examination and regulation of all banks of deposit, be amended to require "that all banks with deposits transferable by check or used as a circulating medium maintain an amount equal to a specified percentage of its own deposits in a reserve account at the Federal Reserve Bank of the district in which it is located" [p. 352]. He also would "extend all of the privileges now associated with membership to all insured commercial banks," including access to the discount window and to Federal Reserve facilities [p. 352].

When the history of membership in the Fed is reviewed . . . , the merits of Warburton's recommendation are enhanced. Membership in the Fed by individual banks is almost an accident of history that stemmed from the reluctance of Congress to create a central bank. The national banks joined because they benefited from lower cash reserves. The large state chartered banks joined because they benefited from Federal Reserve check clearance facilities that enabled them to compete in correspondent banking and from lower than market interest rate loans, and because they were less able than smaller banks to withstand political pressure during the First World War. But since the creation of the FDIC and the recognition that the Federal Reserve is the nation's central bank, whose actions affect all banks and indeed the entire economy, the Fed's organization as a very large bank "owned" by its members is meaningless if not ludicrous.

Some arguments against abolishing membership should be considered. One is that the Fed must have supervisory control over member banks to enable it to determine the credit that should be extended via the discount window and to provide it with continuous information on the interactions of monetary policy actions and the conditions of individual banks. Presumably, bank examination by the Federal Reserve's examiners is required for these purposes. This argument, though, is not based on good reasoning and is contrary to evidence. The Fed's role as a lender of last resort is not limited to the state chartered member banks that its personnel supervises. The Comptroller of the Currency supervises the national banks, who comprise the overwhelming majority of member banks. There is no reason for the Fed not to rely also on examinations conducted by the FDIC. The value of information gathered and transmitted by bank examiners about the effects of monetary policy on banks and about changes in the economy as reflected in changes in the quality of bank credit is not supported by research findings. Benston and Marlin[1974] examined this hypothesis empirically with all of the available data on examiners' reports of substandard loans. They find that changes in substandard loans, the key variable that bank examiners use as a measure of credit quality, is unrelated to changes in the economy or of monetary policy. Indeed, they question the meaningfulness of the bank examiners' evaluations of credit quality for any purpose of economic analysis. In addition, the Fed's examiners and supervisors are in contact only with a minority of commercial banks. If the monetary authorities wish to use information on banking operations, it would be preferable for them to request this information from the Comptroller of the Currency and the FDIC.

The second argument against abolishing membership is that the Fed might lose an important constituency—member banks. Few organizations choose to divest themselves of allies. However, voluntary divestiture appears to be occurring in any event. Therefore, it might be in the Federal Reserve's interest to restructure its organization in a manner that is consistent with its fundamental function as a central bank.

Recommendations

The analyses and data presented lead to the following recommendations:

1. Banks and other financial institutions with deposits transferable by check, negotiable orders of withdrawal, or otherwise used as circulating medium (bank money) should be required to maintain reserves at a Federal Reserve Bank at rates that are the same for all institutions. This requirement is dictated solely to give the Federal Reserve possibly better control over the money supply, which control is its primary responsibility.

2. Reserves should not be required against savings and time deposits, so long as they are not readily transferable and, therefore, do not serve as part of the circulating medium. (NOW accounts, therefore, would be classified as deposits subject to reserve requirements.) Required reserves against these deposits not only complicates the control that the Fed can exercise over the money supply but also results in an inequitable and inefficient tax on a specific form of savings provided by some institutions. (However, it should be noted that the definition of the money supply is an empirical matter that is not yet decided.)

3. The Federal Reserve should institute other reforms of the reserve requirement system (such as abolition of reserves against U.S. government deposits and a change from the lagged reserve competition scheme) that serve to make control of the money supply more difficult.

4. Reserves required against demand deposits (and other deposits that are used as circulating medium or that empirical analysis indicates should be included in the money supply) and held at the Federal Reserve banks may be entirely invested in U.S. Government obligations, as described in the proposal of the FRBKC [1977] (outlined above). This procedure would make reserves earning assets. The interest earnings on the invested reserves would compensate the users of bank-money (via the institutions) for having to keep some of their deposits (that otherwise would have been invested) at the Federal Reserve

banks to aid the Fed in its control over the money supply. The amount of the reserves that can be invested for the benefit of the institutions (and hence for users of bank-money) should not be limited, since there is no basis for believing that the cost to the users of bank-money differs according to sizes of the bank in which they have their accounts.

5. Explicit interest payments on all deposits (demand and time) should be uncontrolled. In this way the users of bank money will be assured of receiving the benefit from the removal of the tax on required reserves. An additional, related change would permit all chartered financial institutions to offer the public third party payment services (with uniformly assessed reserves kept at the Federal Reserve Banks). These changes would not only be equitable (particularly for smaller depositors), but would improve the efficiency of the banking system.

6. The Federal Reserve should make all of its payments facilities and other services available to all financial institutions on a fee basis, such that the cost of operating the facilities is self-supporting. This change would permit competing institutions equal access to this essentially public facility. Charges for the services on a self-supporting basis would work to improve efficiency by weeding out operations that are not worth the cost to users and by encouraging the Fed to develop services for which there are demands. It also would enable alternative arrangements, such as correspondent banking services, to compete. (The Fed still would have an advantage unless it could be required to earn a market rate of return on its investment.)

7. Membership in the Federal Reserve should be abolished. National banks would continue to be supervised by the Comptroller of the Currency. All state chartered banks would continue to be supervised by their respective states and the FDIC would examine all state banks rather than only nonmembers. Membership in the Federal Reserve is an anachronism with present-day dysfunctional effects. It serves to discriminate in favor of some users of bank money and/or owners of bank stock. Membership also causes the Fed to concoct procedures and regulations designed to placate banks that might withdraw from the System. Not only are these often discriminatory against banks that are unlikely to leave (and, hence, against their depositors), but they increasingly serve to complicate the Fed's control over the money supply and hence divert it from its primary function.

8. The right to borrow from the discount window should be made available to all institutions that maintain reserves with the Fed. The rate charged should be tied to and be greater than a market rate, such as the Treasury bill rate, so that banks do not have an incentive to borrow except for emergencies.

I suggest that these changes are supported by the available data and are long overdue. Were they instituted, they would increase the equity among users of financial services and among the institutions that provide those services, increase the viability of the dual banking system, and improve the Federal Reserve's control over the money supply and enable it to carry out its other, vitally important functions with fewer distractions.

REFERENCES

BENSTON, GEORGE J. 1964. "Internal Payments on Demand Deposits and Bank Investment Behavior." *Journal of Political Economy* LXXII (October), pp. 431–49.

————. 1969. "An Analysis and Evaluation of Alternative Reserve Requirement Plans." *Journal of Finance* XXIV (December), pp. 849–70.

————. 1972. "Economies of Scale of Financial Institutions." *Journal of Money, Credit and Banking* IV (May), pp. 312–41.

————. 1973. "The Optimal Banking Structure: Theory and Evidence." *Journal of Bank Research* 3 (Winter), pp. 220–36.

————, and JOHN TEPPER MARLIN. 1974. "Bank Examiners' Evaluation of Credit: An Analysis of the Usefulness of Substandard Loan Data." *Journal of Money, Credit and Banking* VI (February), pp. 23–44.

BOARD OF DIRECTORS OF THE FEDERAL RESERVE BANK OF KANSAS CITY. 1977. *A Proposal For Enhancing the Attractiveness of Membership in the Federal Reserve System,* June.

BOARD OF GOVERNORS OF THE FEDERAL RESERVE SYSTEM. 1948. *Thirty-Fifth Annual Report of the Board of Governors of the Federal Reserve System.* Washington, D.C.

BRIMMER, ANDREW F. 1966. "Reserve Requirements, Nonpar Banks, and Membership in the Federal Reserve System," Federal Reserve Bank of Minneapolis *Monthly Review,* Supplement (July), pp. 2–11.

BURNS, ARTHUR. 1977. "Statement before the Subcommittee on Financial Institutions, Committee on Banking, Housing and Urban Affairs, United States Senate, June 20, 1977." *Federal Reserve Bulletin,* July, pp. 636–43.

CARSON, DEANE. 1964. "Is the Federal Reserve System Really Necessary?" *Journal of Finance* XIX (December).

————. 1973. "Should Reserve Requirements be Abolished?" *The Bankers Magazine,* Winter.

COX, ALBERT H., JR. 1966. *Regulation of Interest on Bank Deposits.* Michigan Business Studies, Vol. XVII, No. 4.

COX, WILLIAM M., III. 1977. "Small Banks and Monetary Control: Is Fed Membership Important?" Federal Reserve Bank of Atlanta. Working Paper Series, January.

DEWALD, WILLIAM G. 1972. "The Required Reserve Rates for Member Banks." *Bulletin of Business Research,* pp. 1–7. Center for Business and Economic Research, Ohio State University, XLVII (September).

FEDERAL RESERVE BANK OF SAN FRANCISCO. 1977. *Twelfth District Members—Banks Opinion Survey on Federal Reserve Membership.* Unpublished report, June.

FRASER, DONALD R., PETER S. ROSE, and GARY L. SCHUGART. 1975. "Federal Reserve Membership and Bank Performance: The Evidence from Texas." *Journal of Finance* XXX (May), pp. 641–58.

FRIEDMAN, MILTON. 1960. *A Program for Monetary Stability.* New York: Fordham University Press.

FRODIN, JOANNA. 1977. "The Tax/Subsidy Relation between Member Banks and the Federal Reserve System." Unpublished manuscript. Wellesley College.

FULMER, JOHN. 1974. "The Effect of Federal Reserve System Membership on the Earnings of Commercial Banks in South Carolina." *Journal of Bank Research* 4 (Winter), pp. 314-25.

GILBERT, ALTON. 1973. "The Effects of Lagged Reserve Requirements on the Reserve Adjustment Pressure on Banks." *Financial Analysts Journal* XXIX (September/October), pp. 34-43 and "Appendix," pp. 88-89.

GILBERT, ALTON R. 1976. "Recent Changes in Reserve Requirements: An Example of Contradictory Regulations." *Federal Reserve Bank of St. Louis Review* 58 (March), pp. 2-7.

———. 1977. "Utilization of Federal Reserve Bank Services by Member Banks: Implications for the Costs and Benefits of Membership." *Federal Reserve Bank of St. Louis Review* 59 (August), pp. 2-15.

GILBERT, GARY G., and MANFERD O. PETERSON. 1974. "Reserve Requirements, Federal Reserve Membership and Bank Performance." Financial and Economic Research Series, Division of Research, Federal Deposit Insurance Corporation, Working Paper 74-8.

———. 1975. "The Impact of Changes in Federal Reserve Membership on Commercial Bank Performance." *Journal of Finance* XXX (June), pp. 713-19.

GOLDBERG, LAWRENCE G., and JOHN T. ROSE. 1976. "The Effect on Nonmember Banks of The Imposition of Member Bank Reserve Requirements—with and without Federal Reserve Services." *Journal of Finance* XXXI (December), pp. 1457-69.

———. 1977. "Do State Reserve Requirements Matter?" *Journal of Bank Research* 8 (Spring), pp. 31-39.

HOSKINS, W. LEE. 1975. "Should the Fed Sell Its Services?" *Federal Reserve Bank of Philadelphia Business Review,* January, pp. 11-17.

KLEIN, BENJAMIN. 1977. "Determinants of Membership in the Federal Reserve System," Unpublished manuscript. University of California, Los Angeles.

KOPECKY, KENNETH J. 1978. "Nonmember Banks and Empirical Measures of the Variability of Reserves and Money: A Theoretical Appraisal," *Journal of Finance* XXXIII (March), pp. 311-18.

KNIGHT, ROBERT E. 1970A. "Correspondent Banking, Part 1: Balances and Services." *Federal Reserve Bank of Kansas City Monthly Review,* November, pp. 3-14.

———. 1970B. "Correspondent Banking, Part II: Loan Participations and Fund Flows." *Federal Reserve Bank of Kansas City Monthly Review,* December, pp. 12-24.

———. 1974A. "Reserve Requirements, Part I: Comparative Reserve Requirements at Member and Nonmember Banks." *Federal Reserve Bank of Kansas City Monthly Review,* April, pp. 3-20.

———. 1974B. "Reserve Requirements, Part II: An Analysis of the Case for Uniform Reserve Requirements." *Federal Reserve Bank of Kansas City Monthly Review,* May, pp. 3-15, 24.

———. 1976. "Account Analysis in Correspondent Banking." *Federal Reserve Bank of Kansas City Monthly Review,* March, pp. 11-20.

———. 1977. "Comparative Burdens of Federal Reserve Members and Nonmember Banks." *Federal Reserve Bank of Kansas City Monthly Review,* March, pp. 13-28.

KREIDER, LAWRENCE E. 1976. *Optional Affiliation with The Federal Reserve System for Reserve Purposes is Consistent with Equitable Treatment Between Banks.* Conference of State Bank Supervisors, Washington, D.C.

LE MAISTRE, GEORGE A. 1977. "Statement on Consumer Financial Services Act (5.2055)." Presented to Subcommittee on Financial Institutions, Supervision, Regulation and Insurance, Committee on Banking, Finance and Urban Affairs. House of Representatives, September 7.

MAYER, THOMAS. 1966. "Interest Payments on Required Reserve Balances." *Journal of Finance* XXI (March), pp. 116–18.

MAYNE, LUCILLE S. 1967. *The Effect of Federal Reserve System Membership on the Profitability of Illinois Banks.* Center for Research of the College of Business Administration, The Pennsylvania State University, 1961–63.

———. 1976. "Deposit Reserve Requirements: Time for Change." *Journal of Bank Research* 6 (Winter), pp. 268–74.

PAULUS, JOHN D. 1976. "Effects of 'NOW' Accounts on Costs and Earnings of Commercial Banks in 1974–75." Staff Economics Studies. Board of Governors of the Federal Reserve System, September.

———. 1977. "The Burden of Federal Reserve Membership, NOW Accounts, and the Payment of Interest on Reserves." Federal Reserve Board, Division of Research and Statistics. Unpublished paper, June. (Other contributors are Edward Ettin, Stephen Axelrod, James Brundy, Milton Hudson, John Williams, John DuBois and David Reifschneider).

PETERSON, MANFERD O., and HUGH S. MC LAUGHLIN. 1975. "Reserve Requirements and Federal Reserve Membership." Financial and Economics Research Section, Division of Research. Federal Deposit Insurance Corporation. Executive Summary 75-2.

PHAUP, MARVIN. 1973. "The Effect of Federal Reserve System Membership on Earnings of Fourth District Banks, 1963–1970." Federal Reserve Bank of Cleveland. *Economic Review,* January–February, pp. 3–18.

PRESTOPINO, CHRIS JOSEPH. 1976. "Do Higher Reserve Requirements Discourage Federal Reserve Membership?" *Journal of Finance* XXXI (December), pp. 1471–80.

QUICK, PERRY. 1977. "Nonmember Bank Reserve Requirements." Appendix A to John Paulus. "The Burden of Federal Reserve Membership, NOW Accounts, and the Payment of Interest on Reserves." Federal Reserve Board, Division of Research and Statistics, June.

REINHARDT, C. HENRY, JR. 1942. *Membership of State Banks in the Federal Reserve System.* An essay prepared for the Graduate School of Banking at Rutgers University.

ROBERTSON, ROSS M., and ALMARIN PHILLIPS. 1974. *Optional Affiliation with the Federal Reserve System for Reserve Purposes Is Consistent with Effective Monetary Policies.* Conference of State Bank Supervisors, Washington, D.C.

ROSE, JOHN T. 1976. "Bank Capital Requirements and the Cost of Federal Reserve System Membership." Unpublished paper, August.

ROSE, PETER S. 1976. "Exodus: Why Banks Are Leaving the Fed." *Bankers Magazine,* Winter, pp. 43–49.

———. 1977. "Banker Attitudes toward the Federal Reserve System: Survey Results," *Journal of Bank Research* 8 (Summer), pp. 77–84.

TOLLEY, GEORGE. 1957. "Providing for the Growth of the Money Supply." *Journal of Political Economy* LXV (December), pp. 465–85.

VARVEL, WALTER A. 1977. "The Cost of Membership in the Federal Reserve System." Federal Reserve Bank of Richmond. March, Working Paper 77-1.

WARBURTON, CLARK. 1963. "Nonmember Banks and the Effectiveness of Monetary Policy,"
Research Study Three in *Monetary Management* (prepared for the Commission on
Money and Credit). pp. 317–59. New York: Prentice-Hall.

WINGFIELD, B. MAGRUDER. 1941. "Deterrents to Membership in the Reserve System." In
Banking Studies, Staff Board of Governors of the Federal Reserve System.